The Particulars of Rapture

The Particulars of Rapture

REFLECTIONS ON EXODUS

Avivah Gottlieb Zornberg

IMAGE/DOUBLEDAY

New York London Toronto Sydney Auckland

AN IMAGE BOOK
PUBLISHED BY DOUBLEDAY
a division of Random House, Inc.
1540 Broadway, New York, New York 10036

IMAGE, DOUBLEDAY, and the portrayal of a deer drinking from a stream
are trademarks of Doubleday,

a division of Random House, Inc.

Book design by Pei Loi Koay

The Library of Congress has cataloged the hardcover edition as follows:

Zornberg, Avivah Gottlieb.
The particulars of rapture/Avivah Gottlieb Zornberg.—1st ed.
p. cm.
Includes bibliographical references and indexes.
1. Bible. O.T. Exodus—Commentaries. 2. Midrash.
3. Bible. O.T. Exodus—Criticism, interpretation, etc.,
Jewish. I. Title.
BS1245.3.Z67 2000
296.1'4—dc21
00-024156

ISBN 0-385-49153-0

PRINTED IN THE UNITED STATES OF AMERICA

November 2002

FIRST IMAGE BOOKS EDITION

1 2 3 4 5 6 7 8 9 10

Two things of opposite natures seem to depend
On one another, as a man depends
On a woman, day on night, the imagined

On the real. This is the origin of change.
Winter and spring, cold copulars, embrace
And forth the particulars of rapture come.

—WALLACE STEVENS,
"NOTES TOWARD A SUPREME FICTION"

Contents

The Particulars of Rapture

Introduction

Some books cannot be taken by direct assault;
they must be taken like Jericho.

— ORTEGA

Since these essays on Exodus are largely concerned with the interpretation of the narrative as it is found in midrashic sources, I would like to introduce them by offering a working definition of "midrash" and—perhaps more to the point—a personal meditation on the midrashic model for reading texts. My working definition—with all due caveats, acknowledging the essentially undefined nature of the term[1]—would be this:

> Midrash, derived from the root *darash*, "to seek out" or "to inquire," is a term used in rabbinic literature for the interpretive study of the Bible. The word is used in two related senses: first, to refer to the results of that interpretive exegesis; and, second, to describe the literary compilations in which the original interpretations, many of them first delivered and transmitted orally, were eventually collected.

These essays on Exodus make extensive use of some of these midrashic collections, notably Midrash Rabbah and Midrash Tanchuma. In addition, Rashi, the great French eleventh-century commentator on the Torah, includes in his text a significant selection of midrashic interpretations; often, I refer to Rashi's versions, where they offer interesting nuances on the original sources. Since Rashi's commentary has been absorbed into the bloodstream of Jewish culture, his midrashic material has become a kind of "second nature" in the traditional reading of the biblical text.

Before turning to a more personal view of the nature of midrashic reading, some technical observations are in order. These essays are based on the literary and liturgical device of "Parshat ha-Shavua," or "the Parsha": the Bible is read in Synagogue in weekly sections, so as to be completed in yearly cycles. Each Parsha is titled after a significant opening word. This device constitutes a way of living Jewish time; each week is saturated, as it were, with the material of that particular biblical section. One thinks, one studies, one lives the Parsha. If one is a teacher, this process is intensified. It is as a result of years of teaching the Bible in this form that I have come to articulate the ideas in this book.

Since on one level, then, this book began life as oral presentations, delivered to a wide range of students, of all ages, backgrounds, and intellectual habits, these essays remain separate attempts to engage with a particular literary unit, the Parsha of the particular week. They address themes that arise compellingly from the Torah text, often from the midrashic or other interpretations of the text. On another level, however, they flow into one another, engaging with the narrative of the Exodus as a whole, and addressing the themes of the grand narrative: redemption, revelation, betrayal, and the quest for "God in our midst."

In my approach, the biblical text is not allowed to stand alone, but has its boundaries blurred by later commentaries and by a persistent intertextuality that makes it impossible to imagine that meaning is somehow transparently present in the isolated text. Such an approach represents perhaps the greatest difficulty for the modern reader. It continues, in a sense, the rabbinic mode of reading, where "the rabbis imagined themselves a *part* of the whole, participating in Torah rather than operating on it at an analytic distance . . . [I]t follows that the words of interpretation cannot be isolated in any rigorously analytical way from the words of Torah itself."[2] Elliot Wolfson articulates this reading practice: "the base text of revelation is thought to comprise within itself layers of interpretation, and the works of interpretation on the biblical canon are considered revelatory in nature."[3]

The blurring of boundaries between revelation and interpretation, between the written and the oral Torah, is a fundamental mode of the rabbinic imagination. In this book, I have adopted this mode. I confess to a perhaps naive sense of the naturalness of this mode. However, as I invite the reader to enter the world of midrashic reading, I would like to offer an account of my reading practice, of how I understand the midrashic enterprise.

Central to this enterprise is the telling of stories that fill in gaps in the written biblical text. For instance, the midrash that, in a sense, engenders this book—about women's play with mirrors and the "secret of redemption"[4]—intends to explain a mysterious verse at the end of Exodus: "He made the laver of copper and its stand of copper, from the mirrors of the women who thronged, who came in throngs to the entrance of the Tent of Meeting" (38:8). The reader is baffled: *Which* mirrors (*the* mirrors)? What is the purpose of this specific gift to the Mishkan (Tabernacle)? Why is the expression *tzava*—to throng, to proliferate—repeated? Why is this particular copper contribution singled out from the larger mass of copper donated to the Mishkan? The midrash offers a narrative and, consequently, an interpretation of the enigmatic text: The women *created* the hosts, the throngs of Israel by their play with mirrors. As the midrash puts it: "It was all done with mirrors!"

Such a narrative spins away from the biblical text; in a sense, it seems unrooted, fantastic. Yet close study of the midrash reveals multiple skeins of connection, a network of textual roots within the language of the Bible. And—perhaps more importantly—the midrash offers an answer to a repressed question: How are this people to be redeemable? Can they be imagined as, in some sense, generating their own freedom? If we make use of the classic image of birth, must we have recourse to a forced birth, a forceps delivery, in imagining the relations of God the "midwife" and the newborn?[5] Or is there some way of catching the elusive moment of inner transformation that creates human possibility where before there was only necessity? The "secret of redemption," as the Rabbis call it, is the real problem at the heart of this midrash.

While the question of "redeemability" is repressed in the biblical text, it is articulated in many midrashic sources, and it emerges significantly in Rashi's commentary. Here, I would like to claim that this articulation of the repressed is the genius of midrashic narrative. Adopting the psychoanalytic model, I suggest that the *peshat*, or plain meaning of the text, functions as the conscious layer of meaning; while the midrashic stories and exegeses intimate unconscious layers, encrypted traces of more complex meaning. The public, overt, triumphal narrative of redemption is therefore diffracted in the midrashic texts into multiple, contradictory, unofficial narratives which, like the unconscious, undercut, destabilize the public narrative.

The result is a plethora of possible stories of redemption. Some of these will be attributed to "the enemy": they are false, adversarial narratives,

Egyptian narratives, narratives of obtuse misunderstanding. These counter-narratives, the demonized expression of unthinkable thoughts, construct the official Israelite history of the Exodus as incomplete, inflated, or mythic invention. In chapter 3, I discuss the problem of such counter-narratives and the implications of the Rabbis' willingness to articulate them.

Most significant, however, is the midrashic hospitality to the very concept of multiple alternative narratives. Time and time again, the magisterial biblical history of the Exodus is fractured in these midrashic versions. Moreover, the biblical text itself seems to give warrant for such retellings. Several times, the Torah itself emphasizes the importance of telling the story to one's children and grandchildren. At certain moments, this imperative to narrate the Exodus becomes the very purpose of the historical event: it happened so that you may tell it. At the heart of the liberation account, indeed, God prepares Moses with a story to tell a future child; this rhetorical narrative, astonishingly, *precedes* the historical narrative of liberation.

One might perhaps assume that these stories of the future are standard retellings of the biblical narrative. Not so: the biblical text itself includes four versions of the narrative to respond to four hypothetical questioning sons of the future.[6] These become typologies of four sons, who are later characterized in the Haggadah—read each year on the night of Passover—as the wise, the wicked, the simple, and the one who does not know how to ask. Even in the biblical sources, where the four passages are dispersed, the *difference* between the four versions is remarkable. In the Haggadah, this difference is presented as a psychological response to different types of child; but even the biblical text seems to offer an invitation to modulate the story to meet varying rhetorical ends.

If the stories of the future are to be multiple, responsive to time and place and temperament, then the midrashic narratives exemplify this diffraction of the original narrative at its most radical. Essentially, I suggest, they raise both philosophical and psychological questions: about metaphysical truth and about the nature of the self. The notion that knowledge of reality is singular, absolute, static, and eternal is tested in these midrashic narratives of the foundational events in Jewish history. The midrashic versions convey a plural, contextual, constructed, and dynamic vision of reality. The "Platonic ideal" in the history of philosophy is described by Isaiah Berlin: it posits

> . . . that all genuine questions must have one true answer and one only, all the rest being necessarily errors; in the second place, that there must be a dependable path towards the discovery of these truths; in the third

> place, that the true answers, when found, must necessarily be compatible with one another and form a single whole, for one truth cannot be incompatible with another—that we knew *a priori*. This kind of omniscience was the solution of the cosmic jigsaw puzzle.[7]

As against this view, which obtained in Western philosophy till the late nineteenth century, the midrashic literature presents a heterogeneous, even—consciously and ambivalently—a heretical multiplicity of answers.[8] Exodus as a narrative that consistently deploys the "omnipotence effect," to use Meir Sternberg's term, is significantly diffracted by the many counter-narratives that the midrash generates from within the triumphal and unequivocal master story. "What really happened in Egypt?" becomes a less important question than "How best to tell the story? Where to begin? What in the master story speaks to one and therefore makes one speak?"

The psychological dimension of these counter-narratives is no less crucial. Diffracted narratives interrogate the nature of the self. The American psychoanalyst Stephen Mitchell describes one facet of the problem:

> People often experience themselves, at any given moment, as containing or being a "self" that is complete in the present; a "sense of self" often comes with a feeling of substantiality, presence, integrity, and fullness. Yet selves change and are transformed continually over time; no version of self is fully present at any instant, and a single life is composed of many selves. An experience of self takes place necessarily in a moment of time; it fills one's psychic space, and other, alternative versions of self fade into the background. A river can be represented in a photograph, which fixes its flow and makes it possible for it to be viewed and grasped. Yet the movement of the river, in its larger course, cannot be grasped in a moment. Rivers and selves, like music and narrative, take time to happen in.[9]

The "self" that was liberated from Egypt—whether we consider the people as a psychological unit, or imagine an individual participant in the Exodus—experienced a limited, fragmentary version of events and a provisional sense of his or her own self. It is precisely through narration, by fulfilling the biblical imperative to tell the story, by the continuing interaction between parents and children, that transformed versions of self and of the meanings of liberation will be generated.

In *The Magic Mountain*, Thomas Mann discusses the use of narrative to experience the self in time:

> [T]ime is the medium of narration, as it is the medium of life. Both are inextricably bound up with it, as inextricably as are bodies in space. Similarly, time is the medium of music; music divides, measures, articulates time . . . Thus music and narration are alike, in that they can only present themselves as a flowing, as a succession in time, as one thing after another; and both differ from the plastic arts, which are complete in the present, and unrelated to them save as all bodies are, whereas narration—like music—even if it should try to be completely present at any given moment, would need time to do it in.[10]

Narrative needs time to do its work, to renegotiate the sense of total presence and fullness that the self craves. This, I suggest, is the core tension that the midrashic narratives express. By intimating unconscious conflicts about living in time, about the self as multiple, diffracted, discontinuous, the midrash often confronts the apparent simplicity of the biblical narrative with a more complex and nuanced notion of the self.

In the midrashic account of the Exodus, these conflicts come to a head in the narrative of the Golden Calf.[11] Here, the dilemmas of temporality are figured in grotesque and yet inevitable form. Moses' "lateness" in descending the mountain precipitates a panic response whose shock waves spread wide and deep. In the midrashic versions, and in commentaries profoundly influenced by these versions, all the certainties of liberation, on the psychological as well as the historical and philosophical planes, are destabilized. Possible demonic narratives are released that will shape the nightmares of the future. The people experience the whips and scorns of time; the melancholy of those who do not know, in Julia Kristeva's expression, "how to lose"; the insecurity of those who require certainty and yearn for total presence, who are, as one nineteenth-century Chasidic thinker has it, impatient with that need for *prayer* that is the posture of those who live within the veils of time.[12]

For the midrash to read in the biblical text such intimations of the unconscious life of a people becomes legitimate, in view of one necessary assumption of the rabbinic mind: the implied author of the Torah is God. As Daniel Boyarin succinctly puts it: "This is not a theological or dogmatic claim but a semiotic one . . . If God is the implied author of the Bible, then the gaps, repetitions, contradictions, and heterogeneity of the biblical text must be *read* . . ."[13] The midrashic search for multiple levels of meaning, the attempt to retrieve unconscious layers of truth, is warranted by the assumption that, as God's work, the Torah encompasses all. "Turn it, and turn it, for all is in it," says Ben Bag Bag,[14] using the image of the plow turning the earth, breaking, transforming, reversing, subverting. Two thousand years later, such an image of excavation becomes the informing image in Freud's project: to unearth the repressed life that is encrypted within the human experience. The psychoanalytic project, like the midrashic one, represents a dissatisfaction with surface meanings, and a confidence that rich if disturbing lodes seam the earth's depths. The activity of the plowman is not only legitimate but imperative: in this way, the interpreter responds to the claim of God's text.

At this juncture I would like to discuss one specific example of the midrashic retrieval of unconscious traces from within the biblical narrative. By contrast with the Genesis sagas, the absence of women from the narrative of Exodus—and indeed from all the later books of the Bible—is quite striking. This is not, of course, a total absence. There is the opening sequence in which women figure prominently: Jochebed, Miriam, Pharaoh's daughter, the midwives, Moses' wife, Zipporah. All are related to the theme of birth, all are dedicated to what Vaclav Havel calls the "hidden sphere" that endangers the totalitarian structure: to the baby crying within the brick.[15] Once this theme has been established within the biblical text, however, women essentially disappear. Miriam makes a brief reappearance, singing and dancing at the Red Sea, and later, in Numbers 12, she is afflicted with leprosy for maligning her brother Moses. Aside from this, there is one significant biblical moment devoted to women: in Numbers (27:1–12), the daughters of Zelofhad successfully claim a share in their father's inheritance. A minor reference to women places them among the "wise-of-heart" who weave cloth for the Mishkan (Exod 35:25–26).

The omission of women from the narrative can, of course, be seen as simply that—an omission, a lack of specific interest in the feminine, which is absorbed into the larger body of the "children of Israel." However, Rashi precedes the feminist movement by many centuries when, in an extraordinary midrashic comment, he excludes women from the most intense moments in the biblical drama: they simply did not participate in the major rebellions of the people in the wilderness. Rashi comments on the final census of the people before entering the Holy Land:

> "In this [census], no man survived from the original census of Moses and Aaron, when they had counted the Israelites in the wilderness of Sinai"

> (Num 26:64): But the women were not subjected to the decree against the Spies, because they loved the Holy Land. The men said, "Let us appoint (*nitna*) a leader to return to Egypt" (14:4); while the women said, "Appoint (*t'na*) for us a holding among our father's brothers" (27:4). That is why the story of Zelofhad's daughters is narrated directly after this.

Rashi's point is simple but revolutionary in its implications. Taking "man" literally, he limits the destruction of a generation, in punishment for the sin of the Spies, to the males only. While all the *men* over twenty died in the course of the forty years' wandering, the women survived—because, unlike the men, they loved the Land of Israel.

Rashi's midrashic claim is provocative in the extreme. With barely a hint in the text to support him, he presents a startlingly asymmetrical demographic image of the people who entered the Holy Land, with women in the large majority. His basis in the text is the expression "No *man* survived . . ." and the fact that the story of the daughters of Zelofhad, who were inspired by love of the Land, immediately follows: the sequence invites the reader to notice that these women and the rebels involved with the Spies use the same word (*t'na/nitna*) to opposite effect.

The compelling implication of Rashi's comment, however, is not the demographic one. Rather it is that the absence of women from the text does *not* necessarily mean that they are assimilated into the general "children of Israel," as the plain meaning (*peshat*) of the text might indicate. Women have a separate, hidden history, which is not conveyed on the surface of the text. This history is a faithful, loving, and vital one, which excludes them from the dramas of sin and punishment that constitute the narrative of the wilderness. Indeed, Rashi's midrashic source includes *both* the major crises in the wilderness as dramas in which women were not incriminated:

> In that generation, women would repair what men tore down. For you find that when Aaron said, "Break off your golden earrings [to make the Golden Calf]," the women refused and protested, as it is said, "The whole people broke off the golden rings from their ears" (Exod 32:3). The women did not participate in the making of the Golden Calf. Similarly, when the Spies slandered [the Holy Land], and the people complained, God issued His decree against them for saying, "We cannot go up against the people . . ." (Num 13:31). But the women were not part of that movement, as it is written, "No *man* of them survived . . ."—no *man*, not no *woman*, since it was the men who refused to enter the Holy Land, while the women approached Moses to ask for an inheritance (27:1).[16]

Women emerge as exemplary in this midrash: they repair what men have torn down, they reaffirm the value of love of the Holy Land and loyalty to the one God that men, in the rebellions of the Spies and of the Golden Calf, have eroded. This admirable history of women, however, is found only in the midrashic texts. Within the biblical narrative it is barely intimated. The implication of this is profoundly paradoxical. In the written text, the absence of women would seem to imply that they are included in the large dramas of the Israelites in the wilderness; it is precisely in the midrash that women figure as having a separate, hidden history. In effect, the midrash makes the reader aware of a mistaken reading: all along, women have been *really* absent, *really* elsewhere. An alternative history, the midrashic history of women, would take us, at least at the most significant moments in the narrative, beyond the margins of the biblical account.

Women's story can be seen, then, at least at certain critical junctures, as the repressed narrative of the biblical text. Midrash retains the traces of that narrative and brings it to consciousness, with marked effects on the manifest level of meaning. All the midrashic narratives about women, indeed, can be registered in this way: the women's mirror-play with their husbands in Egypt; the rich material on the experience of women at the Red Sea and on Miriam's song/dance; Miriam's well and its disappearance; and the strange emphasis on the female role in Korah's rebellion.[17] All construct a counter-reality to the one officially inscribed in the Torah; all expose a complex ferment disguised by the lucidity of the text. Like the unconscious in the psychic economy, women remain a latent presence in their very absence; they represent the "hidden sphere" which must remain hidden if it is to do its work with full power, but which must be revealed in some form if that work is to be integrated.

If women serve as the unconscious of the biblical story, the place where they come to light is the midrashic narrative. We have suggested that midrash articulates the unconscious of the text: the hidden narratives, almost entirely camouflaged by the words of the Torah, emerge from the spaces, from the gaps in meaning, from the dream resonance of those words ("No *man*, not no *woman* . . ."). This tradition of reading is intensively developed in a later period by the chasidic masters, who treat the midrashic texts as having, in their turn, emerged into conscious meaning, and who play with the latent meanings within and between those texts.

Ultimately, conscious and unconscious layers of meaning inform one another; the written and oral Torah are not separated by an impermeable wall. The conscious level alone, the written text with its plain meaning, the undifferentiated history of the Israelite people in the wilderness, would provide a sterile version of the Exodus. It is the interplay of conscious and unconscious motifs that makes for the grand narrative, which is capable of providing the matrix within which future narratives can take shape. The "particulars of rapture," in Wallace Stevens's phrase, can evolve only where

Two things of opposite natures seem to depend
On one another, as a man depends
On a woman, day on night, the imagined

On the real. This is the origin of change.
Winter and spring, cold copulars, embrace
And forth the particulars of rapture come.

—WALLACE STEVENS, "NOTES TOWARD A SUPREME FICTION"[18]

The grand narrative of the Exodus, then, must be a midrashic narrative in which the hidden, the repressed, can be at least partially witnessed. If the Exodus is to be a narrative for all times and all places, as Sefath Emeth, for example, claims,[19] it must be capable of particular reincarnations through time. As in Roland Barthes's famous example of those names of countries which cover the map in such large capitals that they become effectively invisible, the Exodus has come to constitute the very framework of Jewish perception and, for that very reason, is only partially visible.

This metanarrative of the Exodus is the subject of a lyrical passage in R. Kook's *Olath Re'iya*:

> The Exodus was such an event as only a crudely superficial eye could read as an event that happened and ended, and that has remained as a magnificent memory in the history of Israel and in the general history of mankind. But in reality, with a penetrating consciousness, we come to realize that the essential event of the Exodus is one that *never ceases at all.* The public and manifest revelation of God's hand in world history is an explosion of the light of the divine soul which lives and acts throughout the world and which Israel, through its greatness and training in holiness, merits to disseminate powerfully through all the habitations of darkness to all generations. The essential work of the Exodus continues to have its effect; the divine seed which achieved Israel's redemption from Egypt is

still constantly active, in the process of becoming, without interruption or disturbance.[20]

All the life of the worlds, of individuals and nations, all power of generation and regeneration, can be read in the metahistory of the Exodus. For R. Kook, the first chief rabbi of the restored State of Israel, it is the organic connection between the "explosion" of particulars and the rapture of the Exodus that is accessible to the penetrating consciousness. The Exodus has no end and no limit. Such a view sets itself firmly against the historicizing consciousness, which Susan Sontag has characterized as the "predatory embrace" of the modern period, "the gesture whereby man indefatigably patronizes himself . . . More and more, the shrewdest thinkers and artists are precocious archaeologists of these ruins-in-the-making."[21]

From R. Kook's perspective, the original liberation from Egypt participates in a continuum of sunbursts: the history of man's possibilities is not exhausted. Indeed, in the tradition of Chasidic thought from which he draws his inspiration, the original Exodus need not even be regarded as the overwhelming epic event that reduces all future experiences of liberation to pale replicas. Precisely the opposite dynamic may be true: the people who left Egypt were perhaps *unfit* for redemption, incapable of hearing God's word in any real fullness. Their hopes in leaving the land of terror were shriveled by the cramped conditions of their nurture; they were cramped hopes, Egyptian-shaped hopes. Like the patient entering analysis, who can have only a distorted view of the process awaiting him, of the way in which it will expand the underlying structures of experience, the Israelites leave Egypt

more like a man
Flying from something that he dreads than one
Who sought the thing he loved.

—WILLIAM WORDSWORTH, "TINTERN ABBEY"

And like the analyst whose hopes for the patient are radically different from those of the patient for himself, God begins a process with His people in a stage of arrested development, a process that will lead them into fuller, unimagined life.

However, in this scenario, in which God's hopes and the people's hopes are profoundly different, there is a hidden assumption about the arrested "truer self" of Israel, the self that harks back to the foundational narratives of Genesis. Both analyst and patient share a hope for the unfolding of that truer self. But such a shared hope is at first almost invisible; only the discordance is visible.

Intensely challenging passages in Chasidic literature tell of the development of that divine seed in history. Later narratives of the Exodus complete and compensate and restructure the inadequacies of the historical event as the people first lived it. Redemption is engendered by the changing stories of redemption that, with richer idiom, amplify the particulars of rapture.

Sefath Emeth, for example, addresses the unconsummated experience of the historical Exodus.[22] Telling the story of the Exodus is so imperative because of the *chipazon*, the panic haste, in which the original generation left Egypt. The existential quality of the historical Exodus, that is, reflected a rawness, an immaturity of spirit that later narratives, in some sense, will bring to ripeness.[23] In this way, Sefath Emeth beautifully explains the people's "deafness" to the possibility of redemption: "And they could not hear Moses for shortness of spirit and hard labor" (6:9). What they are unable or unwilling to hear is God's promise couched in four synonyms for redemption ("I shall release . . . I shall save . . . I shall redeem . . . I shall take you to Me as a people . . ." [6:6–7])—the classic *arba leshonot geulah* (four languages of redemption). "And *therefore*," writes Sefath Emeth, "we must now tell the story of the Exodus!"

The paradox is compelling: out of the inadequacy of the historical event as it was registered by those who lived it is generated "Torah for all generations," each with its own language, its own existential framework for conceiving of redemption. Each generation thus has an exclusive opportunity to reorganize, reorder (*seder*—order—is the theme as well as the name of the Passover night) what originally was inchoate, disoriented. So "the story of redemption is constantly being revealed," as a fuller, more complex sense of self yields richer understandings of the master-narrative.

The four languages of redemption, then, represent the infinite particular idioms that will inform the narratives of the future, which will continuously articulate aspects of what was only implicit in the original event. In the context of an uninterrupted interaction with the master narrative, the people will engender forms of testimony to God's redemption that are not merely restatements of the known, but testings, trials of self and world that give birth to new structures of knowledge. Like the technique known as "remastering," in which precious original musical performances are liberated years later from the limitations and distortions of primitive recordings, the later languages of redemption seek to liberate an original divine impulse in an unprecedented manner.[24]

Such a concept of narrative cuts away the security of an ideal original narrative. Indeed, in a rather disconcerting sense it dismantles the very platform that the original narrative uses to do its work: a privileged story of redemption replete with miracles, an inspired and infallible leader whose every word comes from God. The issue is not the objective truth of these ideas, but the people's need to wean themselves of the infantile longings that have invested Moses with such powerful transferential significance. The power of the transferential fantasy helps to move the patient towards healing; but, at a more mature stage, the fantasy must be dissolved. The anguish of this paradox is the subject of chapter 9: in the light of a comment by Meshech Chochma[25]—Talmudist and contemporary of Freud—Moses' "transferential" role becomes the latent theme of the Golden Calf episode.

If fuller and richer languages for redemption are to evolve, fantasies that fetishize the past must be relinquished. The "particulars of rapture" can come forth only when "Two things of opposite natures" interplay. This is where the midrashic mode is powerful. Here, past and present interact: the original text of *Exodus* and the narrative that will endow that matrix with generative force. Here is the mutual dependence—"as a man depends On a woman" (Stevens); for without the black-on-white words of the scriptural narrative nothing can be generated, but without the evolving "languages," idioms of redemption, the foundational rapture recedes beyond recall. Or, more importantly: a strong written narrative endows the future with a structure of meaning; but it is the *weakness*, the gaps, the "unthought known" (Christopher Bollas's expression) in that narrative that paradoxically invites the future to discover the primordial energy repressed in the text. As we have seen, it is the Israelites' *inability* to appropriate their own redemption that makes redemption a matter of endless testimony.

In this sense, I have suggested that there are two narratives of Exodus: the narrative of the day, and the narrative of the night (see chapter 3). The day-narrative tells of the public, manifest, consciously perceived and transmitted liberation from Egypt; the night-narrative tells of *chipazon*, of panic haste, of unassimilated experience, as it tells also of God who "leaps" (*pasach*)—a lurching, syncopated movement—over houses, creating gaps for liberation. It is this second narrative that engenders questions and multiple, not always harmonious narratives. This narrative, too, is the domain of the unconscious, of midrashic counterworlds that endow the manifest world of the biblical text with depth and vitality.

The most potent image for the interaction of opposites that I am trying to convey remains the erotic one: ". . . as a man depends On a woman . . . This is the origin of change." It is for this reason, it seems to me, that the midrash is fascinated by that alternative world of the feminine, which must not be revealed, but which must be intimated. The mirrors in which women play with their husbands, "swinging them with words,"[26] remain, for me, the most evocative symbol of redemption. Here is the mode of infinite possibility, of six hundred thousand babies at a birth—and it is all done with mirrors. A river of coruscating souls, endlessly varied, shimmers forth from these mirrors: who can predict the force of these particulars of rapture? And yet, Moses' voice, suspicious, fastidious, is retained as a counterforce in the midrash. The effect is of an almost unbearable tension: even as God chides Moses, supporting the women with their mirror play, the values of *gezera*, of what must be, of order and consciousness and control, are not totally neutralized.

Freedom and law, possibility and necessity: these are the poles between which the electric current of redemption must run, if the particulars of rapture are to come forth. In terms of reading practice, this means a dialectical tension between *peshat* (plain meaning) and midrashic narrative. In philosophical or psychological terms, this means an awareness of the tension between "finitude and infinitude," to use Kierkegaard's expression.

The central issue for Kierkegaard, and for readers of Exodus, is freedom: "freedom is the dialectical aspect of the categories of possibility and necessity."[27] Each mode has its own danger, its form of despair. On the one hand, there is "[t]he fantastic . . . which leads a person out into the infinite in such a way that it only leads him away from himself";[28] in its relation to God, as well, "this infinitizing can so sweep a man off his feet that his state is simply an intoxication. To exist before God may seem unendurable to a man because he cannot come back to himself, become himself."[29] On the other hand, there is another kind of despair which "seems to permit itself to be tricked out of its self by 'the others' . . . such a person forgets himself, forgets his name divinely understood."[30] This second despair, the despair of finitude, is entirely unregarded in the world: this is the pathology of the *gezera* modality, which is vindicated by all the prudential wisdom of the world:

> For example, we say that one regrets ten times for having spoken to once for having kept silent—and why? Because the external fact of having spoken can involve one in difficulties, since it is an actuality. But to have kept silent! And yet this is the most dangerous of all . . . Not to venture is

> prudent. And yet, precisely by not venturing it is so terribly easy to lose what would be hard to lose, however much one lost by risking, and in any case never this way, so easily, so completely, as if it were nothing at all—namely, oneself.[31]

Between silence and speech, silence is the more dangerous: its very safety endangers the self. Through such paradoxes, Kierkegaard conveys the difficulties of the dialectic: between finitude and infinitude, possibility and necessity, the human being struggles for an authentic freedom.

This struggle, I suggest, lies at the very heart of the project of reading Exodus.[32] Between the self that is and the self, or selves, that may be, the particulars of rapture are always being reborn. It is for this reason that the Exodus, and the Passover[33] festival that celebrates it, focuses so compellingly on telling and retelling the story. It is only by taking the real risks of language, by rupturing the autistic safety of silence, that the self can reclaim itself. To venture into words, narratives, is to venture everything for the sake of that "self before God."[34]

And yet—and here, the dialectic becomes most painful—perhaps all the many words of the Exodus narrative, of the narratives of the future, specifically of the Seder night, all in a sense weave endlessly around the inexpressible heart of the matter. As though by indirections to find direction out, we talk and we tell at such length because we cannot articulate what is essential. We cannot pluck out the heart of the mystery. Perhaps all the narratives in the book of Exodus are externalized versions of an intimate story more truly told in The Song of Songs. This, at least, is the midrashic view of the matter. The longing, the dynamics of desire: this is the subject of Exodus.

So we speak and unpack our hearts with words, knowing that the essential longing is enthralled in silence. R. Hutner[35] writes of this tension, of the repressed desire like an erotic longing that, inexpressible, erupts in displaced forms. These complex eruptions of language are the progeny of a great silence.

Ludwig Wittgenstein said, "Whereof one cannot speak, one must be silent." R. Hutner describes the Jewish practice of a kind of verbal catharsis that resembles the Freudian; his version might be, "Whereof one cannot speak, one must say everything." Commenting on the *lechem oni*, the bread of affliction (i.e. the matza) eaten on the Seder night, he bases his essay on the Talmudic expansion: "bread to which *one responds with many words*" (a pun on *oni* [affliction] and *onin* [response]).[36] These many words of the Seder night, of the continuing narratives of Exodus, represent an absence, an unattainable longing for full presence. The molten core of the self remains unreleased, unspeakable. *Therefore*, the cascade of language, ideas, images, which, by displacement, evoke a speechless passion. On Passover, the mouth speaks (*peh sach*): all the particulars of rapture intimate an absolute desire.

R. Hutner's account has a somber, almost tragic resonance. Ultimately, there is no expressing the heart of the matter. All the coruscations of possibility, all the midrashic versions of an original moment of liberation, all leave some core self still in prison, still in Egypt (*Mitzrayim*), still constrained in narrow places (*meitzarim*). All the mirrors of all the women cannot offer total liberation.

And yet, even in R. Hutner's somber account, there is the moment of surprise: language is the very means by which the imprisoned heart gains freedom. As in the psychoanalytic model, speaking of many things, one comes by indirection at the core. This generation of truth through language, the experience of speaking beyond one's means, has an unwitting character. It happens in the interaction between two people: "one does not have to *possess* or *own* the truth in order to effectively *bear witness* to it."[37]

Language as testimony, then, can give access to the hidden passion; in a sense, the "many words" of the Exodus narratives beget that passion. This experience is, one might say, the very taste of freedom:[38] the taste in the mouth that is impossible to communicate to those unfamiliar with it, and that makes one willing to become a medium of testimony.

I think of midrash with its "many words" concealing/revealing a central mystery as offering a bridge between old hopes and the fullness of an unknown future identity. New narratives of redemption create the very freedom that the original protagonists could not "hear." The old hopes, as Wordsworth intimates, are born from dread. The midrashic mode offers a transformation of those old hopes and a new way of imagining the self. And the quest for such transformation continues to inform the reading practice and the spiritual hopes of those who enter this world of Exodus. This, at any rate, has been my quest in this book. I ask not to share the "secret of redemption"—that is far beyond my reach; but to find those who will hear with me a particular idiom of redemption. And within the particulars of rapture to hear what cannot be expressed.

I Shemoth

THE MIRROR OF REDEMPTION

[Exodus 1:1–6:1]

1. *Fit for Redemption? The Human Context* 

Israel and Egypt: The Mosaic Distinction

In Jewish tradition, the Exodus from Egypt marks the birth of the Israelite nation and religion. Conceptually, it marks a basic separation between cultures: a distinction between true and false in religion that Jan Assmann, in *Moses the Egyptian*, calls the Mosaic distinction: "The space severed or cloven by this distinction is the space of Western monotheism."[1]

How was this distinction conceived? What are the symbolic values attached to each of the two figures, Israel and Egypt? Underlying the issues of truth and falsehood, the Mosaic distinction, in its more profound ethical dimensions, attributes psychological and spiritual values to each figure. The stakes of redemption, of birth to a full selfhood, are large: the issue is not narrowly theological but rather is related to all that makes individual and collective life fruitful or sterile.

Particularly in the midrashic sources and in Chasidic texts, questions as to the inner meaning of redemption generate a construction of Egypt as the world of constriction, paralysis, and silence. The pun often found in Chasidic writings associates *Mitzrayim* (Egypt) with *meitzarim* (straits).

Egypt becomes a country of the spirit, constricted and, in a real sense, inescapable.

This is the fundamental issue of the Exodus: how to be redeemed when Egypt, that enervating soulscape, has one in its pincer grip? From such a perspective, Israel in Egypt *cannot* be redeemed; no separation is possible—in the same way as, in terms of mythic thought, the baby held in the womb *cannot* be born, must remain monstrously but all-too-plausibly immobilized forever.

The peculiar suffering of such inertia haunts the midrashic accounts of the time before the Exodus: "No slave ever escaped from Egypt" (Mekhilta). What makes release possible, or, in midrashic language, what makes the people *fit* for redemption? What is the turning point in the history of this unarticulated misery? And what, again in midrashic language, is the *secret* of redemption?

"And they swarmed . . ." —Blessing or Critique?

Exodus, the book of Exile and Redemption,[2] begins with a list of names:

> These are the names of the sons of Israel who came to Egypt with Jacob, each coming with his household: Reuben, Simeon, Levi, and Judah; Issachar, Zebulun, and Benjamin; Dan and Naftali, Gad and Asher. The total number of persons that were of Jacob's issue came to seventy, Joseph being already in Egypt. Joseph died, and all his brothers, and all that generation. (Exod 1:1–6)

These are the dead; listed, to tell the reader that they are no more. In Jewish tradition, the book is called The Book of Names: the reference is clearly to the names of the children of Israel, those individuals who, in a moment in history, went down to Egypt and died there, together with their brother, Joseph, who had preceded them.

What follows, however, on this meticulous listing of the dead, is an explosion of life, an almost surrealistic description of the spawning of a nation:

> And the children of Israel were fruitful and swarmed and multiplied and increased very greatly, so that the land was filled with them. (1:7)

Nameless, faceless, these too are the "children of Israel." How are we to read this description of their anonymous fecundity? There are two possible understandings. On the one hand, this is a celebration of fullness, of life burgeoning and uncontained. This reading would be a fulfillment of God's promise to Jacob: "Fear not to go down to Egypt, for I will make you there into a great nation" (Gen 46:3).[3] The redundant expressions of fertility have been read as denoting multiple births, healthy development, absence of fetal, infant, or adult mortality.[4] In the midrashic readings, there is a miraculous, even a whimsical sense of the outrageous victory of life over death: these, for instance, take the six expressions of fertility (they were fruitful, they swarmed, they multiplied, they increased, very, very much) to indicate that each woman gave birth to sextuplets ("six to a belly").[5]

The affirmation of life contained in these pounding synonyms intimates, in its very excess, a transcendent order of meaning: "Even though Joseph and his brothers died, their God did not die, but the children of Israel were fruitful and multiplied . . ."[6] The midrash here wants to decipher the cascade of births not only as blessing but as the "survival of God." The generation that connects with the meaningful past is all gone. But in some way that is not fully explained here, God expresses His undimmed vitality in the language of physical fertility.

An alternative reading of this passage, however, would take its cue from the ambiguous expression *vayishretzu*—"they swarmed." This can mean the blessing of extraordinary increase;[7] but it connotes a reptilian fecundity, which introduces a bizarre note in a description of human fertility.[8] In this second view, *vayishretzu* is a repellent description for a family fallen from greatness.

Seforno, the sixteenth-century Italian commentator, articulates this tragic historical reading most clearly. At first, he writes, there were individuals, named, highly evolved persons, who went down to Egypt. Immediately upon their deaths, names cease. What we have is masses of unindividuated "insect-like" conformists, whose whole effort is to assimilate to their surroundings, and whose unconscious drive is for lemming-like suicide:

> After the seventy original immigrants had died, they inclined toward the ways of *sheratzim*, of reptiles (an uncomplimentary reference to the pagan nations, whose concerns are entirely this-worldly). They ran through their lives in a headlong rush towards the abyss (a pun on *sheratzim/she-ratzim* = "those who run.") (1:7)

An existential failure is marked here: the grandchildren of Jacob have already lost their distinctness, their names, their sense of purpose.[9] They have assimilated themselves entirely to the surrounding culture. One significant detail that recurs in many midrashic sources is that the Israelites in Egypt stopped circumcising their children.[10] The sages read this drive to assimilation as, in effect, a death wish. Ironically, as both Seforno and his midrashic source point out, the Israelite assimilation project backfires, as it turns Pharaoh against them. Having abandoned their tradition and individuality, they at least share the blame for the fact that Pharaoh no longer recognizes them as Joseph's kin. Seforno tells a tale of justified persecution—not to exonerate Pharaoh, but to ground events in the history of a people who have, in two generations, lost their claim to their own names, and whose swarming is not a token of blessing, but a symptom of alienation from that true self that even a Pharaoh will acknowledge.

Seforno's reading, rooted as it is in traditional rabbinic commentaries, is deeply disturbing. For one thing, it stands against the more often quoted, certainly more consoling rabbinic sources that declare that the children of Israel in Egypt remained essentially untouched by their environment.[11] Particularly in matters of language—naming themselves and their world—as well as in their clothing, they held to their own identity. Even on the question of circumcision, there are midrashic sources that make precisely the opposite claim: that they never totally abandoned this fundamental covenantal practice.[12]

In addition to the problem of conflicting sources, there is the larger question of narrative meaning. What does Seforno gain by making the story one of guilt and punishment, within the evolving sense of self of the Jewish people? Surely Pharaoh is the unmitigated villain of the piece. Surely his story is one of unwarranted, fantastical malice and cruelty against a people whose only narrated sin is their fertility. ("Come, let us deal shrewdly with them, so that they may not increase; else in the event of war they may join our enemies in fighting against us and leave the country" [1:10]).

Seforno's reading of the people's "swarming" (*vayishretzu*) may seem to give some theological rationale for Israelite suffering. But this is not a necessary move. For, arching over most of Genesis, there is the unfulfilled decree—the *gezera*, as it is often called—of God's address to Abraham: "Know well that your offspring shall be strangers in a land not theirs, and they shall be enslaved and oppressed four hundred years . . ." (Gen 15:13). By the beginning of Exodus, the time has come for the decree to be applied, the time for alienation, for slavery, for oppression. Why, then, does Seforno introduce a motif of Israelite responsibility for the suffering that is decreed?

To this question, there is, of course, no unequivocal, historical answer. Perhaps the value of such a question lies simply in its pointing to a choice of interpretation. Seforno, we become aware, has constructed a narrative of failure, guilt, punishment, where the biblical text seemed to give us only the facts of suffering. His choice closes off certain kinds of understanding of history, of the lives of individuals and nations. Lawrence Weschler, in his study of the nature of modern totalitarianism, *Calamities of Exile*, notes that a position that insists on asserting one's own responsibility for a given situation "has heuristic value: it makes possible a future politics that otherwise might become lost in a bottomless sense of victimization and despair."[13] Concentrating on responsibility for one's own predicaments creates an emotional world in which inner growth becomes imaginable. In adopting this view of Israelite suffering, therefore, Seforno opens up difficult kinds of understanding. He invites us to reflect on the ways in which slavery, persecution, alienation—even when they are functions of a divine "edict"—are generated by human beings, in the freedom of their own narratives. And—in the same vein—on the meanings of redemption, exodus, freedom. In doing this, he stands in a tradition of commentators who read the Exodus narrative psychologically, spiritually, from the point of view of the victim who seeks redemption, in the intimate as well as the political sense.

Anonymity and Silence

The particular form of inadequacy that Seforno singles out has to do with names and anonymity. The names that begin—and entitle—the book are a marker for loss, as the narrative begins to tell of the nameless. Moses' parents are conspicuously unnamed at first mention—a "man from the house of Levi" and a "daughter of Levi." Pharaoh's daughter is likewise anonymous. Cumulatively, a world is composed where even the heroes have a faceless, unindividuated quality.

The other feature of the "anonymity" that characterizes the opening of the narrative is the silence of all voices but Pharaoh's. Implicit in Seforno's reading of the "swarming" modality is a vision of a primal, pre-linguistic stage of evolution, of masses of proliferating, reptilean creatures, who utter no response to Pharaoh's scheme, but move in a compelled surge towards the abyss. Language has failed; even the suffering, the harsh labor, the bitterness of their lives elicits from them no protest, not even an audible groan—no expression of awareness, of memory, outrage, or hope.

In this silence, the paradox of fertility is emphasized: "the more they were oppressed, the more they increased (*ken yirbeh*) and spread out, so that the Egyptians were sickened by the Israelites" (1:12). To the Egyptians, there is something repulsive about the silent fecundity of this people. Contrary to normal behavior patterns, harsh treatment, exhaustion, the unbearable weight of Egypt's burdens only serve, apparently, to make them reproduce at a faster rate.

Rashi comments: "This is the Holy Spirit speaking: 'You say, "Lest they increase," (*pen yirbeh—[1:10]*) but I say, "So they shall increase!" (*ken yirbeh*)'." The policy of persecution, Rashi reminds us, is expressly intended to prevent fertility. God is opposed to this—a head-on clash between intentionalities. For Rashi, the future tense (usually translated as the past continuous—"So they would increase") is the unheard idiom of God, whose words give meaning to the silent surge of reproduction. In the world of Egypt, however, His intentions are muted, find no resonance; only the alert midrashic reader may respond to the willful play of tenses in the text—"Let us see whose word will stand, Mine or yours . . ." adds Rashi's midrashic source.[14] Human language, Pharaoh's monologue against life, is challenged by the unheard word of God, working through unconscious flesh.

The Midwives' Rebellion

The first to speak back to Pharaoh are the technicians of birth, the midwives. Emerging from the anonymous, silent masses, ambiguous in their identity (midwives to the Hebrew women, or Hebrew midwives?), they are named and involved in dialogue with Pharaoh. What compels them to speak is their disobedience to Pharaoh's decree ("When you deliver the Hebrew women, look at the birthstool: if it is a boy, kill him; if it is a girl, let her live" [1:16].) Pharaoh's tone is the tone of *gezera*, edict: unequivocal, surgical in its categorization of possibilities. The command is to kill: the alternative—in the case of a girl baby—is *vachaya*—"let her be, let her live." The pivotal verb is "look": Pharaoh commands them to *see difference*, to analyze the situation in the very thrust of birth. This kind of seeing—boy/girl; death/life—is essential to the mode of *gezera*, of edict. The word, *gezera*, is, in fact, rooted in the verb "to cut," in the notion of separation, difference, analysis.

The midwives' disobedience is described with an idiom that has never before appeared in the Torah in just this form: "they feared God." We remember that Abraham, after he is released from the trial of the Akeda, the Binding of Isaac, is called a God-fearing person (Gen 22:12). The midwives, however, enact fear of God: they "do" it. Using the verb form—"they feared God"—conveys the sense of a moral act, that mobilizes the energy "not to do what the Egyptian king had told them; they let the boys live" (1:18).

This active "fearing God," which generates life for the boy babies is, essentially, a refusal to see as Pharaoh sees, to see difference. Traditionally, they are understood to have nurtured the babies, providing them with food and water (Rashi). This "fear of God" is a classic, heroic response to the edicts of tyrants. As Or HaChaim suggests, the very extremity of the edict forces a new moral vision upon the midwives, a radical choice between life and death. Disobedience to Pharaoh becomes more than merely a refusal to kill, it becomes a total dedication to nourishing life. The narrative has conveyed, in mid-flight, as it were, the very moment of "fearing God," its free assumption of responsibility.

Pharaoh then reproaches them, not with negligence, but with giving, preserving life. And it is at this point that the first words of resistance in Exodus are spoken. Against the absurd reproach of Pharaoh ("Why have you done this thing, and kept the children alive?"), against the unself-conscious brutality of Pharaoh's implicit question: "Why life?" they answer: "They (the Hebrew women) are vigorous—*chayoth*, lively: before the midwife can come to them, they have given birth." In terms of the Hebrew idioms used, their answer is: "These women are alive: before the birth-aide can come, they give birth."

Some radical, irreducible confrontation is marked in these first words against Pharaoh. To speak against the *gezera* is, in a real sense, impossible. The only appropriate response to a *gezera* is silence. To utter words is to create an alternative world, a world of undifferentiated life. This is, indeed, the claim of the Hebrew midwives: the Hebrew women are *not like* the Egyptian women; an alternative realm to Pharaoh's "Egyptian" realm is sketched in their words. In this Hebrew women's world, life and birth happen irrepressibly.

Moses' Early Life

Pharaoh's next move is to command the public murder of boy babies: they are to be thrown in the river. And the next words spoken are those of

Pharaoh's daughter, when she opens the casket where the infant Moses is hidden: "This must be a Hebrew child" (2:6). Her words are not apparently expressive of any particular emotion—simply a phrase of identification. The baby's sister hears her words, as she waits at a distance "to know what would befall him" (2:4). She immediately enters into a conversation with the princess about a wet nurse for the baby. She brings her mother, who is commissioned to nurse her own child.

This passage, with its detailed discussion of the nursing arrangements for the infant Moses, seems unnecessarily florid in a narrative that is otherwise quite sparing of detail. However, although apparently of purely technical interest, this passage, with its short, practical interchanges between women, focuses our attention on the necessities of life. What is needed for the survival of the infant in a culture of death is not simply a private maternal breast—the child cannot be hidden beyond the earliest phase of life—but a discourse between those who are moved to dangerous words about nurturance.

This is a conspiracy of three women, who return the baby to the mother's breast, its natural place; only by *speaking* of nursing does this most natural function become possible. From the princess's viewpoint, this is clearly a "nursing-for-me." ("Take this child and nurse it for me . . ." [2:9]). The wet nurse is serving as an aide to her, in her desire to bring life out of the destructive waters.

This episode turns, we notice, on a specific way of seeing: the princess "*saw* the basket among the reeds . . . When she opened it, she *saw* that it was a child, a boy crying . . ." (2:5–6). The next episode gives us Moses' first significant act as an adult, also in terms of a way of seeing:

> Some time after that, when Moses had grown up, he went out to his kinsfolk and *saw* their burdens. He *saw* an Egyptian beating a Hebrew, one of his brothers. He turned this way and that, and he *saw* that no one was about, and he struck down the Egyptian and hid him in the sand. (2:11–12)

"Moses had grown up"—this is the second use of the verb: the first, in the previous verse, had indicated a process of development ended in weaning and in the princess's assuming the maternal role (2:10). Now, again, a phase of growth is indicated in his emergence from the palace, to see the sufferings of his brothers. The phases of growth have a paradoxical symmetry. To become *gadol*—great, grown—means to come to the end of a stage of development, to become capable of confronting new experiences. Moses leaves his birth-mother, the nursing breast, and moves to the princess's palace; Moses later leaves that palace, and is able, strangely, to recognize in the brutalized slaves outside, his own brothers.

"He saw their sufferings"—what they had to bear, the weight of their existence. Rashi comments: "He gave his eyes and his heart to be distressed over them." Moses seeing is Moses allowing himself to be affected, to suffer with those who are unexpectedly called "his brothers." This kind of seeing is contrasted with the seeing essential to Pharaoh's edict: "Look at the birth-stool . . ." (1:16). Pharaoh's was a seeing of disjunction and difference; while Moses' first significant act of maturity is an act of empathy with those who seem, physically, socially, and existentially, so different from him. He looks at those crushed under Egyptians' burdens with what Jorge Semprun calls a "pure fraternal gaze."[15]

It is on the basis of that vulnerable empathy that he then "sees" the Egyptian taskmaster battering one of his "brothers": sees, that is, the axis of difference now running between those who inflict cruelty and those who suffer it. It is then, for the third time, that he "sees that there was no one about, and he struck down the Egyptian" (*vayach*—the same verb as described the Egyptian striking the Hebrew). This third "seeing" conveys the unavoidable responsibility to act on the basis of a complex empathy.

Fit for Redemption?

On the following day the episode reaches its climax: Moses tries to prevent violence between two Hebrews (now no longer described as his brothers). He is taunted:

> "Who made you chief and ruler over us? Do you mean to kill me as you killed the Egyptian?" Moses was frightened, and thought, "Then the matter is known!" (2:14).

The reason for his fear is evident: in spite of his original caution, his killing of the Egyptian has become public knowledge. And indeed in the next verse we read that he has to flee Pharaoh's death warrant. But why does the narrative linger over the dialogue between Moses and the menacing Hebrew? And, in particular, why that response of Moses to his threat: "Then the matter is known!"? The narrative would have read quite smoothly without those three Hebrew words; Moses' fear is sufficiently explained in the text.

At this point the midrash interleaves a theme that we shall encounter time and time again. Rashi integrates this theme consistently into his commentary:

> *Moses was afraid*: He was anxious because he saw among the Israelites wicked people, informers. He said, "I am concerned that they may not be worthy (*ra'uy*) to be redeemed."

> *Then the matter is known:* "The matter I was perplexed about: how did Israel sin, more than all the seventy nations, that they are oppressed with harsh labor? But now I see that they are worthy (*ra'uy*) of it."

These are Moses' first words. In Rashi's reading, they reveal a Moses who has been silently perplexed over the meaning of the suffering he witnesses: why do the Israelites deserve their suffering? He has a moment of insight, shedding light on an old enigma. He realizes that wicked Israelites have spread the word about his killing of the Egyptian. It is this discovery of moral corruption among his people that causes him fear, or anxiety: "Perhaps they are not fit for redemption . . . Now I see that they are fit for slavery."

The question that preoccupies Moses is of the "fit" status of the Israelites. The word *ra'uy* means "fit," "worthy," literally "to be seen as . . ." Moses is engaged in an effort to see his reality with a kind of moral harmony. When he realizes that malicious tongues among his own people have informed on him, he finally sees a sinister fitness in their suffering.

The problem of seeing is submerged here into the language of the midrashic text: "He was anxious when he *saw* among the Israelites wicked people . . . I *see* they are fit for slavery . . ." The Sages are obviously focusing on an eternal problem of Jewish theodicy: why the Jews have been singled out for persecution throughout the ages. Moses becomes the first anguished questioner in an unending chain of questioners of the meaning of Jewish history. Strikingly, the Sages depict him as justifying the Israelite slavery in moral terms. In their reading Moses is gripped by a radical anxiety: perhaps redemption cannot happen, perhaps they are essentially unsuited to freedom, are even suited to slavery.

What Moses sees with such anxiety is the phenomenon of "wicked informers." This perception is expressed even more powerfully in Rashi's source in Shemoth Rabba (1:30): "He would ponder in his heart and say, 'There is *lashon hara*, evil talk, among them—How shall they be worthy of redemption?' " Clearly, the midrash does not speak only of a few "wicked informers," but of a characteristic—evil talk—that prompts a question about the very possibility of redemption. In both the midrash and Rashi's version, there is an emphasis on Moses' long preoccupation with the question of Israel's suffering, and on this as a moment of insight. "Then the matter is known!" translates then almost as a confirmation of a suppressed anxiety. Now, Moses knows what he has suspected earlier, when he turned this way and that: that something is rotten in the language-state of his people. In this reading what concerns Moses is not his own immediate danger—that is a separate strand of the narrative—but a way of seeing his people that makes redemption incongruous to their reality.

The Possibility of Redemption

Moses' skepticism about the people is a thread that runs through midrashic commentary on Moses' early life in Egypt. It comes, indeed, to constitute a philosophical underpinning to the whole Exodus narrative. At the Burning Bush, for instance, Moses' first response to God's mission is: "Who am I that I should go to Pharaoh and free the Israelites from Egypt?" (3:11). Rashi divides this into two questions:

> "*Who am I. . . ?* Of what importance am I, that I should speak with kings?
>
> "*And that I should free the Israelites. . . ?* Even if I am of some importance, how have the Israelites deserved a miracle, that I should free them from Egypt?"

Moses resists God's invitation to mediate redemption: neither he nor the people are fit for this new stage of experience. God answers Moses, on his second, more puzzling objection; after all, why would Moses be portrayed as skeptical about the people, when the very basis of his relations with them is clearly compassion and outrage at their pain? "This shall be a sign for you that it was I who sent you: when you free the people from Egypt, you shall worship God at this mountain" (3:12). Rashi comments:

> About your question: how do the people deserve to be freed from Egypt?—I have a great thing/word (*davar*) about this liberation, for they are destined to receive the Torah at this mountain three months after their liberation from Egypt.

The "merit for redemption" that Moses feels they lack is strangely invested in the future: the fact that they *will receive* the Torah at this mountain. God has a *davar gadol*—a "great thing," a secret knowledge that finds intimations of the future in the present. The experience of exodus will bring to fullness what is now indescribable.

In logical terms, God does not answer Moses' objection about the people's merit. But Rashi picks up this motif again shortly afterwards, to devastating effect. A debate ensues, between Moses and God, on the question of whether the people will "listen to his voice," will believe Moses' message of redemption. God promises, "They will listen to your voice" (3:18); He depicts the future history of exodus, culminating even in the silver and gold and spoils that the Israelites will ask of their Egyptian neighbors.

In response, Moses denies the premise, the foundation of the whole story of redemption: "Moses spoke up and said, 'But they will not believe me and will not listen to me; for they will say, God never appeared to you' " (4:1).

This is a moment of extraordinary tension, of unprecedented tonality, in the biblical record of human relations with God. This "most humble of men upon the face of the earth"[16] flatly contradicts God's scenario for the future. So convinced is he of his own and his people's inadequacy—his to make himself heard, theirs to respond to such a message[17]—that he simply contradicts God's version of the future.

At this point, indeed, the midrash detects a crisis of divine displeasure: God punishes Moses for his radical and, as we have seen, ongoing skepticism about the people's redeemability. The credentials that God gives Moses—the rod that turns into a snake, the hands that turn leprous—are read in the midrash as signs that Moses has spoken slander (like the snake in the Garden of Eden, like the victim of leprosy, the biblical skin disease, traditionally associated with the sin of slander).[18]

Again, Rashi includes this midrashic motif in his commentary:[19]

> *"What is that in your hand?" Mahzeh* (what is that) is written in one word, so that we read it to mean, "From what is in your hand (*mizeh*) you must be punished, for you have been guilty of suspecting the innocent."
>
> *"And it became a snake"*: He hinted to him that he had spoken slander about Israel, that he had adopted the manner of the snake. (4:2–3)

Moses now stands accused by God of that very sin of slander that he had previously criticized in the Israelites. He has contradicted God's narrative of redemption, but it is not on grounds of *lèse majesté* that God faults him.

Rather, God expresses His displeasure with Moses' account of his people. In Rashi's reading, the expression *choshed bekesherim*—suspicion of the innocent—indicts Moses for a false assessment of the people. Indeed, the narrative goes on to "vindicate" God; ". . . and the people did believe, and they listened to the message that God had taken note (*pakad*) of the Israelites, and that He had seen their affliction, and they bowed down . . ." (4:31). But if Moses is simply wrong in characterizing them as nonbelievers, why does the midrashic narrative keep harping on the theme of the people's inadequacy for redemption? We shall see more examples of this theme shortly.

Here, it is important to notice that the basis for God's promise that the people will listen to Moses is a highly specific use of language: they respond to the message that "God had *taken note*"—*pakad*—of them. These were God's words: "Go and assemble the elders of Israel and say to them: The Lord, the God of your fathers, the God of Abraham, Isaac, and Jacob, has appeared to me and said, 'I have *taken note* (*pakod pakadti*) of you and of what is being done to you in Egypt' " (3:16). Rashi, quoting the midrash, sees the *pakod pakadti* formula as the linguistic key to redemption: "In this wording, they are redeemed." These are, in fact, the key words used twice by Joseph to signify God's promise of redemption:

> "God will surely take notice (*pakod yifkod*) of you and bring you up from this land to the land that He promised on oath to Abraham, to Isaac, and to Jacob." So Joseph made the sons of Israel swear, saying, "When God has taken notice (*pakod yifkod*) of you, you shall carry up my bones from here." (Gen 50:24–25)

Midrashic narratives read in this expression a kind of cypher, a secret code that will validate Moses' message. If such a pass-code is needed, presumably there will be many false messages of redemption: a filtering system is necessary. Here, however, Moses fears an apathetic skepticism; the people will be unable even to concentrate on words of hope. The code words are needed for the opposite reason, therefore: to give plausibility to an unimaginable hope.

There is, of course, a paradox inherent in the very idea of a published secret code: what is to prevent any impostor from using the code and claiming prophetic privilege? One of the midrashic passages that narrates the story of the code sharpens and amplifies our question:

> The letters were given over to Abraham, who gave them to Isaac, who gave them to Jacob, who gave them to Joseph, who gave them to his

> brothers, one of whom, Asher, son of Jacob, gave the secret of redemption over to Serach, daughter of Asher. So when Moses and Aaron came to the elders of Israel and performed the signs (*othoth*) before their eyes, the elders went to their elder, Serach, daughter of Asher, and told her: "A man has come who has performed certain signs before our eyes." She told them: "There is nothing to these signs!" They then said: "But he told us, *Pakod pakadti*—'God has surely taken notice of you . . .' " She responded: "That is the man who is destined to redeem Israel from Egypt. For that is what I heard from father: '*Peh, Peh*—as it is said, *Pakod pakodti*—I have taken notice of you.' " Immediately, the people believed in God and in Moses, as it is said, "And the people believed, when they heard that God had taken note—*pakad*—of the children of Israel." (4:31)[20]

One elderly woman is depicted as the repository of the "secret of redemption." Spanning generations, transgressing the normal limits of a life experience, she retains a rudimentary memory-trace from her father (*Abba*—the intimacy of the expression instantly transforms the venerable matriarch into a child at her father's knee). This is all that remains of the promise of redemption, as Joseph had reported it.

In the midrash, the tradition of the promise had begun even before Joseph—with Abraham and Isaac. But where did Abraham and Isaac show knowledge of this formula? In the story of Isaac's miraculous conception and birth, after a hundred years of sterility: "The Lord *took note* of Sarah as He had promised. . . Sarah conceived and bore a son to Abraham in his old age . . ." (Gen 21:1–2). This is a dreamlike association, of course, because the word is not used, on a conscious level, as part of this transmission of the "secret of redemption." And yet the association is not to be dismissed: the resources of the word *pakad* that have to do with pregnancy and birth.[21] These will become important in our reading later.

2. *Pain and Empathy: The Fate of the Individual*

The Turning Point

We have, then, a puzzle about "fitness," about the very possibility of a human context for redemption. A turning point in the narrative occurs when, at the end of the second chapter, Pharaoh dies:

> A long time after that, the king of Egypt died. The Israelites were groaning under the bondage and cried; their shriek for help from the bondage rose up to God. God heard their moaning, and God remembered His covenant with Abraham and Isaac and Jacob. God looked upon the Israelites, and God knew. (2:23–25)

Four synonyms for crying are used here: *anacha*, *za'aka*, *shav'a*, *na'aka*. In response, God—never mentioned till now—hears, remembers, sees, knows. There is a sense of a violent opening of the channels linking God and the world. This is signaled, in human experience, by a sudden outbreak of wailing, screaming, groaning, howling, after the silence of the early phase of the narrative. From God's viewpoint, the narrative describes a moment of transformation: God, in one instant, focuses His awareness of them, He "no longer hides his eyes," as Rashi puts it (2:25). Ramban elaborates:

> Now God heard and saw them, He no longer hid His face from them . . . And God knew "For I know their pain" (3:7). For even though the time of God's decree (of slavery) was over, they *were not fit to be redeemed*, as we find clearly in Ezekiel 26. It was, however, only because of their cry that He received their prayer in His compassion.

In this important passage, Ramban defines the turning point in the history of the Exodus. Basing himself on Rashi, he reads the verbs of God's attention to the people ("He heard, He saw . . .") as indicating that, till now, there has been a "blocking" of God's attention. This daringly anthropomorphic notion—which Ramban refers to in the classic form as the "hiding of His face"—conveys most powerfully the human experience of being abandoned by God. To suffer grinding, senseless labor, to lose one's babies to the river, is to know the world as one where God indeed seems blind and deaf and unknowing. Ramban, however, gives the idea of God's apathy a status that is not merely a projection of human experience: it has an objective force, something "really" changes in God's relation to His people. When He no longer hides His face, history changes; redemption becomes possible.

This moment Ramban describes as fraught with tension. For the people are not "fit to be redeemed." On some intimate, undescribed scale of measurement, contrasted with the objective passage of time (the four hundred years of the decree to Abraham have passed), the people are "unripe" for redemption. Ramban gestures at one of the later Prophetic texts, in which the Jewish people have traditionally read their callowness, their deep unreadiness:

> I said to them: Cast away, every one of you, the detestable things that you are drawn to, and do not defile yourselves with the fetishes of Egypt—I am the Lord your God. But they defied Me and refused to listen to Me. They did not cast away the detestable things they were drawn to, nor did they give up the fetishes of Egypt. Then I resolved to pour out My fury upon them, to vent all My anger upon them there, in the land of Egypt. But I acted for the sake of My name, that it might not be profaned in the sight of the nations among whom they were. For it was before their eyes that I had made Myself known to Israel to bring them out of the land of Egypt. (Ezek 20:7–9)

In this version of the Exodus narrative, the people had responded with apathy to God's offer to free them from Egypt. Rashi comments that it was Aaron who had conveyed to them God's offer of redemption and His commands to rid themselves of their idols: Aaron had served as prophet before Moses' encounter with God at the Burning Bush. The people's rebellion—the expression of their "unfitness for redemption"—is given in the form of negatives: fundamentally, they "did not want to listen to Me." The effect is of an apathy, a lack of response. It is as though God had not spoken, since they are deeply unwilling to listen.

Ramban evokes Ezekiel's account of the prehistory of redemption, in order to dramatize the mysterious turning of God to His essentially unredeemable people. In this impasse, with a people anesthetized and a God with His face turned away, there appear the words of perception, of attention: "God heard . . . God remembered . . . God saw . . . God knew." What did God know? In theological terms, the sentence hangs precariously on the verge of impropriety. What was it that God only now heard, saw, remembered, knew? Ramban's answer is to quote God's own words to Moses at the Burning Bush: "I know their pain" (3:7) and to assert that it was the people's crying that had changed God from dispassion to compassion. This change—the human cry, the divine involvement in pain—is what makes redemption possible.

This passage represents a sudden diversion from the plot-sequence. Moses has just had his first child in Midian. He is about to encounter God at the Burning Bush. And intervening in the press of the story come these sentences, repetitious, synonymous, about crying and about God's compassion. Far from the realistic surface of the narrative, this passage speaks of God in heightened, stark language, using the basic words that describe human perception; His name is repeated four times, in a ground bass. The passage also speaks of human beings in a strangely rich language, exploring the resources of synonymy, of words for wordless cries of pain. Why does this passage turn the narrative towards redemption?

The immediate occasion of the people's crying is, of course, the death of Pharaoh. What is the logic of such tears at the death of a tyrant? The commentaries speculate: Perhaps they had hoped for amnesty and are disillusioned (Hizkuni). Perhaps only in the official mourning period for Pharaoh do they have the leisure to contemplate their own anguish (Ha-Amek Davar). Most important for our purposes is the redemptive effect of their cry. Ha-Amek Davar writes of the way in which an inchoate groan of pain becomes a protest, an interrogation of God: what will be the end of this?

The final point of the process is, "Their shriek for help from the bondage *rose up to God*"—that is, the cry is transmuted into a prayer. Out of the brutalized silence rises the cry which is one of the essential links in the story of redemption.

In the short summary-narrative of the Exodus, which is spoken by every Israelite at the moment of delivering his first fruits to the Temple, this moment of crying will be crucial:

> We cried to the Lord, the God of our fathers, and the Lord heard our plea and saw our plight, our misery, and our oppression. (Deut 26:7)

What is the function of this cry? Sefath Emeth describes the therapeutic process in these terms: "Before this, they were so deep in exile that they did not feel they were in exile. Now that they understood exile and groaned, a little redemption began . . ."[22] The basic requirement of freedom ("redemption") is the awareness of "exile," the groan of conscious alienation. To be in exile and not to feel it—this needs a "great salvation."

In similar vein, another nineteenth-century Chasidic writer, Mei HaShiloach, writes of the releasing power of the groan:

> Immediately, as their cry rose up, salvation began. Till then, they had not had any arousal to cry and to pray. But since God wanted to save them, He roused in them a cry—and that is the beginning of redemption. For before God wants to save, one does not see one's own lack, one is unaware of what one has not. But when God wants to save, He shows one

the root of one's lack, so that one sees that all the complexity of one's needs is rooted in this basic lack. And He gives one the power of prayer, of crying out to God. One begins to rage to God about it . . .[23]

Here, the sense of anguish is God's gift, the beginning of redemption. Dulled, acquiescent, walled up in their clogged senses, the Israelites are unredeemable. Another way of saying this is to say that God "does not want to save them." God and the human mirror each other. When God does want to save, this is experienced by the human being as a most intimate pain of lack, that organizes the diffuse sensations into the coherence of a cry. The human rage that shakes the dulled world is a divine power within the human being.

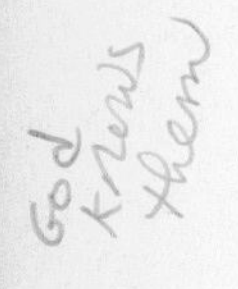

The pain of not-having emerges in a cry: this is the moment of transformation when the people become redeemable. Then, God knows. What He knows, says Ramban, is what He tells Moses He knows, at the Burning Bush: "I know their pain." This is the core sentence, in which God explains His transformed awareness of the people's suffering; *because* of this, God decides to save them. Rashi reads this sentence in the same way as he read the passage about God's response to the people's cries: "This means: I have turned My attention to contemplate and know their pain: no longer will I hide My eyes, not block My ears from their cry."

At the heart of redemption, perhaps a way of describing redemption, this sentence tells of renewed sensibility, a new mode of connection between God and the human. The "knowledge of pain" engenders a cry of consciousness, a movement of compassionate approach in God. Before, there was an autistic "un-knowing," represented by Pharaoh, who "did not know Joseph" (1:8). This Pharaoh's son later expresses his lack of connection, of concern, when he rejects Moses and Aaron's first message: "I do not know God" (5:2). Against him, against the impassive royal mode stands the God who knows human pain, for whom the human body is not an object of alienated apathy, but a register of all human experience, including the encounter with God Himself.

Pain and Empathy

Pain, that most isolating of experiences, in which, according to Elaine Scarry, the world is "unmade,"[24] is precisely where God situates Himself. This is clearly a different kind of language from the language of the philosophers. Here, pain is not to be transcended, but shared. The body is not a collection of nerve centers, each with its own local repertoire of anguish. But a register of the experience of the true self, which can be lost, so that redemption becomes impossible.

A powerful illustration of such a loss is given in the "Gradgrind philosophy," as Charles Dickens describes it in *Hard Times*: "In this life, we want nothing but Facts, sir; nothing but Facts." In one of the most poignant moments in the novel, Mrs. Gradgrind, on her deathbed, is asked by her daughter, Louisa, "Are you in pain, dear mother?" And, victim of her husband's philosophy, answers, "I think there's a pain somewhere in the room . . . but I couldn't positively say that I have got it."[25] Too apt a student of her husband's theories, she has lost her sense of qualitative distinctness, of separate personhood. The body that has lost its own integrity, its sense of proprioception, of owning its own sensations, falls silent, can speak neither to man nor to God. What makes it possible for such a body to begin to feel, to speak and be heard, to hear and be addressed? This is the enigma of redemption; to decode it is to engage with the "secret of redemption," in the midrashic phrase.[26]

When God says, "I know their pain," and when this becomes the underlying *reason* ("because I know their pain") that He gives for opening up channels of connection between Himself and the human being, then the reader is drawn into the paradox of God's *knowing*—that is, God's being intimately involved in human pain. One midrash goes as far as to suggest that God feels the pain that human beings are too inert to feel:

> Since dead flesh does not feel the scalpel, while I do know their pain, which they themselves do not feel.[27]

In an "unphilosophical" move, God identifies Himself with the twitch of involuntary sensation, the basic pain-response. God's feeling human pain becomes a way of speaking of the necessary awakening to self-feeling that must, for human beings, precede redemption. As we saw earlier, in the excerpt from Mei HaShiloach, the ability to cry out is initiated by God within the human. The will to cry, which he calls prayer, is the expression of God's will to save. At root, this is the sensation of pain, which God feels *for* those who are incapable of acknowledging their own pain.

The Hebrew word for pain—*ke'ev* (here, in elaborated form, *mach'ov*), which occurs almost exclusively in the "pain-books" of Job, Jeremiah, Lamentations, and Psalms, is used in Exodus 3:7 for the second time in the

Bible. Its first occurrence (and the only other occurrence in the Pentateuch) is in Genesis 34:25: "On the third day, when they were in pain . . ." Using this expression to prove its point, the Jerusalem Talmud says:

> It does not say: "The circumcized organ was in pain," but "*they* were in pain." This teaches that their whole body was in pain, and from this we learn that we wash the infant's whole body on the third day after circumcision, even if it is Shabbat (when heating water is normally forbidden).

In claiming knowledge of this pain of whole persons, God introduces an idea of integrated being. In the earlier passage, the narrator describes God's entry into the world of sensation, culminating in the enigmatic: "God knew." It is God, and God alone, who sees, hears, remembers, knows. His name is repeated four times, without the palliative effect of pronouns. This is an unusual—and inelegant—usage in biblical Hebrew.[28] It indicates that a new factor has entered the world of slavery; it is called God (*elohim*), and it works as perception of pain. And it is because of this new awareness that words of salvation become possible: "I know their pain—*Therefore*, I have come down to rescue them . . ." (3:7–8).

Moses Questions God's Empathy

Moses is commissioned to carry God's words to Pharaoh and to the Israelites. We have seen how Moses' resistance is amplified and intensified in midrashic commentary: "Who am I? . . . What is Israel's merit. . . ?" (3:11). We have seen him skeptical about the possibilities of redemption, as he contradicts God's assurances: "But they will not believe me . . ." (4:1). And then, in an astonishing turn, we read of his reaction after carrying out the first stage of his mission: he has challenged Pharaoh to release the people, and Pharaoh has increased his demands on the slave laborers; now, they themselves must collect straw for the brick making and still meet the same daily quotas. Confronted by their misery and anger, Moses turns to God: "O Lord, why have You done evil to this people? Why did You send me? Ever since I came to Pharaoh to speak in Your name, he has brought more evil on this people, and still you have not saved Your people" (5:22–23).

Essentially, Moses is questioning God's promise to save. His protest recalls the midrashic theme, in which Moses questioned the selection of his people for suffering. Now, his protest is explicit in the biblical narrative, and sharper, because God has specifically commissioned him to proclaim an end to the suffering, which has only increased.

In an obvious way, Moses' protest is understandable. And yet—as several commentators note[29]—his disappointment is rather strange, since God had clearly warned him that Pharaoh would not immediately yield to his demands. Indeed, Rashi[30] quotes the midrash to suggest once again that God punishes Moses for his lack of faith in redemption. This time, the ultimate disappointment of his life—that he never enters the Promised Land—is traced back to this moment of passionate protest about God's unfulfilled promises. Moses' protest here is thus read as yet another example of an ongoing skepticism about redemption—this time directed squarely against God Himself. What moves him to this pitch of exasperation, in which he twice associates God with the word "evil" and deplores his own involvement in what he depicts as an abortive mission?

One answer is given in Shemoth Rabba (5:27):

> Rabbi Akiva said, "I know that You will save them. But what do You care about those who are set under the building!" At that moment, the divine attribute of justice sought to injure Moses. When God saw that it was for the sake of Israel that he spoke, the attribute of justice did not injure him.

In this reading the issue is not whether God *can* save. Rather, Moses' question is about God's concern for those who are already dead, immured in the buildings of Egypt. This horrifying midrashic motif—that the Egyptians literally built babies into the walls of their buildings—is given an absolute prominence here: it becomes the basis of Moses' most violent protest. He accepts that God will fulfill His promise to free the people. What he cannot bear is God's apparent callousness about each individual life, about those many who die on the way to redemption.

The Egyptian Building Project

Building is, of course, the essential Egyptian project. The lives of individual slaves have a merely instrumental, quantifiable value. Moses' cry to God is, the midrash explains, "for the sake of Israel": it is not primarily about God's glory, or about faith in God's promises. Rather, it is about the empirical limits of compassion in the world of suffering. What about those who are already dead? What about their individual pain, their unassuaged despair? What can redemption do for them? They have now become part of the Egyptian project, in which individual human pain has no meaning. Moses audaciously implies in his question, "Why have You done evil to this people?" that God, like Pharaoh, is concerned only with the larger structures of history, the ultimate redemption. In this reading, Moses' "Why? . . . Why? . . ." addresses the most radical question about God's concern for human life.

Another midrash on the same savage theme of immurement focuses on the Egyptian building project:

> Said Rabbi Chama bar Chanina: When Israel went out of Egypt, the Egyptian guardian angel rose up and prostrated himself before God. He said, "Master of the universe, You created Your world by the attribute of mercy and You are powerful in might." Immediately, God called all the guardian angels of the nations, and He explained the case to them. He said, "Now you judge between him and Me. For at first My children went down to Egypt simply for a temporary stay . . . Then Pharaoh arose and subjected them to slavery. At first, he made them shepherds . . . ; *then he made them builders*, as it is said, "He built store-cities—*to inhibit them from procreating*." Then he decreed, "Every boy that is born shall be thrown into the river." Then, he decreed, "If it is a boy, you shall kill him." The Egyptian guardian angel replied, "Master of the universe, Justice is yours, and yours is truth. But if You please, save Israel, but do not destroy Egypt!"[31]

The midrash first focuses on the fact that Pharaoh makes the Israelites into *builders*: this is his first significant move in his policy of destruction. This midrash does not speak of slavery or physical suffering. Apparently, merely to make them builders is to reduce their capacity for childbearing—that is, to decimate their numbers. The logical next step is to throw their babies in the river; and then for the midwives to kill the male babies. The obvious reversal in the order of events—the midwives' story in fact preceded the orders to throw the babies in the river—creates an effect of greater emphasis on the first decree, making builders of the Israelites.

The Egyptian building project—the "store cities," as they are called—is the subject of rather startling midrashic punning:

> Rav said: They are called *miskenoth* (1:11), because they endanger (*misaknoth*) their owners. Samuel said: They are called *miskenoth*, because

> they impoverish (*mimaskenoth*) their owners . . . Anyone who is engaged in building becomes poor . . .[32]

To be a builder is presented in these midrashic sources as a condition of physical and economic hazard. Primarily, this is the Egyptian condition. Whatever positive connotations the notion of building may have are neutralized in these passages. Instead, a sinister value is associated with the building idea. The Egyptians are the archetypal example of this, but when they want to destroy the Israelites, specifically to prevent them from proliferating, from "being fruitful and multiplying" to use the classic expression spoken by God to Adam and Eve, they make builders of them, too.[33] Building as opposed to childbearing; *binyan* as opposed to *banim*. The tension is awkward, since the Hebrew words may well derive from one another: *banim*, one's children, are the most intimate building blocks of one's life. And yet, in the context of the Egyptian world, *binyan*, building, is set at odds with *banim*. One midrash even declares flatly: *binyan* precludes *beracha* (blessing—a classic synonym for children).

> Said Rabbi Joshua ben Levi: When the angel, Michael saw that the angels of the nations were supporting the Egyptian case, he made a sign to the angel Gabriel, who flew to Egypt in one swoop, and extracted from a building one brick with its clay and with one baby that they had wedged into the building. He stood in the presence of God and said, "Master of the universe, this is the story of how they enslaved Your children." When the Attribute of Justice saw this, she said, "Do justice to Your children in Egypt, for most of them are guilty." Immediately, Egypt drowned in the Red Sea, as it is said, "You make Your steeds tread the sea, stirring the mighty waters" (Hab 3:15). [Literally, "the heaps—*chomer*—of the many waters"; the word *chomer* can also mean "clay," which leads to the midrashic reading:] *that clay which Gabriel brought caused the Egyptians to drown.*[34]

In the second part of the above midrash, the angels were defending the Egyptians: It is true that they made builders of the Israelites, thereby reducing their fertility,[35] that they killed babies at various stages of development—nevertheless, "Save the Israelites, but don't destroy the Egyptians." The angel, Gabriel, reacts with one simple, terrifying gesture. As though to say, "Look at the true implications of the Egyptian enterprise," he flies "in one swoop" to Egypt and extracts one brick with its mortar and one baby that had been assimilated into the structure. The Hebrew word, *lehashkia*, means to be submerged, to become part of a larger whole, to be merged, mixed up beyond recognition. Holding the brick, Gabriel stands before God: "This is the mode of their enslavement of Your children." This is the *coup de grace* for the Egyptians; after this, their fate is sealed. It is the clay, the mortar that Gabriel brings into God's court—there is no need to mention the baby, whose image is branded into one's imagination—that condemns them.

The midrash has deconstructed the building world of Egypt to the issue of clay, mortar, and bricks. Phenomenologically, this is the meaning of the slavery of Egypt: "They embittered their lives with harsh labor, with clay and with bricks . . ." (1:14). Building endangers those who are involved in it: "Through those cities and that labor, the Egyptians were endangered and ended up drowned in the Red Sea."[36] Ultimately, the midrash grotesquely suggests, building projects end up with babies being wedged into the walls.

These associations at first seem overwrought. Yet, relentlessly, the midrashic sources confront the horror of this imagery. A similar midrash, of almost unbearable poignancy, is given in Pirke d'Rabbi Eliezer:

> Said Rabbi Akiva: Pharaoh's police would strangle the Israelites in the walls of the buildings, between the bricks. And they would cry out from within the walls and God would hear their moaning, as it is said, "And God heard their moaning—*na'akah*—and God remembered His covenant . . ." (2:24)
>
> Then, they no longer gave straw to the Israelites . . . so that they would search for stubble in the desert, using their donkeys and their wives and sons and daughters to trample the clay to make bricks. And the harsh stubble would prick their heels, so that their blood would mingle with the clay. Rachel, granddaughter of Shutelach, who was about to give birth, was trampling the clay with her husband and the baby came out of her womb and was mingled into the brick . . . Then her cry rose up before the Throne of Glory, and the angel, Michael, came down and took the brick in its clay and brought it up before the Throne of Glory. That very night, God revealed Himself and smote all the first-born of Egypt . . .[37]

The very act of making bricks involves the suffocation of the Israelites. Here, we notice, babies are only the most extreme, the most pathetic case; at first, there is a more general statement about "Israel being suffocated in the walls of the buildings." The cries that God hears—those cries that we have called "the beginning of salvation," the very awareness of pain, of need—here become the strangled cries of those buried in the walls. *Na'akah*—the form of crying that God hears—is understood as the voice of the *nechenak*, the suffocated.

The second part of the midrash touches on the horror at the very limits of language. The cry now is the cry of outrage at the unimaginable, at what Arthur Cohen calls the *tremendum*, that which refuses to be held in the mind. There is a pitch of suffering that produces a cry that pierces to the heart of the heavens.

Such cries change reality. In the first part of the midrash, an ambiguity haunts the words: "God hears the strangled cries of the moment of death" shades off into: "God hears the ghostly cries of the dead, wailing from the walls." Those who are lost, beyond hope, "wedged into the walls"—those were, we remember, the burden of Moses' protest to God: "Why have You done evil to your people? . . . What do You care for those who are sunk beneath the building?" At the heart of Moses' skepticism about redemption lies a question—not about God's power to liberate nations, on the historical plane—but about His concern, His love for those who are crushed, sunk into the larger structures of history.

His question "for the sake of Israel" notably ignores any resort to the comforts of worlds beyond this, to transcendent rewards and revisions of reality. With an almost brutal literalness, Moses deconstructs the meaning of redemption, subverts its power to resolve meaninglessness. Taken on this level, his protest, because of its passionate concern for individual pain, both exposes him to divine anger and grants him immunity from that anger.

The quintessential man of God interrogates God's silence: Does God hear the cries of the strangled, those wedged into the walls?

The Despair of the Dry Bones

The lost ones function as a dream-image representing the deathly despair of the people before redemption. This is Ramban's reading of the passage about the groans and cries of the people:

> *The king of Egypt died and they groaned:* it is normal for those who are subjected to a tyrant to look forward in hope to the day of his death. But when they saw that the king was dead, they groaned deeply at the prospect of a worse ruler, more vicious than the previous one. For they said "Our hope is lost, we are cut off"; (Ezek 37:11) and preferred death

to life. This is the meaning of *na'akah:* "they groaned with the groans of one struck down." (Ezek 30:24)

What God hears is the death-cry of the people; existentially, this means the cry of those who hope for nothing. This cry says: "Our bones are dried up, our hope is lost; we are cut off." Ramban quotes from Ezekiel's vision of the valley of dry bones to describe the reality of Israelite existence before redemption. On several occasions, Ramban emphasizes the sheer devastating *length* of the time of exile. For example, Moses' protest to God: "Why have You done evil to Your people? . . . You have not saved them . . ." (5:22–23) is a response to the silence of God, as day follows day, in mounting pain. Warned that Pharaoh would not immediately yield, he had nevertheless expected a certain rhythm of redemptive signs. The reality that he shares with his people is one of suffering unabated through time.

This condition, for which Ezekiel's vision of dry bones stands as paradigm, is also, in Ramban's rhetoric, the condition of his—and the contemporary Jewish—exile. In his introduction to the last Portion of Genesis (*Vayechi*), Jacob's descent to Egypt becomes a paradigm for the unwitting, supposedly short-term exile after the Roman conquest of Palestine. He writes poignantly of the unexpected length of this exile, the sense of "endlessness": ". . . and we are in it like the dead who say: Our bones are dried up, we are cut off . . ."

The dry bones speak, as bodies speak, when God hears their message. The bones say, "We are dried out; we are cut off." This is a literal translation of *nigzarnu lanu*—we are the victims of *gezera*, of the large edicts of history. These bones, says God, are the whole house of Israel. One traditional commentary evokes the theme we have been exploring: "Those who have died in exile say, 'By the time redemption comes, we shall already be dead and our bones dried up. So our hope for redemption is gone; since we are cut off, isolated, we will not be part of the society of those who will see redemption.' This is as if to say, 'In that case, what good is redemption to us?' "[38]

The despair expressed here is of those who believe that God will save, but that they personally will not live to see it. The voice of the dry bones is the voice that, unphilosophically seized by the terror of death, cries, "Me! Me! Me!" Franz Rosenzweig begins *The Star of Redemption* with an ironic response to philosophical dualism:

> Why should philosophy be concerned if the fear of death knows nothing of such a dichotomy between body and soul, if it roars Me! Me! Me!,

> if it wants nothing to do with relegating fear onto a mere "body"? Let man creep like a worm into the folds of the naked earth before the fast-approaching volleys of a blind death from which there is no appeal; let him sense there, forcibly, inexorably, what he otherwise never senses: that his I would be but an It if it died; let him therefore cry his very I out with every cry that is still in his throat against Him from whom there is no appeal, from whom such unthinkable annihilation threatens—for all this dire necessity philosophy has only its vacuous smile.[39]

Philosophy's "vacuous smile" confronts the fear of death, which is always personal. What good then is redemption? The "hard summons [of death] sounds unbroken even out of the mist with which philosophy envelops it."[40] God's answer to Ezekiel is given expressly to an uncompromised despair that He alone fully hears. It is because He hears it, that He tells Ezekiel: "*Therefore*, prophesy and say to them, Thus said the Lord God: I am going to open your graves and lift you out of the graves, O my people, and bring you to the land of Israel . . ." (37:12).

The bones say: "We are cut off—by the *gezera*—by the razor-sharp edge of necessity. Of what use to us is the redemption of others?" Death is not denied, it is not Nought.[41] Implicit in their words is a sense of time as sweeping all before it.

In an eloquent essay, John Berger writes of the "finality of modern despair," which translates the figure of death into scientific principle:

> In most earlier cosmogonies . . . time was cyclic and this meant that the 'ideal' original state would one day return or was *retrievable* . . . With entropy and the nineteenth century view of time, we face only the irretrievable and only dissipation . . . The sexual thrust to reproduce and to fill the future is a thrust against the current of time flowing towards the past. The genetic information which assures reproduction works against dissipation . . .[42]

The force of entropy as a modern concept is a notion that I would like, anachronistically, to borrow, in order to sharpen my reading of the Ezekiel passage, and, through it, of the Egyptian despair. Berger writes of the reproductive thrust as a force that moves against the force of entropy, with its envisaged end, termed "heat death." In the "dry bones" passage, the loss of hope, the bone-dryness that speaks of being irretrievably cut off, is countered by God's words about an opening of graves, a movement upwards.

On one level this is the expected language of redemption. Defying the limits of experience, this language reverses entropy, desiccation, dissipation. Unimaginably, redemption will reverse time's arrow: what is closed will be opened, what is sunk below will be raised up. But the climax, the essential promise of redemption is paradoxically one about human understanding: "You shall know that I the Lord have spoken and have acted" (37:14). Twice, after all the apocalyptic miracles, God's promise focuses on knowledge. Redemption will not be a mechanical matter of reassembled bones, even of reanimated bodies, robot-like returned from the grave—"The breath entered them, and they came to life and stood up on their feet, a vast multitude—*chayil gadol meod meod*" (37:10). Starkly restored to life, such bodies, without knowledge of God, are still essentially dry bones and speak the language of dry bones, eternally crying: "Me! Me! Me!" in the terror of death.

The only answer that God has for the quaking bones is the promise of knowledge: "You shall know that I am the Lord . . . you shall know that I the Lord have spoken and acted" (37:13–14). Within the limits of Ezekiel's vision, this remains an unfulfilled promise. There is no transformation of consciousness: the words are of promise, of desire for such a transformation. When Ramban uses Ezekiel's vision to read the condition of Israel in Egypt—or, indeed, the condition of contemporary Jewish reality—he deploys an imagery of spiritual death. It is the death-cry (*na'akah*) of the people that God hears. Such a cry, we suggested, is the beginning of redemption, the first sign of consciousness of what is lacking. What force is it, indeed, that can reverse the inevitable thrust of entropy? How is resurrection, redemption to be realized, in the experience of a people who sense themselves "cut off"? "You shall know that I am the Lord . . ." said God to Ezekiel. What, in the narrative of the exodus from Egypt, translates as this necessary transformation of consciousness?

The Egyptian Disease

When Moses first appeals to Pharaoh to release the Israelites, Pharaoh answers: "Who is the Lord (Hashem)? . . . I do not know Hashem" (5:2). In mock-naive mode, the midrash relates how Pharaoh sends for his reference books, his encyclopedias of divinity, to look up this new God of the Hebrews:

> "Who is Hashem that I should listen to his voice, when He does not even know enough to send me a crown on the royal birthday. [Pharaoh is celebrating his position as king of the world.] You come to me with words?!"

He examined his deity-lists without success. Moses and Aaron then mocked him: "You fool! these deities are dead, while our Hashem is alive and reigns for ever!" This is like a foolish servant who looks for his master—a priest—in a cemetery. "You fool!" people tell him, "Who ever saw a priest in a cemetery?" [In Jewish law, priests are forbidden any contact with death].[43]

Pharaoh's ignorance of Hashem—his failure to know Hashem—is a sign of his emotional obtuseness: he is looking in the most inappropriate place, in texts, lists of deities. But this God is a living God, not to be found in texts, not to be mastered by Pharaoh. He is to be encountered in the challenge of "words," of language that asks for responsive language, that requires a "listening to the voice" of the speaker, in all its human resonance. To "know" Hashem, then, demands a vulnerability, even a "not-knowing," that is the mirror-image of God's "knowing the pain" of human beings. Knowledge of this kind is clearly not in Pharaoh's repertoire. Impassive, he is characterized by repeated references to his hard, dense, impenetrable heart. Even the plagues that will later wreak havoc with Egypt will elicit from him an almost catatonic response: "Pharaoh turned and went into his palace; and paid no attention (literally, "no heart") even to this" (7:23).

With an unnerving symmetry, the Israelites, too, are described as apathetic and affectless in their misery; they are not fit for redemption, incapable of breaking out of their stony silence, of listening, of knowing. This is the Egyptian disease, it seems: in cabalistic sources it is termed *galuth hadibur*—the exile of language. So convinced is Moses that they are unredeemable, that he contradicts God's narrative of a redeemed future: "They will not believe me, nor will they listen to my voice . . ." (4:1). They are incapable of listening to a new voice.[44]

The irony is that Moses, too, is accused, through the emblematic imagery of snakes and leprosy, of slandering the people whom he had found "unfit for redemption," because of their own tendency to slander. Misuse of language apparently disqualifies one for redemption: it is an expression of the disintegrated self, of a fragmented bone-dry reality.

In Christopher Bollas's terms, what has failed is that personal idiom that expresses the vitality of the subconscious life.[45] *Lashon hara*, "evil language" closes off that dissemination of meanings and associations that engenders an inward sense of rich experience.

> It is entirely a matter of whether one can or cannot experience a psychically intense moment and then, crucially, whether one can be lost in thought

> when the nucleus of the experience explodes along fissures of separating and dividing interest . . . the fundamental agency of change in a psychoanalysis is the continuous exercise of this freedom [of free association], which ultimately deconstructs and disseminates any narrative action.[46]

The misuse of language that is called "evil talk" ends that movement outwards into the world in which the self's idiom is deployed in the object world. Slander represents an obsessively private world of language, shot through with inviolable anxieties: an unfree condition in which language is impoverished. In the audacious midrashic narrative, Moses presents the same pathology as his people; his view of them is diagnosed as slander; he finds the serpentine emblem of death in his hands, his skin is covered with the scaly carapace of leprosy.

The "Unseen Eyebeam"

The beginning of Exodus, then, gives us a panorama of autistic, sealed selves, incapable of knowledge. God Himself, at first absent from the narrative, appears at the end of chapter 2, characterized as the One who breaks through the apathetic un-seeing, un-hearing, un-knowing of His own past. Simultaneously, the people find a voice for anguish, which "rises up" to Him. Immediately after this turning point, He calls to Moses at the Burning Bush. His characteristic is empathetic relationship: "I have indeed seen the affliction of My people in Egypt and have heard their cry because of their taskmasters; I know their pain" (3:7).

What is it, in the uninhibited anthropomorphism of this passage—which Rashi amplifies: "I shall no longer hide My eyes, nor block My ears to their cries"—that allows the ice of apathy to dissolve? The dynamic of this moment of revelation is the subject of a powerful comment by Rashi on a passage in *The Song of Songs* (2:8):

> *The voice of my Beloved, here he comes:* here, the poet returns to the beginning of Jewish history, to describe how God took note (*pakad*) of them in Egypt, with an expression of love. "The king brought me into His inner rooms" (1:4); my Lover drew me after him. This is how it happened: I had given up all hope (literally, "I spoke despair") of redemption before the end of the four hundred years foretold to Abraham (Gen 15:13). Then, came the voice of my Beloved, before the assigned time: "There He stands be-

> hind our wall, gazing through the window, peering through the lattice." (Song 2:9) I thought myself doomed for many days, but He let me know that He was standing and looking through the heavenly windows at my fate: "I have indeed seen the affliction of my people." (Exod 3:7)

The effect of the Lover's eyes on the beloved breaks the trance in which she is held. Conscious of being seen by God, the people move in an instant from paralysis to a fascinated awareness of a new mode of being: "Draw me after You, let us run; the King has brought us into His inner rooms" (Song of Songs 1:4). Here begins a process that reaches its climax at Mount Sinai. It is born in a moment of intimate self-consciousness: the beloved knows she is being looked at, though she cannot see her Lover's gaze (He "peers through the lattice . . .").

Interleaving the Song of Songs and the Exodus narrative, Rashi strikingly amplifies the obvious meaning of God's opening words at the Burning Bush: "I have *indeed seen* the affliction of My people." What is being seen is not primarily the suffering but the beloved herself in all her unthought possibilities. Similarly, in the following midrash, the doubling of the verb "to see" ("I have indeed seen" literally reads as "I have seen, seen") complicates the meaning of God's gaze:

> "I have seen/see the affliction of My people:" God said to him: "Moses, you see with a single vision, while I see with a double vision. You see them arriving at Sinai and accepting My Torah; while I see them accepting My Torah—that is one vision—and I also see them making the Golden Calf—that is the second vision (as it is said, "I have seen this people, and behold it is a stiff-necked people" [32:9]). When I come to Sinai to give them the Torah, I shall descend in My carriage drawn by four animals (one of which is the calf or ox—see Ezekiel's vision [1:10]); they will look at Me and pull one of the animals out of harness and make Me angry with it."[47]

God has eyes to see what no human being can see: the best and worst roles that the people will play. The doubled verb for seeing gives an impression of stereoscopic vision: a depth of field accessible only to Him. Most significantly, knowing they are the object of this penetrating comprehensive gaze frees the people from the invisibility of their Egyptian fate, of being submerged under the building. This sense of being seen is the pure experience of redemptive love:

And the unseen eyebeam crossed, for the roses
Had the look of flowers that are looked at.

—T. S. ELIOT, *BURNT NORTON*

Rashi describes their unredeemed condition in the words, "I spoke despair . . ." These words are an idiom that suggests something more precise than a *mood* of despair. They are used by Jeremiah, for example, to describe the people's inability to repent, to "return to God": *"Ve'omru no'ash*—they will say, 'It is no use. We will keep on following our own plans; each of us will act in the willfulness of his evil heart' " (Jer 18:12). God here predicts that their response will be a kind of autism: they will simply continue walking in the wake of their own thoughts, sunk into the old structures, like Winnie-the-Pooh pursuing the fabulous Heffalump round and round the same tree.

3. *Against Automatism: The Hidden Sphere*

The Hidden Sphere

To help them break loose, become redeemable, while in bondage in Egypt, God lets the Israelites know that, invisible to them, there is a gaze, expectant, seeing in them all possibilities. The trance, the moral apathy from which they suffer, has been much described in our century. Nadezhda Mandelstam, for instance, writes of the

> sickness—lethargy, plague, hypnotic trance or whatever one calls it—that affected all those who committed terrible deeds in the name of the "New Era." . . . They . . . imagined that time had stopped—this, indeed, was the chief symptom of their sickness. We had, you see, been led to believe that in our country nothing would ever change again.[48]

She writes of the persecutors; but the "sickness" of which she writes, the belief that "nothing would ever change again," was the fate of *all* those trapped within the system that she describes. To be able to think in any other way becomes almost a definition of freedom, of good health.

What Stalinist Russia has in common with the Egypt that oppressed the

Hebrew slaves is adumbrated in Vaclav Havel's classic essay, *The Power of the Powerless*. Havel, one of the signatories of Charter 77, writes of the "post-totalitarian" state, a modern phenomenon, set in the historical contingencies of contemporary society. His description, in its very banality, its lack of overt sadism, evokes a core-reality of all states where the truth of the individual is submerged within the system.

He begins with a banal example: the manager of a fruit-and-vegetable shop places in his window, among the onions and carrots, the slogan, "Workers of the World, Unite!" The worker does this simply, "because that it is the way it has to be." In Rabbinic Hebrew, the term for that is *gezera*—the cut-and-dried "way it has to be."

> The system reveals its most essential characteristic to be introversion, a movement toward being ever more completely and unreservedly *itself* . . . the social phenomenon of self-preservation is subordinated to something higher, to a kind of blind *automatism* which drives the system . . . [and which] will always triumph over the will of any individual.[49]

In such a system, individuals must "live within a lie . . . [they] confirm the system, fulfill the system, make the system, *are* the system" (31). All the slogans form part of the panorama of everyday life; "everyone in his or her own way is both a victim and a supporter of the system" (37) . . . Most important,

> there is obviously something in human beings which responds to this system, something they reflect and accommodate . . . Human beings are compelled to live within a lie, but they can be compelled to do so only because they are in fact capable of living in this way. (38)

The condition Havel diagnoses is, at base, a "pre-political" condition; and he insists that to cure it a "pre-political" response is necessary, one in which individuals "live within the truth," and simply "*are* what they are" (56). "Dissidence" is, therefore, an expression he is uneasy with: he speaks not out of a profession but out of an existential attitude. Living within the truth, as an open, political mode, is an expression of a "hidden sphere":

> It is from this sphere that life lived openly in the truth grows; it is to this sphere that it speaks, and in it that it finds understanding. This is where the potential for communication exists. But this place is hidden and

> therefore, from the perspective of power, very dangerous. The complex ferment that takes place within it goes on in semi-darkness, and by the time it finally surfaces into the light of day as an assortment of shocking surprises to the system, it is usually too late to cover them up in the usual fashion. (41)

"Living within a lie" is a denial of responsibility, it is a token of a demoralized person. "The system depends on this demoralization, deepens it, is in fact a projection of it into society" (45). Living within the truth, on the other hand, is a moral act, uncalculating, generously responsible. The hidden ferment in the semidarkness is "difficult to chart or analyze." When it bursts through the moribund surface of life within the lie, it has a shock effect on those embedded within that system.

Havel is clearly portraying the cultural and political world of "post-totalitarian" Czechoslovakia; specific characteristics of modern society nurture the "automatism" he describes. And yet, it is uncanny to notice the universal phenomenological aspect of his description. An automatism, in which the possibility of living within the truth has been driven underground, into a "hidden sphere": this, existentially, is what Egypt (Heb. *mitzrayim* similar to *meitzarim*—that "world within straits") represents, in the midrashic readings we have explored. Here, the individual is "built into the building." The symbolism of the death-cries of those who protest, as they are immured, is quite blatant. All who are involved in "building" *become* the system, serve its automatism.

Pharaoh initiates his sophisticated plot, which includes in its more desperate range submerging babies in rivers, by making *builders* of the Israelites. To build, in this sense, is to shore up the system;[50] ultimately, it is to be impoverished, endangered. The structure, the "way it has to be," reveals, in the most macabre forms, its moribund dimension: it denies the very possibility of procreation, of the "hidden sphere of life," both in its biological and its existential modes. We remember John Berger: "The sexual thrust to reproduce and to fill the future is a thrust against the current of time flowing towards the past . . ."[51] The effect of Egypt, *mitzrayim*, on language is, likewise, to erode meaning, communication, in the interest of slogans that no one reads, or even sees. Language is absorbed into the panorama of "the way it has to be"—the "auto-totality of society."[52]

In the midrashic narratives of Egypt, the centrality of the *gezera*—Pharaoh's edicts—suggests the mode of "automatism," of which Havel writes: Pharaoh issues uncompromising orders that leave no room for play, for invention. One of his most effective edicts is the one that "cuts off" men from women. In the midrashic reading to which we shall soon return, men's work in the field necessitates their sleeping there at night, so that, in the physical and biological sense, they are prevented from union with their wives. The force of *gezera* thus drives the root-words apart: *binyan* (building) from *banim* (children).

Ironically, when God rewards the midwives for their nurturing of life, "He made them *batim*—houses" (1:21). (The word is related to the concept of building.) But these are not the houses of the builder, those sinister structures that menace the "hidden sphere" of life, the complex, secret ferment that goes on in the semidarkness. Rather, says Rashi, quoting the midrash, the "houses" of God's gift are dynasties of monarchy, of priesthood. There will emerge from these two women the very issue of that secret ferment, that creation of more life—offspring who will discover the natural form of their own being: priesthood, monarchy, embodied in flesh and blood.

The Raucous Cry

Babies, not bricks. Consider the anarchic force of the baby Moses crying in his casket in the river. His mother, knowing that she can hide him no longer, sets him in a box, and exposes him to the chances of the river. In a sense she thereby obeys Pharaoh's decree "to throw the baby boys into the river." But the imagery compels our notice: we expect the baby container to be a cradle, however the word for it is *teva*, box;[53] it is coated in clay; it represents a brick. And set within it is a baby, aggressively, almost grotesquely, giving voice. Only when the princess has opened the brick, "behold, a boy (*na'ar*) is crying," (2:6) she is assailed by the premature coarseness of a boy's voice in the infant body. This is the midrashic comment on the word *na'ar*, boy, uncanny in its imaginative force: "But if you read *na'ar* like that, you are making Moses repulsive," says Rabbi Nehemia;[54] so that we receive the full shock of the precocious voice that emerges from the semidarkness, the voice that shocks the system.

By a kind of "syncope," the measured predictability of time is suspended, in this image of the "boy crying" in the brick. His voice thick with life, Moses earns the princess's pity. (The word used here for pity, *chemla*, connotes a compound of admiration and regret at waste.)[55] Suddenly, the "secret of redemption" has burst through the moribund surface. But it is she who has opened the brick—she who "saw it, took it, opened it—and [again] saw it, the child" (2:5–6). Rashi gives great credit to her way of seeing: she "sees It, the Presence of God, *with* the child." Her way of seeing makes room for the "hidden sphere," for the "complex ferment" that is the Presence of God, for the crying voice of a child.

Perhaps this scene gives us an intimation of the "secret of redemption." The paradox of secrets is this: secrets are to be revealed; secrets are to remain hidden. The hoarse cry of a boy, precociously vital, cracks the moribund surface, the living within the lie, the need to control, to perpetuate the "way it must be."

As a full-grown man, Moses says to God, "I am heavy of mouth, heavy of tongue" (4:10). He expresses a difficulty with expression: heaviness hangs on his tongue, in his mouth. Traditional commentaries have understood this as any one of a full range of physical, psychological, and cultural impediments: Moses has a stutter, he does not speak Egyptian well, he has no gift of eloquence. One midrashic source strikingly focuses on Moses' sense of *heaviness*:

> Moses answered God: Master of the universe, You tell me, "Go down to Egypt and free six hundred thousand people from under the burden of Egypt." If You were to tell me to free a hundred or two hundred people, it would still be hard (*kasheh*) for me; and You tell me to free six hundred thousand! And if the slavery had lasted only a year or two, then there would be no difficulty in freeing them; but they have been enslaved for two hundred and ten years! Pharaoh will say, "If a slave worked for ten years, and no one objected, how can someone turn up and free him? Or if one worked a vineyard for ten years, and no one objected, how can someone turn up and free him?" Master of the universe, heavy and grave are these things that You tell me, for heavy of mouth and heavy of tongue am I.[56]

In this midrash, heaviness is the experience of being overwhelmed by that which dwarfs individual dimensions. A vital potency is encumbered by sheer numbers: "You charge me with the task of levering out from under the weight of Egypt six hundred thousand bodies! Even a hundred would be unbearable!" In a similar vein, "after two hundred and ten years of unprotesting subjection to the system, the weight of silence has accumulated: who can break it now?" Language is dragged down by the enormity of the experience of living, over time, "within the lie." For God's charge to Moses had always been, in some radical sense, a matter of language: essentially, it is Moses' words that will free the Israelites.[57] His intimate sense of impediment is a most personal response to the formidable project of redemption. As Havel observes:

> the more complex the mechanisms of power become, the larger and more stratified the society they embrace, and the longer they have operated historically, the more individuals must be connected to them from outside, and the greater the importance attached to the ideological excuse.[58]

The real issue will be ideological; it will have to do with the use of words, with their power to pry the individual out from under the complex and cumulative machinery of the system. The difficulty of finding a language for liberation has already been indicated in the wordless cries and groans of the national awakening. Like the baby in the brick, all the people find a genuine voice in pain and dissonance. In *Dr. Faustus*, Thomas Mann writes of a condition in which the only way to express a spiritual truth is through raucous disharmony:

> The whole work is dominated by the paradox (if it is a paradox) that in it dissonance stands for the expression of everything lofty, solemn, pious, everything of the spirit; while consonance and firm tonality are reserved for the world of hell, in this context a world of banality and commonplace.[59]

Icons of Fear

Egypt is the "world of hell," dense, retentive, antagonistic to the "hidden ferment," moribund. In terms of sound, this excludes raw, authentic language. In visual terms, it expresses itself in formal, geometric works of art.

Here, for instance, is Max Raphael, in *Prehistoric Pottery and Civilization in Egypt*:

> The beginnings of pottery were rooted in necessity, the beginnings of its ornamentation were rooted in mathematics, in the sense that there was a *will to abstraction*, i.e. to achieve a certain *detachment* from the physical quality of the object, to distil and bring forth from amorphousness something *simple, limited, fixed, enduring, and universally valid.* The neolithic artist wanted a world of forms illustrating not *changeable and transient* activities and events . . . but rather the relations of people to one another and to the cosmos within an *unchanging system.* The intention was not to suppress the content of life but to *dominate* it, to compel it to surrender its physical ascendancy to the power of creative will—to man's *drive to manipulate and refashion* his world. (My italics.)[60]

Read writes persuasively of the motif of taming animals, in patterned, symmetrical, duplicated, or reversed images that avoid the vital image and can be read as a symbol of man's magical power.

> But observe what had happened: not only had the wild animals been tamed, but the wild imagination of man himself had been tamed. It had been compelled to surrender the direct, eidetic image of the phenomenal object, and to create in its place a formal composition.[61]

Read goes beyond description and attempts to explain "why man should have been content to abandon the vital image."[62] His diagnosis emphasizes the effect of fear, as the emotion that inspires nonrepresentational art: "fear of the unknown, fear of events for which they have no causal explanation . . . Fear breeds secrecy, a desire to communicate in a language that is not understood by the uninitiated—by the hostile forces." Such a secret language, the "whole magic lore of geometric signs," emphasizes human power, but represses all that terrifies it.

The desire to dominate the amorphousness of the world, to assert technical, or magical, control is expressed specifically in this period through work *in clay*, in the "clay, mortar and bricks," which, in the biblical account, constitute the essence of Egyptian slavery. I am suggesting, like Read, that the bricks, the clay, the formal structures are a way of "thinking in pictures": they are icons of fear. In the midrashic sources, the clay, the material of human creativity, is formed into rigid, life-stifling bricks. The rigidity of the building-blocks paradoxically evokes the amorphous, filthy piles of stuff of which it is composed. The ambiguous terror of mud is indicated in the midrashic moral symmetry: those who enslaved others in mud and bricks are ultimately *drowned in mud*.[63]

The Vision of Possibility

As against this Egyptian model, Read quotes from Max Scheler, on the "mission of all true art":

> not to reproduce what is already given (which would be superfluous), nor to create something in the pure play of subjective fancy (which can only be transitory and must necessarily be a matter of complete indifference to other people), but to press forward into the whole of the external world

> *and* the soul, to see and communicate those objective realities within it which rule and convention have hitherto concealed.

Poets do not merely express common human experiences, but

> soar above the prevailing network of ideas in which our experience is confined, as it were, by ordinary language; they enable the rest of us to *see*, for the first time, in our experience, something which may answer to these new and richer forms of expression, and by so doing they actually *extend* the scope of our *possible* self-awareness.[64]

The language of art enlarges, makes the hidden visible. It is this power of language, not merely to reproduce the given, to contribute to the "automatism" of the structure, but to speak for the "hidden sphere" of life, that Moses recognizes—and doubts in himself. For the resistance, within and without, to such a liberating voice is formidable. The words for Pharaoh's heart—*kasheh*, *kaved*, *chazak*, hard, heavy, dense[65]—are the words for "what is already given," for "the way it must be." They express the density, the cumulative weight of the past, of the system. The individual voice has no power against them. That, at least, is the almost palpable sensation in the mouth of the one who is to counter-say them.

These are the words for the *gezera*, the edict—the *schwer*, heavy words of which Milan Kundera writes: *"Muss es sein? Es muss sein."* (*"Must it be? It must be."*)—and which became the motif of the fourth movement of Beethoven's last quartet, Opus 135. Earlier, Kundera explains, the composer had used the three-note motif in a canon with a jocular reference to the necessity of paying a debt; now, some think, they acquired for Beethoven a "much more solemn ring; they seemed to issue directly from the lips of Fate . . . German is a language of *heavy* words. *'Es muss sein!'* was no longer a joke; it had become *'der schwer gefasste Entschluss'* (the difficult or weighty resolution)."[66]

The question about the *gezera*, about necessity, about the fatality of human existence receives its grim answer in Beethoven's music: *Es muss sein.* But Moses must find words for another answer. At first, in his doubting questions about himself, about his people, even about God Himself, there is a respect for the harsh weight of the *gezera*. The people are not *ra'uy*—not fit for redemption. Literally, they cannot be *seen* in that "complex ferment" of the inner sphere, which will make it possible for them to "live in the truth." He cannot *see in them* that mode of being that is called redemption.

For lack of this vision, how can he speak words that will enlarge, make real the vision of possibility?[67]

4. *The Secret of Redemption: A Tale of Mirrors*

The Secret of Redemption

The "secret of redemption," in its technical, coded form, consisted, we remember, of the words, *pakod pakad*—"He has taken notice . . ."—see above, pp. 29–30. The one who knows the words will be the accredited redeemer. For Serach, the wise matriarch, this secret is reducible to "letters": in these letters, she hears the reconstituted words that represent redemption. The letters are *peh peh*, labials, panting, rudimentary sounds. They evoke the panting cries of the laboring woman. Rashi puts us in mind of these cries, when he treats the name Puah (one of the midwives) as a professional reference: identified in the midrash with Miriam, she is named for the panting breaths of the laboring woman, or the coaxing talk of the midwife (1:15). The name is an onomatopoeia, conjuring the sound-world of birth.

The letter *peh* is the same as the word for mouth, the site of language; that is, the place where redemption is constructed or suffocated. One who comes uttering these letters will, in the future, redeem, says Serach. And in saying so, in recognizing the letters, in decoding the secret signs, she makes redemption real in the world. The midrash subtly registers her sensibility, by using the two expressions, *othoth* and *othioth*. Of the signs, the miracles, the *othoth*, she declares dismissively, *ein bahem mamash*—"There is nothing solid in them." Only letters, *othioth*, the fluid shapings of language, only they have substance. Paradoxically, she declasses the miracle, and gives prestige to the letter, to the lips, the mouth.

The key to redemption is hers, but she is absent from the surface of the biblical narrative. The midrash detects her, extracts her from the "inner sphere," has her construct redemption. In this role she becomes not merely a custodian, but an agent of redemption.

A Tale of Women

However, a classic statement in the Talmud singles out that human group, quite visible in the biblical narrative, to which she belongs: "In reward for the righteous women of that generation, Israel was redeemed from Egypt."[68] Redemption, says the Talmud, came only because of "righteous women." In the narrative, we can think of the righteousness of Jochebed (Moses' mother) and Miriam, of Pharaoh's daughter, of the dissident midwives. But the Talmud seems to speak of something else, something that many women shared, without which the people would not have been redeemed. This "secret sharing," connoted by Serach, whose words create redemption, characterizes, I would suggest, all the righteous women of the time. What is it that, working in the semidarkness of Havel's "inner sphere," emerges with such explosive force as to shock the system of Egypt?

The Talmudic answer is the narrative that follows the statement. This is a narrative about women who feed and comfort their husbands in the field, have relations with them there, and bear children. That is, they defy the *gezera* of Pharaoh in the most literal sense, by being fruitful. Their answer to the decree is the answer of the body—sexuality, pregnancy, birth, nursing—assisted by God Himself. They act as God had done at the beginning of time, they create and nurture life: that is, in the simplest sense, the meaning of redemption. They live within the truth.

Another version of this midrash, however, gives us, I suggest, an answer of greater imaginative power:

> *"These are the records* (pikudei) *of the Tabernacle":* You find that when Israel were in harsh labor in Egypt, Pharaoh decreed (*gazar*) against them that they should not sleep at home nor have relations with their wives. Said Rabbi Shimeon bar Chalafta, What did the daughters of Israel do? They would go down to draw water from the river and God would prepare for them little fish in their buckets, and they would sell some of them, and cook some of them, and buy wine with the proceeds, and go to the field and feed their husbands, as it is said, "In all the labor in the field." (1:14) And when they had eaten and drunk, the women would take the mirrors and look into them with their husbands, and she would say, "I am more comely than you," and he would say, "I am more comely than you." And as a result, they would accustom themselves to desire, and they were fruitful and multiplied, and God took note of them (*pakad*) immediately.

> Some of our sages said, They bore two children at a time, others said, They bore six at a time, yet others said, They bore twelve at a time, and still others said, Six hundred thousand . . . *And all these numbers from* the *mirrors* . . . In the merit of those mirrors which they showed their husbands to accustom them to desire, from the midst of the harsh labor, they raised up all the hosts, as it is said, "All the hosts of God went out of the land of Egypt" (12:41) and it is said, "God brought the children of Israel out of the land of Egypt in their hosts." (12:51)
>
> When God told Moses to make the Tabernacle, the whole people stood up and offered whatever they had—silver, gold, copper, etc.; everyone eagerly offered their treasures. The women said, "What have we to offer as a gift for the Tabernacle?" So they brought the mirrors to Moses. When Moses saw those mirrors, he was furious with them. He said to the Israelites, "Take sticks and break their thighs! What do they need mirrors for?" Then God said to Moses, "Moses, these you despise! *These mirrors raised up all those hosts in Egypt!* Take them, and make of them a copper ewer with a copper stand for the priests to sanctify themselves—as it is said, 'And he made the ewer of copper and its stand of copper, of the mirrors of those who created hosts. . .'" (38:8) [This is a free, midrashic translation of the verse.][69]

The midrash gains its momentum from the opening *gezera*: Pharaoh issues a decree, a cut-and-dried (the root of *gezera* means "to cut") formula that will separate men from women. In the context of the biblical narrative, the purpose is clear: ". . . so that they may not increase . . ." (1:10). Pharaoh has cut off the possibility of natural increase among the Israelites. But the midrash does not emphasize the effective purpose of the edict: merely that couples are sexually separated, since the husbands may not sleep at home.

The women enter the narrative as a question: "What did the daughters of Israel do?" The assumption is that the women, who are not most directly affected by the edict (since it is the men who are the laborers and who are prevented from going home at night), will adopt some measure against it. Since the edict is one of separation, of effective sterilization, the women's efforts naturally tend towards reunion. The little fish, archetypal symbols of fertility, become clear sexual signs, as they providentially swim up in the women's buckets. They are transformed, in the most pragmatic way—through cooking and the cash nexus—into a nourishing and stimulating meal for the exhausted husbands in the field.

It is striking that God appears twice in this narrative: first, He provides the little fish, the most "natural" of events. Thereafter, the women's planning takes over, the conscious use and reconstruction of the natural into the shape of desire. Having fed their husbands, the women contemplate themselves with their husbands as a couple in "the mirrors," which are described with the definite article, though we have not read of them till now. What follows is an intimate scene of erotic "boasting," shockingly unconventional in sentimental terms. Instead of praising each other, each praises her/his own beauty, by comparison with the other. This "mirror work" produces desire and procreation; through processes that are complex and willful, they are "fruitful and multiply," fulfilling the original blessing/command to humankind (Gen 1:28; 9:7).

And God acts a second time: He "takes notice"—*pakad*—of them. This one word, here most clearly signifying the mysterious gift of pregnancy, gathers multiple resonances. Its first use in the Torah was to narrate Sarah's pregnancy, after years of barrenness (Gen 21:1). God's promise of redemption—*pakod yifkod*—is fulfilled here, in the most "natural" mode imaginable. For what could be more "natural" than the women's conceiving, after they are reunited with their husbands? It is as natural as the shoals of fish that swarm up in the women's buckets. And yet in these two moments, particularly, in the fishing and in the conceiving of many children (and the midrash reminds us that the same word is used for both—*vayishretzu*—they "swarmed"), God enters the narrative, and gives a surrealistic turn to the natural events: fish-becomes-wine-becomes-desire, and babies are born in multiples of (perhaps) six hundred thousand. Why does the midrash require God here? Why does it bring into play the epic resonance of *pakod yifkod*, of the "secret of redemption"? And why the mirrored narcissism of the couple at the visual heart of the midrash? On the "plot" level, it would have been sufficient to have the women feed their husbands well, in order to achieve reunion and fertility.

The end of the midrash emphasizes the enigmatic character of events. The extraordinary fertility of the women leads to the Zen-like statement: "All these numbers were from the mirrors." The midrash deflects our attention from the "natural" level of reading, from the normal strategies of arousal of desire, the aphrodisiac function of wine and fish, although the calculated preparation of these delicacies was the opening subject of the narrative. Essentially, claims the midrash, it was all done with mirrors. And finishes with a bizarre dialogue, in which Moses violently deplores the women's gift of these same mirrors to the Tabernacle, while God overrides his objections: "these mirrors raised up all the Israelite hosts in Egypt."

Subtly, the midrash yields its meanings. The mirrors are not simply the means by which women adorn themselves, set in motion the processes of desire, procreation, the creation of a nation. A much larger claim is being made: through these mirrors, each woman conceived *six hundred thousand* babies at a time. These mirrors, when God asks for gifts to the Tabernacle, to create sacred space, are *all the women have.* In Rashi's version, God concludes: "These mirrors are more precious to Me than any other gift."[70]

Moses' anger at the apparent frivolity, the inappropriate sexual associations of the gift, makes it clear that the gift is not a "giving up" of vanity.[71] It becomes an installation at the liminal point of entry into the sacred space: the mirrors are used to plate the priestly ewer, where hands and feet are washed. Giving their mirrors for this purpose, the women are making no ascetic immolation of the accoutrements of desire: Moses' outraged rejection indicates this quite unmistakably. "Break their thighs," expresses an anger at sexuality that transgresses boundaries. It is God who speaks for the women and their mirrors: "the mirrors *raised up* the hosts of Israel." The verb *he'emidu* is often used to mean "beget," so that God actually says: "These mirrors *begat* the hosts of Israel." It was all done with mirrors!

Mirror Work

The most direct effect of the mirrors, in the words of the midrash, is desire ("And they accustomed themselves to desire . . ."). The drama, the action of husband and wife in front of the mirror, the four faces speaking, challenging, affirming beauty, creates a culture of desire. For one of the most arresting phenomena in the narrative is its fusion of intimacy and the most public perspective. The subject is the relation between husband and wife, in its most delicate moment; but in watching the couple in front of their mirror, we see multiple mirror reflections of the scene. Every woman in Israel is enacting the same drama. Our subject is not one particular woman, one extraordinary heroic figure, but "the daughters of Israel," a title that gives honor and propriety to their acts. Strangely, there is a chaste, impersonal quality to the narrative: it tells, essentially, the story of redemption: "In reward for the righteous women of that generation, Israel were redeemed from Egypt" (B. Sotah 11b). In this way a nation of six hundred thousand men was formed: this is the demographic, public product of the story. But, at the same time, each individual woman is described as having given birth to six hundred thousand. The very thought concentrates the mind wonderfully!

The enigmas of the story clearly center on the mirror. What is its role here, in creating desire, fruitfulness, and the *pekida*, the transfiguring presence of God? Each woman says, "I am more beautiful than you." She initiates the boasting game. The midrash may well be evoking the verse from The Song of Songs: "I am black but beautiful—*na'avah*" (1:5). The word for beauty is the same as the one used in the midrash—*na'eh*—comely, harmonious. Literally, the verse reads, "I am black *and* beautiful," but since there is no alternative mode of indicating the disjunctive "but," a teasing ambiguity destabilizes the text. Clearly, in context, blackness is a reason for shame:[72] here, the beloved proudly claims a paradoxical beauty despite/within her swarthiness. This is no primary narcissism; but the difficult project of seeing beauty in the blackened self.

Classic midrashim tell of the beauty that God sees in His people, in their very blackness. In Rashi's commentary, for instance, although the lover has abandoned her because of her blackness, she asserts her *structural* beauty: the blackness is mere sunburn, but her limbs are well made. By analogy, even if her deeds are ugly, she affirms a true self, a genetic identity, in which beauty is always potential. To assert this, she must draw, not on the assurances of a lover, but on her own awareness of beauty-within-blackness.

She says: "I am more beautiful than you," not "You are more beautiful than I." Her boast, delivered as they gaze together at their reflection in the mirror, is a challenge to her husband, grimy with clay and mud, to see beauty within that blackness. What she initiates is a dynamic, loving game. What she says is not a statement of fact, but a performance of transformation. Against the *gezerah* of Pharaoh she sets up the mirror of desire. The hosts of Israel, the secret of redemption: it is all done with mirrors.

The peculiar nature of this gift of the women to the Tabernacle is discussed by Ramban.[73] Why was Moses so angry at this particular donation? After all, the women gave other female items associated with narcissism and sexuality—jewelry of all kinds. Ramban answers that the other gifts were melted down, gold, silver, copper, to make the accessories of the Tabernacle. Only the mirrors were preserved as mirrors and used for one specific object—the ewer. The burnished copper, "very beautiful," Ramban notes, was assigned to this one purpose, and so remains as an unmitigated reminder of the mirrors and their original uses, with all the erotic associations that Moses deplores. The ewer, at which priests consecrate themselves to the service of God,[74] retains the reflective surfaces, the form and function of the original gift.

There are even fascinating speculations in the midrashic literature that the ewer served as a kind of mirror-system, like a periscope or a telescope, giving people a view of the interior of the Tabernacle, for example.[75] Mirrors thus function to allow vision at oblique angles, round corners, at a distance. With all the distortion of mirrors of that period (polished copper, we remember[76]), we may say that they function as revealers of the inaccessible: one's own face, the banned interior of the Tabernacle. They offer, in a sense, a counterworld to the world of the *gezera*, of the "way it has to be." The natural limitations of vision are challenged and deflected by this instrument that distorts reality (even modern mirrors retain the right-left reversal) in order to extend perception.

A similar point is made by Rashi, in a comment on Isaiah 3:23. Here, mirrors are referred to as *gilyonim*—"revealers." Since this expression never recurs, Rashi explains: "These are mirrors, called so because they reveal the forms of the face." The plural perspectives of the mirror—each movement of the head produces a different form in the mirror—yield a shifting, multiple revelation of the self.

In *The Unbearable Lightness of Being*, Milan Kundera uses the mirror as the means by which lovers explore unexpected possibilities. Sabina "looked into the mirror with the same long questioning stare, training it first on herself, then on him."[77] A bowler hat reveals the abyss between them, since it was a motif in her previous love relationship with Tomas, and its multiple meanings are meaningless to her present lover. Originally, it had evoked laughter and a strange excitement: "Is excitement really a mere step away from laughter?"[78] The mirror, opening up possibilities, raises questions about the *gezera*, about the restricted, cramped experience of what has to be. It also painfully reveals the loneliness of unshared idioms of love.

Mirrors, as Rashi comments on the women's gift to the Tabernacle, are used by women to adorn themselves. It is this possibility of self-adornment, of costuming, that is the gift of the mirror. The effect can be jocular, it can signify violence, or humiliation, as in the Kundera scene. The basic assumption is that this activity belongs to the realm of the *yetzer hara*, the evil inclination, as Rashi points out; that is, self-costuming, cosmetics, self-decoration are a masking of the true face, they are used to deceive, to seduce. And yet, in our midrash, God vindicates the mirror and its costuming function against Moses' predictable indignation. For the mirror is used against the *gezera;* when a couple gazes into it, it generates redemption.

Many things can function as mirrors, can reveal the human face, in all its possible forms, to itself. To this end the work of art has traditionally been described as a mirror. In the English Renaissance, indeed, this became something of a cliche: the literary device of the *Mirror for Magistrates*, for instance, became a popular moral genre. More famously, Hamlet exhorts the players, as they rehearse their play, to "hold as 'twere the mirror up to nature."[79] The play is to present a version of reality—but only "as 'twere"; it is to be a stylized rendering of the murderous act in which Claudius is to recognize himself. Similarly, when he attempts to touch his mother's moral imagination, he shows her a diptych, twin portraits of his father and his uncle, her past and her present husband. They are "a glass Where you may see the inmost part of you."[80] Looking outwards at this "glass" is in some deflected, undefended way to see one's own face; for Gertrude, it is to be shocked out of the lie she has been living.

Lionel Trilling notices that the manufacture of mirrors in the eighteenth century coincides with that point in history when "men became individuals." This he defines as the ability to imagine oneself in more than one role:

> The individual looks into mirrors, larger and much brighter than those that were formerly held up to magistrates. The French psychoanalyst Jacques Lacan believes the development of the *"Je"* was advanced by the manufacture of mirrors: again it cannot be decided whether man's belief that he is a *"Je"* is the result of the Venetian craftsmen's having learned how to make plate-glass or whether the demand for looking-glasses stimulated this technological success. If he is an artist the individual is likely to paint self-portraits; if he is Rembrandt, he paints some threescore of them. And he begins to use the word "self" not as a mere reflexive or intensive, but as an autonomous noun referring, the O.E.D. tells us, to "that . . . in a person [which] is really and intrinsically *he* (in contradistinction to what is adventitious)", as that which he must cherish for its own sake and show to the world for the sake of good faith. The subject of an autobiography is just such a self . . .[81]

The Mirror Stage

Trilling's reference to Lacan evokes the French psychoanalyst's important theory of the mirror. Lacan writes of the formation of the "Je," as experienced in psychoanalysis, which "leads us to oppose any philosophy directly issuing from the *Cogito.*" It is not pure thought that defines Being ("I think, therefore I am"—[Descartes]), but the ability of the human infant to recognize his own image in the mirror (the *aha*—realization), to play with his reflection: "a startling spectacle," writes Lacan:

> Unable as yet to walk, or even to stand up, and held tightly as he is by some support, human or artificial . . . , he nevertheless overcomes, in a flutter of jubilant activity, the obstructions of his support and, fixing his attitude in a slightly leaning-forward position, in order to hold it in his gaze, brings back an instantaneous aspect of the image.[82]

This "mirror stage" constitutes the transformation that takes place in the subject when he assumes an image, an "Ideal-I": "the subject anticipates in a mirage the maturation of his power." "Still sunk in his motor incapacity and nursling dependence," he experiences a "jubilant assumption of his specular image," a gestalt, an imago, that is "capable of formative effects in the organism." Lacan cites a biological experiment, which shows that "it is a necessary condition for the maturation of the gonad of the female pigeon that it should see another member of its species, of either sex; so sufficient in itself is this condition that the desired effect may be obtained merely by placing the individual within reach of the field of reflection of a mirror."

> The *mirror stage* is a drama whose internal thrust is precipitated from insufficiency to anticipation—and which manufactures for the subject, caught up in the lure of spatial identification, the succession of phantasies that extends from a fragmented body-image to a form of its totality that I shall call orthopaedic—and, lastly, to the assumption of the armor of an alienating identity, which will mark with its rigid structure the subject's entire mental development.[83]

The movement from fragmented body (*corps morcelé*) to "orthopaedic totality" is traced by Jane Gallop in her study, *Reading Lacan*.[84] In her reading, the mirror stage is crucial since it is not only the individual's *future* that is created in anticipation, but his *past*, the body in bits and pieces, that is also retroactively imagined, perceived for the first time in the illusory mirror moment, when the body seems to become coherent. Anticipation creates an awareness of the *corps morcele* that must come *after* the mirror stage.

Since the entire past and present is dependent upon an already anticipated maturity—that is, a projected ideal one—any "natural maturation (however closely it might resemble the anticipated ideal one) must be defended against, for it threatens to expose the fact that the self is an illusion done with mirrors."

Gallop quotes a later article of Lacan, to focus the paradox of the mirror stage:

> This illusion of unity, in which a human being is always looking forward to self-mastery, entails a constant danger of sliding back again into the chaos from which he started; it hangs over the abyss of a dizzy Ascent in which one can perhaps see the very essence of Anxiety.[85]

Self-mastery is, in some unavoidable sense, the realization of the falsity of the self. And yet, there is the infant's *jubilation.* In spite of the anxiety of the "dizzy Ascent," in spite of the risk of "sliding back again into . . . chaos," there is that "fleeting moment of jubilation" (Gallop) on the threshold of selfhood. This moment, then, is a "brief moment of doomed glory," like that of Adam and Eve, expelled from paradise into history: anticipating mastery, they actually gain a "horrified recognition of their nakedness."

The Paradox of Redemption

Like Adam and Eve, and the mirror-stage infant, we have the Exodus midrashic couple in the mirror. In a moment of illumination, they laugh at the anticipated beauty of their being. Inspired by the truth of her "inner sphere," the woman challenges her husband to recognize the mirror image of his own beauty. In this way the couple are "precipitated from insufficiency to anticipation." This is the secret of redemption: they are "thrown forward into history."

The tragic dimension of the experience, however, as Gallop points out, is that, like the infant, the couple have "assumed by anticipation a totalized mastered body." They must therefore retroactively perceive their own inadequacy. A vision of wholeness will give birth to the infinite variations of the whole Jewish people (the mythic six hundred thousand births); each woman senses the intimate immensity of the resources of self and other. But the new awareness that is redemption inevitably brings with it an awareness of the body "in bits and pieces." For it is, in essence, a moment of self-delusion, of captivation by an illusory image. Both future and past are thus rooted in an illusion.

Inevitably, we are confronting the radical questions raised earlier (pp. 25–27) about whether the people are fit for redemption. Are they *re'uyim*, literally, are they "see-able" as redeemed? The power of the midrash lies in its affirmation of a transformative vision that anticipates a future beauty and thus reconstructs the past. This is the "secret" of the women, as they place the "inner sphere," the intimate arena of their love-relations with their husbands in the mirror of their desire. In doing this, they defy the *gezera*: instead of that which must be, there are multiple possibilities, jubilant, polymorphous, anticipatory:

> Sublimated forms of love—political, social, religious, cultural—reclaim a totality on a historical as well as a personal scale. But in every form of love a past and a future are grasped as if present . . . What is *ahistorical* is the need to hope. And the act of hoping is inseparable from the energy of love, from that which "holds," from that which is art's constant example.[86]

At the same time, there is a recognition of the illusory image, the "horrified recognition of . . . nakedness," with the anxiety at "sliding back again into . . . chaos," of which Lacan writes. The self is not yet mastered, the body is still—and especially now, retroactively—"in bits and pieces."

The paradox of redemption, therefore, is a tragic one. When Moses, with perhaps unparalleled savagery, cries out, "Break their thighs," he does so out of this anxiety of the *gezera* mind. Things are what they are; to pretend otherwise, to anticipate, to create counter-realities is to assume a posture of mastery that is not justified. In the house of mourning, according to Jewish tradition, the bereaved cover the mirrors. Without illusion, without anticipation, we accept the *gezera*, the reality of the human condition, as God has imposed it upon us.

And yet God defends the women's mirror-practice; with all the anxiety that will ensue, the women, each in her intimate sphere of mirror work, have modeled redemption. Perhaps for this reason, the language of the midrash associated God's name with the most natural gestures in the narrative: the surge of the little fish into the women's buckets, the multiple births. Excessive, surrealistic, they offer access to the "secret," inexplicable knowledge that is called *peh peh*: *pakod pakad*.

The Midwives Mirror Abraham

One example from the biblical narrative: "The midwives feared God and did not do as the king of Egypt had told them; they let the boys live" (1:17). As we have seen, the midrashic tradition understands them to have acted in unexpected, life-nurturing ways: not only do they not obey Pharaoh, they do something that is called "fear of God." The midrash formulates this in a startling way:

They modeled their conduct (literally, they adorned themselves) on that of their progenitor, Abraham, of whom God testified, "For now I know that you are a God-fearing man (Gen 22:12)." They said, "Abraham, our ancestor, opened an inn where he fed all wayfarers, men who were uncircumcised; and, as for us, not only have we nothing with which to feed them, but we are even to kill them! No, we will keep them alive!" When Pharaoh saw that they did not fulfill his decree, he summoned them . . .[87]

The midwives' leap of faith gains its momentum from an act of costuming. They contemplate "self and Abraham"—a diptych—and will themselves to "enact Abraham." They "adorn themselves"—*kashtu;* the same root as Rashi used dismissively for women's mirror-narcissism is used here to convey the assumption of a role, the use of art to reach to the "inner sphere" of truth. The word *kushta*, ironically, means "truth" in Aramaic. The midwives find an inaccessible layer of integrity through a decisive act of mirroring. In doing this, they anticipate "natural maturation"; they anticipate, in fact, a newly humiliating awareness of their "bits and pieces" reality: "We are even to kill the babies!"

The act of preserving, nurturing life is made equivalent to "fearing God." The midwives construct this as the defining act of Abraham's life: a deliberate misreading of the text, since Abraham's "fear of God" is, as the midrash itself notes, a function of the Akeda test. "Now I know that you are a God-fearing man, for you have not withheld your son, your only one from Me" (Gen 22:12), says the angel, after the test is over and Isaac is released. In the midrash, the God-fearing attribute of Abraham is transplanted to different soil. He invested actively in human lives of all kinds, in fulfilling the needs of travelers (the type of the vulnerable, physically needy other): how can the midwives face themselves in the mirror, if they refuse to assume the same role?

It is interesting to notice that the two midwives, Shifra and Puah, are considered by Ibn Ezra to represent a large group of working midwives serving the population of Israelite women. They were perhaps the state fiscal administrators of the midwives' guild.[88] The effect of this speculation is to make the midwives' reaction to Pharaoh's *gezerah* not an exceptionally heroic one, but rather one shared by the whole body politic of Hebrew midwives.

This stage in the formation of the *"Je,"* the Ideal-I of the people, is experienced, then, on the microscopic level, couple by couple. Against the *gezera*, the edict proclaiming what must be, against the actual immaturity, unfitness of the people, the women construct the surrealistic image of babies streaming from mirrors, propelled by desire. The tragic dimension of the mirror stage will haunt the people, couple by couple, individual by individual, for the whole forty years of maturation in the wilderness. For the world of *gezera* is not to be cheated by the radical jubilations of redemption. During their protracted travails in the wilderness, the people will play out the tensions of redemption anticipated and paradise lost.

A Decree Harder than Pharaoh's

For now, however, there are intimations of the revolutionary potential of the mirror stage. In the following midrash, the mode of *gezera* is extended into the world of the Israelites:

> Puah was so named because she lifted up her face (literally, "made her face appear") against Pharaoh and turned up her nose at him, saying, "Woe to this man when God comes to exact His retribution!" . . . Puah, because she lifted up her face against her father. Amram was at that time the head of the Sanhedrin, and when Pharaoh decreed, "If it is a boy, kill him," Amram said, "The Israelites beget children for nothing," and immediately separated from his wife, had no intercourse with her, even divorced her when she was three months pregnant. Then, all the Israelites arose and divorced their wives. His daughter said to him, "Your decree (*gezera*) is harsher than that of Pharaoh; for Pharaoh decreed the elimination of the male children only, while you decree the elimination of male and female alike. Besides, Pharaoh is wicked, so it is doubtful whether his decree will be fulfilled, but you are righteous and your decree will be fulfilled." So he took his wife back and was followed by all the Israelites, who also took their wives back. That is why she was called Puah, becaused she lifted up her face against her father.[89]

Miriam defies her father. He is a figure of authority, not only as father but as head of the Israelites' court of justice, the Sanhedrin. His reaction to Pharaoh's *gezera* is, essentially, to issue his own *gezera*, which, in a paradoxical sense, underwrites, even exacerbates Pharaoh's. His daughter mobilizes the power of her face and voice to speak of the destructive effect of her father's *gezera*: it is more *kasheh* than Pharaoh's, she says, using the routine adjective that describes the nature of all *gezeroth*—hard, irresistible, making redemption impossible. It seems that not only the wicked make *gezeroth;* the righteous, too, deal in "what must be," "the way it has to be."

The irony of Miriam's comment is courageous and finely honed. For her father's decision, his decree of effective sterilization, is surely a serious response to Pharaoh's genocidal plan. "We beget children for nothing," her father says: ultimately, all our attempts to "anticipate" and create the future are pointless. There is a weight to his decision; just because he is a righteous man, it is not arbitrary, but judicious. Objectively, his daughter brings him no news when she says his decision condemns daughters as well as sons. Indeed, in other versions of this midrash, serious credit is given to his decision, as well as to its reversal:

> God said to Moses: The merit of Amram, your father, protects you, because he did a great thing in Israel. When the Egyptians laid harsh labor upon the Israelites, and drowned them in the river, they said, "We marry and beget children, and the Egyptians drown them in the river. Why do we tire ourselves out for nothing?" Then Amram arose and did a great thing in Israel, and thereby reflected the will of God. He divorced his wife, who was three months pregnant. And three months later, he remarried her, as it is said, "A man from the house of Levi went and married the daughter of Levi . . ." (2:1)[90]

A striking detail in both versions is the fact that his wife, Jochebed, is three months pregnant when he divorces her. The act of despair is timed providentially, so that the redeemer is already conceived. But from the human point of view, the decision to divorce, to prevent future births, is a rational, a fully serious one, which God Himself, rather mysteriously, calls a "great act." And yet, to balance it, there must be an act of remarriage, a nonrational celebration of life, in spite of the *gezera.* Perhaps, after all, *this* is the "great act" of which God speaks?—not the divorce but the remarriage? Or both together, the tension of *gezera* and desire, held in love?

> . . . the totality which love has to continually reclaim is precisely the totality which time so convincingly appears to fragment and hide. Love is a reconstitution—in the heart as much as in the mind—of that "holding," of that Being, which occurs in the momentary equilibrium created by the opposing forces of sexuality and time.[91]

In Midrash HaGadol and other versions of this midrash, there are angels dancing beside the wedding canopy in its triumphal procession, singing, "O joyous mother of children . . ." But Jochebed is already pregnant, the remarriage is not a necessary, practical measure to ensure the birth of the redeemer; it is simply a gratuitous celebration, a vindication of that hidden sphere for which Miriam-Puah speaks.

The role of Miriam varies in the different midrashic texts. In Midrash HaGadol, she is absent; the dialectic of Amram's divorce and remarriage is not blurred by any intervening voice.[92] The greatness, the merit, are his alone. In most other versions, however, it is Miriam who speaks the counter-truth to the truth of the *gezera*. Hers is the credit for the redemptive idea of remarriage; it is she who articulates, by face and voice, the limitations, the deathliness of the *gezera*. As we have suggested, this cannot constitute any great revelation for Amram. Naturally, he must know the logical implications of his own decree. But she makes fully visible to him the radical meaning of *gezera*, in its most virtuous form.

Amram follows his daughter's advice; although she does not articulate it, her advice is implicit in her comparison of her father with Pharaoh.[93] The consequences are narrated with conscious irony in the Talmud:

> Miriam would prophesy, "My mother will give birth to a son who will save Israel." When Moses was born, the whole house was filled with light. Her father arose and kissed her on her head and said, "My daughter, your prophecy is fulfilled." But when the baby was thrown into the river, her father arose and tapped her on her head and said, "My daughter, now where is your prophecy?" So it is written, "His sister stationed herself at a distance to know what would become of him—what would become of her prophecy."[94]

In the *gezera* view of the world, reality is perceived in freeze-frame mode. Things are what they are, what they must be. There is no other basis for decision, for evaluation. Now, there is one more baby bound for the river—that is the effect of Miriam's prophetic speech.

She alone stands expectant, waiting on knowledge—*lede'ah* the word is the same as the one that brings to a head God's awareness, His empathy for what has previously been overlooked in his people: *Vayeda elokim*—"And God knew" (2:25). It is the word that is used to describe Pharaoh's essential failure: the first fact we are given about him is that "he did not know (*lo yada*) Joseph" (1:8). On one view,[95] indeed, this is the same Pharaoh as the one who did not know God: "Who is Hashem, that I should listen to His voice to free Israel? I do not know Hashem . . ." (5:2). In this view, "not knowing" constitutes a failure in responsibility, a refusal to respond to the challenge of the other. This is intimated in the midrashic comment on "Pharaoh who did not know Joseph": He made himself *as though he did not know.*[96] The way of those who live in the *gezera* mode is to limit knowledge, vulnerability, empathy; the verbal link with "I do not know Hashem," intimates what knowledge of Hashem might demand. And Miriam, waiting on knowledge, anticipates that maturation of a vision.

5. *Infinitude and Finitude: Staging Redemption*

The Mirror and the *Gezerah*

Ultimately, the problem of the *gezera* mode and the redemptive mirror work of the women affects the largest questions. For the *gezera* is of course one of the modes of God Himself. It would be inadequate to the complexity of the issue to idealize the women's mirror work, the culture of desire that is their project, as though it represented a total value. The redemption that comes of mirrors, as we have seen, bears with it anxiety, the awareness that all can be lost, the fear of "sliding back again into the chaos."[97] This, in fact, is precisely the dynamic that will possess the Israelites in the wilderness. The moments of loving, transforming vision will be succeeded by moments of anger, of regression, even of hatred. The experience of such different moments will generate different histories of exodus: histories of redemption, histories of chagrin.

It is true that God vindicates the women and their mirrors against the violent anger of Moses. All the hosts of possibility are created by mirrors. The delicate workings of the "inner sphere" create new life; they are the very stuff of redemption. And yet, as always in the powerful midrashic narratives of confrontation, Moses' anger finds a voice that is not suppressed by the ultimate judgment of God. The dialogue is preserved intact.

For Moses speaks for one dimension of the way that God Himself rules the world. This dimension, which is called *gezera*, is the cause, strangely, of the whole Egyptian exile. This is "the edict of the Covenant between the Pieces": God told Abraham, "Your seed shall be sojourners in a land that is not theirs, and they shall enslave them and afflict them for four hundred years . . ." (Gen 15:13). The rest of Genesis and the whole of Exodus are the playing out of that *gezera*. See, for instance, Ramban's introduction to Exodus: "This book is devoted to the narrative of the first exile, which was decreed (*nigzar*) explicitly, and of the redemption from it . . ." And see, also,

Ramban on the beginning of the Joseph saga, in which personal, family passions will flesh out the fulfillment of God's "plot":

> *A man found him wandering in the field: . . .* This teaches us that the *gezera*, the edict, is true and all human ingenuity is in vain (to evade God's intent).[98]

From this theological perspective, there is only the *gezera* of God, His decree, in all its steely hardness. Even when Joseph feels at his most free, events are arranged in such a way as to determine his actions.

Maharal, indeed, presses the point home, by reversing our normal ways of reading narrative. It is not, he claims, that the brothers' selling of Joseph eventually brings punishment on the whole family—slavery in Egypt. Rather, it is the *gezera*, God's decree to Abraham, that "causes" the brothers to sell Joseph! Maharal goes so far as to exonerate the brothers from blame: Joseph sends a coded message to Jacob, assuring him that the whole tragic history is a *gezera* from heaven—the inexorable working of destiny.

This strictly providential view of history leaves little room for the individual freedom, the complex ferment of the inner sphere, of which Havel writes. When Moses is angry with the women and their mirrors, he sees the world as shaped by the *gezera;* and God presses him to recognize the cost of his perspective: "These you despise. . . ?! These mirrors begat all those hosts in Egypt!" What makes this doubly difficult for Moses is that the authority for his *gezera* is God, the very Being now telling him to rethink his reality. God's rhetorical question challenges him to perform the most difficult task, to change a well-founded, totally structured way of looking at reality. To such a totalizing gaze, the people are unworthy, the mirrors are a malapropism in the sanctuary of God.

The *gezera* world has the weight of experience, of memory, of astute observation behind it: inevitably, it cramps the free play of imagination. In an evocative use of the word *gezera*, for instance, Rashi declares: "A *gezera* has been enacted that the dead are forgotten from the heart at the end of twelve months."[99] More than simply a statement about what invariably happens, Rashi's comment indicates how inexplicable, from a private human perspective, such a forgetting is; nevertheless, since it is part of God's dispensation in the world, that it is invariable and even, in some sense, benign. In the Genesis narrative that is the basis of Rashi's comment, Jacob refuses to be comforted for the disappearance of his son Joseph. Why does the usual *gezera* of ultimate forgetting not give him relief? Because it applies only to those who really are dead, while Joseph, unknown to his father, is alive. Implicit in this strained logic is the suggestion that Jacob cannot be comforted because he knows, in some subconscious sense, that Joseph is not dead.[100] But even if he were dead, the mechanism of comfort-forgetting remains a dispensation that is bizarre to the sensibility of the "inner sphere." Hard-edged, it protects the world against luxuries of grief. But in its concern for the structure, for the *binyan*, it silences the cry of the individual, the possibility of pain and of blessing.

Ezekiel's dry bones cry out, "We are cut off—*nigzarnu lanu*—We are the victims of the *gezera* perspective, we are those who die before redemption comes." Ramban, we have seen, identifies the Israelites in Egypt with this bone-dry despair. And women, righteous women of that time, wield mirrors to make rebirth possible. God vindicates them, but Moses' voice is not censored out of the narrative. For Moses' anger is part of the tension in which the identity of the people will be formed. It is the same anger that protested that the people are unfit for redemption. It is the same anger that declared, "Please, O Lord, I am not a man of words . . . I am heavy of mouth and heavy of tongue" (4:10). A stern realism, a recognition of human limits, characterizes these speeches. But also anger, the anger of one who will not ask for miracles, for transformations.[101]

Emmanuel Levinas writes:

> The language of the Old Testament is so suspicious of any rhetoric which never stammers that it has as its chief prophet a man "slow of speech and of tongue." In this disability we can see more than the simple admission of a limitation; it also acknowledges the nature of this kerygma, one which does not forget *the weight of the world, the inertia of men, the dullness of their understanding.*[102] (Emphasis added)

The weight, the inertia, the dullness—all dimensions of a *gezera* world—proclaim an unredeemed people, a people who, properly speaking, are "unfit for redemption." Transformation is the need of the hour, a dynamic process that will, in R. Hutner's phrase, "create the face of one who *can receive . . .*"[103] Such a face, transformed from within, that can receive others, that can receive God, and His Torah, is molded by that which engages with the *kasheh*, the *gezera*: by questions (*kushiyoth*) that open one to answers. Ultimately, a therapeutic narrative of the Exodus will develop out of the answers to these questions.

"I SHALL BE WHAT I SHALL BE . . ."

In a subversive sense, Moses is allied with Pharaoh, king of the *kaved* (heavy), the *gezera*, the intransigent; but also with Amram, and with a dimension of God Himself. Yet here, in the mirror-midrash, God Himself challenges him to interrogate "the way it must be." This paradoxical confrontation can perhaps be traced back to the opening dialogue at the Burning Bush. Moses asks God, "When they (the Israelites) ask me, What is His name? what shall I tell them?" (3:13). God's answer is: *ehyeh asher ehyeh*—"I shall be what I shall be." This enigmatic answer has generated countless divergent interpretations; to quote a classic midrashic figure of speech—How many pens have been broken, how much ink spilt, to explain this sentence!

Rashi's comment increases complexity: "I shall be with them in this anguish as I shall be with them in future crises of slavery!" On this reading, God defines Himself as the God of continual redemption; implicitly, catastrophically, God intimates that Jewish history will be one of continual crises. There will be other slaveries, other redemptions. The implications of this reading, which Rashi quotes from the Babylonian Talmud,[104] are so somber that Moses is instructed to tell the people only of the immediate redemption, the first *ehyeh*: "Tell the children of Israel, *Ehyeh* has sent me to you . . ." (3:14). The full meaning of God's identity as redeemer is veiled; as far as the people are concerned, "Sufficient unto the day is the evil thereof."

Maharal[105] takes the inner logic of God's self-naming a stage further. God's being is a being-with—"I shall be-with you." It will always respond to the need of the human, to the specific quality of the human cry. The particular idiom of a particular time, a particular place, a particular conception of God will draw forth an answering sense of redemption. From Moses' viewpoint, this name of God is no name at all: it yields nothing constant, nothing knowable through all vicissitudes. It is contingent, the very figure of human desire—a fluid, dynamic name, it expresses the First Person form of God's Name (some read the Tetragrammaton as the third person form of the verb "to be"), addressing the human, involved in dialogue with the human. It changes constantly, as human beings find and lose relationship with Him. This periodicity implicitly contains within itself the idea of continual "slaveries"—periods of catastrophe and subjection.

The human experience of redemption, then, will be episodic; it will remain a problematic existential desire. Even after this first redemption, the human being remains the "center of surprise in creation," calling out, responding in ways that defy all "dogmatic encystment."[106] God names Himself in terms of that evolving human capacity:

> What is the meaning of *Ehyeh asher Ehyeh*—"I shall be what I shall be?" "As you are with Me, so I am with you. If they open their hands to give charity, so I shall open My hands, as it is said, 'God shall open for you His goodly treasure.' " (Deut 28:12)[107]

In a similar vein, the opening of the Ten Commandments is read by Mei HaShiloach: "I am the Lord your God." The word for "I" is *anochi*, rather than *ani*, an alternative form. *Anochi*, comments this Chasidic writer, contains the letter *chaf*, which means "like, as if": as a prefix, it has a modifying, approximating effect. This introduces into the very basis of the Ten Commandments a tonality of incompleteness, of human work of discovery still to be done. Multiple possibilities are held within the Torah text, a tension of evolving revelations; with each new understanding will come a realization of the benighted "un-revelation" of the previous stage. As with the infant in the mirror, the "Je," the *anochi* of present mastery is always a matter of anticipation and always creates a past of "bits and pieces," of incoherent mastery (Lacan's "corps morcelé").

For this reason, the next Commandment exposes the negative dimension of human mastery: "You shall not make for yourself a graven image . . ." The Zohar reads: "Do not construct for yourself other Torahs." It stands against the construction of absolute systems, cut in stone, claiming eternal validity. Only the Torah can claim such immaculate perfection; but even the Torah, as we have seen, is to be understood by human beings, in a mode of evolving revelation. In its absolute dimension, beyond human reach, the Torah is called "the Torah of Moses our Teacher" so that once again we are reminded of the tension between Moses and that dimension of God which invites continuous revelation.[108]

A Necessary Tension

This tension, best exemplified in the mirror-midrash, makes it impossible for us to lapse back into our monochrome mode of vision. When Moses argues repeatedly that the people are unfit for redemption, he is forced to look in the mirror. His insistence that he is overwhelmed, that his mouth and tongue cannot bear the weight, the resistant hardness of reality, is answered by the loving intimacy of the women playing with mirrors. God compels his gaze upon the redemptive rewards of desire. He justifies the women: from the "hidden ferment" of the inner sphere emerges a force that will shatter systems and generate "hosts of Israel." But in justifying the hosts of desire, the "hosts of God," as the Torah names them (12:41), God yet addresses Moses with a certain tenderness, which the midrash subtly suggests in the use of the vocative: "God said to Moses: 'Moses, these you despise. . . ?' " Reproach is implicit, but also love.

It is as though God acknowledges, even as he corrects Moses, that, without Moses' form of sensitivity to the *gezera*-mode, there will be no *torath moshe*, no tension between what is and what may be. All the power and beauty of the culture of desire arises from that sustained tension. The mirrors become pregnant in their brilliance when they achieve difficult unions. When all merges into all, desire fails and vision becomes banal. The tragic moment of Lacan's mirror stage, like the moment of expulsion from Eden, fuses jubilation and anxiety. Moses' reaction of outrage preserves that moment from kitsch, the bane of transfigurative experience.

For the mystery of such experience has at its core the *kasheh*, the harsh, the irresistible, the difficult intimately involved with the desirable. The Sages reflect on the body of the woman in childbirth: "God makes her limbs *hard as stones* when she sits on the birth-stool, else she would die . . ."[109] The adventure of birth is to be undertaken in a spirit of hard, gem-like clarity. The woman's body becomes *stony;* only so, can she survive. Births of all kinds, one might say, demand this quality of stoniness, of *avanim.* The wordplay between *avanim* (stones) and *banim* (babies) is not trivial, suggesting the paradox of hardness and softness, death and life, masculine and feminine.[110] Restraint, discipline, a total dedication, a hard energy are associated with the female:[111] Jeremiah speaks of those who "say to the stone, You gave birth to me" (2:27). An uncanny, unsentimental image: the lapidary intentness of the body giving birth. "Or else she would die": the hardness is vital, brings her through the terror of creation.

The tactile sense of the *kasheh* is ultimately associated, in a context that seems quite uncomplimentary, with the very nature of the Jewish people. Resistant, insensitive, rigid—stiff-necked (*kesheh oref*)—they are described by God after the sin of the Golden Calf. But in an unexpected midrashic turn, one of the Sages praises the virtues of the stiff-necked: "You think it is a vice of the Jewish people? But really, it is a virtue, since it makes them capable of enduring martyrdom, rather than abandon their faith."[112] Historically, the Sages recognize, the stiff neck has proven itself an organ of spiritual survival.

The Tension of Exodus

Ironically, the Exodus narrative associates this life-preserving facet of the *kasheh* with everything that seeks to prevent birth, release, redemption. This brings us full circle to the central question we have been exploring: the unfitness of the people, Moses' continuous and disenchanted eyeing of their—and his—unreadiness for redemption. This habitual response on Moses' part runs counter to the compassion for his people that is evident from the first description of his adult consciousness: "Moses grew up, he went out to his brothers, and he saw their suffering . . ." (2:11). His eyes dwell on their suffering, on what they have to bear. From the beginning of his narrative, an immediate empathy permeates his thoughts and actions. In a sense, this is the foundation for all the tension of his relation with the people in the future: in his angriest moments, the infrastructure of empathy is a given. Why, then, does he speak so carpingly of them—to the point where God marks his skin with the snakelike, leprous transformations of the slanderous?

Sefath Emeth offers an arresting view of Moses' dynamic with God.[113] Moses speaks "face to face" with God. This means that he speaks not so as to have the final word, but so that the essential words can be spoken by God. Moses, sensitive to that dynamic moment in all relationships which changes reality, enters into a kind of mirror-game with God: "How are they fit for redemption?"—the skeptical question is intended to challenge God into expressing a vision of their fitness. God answers with a vision of the people in anticipated beauty: in the future, they will serve Him on this same mountain, they will become capable of saying, with a mature faith, "We shall do and we shall hear."[114] In a version of the mirror stage, the "drama whose internal thrust is precipitated from insufficiency to anticipation," God anticipates the maturation of the people's power. But in the anthropomorphic temerity of Chasidic thought, it is Moses who has allowed, invited, *provoked* God into this generous vision of mastery and wholeness.

In this reading, Moses sets the stage for divine redemption. The hardness, the objectivity, the way it has to be—these must be uttered, so that the mirrors can be mobilized in contradictory, visionary love. An alternative scenario might have been to let God speak first, express anger, criticism of the people, and then for Moses to defend the people and point out their potential. This is the dynamic between Moses and God at important later points in the narrative. Here, however, at the very foundation, he stages rather than argues for redemption, as do the women with their mirrors of desire. Responding to God's approach, he speaks first, devil's advocate, rational spokesman for entropy. He creates an imbalance, a vacuum, out of which God can contradict him, speaking for anticipation, for the beauty that will be.

An audacious game. In the subtle reading of Sefath Emeth, Moses' anger with the people has about it a quality of role-playing. Someone has to speak for the *kasheh* dimension. Moses performs a cathartic act to make space for God's love to appear. In the same complex passage, Sefath Emeth reads the midrashic comment on God's anger at the sin of the Golden Calf. God says to Moses: " 'Return to the camp': If I am angry, and you are angry, then who will bring them close?"[115] And Sefath Emeth turns the screw one more turn: it is Moses who has staged the situation, by enacting alienation, withdrawing from the camp . . . *so that* God will break the impasse of too much anger.

What is important in both situations is that the exchange brings human beings closer to God. Moses' project is not the description of reality; it is bringing the godly into contact with the lives of his people. By playing devil's advocate, Moses makes closeness possible. Now it is God Himself and not merely Moses who will utter the redemptive vision.

In the end, the anthropomorphic midrashic and Chasidic narratives must translate back into human experience. If Moses attacks the people for unfitness, himself for inadequacy, it is in order to model the real risks of redemption. In the narrative of the Exodus, both he and they will pay the price of precipitate redemption, of the generous mirror imagination. To quote Berger again:

> . . . in every form of love a past and a future are grasped as if present. The momentary "holding," seized by the imagination through the energy of love, realizes a whole, which is outside time . . . To ask whether love has or has not an objective existence is to ask a somewhat mechanical question, for it ignores that what we feel can be a response to what approaches us . . . in both time and space . . . This "approaching" has al-

ways been recognized by artists and in the modern era has been termed inspiration.[116]

Approached by God's presence, there is a "momentary holding," followed by much doubt, much anger, many struggles to reconstitute that loving vision that is "outside time"—to make it authentically contain all, even the world of time. For this project, both mirrors and edicts will be necessary; both narrative and law; both the visionary women and the austere Moses. But revelation sparks precisely in the encounter of opposites.

Two things of opposite natures seem to depend
On one another, as a man depends
On a woman, day on night, the imagined

On the real. This is the origin of change.
Winter and spring, cold copulars, embrace
And forth the particulars of rapture come.[117]

Often abrasive, never simple, the drama of Exodus, ranging over forty years, will play out the implicit tensions of these modalities. This will not be a morality play, with good and evil forces allegorically figured in different protagonists and predictably arrayed on the stage. Moses, single-minded "man of God," is chosen for his role because he "turned aside to see" the Burning Bush. According to one radical midrash, "Moses craned his neck to see": this "turning" is a torsion of the neck, a deliberate motion out of the straight, the stiff:

> Moses said, Let me turn aside to see . . . Rabbi Jonathan said, "He took three steps;" Rabbi Simeon ben Levi said, "He took no steps, but he twisted his neck. God said to him, 'You went to trouble to see—as you live, you are worthy that I should reveal Myself to you.' " Immediately, "God called to him from the midst of the burning bush . . ."[118]

God chooses to reveal Himself to Moses, because he has "gone to trouble to see." As against Rabbi Jonathan's spatial reading (three steps constitute the movement into a different space), Rabbi Simeon condenses Moses' movement to a "twist of the neck." Subtle, minimalistic, Moses' gesture realigns his whole being, puts it into intimate relation with that which has approached him. Such a gesture involves "trouble," a deviation from the obvious. For Rabbi Simeon, it is his capacity to "twist his neck," to turn his face in wonder and questioning, that brings him the voice of God.

The neck in torsion—an image for desire, a counterimage to the stiff-necked intransigence of those who set themselves against the new. Within Moses himself, within his people, within the Egyptians, even within the representations of God in the narratives of redemption, the tensions of Exodus will seek resolution, the momentary equilibrium that again and again is to be lost and reclaimed.

2 *Vaera*

THE EXILE OF THE WORD

[6:2–9:34]

1. *Resisting Redemption: Moses*

The Crisis of Redemption

The first stage of the redemption has ended, it seems, in failure and frustration, with Moses protesting to God. Under pressure from a brutalized people, who question the authority by which Moses and Aaron have provoked Pharaoh to harsher policies, Moses cries out, "Since I have come to Pharaoh to speak in Your Name, he has dealt worse with this people; You have not saved Your people" (5:23).

In a subtle movement, he speaks first of "*this* people," and then of "*Your* people." "This people" has an alienated ring: the people become an object of discourse. "Your people," on the other hand, suggests relationship, God's concern for human life. It recalls the form that God uses when he first speaks to Moses at the Burning Bush: "I have indeed seen the affliction of *My* people . . ." (3:7). Perhaps Moses is quietly quoting God back to Himself, as though to say, "Where now is that empathy of which You spoke so emphatically. . . ?" That is, the radical nature of Moses' protest lies not so much in its description of objective fact—"things have got worse instead of better"—as in its tone of disillusion and irony.

This is, undoubtedly, a dangerous moment in his relation to God. God has made promises, has, essentially, told a story that begins in empathy and ends in a land flowing with milk and honey. Now, Moses reports a different, a demonic narrative, in which events turn towards tragedy—a narrative of evil, failure to save, the perverse effect of his mission. In this micro-narrative, God's empathic declarations are placed in ironic quotation marks: "You have in fact not saved 'Your people.' "

The situation, then, is not a promising one. In Rashi's words, Moses has spoken harshly to God. God responds by reaffirming His promises, and by emphasizing His Name: "I am Hashem" (6:2). He links His commitment to save the people with his unfulfilled promises to their ancestors, Abraham, Isaac, and Jacob. There is even, perhaps, an answering irony in God's words, "I, too, have heard the moaning of the Israelites" (6:5)—"you are not the only sensitive observer on the scene!"[1] But, at their core, God's words are a renewed message to the people: a narrative of insistent, dynamic hope, with four verbs of redemption that lead the imagination from past to future: "I will free you from the labors of the Egyptians; I will save you from their bondage; I will redeem you with an outstretched arm and through great acts of judgment; I will take you for Me as a people . . ." (6:6–7).

This is the message that Moses brings to the people. But, once again, there is the paralyzing jolt of failure. All God's bounteous synonyms for redemption are met with blankness: "Moses spoke thus (*ken*—in just this way) to the children of Israel, but they did not listen to Moses, out of shortness of spirit and hard labor" (6:9). The narrative grinds heavily to a halt.

Apparently changing direction, God now tells Moses, "Go speak to Pharaoh, king of Egypt, that he may send the children of Israel free from his land" (6:11). Moses answers: "The children of Israel would not listen to me; how then should Pharaoh listen to me—and I am of uncircumcised lips!" (6:12).

Moses' answer, which again seems to bring the narrative to an impasse, is one of the classic examples of *kal vachomer*—the *a fortiore* argument—in the Torah. This is the argument from a minor to a major premise, as in Genesis 44:8: "Even the silver that we found in the mouths of our bags we brought back to you from the land of Canaan—how then could we have stolen any silver or gold from your master's house!" Here, too, the logic is clear: if Israel, who have every reason to desire to hear of redemption, have refused to hear me, then how can I expect Pharaoh, whose vested interests are clearly massed against me, to listen to me? At this point, Moses adds the *coup de grace* to his narrative of futility: ". . . and I am of uncircumcised lips."

Reverting to his original resistance at the Burning Bush, he speaks of himself as one who cannot speak. How, then, can he expect Pharaoh and—in retrospect—the Israelites, too—to listen?

The crisis in the drama of redemption enters its most fraught moment. It could be sketched with a kind of structural simplicity: God's will, His message of redemption, is blocked by all three human protagonists: by Pharaoh, by the Israelites, and by Moses himself. Pharaoh and the Israelites are described as "not listening." The formula, *lo shama* ("he did not listen"), indeed, will become the leitmotiv of the plague-narrative. Repeatedly, Pharaoh's surrender to God will be neutralized in these words. An essential deafness inheres in Pharaoh's persona. But the Israelites, too, as we have just noticed, are described in terms of deafness (6:9, 12). Their deafness is contrasted with Pharaoh's only in being accounted for: it is a product of "shortness of spirit and hard labor." What this diagnosis may mean, as well as the enigmatic quality of Pharaoh's deafness, are subjects I explore in this chapter.

Before I turn to them, however, let me emphasize that Moses, too, belongs to the complex party of those who block God's message of redemption. In his protest, in his ironic interrogation of God's narrative, in his questioning of the people's "fitness for redemption,"[2] he essentially refuses the role to which God has called him.

The heart of his refusal is in these last words: ". . . I am of uncircumcised lips." Their power and poignancy can be estimated if one asks why he uses this particular form of *kal vachomer* logic, moving from minor to major conclusion: if the children of Israel would not listen, how can I expect Pharaoh to listen? A simpler argument might have been to speak of Pharaoh's proven obduracy: Moses and Aaron have already experienced his willful deafness ("Who is God that I should listen to His voice?" [5:2]). Indeed, this deafness had resulted, as we have noticed, in a tragic tightening of the stranglehold of slavery. Why, then, should he listen this second time?

This, however, is not the argument that Moses uses. In his words, the real pain emerges with great lucidity: it is a "hearing problem" that besets him. To put it very simply, Moses is saying, "I cannot make them listen—I am of foreskinned lips."[3] What he is expressing is a sense of impotence: "I am incapable of communicating with either of my two audiences—the evidence is devastatingly clear, if even those who have an interest in hearing me will not listen!"

The complexity of Moses' complaint is given additional resonance in the reading of Sefath Emeth.[4] Here, Moses links the "deafness" of both Pharaoh and the Israelites with his own "foreskinned" lips: "*because* they would not listen, *therefore* I am of foreskinned lips." Speech, we normally affirm, creates listeners (or fails to create them). Here, the converse truth is affirmed: it is the listener who creates the act of speech. The prophet prophesies by dint of the listening of his people. As long as there is no one to listen to God's word, language impotently stutters. In this vein, Sefath Emeth reads the prophetic call: "Listen, my people, that I may speak" (Ps 50:7)—"Your listening will enable me to speak."

The pathology described here is what the Zohar calls the Exile of the Word. The dynamic of language, of communication, has failed. In the Zohar, this failure is the profound meaning of exile; it encompasses the inability to hear and the inability to speak. Moses' speech problem, in this context, is to be understood as a function of a deeper cultural rupture. The ears of this generation do not, cannot respond to living language. For this reason, Moses will not, cannot speak.

The impasse of this moment, in which all protagonists close out the word of God, is the essential dilemma of redemption. I would like to explore this "crisis of language," in which human beings seem to form a phalanx to resist God's narrative. Moses, the Israelites, and Pharaoh are strangely matched in a common resistance. The situation has a surrealistic, even a subversive quality: without villains or heroes, beyond good and evil, defying resolution.

The most radical imagery used by the midrash to portray this impasse is of stalled birth: what if the baby refuses to leave the womb, if the mother's body refuses to release, if the natural processes will not proceed to their natural conclusion?

> "Has God ever ventured to go and take Himself one nation from the midst (*kerev*) of another?" (Deut 4:34) What is the force of "one nation *from the midst* (from the innards [*kerev*]) of another nation"? Like a person who extracts the foetus from the bowels of the mother animal, God brought Israel out of Egypt, as it is said, ". . . the *innards* (*kerev*) and the entrails." This is clearly stressful for the delivered (the fetus): how do we know that it is also stressful for the deliverer? As it is said, "God took you and brought you out from the iron blast furnace" (4:20)—like one who extracts gold from fire, without tongs or gloves . . .[5]

A forceps delivery is the violent resolution to the stalled birth: God forcibly removes His people, torpid, assimilated to the fetal condition, from the deathly hold of the Egyptian mother-body. This solution, however, as the midrash itself—modulating from the birth-imagery to the imagery of gold-smelting—remarks, is *tza'ar la-nishmat ve-la-shomet*: it means stress for both deliverer and delivered. Both God and Israel would emerge from the redemptive moment bearing the marks of trauma. (The notion of God's "trauma" is a radical component of midrashic and Chasidic thinking: God's suffering registers the pain of a world out of joint, even as it intimates the possibility of a healed condition.)

This midrash evokes the question of an alternative narrative: is there any other solution to the problem of impasse, of stalled birth, than the invasive solution of a forceps delivery? Is the Exile of the Word a fate for which there exists a more organic form of release?

Our way in to this "crisis of language" is the midrashic reading of Moses' resistance. Then I will explore the "deafness" of Pharaoh and the Israelites. Finally, we return to Moses and his most enigmatic embodiment of speech-problem and speech-therapy, as we find it in midrashic and Chasidic sources.

Moses—an Oedipal Resistance?

In Moses' case, the refusal to speak goes back to the Burning Bush. According to midrashic tradition, Moses resists God for *seven days* at the Burning Bush: "Please, my Lord, no man of words am I, neither yesterday nor the day before, nor since You have spoken to your servant, for heavy of mouth and heavy of tongue am I" (4:10). Finally, after God has promised to "be with your mouth, to teach you what you will speak" (4:12), Moses obdurately replies, "Please, my Lord, please send by whose hand You will send!" (4:13). At this point God becomes angry with Moses: "God's anger burned against Moses and He said, 'Is there not Aaron your brother, the Levite—I know that *he* can speak, yes, speak well . . .' " (4:14).[6]

Clearly, Moses' resistance angers God. Rashi explores Moses' final tautological "Send by whose hand You will send!"; protest, which sparks God's rage:

> "Send by whose hand You will send:" by the hand of the one You are accustomed to send by—that is, Aaron.
>
> "God's anger burned:" R. Joshua ben Korha said, Every time anger is mentioned in the Torah, its effect is specified. Here, there is no description of

> its effect. But "Is there not Aaron your brother, the Levite . . ."—he was destined to be the Levite, not the priest, while the priesthood was destined for your descendants. Now, he will be priest and you merely Levite . . . (4:13–14)

A hidden psychological motif is detected and isolated: Moses' relation with his older brother Aaron. If we glance back at Rashi's commentary on 4:10, the oedipal dilemma becomes vivid:

> "Neither yesterday nor the day before:" [After seven days of resistance], when Moses added, "Send by whose hand You will send," God became angry with him and he accepted the mission. All this resistance was because he did not want to assume greatness over his brother, who was older than him and already a prophet . . .[7]

From Rashi's perspective, Moses' problem is his reluctance to usurp Aaron's position in the family and in the community. Rashi's emphasis is on the question of greatness (in age and in power). To assume power over one's elder brother carries with it associations of sacrilege, of peril, of dire disruptions of order. This remains true despite the many violations of the norm that inform the Genesis narrative: as Robert Cover has shown, these retain their subversive force, without eroding the shared universe of values and practices that is the law; only a conviction of divine destiny can overturn it. Lacking such conviction, Moses is reluctant to cross the "great fault-line in the normative topography of the Israelites."[8]

Is this a virtuous reluctance on Moses' part? Several midrashic sources clearly indicate that it is. One source[9] articulates Moses' dilemma in moral, transgressive terms: as against the notorious sibling struggles of Genesis ("You find that all brothers hate one another . . .")—Cain and Abel, Ishmael and Isaac, Esau and Jacob, Joseph's brothers and Joseph—the relation of Moses and Aaron is one of mutual concern: "they rejoiced in each other's greatness." And Moses refuses God's call because "All these years, Aaron my brother has been the prophet; and now I should trespass on my brother's territory and distress him!" God's answer reassures Moses: Aaron is quite unselfish and will "rejoice in his heart" (4:14), will be genuinely happy at Moses' call. The midrash gives us a new model for brotherly relations, an idyll of mutual love uncontaminated by egoism.

This midrashic motif, which throws benign light on both Moses and Aaron, is the most common way of understanding Moses' altruistic refusal of God's mission. Rashi cites the tradition: Aaron will be rewarded for his lack of pettiness; he will be invested with the priestly breastplate, the *choshen*—that loving heart will be covered with the lights (the *urim vetumim*) of oracle.

But here is the rub: in Rashi's reading, Moses loses his priestly role, in token of God's anger. This is the effect—the *roshem*, the trace—of God's anger: that priesthood will not come of him. It seems that Moses' respect for his brother, his reluctance to trespass, is not unequivocally virtuous. In Rashi's reading, it arouses God's anger and eternally deprives Moses of the priestly function.

This theme of God's displeasure with Moses' resistance would be quite comprehensible, if Rashi had not introduced the oedipal theme. For, as we have noticed, the midrashic sources tend to read Moses' hesitation to trespass on his brother's privileges as virtuous. One more midrash will amplify this perception of the relations of the brothers:

> "And it was on the eighth day . . ." (Lev 9:1) Our Sages said, All seven days that Moses was at the Burning Bush, God continuously urged him, "Go on My mission," and he answered, "Send by whose hand You will send!" This was repeated on each of the seven days. God said to him, "I am telling you to go, and you say, 'Send by whose hand You will send!' As you live, tomorrow I shall pay you back. When the Tabernacle is completed, you will assume that you are to serve as High Priest; and then I shall say to you, 'Call Aaron to serve as the High Priest!'" So it says, "Moses called Aaron and his sons . . ." (Lev 9:1) Moses said to him, "So did God command me, to appoint you High Priest." Aaron replied, "You have labored over the Tabernacle, and I become High Priest!" Moses answered him, "As you live, even though you have become High Priest, it is as though I had become High Priest. Just as you rejoiced over my rise to greatness, so I rejoice over your rise to greatness . . ." . . . Moses had said [at the Burning Bush], "Please, my Lord—You are bringing an outcry upon me, for my brother is older than I—and I should go to Pharaoh! . . . " God had answered, "As you live, you are right—he is older than you—but nevertheless, when he sees you he will rejoice in his heart . . ." . . . So all seven days that Moses was occupied with the Tabernacle, he sprinkled the blood and performed the priestly rituals; till God said to him, "What do you think, that you have become High Priest? Call Aaron and his sons that they may serve as priests . . ."[10]

Here, Moses' altruism is celebrated, as he accepts the full implications of his loss of priesthood. The fact that he has worked so hard for the Tabernacle, specifically that he has acted as High Priest during the seven days of consecration, expresses an existential bond with the role that he has lost. These seven days, as the midrash notes, represent a kind of poetic justice: for seven days, Moses resisted God's call at the Burning Bush; now, for seven days, he imagines himself as filling a role that he will then be forced to relinquish. Aaron feels the sting of irony for his brother: *"Now,* after all this, *I* become High Priest!" But Moses reciprocates Aaron's selfless joy: "it is as though I had become High Priest."

In this midrash, the balance of value and feeling is exquisite. Rashi had quoted an alternative midrash[11] about the "effect," the "trace," of God's anger in the narrative. Moses loses the High Priesthood: that is the "evidence" of the state of God's emotion towards him. Who is aware of such a "trace" of divine anger in human experience? Surely only Moses himself. For the reader, the most obvious understanding of the verse (4:14) is simply that Aaron will speak instead of the "foreskinned" Moses. Only the fine-tuned midrashic ear detects in the phrase "Aaron the Levite" an intimation of crisis: "Aaron *was to have been* merely a Levite, but will now assume your priestly privilege" (Rashi). Only in his most intimate sense of self, Moses knows that he has been divested of a potential role, of a way of being in the world that *might have been his.* The notion of God's anger conveys the idea of a narrative mis-told, of a failure to listen to God's narrative.

In the Tanchuma version, this dynamic of anger and poetic justice is fleshed out considerably. Moses' plea, "Send by whose hand You will send!" becomes the refrain of all seven days at the Burning Bush. In Rashi's view, Moses' resistance has, we remember, an oedipal core: how can he usurp the rights and the status of the *gadol*, the older, established leader? God's revenge ("I'll pay you back . . .") is painfully symmetrical: for seven days Moses will act in complete comfort in a role that he imagines to be his own—only to be shocked into a sudden awareness that he has been trespassing, if only in imagination, on his brother's prerogative. His reaction is commendable: an altruistic joy at Aaron's appointment that parallels Aaron's previous joy at his own appointment to prophecy.

But the larger thrust of the midrash expresses the tragic *wrongness* in Moses' steadfast refusal of God's mission. He reacts to his loss with equanimity, as though to deny any sense of deprivation: "It is as though I had become High Priest." But God's words testify to another truth: "As you live, I shall pay you back . . ." He has refused greatness: there is a price to pay for such refusals, which even modesty and brotherly altruism cannot entirely blur.

The midrash expresses a difficult ambiguity. Moses is right to resist God's call; Moses is wrong to resist God's call. God's words have, perhaps, a tinge of irony: "You are right . . ." Strictly speaking, Moses' oedipal response, piously altruistic, is impeccable. And yet, there is something about the call to greatness that is not ignored without peril.

God's anger remains mysterious. This is, indeed, the first time in the Torah that God is described as being angry. Rashi, in his selection of sources, conveys a sense of the moral and imaginative complexity of the situation. How is God's anger, in fact, to be imagined? Particularly if we adopt Rashi's oedipal reading, Moses seems to have good reason for refusing the offered role. His sincerity is proved by his later serene response to his brother's promotion. And yet there is a moment of profound disruption: Moses stands against the will of God and refuses to speak. Rashi's reading—the oedipal taboo—does not serve to justify Moses in the face of God's anger.

One might say that there is a sense of the hidden, the unexpressed, in this drama of resistance. Just as Rashi's reading intimates that it is the brothers' relationship that explains this resistance—a perception not at all blatantly obvious in the text—so, I would suggest, the very reference to the uncanny relationship that we now call the oedipus complex is a way of indicating the largest, the most inchoate experiences of resistance. Moses' sensitivity to the claims of the *gadol*, the older brother, the father, is, perhaps, a displaced sensitivity to the hidden father of his life—Pharaoh himself.

For Moses' relation to the Egyptian king is bizarre in the extreme: adopted son of Pharaoh's daughter, he is, effectively, grandson to Pharaoh—a dimension of the narrative that is never conspicuous. For this very reason, one might say—precisely because the Torah text does not draw attention to this paradoxical intimacy between the major antagonists—we should become alert to what lies just beneath the explicit, conscious level of the narrative. The fact that Moses finally kills Pharaoh[12] at the Red Sea—an oedipal act, in the clearest sense—is blurred in many ways: in entering the Red Sea, he acts at the command of God;[13] Pharaoh is not his father,[14] but his grandfather; Pharaoh is not literally his grandfather. But the radical tension between the antagonists is fed by the fact that Moses has a dual identity, Egyptian and Hebrew: if he is son of Amram and Jochebed, he is also son of Pharaoh.

This paradox lies at the heart of the narrative. In his infancy, according to a famous legend,[15] Moses was the object of an infanticidal attempt by Pharaoh. At three years old, he took Pharaoh's crown from his head and put it on his own. Pharaoh's advisers, led by Balaam, urge that the child be put to death. Clearly, his gesture is one of usurpation—he aims, like all his Israelite ancestors, to overthrow the superior, the elder rival. The angel

Gabriel, disguised as one of the Egyptian sages, proposes a test to determine if there is precocious intent behind the infant Moses' act. An onyx stone and a burning coal are placed before him: if he reaches for the coal, brighter but worthless, he will prove that he is just an infant, attracted to the shiny; if he reaches for the valuable stone, he will prove his precociousness and the sinister nature of his self-crowning. Moses, who is indeed precociously wise, and destined to overthrow Pharaoh, reaches for the stone. But Gabriel supernaturally diverts his hand towards the coal; he burns his hand and puts it instinctively to his mouth, burning that as well. This gesture saves his life, and also explains how he becomes "heavy of mouth and heavy of tongue."[16]

As Robert Paul suggests, Moses' "speech-defect" thus can be understood as the "scar" left by a failed infanticidal attack, like Oedipus's wounded feet. He has survived his "father's" fatal attack; later he will kill this father at the Red Sea. In the interim, Pharaoh will again seek to kill him, in punishment for killing the Egyptian taskmaster (2:15). Two "paternal" attacks on his life provide the filicidal justification for his own ultimate act of "parricide."

The notion of the "scar," however, is the most compelling aspect of the midrash. Moses' "heaviness" with language will be, we recall, his main explanation for refusing God's mission. Moses' infant gesture—angel-guided—disguises the genuinely oedipal intimation: he will indeed overthrow the *gadol*, the source of all decrees, of all that is *kasheh* and *kaved*—dense and irrevocable. The anxiety that accompanies such an intimation leads to a lifelong preoccupation with his burnt mouth, with the repressed memory of the danger of expressing inner power.

In a self-preserving gesture, the adult Moses speaks of his own *keveduth*, heaviness, of his problematic knowledge of his own power and powerlessness. And God is angry. In an act that would seem to pacify Moses' anxiety, God appoints Aaron as "speaker," expressing unequivocal power. But this is an act of *anger*, as the text points out. Moses' "scar," his deep awareness of the ambiguities of language, has alienated him, in some palpable way, from God.

The reason for God's anger is expressed most crushingly in a series of midrashic responses to this passage.[17] In no fewer than nine parallel passages, the logic of God's anger is spelled out. Three of these passages read as follows:

> R. Yehuda said: God said to Moses, "I am master of the universe, I am full of compassion, I am reliable in paying reward, My children are en-

slaved by human beings—and you say to Me, Send by whose hand You will send!"

R. Nechemia said: God said to Moses, "The anguish of My children in Egypt is revealed and known to Me, as it is said, 'God saw the children of Israel, and God knew.' My children dwell in anguish and you dwell at ease; and I seek to set them free from Egypt—and you say to Me, Send by whose hand You will send!"

R. Yossi Haglili said: God said to Moses, "My children in Egypt deserve total destruction, as it is said, 'I said to them, Each of you throw away the detestable things that you are drawn to, and do not defile yourselves with the fetishes of Egypt . . . But they defied Me and refused to listen to Me.' (Ezek 20, 7–8) But I have decided to act for the sake of My great Name, so that it is not profaned . . . and I seek to set them free from Egypt—and you say to Me, Send by whose hand You will send!"

In these passages, the drama of confrontation between God and Moses is unparalleled in any later dialogue. As opposed to the conventional dynamic between Moses and God—in which God's anger is turned against the people, while Moses argues in their defense—here, God repeatedly echoes the ground-bass theme—Moses' obdurate formula, "Send by whose hand You will send"—in a tone of outrage. For the bare truth is that Moses has set himself against redemption. God describes Himself as moved by humanly imaginable emotion—by compassion, by loyalty to His promises to Abraham, Isaac, and Jacob, even—in the last passage and in others not quoted here—by the sheer freedom of His desire to redeem, in a situation where justice and logic offer no support. And Moses resists, delegates, tries to shrug off the mission. The refrain of each passage, "And you say, Send by whose hand You will send!" expresses a divine bafflement, which is a rhetorical move to focus our attention on the strange inadequacy of Moses' response. There is a mystery here. In a later passage in the same midrash, God even speaks of *gezera*—of the decree by which God declares that He will act to deliver the Israelites out of the hands of their enemies. Against the urgent imperative of redemption, overriding all quibbles of reason and morality, Moses, inexplicably, refuses his cooperation.

The climax of the midrash is reached in the following passage:

R. Akiva said: God said to Moses, "By speech, and by decree, and by oath, it is decided by Me that you shall not enter the Holy Land." So God says,

> "Therefore you shall not bring this community into the Land . . ." (Num 20:12); "therefore" indicates an oath . . .

Moses' opposition to God's redemptive will is so outrageous that God swears on oath (the evidence for this claim comes from a later verse, where God explicitly bars Moses) that he will not enter the Holy Land. On this midrashic reading, the decree against Moses is in place from this early stage in the history of the Exodus.

A complicating element here relates to Moses' complaint about the failure of his first attempts to achieve freedom for his people. They represent God's answer to Moses' cry of "Why have you done evil to this people?" (5:22). Included in God's words, however, is Moses' earlier protest, at the Burning Bush—"Send by whose hand You will send!" (4:13). The two passages are brought together in an unexpected way: the earlier one expressing Moses' refusal of the mission, the later one protesting at its failure. And God's anger in the earlier scene is transferred to this later one, so that a kind of "double-exposure" effect is achieved. God's determination to ban Moses from the Holy Land is located, in a midrash that Rashi quotes, in the later scene.[18] But a classic midrash actually makes Moses aware, from the time of the earlier confrontation, that he will not lead the people into the Land. This is Rashi's version:

> "Send by whose hand You will send" (4:13): By the hand of someone else whom You will choose to send. I am not destined to bring them into the Land and to be their future redeemer: You have many messengers.

In this alternative explanation of "Send by whose hand . . ." Moses is skeptical about his own adequacy to consummate the mission. God's will is incalculable: Moses senses from the time of the first call that his own resistances will disqualify him from completing the mission. In a sense, this is beyond his own determination. Even if he accepts the mission—as he does, after the Burning Bush—the undercurrent of resistance will continue. And God will "decree," "swear on oath"—translate that resistance into a limitation of achievement. This is not a matter of punishment, but of *gezera*—a reflection of how it must be.

Moses' refusal to speak is his most intimate expression of this resistance. And again, the fact that he reverts to this theme after God's renewed assurances (6:2–8) suggests quite clearly that we are dealing with a phenomenon that defies obvious solutions. It is true that he does obey God and convey His message to the people; but the desperate conclusion he draws from his failure has an almost triumphant note: "*Hen*—You see! the children of Israel did not listen to me. . . !" (6:12). A deep pessimism is vindicated.

Moses—The Imperative of Language

Ramban's reading of this crisis is illuminating (6:13):

> After Moses' protest ("See! the children of Israel would not listen to me . . ."), God commanded both Moses and Aaron to speak to the people and Pharaoh. Moses then thought that they would both prophesy and perform the signs, in the presence of the Israelites and of Pharaoh: only one would speak, as is customary in such cases. With this, Moses was appeased. But then, God again said to him, "I am God (6:29) [who appeared to you alone to speak in My Name.] So speak to Pharaoh whatever I say to you . . . [for all the words will be addressed to you and not to Aaron—you are the one I have made My messenger to Pharaoh."] Moses answered again, "I am of uncircumcised lips." (6:30); and God replied, "See, I have made you a god to Pharaoh (7:1): [You will charge Aaron with my messages, without Pharaoh hearing you. Aaron will act as your agent and communicate your words, just as God charges the prophet to communicate and castigate."] This was great prestige for Moses, which he achieved through his modesty, in his embarrassment in speaking with "uncircumcised lips." That is why it says, "The man Moses was very great in the land of Egypt in the eyes of Pharaoh's servants and in the eyes of the people:" (11:3) poetic justice, since he was afraid of being despicable in their eyes.

In Ramban's reading, the lines are drawn differently: Moses' resistance is virtuous, an expression of modesty, fear of trivializing God's message. God supplies Aaron as an aide, but his function is different from what Moses at first assumes. He cannot be the sole speaker, the one to express God's message. For—and this, it seems, is the central point—Moses alone saw the vision at the Burning Bush: to him, alone, God has spoken. Aaron can speak only at one remove from the source—inspired by Moses' words, delivered in an undertone, Aaron can broadcast them to Pharaoh.

In this reading, Moses' greatness is unshadowed. His resistance is morally justified, even rewarded. But the problem of language is given large resonance: there is no escape from the imperative of language, because only he has seen and heard. The burden of revelation lies directly on him: only he can speak of what he knows. This means a project of translation: he must make God's words heard by others. This is the essential role of the prophet, even of the quintessential "man of God," Moses, to whom God says, "I will be with your mouth; I will teach you what to say" (4:12).

To speak always means to translate, to transform; even the most faithful translations are betrayals: *il traduttore e traditore*—"To translate is to betray." In its original form, God's presence, His meanings, had come to Moses as what George Steiner calls "the great tautology": "I am what I am."[19] Steiner writes of the implications of tautology for language:

> In pre-lapsarian discourse, name and object, the signifying and signified, match exactly. There is no gap for involuntary misprision. Verbal falsehood is excluded from a grammar which, even more precisely than in the equation which the early Wittgenstein posits between the limits of language and those of our world, maps being and experience totally. Designation and corresponding essence are made one—their relation is tautological.[20]

In the descent into the fallen world, involving human perspectives, impurity, fictions of all kinds, " 'the words of the tribe' (Mallarmé's phrase) can never be made altogether pure again . . . the incarnate tautologies between word and object leak."[21] On Schoenberg's *Moses und Aron*, Steiner comments:

> human speech represents, it images. Such representation and imaging falsifies revealed, absolute truths. Specifically, this falsification by virtue of imagery violates those prohibitions on the making of images decreed by the Mosaic God precisely so that the abstract and moral verities of God's legislation may not be vulgarized and distorted. . . . Schoenberg does not set to music the "I am" but lets Moses spell out the litany of its inaccessibility . . .
>
> *Inconceivable because invisible;*
> *because immeasurable;*
> *because everlasting*
> *because eternal*
> *because omnipresent;*
> *because omnipotent.*[22]

Schoenberg's work ends, incomplete, with Moses' despairing cry:

None can, none may give Him utterance.
Oh, Word, Word, Word, that I lack!

The work remains a fragment; this, too, intimates the inaccessibility of the divine words.

Ramban gives us a Moses who is rightly "modest" about his ability to communicate God's word; but who nevertheless cannot be absolved from his responsibility. He cannot delegate Aaron, who has not heard the "great tautology" of the *Ehyeh*—"I shall be what I shall be." Only Moses is in a position to assay the wracking act of translation: in Ramban's reading, God's concession is to limit his task to an "undertone" communication to Pharaoh. Moses is the bridge-builder, the pontificator, in the literal sense, between God and the human. A minimum of translation is ineluctably his; Aaron will then take over, he will exploit the full resources—in Steiner's terms, the fictionality—of language to impress Pharaoh and the Israelites.

Implicit in Ramban's reading is the complex notion of the treachery of language—and its inevitability. Apparently, Ramban is not interested—as Rashi is—in the psychological underpinnings of Moses' refusal; he makes, for example, no comment on God's anger. Moses' refusal is simply a consistent expression of the fact that he is "more modest than any human being on the face of the earth."[23] His silence in Pharaoh's presence will give him prestige—"like a god"—precisely because it represents the inaccessibility, the perfection of the god.

Even in Ramban's reading, however, Moses' inhibition about language is put down to a *fear* of being despicable in the eyes of Pharaoh. This is psychological language; Ramban clearly approves of Moses' reluctance, but his reference to fear leads us back to a questioning of Moses' resistance. It is somewhat reminiscent of Kafka's story about Abraham, who is afraid to obey God's command:

> he would make the sacrifice in the right spirit if only he could believe he was the one meant. He is afraid that after starting out as Abraham with his son he would change on the way into Don Quixote . . . An Abraham who should come unsummoned! It is as if, at the end of the year, when the best student was solemnly about to receive a prize, the worst student rose in the expectant stillness and came forward from his dirty desk in the last row because he had made a mistake of hearing, and the whole class burst out laughing.[24]

Moses' "fear of seeming despicable" is not remote from the oedipal anxiety, the problem of being called to greatness, with its fearful fantasy of ridicule, the always-possible "mistake of hearing" from which Kafka's Abraham suffers. This is the problem that brings Ramban and Rashi together. Ramban calls it "modesty," justifies it, rewards it. But the shame that he describes can perhaps be viewed through the prism of Walter Benjamin's discussion of this motif in Kafka:

> "It was as if the shame of it was to outlive him." With these words *The Trial* ends. Corresponding as it does to his "elemental purity of feeling," shame is Kafka's strongest gesture. It has a dual aspect, however. Shame is an intimate human reaction, but at the same time it has social pretensions. Shame is not only shame in the presence of others, but can also be shame one feels for them . . . "He feels as though he were living and thinking under the constraint of a family . . . Because of this unknown family . . . he cannot be released."[25]

The atavisms of the swamp world that Benjamin sketches generate in Kafka a *human shame*. Perhaps one can read in Ramban a similar notion of a shame, a modesty one feels "under the constraint of a family." This is the heaviness of mouth and of tongue, the uncircumcised lips—the sense of impedimenta, grotesquely retarding one's ability to shape one's lips to the words of eternity. Moses' shame, his fear, then, would be, in Benjamin's words, his "strongest gesture," a token of an awareness where others experience nothing but oblivion.

At the same time, however, Moses emerges even from Ramban's account as a victim of fear, incapable of meeting the demands of the hour. This critical perspective on Moses reaches its most acute expression in the enigmatic episode at the "hotel":

> At a hotel (*malon*) on the way, God encountered him and sought to kill him. So Zipporah took a flint and cut off her son's foreskin, and touched his legs with it, saying, "You are truly a bridegroom of blood to me!" (4:24–25)

Why does God "attack" Moses in this uncanny way? The Talmud speaks of his "negligence" (*nitrashel*) in circumcising his infant son;[26] for this, he is swallowed by a serpent from the head down, and from the feet up, to the site of circumcision on his own body.[27] Zipporah reads this macabre event as a diagnostic drama and immediately circumcises the baby. I suggest that the repressed meaning of this narrative lies in a play on the word *milah*—"circumcision"—which, in Rabbinic Hebrew, also means "the word," "language." It is Moses' crisis of language that provokes God's attack—significantly, in a *malon* (hotel)—another pun on *milah*. The real issue is Moses' continuing resistance to language, to entering the world of others. The uncircumcised baby, foreskin uncut, is a figure for Moses himself, "of uncircumcised lips," resisting the embarrassments of language.[28]

2. *Resisting Redemption: Pharaoh*

Pharaoh—Catatonic Silence

The resistance to God's message in the other protagonists of the narrative, Pharaoh and the Israelites, bears further exploration. In Moses, as we have seen, this resistance—the refusal to speak—is an undercurrent that constantly reemerges, despite apparent acquiescence, despite God's reassurances, despite even the ethical and theological demands of the situation. He himself classes his own resistance with that of Pharaoh and the Israelites: "Here, if the children of Israel do not listen to me, how will Pharaoh listen to me?—and I am of foreskinned lips!" We have seen the Sefat Emeth's suggestion that his own failure may be the *product*, rather than the cause of theirs: their failure to listen has demoralized him as a speaker. The situation described in this way gives great power to the act of listening.

In the case of Pharaoh, in each of the early plague-episodes, his response to each assault becomes a formula for "deafness": "He did not listen to them, as God had said."[29] After the second confrontation, when Moses and Aaron perform the wonder of the stick transformed to a snake, God sends Moses with a message announcing the first plague: "Say to him, The Lord, God of the Hebrews has sent me to you, saying, Send My people free, that they may serve Me in the desert: but here, you have not listened till now" (7:16).

This clearly refers back to the original message. God now summarizes the situation at its most essential: "You have not *listened* till now." This can be taken idiomatically as meaning, "You have not obeyed Me." Rashi's midrashic reading seems to follow such a translation:

> "Till now—*ad koh:*" till you hear from Me about the plague of the first-born, which will begin with the word, *koh—koh amar adonai*—"thus says God." (11:4)

Rashi understands Pharaoh's disobedience to be not merely a temporary affair, but one that will endure to the very end of the bombardment of divine plagues. Even where the text does not specifically say so, Pharaoh's identity will remain obdurately one of a "non-listener."

Ramban investigates the meaning of Pharaoh's "non-listening":

> "Here, you have not listened . . ."—Because God was about to inflict the first plague upon him, He told him that his wickedness was to blame, that he did not listen to the commandment of his Creator. Now, Pharaoh did not tell them *explicitly* that he would not listen or set them free—except for the first time, when he said, "Who is God that I should listen to Him, to set Israel free. . . ?" (5:2) He did not reprove them, but *listened to their words in silence.* For he was afraid of the plagues from the time that they performed the wonder of the alligator that swallowed the Egyptian staffs. In the first plagues, he had his magicians attempt to duplicate their acts—to prove that these were merely witchcraft. So in fact he was afraid and reacted to fear by strengthening himself—that is the meaning of "Pharaoh's heart was strengthened." (7:22)

The hypothesis that the wonders and the plagues are merely witchcraft provides Pharaoh with a source of courage and resilience: witchcraft, after all, as a number of midrashim point out, is almost a cottage industry in Egypt.[30] The peculiarity of these early episodes between Moses and Pharaoh is the *speechlessness* of Pharaoh's defiance: he "listened to their words in silence." His resistance is passive; in the final analysis, such a listening is equivalent to "not-listening." In his silent obduracy, he expresses the meaning of "not-listening." Ramban presents Pharaoh as refusing language. Fear freezes him in a catatonic silence, he does not express even resistance to God's word. The medium is the message: a deaf-and-dumbness enacts a moral autism.

In Ramban's description, "You have not listened till now" begins by meaning, "You have not done the right thing till now—that is, not listened to Me, not obeyed Me"; and moves to meaning, "You have been invested in a hardening crust of not-listening, expressed in not-speaking." The hardening agents include the periodic morale boost that comes from the magicians and their early attempts to duplicate Moses' signs and plagues. Pharaoh alternates between fear and the momentary courage he draws from the apparent success of his magicians.

This alternation increasingly anesthetizes him to a point where he becomes, in his very being, a creature of refusal. This is Rashi's reading of 7:27:

> "And if you refuse to send them free:" If you are a *refuser*—this form of the verb (*ma'en*) is adjectival, where a person is described by his acts, like *shaket* (quiet), *shalev* (peaceful).

In a grammatical comment, Rashi gives us a lightning-sketch of a Pharaoh who absorbs the black energy of nay-saying into himself, so that he has become its very embodiment. Dense, impenetrable, speechless, he betrays no flicker of response; he is impacted in silence. God had foretold that it would be so: "Pharaoh will not listen to you" (7:4). In this reading, this means more than: "he will not do as you wish." It indicates a growing, willed incapacity to hear and to speak.[31]

In a brilliant reading, Ha-amek Davar in fact suggests that God here sketches the whole progress of the plagues: "the day will come when Pharaoh will literally refuse to listen to you—before the plague of the first-born" (7:4). On that day, Pharaoh says, "Do not see my face again" (10:28), and dismisses Moses in anger. That overt anger and verbal rejection will represent a crack in Pharaoh's impermeable silence. The hardening process receives its fatal setback in this final moment of explosive fury, which leaves him suddenly vulnerable to pain.

Pharaoh as refuser, nonporous, inaccessible, blocked by fear, is the subject of the Or HaChaim's description, too:

> "Pharaoh's heart has become heavy." (7:14)—he is not sufficiently affected even to respond negatively to the plagues, so that God has to explain to Moses the meaning of his silence: "He has closed up his heart, he refuses to set the people free."

Pharaoh—The Unbearable Lightness of Being

Pharaoh as impassive, enigmatic, represents a certain Egyptian ideal: the Sphinx, inexpressive, above human discourse. Ramban detects in this persona the effects of fear. In a similar vein, Rashi quotes the bizarre midrash about Pharaoh's early-morning expeditions to the river:

> "Look, he goes out to the water:" (7:15)—to perform his bodily needs. For he would make himself into a god, claiming that he had no bodily needs (lit., "did not need to clear his bowels"); he would rise early in the morning, and go out to the Nile to perform his needs there.

Pharaoh constructs himself as a god, without needs. In the midrashic expression, he is *eino machnis ve-eino motzi*, he takes in nothing and evacuates nothing. He neither eats nor eliminates waste matter. That cycle, depending on a vital traffic through the orifices of the body, is denied by one who claims to be above change, beyond the cycles of in and out, hunger and fullness, the vicissitudes of time and bodily state.

The euphemistic shorthand idiom for the natural process that Pharaoh denies is the word, "needs." Since Freud, many thinkers—among them, Norman Brown and Ernest Becker—have discussed the peculiar implications of "anality" for human experience. Natural body functions are the most disturbing blow to the child's illusion of "godlikeness"—the "causa sui" project, as Becker, quoting Spinoza, calls it: the fantasy that one's individuality is total and integral engenders suspicion of the body, in its vulnerability, as well as of the female and the species-role.[32] Underlying this fantasy is the fear of death: the shocking knowledge, as Montaigne puts it, that on the highest throne in the world man sits on a part of his anatomy that signifies excretion, dependence, lack of control, need.[33]

What Pharaoh denies is the unbearable lightness of being: the meaningless movement of fluids and solids that marks human life. Kundera's word, "lightness," is the word the midrash uses to describe Pharaoh's condition: in the moment of defecation, he stands in *kalon*, in shame, whose root is "lightness."[34] This is the moment of "neediness," that he must hide at all costs: for to recognize one's lightness is to experience a radical and unbearable shame. To acknowledge the apertures in one's body—the openings and cavities for which Jews traditionally thank God after each experience of the natural physical process—is to surrender the claim to immortality. We remember Kafka and his concern with shame, a concern that Walter Benjamin termed his "strongest gesture": the honest recognition of a complex and mortal humanity, subject to fluctuation, in its essence neither lordly nor metaphysical. Pharaoh's response to such a surrender is to make himself as *kaved*, as heavy, dense, significant, and impregnable as possible: in fact, to make himself a god.

Pharaoh—The Yearning for Impermeability

In descriptions of Pharaoh, the midrash often quotes a verse from Ezekiel (29:3): "Behold, I am against you, Pharaoh, king of Egypt, mighty monster, sprawling in its channels, who said, My river is my own; I made it for myself . . ." Rashi's comment is that Pharaoh feels no need of life-sources beyond himself: need not look upwards for rain, for instance: "I have increased my power through my own wisdom . . ." This is the "causa sui" fantasy, in full-fledged form. Pharaoh conceives of himself as generating his own greatness. In midrashic literature, Pharaoh becomes a prototype of the pathology of arrogance. But the point that strikes us forcefully is the fear of vulnerability that lies at the heart of such arrogance.

To deny mortality means, in terms of inner body-imagery, to close the body, its exits and entrances, to become nonporous.[35] The child who first discovers his own fallibility becomes a "philosopher of the human condition,"[36] experiencing man's horror of his own basic animal nature. One response is to attempt to overcome the ensuing conflict by "narcissistic inflation"—the "project of becoming God—in Spinoza's formula, *causa sui*," which Norman Brown sees as the essence of the Oedipal complex.[37]

Pharaoh, I suggest, closes in the same way all the apertures of his body—including ears and mouth. He will not listen and he will not speak: only so, can his *keveduth*, his impermeability, be properly protected. "Not hearing," in this sense, is not a primary, "natural" event; rather, it represents a deliberate movement to block the ears and stifle an instinctive response.

This is a philosophy of "not hearing," which, in Michael Walzer's words, "represses instinct and moral value at the same time." Walzer quotes a passage from Rousseau's *Discourse on the Origin of Inequality*, to make the paradoxical point:

> the "tranquil sleep" of the philosopher is suddenly disturbed by cries for help. He hears the cries but cannot be torn from his bed. A murder may with impunity be committed under his window; he has only to put his hands in his ears and argue a little with himself to prevent nature, which is shocked within him, from identifying itself with the unfortunate sufferer. Uncivilized man has not this admirable talent; and for want of reason . . . is always foolishly ready to obey the first promptings of humanity.[38]

A perversely "civilized" response is described here. Walzer sees it as the operation of the "critical 'I' . . . a calculating and prudent watchfulness, wary of the traps of sentimental goodness." The philosopher goes back to sleep, contented with himself, having argued himself out of a sense of guilt. The complex picture that emerges is one where the "critical 'I' " can work to confirm or to repress a primary sense of guilt. It is composed of "different critics making different claims on behalf of different and often inconsistent notions of a more perfect self."[39] If Milton's God speaks of having placed within human beings "My Umpire Conscience" as His sole representative, the secular psychological experience, Walzer argues, is haunted by internal disagreements, a dissonant chorus of critics: "conscience is itself divided."[40]

Pharaoh, I suggest, brings to felt experience the problems of the "critical 'I'." If the Torah describes him as a "non-listener," this evokes precisely the confusing sense of a "calculating and prudent watchfulness," which refuses to allow the "perdurable"[41] self to be affected, to be weakened. Pharaoh is ruled by an inner "umpire," a conscience of sorts. Clearly, in the moral dynamics of the biblical narrative, he has silenced the true voices of Moses and Aaron, bearing God's message.

And yet, the repeated phrase, "He did not listen to them, *as God had said*," has a strange and paradoxical effect. On the one hand, Pharaoh repeatedly blocks out God's message, in a controlled frenzy of fear. In doing so, he hardens himself, making himself ultimately incapable of hearing, responding, yielding to a knowledge that would diminish his beleaguered self. This is the most plausible understanding of the modulated expression that ends the narratives of each of the last five plagues: "And *God* hardened his heart. . ." He has put himself beyond possibility of change. Like Macbeth who, after his crime, finds himself *unable* to utter "Amen," in response to the guards ("But wherefore could not I pronounce 'Amen'?" [*Macbeth*, II.ii.32]). Pharaoh is ultimately imprisoned within the world of his own critical choices.

On the other hand, however, the repeated reminder that God had predicted this process in Pharaoh evokes an irrational sense that God is behind Pharaoh's "not-listening." Pharaoh's "critical 'I'," in Walzer's formula, resists weakness, sentimentality, erosion of his "perdurable" self. "As God had told them," conveys a possible notion of a perverse legality in Pharaoh's perspective, an imaginable blueprint for selfhood: heaviness, density, the closed body.

Dimly, one can conceive of such a fantasy: the Uroboros, the primal dragon of which Erich Neumann writes in the first chapter of *The Origins and History of Consciousness;* the serpent coiled in on itself, total, self-sufficient, the "tail-eater," symbolic of the "swamp stage," described by Bachofen: a world in which every creature devours every other, in which the polar tension of the sexes is still in abeyance; a perfect circle, hermaphrodite, containing all contraries, beyond time and space. In Neumann's description, this symbol, existence in the Uroboros, rests on a collective basis, corresponding to the infancy of mankind and of the child.

Pharaoh unhearing, unspeaking, orifices sealed, represents a powerful longing, the "desire to remain unconscious," as Neumann terms it, only to correct himself: "even this is a false formulation, since it starts from consciousness as though that were the natural and self-evident thing. But fixation in unconsciousness, the downward drag of its specific gravity, cannot be called a desire to remain unconscious; on the contrary, *that* is the natural thing . . . one is primarily unconscious and can at most conquer the original situation in which man drowses in the world, drowses in the unconscious, contained in the infinite like a fish in the environing sea."[42] Or like the river monster in Ezekiel, sprawling in its channels: "My river is my own; I made it for myself."

As against this image of the self-contained body, God's message presses for hearing and response, for an acknowledged vulnerability, insecurity, anxiety. "Neurosis," writes Herbert Fingarette, "is precisely the disease of uncontrollable 'willfulness' . . . [it] is in fact a form of obstinate refusal to face anxiety openly and explore its quality and source . . . it is passive in the sense of rigidly avoiding something."[43] Therapeutic openness, on the other hand, is expressed in a willingness to face the unknown. These two modes are both forms of passivity: neurotic passivity and therapeutic passivity.

In similar vein, Sartre writes of the lapidary hardness of the anti-Semite:

> How can anyone choose to reason falsely? It is simply the old yearning for impermeability . . . there are people who are attracted by the permanence of stone. They would like to be solid and impenetrable, they do not want change: for who knows what change might bring? . . . It is as if their own existence were perpetually in suspense. But they want to exist in all ways at once, and all in one instant. They have no wish to acquire ideas, they want them to be innate . . . they want to adopt a mode of life in which reasoning and the quest for truth play only a subordinate part, in which nothing is sought except what has already been found, in which one never becomes anything else but what one already was.[44]

This yearning for impermeability is, as Mary Douglas points out, in us all.

> It is part of our human condition to long for hard lines and clear concepts. When we have them we have to either face the fact that some realities elude them, or else blind ourselves to the inadequacy of the concepts.

Pharaoh, then, resisting penetration and expression, becomes a mythic representation of a universal yearning, which has in it something of God—twisted and overgrown to pathological dimensions, inappropriate to one who is not God.

I am suggesting that Pharaoh becomes a demonic expression of the human desire to be unchanging and invulnerable, like God. The power of this idea is rooted in the knowledge that it is not unequivocally evil. When God decides to expel Adam and Eve from Paradise, for instance, there is a compelling ambiguity in a traditional reading of God's speech: "And the Lord God said, 'Now that the man has become like one of us, knowing good and bad, what if (*pen*) he should stretch out his hand and take also from the tree of life and eat, and live forever!' " (Gen 3:22). The word *pen*—"what if . . ."—is translated in the Targum as *dilma*: this sometimes has a negative connotation ("lest"), but sometimes is quite neutral ("perhaps.") On this latter reading, God does not regard such an eventuality—that the couple will eat of the Tree of Life and live forever—as totally unthinkable. It is a possibility that is built into the nature of things.

Rashi also narrows his definition of the evil that God prevents by expelling Adam and Eve from Paradise: "if they do eat, they will live for ever—which will plausibly deceive later generations into thinking them gods." It is not eternal life, or the desire for it that is evil: but the ambition to *become God.* Chasidic sources even read this as containing a veiled promise for the future. When human beings will have worked through the pathological aspects of their desire to be gods, this verse will become prophecy: they will genuinely become godlike, in the positive sense, combining the fruits of the two trees: knowledge of good and evil with eternal life.

PHARAOH—"AND GOD HARDENED PHARAOH'S HEART . . ."

The nuances are subtle and, indeed, largely undefined. In Pharaoh's case, not-listening becomes a fatal reflex, closing him to vulnerability and to growth. Nevertheless, it is based on a horror and a desire that are not alien to human experience.

The process by which he moves from hardening his own heart to God's hardening his heart (in general terms, this happens after the first five plagues) is essentially a mysterious one. A stamina of endurance possesses Pharaoh: to the bystander, there is an unnatural, compulsive quality about this refusal that is, perhaps, as Shadal and Cassuto suggest, the idiomatic meaning of the formula: "God hardened his heart": where God is described as the cause of human emotional responses, the effect is to suggest an *unaccountable* human reaction.[45] On such a reading, Pharaoh increasingly strikes the reader with a kind of appalled fascination as he compulsively resists the bombardment that should have defeated him. What demonic strength possesses him? "I shall strengthen his heart" (7:3); "God made his heart impenetrable": these expressions only serve to underline the mystery of human self-destruction.

We notice that with the progress of the plagues, the phrase, "Pharaoh did not listen to them . . ." disappears from the Torah. It is absent in the fourth plague, reappears in the sixth, and does not recur. Without being overly systematic, I would suggest that the sixth plague (boils) represents the crisis of the narrative: the turning point, where God's role in Pharaoh's resistance begins.[46] At this juncture, the expression *lo shama*, "he did not listen . . ." is used for the last time, in a last flare-up of deafness, after two plagues where no mention is made of it. This plague is characterized by the explicit failure of Pharaoh's magicians to duplicate Moses' miraculous feat. This represents the final breakdown of Pharaoh's belief system.

In Ramban's reading, the magicians, whose early success in duplicating the plagues gave support to Pharaoh's obstinacy, are trounced from the plague of lice (the third plague) onward ("The magicians did the like with their spells to produce lice, but they could not" [8:14]). At the sixth plague, however, the plague of boils, they too are affected; and, in sheer shame, are unable to appear in public: "The magicians were unable to confront Moses because of the inflammation, for the inflammation afflicted the magicians as well as the other Egyptians" (9:11).

> They were ashamed and confounded and embarrassed since they were full of boils and could not preserve themselves. So they did not enter the king's palace, nor did they appear before Moses in the streets, but stayed closed in their houses.

After this point, when the last vestige of rationalization has disappeared, Pharaoh has only the mysterious momentum of his own impulses to drive him.[47] The Torah no longer describes him as *lo shama*, as not hearing, since the "critical 'I' " of inner conflict is silenced. There is no more refusal, no more sealing of the vulnerable apertures. What remains is a kind of autism, almost pitiable in its irrationality.[48] The change happens gradually. At the climax of his magicians' shame, when only God's hardening Pharaoh's heart can account for his unaccountable stubbornness, *lo shama* is affirmed for the last time (9:12). Paradoxically, this represents a last flicker of conflict: "He refused to be affected . . ." Then, a kind of spiritual *rigor mortis* sets in. Till the ninth plague (darkness), he neither hears nor speaks, as he denies the Israelites freedom at the end of each plague. And the text no longer even speaks of his deafness, his dumbness.

3. *Resisting Redemption: The Israelites*

The Israelites—The Egyptian Disease

There is a provocative midrashic tradition that focuses on the boils, with the shame attendant on them. The claim is that the boils are never healed. The magicians can make no more public appearances, because they bear, full-blown on their skin, the marks of disease.[49] This tradition relates this episode to the baneful words of the Covenant: "God will smite you with the Egyptian boils . . . which are incurable . . ." (Deut 28:27). This specific pathology is characterized by *incurability.* This motif is repeated a few verses later: "God will smite you with malignant boils on knees and thighs—which are *incurable*" (28:35).

Over forty years in the desert, the people clearly remember the peculiar horror of this skin disease, for which there is no healing. This, of all the plagues, leaves a trace in Israelite folk memory.[50] There is an echo of it even in Job's sufferings, when Satan is given permission to inflict boils on Job. After losing his children and his wealth, this might seem like an anticlimax. But Satan knows otherwise: " 'But just stretch out Your hand and touch his person, his flesh—See if he does not blaspheme against You!' And Satan smote Job with evil boils, from the sole of his foot to the top of his head" (Job 2:5–7). The last phrase is quoted from the Deuteronomy description of the incurable Egyptian disease (28:35). This stage of Job's sufferings is overwhelming: in Satan's view, as well as in the reaction of Job's wife, blasphemy and death are preferable to its endurance.

Egyptian boils have thus become a byword for relentless pain, invasive of the most intimate sense of self ("Touch his person, his flesh—*atzmo, besoro*"—the same dimensions of the self that Adam marvels to see incarnated in Eve, beyond the boundaries of his own flesh, same yet other). There is a subtle indication in Deuteronomy 7:15 that the Israelites too know of this disease, in their own flesh: "And God will remove from you all sickness; and all the malignant diseases of Egypt, *which you know*, He will not inflict upon you, but will inflict them upon all your enemies." The reference to the Egyptian disease is left unspecified, but clearly it has been experienced by the Israelites as well. God promises to *remove* it, that is, to cure, rather than to prevent its ever affecting them.

Immediately after the Exodus from Egypt, indeed, God had made a paradoxical promise to the people, on this very issue. The people had been led across the Red Sea, where the Egyptians drowned. They had complained about the bitter water, and it is sweetened by a tree being thrown into it: "He said, 'If you will listen to the Lord your God diligently, doing what is upright in His eyes, giving ear to His commandments and keeping all His laws, then I will not bring upon you any of the diseases that I brought upon the Egyptians, for I the Lord am your healer' " (Exod 15:26).

The fundamental condition for God's promise is an act of *listening*: if they listen, then they will be immune to the Egyptian disease, "for I the Lord am your healer." The last phrase has occasioned surprise; as the Talmud puts it, "Since He will not inflict disease—what need is there for healing?"[51]

Rashi gives two answers to the same question:

> "I will not bring upon you:" and if I do bring them upon you, it will be as though I had not, for I the Lord am your healer. That is the midrash (Mechilta). The *peshat*, primary, contextual reading is that I the Lord am your healer—teaching you Torah and commandments, so that you may be preserved from these diseases—like a doctor who tells his patient, Do not eat foods that make you liable to get sick. That is the effect of giving ear (*izoon*) to the commandments, as it is said, "It will be a cure for your body." (Prov 3:8)

The second answer, the *peshat*, refers to preventive medicine: a healthful regime of Torah and mitzvoth will create an inner balance, that will immunize against disease. The first explanation is less harmonious, less elegant: "I will not inflict the Egyptian disease upon you—and if I do, it will be as though I had not, for I am your healer . . ." The awkwardness here is striking. Why, in fact, does Rashi resort to a second explanation, when the *peshat* (God as preventive healer) seems so satisfactory? Rashi's source in Sanhedrin 101a suggests an important answer to this question:

If you listen, I will not inflict the Egyptian disease. If you do not listen, I will inflict it—*but nevertheless I am your healer.*

God's condition with the people is analyzed for both possible eventualities. Their listening will result in perfect health; but even if they do not listen, and have to suffer the Egyptian disease, God makes a most significant promise. He opens up the prospect of *refuah*, of healing. This possibility goes against the grain of the Egyptian pathology, in its very definition: "it cannot be cured." God here introduces a motif that is of the utmost relevance to the question of redemption. What is to happen if physically, or spiritually, the people betray symptoms of the Egyptian disease? God offers cure, on the realistic premise that illness cannot be entirely avoided. In physical terms, the capacity of the body to cure itself is the very condition of health; the ability of doctors to assist in this process one of the major achievements of civilization. In spiritual terms, too, the capacity of the organism to deal with melancholy, conflict, challenge is a better indication of vigorous health than any measures to prevent sickness.

The Egyptian sickness—the boils in skin and flesh—is related to the question of listening. A basic indisposition to listen is Pharaoh's pathology. A misalignment of the borders of his body, a fantasy of total control, without entry or exit ("No slave ever escaped from Egypt"), erupts in a malignant thickening, a deadening of the body-limits that are constituted by the skin. His magicians, whose culture of witchcraft supports Pharaoh's defiance of God, are afflicted with these miserable boils, which express a kind of "thick skin" obstinacy.

The striking suggestion that emerges from the sources we have just explored, however, is that this psychosomatic condition will come to represent for the Israelites the most radical problem in their experience: the problem of *teshuva*, of repentance. For them, the major spiritual project will be that of *refuah*, of healing: of how to deal with that deafness which cannot be prevented. In the Egyptian model, this deafness is, as we have suggested, paradigmatic. To hear is to open oneself up to vulnerability, change, contingency. The Egyptian solution to the *causa sui* dilemma, the "narcissistic inflation" that attempts to overcome the conflict of ambivalence, turns out to be pathological. But it is not, it seems, confined to Egyptians. The Israelites also do not listen. God's promise here, therefore, is of the greatest importance; the Israelites will have the capacity to be healed of their perhaps inevitable sicknesses. This, possibly, is a way of defining the very purpose of Torah teachings: to prevent sickness, but, more importantly, to teach the people how to recover equilibrium.

The Israelites—The Possibility of Healing

The midrash identifies the Egyptian boils with the leprosy that afflicts Moses, when he resists God's mission at the Burning Bush:

> Moses put his hand into his bosom and brought it forth leprous as snow. They [the magicians] too put their hands in their bosoms and brought them out leprous as snow. *But they were not healed till the day of their death.*[52]

The sign that Moses is taught to perform is immediately imitated by the magicians—as, indeed, they imitate all the early plagues. The triumph of their success is marred, however, by the fact that they cannot revert to health. From this point on, they are afflicted with leprosy/boils. All the other plagues are resolved back to normality, but the boils will leave the magicians scarred by the original pathology, for which they have found no cure. Ramban, we remember, reads this crisis of Egyptian defeat as one of "shame": they "were unable to confront Moses because of the inflammation . . ." (9:11). Their sealing of the vulnerable, changing body, with its apertures, its traffic in and out, is confirmed in a humiliating blanched crust of death.

The symbolism attaching to Moses is equally arresting. He is not immune to the problem of deafness and dumbness. (We will return to his narrative later.) But we remember the "scar" left on his lips by the burning coal. And we notice that his hand, shifted out of true by the angel, brought the coal to his lips; and that this hand later experiences the Egyptian disease, the leprosy/boils. What differentiates Moses from the equally afflicted Egyptians, in this latter narrative, is the experience of *healing.*[53]

Related to this point is Winnicott's observation that "babies are constantly being *cured*" or "mended" by the "good-enough" mother.[54] Infant distress at the absence of the mother is normally not allowed to reach the point of trauma, the "break in life's continuity" that is madness, in Winnicott's terms. Constantly, mothers engage in a healing, "localized spoiling that mends the ego structure [and] reconstitutes the baby's capacity to use a symbol of union; the baby then comes once more to allow and even to benefit from separation."[55]

Winnicott's evocative sentence generates an important and seminal discussion of the benefits of separation, the creation of the "play-area," where separation may become a form of union. In similar terms, I would suggest that in the early development of the Israelites—in the Exodus narrative, which covers the birth and infancy of a nation—the important issues are those that deal with separation, trauma, and the danger of madness. And that the "secret of redemption" has much to do with the capacity of the infant to develop healing-strategies, the "play-area" in which growth can happen.

The Israelites—The Breathing Problem

For this to be possible, God—like the mother in Winnicott—must constantly "mend the ego structure" of a people who are described, in terms quite equivalent to those used of Pharaoh, as "not listening": "They did not listen to Moses, out of shortness of spirit and out of hard work" (6:9). The difference in rhetoric here is striking: the double phrase *explaining* the people's "deafness." *Kotzer ruach*, literally, "shortness of breath," can be translated "impatience." This is Rashi's comment: "They did not accept consolation. Anyone who is distressed in spirit and short of breath and cannot take deep breaths . . ."

The people cannot listen to consoling narratives; this is connected to physical and emotional causes. A psychosomatic condition, in which deep breathing becomes impossible, inhibits one from taking in words of consolation. The description here is of a most intimately painful experience, a subjectively felt condition: the inability to take in air and consolation. The Targum emphasizes this dimension when it translates: "They could not accept Moses' words, because of emotional pressure and work that was hard *for them.*" It is not the objective difficulty of the slave labor that explains their unresponsiveness: but an inner sense of the *kasheh*—the hard, the heavy, the dense, the implacable.

The sense of pressure that inhibits deep breathing is notoriously only aggravated by shallow breathing. "If only they could take one deep breath," we may think; the vicious cycle would then be broken. But this is precisely the problem: the psychosomatic condition represents a kind of "double-bind" situation. As Sefath Emeth puts it, in the passage we quoted earlier:

> Language was in exile, as long as they refused to receive the word of God, were not prepared to hear it. In the midrash, we find: "They did not listen—because *it was hard for them* to separate from idolatry, as it is written, 'They did not cast away the detestable things they were drawn to.' " (Ezek 20:8) *Avodah zarah* should be translated here, not as "idolatry," but,

> literally, as work which was strange to them. For, in order to hear, one must be clear of all obstructions—as it is said, "Listen, oh daughter . . . and incline your ear, and forget your people and the house of your father." (Ps 45:11) This is the essence of exile, even now, that one cannot clear oneself of distractions and forget the vanities of the world, so that one's heart is clear to hear the word of God, without foreign thoughts—as it is said, "You shall not go astray after your heart." (Num 15:39) And that is what is meant by, "They did not cast away the detestable things they were drawn to—and *therefore* they did not give up the fetishes of Egypt." If they had been prepared to hear the word of God, they would have been redeemed immediately.[56]

The double bind is that although the capacity to hear the word of God, to take the deep breath, is the very condition of redemption, it is only after redemption that one is equipped to hear, to breathe. The passage continues to explain the daily utterance of the *Shema* prayer, in terms of this paradox. "Hear, O Israel, the Lord our God, the Lord is one": we call Israel to hear the revelation of "God is one," which is the message of Sinai. But, in order to hear, we must clear ourselves of obstruction, open ourselves; for that reason, we read the narrative of the Exodus, culminating in the Song of the Sea, *before* reading the *Shema* prayer. The Exodus thus becomes the therapeutic paradigm for preparedness—the catharsis that frees us to hear.

For the Sefath Emeth, the act of reading the Exodus narrative is the act that enables us to hear. But, we may ask, how did the generation of slaves, without a narrative in hand, ever break free of the paralysis that constricts body and breath?

In another passage, Sefath Emeth confirms the poignancy of the situation. After God has commanded Moses to convey to the people the future narrative of redemption, the people may not listen; but this is excused as a kind of involuntary condition that is the effect of exile. Subtly, the verse is read to suggest the great desire of the people to hear, to accept: "they *could* not listen to Moses, though they yearned to do so . . ." Imprisoned in a condition called in the Zohar the "exile of language," they yearn for release.[57]

It is this condition that Moses refers to in his famous *kal vachomer*, the *a fortiore* argument: if the Israelites would not listen to me, how can I expect Pharaoh to listen? The people's "not listening," becomes, in a comment of Mei HaShiloach, the nub of God's answer to Moses, after his original complaint: "Why have you done harm to this people?" (5:22). God's answer is "I am Hashem" (6:2). The people, unresponsive, prove God's point: they are not yet prepared for redemption. Unlike Moses, who, in the midrashic narratives, articulates this in words, God demonstrates it, through the spontaneous freedom of human response. In this daring reading, the dynamic is not one of promised redemption ("I shall set them free"), followed by setback ("They did not listen . . ."). But rather of a message floated as a test-balloon: what are the people's capacities for that essential act of *hearing?* Their failure, then, is precisely the subject of the opening of this Parsha. Redemption will have to grow out of unreadiness, trauma, discontinuity.

As with Lacan's mirror-stage, the infant is "projected" into history. This is a moment in the natural maturation process, in which the infant "anticipates the maturation of his power": In a sense, the self is an illusion done with mirrors, since any maturation simply reveals a previous immaturity; at each stage, therefore, there is a natural resistance to that maturation which will reveal the hollow ground, the anticipated fantasy on which one had built the earlier self.

The Israelites—Where to Begin?

The real question is "Where to begin?" How is the "exile of language," which includes both hearing and speaking, to be treated, so that redemption, growth, can happen? The problem of exile is not a superficial one: not a matter of a mature self, ready for freedom, the Egyptian disease merely a mask to be stripped off. Rather, exile cramps and inhibits the most fundamental vital processes: breathing, hearing, speaking, being consoled.

God knows of this immaturity in the people. However, the idea of a "natural maturation," which Mei HaShiloach seems to espouse—they are "not yet" fit for redemption—is made problematic by his use of the verse from Song of Songs: "He leaps over the mountains, He springs over the hills," (2:8) a verse which traditionally has encoded the idea of *anticipation*, of projection into history.

In the simplest sense, of course, what inhibits the people from listening to Moses, from "accepting consolation," is the weight of the past. It is the experience of things getting worse since Moses' first appearance that makes them unable to listen further.[58] A narrative of despair blocks out the sound of a narrative of hope. To be able to hear God's promise, they must, in the words of Sefath Emeth, be "clear of all obstructions." A narrative, even one based on the most empirical data, can be an obstruction, creating dizziness, imbalance.[59] There is a problem in basic trust, to use Winnicott's term, which generates narratives of despair and inhibits the development of narratives of hope.

Here, too, as with Pharaoh's "deafness," fear is a potent agent. It produces rigidity, willfulness, the illusion of autonomy. This is the result of Pharaoh's tightening his stranglehold upon them. In a most effective gesture, Pharaoh refuses them straw and demands the same daily quota of bricks. He brings a weight of labor down upon them, which, quite literally, makes it hard for them to breathe: "The same quota of bricks as they have been making up to now you shall impose upon them; you shall not reduce it. For they are shirkers (*nirpim*); that is why they cry, Let us go and sacrifice to our God! Let heavier work be laid upon the men; let them labor at it, and not pay attention (*yish'u*) to false words" (5:8–9).

There are two unusual words in this passage, which will lead us further in interpreting these verses. One is *nirpim*, here translated "shirkers" (JPS); the other *yish'u*, here translated "pay attention." *Nirpim* is translated in the Targum *batlanin*—lax, idle; in Rashi, as "work-shy—that is why their hearts turn towards idleness . . . *nirpim* means that the work is *rafui*—loose, lax in their hands, they are flaccid, the work falls away from them."

Pharaoh's contempt is directed at the looseness, the softness that are connotations of the *rafeh.* He prescribes a corrective heaviness, firmness, pressure ("Let heavier work be laid upon them!"), that will have the hand firmly gripping. This, of course, is the perspective of the Pharaoh whose modality is *kasheh, kaved, chazak*—the terms for the hardening of his heart that are repeated throughout the narrative. But it is interesting that the word *rafeh*, which draws such scorn from him—lax, loose—is related to the word *rapeh*, to heal.

This perception gains significance as we look at the second unusual word in Pharaoh's speech, *yish'u*—"let them not *pay attention* to false words." This is normally translated, "Let them not *regard* lying words," and involves a play on words: "*Ya'asu*—let them labor . . . *ve'al yish'u*—and let them not regard . . ."[60] Rashi, however, rejects this translation, on the grounds that the preposition *be*—"in"—is inappropriate to it. (The normal preposition would be *el* or *le*—to pay attention *to*, not *in*.) He therefore translates:

> "Let them not contemplate and speak constantly of windy words (lit.), saying, Let us go sacrifice . . ."

Rashi asserts that *yish'u be* . . . means to be involved in discourse. In this reading, Pharaoh cannot tolerate a burgeoning culture of thought and discussion about what he contemptuously calls, in Rashi's terms, "windy words." The word for "wind"—*ruach*—is, of course, also the word for "spirit"; so that there emerges from this text in Rashi a fine ambiguity: what to Pharaoh is wind, falsehood, is, in another context, the life of the spirit. What Rashi emphasizes in his translation is the life of language. It is this that Pharaoh calls idleness, laxness. It requires a certain loosening of contact with reality, indeed with labor.[61] This condition, called in Hebrew *batala*, is the very ground of culture. Pharaoh's word, *nirpim*, also brings into play, as we have noticed, the idea of healing. Implicit in Rashi's reading is Pharaoh's awareness of the danger of words: of a possible therapeutic movement among the people that may bring about a renaissance of language. Pharaoh's concern is to bring a harsh weight of labor down upon their hands, leaving no free time or space for the obsessions of the spirit.

The Israelites—The Subversive Scrolls

Behind this translation in Rashi lies an evocative midrash:

> Pharaoh said to them: "Why—*lamah*—do you distract the people from their tasks?" (5:4)—You are *lamah* and your words are *lamah* [pointless, empty rhetoric], as it were. Go home to do some work—"Let heavier work be laid upon the men and let them keep at it and not pay attention to false words." What is *yish'u*? They had scrolls in their possession, with which they would *play* (*yishta'ash'u*) from Shabbat to Shabbat: these declared that God would redeem them. So Pharaoh said to them, *Al yish'u*—Let them not *play* . . . ; that is, let them not rest [on Shabbat] . . .[62]

The scrolls are a weekly source of *sha'ashu'a* for the enslaved people. A text, rolled up in light, portable form (almost with "softcover" accommodation to the reader), provides them with delight, pleasure, entertainment—all these are idiomatic translations for the word, *sha'ashu'a*. But the word has at its root the word *sha'a* (*al yish'u*)—to pay attention; in its doubled form, this becomes *sha'ashu'a*, which means play, the diffuse attention to multiple aspects of an object. It is, then, the experience of *play* with a text in which God is the redeemer that angers Pharaoh and leads to an intensified burden of work.

The use of this word in the midrash is quite remarkable, evoking as it does the passionate verse in Psalms 119:92: "If Your Torah had not been my plaything—*sha'ashu'ai*—I should have perished in my affliction." The Torah as "play-object"; the phrase is found several times in the Tanach. But the issues are not frivolous; as the Psalmist expresses it, this play-activity is a matter of life and death. It is the secret of survival, enigmatic, never fully understood.

In our midrash, the scrolls serve as rudimentary, pre-Torah texts—pretexts for interpretation, speculation, delight. Reading is not, we notice, the operative word here; there is an active, energetic, even erotic modality, that Pharaoh recognizes in all its dangerous "lightness": "Let *heavier* work be laid upon them," is his appropriate response. "You are a *lamah* (*"Why?"*) and your words are a *lamah*," introduces the midrashic drama. Pharaoh displays his contempt for discourse, for that play of the mind that Moses' message invites. *"Al yish'u—Let them not play*, let them not rest"—literally, "draw breath"; let them take no time for that deep luxurious breathing which generates the life of philosophy, art, dream. He condemns that gesture of *she'iya*, which is "taking time out" from the rigors of necessity; the use of *penai*, time and attention cleared from what-must-be.

Such time—the time of Shabbat—is time cleared-for-play. In *Playing and Reality*, D. W. Winnicott describes the site of cultural experience, the potential space that opens up, as the infant begins to move away from the mother into the world of objects. Here, the infant discovers objects that become symbols of the lost unity with the mother. "It is at the place in space and time where and when the mother is in transition from being (in the baby's mind) merged in with the infant and alternatively being experienced as an object to be perceived rather than conceived of."[63] For the Israelites, the trauma of Egypt has meant a break in the natural continuity of their cultural and religious growth. Their ancestors, Abraham, Isaac, and Jacob, were mythically viewed as being "merged" with God, having total faith in God's promises, with no experience of alienation. After the trauma, the threatened "madness" of Egypt, a forced birth into separate existence takes place. Now they must learn to use objects that symbolize the union of two now separate things. The "Shabbat scrolls" are such objects: in "playing" with them, the people will begin to symbolize—in words, primarily—that primal union with God that is now lost.

The idea of play in Winnicott's discussion is beautifully illumined by the image he cites from Marion Milner: "the tremendous significance that there can be in the interplay of the edges of two curtains, or of the surface of a jug that is placed in front of another jug."[64] Infinite variability, the

Torah's "seventy faces," the characteristic of the play-area, contrasts with "the relative stereotypy of phenomena that relate either to personal body functioning or to environmental actuality."

Such interplay between subjective and objective experience, between separateness and union, originality and the acceptance of tradition, is the basis of the notion of the Oral Law. The implication of the midrash is radical: even before the Written Torah is given to the people at Mount Sinai, they have begun to cultivate the capacity for interpretation of scroll-texts that speak of redemption. It is this capacity that, implicitly, will "cure" them for redemption. Pharaoh's anxiety is justified. His decree, depriving them, simply, of *time* (not of the scrolls) is all too effective.

In this banned activity, the play with the scrolls of redemption, the mode of *reverie* is significant. W. R. Bion writes of the incapacity for reverie which is found in the psychotic, along with incapacity for "attention, passing of judgment, memory, and dream-pictures":

> But this in turn means that he destroys the capacity for thought which is essential to action in reality and which makes bearable the frustration—an essential concomitant of the interval between a wish and its fulfillment. So the psychotic's attempt to evade frustration ends in producing a personality more than ever subject to frustration without the softening or moderating mechanism that would have been available through . . . thought. In consequence he is more than ever intolerant of a frustration that is more than ever intolerable. And thus a self-perpetuating situation is created in which more and more frustration is produced by more and more effort devoted to its evasion by the destruction of the capacity for dreaming which, had he retained it, might have enabled him to moderate frustration.[65]

Frustration is fed by the incapacity for reverie. Bion's terms can be related to the midrash we are considering. Reverie, I suggest, is one form of *sha'ashu'a*, which makes bearable the interval between the wish for redemption and its fulfillment. To have that avenue blocked off is to become increasingly frustrated: the state of feeling that the Torah describes as *kotzer ruach*—shortness of spirit. Ultimately, the psychotic intolerance of frustration makes for intolerance of reality: the people, unable to breathe deep, to engage in healing reverie, become incapable of *hearing* the words of Moses.

This "self-perpetuating situation," then, is what the people's deafness implies. In inhibiting them from reverie, from play, from breathing deep, Pharaoh deprives them of the vital capacity to tolerate, to *modify*, in Bion's expression,[66] frustration. In the Tanchuma passage, *al yish'u* represents a decree against reverie, against the complex activity of *sha'ashu'a*, which, in Bion's view, itself carries "an element of frustration." The resulting paradox is that "excessive intolerance of frustration short-sightedly leads to the attempt at evasion of the frustration intrinsic to the task of modification of the frustration." For Rashi, this is best understood as the activity, the play of language: "Let them not engage in windy/spirited words about redemption . . ."

4. *Resisting Redemption: Moses Again*

Moses—The Imperative of Birth

Moses' resistance to speaking God's message is predicated, we remember, on the deafness of the people: "The Israelites would not listen to me; how then should Pharaoh listen to me—and I am of uncircumcised lips!" (6:12). The logic of his cry is palpable. He inhabits a world in which language has lost its power. A kind of psychosis pervades Egypt. Healing, redemption are ruled out by the nature of the disease. Without the Shabbat reverie on the scrolls of redemption, there is no germ of possibility, no inner energy to moderate the frustration of reality. Moses' *kal vachomer* is lucid: if the Israelites have been sealed from the world of play and therefore of reality, how can he expect to communicate with the master of heaviness himself?

". . . and I am of uncircumcised lips": we remember the Sefath Emeth and the vicious circle of failed language. If they cannot listen, then I am no prophet. Words that fall on deaf ears are not, with any meaning, language. The ears of the people—and obviously therefore of Pharaoh—are filled with data that make his words inaudible. The resulting sensation is felt physically in Moses' mouth—"I am of uncircumcised lips." The grotesque imagery of the foreskin blocking the opening (Rashi) conveys an experience of the heaviness that is the incapacity to play:

> What is the source of our first suffering? It lies in the fact that we hesitated to speak . . . It was born in the moments when we accumulated silent things within us. The brook will nonetheless teach you to speak, in spite of sorrows and memories, it will teach you euphoria through

euphuism, energy through the poem. It will repeat incessantly some beautiful, round word which rolls over rocks.[67]

Gaston Bachelard, in this lyrical passage, describes quite precisely "our first suffering." Moses' experience of the "uncircumcised lips," the "heavy mouth and heavy tongue," is this accumulation of silent things within him. His own experience of speechlessness is a mirror of the deafness around him. This pressure of silent things is, as Bachelard perceives so poignantly, suffering.

It is also, ultimately, destructive. As George Steiner notes, Cordelia's "asceticism, her refusal of the mendacities of speech, prove murderous . . . We empty of their humanity those to whom we deny speech . . . There is a terrible, literal image in 'stone-deafness,' in the opaque babble or speechlessness of the 'stoned.' Break off speech to others and the Medusa turns inwards."[68]

Steiner's images of stoniness are an essential element in the biblical dilemmas of redemption. Inability to speak is both "first suffering" and ultimate petrifaction: "the Medusa turns inwards." Redemption begins here.

Moses' self-description, "of uncircumcised lips," indeed, can perhaps be read not as rebellion but as soliloquy. Two commentaries suggest this reading. Or Hachaim reads the enigmatic word *lemor*—"Moses spoke in the presence of God *lemor—saying* . . ." (6:12)—to indicate that he spoke as one who complains to himself about his own failure. His purpose in speaking is not to oppose God but to bewail himself—*"for the sake of saying."* Similarly, Ha-amek Davar reads Moses' speech *"in the presence* of God":[69] "he spoke to himself, and God heard his anguish. If God had not responded, Moses would have obeyed His command."

These readings pick up the theme of Bachelard's "first suffering." Moses expresses the felt pain of Egypt, the Exile of the Word. Previously, as we have seen, he resisted God's mission out of a respect for the elder brother, the father, the system of Egypt. To be called to greatness is to be required to be born. In this intimate narrative, Moses represents the imperative of Exodus: the difficult imperative of birth and growth of the self.

The first verbs that are used of Moses are "crying" and "growing": "And behold the boy was crying . . . And the child grew up . . ." (2:6,10). The history of Moses interrogates the meanings of the growth to greatness. How and when does Moses really become a prophet—indeed, in Jewish tradition, *the* prophet? At the age of eighty he begins a process of growth.[70] The midrash calls him a "novice in prophecy."[71] He is introduced, that is, as the paradigm of the "not yet" situation. His unreadiness destabilizes God's promises of redemption; but his questions about the power and authenticity of language are the necessary questions of one who has doubts about the impiety implicit in the very process of growing.

We noticed earlier that God's response to Moses' motif of "Send by whose hand You will send," was anger. We saw, too, how the midrash identifies Moses' resistance and God's anger as reemerging in 5:22–6:12; Moses is banned from entering the Holy Land because of it. Ultimately, with all the virtuous implications of modesty and concern for his brother, there is a wrong in Moses' resistance to God's call to greatness. He has set himself against redemption. ("I am God—ready to redeem . . . and you say, 'Send by whose hand You will send!' ")

Technically, and in terms of later legal categories, he is a "prophet who has suppressed his prophecy." The Talmud gives an arresting interpretation of Deuteronomy 18:19: speaking of the phenomenon of the false prophet, God says, "And it will be that if someone (*ish*) does not listen to My words which he will speak in My name, then I shall require it of him." Most obviously, this refers to one who disregards the prophetic word: *ish* (the "someone who does not listen") is not identical with the one who "speaks in My name." But the Talmud adds: "This refers also to the prophet who suppresses his own prophecy, and who transgresses against his own words."[72]

In a reflexive move, the prophet himself becomes the one who refuses to listen—either in the sense of obeying his own words, or in the sense of suppressing his prophecy—that is, of silencing his prophecy, so that it cannot be heard.[73] In order to be audible, the prophet must first hear his own words, which are God's words. One who silences this voice—"I will require it of him." The Talmud reads this as punishment "at the hands of Heaven"—not in the human court of law. In other words, such suppression of the voice within is a violation of authenticity, answerable to God alone.

In the same way, Moses' refusal to speak can be understood, at root, as a refusal to hear. God's anger is directed against a prophet who refuses to grow into prophecy, who does not even, as Ramban points out, *ask to be cured* of his speech problem: "so great was his desire not to go on the mission, that he did not pray to God to remove the heaviness of his mouth . . . And, since he did not pray, God did not want to heal him."[74]

Moses' reluctance to be healed is met at this stage (at the Burning Bush) by God's determination to send him on his mission in his "heavy" state. Unhealed, Moses bears the "scar" of the fiery coal, with which he branded himself in his infancy. Perhaps it is this scar that he values, the scar that closes his mouth to the duplicities of language. God is displeased; but can use him, in spite of his reluctance. In this way, the real question of healing is held in abeyance; one who values the sickness cannot be healed. And by the time Moses speaks his soliloquy, as we have termed it, about the deaf-and-dumb condition of Egypt, the Israelites, and himself (6:12), his suffering is driven inwards. He speaks to himself, no longer resists his mission; and God responds nonpragmatically, not in order to achieve His will, but in tenderness to his suffering.

Reluctance to be healed, to be born into language: this is the theme that Maharal elaborates in an extrordinary passage in *Gevurot Hashem*, chapter 28. His subject is Moses' speech defect. He relates this to a famous midrash[75] which describes the birth of the infant: an angel comes and strikes the infant on its mouth and makes it forget the whole Torah it had known in the womb. Thereafter, through the use of language, the human being reconstructs the forgotten Torah.

The gift of language, that is, constitutes the final act in the creation of the child. Spirit and body are fused together in the faculty of speech. The stroke of the angel (which imprints the cleft above the lips) is the *coup de grace*, the concluding tap of the artist's chisel. For the new human being, it is the gift of language that consummates him as human, and, at the same moment, makes him forget the totality of his knowledge.

Maharal applies this midrashic model to Moses. Attached to totality, he is not truly born into the human condition. The angel, as it were, never touched his mouth, which remains heavy, closed, guarding the secrets of another world. There is a purity in this portrait of a man, remote from human language, close to the transcendent world that defies representation. But, equally, this is an unfinished man: some descent into the treacheries of language is demanded of him. Instead of the cleft on the lips, he carries the scorch-mark, the brand of another angel. Saved from death, he bears in his mouth the weight of accumulated silent things.

Moses—Two Narratives

Implicit in this portrait of Moses is the tension between two narratives: one of greatness, selfless concern for his brother, a vision of totality (the whole Torah in its entirety), that makes him unique among human beings; and the other of God's anger, the suppression of the prophetic voice, the refusal to be healed, the "first suffering" that comes of the "accumulated silent things." This tension is not, perhaps, unbearable. In ways that are related to the lyrical pedagogy of which Bachelard writes, the Chasidic sources suggest resolutions: "The brook will nonetheless teach you to speak, in spite of sorrows and memories, it will teach you euphoria through euphuism, energy through the poem . . ."[76]

On the problem of deafness Rabbi Nachman of Bratzlav writes:

> Our Sages wrote on the verse, " 'Their fruit will serve for food and their leaves for healing—*le-terufah:'* (Ezek 47:12)—*lehatir peh*—the leaves will release the mouth of the dumb and release the mouth of the barren." For it is by arousing people from their sleep by story-telling—which is the meaning of "their leaves for healing"—that the mouths of the dumb are released (lit., loosened). Before, when they were asleep, they could not hear the words of arousal spoken by the sage but were as though deaf, completely unhearing. Because of this, it was impossible for them to speak, for this is the condition of a *cheresh*, a deaf-mute—because he does not hear, he cannot speak. But now, when the sage arouses him to hear his words, then he can also speak. That is the meaning of "loosening the mouth of the dumb;" also of the verse, "Open your mouth to the dumb." (Prov 31:8) As a consequence, the mouth of the barren is also loosened. This power of language, so constricted for so long, while they were deaf-mutes, now emerges with great force, which affects also the procreative organs. . . It is important to see that the language organs should be close to the procreative organs, so that the latter can receive the power of language. In this way, one avoids the situation of "You are close to their mouth, but far from their kidneys . . ." (Jer 12:2) Therefore, the language organs and the procreative organs form a single category, language affecting procreation.[77]

Rabbi Nachman weaves a complex and enigmatic interpretation of the verse from Ezekiel. Stories have the power to free (loosen) and thereby heal those who are deaf and dumb, so that they learn to speak; the effects of this "loosening of the mouth" are felt in the procreative area, as well. In a sense that goes beyond the historical relation between deafness and dumbness (there was no way of learning language if one could not hear), the pathology of dumbness, of constricted speech, is connected here with the inability to hear, to be aroused by the words of the Sages. Clearly, a physical condition is the basis, in Rabbi Nachman's rhetoric, for a description of an emotional, even a spiritual pathology: the deafness that we have been exploring in this chapter.

In Rabbi Nachman's mapping of the human body, ear, mouth, and procreative organs are integrally connected. A certain energy is either manifested or constricted. The problem is one of *relaxing*, loosening what is cramped. He quotes from a discussion in Sanhedrin (100a) about Ezekiel's vision of the end of days: " 'Their fruit will serve for food and their leaves for healing.' One sage said, 'For relaxing the mouth of the dumb'; while the other said, 'For relaxing the mouth of the barren.' " Language and sexuality are linked, in Rabbi Nachman's mapping; a confident, expressive energy animates the body in all its creative functions.

In the section we omitted from his discussion, he quotes: "Those who hope for God shall renew their strength" (Isa 40:31). It is the indefinable experience of "hoping for God"—basic trust, as Winnicott calls it—that determines the freedom and energy with which the individual acts in the world. In this sense, Rabbi Nachman emphasizes the vital relation of language, hearing and speaking, to sexual and emotional life. Jeremiah describes the pathological alternative condition, "You are close to their mouth, but far from their kidneys"; this "dissociation of sensibility," to borrow a phrase from T. S. Eliot, that divorces intellectual from physical experience, runs counter to a natural and desirable integration.

According to Rabbi Nachman, pathology in this area is to be healed primarily by a therapeutic treatment of the *ear*: by telling stories that will arouse the sleeping self. One might return to the idea of reverie: a capacity of imagination, which can be entirely stifled, must be liberated. On this depend expressiveness and creativity, on all levels; and the means to achieve this awakening of imagination is by the telling of stories. For the characteristic of stories is that they have endless facets of meaning;[78] they gain admission to our inner world because they are polymorphous, plastic, familiar and strange at the same time. Once within, they begin their work, turning around and around, inviting us to play with their meanings. They are the scrolls of redemption, light, subversive, generating life.

For Rabbi Nachman, the idea of bibliotherapy—the release of energy on all levels by listening to stories—is indicated in the Talmudic pun on Ezekiel's word, *terufa*. Rabbi Nachman is not discussing Moses, specifically. In the following midrash, however, Moses becomes the classic example of the problem we have been discussing, the problem that Bachelard called "our first suffering":

> God said, See the language (*lashon—tongue*) of Torah, how precious it is, for it cures the tongue! How do we know this? For it is written, "The tree of life heals the tongue." (Prov 15:4) The tree of life is none other than the Torah, as it is said, "It is a tree of life to those who hold on to it."

> (Prov 3:18) And the tongue of Torah releases the tongue. Know that in future time, God will raise up excellent trees from the Garden of Eden. What is their excellence? That they heal the tongue, as it is said, "All kinds of trees for food will grow up on both banks of the stream" (Ezek 47:12) [*al sefato* translates as "bank" and as "lip"]. How do we know that they will heal the tongue? It is said, "Their leaves will serve for healing." (ibid.)—*terufah:* R. Yochanan said, This means for food [from *teref*—instantly ripening fruit]. R. Joshua ben Levi said, "Anyone who is dumb and eats of it heals his tongue. He polishes his tongue on the words of Torah, as it is written, 'On this side and that they are written' (Exod 32:15)—*mizeh umizeh*—the same expression as Ezekiel uses about the healing trees that grow 'on both banks.' "
>
> R. Levi said, Why should we learn from another place, when we can learn from its own proper place? Moses, before he came to merit the Torah, was described as "not a man of words." But when he came to merit the Torah, his tongue was healed and he began to speak words: "These are the words that Moses spoke . . ." (Deut 1:1)[79]

R. Levi reads the essential story of Moses as one of language acquisition. All the evidences from Proverbs, from Ezekiel, that the Torah cures the problem of the tongue become unnecessary, in his view, if we study this one single case history. His is the archetypal case, asserts R. Levi: when he merited Torah, the words began to flow. But, of course, the converse is also true: by exploring the complex readings about language, we are better able to understand Moses' particular problem.

Ezekiel's trees of ultimate redemption bring this specific kind of healing, the *terufa* (a hapax legomenon—that is, the sole occurrence of this word in the Tanach). Torah, the tree of life, its very *language*, its *tongue*, rubs against the human tongue, polishes it this way and that, loosening it for expressive use. The extraordinary play on the word *lashon*—tongue—yields a language on which the human tongue learns to glisten; human language becomes liquid and clear. There is an abrasive meeting of tongue and tongue, which multiplies meanings and refurbishes language with complex sources, "from this side and that."

The imagery here is hard, steely, glistening. But before this "polishing" process can happen, the tongue must be cured: that is, relaxed, released, from the spasm of inhibition that is portrayed as primary. This is Bachelard's "first suffering . . . the fact that we hesitated to speak . . . It was born in the moments when we accumulated silent things within us." For Bachelard, healing comes from the brook: "it will teach you euphoria through euphuism, energy through the poem. It will repeat incessantly some beautiful, round word which rolls over rocks."[80] That is, the human reverie, taking in and disseminating the power of the brook, will work through the accumulated mass of "sorrows and memories," make them liquid and speakable.

For Rabbi Nachman, the midrashic idea that the words, the tongue of Torah has power to release the human tongue—and, with it, all the pent-up energies of sexuality—is a similarly experiential idea. In his text, muscles and nerves are the infrastructure of his mapping of body and spirit. Some event must happen to this paralyzed organism: in his idiom, the event is the narrative that seizes the imagination, that invites the telling of narratives. The burden of this redemptive narrative is "hope for God"; its effect is a therapeutic generation of endless stories, creating and procreating.

Basic to Rabbi Nachman's vision is the Talmudic imagery of loosening, releasing. The midrash uses the word *terufa* enigmatically. Sound and meaning play with each other. But, at its core, the word *rafeh*, healing, embodies the notion of softening, relaxing—as in the process of "curing" leather, or of working with metal. Rabbi Nachman's discussion uses this as the central tactile image for healing: opening the closed, softening the hard, allowing life to flow where previously there was constriction.

Moses—The Power of Narrative

According to R. Levi's words, Moses is *mekomo*, the *locus classicus*, the prototype for understanding therapeutic change of this kind. His story condenses the larger therapeutic story of Israel, released from Egypt. On this conceptual level, the Zohar reads the narrative of the Exodus. Egypt, *Mitzrayim*, is the place of *meitzarim*, of constriction, the place of *galuth hadibur*, the Exile of the Word. Here, a kind of fatal sleep dulls the senses and makes listening impossible. What can rouse the sleeper? The general torpor affects all—from Pharaoh to the Israelites to Moses himself. It takes many forms, but underlying all is fear—fear of death, fear of life. It is this fear that makes hearing, reverie, and speech impossible: a defensive rigidity that narrows the channels and closes the apertures.

The cure is to be Torah. When Moses "comes to merit" Torah, words rush to his lips. But how does one "come to merit" Torah? How does one come at redemption, if it is not already within? Rabbi Nachman answers: listen to stories about hope for God. Off guard, one will be infiltrated; almost unconsciously, one will begin the process of incorporation, of making Torah one's own. Seventy languages will be released, multiple understandings and constructions.

The power of narrative to generate worlds becomes, in this reading, the way to redemption. In the Exodus story, of course, there is constant reference to the fact that the purpose of the story is "so that you shall tell the tale . . ."[81] The logic is challenging: God foretells redemption; redemption happens and is narrated in the Torah, *so that* all future generations will go on narrating. The crucial moment is the moment when a stupefied nation is aroused to listen and to tell; the health and vigor of individual and people will be indicated by their capacity to tell the story of redemption.

Ha-amek Davar offers a comment on this storytelling faculty as the very experience of redemption. In the Haggadah, read on the Seder night, the first night of Passover, the phrase occurs: "whoever tells the story at greatest length, that is the most praiseworthy." He comments: the elite among the people are those whose sensibility to the wonder of redemption is most acute and who therefore have *most to tell* about the Exodus. The development of such an elite is the final stage of redemption—beyond the four stages of national redemption, listed in the passage at the beginning of our Parsha: "I shall set free . . . I shall save . . . I shall redeem . . . I shall take unto Me . . ." (6:6–7). The final verb is "And you shall know . . ." (6:7): this represents the high consciousness of the few, who fulfill the spiritual purpose of Exodus in their complex, elaborate narratives.[82]

Moses—Obstacle and Desire

Narrative as therapeutic procedure: the notion evokes the psychoanalytic project. If we are to take this seriously, then we must say that a people are to be released from cultural and sexual paralysis through a version of Freud's "talking cure."[83] But again, the question recurs: how is the paralyzed tongue released, so that it can speak the language that releases it?

For this, there is one prerequisite: the force of desire. It is desire that, in Rabbi Nachman's terms, clears the throat of its pent-up words, of that hoarseness that makes articulation difficult. This is *Mitzrayim* (Egypt)—*meitzarim bagaron*—the constriction in the throat that he calls (in Yiddish), *heizerik* (hoarseness). All the "accumulated silent things within us" are backed up in the congested throat: the "sorrows and memories . . ." What is needed is the addition of vowels to those dry congested consonants: the fluid movement that gives life to the dead letter, and that makes language and therefore thought possible.[84]

These vowels—the *nekudoth*—represented in Hebrew orthography as dots (and dashes) which connect, like the sound of a brook, consonant to consonant, are celebrated as the "dots of desire." In a deliberate misreading of The Song of Songs (1:11), Rabbi Nachman translates *nekudoth hakesef*—"the silver spangles"—as "dots of *kisufin*, of yearning." Without the forward motion of desire—like vowel-sounds transforming the glut in the throat into the fluidity of words and sentences, thought and feeling—it is impossible, he asserts, to speak, or, indeed, to do anything.

Primary, therefore, to language, or to any human act, is desire. Here, Rabbi Nachman's thought makes a paradoxical leap: desire is generated, precisely, by obstacles. Particularly when an important task is to be performed, he writes, when much energy of desire is necessary, God sets in place obstacles to sharpen that desire. He describes the classic reaction of the child to the object that is hidden from him: the *fort da* model that Freud discussed as so significant in the early experience of desire. "This obstacle is there for the sake of the desire," writes Rabbi Nachman. The relation between taboo and passion is a psychological commonplace; that same passion Rabbi Nachman would claim for the world of holiness.

The paradoxical power of obstacles is the subject of an essay by Adam Phillips. He quotes Sartre (in *Being and Nothingness*): a walker is confronted with an overhanging cliff face:

> For the simple traveler, who passes over this road and whose free project is a pure aesthetic ordering of the landscape, the crag is not revealed either as scalable or not scalable; it is manifested only as beautiful or ugly.

And comments:

> If I am simply on a walk, the rock face is an obstacle; if I am a painter, it is not. But the absurd—the psychoanalytic—possibility that Sartre does not consider is that I may realize I am on a walk only when I perceive the cliff as an obstacle. That is to say, the only way to discover your projects is to notice—to make conscious—what you reckon are obstacles . . . The desire does not reveal the obstacle; the obstacle reveals the desire. And if only it was as simple as this we could say to our patients, or to ourselves, "Tell me what your obstacles are, and I will tell you what you desire."[85]

It is the obstacles that keep the fires stoked; without them there is "merging or incest, and so the death of desire; and obstacles without desire are literally unthinkable, or surreal like Magritte's doors suspended in the air." From this, he concludes that "there must anyway be a wish for obstacles as unconscious mnemonics of desire. The obstacle reminds me of what I want, in one part of my mind, to forget."[86]

The wish for the obstacle is, I am suggesting, indeed a version of the wish for desire. A people exiled from language love their own constriction, because it reminds them of yearning. The dynamic of the Exodus from Egypt, therefore, on all its levels, is one of friction and relaxation, obstacle and desire. The Chasidic reading of "The children of Israel did not listen to Moses," we remember, included the notion of the "desire to hear," the frustration which becomes the energy that generates redemption.[87] It is precisely the difficulty of redemption that arouses this longing.

MOSES—THE WOUNDED HEALER

Phillips writes of the need to articulate a "vocabulary of impediments," if development is to be conceivable: the obstacle reveals the desire. Perhaps it is Moses' final articulation of his speech problem *as impediment* ("I am of uncircumcised lips . . .") that offers him the key to desire: after this, he never complains again of such a problem. As with the infant who is born into language, it is forgetting, loss, the trauma of the angelic tap on the mouth, that impels him through the straits and into the world of others.

If this is the underlying drama of the Exodus, if the sickness, the paralysis contains the elements of healing, then it is Moses, the leader, the peerless teacher, who brings the people to redemption. Ultimately, this description of his role will be paramount: he is the quintessential teacher—*moshe rabbenu* (Moses our teacher). In order to achieve his pedagogical task—in his case, perhaps in all cases, also a therapeutic task—he must know, in more concentrated form, the difficulties, the suffering that he is to heal. The language problem is peculiarly his: "Oh, Word, Word, Word, that I lack!" cries Schoenberg's Moses. His impediments, the "unconscious mnemonics of desire" (Phillips), constantly evoke that desire for healing which is complicated by the reluctance to be healed. This dilemma is never entirely resolved, even in the glistening encounter between tongue and Torah.

The healer must know the deepest loneliness and pain of his patients.

Elias Canetti writes of the initiation of the healer among the Aranda in Australia:

> [he] wanders away to the mouth of the cave where the spirits dwell. Here, first of all, his tongue is perforated by a lance thrown at him by one of the spirits. He is quite alone and it is part of his initiation that he should feel great fear of the spirits. The courage to endure loneliness, and this in a place of particular danger, is one of the qualifications of his profession . . . In this way he is strengthened for his role, but from *within;* his new power originates in his intestines. He must have been dead before he can begin to exercise it, for death makes possible the complete penetration and exploration of his body. His secret is known only to him and to the spirits; it lies within his body.[88]

It is noticeable that preparation for the life of healing—and teaching—involves fear and courage, loneliness, the disabling of the tongue, and an entire inner transformation, a replacement of his inner organs, a death and rebirth. It is such intimate interrogation of his whole being that initiates the healer, puts him in contact with powers of teaching, in the largest sense.

5. *Exile and Redemption: An Eternal Tension*

Exodus: The Moment of Danger

The motif of Moses' speech difficulty represents, I suggest, an initiation of this sort: one peculiarly adapted to the project of his generation. In Chasidic thinking, however, the historical view is not the important one. In the work of Sefath Emeth, for example, the dynamic of Egypt is an eternal one: "The truth is that at all times there is *mitzrayim*—Egypt/constriction—for every person in Israel. That is why we mention the Exodus, liberation from *mitzrayim*, every day. And, in as much as we know and remember that God released us, there is no need for us to be, in literal fact, within the straits of *mitzrayim*—for the exodus is evoked in us at all times."[89]

For Sefath Emeth, the tension of exile and redemption is always present. Too great confidence about accomplished redemption cuts one off from God, the redeemer; actual suffering, on the other hand, also prevents one from hearing His word. The key to the paradox is narrative: the effort to retain the moment of redemption, to remember it and to know it. For this, the dynamic of listening and speaking, on the one hand, and of the Exile of the Word, on the other, must remain potent.

The world of *Mitzrayim*, of Egypt, dominated by an unhearing, unspeaking Pharaoh, becomes the environment of imagination. The narrative of redemption repeats constantly, "at all times." The complex dynamics of Moses—who is "not a man of words," and yet comes to "speak so much"[90]—compels and resists systematic resolution.

In the Chasidic perception, Egypt has not been defeated. "To articulate the past historically," writes Walter Benjamin, "does not mean to recognize it 'the way it really was' (Ranke). It means to seize hold of a memory as it flashes up at a moment of danger."[91] Egypt is the eternal "moment of danger." To tell of release and freedom—the narrative of hope—a continuing dialectic is necessary.

It is not, Kierkegaard notes, "that [faith] annihilates dread, but remaining ever young, it is continually developing itself out of the death-throe of dread."[92] The story of the Exodus, the eternal tension between faith and dread, is destined to be retold continuously, as it is reenacted continuously.

The Psalmist provides poignant testimony to the eternity of the Egyptian anguish and release. In Psalm 81, God reminds His people of how He saved them from the suffering of Egypt:

"I relieved his shoulder of the burden, his hands were freed from the basket. In distress you called and I rescued you. I answered you from the secret place of thunder; I tested you at the waters of Meriba" (81:7–8).

According to Rashi's reading, the people called to God in an intimate cry of despair, while He responded publicly, prodigiously, thunderously. The reference to the test at Meriba Rashi reads: "I answered you . . . even though it was clear to Me that you would rebel at Meriba." In other words, God's redemption contains within it the knowledge of continuing tension.

The climax of the Psalm follows:

> Hear, My people, and I will testify against you; Israel, if you would but listen to Me! You shall have no foreign god, you shall not bow down to an alien god. I am the Lord your God who brought you up from the Land of Egypt; open your mouth wide and I will fill it. But My people would not listen to Me, Israel would have none of Me (lit., "did not want Me.") So I let them go after their wilful heart, that they might follow their own devices. *If only My people would listen to Me*, if Israel would follow My paths, then would I subdue their enemies at once, strike their foes again and again. Those who hate the Lord shall cower before Him; their doom

shall be eternal. He fed them the finest wheat; I sated you with honey from the rock. (81:9–17)

God's appeal to His people is that they hear Him: "Hear, My people . . . If only My people would listen to Me . . ." After all His redemptive work, surely this is a justified claim. Even now, after all the history of deafness, of rejection, if only they would listen. In Rashi's reading, both poles of the paradox are contained: the logic of God's claim to their loving response, and the empirical irony of their freedom expressed in not-hearing, not-wanting Him. The reference to those who "hate the Lord" is obviously a reference to the enemies of Israel: God offers to destroy them totally, if His people return to Him. But perhaps there is a veiled, unspeakable reference to Israel themselves; those who "do not want God," are identical with those who "hate the Lord."

What God wants of His people is their hearing; but, also, their "open mouths": "Open your mouth wide and I will fill it." Rashi: "To ask of Me all the desire of your heart." The oral imagery—the mouth wide open to be fed—is transformed into the verbal demand of the mouth, articulating its desires. What God wants is a hunger that has been worded. An awareness of desire, of emptiness; and a narrative that connects this with a history, in which God is the source of the most basic satisfactions of the mouth.

Exodus: Honey from the Rock

The memory of redemption is essentially this: "He fed them the finest wheat; I sated you with honey from the rock." Honey from the rock: the phrase is evocative of the antinomies we have been exploring—the soft and the hard, the fluid and the rigid. These antinomies enter into a dialectic of redemption in the Egyptian story.

At the end of his life, Moses sings of God's work in Egypt: "He suckled them with honey from the crag, and with oil from the flinty rock."[93] The Talmud tells the most intimate tale of redemption, a tale of desire, pregnancy, and birth. And of suckling: "God's angel would give the newborn babies two smooth pebbles from one of which they suckled oil and from the other honey—as it is said, 'He suckled him with honey from the crag, and with oil from the flinty rock.' "[94] Oil and honey flowed from the stones of Egypt, like milk from the mother's breast. Stones and breasts; milk, honey, oil from the rock. These are the uncanny memories of Israel in Egypt.

Mother and baby blissfully merged; flinty rejection, deafness. So it was then, and so it continues. Only in language, in narrative, can the tension be contained. "Open your mouth wide and I will fill it." The mouth of which God speaks is not that blind mouth of infancy. There is an adult choice here, a conscious will to open, to utter desire. This means to recognize, in separateness, the Other who is the redeemer. Here is the world of language, which offers an alternative to Egypt, *Mitzrayim.* Here, at least, is Bachelard's brook, which "will repeat incessantly some beautiful, round word which rolls over rocks."

3 *Bo*

THE NARRATIVE OF THE NIGHT

[10:1–13:16]

1. The Omnipotence Effect: Narrative and Counter-Narrative

The Purpose of Narrative

The Parsha begins with the formulaic command by God to Moses, introducing the eighth plague, the locusts:

> Then God said to Moses, "Go to Pharaoh. For I have hardened his heart and the hearts of his courtiers, in order that I may display these My signs among them, and that you may recount in the hearing of your sons and of your sons' sons how I made a mockery of the Egyptians and how I displayed My signs among them—in order that you may know that I am God." (10:1–2)

The logic of God's call here seems opaque: Moses is to go to Pharaoh, presumably to warn him of the next plague, *because* God has hardened Pharaoh's heart? This is the only time that God, in His own voice, announces that He has interfered with Pharaoh's heart: all other descriptions report such divine intervention in the third person narrative voice ("God hardened his heart."). This use of the first person, here, is paralleled only by God's foreshadowing of the plague-history in 7:3: "And I shall harden Pharaoh's heart . . ."

The use of the first person voice of God, telling and foretelling the plague story, has the effect of explaining a cryptic sequence of events. Here, God explains why Moses should persist in warning Pharaoh, in spite of the clear evidence that Pharaoh is impervious to all appeals. The evidence is that, even after he has apparently yielded, with an unprecedented confession ("I stand guilty this time. God is in the right, and I and my people are in the wrong" [9:27]), as soon as he sees the hail stop, "he hardened his heart and reverted to his guilty ways . . ." (9:34). After such a moment of radical disappointment, Moses is convinced that even unbearable suffering will not release Pharaoh's stranglehold on the Israelites.[1] In this impasse, God has to justify Moses' continuing to warn Pharaoh of the impending plagues.

On this reading, then, a point of absurdity has been reached. Although God has told Moses from the beginning that "Pharaoh will not listen . . ." it is only now, before the locust plague, that Moses experiences the full sense of fatality. God then explains: "For *I* have hardened his heart . . ." In all this insane stubbornness, there is something of God—something inexplicable in other terms.[2] Beyond reasonable diagnosis, Pharaoh's behavior has been *engineered*, so that certain purposes may be achieved. These purposes are "to display these My signs among them" and "so that you may recount in the hearing of your sons and your sons' sons how I made a mockery of the Egyptians . . ."

God's explanation to Moses seems to justify continuing the drama of warning—resistance—yielding—refusal, on the grounds that ultimately this will constitute a narrative for his children and grandchildren. The narrative is to be extended, without hope of effecting change in Pharaoh, for the sake of the narrative which Moses, personally, will tell his son and grandson.

Seforno softens the harshness of such a reading by suggesting that God gives Pharaoh strength to resist the impact of the plagues, for the sake of the signs that may bring about repentance in *other* Egyptians—as well as for the Israelite narrative of "My greatness and My goodness." Possibly, Moses' warnings, his repeated predictions of miracles, precisely fulfilled, will have an effect on "some" of the Egyptians, who will allow themselves to become aware of "My greatness."

The distinction in Seforno's reading, between the reactions of the Egyptians and of the Israelites to the plague narrative, is pointed: the Egyptians may repent, out of a sense of God's "greatness"—that is, His power; the Israelites will come to recognize His "greatness and *goodness.*" In this narrative, the obvious suffering, repeatedly endured by the Egyptians, is an intensifying serial demonstration of God's good intentions towards His persecuted people.

The humanitarian point that Seforno makes is that the Egyptians, too, are being addressed by this extension of the plague narrative. They remain subjects, capable of change. Pharaoh, personally, may be beyond redemption, but to persist in warning him is not entirely futile. It will create more, and perhaps more effective signs, indications that may convince some Egyptians to repent.

Aside from this characteristically humane reading by Seforno, the general thrust of the passage is stark and unequivocal: it is the Israelites whose narrative of God's power and goodness will be constructed by the repeated cycle of warning—resistance—yielding—refusal. For the sake of this narrative—or, more exactly, for the sake of Moses' magisterial narrative to his son and grandson—he must renew the perverse cycle, waste words of warning that he knows will not be heard.

The Omnipotence Effect

This narrative, centering on what Meir Sternberg calls the "omnipotence effect," plays out for all to see the full implications of God as Omnipotent Creator. God manifests His power, manipulating the Egyptians for the good of the Israelites: "The plagues thus come as an object lesson to three different audiences, whom he himself enumerates to Moses: 'Pharaoh and his servants,' 'you,' 'thy son and thy son's son,' all needing to 'know that I am the Lord' " (Exod 10:1–2).[3] The past is organized into a rhetoric of faith: time and time again, God foreshadows the plagues, and time and time again, His will is executed.

In Sternberg's analysis, however, this very repetition, which involves a delay in the final redemption, might be used to tell a counter-narrative of divine weakness. It is to forestall such a reading of events that God preannounces His intention to harden Pharaoh's heart. The effect is that "the potential weakness turns into a source of rhetorical strength, because notice ushers in a double demonstration of omnipotence—over the workings of the heart as well as of nature."[4] By such devices as repetition, too, the narrator elicits possible counter-narratives of weakness ["Why did He protract the drama of the Exodus, when He might have overwhelmed Pharaoh in one omnipotent act?"]. This then becomes a strategy to vindicate God's power. The counter-narratives, the "jarring and inimical views" of God's power in the world, are brought out into the open, "through a dramatic voice that can suitably be dealt with in context, notably by subjecting that misbeliever to a process of discovery that ends in retraction and alignment. Dissonant voices are thus manipulated rather than eliminated in the interests of persuasive harmony."[5]

This harmonizing of dissonant voices (Sternberg brings the example of the skeptical laughter of Abraham and Sarah at the promise of a son) echoes a necessary process in the reader, too. Any skepticism in the reader is worked through to the ultimate triumph of the narrative of faith. A sequence of signs, precisely predicted as to time and place ("spatiotemporal bounding," in Sternberg's term) increases the "credit for control . . . in direct proportion to the risk of failure."[6] The land of Goshen is exempted, the plague will come "by tomorrow"—all observers must be struck by the impressive repertoire that God stages so publicly before the eyes of the people.

In Sternberg's account, this last point is of great significance. Sight, the public testimony of the Israelite audience, generates faith and knowledge. From the beginning of the narrative, the people belie Moses' skepticism ("Indeed, they will not believe me . . ." [4:1]), by their response to his transforming the rod into a serpent, "before the eyes of the people; and the people believed . . . and they bowed low in homage" (4:31). The very last words of the Torah tell of "all the signs and wonders . . . and all the mighty power and all the deeds of great terror which Moses wrought *before the eyes of all Israel*" (Deut 34:11–12). At Mount Sinai, the people "*saw* the sounds" (Exod 20:15). At the Red Sea, the people "*saw* (*va-yav*) God's great hand acting against Egypt, and the people feared (*va-yire'u*) God, and they believed in God and in Moses, his servant" (14:31). Seeing is not just believing, but *yir'ah*, existential submission to God's power. Moses reverts to this theme in his final speech, when he reminds them of "the things your eyes have *seen*" (Deut 4:9), and urges them to communicate their eyewitness account to posterity. Remembrance, narrative are produced by empirical experience. This, together with an impressive repertoire of other narrative stratagems, most effectively stages the "omnipotence effect."

Sternberg's account, dazzling in its details and its thickness of specification, gives us a narrative of unambiguous enthusiasm for God's omnipotence, a narrative in which all jarring voices have been manipulated into harmony. By the use of an entire repertoire of structural, psychological, and semantic devices, all the claims of God triumph, while the counterclaims of skepticism are silenced. This is the narrative that will be transmitted to children and children's children.

The Weight of Counter-Narratives

There is, however, something much too totally harmonized about this version of the Exodus story. The counter-voices have been silenced by the triumphant master-narrative. Sternberg's emphasis on the visual, public status of miracles and plagues, for instance, as engendering an unequivocal faith, ignores the skeptical narratives that surround each description of eyewitness experience.

For example, after the original description of the rod-serpent miracle ("before the eyes of the people; and the people believed . . ." [4:31]), there follows the Israelites' attack upon Moses and Aaron, on the failure of their first appeal to Pharaoh ("May God look upon you and punish you for making us loathsome in the eyes of Pharaoh" [5:21]). Here, the narrative is impressed with the sign of failure, the "repulsion" (lit. "the stink") which results from *being seen* by Pharaoh as ineffective rebels. Public testimony of a most ungratifying sort now speaks against the claims of faith.

This is followed by the refusal of the Israelites even to listen to Moses, "because of shortness of breath and harsh labor." The question is, what happens to such skeptical counter-narratives? Are they presented only in order to raise the handicap, as it were, and make God's prodigious power seem even more "incredible," in the idiomatic sense? This is Sternberg's argument. I should like to take a different view, one that distributes rather differently the relative weights of narrative and counter-narrative.

Seeing as Appropriation

If we take Sternberg's example from Deuteronomy, for instance ("the things your eyes have seen . . ." [4:9]), we have the case, apparently, of eyewitness testimony to the total power of God, which, in sheer gratitude and awe, is to be transmitted in story to posterity. The fact is, however, that the people Moses is addressing at this point, forty years after the Exodus, did not themselves witness the events of Sinai; there are no adult survivors of that time, by virtue of God's edict after the sin of the Spies.[7] Moses, in addressing the second generation, is addressing those who are "dystemporaneous" with him (to use Michael Fishbane's expression), not the adults who actually left Egypt with him.

Here is a strange ambiguity: on the one hand, he speaks to them as contemporaries, witnesses with him of "the things" of Sinai, who must testify to their children "who did not know" these things (31:13); while, on the other hand, the larger narrative has made it very clear that those whose eyes saw the Revelation at Sinai have fallen as carcasses into the sand, over the forty-year interim. What, then, is meant by Moses' injunction: "But take utmost care and watch yourselves scrupulously, so that you do not forget the things that your own eyes have seen . . ." (4:9)? It is true that, in a secondary sense, "you" refers to the transpersonal reader throughout the ages; but the primary reference is to a generation who, themselves, have not seen.

The Jerusalem Talmud adopts a metaphorical reading of the phrase, "that your own eyes have seen": "One who internalizes his learning does not quickly forget it."[8] "Seeing" becomes a word for inner clarity, for a profound internalization of what one has learned. Our verse becomes a proof-text for the importance of such a spiritual-intellectual process, precisely because the literal meaning of "you saw with your own eyes" has been abandoned. Since Moses' audience consists of those who did *not* see, what makes them guardians of the narrative and tellers to the future is a *verbal* process of learning and appropriating the Torah. The effect is a kind of "seeing the sounds, the voices" (Exod 20:15), which recalls the paradox of Sinai itself, where the people are described as "seeing the sounds."

Ultimately, such a reading gives great weight to personal construction of meaning, the inner processes by which ideas are appropriated. This would be true for the generation that Moses addresses before his death; but, by extension, perhaps, even the generation who stood at Sinai, those who saw, were also engaged in the act of appropriation, of interpretation, that makes forgetting harder. Even in the presence of Revelation, it is necessary to "see the sounds," to interpret, internalize what is learned.

The Eyewitness Experience as Illusion

To suggest this is to erode the absolute and manifest quality of the eyewitness experience. Rather than understanding the recurrent expression "before the eyes of the Israelites" to convey incontestable evidence for the claims of faith, I suggest that, conceivably, "before the eyes," qualifies, diminishes the authority of perception. When, for instance, Joseph, in the course of tormenting his brothers in his guise of arbitrary tyrant, throws his brother Simeon into prison as hostage for their return to Egypt, the narrative emphasizes: "He imprisoned him *before their eyes*" (Gen 42:24). Rashi comments: "He only imprisoned him before their eyes: as soon as they left, he freed him and gave him food and drink."

"Before their eyes" intimates illusion; it is performed for effect. This act of arbitrary imprisoning ("Your brother—any one—shall be imprisoned . . ." [42:19]) is read midrashically as a facade, covering a specific choice (Simeon had been the ringleader of the brothers' fratricidal intent) and magnanimous forgiveness. This midrashic reading of "before their eyes," is given force by the first part of the verse: "He turned aside from them and wept . . ." These tears, the first of many to be shed by Joseph, introduce a narrative of self-division, a dissonance between Joseph's behavior and his inner life that will characterize him to the very end of Genesis—even beyond his final harmonizing declaration (50:19–21), signaled by a final significant paroxysm of tears.[9]

Such a reading of "before their eyes," can be applied to other uses of the idiom. Moses performs the signs—the rod turning into a serpent—"before the eyes of the people." Possibly here, too, there is a suggestion of the performer's art. The "signs" were, after all, a concession given to Moses, when he could not believe that the people were capable of believing: "They will not believe in me and they will not listen to my voice" (Exod 4:1). God meets his anxiety by seizing on available "props": the stick, the hand that dies and is restored to life. These signs are given as psychological insurance: surely the people will listen to these voices—if not to the one, then to the other (4:8). The signs, in other words, are rather flamboyant concessions, theatrical demonstrations of power, whose very conclusiveness is their weakness. This solution to the problem of belief is a makeshift, ultimately spurious one. Moses' complaint—precisely, "They will not listen to my voice—*be-koli*—intently, to all the implications of my message"[10]—expresses a radical failure in the kind of face-to-face attention that must underlie belief. To resort to marvels and transformations is a descent to a more facile mode of communication: on this level, they merely respond to "the voice of the sign—*lekol ha'oth,*" in its most unequivocal and undemanding form.

A further possibility in reading this passage is raised by the comment of the Talmud:

> It is revealed to God that Israel are believers. So He said to Moses: Israel are believers, children of believers, as it is written, "The people believed . . ." (4:31)[11]

This comment throws the burden of unbelief squarely onto Moses. The people's capacity for belief is more highly evolved than is suggested by the rather tawdry signs and wonders. It is Moses whose skepticism has to be allayed, by providing him with an arsenal of signs—"before their eyes," for instant visual effect.

The phrase "before their eyes" thus introduces the nuance of the illusory, the too-immaculate facade. It bears a cautionary resonance, reminding us of a particular, limited perspective. When Moses goes up Mount Sinai, for instance, to receive the Torah, we read: "The vision of the glory of God was like a consuming fire before the eyes of the children of Israel" (24:17). All the people see is the consuming fire, which bars access to the mystery of Moses' encounter with God. Moses, by contrast, comes "into the midst of the cloud": he enters with his whole being and traverses the cloud to a condition that can be indicated in language only by the word, "to be": "And Moses *was* on the mountain forty days and forty nights" (24:18).

Similarly, "before the eyes of all Israel," inscribed as the very last words of the Torah, frame Moses' life history, his acts performed with a "strong hand," in the fearsome wilderness. In a challenging final comment, Rashi concludes his text on the Torah:

> Before the eyes of all Israel: this refers to his inspiration to break the Tablets before their eyes, as it is said, "I broke them *before your eyes*" (Deut 9:17). God agreed with his decision, as it is said, "the tablets which (*asher*) you broke" (10:2)—"Congratulations (*yishar kochacha*) that you broke them!" (Rashi: Deut 34:12)

Here, "before the eyes of all Israel" is decoded as a reference to Moses' breaking of the Tablets (also "before their eyes"). This act is applauded by God and inscribed into the last words of the Torah—as Moses' finest hour, as it were. Moses' courage in performing such an iconoclastic act—literally breaking the image, the one physical evidence of revelation—is suggested by the words *nessa'o libo*, "his heart lifted him up." He was inspired to an extravagant deed that, retroactively, is recognized as his masterpiece. The paradox is, of course, that *before the eyes* of all the people, he shatters the one visual manifestation—written by the finger of God—that Moses has brought back from the invisible world. In one phrase, Moses' essential lifework is caught in all its dialectical tension. He has enacted for the people the perilous claim of the visual and its vulnerability—but this enactment has itself been visual. It has been, to use Susan Handelman's expression, a "staging" of ongoing unconscious conflicts. Handelman writes:

> When something is staged, it is put into motion, re-created, transformed . . . [In psychoanalysis, the] analyst becomes a screen onto which

> are projected the patient's unconscious conflicts, and these are then *re-enacted* in the relation with the analyst . . . So perhaps we could further say that the knowledge produced out of the teaching relation is a knowledge that is "staged."[12]

Earlier, Handelman quotes Roland Barthes, in an unexpected analogy. He compares the teacher, not to the psychoanalyst, but to the patient:

> For the *patient* talks compulsively to the silent audience of the analyst, like the teacher talking compulsively to the class . . . "the teacher is the one who learns and teaches nothing other than the way he learns. The subject of teaching is an interminable learning."[13]

In the light of this suggestion, we can perhaps say that Moses as teacher (which is, of course, his classic appellation—*moshe rabbenu*) stages for the people the process of learning, works through the conflicts evoked by such fraught objects as "stone tablets, inscribed by the finger of God," placed in juxtaposition with a calf made of gold jewelry.[14] Moses' "interminable learning" is sealed by the words, "before the eyes of all Israel." The eyes of the people, their limited perspectives, have allowed them to share in a "pedagogical moment," in Handelman's phrase, a process of learning that is an unfolding, a generating of knowledge, that is aware of its own involvement.

This notion of the role of the visual is, of course, quite different from Sternberg's description of the "essential observability of the marvel and its role as persuasive sign."[15] In Sternberg's account of the rhetorical effectiveness of the narrative, God's omnipotence receives the widest public testimony, through the plagues, the miracles of Egypt, and the revelation at Sinai. In counterpoint, I would emphasize the skepticism implicit in texts about things seen, wonders staged so dramatically that none could deny them. There is a sadness about the constant appeal to the eyes, to eyewitness as basis for faith.

If the purpose of the plagues is to become narrative, this will not be a mere transcription of the manifest power of God, observed by all, Egyptian and Israelite alike. It will be a self-conscious account, personal to each father-son dyad, of the unfolding conflicts generated by memory. Telling will be performative, a mode of access to meanings beyond one's means.[16]

The Sadness of the Eyes

In a poignant essay, John Berger writes of the "sadness in Monet's eyes." The painter, whose early work[17] led to the coining of the term "Impressionist," introduced a new melancholy into painting. It is this sadness that Berger describes: from Monet, the history of painting "had henceforward to admit that every appearance could be thought of as a mutation and visibility itself should be considered flux."[18] The insubstantiality of the painting method reflects a scene that is "makeshift, threadbare, decrepit. It is an image of homelessness. Its very insubstantiality makes shelter in it impossible. Looking at it, the idea occurs to you of a man trying to find his road home through a theater decor."[19]

The effect of such a painting, unlike previous paintings which allowed the viewer to *enter into* them ("A painting created its own time and space which were like an alcove to the world . . ."),[20] is that *"you are compelled to recognize that it* [the subject] *is no longer there."*[21] Each viewer remains alone with her memories; "an impression . . . is what is *left behind* because the scene has disappeared or changed."[22] "What you receive is taken from what happens *between* you and it."[23] The concern of the painter is with "the desperate wish to save *all*, which makes it such an amorphous, flat (and yet, if one recognizes it for what it is, touching) image."[24] Such a concern left both painter and viewer "more alone than ever before, more ridden by the anxiety that their own experience was ephemeral and meaningless."[25]

I take the "sadness in Monet's eyes" as an emblem for the melancholy project of narrative. The original experience of the signs and miracles may have been overwhelming. But when the Torah repeatedly urges their transmission to the future, in the form of narrative, triumphant simplicities disappear in the dazzle and blur of memory. The question arises: "Whose narrative?" The fact that in every Jewish household there is enacted on the Passover night the fourfold drama of alternative narratives (the "four sons" questions and the father's answers) makes obvious that this question (Whose narrative?) admits of no final, or total, answer. But we will return to these four narratives, to these outlined formulas of response to the possible challenges of the future.

Multiple Narratives

"You are compelled to recognize that it is no longer there": that is the melancholy of impressionism, according to Berger. And indeed, when the Torah records God as saying, "because I have hardened his heart," the midrash takes this "first person" explanation of the logic of events and opens up a vista of multiple narratives:

> Said R. Yochanan: This provides a pretext for the heretics (lit., an opening of the mouth), to say, "It was impossible for Pharaoh to repent, since it says, 'I have hardened his heart.' " R. Shimeon ben Lakish answered him: Let the mouths of heretics be sealed—"God gives pretexts for mockery to those who are mockers" (Prov 3:34). God warns a person the first time, the second, and the third; if he does not change his ways, God then locks his heart against repentance, in order to make him pay for what he has already done wrong. God sent five warnings to the wicked Pharaoh and he paid no attention; then God told him, "You have hardened your heart—I am now adding impurity to your impurity."[26]

R. Yochanan is perturbed at the way in which such an admission by God ("I have hardened his heart") opens up, offers an "opening of the mouth"—*pitchon peh*—to possible counter-narratives. Heretics will have a field day, since the Torah itself provides them with evidence for skeptical narratives. If it was impossible for Pharaoh to repent—obviously a theologically offensive notion—the plague story becomes a narrative of vengeful abuse, of a morally paralyzed victim bombarded by all the armaments of a powerful but immoral deity.

R. Shimeon ben Lakish responds by closing the narrative-repertoire of the heretics—*yisatem pihem*, let their mouths be sealed. He has a "conclusive" argument that will allay R. Yochanan's concern: God may plausibly be understood to "lock up the heart of the wicked," to make repentance impossible, when a habit of scoffing has become second-nature. After five rounds of obstinate refusal, Pharaoh has no ground for complaint when God "adds impurity to his impurity": in other words, God's role is simply to allow the naturally intensifying effects of insensibility to prevail. R. Shimeon has disposed of a challenging counter-narrative, thus vindicating the moral standing of the authoritative story.

Perhaps we may carry the implications of this dialogue a stage further.

R. Yochanan is concerned at the "opening" that God's own words provide for disturbing counter-narratives. The irony is manifest: God's own narrative cannot seal history against the corrosive effects of other jarring voices. R. Shimeon harmonizes the critical, moral voice: he takes it into account, and thereby enriches the magisterial narrative. Paradoxically, just because of the attack, God's words about hardening Pharaoh's heart undergo a kind of opening, an unfolding of meaning. Now this hostile voice is silenced, it is integrated into the midrashic narrative.

For R. Shimeon, we are left with one narrative, that has swallowed up, metabolized its rivals. But has R. Shimeon totally neutralized R. Yochanan's reading? Is it nevertheless possible that the text of the Torah, even the words attributed to God Himself within the text, may open up opportunities for alternative, subversive readings? On one level, one might answer: "No! The problem raised by God's hardening Pharaoh's heart has been satisfactorily resolved by R. Shimeon—now, both Pharaoh's heart and the mouth of the subversive questioner are closed." This would be to see R. Shimeon's problem as totally harmonized by R. Shimeon's answer.

There is, however, an alternative model for the discussion between them: the model of endless questioning, in which an answer does not totally silence the questioner. Such a model would leave R. Yochanan with multiple possibilities for reinforcing or sharpening his question—precisely *because* an answer, only partially convincing, has been articulated.

In our midrash, the implications of such a model are provocative. The sense that, in spite of R. Shimeon's answer, God's hardening of Pharaoh's heart remains problematic, would open up further discussion, which in turn would undermine future total answers. But we must notice that this model for the relation between questions and answers would reinforce the idea that the text of the Torah does provide *pitchon peh*, narrative opportunities for heretics—that there is no final answer that would censor their alternative narratives. The Torah, even God's quoted words, gives rise to interpretations that radically contradict its own master-narrative, and that cannot, moreover, be totally repudiated by its accredited expositors.

The Work of Questioning

Questioning that spawns further questioning in an endless flow of narratives indeed leaves the door open to heretics. Nonetheless, this notion will be important as we turn shortly to study the rabbinic texts on Exodus that deal with alternative narratives. I would like, first, however, to look at a fascinating midrash-sequence that articulates the issue of *pitchon peh* in all its complexity. The subject of the midrash is God's statement at the end of the Creation story: "Let us make man in our image . . ." (Gen 1:26). The plural form used by God (*us*) leads R. Shmuel bar Nachman to narrate a dialogue between God, the author of the Torah, and Moses who takes dictation from him:

> When Moses was writing the Torah and was describing the creation work of each day, he reached this verse: "God said, Let us make man in our image, after our likeness." He said, Master of the Universe, why do You give heretics an opening of the mouth (*pitchon peh*)? God answered, Write, and whoever wants to read wrongly will read wrongly. God went on: Moses, from this human being that I have created I will raise superior and inferior descendants. If a superior considers consulting with an inferior, he may say, "Why do I need to consult someone less important than I?" Then he can be told, "Learn a lesson from your Creator who created upper and lower worlds, but when He came to create the human being, He consulted the angels." R. Levi said: This is not about consultation. This is analogous to a king who was walking in the palace courtyard and saw a hewn block lying there; he asked, "What shall we do with it?" Some answered, "Baths;" others answered, "Palace mansions;" the king then said, "An image of the king I shall make of it." Who could stop him?[27]

It is noticeable that in R. Shmuel's dialogue, it is Moses himself who takes up the role of disturbed and disturbing questioner: his relationship to God includes this dimension of "His Majesty's Loyal opposition."[28] He is pained by the opportunity that God's text gives to heretics to challenge the belief in monotheism. Perhaps the fact that only in the creation of man does God use the plural form sharpens Moses' question, since clearly the plural is not simply a routine stylistic form, the *pluralis maiestatis*.[29] God's answer is twofold. First, "Write, and whoever wants to read wrongly will read wrongly." There is no way of sealing the text against misinterpretation; even more, the question of will, of desire, is relevant to interpretation. The reader of this text, or of any text, comes with a grid of prejudices and expectations that inform his reading.

God then offers an interpretation of the problematic plural: He is teaching human beings, who are the present subject of creation, the virtue of humility, of consulting with one's inferiors. This interpretation might plausibly silence Moses' objection to the text. But the midrash does not end there, but goes on to quote R. Levi's criticism of the humility notion. In other words, Moses' question retains its disturbing force, which is recognized in God's first answer: "Whoever wants to read wrongly will read wrongly."

The midrash takes up the question again:

> Said R. Simlai, Wherever you find *pitchon peh*, an opening of the mouth for heretics, you also find an answer right beside it. So they asked him again [this is the second dialogue between R. Simlai and the heretics]: What is the meaning of "Let us make man in our image, after our likeness"? He replied, What is written after that? It is not written, "And God created (plural) man in *their* image," but "And God created (singular) man after *His* image." When the heretics had left, his students took up the issue: Rabbi, you fobbed them off easily. But how do you answer us? He answered them: In the past, Adam was created from the earth, while Eve was created from Adam. From now on, children will be born "in our image, after our likeness"—not from man without woman, not from woman without man, and from neither without the divine Presence.
>
> They asked him again: What is the meaning of "God, the Powerful One (*El*, *Elohim*—two names for God) is Hashem"? [The verse seems to allow the heresy of two gods] He answered them: The verse does not continue, "*They* know . . ." but "*He* knows . . ." His students then said to him: You fobbed them off easily. But how do you answer us? He answered, All three expressions are names for God (El, Elohim, Hashem)—as people speak of Silogus Caesar, or Augustus Caesar (whose different types of power become generic titles for later rulers).
>
> The heretics asked him again: What is the meaning of "He is a holy God (adjective and noun are written in the plural)"? He answered: But it does not say "*They* are . . ." but "*He* is . . ."[30]

Here the real tension informing the issue is vividly staged. "*Wherever—in every place*—you find heretical openings, you find the answer right there," is a description of desirable order: every problem of *pitchon peh*, of a text that lays itself open to subversive readings, is resolvable, indeed resolved, by the answers given by the Sages, also drawing from the divine text. An example follows: The problem of "Let *us* make man . . ." is countered by the following verse, which speaks clearly of God's act in creating man in *His* image.

This leaves no doubt that God is singular. But this answer satisfies only the heretics, who leave at this point, presumably silenced. The ironic point of the midrash is that it is R. Simlai's own students who persist in the question, sardonically dismissing the facile solution just offered: "How do you answer *us*?" A proper answer must engage not only with the question but with the *questioner*. And they receive another answer, alluding to the complex forces behind human creation—man, woman, and God's Presence.

This pattern is repeated twice more: a grammatical answer is given that reinforces the orthodox understanding of God's unity; the students hold out for a better answer, and are answered on a different level.[31]

The midrash can be read in at least two ways. One way would be to assume that the students are simply better readers than the heretics, less likely to be fobbed off by a partial answer. (For instance, they notice that God's creating man in *His* image does not really deal with the question: why, nevertheless, is the plural form used in the previous sentence?) As better readers, they are clearly applauded by the midrash. Such relentless questioning is a way of getting an answer that will cover all aspects of the question.

Another way of reading the midrash, however, makes the Torah text more ambiguous, readable on different levels. The students' persistence is provoked not by some obvious problem of accuracy or consistency in R. Simlai's first answer, but by the limited thrust of that kind of answer. They demand—and are given—an answer that does not ignore the disturbing philosophical and theological implications of the plural form. The students do not regard a grammatical, technical answer as satisfactory—especially as it fails to cover all references to God as plural.

In this second reading, the technical answer only serves to point up its own inadequacy. Now we have a text in which some verbs are singular, others plural. The students ask for a way of harmonizing voices into a new perspective that recognizes plurality as indeed a facet of the human experience of God's creation.

In both these readings, the original assertion of R. Shmuel is validated: there is an answer, repudiating the subversive questions of the heretics. But the more seriously the question is taken—more seriously, ironically, than the heretics themselves realize—the better the answer will be. Those who are trained by the Sages—initiates in the work of questioning—will generate answers that before were never framed.

Here, we are on the verge of a third, more disturbing reading. Perhaps the answer that will close the mouth of the heretic does not exist? Perhaps each successive question will deepen the sense of disorder and bring into being new, but provisional answers? What we read in the midrash, therefore, has no closure: the students are not totally answered. The drama staged here is an exemplary drama, modular, to be replicated and continued.[32]

In terms of the teacher-student relation, the question-answer model mirrors the tension in the subject under discussion: God as singular or as plural. One response is technical, pointing to textual evidence for His singularity. A second response is to acknowledge and interpret plural forms in theologically harmonious ways. A third response would mirror the undecidability of the question; it would regard all harmonizations as provisional and humanly constructed, and would retain a sense of the "hard kernel" of the unanswerable in the text: the residue of all answers.

This "hardness" (*kasheh*) is the core-idea of the *kushiya*: the question, in Rabbinic Hebrew. Hardness is fraught with mystery and pain.[33] It resists language; it is, to use Slavoj Zizek's expression, the "rock of the Real," which "resists symbolization," which "persists as a surplus and returns through all attempts to domesticate it, to gentrify it."[34] A true *kushiya* has something of the Sublime, in Kant's sense: it disturbs order, it is limitless, terrifying—and yet evokes its own kind of pleasure, even of enthusiasm.[35] The kind of question that we are describing touches on issues that defy "gentrification," that relate to desire, and thus retain their protean force in the face of all answers. The plurality of God is one such question; the hardening of Pharaoh's heart is another.

"To question," says Jabes, "is to break with something; it is to establish an *inside* and an *outside*." "Outside, that is to say, outside of order," adds Marc-Alain Ouaknine. And quotes Heidegger: "We go beyond that which is the order of the day. We question over and beyond the ordinary and the 'in-order' that is well ordered in everyday life"; and Nietzsche: "[the philosopher is the] man who never ceases living, seeing, conjecturing, hoping, dreaming of extra-ordinary things . . ."[36]

Turning back now to the Exodus narrative, we can say that God's hardening of Pharaoh's heart may indeed open the mouths of questioners, in the process creating counterworlds, counter-narratives that are never finally harmonized with the master-narrative. We notice, too, that the question of the hardening of Pharaoh's heart relates to the possibility of what is classically called *teshuva*—repentance. The word basically means "response, answer." The "response" of Pharaoh, his answer to the questions, disturbing both to him and to the Israelites, is the central issue of the story. What are his responses to the narrative disorder, the questions, the *kushiyoth*, that God introduces into his world? God comes "with a strong hand," with harsh plagues, that tear the structures of natural order apart. Can Pharaoh's responses, often jarring and hostile to the obvious meanings of the text, be harmonized with those meanings? Or is his physical defeat, overcome by God's power, simply a way of defeating his narratives by brute force?

Suppressing the Counter-Narrative

The existence of counter-narratives, which explain the facts in subversive ways, is constantly referred to in the midrashic commentaries. For instance, when God destroys the firstborn, "from the first-born of Pharaoh . . . to the first-born of the captive in the dungeon" (12:29), Rashi offers two explanations for including "captives" in the general doom:

> Because they rejoiced at Israel's downfall. And also, so that they should not say, Our god brought about this retribution.

The expression, "so that they should not say," is central here; apparently, the captives are killed, in order to suppress a counter-narrative, the story of the avenging god of the captives. Rashi seems to present this as an alternative answer to his first comment: "They rejoiced at Israel's downfall." But we notice that he uses the word "also" (*ve'od*), instead of his customary, "Another explanation" (*davar acher*); the second reason for killing the captives *supplements* the first. And indeed, Rashi's source, Mechilta (Bo 13), presents the two in one seamless narrative:

> How did the captives sin? They were killed to prevent the captives from saying, "Our god brought retribution upon Pharaoh. Their god is powerful (*kasheh*), for he defended them; but our god is powerful too, for the retribution never affected us." This is to teach you that all the decrees that Pharaoh made against Israel were a cause of joy to the captives . . .

From the captives' counter-narrative, one can deduce their enthusiastic assent to all Pharaoh's harsh decrees against Israel. The captives have their own liberation-history, and the Israelites have no place in it. Holding both explanations in focus,[37] one might say that a hostile counter-narrative is suppressed for the obvious purpose of protecting the authoritative Israelite narrative of the Exodus, and that this suppression is justified by the exclusive nature of liberation-narratives.

We return to the expression, "so that they should not say . . ." It is clear that this counter-narrative is to be censored, in anticipation. At the same time, it is obvious that by drawing attention to this censorship, the midrash actually publicizes the counter-narrative. As always when the expression is used, the gesture to censor is a tribute to the force of the subversive narrative. Moreover, this repressed narrative is not only not suppressed, it is not merely the narrative of the Other, but it is actually a way of telling the story that is plausible to all minds. Even the liberation story of the captives raises a question about the many possibilities of interpretation. If this question were easy to answer, there would, of course, be no need to suppress the captives, and, with them, their disturbing narrative.

The Precariousness of Truth

A more subtle example of the problem of the counter-narrative appears in the Rabbinic reading of Moses' final court appearance, to announce the last plague. On the face of it the narrative is disjointed: Pharaoh is infuriated by Moses' refusal to accept his terms (to leave the cattle behind in Egypt), and threatens him with death if he ever again appears in the palace. Moses answers, "You have spoken rightly. I shall not see your face again!" (10:29). What follows is problematic: "And God said to Moses, 'I will bring but one more plague upon Pharaoh and upon Egypt; after that he shall let you go from here . . .' " (11:1).

The simplest reading would be to translate in the pluperfect: "God *had* said . . ." But this would not entirely remove the question about Moses' next speech to Pharaoh, where he foretells the death of the firstborn. Is this, too, in the pluperfect, preceding Moses' demonstrative exit from the court? The end of the passage (11:8), however, narrates Moses' exit again, "in hot anger," and finely juxtaposes it with his challenge to Pharaoh: " 'Then all these courtiers of yours shall come down to me and bow low to me, saying, Leave, you and all the people who follow you! After that, I will leave.' And he left Pharaoh's presence in hot anger."

The play on the word *tzei* ("leave") has Moses stage for Pharaoh, in dramatic miniature—by his own exit from the court—the ultimate exodus of his people—also, ironically, at the behest of Pharaoh. The whole confrontation becomes primarily a personal one (" 'Leave—*you* [*tzei atta*] . . . After that, *I* will leave [*eitzei*].' And he left [*va-yeitzei*]"), sharpening the drama of the face-to-face encounter, and the shifting meanings of seeing (or not-seeing) the face of the other.

However, the sequence of events remains problematic. Is the ending of chapter 10 simply amplified by the longer account of Moses' exit in chapter 11? Or is this a separate message from God to Moses, which requires him to return to court, despite his defiant ultimatum?

This is Rashi's reading (11:4):

> While he still stood in Pharaoh's presence, God's announcement of the last plague came to him. For after leaving the court, he never saw Pharaoh's face again.

Rashi's source in Shemoth Rabba tells the story more fully:

> "He confirms the word of His servant, and the counsel of kings He shall fulfil." (Isa 44:26) Said R. Abbahu: "He confirms the word of His servant:" this refers to Moses, as it is said, "Not so is My servant, Moses" (Num 12:7). How did He confirm his word? When He brought upon them the plague of darkness, Pharaoh began screaming, "Go! Serve God—just leave your sheep and cattle." Moses answered, "As you live, our cattle too will go with us—not one hoof shall remain! . . ." Pharaoh said to him: "How long will you keep coming here? Go from my presence! Beware, never enter my presence again!" And Moses answered, "You have spoken rightly. I shall not see your face again!" Then God said, "What! I still have to inform Pharaoh of one more plague!" Immediately, He leapt into Moses' presence, as it were; He entered the palace for Moses' sake, because he had said, "I shall not see your face again!" and *God did not want him to look like a deceiver.* You find that God had never before spoken with Moses in Pharaoh's house . . . But now God leapt and spoke with Moses, as it is said, "One more plague I shall bring upon Pharaoh." When Moses heard this, he rejoiced, and his status grew, as it is said, "Also the man Moses was much esteemed in the land of Egypt . . ." (11:3). He began to cry out in public, "So says God, At around midnight . . . You said rightly, You shall not see my face again! I shall never come to you again, but you shall come to me . . ."[38]

God leaps into Pharaoh's court (an unprecedented act, as the midrash makes clear: the spiritual ecology of the court is incompatible with His presence). His purpose is that Moses' declaration, "I shall never see your face again!" shall not be belied by events, since he still has to announce the last plague. Before he can leave the court in high dudgeon, therefore, God "leaps"—breaks through the normal processes, precipitates an early announcement of the last plague; and all this in order to save Moses' face, "that he should not look like a deceiver." This would seem to be the important point, that the Egyptians should have no grounds for thinking Moses a deceiver, using words irresponsibly. In order to prevent this happening, God disturbs the natural order, enters the improper space at the improper time, and so "confirms the word of His servant." Moreover, God's message leads Moses to an even more triumphant elaboration of his challenge to Pharaoh: "I shall never come to you again, but you shall come to me!": the midrash has Moses integrate his earlier challenge with his new message.

A similar motif occurs in the same verse, in the anomalous expression, "At *around* midnight . . ." Rashi comments:

> Moses said, "Ka-*chatzoth*—At *around* midnight," which means "approximately, either before or after midnight:" He did not say, "Ba-*chatzoth*—Exactly at midnight"—so that Pharaoh's astrologers *should not make a mistake and say, "Moses is a deceiver!"*

Moses chooses an awkward expression, *ka-chatzoth*, "approximately," in order, again, not to be seen as a deceiver. Although he knows exactly when midnight is, his language is based on the possibility of error. Moses here exemplifies the principle articulated in the source-midrash: "Teach your tongue to say, 'I don't know,' lest you be exposed as a liar."[39]

The essential point about this reading is the precariousness of truth. The slightest of time-gaps—an error of milliseconds in the Egyptian calculation of mean time—will give them grounds to belie Moses' whole story. Although Moses, and certainly God, knows the precise moment of midnight, human language must engage with the approximations and not with the absolute. This is particularly true in speaking about time, where subjectivity is unavoidable. (In the narrative of the night of the plague of the firstborn, the word, *ba-chatzi*—"at exactly midnight" [12:29]—is used, to describe the absolute, divine measurement that is beyond human perception.)

The point is paradoxical, because elsewhere, as Sternberg indicates, the thrust of the narrative has been to demonstrate the exact and publicly witnessed fulfillment of God's foreshadowing, in time and place, and against all odds of improbability. Here, a contrary movement is held in focus: there is no way of absolutely preventing or repudiating the subversive narratives of Egypt. Moses avoids an arrogant exactness of prediction; he adopts a modest skepticism, which in the Talmud becomes exemplary: "Teach your tongue to say, 'I don't know.' " This motif, of the low cognitive profile, counterpointing the precisely articulated foreshadowings at other moments in the drama, does read strangely, in the context of the most manifest redemption in Jewish history. The human modesty recommended here takes account of the narratives and probable mis-narratives of others.

Even God Himself on occasion explains Himself in human language, in an attempt to deal with possible mis-narratives:

> "I could have stretched forth My hand and stricken you and your people with pestilence; and you would have been effaced from the earth. Nevertheless, I have spared you for this purpose: in order to show you My power, and in order that My fame may resound throughout the world." (9:15–16)

God explains to Pharaoh why He has not brought the drama to closure. The need for an explanation is implicit: why is the narrative so protracted, why are the plague-patterns repeated so frequently? Are these a sign of divine ineffectiveness? Is He not *capable* of bringing a resounding defeat upon Pharaoh and his people? God's answer to this unarticulated question is to tell an alternative story, of an easy, plausible destruction of Pharaoh, in the process of the pestilence that struck down the Egyptian livestock. The ease of such a dénouement—it does not require extraordinary divine resources—strengthens the point about God's will: He keeps Pharaoh on his feet for a double purpose—so that he is in a position to witness God's power, and to create a narrative about Him. God wants Pharaoh to come to a personal recognition of His power; it is his narrative that God desires, his awareness that his own starting point—"I do not know God!" (5:2)—has been repudiated.[40] Such a narrative will surely be worth having. The narrative of conversion, then, is God's desire. It justifies the risk involved in the ambiguous, repetitive, and protracted narrative of the plagues—the risk, that is, of generating an adversary narrative, telling of weakness and inability to accomplish His will.

This theme, of God's desire for Pharaoh's conversion-narrative, informs Rashi's reading at the climax of the Exodus:

> "God struck down all the first-born of Egypt, from the first-born of Pharaoh" (12:29): Pharaoh, too, was a first-born and alone survived of all the first-born. Of him, it is said, "I have spared you for this purpose: in order to show you My power . . ." (9:16)—at the Red Sea.

Pharaoh's survival, alone among the firstborn, is, again, ambiguous: it provides a basis for adversary narratives, but is justified by the prize of the narrative he may yet come to tell. Pharaoh's immunity to destruction can, of course, be understood in many ways. Another midrash tells a subtly different story:

> In order to seduce the Egyptian hearts, so that they should say, "Pharaoh is invincible (*kasheh*), for no punishment could touch him". . .[41]

Here, the anomaly of Pharaoh's survival is intended to destroy the Egyptians by confirming their own narrative illusions to the very end: Pharaoh is simply too strong, he is immune to the power of God. This is, of course, a different way of interpreting events; for Rashi, and his source in Mechilta, the idea is to have Pharaoh survive as witness to God's power.

The climactic demonstration of this power is the Splitting of the Red Sea, which Rashi has defined as the objective of Pharaoh's survival. This, in an obvious way, closes off all possible adversary narratives; it determines, one might say, the meaning of the whole story. Even here, however, there is a tradition that claims that there was one survivor of the total devastation: Pharaoh himself.[42] As with the midrashic observation about Pharaoh being a firstborn, this, of course, erodes the "omnipotence effect," as well as reading against the grain of the text. What is gained is a sense of the importance of testimony—and precisely the testimony of the enemy, the generator of powerful counter-narratives.

The Narrative of the Night

In an eloquent essay, Shoshana Felman meditates on narrative as testimony, drawing attention to literary and psychoanalytical sources that emphasize its involuntary, undetermined dimension:

> As a relation to events, testimony seems to be composed of bits and pieces of a memory that has been overwhelmed by occurrences that have not settled into understanding or remembrance, acts that cannot be constructed as knowledge nor assimilated into full cognition, events in excess of our frames of reference.
>
> What the testimony does not offer is, however, a completed statement, a totalizable account of those events. In the testimony, language is in process and in trial, it does not possess itself as a conclusion, as the constatation of a verdict or the self-transparency of knowledge. Testimony is, in other words, a discursive *practice*, as opposed to a pure theory.[43]

Since the notion of testimony is associated with the legal context, Felman points to the legal situation as one where the facts are not clear and where essential elements of the truth are called into question: testimony comes in a context of a *crisis of truth.* Similarly, texts that testify do not simply report facts but "encounter . . . strangeness"; testimony is not a "simple medium of historical transmission," but, in the case, for instance, of Camus' *The Plague*, "the unsuspected medium of a healing."[44]

In discussing Freud's groundbreaking account of the Irma dream, Felman notes that here Freud discovered, in his own experience, the existence of *unconscious testimony;* psychoanalysis recognizes

> for the first time in the history of culture, that one does not have to *possess* or *own* the truth, in order to effectively *bear witness* to it; that speech as such is unwittingly testimonial; and that the speaking subject constantly bears witness to a truth that nonetheless continues to escape him, a truth that is, essentially, *not available* to its own speaker.[45]

On this level of testimony, which Felman terms "the underground of language," Freud encounters Dostoyevsky, whose *Notes from the Underground* bore compelled witness to a trauma that endowed him with a transcendental vision of reality. Now, testimony becomes a mode of

> truth's realization beyond what is available as statement, beyond what is available, that is, as a truth transparent to itself and entirely known, given, in advance, prior to the very process of its utterance. The testimony will thereby be understood, in other words, not as a mode of *statement of*, but rather as a mode of *access to*, that truth.[46]

The witness is now the one who *begets* the truth, through the speech process of the testimony; in Freud's case, he "gives birth to the entire theory of dreams, and to its undreamt of implications."[47] Begetting, giving birth through the testimonial process reveals the gravity of an idiosyncratic, apparently trivial experience, such as dreaming. Unwittingly, through language, the triviality emerges into historical significance.

The sense of the private, the accidental, the unpredictable equally informs the revolutionary poetic testimony of Mallarmé, as he announces the introduction of free verse, with its loosening of the traditional poetic rules, and, in his own words, "discharges himself of the testimony of an accident."[48] Poetry then becomes the *"art of accident";* it "reaches out for what precisely *cannot be anticipated.*"[49] Its newly unsettled rhythms testify also to political and cultural changes.

Mallarmé confesses that "he speaks too soon, before he is quite ready, before he quite knows what his subject is about":

> Such precocious testimony in effect becomes, with Mallarmé, the very principle of poetic insight and the very core of the event of poetry, which makes precisely language—through its breathless gasps—speak ahead of knowledge and awareness and break through the limits of its own conscious understanding. By its very innovative definition, poetry will henceforth speak *beyond its means* . . .[50]

The "accident" will offer the witness unpredictable and untrivial liberations; he will be willing to "become himself a medium of the testimony—and a medium of the accident," to "*pursue the accident* . . . through darkness and through fragmentation, without quite grasping the full scope and meaning of its implications, without entirely foreseeing where the journey leads and what is the precise nature of its final destination."[51]

Felman's rethinking of the notion of testimony answers quite aptly to my sense of the place of narrative in Exodus. When, for instance, God tells Moses that He is complicating and extending the plague narrative, "so that you may tell the story in the hearing of your sons and your sons' sons . . ." (10:2), the imperative of narrative is to find a way, in a "crisis of truth," to beget, to give birth to knowledge. The mode of access is language, which is always "in trial"; not a simple medium of historical transmission but a testimony to unconscious, unpredictable, and potentially liberating meanings. The pursuit of knowledge through the darkness offers an intimate experience of freedom; whether through psychoanalytic free association, in Freud's testimony, or through free verse, in Mallarmé's account, something new is born in the unsettling play of language.

The political liberation of the Exodus is thus realized most intimately in the narratives that will convey the idiosyncratic "otherness" of the subject, its strangeness, its "underground" dimensions. These narratives of the night are to be told between father and son; perhaps, as Felman puts it, "*it takes two to witness the unconscious.*"[52] In this generative, performative narrative, the father does not possess the truth, he is not an eyewitness to historical events, but yet his speech is unwittingly testimonial to a truth that is not entirely available to its own speaker.

These unwitting testimonies will vary, of course, with the teller and with the listener. There is no limit to the versions that may be generated by the historical record. Not all versions are equally good; but, significantly, none can be totally neutralized. In this realm of the narrative of the night, the magisterial narrative story of redemption is destabilized by multiple alternative stories. This is the theme of our exploration: the value with which the midrashic traditions endow this "mirror-world," that begets knowledge unwittingly.

2. *Counter-Narratives of Exodus*

Repudiating the Repudiators

Now, I would like to return to the biblical and midrashic accounts of the balance of narratives. We have noticed that the magisterial narrative of the Torah is haunted by untold stories—briefer, more resounding tales of God's summary power, Egyptian tales of Pharaoh's power, the captives' tales of the power of their gods, rigorously empirical tales that detect anomalies in the master-narrative. It is because there are so many counter-narratives that, according to Ramban, there are so many plagues:

> When idolatry first appeared in the world, in the days of Enosh, opinions became confused. Some denied the existence of God, saying the world pre-dated everything . . . Some denied His knowledge of details of this world, saying, "How could He know? Is there knowledge with the Most High?" (Ps 73:11) Some acknowledge His knowledge but deny His providence, saying, "He has made mankind like the fish of the sea," (Habbakuk 1:14) for which He has no care, and no punishment or reward—"They say, 'God does not see us; God has abandoned the country.' " (Ezek 8:12) But when God singles out a group or an individual and does a marvel for them, changing the normal course of nature, then the repudiation of all these opinions becomes clear to all. For it shows that there is a God in the world, who constantly renews the world, and knows and responds and is omnipotent. And if this marvel is announced beforehand by a prophet, the truth of prophecy, too, becomes evident . . . All these essential beliefs were denied, or doubted, by the Egyptians, so that the great signs and wonders testified powerfully to the belief in the Creator and in the whole Torah.[53]

Here, essentially, is the basis of Sternberg's account. By miracles and wonders, God repudiates all the many misbeliefs in the world. Especially if they are foretold, these miracles demonstrate the truth of the central articles of faith. The purpose of the plagues is thus to repudiate the repudiators.

This sense of the negative, of the need for a miraculous story to counteract the unbelieving accounts of the world, takes Ramban far beyond the limits of the narrative. He continues to discuss the largest theological questions about beginnings and meanings and moral responsibility. To preserve the Israelites' sense of the prodigious redemption from Egypt, God gave them "signs": no longer referring to the wonders, but to acts to be performed by them, in symbolic testimony to the epic narrative—the paschal offering, the phylacteries (the *tefillin*), the miniature case of texts on the doorpost (the *mezuza*)—all to deny any opportunity to the deniers of His narrative.

In Ramban's view, this is the heart of the narrative—not a physical redemption, but an eternal realization of the truth of God's relation to the world. This realization is achieved by repudiating the repudiators. According to Rashi, Pharaoh's moment of defeat arrives when he relinquishes his own narrative and acknowledges the truth of Moses' narrative:

> He cried out to Moses and Aaron in the night and said, "Get up, get out from among my people. . . Go, worship God as you have spoken! Take also your flocks and your herds, as you have spoken . . ." (12:30–31)

> Rashi: *"As you have spoken:"* All shall be *as you said, and not as I said.* Refuted is "I shall not send . . ." Refuted is "Who exactly are those who are leaving?" Refuted is "Just leave your flocks and herds here"—take both your flocks and your herds!

> And what is the second, "As you have spoken"? Your prediction, "You too shall place sacrifices and burnt offerings in our hands!" (10:25)

The repeated expression, "as you have spoken," is read as referring specifically to the debates between Moses and Pharaoh. The first expression indicates a point-by-point withdrawal from Pharaoh's claims to control the future. All his scenarios of control, his reservations, his last-ditch rigidities, all are *batel*, have become as nothing. What remains after all his negations are swept away is the pure and total Moses narrative: "Release My people, that they may worship Me" (7:26)—"Go, worship God as you have spoken!" Even his final quibble about the animals is repudiated: he accepts the theological insult of contributing his own animals to the Israelites, to be absorbed into their sacred narrative—"as you have spoken."

In this contest of narratives, Moses' words have vanquished Pharaoh's. Pharaoh's defeat is signaled in a quasi-legalistic midrash on the same verse: "Get up! Get out from among my people. . .":

> He said: In the past, you were servants of Pharaoh; from now on, you are servants of God! At that time, they said, Praise God! Praise Him, you servants of God!—servants of God and not servants of Pharaoh![54]

This is the moment when the slave-owner hands over control to another slave-owner. Freedom, it seems, is not the issue here. But in the rhetoric of the midrash, this transfer is cause for celebration: "*Hallelujah!*—Praise God!" What is conspicuous, again, is the *negative* force of this acknowledgment. To become a servant of God is read as equivalent to being released from another servitude by Pharaoh himself. It is his words, articulating the end of his claim on them, that creates the new reality of God's claim. This is not only a description of legal identity, but the staging of a new narrative. New expectations come into play. This new narrative, with its new tensions and desires, is what Moses, in the name of God, has been demanding all along: "Release My people, that they may serve Me." In yielding mastery, Pharaoh loses not merely a workforce, but a significant narrative of meaning, a conviction that his words most truly describe the world.

Moses' predictions have all been fulfilled; even Pharaoh's "hardening of the heart"—the most autonomous expression of his spiritual life—is ultimately absorbed into God's narrative. And yet, I would suggest, there are indications in the Torah and in the midrashic traditions that his narrative is not as harmonious as it appears. The jarring voices—the alternative narratives—are not entirely silenced.

Even at the moment of defeat, the midrash detects a flicker of doubt: the Egyptians press the Israelites to leave without delay, saying, "We are all dying!" What might naturally have been read as terrified surrender is instead understood, in Mechilta, as an anomaly in the fulfillment of Moses'predictions:

> "They said, 'We are *all* dying!' " This is not exactly what Moses had predicted, when he said, "*All the first-born* in the land of Egypt shall die." So they thought that in a family of four or five children, only the first-born would die. But they did not know that their wives were guilty of adultery, so all their children were first-born of different fathers . . .[55]

Here, a gap persists between Moses' words and the reality of the night: many die in each household, not only the firstborn predicted by Moses. "We are *all* dying!" becomes a protest by the Egyptians at the *meaninglessness* of events: the master-narrative has apparently collapsed. In Mechilta, there is a suggestion that the Egyptians come to realize the hidden story of multiple firstborn that will harmonize anomalies. Once again, apparently, God's narrative is shown to be triumphant, overriding all adversary voices. It is interesting, however, to notice that Rashi, in quoting this midrash, gives a cryptic brief version, without any resolution: "They said, This is not in accord with Moses' prediction: for he said, 'All the first-born shall die,' while here even the later children are dying, five or ten to a household!"

Rashi's comment leaves the reader with a sense of dissonance, even though the reader is presumed to know the true explanation. By focusing on this dissonance, it deliberately undermines the strength of the narrative of omnipotence. One might wonder what Rashi's purpose is in doing this. And one might suggest that the adversarial narratives are not meant to be quite so totally annihilated. Perhaps Rashi wants the sense of dissonance, of ambiguity, to linger through all the signs and wonders: the question of "Whose narrative?"

Whose Narrative?

Here, we come to the very core, it seems, of the meaning of the Exodus. At the core, there is a tension between the demonstration of God's omnipotence, on the one hand, and, on the other, the resounding voice of Pharaoh, that is never entirely silenced. Its echoes are to be heard throughout the history of Israel, certainly during the wilderness time that is the subject of the remaining books of the Torah. This voice, at its most sinister, articulates a possible, demonic narrative. Here, the question of power, the contest between God and Pharaoh, is no longer the issue. The issue, rather, is one of good and evil:

> He said to them: God be with you, the same as I mean to let your children go with you! See, *evil is facing you!* (10:10)

> Rashi: . . . I have heard a midrashic aggada, that there is a star whose name is Evil. And Pharaoh said to them, I see in my astrological charts that star rising to greet you in the wilderness; and it is a sign of blood and slaughter. And when Israel sinned with the Golden Calf and God

intended to kill them, Moses said in his prayer (32:12): Why should the Egyptians say, "In Evil (*bera*), He brought them out of Egypt." Moses was referring to Pharaoh's prediction, See, Evil (*ra'ah*) is facing you. Immediately, "God repented of the Evil (*ha-ra'ah*)" (32:14) and He turned the blood into the blood of circumcision, when Joshua circumcised the whole people—as it is said, "Today, I have removed the disgrace of Egypt from you" (Josh 5:9)—that is, their prediction, "We see blood upon you in the wilderness!"

What provokes Pharaoh's outburst is Moses' insistence on taking the young children into the desert. Pharaoh responds by speaking of the Israelites' bad faith: they clearly intend to flee, and the evil he refers to is, on a first reading, their covert intentions, which are written all over their faces. This is Rashi's first *peshat* reading, following the Targum.

But Rashi then quotes a midrash that presents Pharaoh's credo, his narrative about Israel and its God. This alternative reading moves the site of the evil from the Israelite plot to flee to the largest arena of historical interpretation. Here, evil and bloodshed loom over Israel's future, so that, in running to the wilderness, they run like lemmings to their doom. And their God is a god of evil, who plans for them, not a divine comedy, but a divine tragedy. It is the Egyptian narrative that Moses refers to, when he pleads with God after the sin of the Golden Calf: Why should You validate their narrative? This argument is the one that convinces God: "God repented of the Evil . . ." God is, as it were, repelled by the distorting mirror of the Egyptian narrative. And the blood foreseen by the astrologers is reframed as the blood of circumcision that precedes the entry of the Israelites into the Holy Land.

The Egyptian narrative has haunted the Israelite consciousness at least until this point: the "disgrace of Egypt" is the disenchanted view of Israelite history that reconstructs all events in a sinister mode. This view is the astrologers' answer to the question: "What do you see as the end of this people?"[56] The question about ending is a serious question: it is essentially about meaning.[57] In quoting the astrologers' reply, Pharaoh is not lying; what they have seen reflects a certain factual truth, as becomes clear when it is "sublimated" into the circumcision-blood. But the Egyptian interpretation transmutes the story of the Exodus and all that follows it into a farcical bloodbath. This is not the Moses story of love, redemption, and promise. It is, rather, a story of hatred, of sinister intent by a god whose relation to the Israelites is one of malice and anger.

That such an understanding of their destiny is plausible is obvious from the bloodlettings of the wilderness. Sufficient blood is shed in massacres and plagues amply to justify the astrologers' vision. And yet, Rashi and his source midrashim write as if only the threat of total annihilation, after the Golden Calf, would justify that demonic vision; and only the blood of circumcision can interpret and exorcise it. But the possible narrative of a hating God indeed remains viable until that general enactment of sacrifice of a most intimate kind; only then, is the terror of the Egyptian narrative transformed into convenantal act. And Moses' own experience of the terrors of the unnerving encounter with the God of bloodshed, in 4:24–26—an encounter that is likewise resolved in an act of circumcision—uniquely qualifies him to narrate the perplexities of the narrative of hatred.[58]

This mass-circumcision in Joshua's time is, of course, a recircumcision. As the narrative in Joshua 5:2–9 tells it, the Israelites who left Egypt were all circumcised, and all died in the desert. Those who were born in the desert survived and were not circumcised. So that not one circumcised Israelite remained when Joshua came to power. The blood of a universal act of recommitment to the Covenant exorcises the baneful vision of the astrologers.

The Narrative of Hatred

That this vision of evil and hatred has penetrated the Israelite consciousness[59] appears most clearly in Moses' retelling of the desert-story before his death, at the end of the forty-year wandering. In a most powerful critique, Moses diagnoses the sin of the people that caused a whole generation to die in the wilderness—the sin of the Spies: "You sulked in your tents and said, 'It is because God hates us that He brought us out of the land of Egypt, to hand us over to the Amorites to wipe us out' " (Deut 1:27).

"God hates us": this is the narrative of hatred in condensed form. The people have never been entirely convinced that God loves them and that His powerful acts, His strong hand and outstretched arm, mean to deliver them to goodness. From the beginning, we notice, it is goodness that God emphasizes to Moses: "I have come down to rescue them . . . and to bring them . . . to a *good* and spacious land . . ." (3:8). But, also from the beginning, there has been an awareness of other ways of telling the story: "Why have You done *evil* to this people?" (5:22); "It is *good* for us to return to Egypt" (Num 14:3); "It is a land that consumes its inhabitants" (Num 13:32). Even Moses' agenda for the Spies includes the essential question: "Is it *good* or *evil*?" (Num 13:19).

This doubt, that haunts the people throughout the redemption and wilderness epochs, is a doubt about being loved. It is significant, therefore, that in Moses' prayer of intercession for his people, he quotes a version of God's attributes that emphasizes love and forgiveness (Num 14:18).[60] Seforno[61] suggests that the people's idolatry in Egypt arouses God's vengeance: this is the guilty narrative that makes the people question God's love at every juncture. Effectively, the people have internalized the Egyptian narrative of blood and revenge, which comes to dominate the evidences of a loving, nurturing God.

The two possible narratives suggest a kind of Zoroastrianism, in which two gods, one of good and the other of evil, are in eternal conflict. Ralbag comments in this vein: perhaps Pharaoh has heard of such a theology and, because of the "signs that God has placed in his midst" (Exod 10:1, 2), identifies Him with the god of evil and darkness. The plausible aspect of this reading lies precisely in Pharaoh's experience of the Israelite God as powerful and tormenting. The live issue, then, is no longer about *power*—God has amply demonstrated His power; it is about goodness and evil, about the difficulty of recognizing one God, of integrating the light and the darkness into a single narrative.

A shift into the psychological mode is Rashi's contribution to the understanding of this issue:

> "Because God hates us" (1:27): He really loved you; but *you hate Him*! As in the popular adage: One expresses what is in one's heart about one's friend as what is in his heart about oneself.
>
> "Because God hates us, he brought us out of the land of Egypt . . .": He brought us out as an expression of hatred! This is like a king who had two sons and two fields, one with its own source of irrigation, and one dependent on rainfall. To the son he loved he gave the irrigated field, and to the one he hated he gave the field that depends on rainfall. Egypt is irrigated land, since the Nile rises and irrigates it; while Canaan depends on rainfall. He took us out of Egypt to give us the land of Canaan.

Here, Rashi defines the spiritual drama of redemption. In his trenchant diagnosis, the problem of hatred is radically a problem of projection; behind the words, "because God hates us," lies the unspeakable question of human hatred. It is an undertow of hatred—not fear, or lust, or fickleness—that has brought the people again and again to think that it is "good that we return to

Egypt." It is this that has issued in the demonic inversion of Moses' narrative: Egypt becomes the "land flowing with milk and honey" (Num 16:13); and that is expressed in language that the Torah calls *dibah ra'ah*—language that scans for evil. Rashi describes the dynamic of projection: the people hate God, and say that He hates them. And then produces a plausible scenario to illustrate their thinking: the beloved son is surely the one who is given the irrigated field—therefore, since Egypt is a good, fruitful land, to be led out of Egypt constitutes a monstrous plot, in which, at best, God designates a parched and fatal country for His unloved son.

The power of Rashi's comment lies in the plausibility of the people's narrative of hatred. Apparently, he means through this story of the fields to expose the projection in the people's thinking: it is their own hatred that blinds them to the true narrative of love. The story of the fields, however, is all too convincing. It avoids melodramatic scenarios of divine vengeance wiping them out in the desert, it simply looks at the two nations, the two countries, and comes to an apparently lucid conclusion about love and hate. And yet, even in this "transparent" situation, Rashi draws attention to the mind of the thinker, who places himself outside the thought, as though the logic of the comparison were quite disembodied, had nothing to do with the perspective of the observer. It is a commonplace to say that even the paranoid has some facts to go on (people really do dislike him!); it is his evaluation of the subjective and objective elements that needs scrutiny.

Rashi's point is essentially about desire, about the effects of desire on assessments of an emotional situation. Those who love God perceive His love, His goodness, His desire. This issue is at least as important as the issue of power in the development of the people's relationship to God. The analogy with the maturing of a human being is perhaps appropriate: in the early stages, dependency and awe at the strength and competence of the parent are dominant; it is only on approaching adulthood, that one comes to see the parent as somehow commensurate with oneself—and it is only then that a loving relationship can develop. Hate is the price paid for a relationship transfixed in fear.

Yochanan Muffs, in his study, *Love and Joy*, shows how strongly the idea of love is related in ancient legal documents, to the notion of "free and uncoerced volition," which gives greater force to a legal transaction. Sadness and anger, similarly, denote unwillingness, mental reservations, grudging will. He studies the same philological phenomena in Rabbinic documents, noting the "social feelings underlying the law." For instance, he notes that "satisfaction" never occurs after "removal"; only after the owner was properly seduced with payments and gifts was he ready to relinquish . . . to "remove himself from" the property, and to "invest the new owner metaphorically with his rights and privileges."[62] Symbolic gestures, such as "jumping out of the property," walking around it, donning the seller's cloak, expressed the mutual satisfaction ("Joy," "love") of the parties.

In our case, there is an unappeased, resentful quality to Israel's relation to God, an inability to recognize goodness and love in His relation to them. That this "hate" is engendered partly by their pervasive understanding that they have merely exchanged masters, while they still remain slaves, is a notion that we shall return to in later chapters.

3. *The Narrative of the Night*

Narrative Dissonance: Exodus by Day and by Night

Here, however, I should like to point to the instability that, from the very climax of the Exodus, marks their experience of redemption. This instability can be described by noticing the ambiguity of the narrative—there are, essentially, two narratives: the Israelites leave Egypt by night; the Israelites leave Egypt by day. Ramban devotes a long passage to this narrative dissonance (12:31). On the daylight Exodus, he quotes Mechilta:[63]

> "[Pharaoh] called to Moses and Aaron in the night and he said, Get up! Get out. . . !:" Moses answered him, We were commanded, "As for you, not one of you shall cross the threshold of your house till morning." Are we thieves that we should leave by night? We shall only leave "with high hand, before the eyes of all Egypt." (Num 33:3)

To leave by night is to be surreptitious, unsure of one's claims, shy of the gaze of others. This narrative must take place in full daylight, challenging all counterclaimants.[64] So powerful is Moses' insistence on leaving only by day that it culminates in the paradox of Pharaoh urging them to leave, while they remain fixed and immovable in their houses, from midnight till daybreak. Pharaoh cries to Moses and Aaron, "Get up! Get out. . . !"—pleading, pressing for them to depart immediately. From the point of view of the victims, the irony is delectable: Pharaoh uses all the habits of authority to pressure the Israelites to leave—"Egypt applied force[65] on the people, impatient to have them leave the country" (12:33). In doing this, he is fulfilling God's prediction: "He will absolutely drive you out of here one and all" (11:1). And the Israelites transcend all vulgar expectations, expressing their freedom by refusing to leave until daylight. This freedom, of course, is in itself paradoxical, since it is grounded in a commandment of their new master.

The freedom that becomes theirs during that night, therefore, is grounded in negation: "Not one of you shall . . ." They hold vigil during the night, belted and booted (12:11), a motionless tableau of "leaving, exodus." At daybreak, they are released into physical motion. But the night intimates a different kind of freedom, paradoxical, uncanny in many of its dimensions.

Seforno articulates the peculiar quality of negative freedom that marks that night. In a fine reading of Moses' last provocation to Pharaoh ("Then all these courtiers of yours shall come down to me and bow low to me, saying, Depart, you and all the people who follow you! After *that*, I will depart" [11:8]), Seforno focuses on the time-gap: "I shall not leave immediately, when you ask me to leave, but *after that*, for I shall wait till morning."

And yet, as Ramban emphasizes, there is also a significant narrative of "leaving by night." "God brought you out of Egypt by night" (Deut 16:1). The night is indeed the time of redemption, as the people hold fast to the words of their new master and stage a tableau of release. The tension inherent in such a scene is palpable, particularly if one bears in mind the shrieks that rend Egypt and that are heard from the interiors of Israelite houses, set in among the houses of death. To leave by day, "with hands high": this is the stuff of epic. But the night is another country. And, I would suggest, the ambiguity of the two redemptions cannot be totally harmonized. What happens during the "night of watching" is not to be assimilated into the daylight perspective—not even in the sense in which, idiomatically, the "day" is the total, twenty-four hour cycle. No totality can contain the knowledge gained during that night.

The Knowledge of the Night

One way of approaching the problem of the Night of Watching is to notice that the last three plagues are plagues of darkness: the locusts "cover the eye of the earth, so that it cannot be seen" (10:5); the plague of darkness, which is *palpable*—" 'the darkness shall be *felt*' . . . they did not see one another, and they could not stand up from a sitting position" (19:21, 23); while the plague of the firstborn happens at midnight, and the word *liela*—"night"—is repeated with a redundant and subliminal insistence.[66]

The difference, most obviously, between light and darkness lies in whether one can see or not. In the first two of the darkness plagues, a kind of blindness is essential to the suffering of the Egyptians. However, in the plague of the firstborn, I would suggest, this blindness is the fate of the Israelites, enclosed in their houses, with the sounds of massacre and mourning in their ears. With blindness, in the account of the locust-plague, comes ferocious "eating": the locusts devour all the remaining vegetation. This is life-threatening behavior indeed! It evokes mythic fantasies of the dark, inhabited by devouring monsters, that go back to the beginning of history.[67] The predator that haunts the night is intimate with human beings, representing an archaic terror:

> It creates a sensation in the mind of being watched by eyes from which nothing can escape . . . No escape is possible for there is no place to shelter. Their memory is infinite and their threat is nameless. The punishment when it comes will be swift, poisonous and ruthless . . . These sensations create in the subject of their implacable scrutiny a feeling of being totally surrounded by irresistible forces which close in on them from all sides like the Iron [Maiden] of mediaeval tortures or the contracting room of Poe's "The Pit and the Pendulum."[68]

This violent fantasy is not remote from the terror of the consuming locusts, or of a darkness in which one is entirely immobilized and helpless. The predatory possibilities of such a darkness are evoked by the classic midrashic narratives, in which the sighted Israelites, carrying their own light-source with them as it were, move in and out of the Egyptian houses, noting all the valuables, making inventories. From the Egyptian perspective, this is clearly an experience of horror.[69]

In addition, Rashi (10:22) cites the midrash that has the plague of darkness endure for *two* three-day periods: in the first, the Egyptians merely "could not see one another": in the second, there was a "double darkness" of absolute immobility—those who sat could not stand, those who stood could not sit . . . This is a depiction of a dehumanized rigidity, a "hardness," that mimics the rigidity of Pharaoh's heart throughout the narrative. There is a horror—even a moral repulsiveness—in such a condition. One can detect in Rashi's account of this darkness a similar sense of bafflement: "Why did He bring darkness upon them?" Rashi asks. The very question is unusual; on no other of the plagues does he ask such a question. There is something about the plague of darkness, about the way it reduces the human being to a blind and paralyzed vulnerability, that defies rational or moral explanation. And, indeed, Rashi's answers to his own question withdraw narrative interest from the Egyptians to the Israelites.[70] In this kind of darkness, one might say, repentance—*teshuva*—becomes impossible. There is no possible response to the terror of such a condition.

The midrashic accounts of the plague of darkness carry us into the world of the uncanny, of the "double darkness." In connection with no other plague is there such a display of imagery, such a sense of a condition indescribable in ordinary language. Indeed, on the surface, this plague seems the most innocuous of all; what are the injuries incurred by three days of darkness? The Torah text certainly does not spell out concrete losses. But the midrash[71] tells of the "palpable" darkness, which is not merely a removal of light: God sends Egyptian guardian angels to punish their protégés and these angels unnaturally add their own contribution to the decreed punishment. They intensify the darkness, giving it a tactile quality. The image of guardian angels turned destructive has a peculiar terror—an image for an immune system run wild.

The next passage in Tanchuma speaks of the "darkness of death" (*tzal-mavet*), as the opposite of order: its origin is in Gehinnam—the inferno. Before death, a person should put his learning in order: "Woe to the house whose window opens out into the darkness!" The proof-text here is an enigmatic verse from Job (10:22), describing the "land of deepest gloom (*tzal-mavet*); all gloom and disarray, whose light is like darkness."

Most poignantly, the midrash elaborates on Job's description of life in the shadow of death—effectively, of the "devaluation of values." Here, there is no guiding ray of light by which to order the darkness. The window, that should open towards the light, receptive to whatever can make the inner world intelligible, receives instead an endless extension of darkness. Clearly, it is the imagining of death and absurdity that creates the uncanny, what Freud called the *unheimlich*, the unhomely, the sense that what should be most familiar, most significant and comprehended, has become malign, engulfing, morbid. This, says the midrash, is the experience of the wicked, totally submerged in the palpable experience of the dark. "And the dark could be felt" (10:21): the dark was "as thick as a coin (dinar)." The idea of a coin on the eyes is another intimation of death, evoking the ritual practice of placing a coin on the eyes of the corpse.

Such a darkness, continuing for three days (or six days, in midrashic readings), is also uncanny, of course, in the simple sense that it disrupts the basic structures of time, as God had promised, after the Flood, that they never would again be disrupted: "So long as the earth endures, seedtime and harvest, cold and heat, summer and winter, day and night shall not cease" (Gen 8:22). An intriguing suggestion is made in Torah Temimah: this darkness was a subjective blindness, experienced by the Egyptians, perhaps a cataract, "thick as a dinar." Such a notion in fact plays out the implication of the midrashic tradition. This darkness is not a prodigy of nature, so much as an inner experience of each individual: a catatonic terror of absolute helplessness. Kabbalistic sources, indeed, connect this plague with the notion of the "band of deadly angels,"[72] that, in the narrative of the Haggadah, is an enigmatic dimension of the plague-story. This darkness is full of the terrors of the night: transfixed,[73] prey to hallucinations, the Egyptians suffer an inward anguish that is quite inexpressible in language.

The *Other* Night

The plague of darkness, then, can be understood in terms similar to those Maurice Blanchot uses to describe "the *other* night."[74] In the "first night," "everything has disappeared . . . Here absence approaches—silence, repose, night":

> But when everything has disappeared in the night, "everything has disappeared" appears. This is the *other* night. Night is this apparition: "everything has disappeared." It is what we sense when dreams replace sleep, when the dead pass into the deep of the night . . . Apparitions, phantoms, and dreams are an allusion to this empty night . . . Here the invisible is what one cannot cease to see . . . Those who think they see ghosts are those who do not want to see the night. They crowd it with the terror of little images, they occupy and distract it by immobilizing it—stopping the oscillation of eternal starting over. It is empty, it is not . . .

In Blanchot's extraordinary description of "the *other* night," we find the midrashic "double darkness." The "first night" can be seen as the completion of the day: it is "another of day's constructions":

> Night is what day must finally dissolve: day works at its empire; it is its own conquest and elaboration . . . Night must pass into day. Night be-

coming day makes the light richer and gives to clarity's superficial sparkle a deep inner radiance. Then day is the whole of the day and the night, the great promise of the dialectic.[75]

"Day is the whole of the day and the night": this is the traditional optimistic Jewish view. The "*other* night," however, is always other: "The trap, the *other* night, is the first night which we can penetrate, which we enter."[76] To advance in this night is to hear, as in Kafka's story, *The Burrow*, the sound of the "other beast," the endless approach, the "vicissitudes of an always more threatening threat":

> He who, having entered the first night, seeks intrepidly to go toward its profoundest intimacy, toward the essential, hears at a certain moment the *other night*—hears himself, hears the eternally reverberating echo of his own step, a step toward silence, toward the void. But the echo sends this step back to him as the whispering immensity, and the void is now a presence coming toward him.
>
> The moment of realization, of surrender, is what he must avoid—
>
> But such prudence is useless here. There is no exact moment at which one would pass from night to the *other* night, no limit at which to stop and come back in the other direction. Midnight never falls at midnight . . .[77]

The moment at which the "*other* night" takes over cannot be prepared for, appropriated into the day's designs. When Moses times the beginning of his people's redemption, the final plague of the Egyptian firstborn, at *kachatzoth*, "*approximately* midnight," he speaks with knowledge of this inability of language to master this moment of transition.

The Night when God "Leaped"

The night of the Exodus is the third and culminating plague of darkness. That it shares characteristics with the previous two plagues is clear. For the Egyptians, darkness is chaos, blindness, death. More strangely, for the Israelites, too, it is terror, imprisonment, blood—as well as redemption. This is the basis of the name of the festival of redemption—Pesach: the paschal offering is named for the *leap*, the overstepping by which God omits the Israelite houses from the general havoc:

> "And I shall pass through the land of Egypt on that night . . ." Like a king who passes from place to place, and in one "passage," and in one instant, all are struck down. (Rashi 12:12)

The drama of that night is an engulfing destruction: it is for this reason, the Talmud asserts, that the Israelites are under house arrest that whole night ("And not one of you shall leave the threshold of his house till morning . . ." [12:22]):

> Once permission has been given to the Destroyer to do damage, he does not discriminate between righteous and wicked.[78]

God's *leap*—His "passing-over"—is the central element in the narrative: "And when your children ask you, 'What do you mean by this rite?' you shall say, 'It is the Passover sacrifice to God, because He passed over the houses of the Israelites in Egypt when he smote the Egyptians, but saved our houses' " (12:26–27).

This leap is narrated, significantly, not as part of the description of the final night, but as part of the body of law that God gives Moses, *before* the night of redemption. Before the real experience of that night, God prepares the people: the blood of the paschal lamb shall be daubed on the lintels and doorposts of each house—"When I see the blood I will pass over you, so that no plague will destroy you when I strike the land of Egypt" (12:13). God will see the blood, which is the sign of the people's earliest involvement in God's law, and will *leap over*, will omit the Israelite houses from the general fate.

This act of *pesicha* (leaping over, omission)—Rashi emphasizes that the Israelite houses were set in amongst the Egyptian houses—is an expression of instability: a general law becomes riddled with so many exceptions as to lose coherence. God interferes, as it were, with the terrible consistency of the Angel of Death, who has been given hegemony over the night. God's movement through Egypt is now characterized, not by the ruthless, unswerving logic of law, but by a responsiveness to the particular, to signs of blood, daubed on Israelite doors. Such a movement is not dignified: *pesicha* is ungainly, limping. The associations are with indecision, disability.[79] Strangely, at the climax of the narrative of omnipotence, after God has demonstrated His total power over Egypt, the word *pesicha* introduces a jarring note.

Rashi takes up one of the disturbing resonances of this declaration by God:

> "And I shall see the blood": Everything is revealed before Him; but God said, I am focusing My eyes to see how you are preoccupied with My commandments, and I shall leap over you. (12:13)

What God will see is not the blood itself, but the human engagement with His commandments. It is this that makes Him *leap*. Rashi quotes a midrash:

> "And the blood shall be *to you* a sign": To you a sign, but not to others. From here we learn that they placed the blood on the *interior* of the house.

The blood, mark of a new involvement in the world of God's laws, is entirely *within* the house. Its capacity to signify, therefore, is all oriented within: "it is a sign to you," says the Mechilta, "but not to *Me;* to you, and not to others." God penetrates surfaces, perceives an intimate inscription of commitment that makes Him leap over this house. He responds not to daubs of blood, but to the human meanings that they represent.

God's leap appears once again—not in the actual narrative of the Exodus, but before it, at the conclusion of the body of laws of chapter 12, where He prepares the people for the narratives of the future. In a strange inversion of order, before the reality of redemption, God tells of the question that will be asked by future generations:

> "And when your children ask you, What do you mean by this rite? you shall say, It is the Passover sacrifice to God, because He passed over the houses of the Israelites in Egypt when He smote the Egyptians, but saved our houses." (12:26–27)

This is the first of four scenarios of encounter between this and future generations: the father and son, the question and the answer. Its focus is firmly set on the paschal offering as the people's response to God's essential act of *pesicha*, the leap. This is how they are to respond to the question of the children: "What do you mean by this ritual, this laborious service (*avodah*—the same word used to describe the slavery of Egypt)?"

The manifest problem, however, is that in Egypt the people sacrifice the lamb *before* God leaps over their houses; only since Egypt is the sacrifice rationally named after God's *pesicha.* The father in future will explain the ritual of sacrifice by naming it, and tracing the name back to God's redemptive "leap." This sacrifice then becomes the definable meaning of the festival and its central ritual. But in "real time," in Egypt, that night of God's syncopated motion had centered on the fulfillments of God's Commandments, the sacrifice of the nameless lamb, the daubing of the door, the consumption of the roast meat, described in great legal detail. The night had been an enactment of a narrative pretold to Moses—a legal narrative, whose nodal points are Commandments, laws prescribed to become a structural network of meaning. These nodal points, Lacan's *points de capiton,*[80] will fix, like the nodal points of a quilt, the sliding meanings of the narrator. Only after they eat of the paschal lamb is it given a name ("It is a paschal offering to God"); and only then does He respond to the "quilting" work of the Israelites by leaping over them, saving them from the general havoc. After this narrative foreshadowing of the night of the Exodus, God tells of its institutionalization as a "festival for God throughout the generations."

In other words, the actual events of the night are essentially not narrated. What we have is God's foretelling, in a legal framework, of the narrative of the night; in this version, the people will sacrifice a lamb—later to be called *pesach*—and God will respond by leaping over their houses. In Moses' words to the people, on the other hand, he tells of the future narratives—the questions and answers—about that night. Here, the causality goes the other way: God leaps over the houses and, in token of His leap, the sacrifice is offered. In the future narrative, ritual commemorates God's leap; in Egypt, God leapt only in response to a human act, generated only by words, the prenarrative, the nodal points of law, the creation of a quilt of meaning.

In Panic Haste

The significance of that night to the Israelites relates to the paradoxes of freedom. They resist the expulsion order of Pharaoh, and remain immobile in their houses. This immobility, miming in an uncanny way the immobility of the Egyptians, during the plague of darkness, is described as a tableau of readiness-to-leave. The manner in which they are to eat of the so-far unnamed sacrifice is *be-chipazon*—in haste; but the word, as translated by the Targum, and by Rashi, has connotations of panic (*behala*), of disorientation. There is a lack of control in this last meal, a sense of Blanchot's "*other* night." Strangest of all, this "panic" eating is commanded ahead of time (12:11): it is a planned panic, inscribed in the laws, essential to what is to be staged on the night of the Exodus. The sacrifice is named *pesach* immediately after this description of staged panic; and only then does God tell of His "leaping" over the houses.

It is as though the manner of eating the paschal sacrifice mirrors, in some essential way, God's act in leaping over the houses. The word *pesach* names the first of the two acts, and foreshadows the second. The important point, however, is that *pesicha*, God's "leap," happens only in God's words to Moses and in Moses' to the people—*before* the night of redemption. The drama of salvation is not narrated in "real time." It is foreshadowed, commanded, and its future appearances in narrative are formulated ahead of time. The questions of unborn children are articulated before the historical reality of redemption is narrated.

The uncanny quality of these temporal inversions is caught up in the "mirror words": *be-chipazon/u-fasachti*—"in panic haste/I shall leap." Both represent the paradox of an already-narrated spontaneity and responsiveness, an improvised, almost ungainly quality, that is described before it happens.

The mode of eating *be-chipazon* is essential to the experience of the night. It is picked up again in Deuteronomy, when Moses teaches the people to "make the *pesach* offering for the Lord your God," for "in the spring month, the Lord your God brought you out of Egypt *by night*" (16:1–3). The laws of the paschal sacrifice follow: "You shall not eat anything leavened with it; for seven days you shall eat unleavened bread, bread of distress—for you departed from the land of Egypt in haste . . ." The haste with which they left Egypt explains the annual observance of the unleavened bread (*matza*). Here, however, the *chipazon* becomes a characteristic of "the *day* of your leaving Egypt." According to a passage in the Talmud,[81] there were two moments in the narrative when "panic haste" was central: one was at night—referred to as *chipazon deMitzrayim*—and was informed by the terrified pressure of the Egyptians on the Israelites to leave the country; while the other was the following day—referred to as *chipazon deYisrael*—the urgent flight of the Israelites by day.

This "haste of the Israelites," which is a question not merely of tempo but of mood, has an ungainly, undignified quality. A provocative suggestion is made by Ha-amek Davar (12:39): "for they could not delay," appears as a redundant statement, in a verse that has already explained why the bread remained unleavened: "for they were driven out of Egypt." The second clause ("they could not delay") describes their own inner panic—quite distinct from the pressure of the Egyptians, which had happened at night. In the daylight Exodus, the Israelites leave in a flurry, afraid that the Egyptians will realize that they have no intention of returning. The key to this anxiety is the fact that, "obeying the word of Moses" (12:35), they have borrowed silver and gold articles and clothing from the Egyptians. This borrowing implies that they will return to Egypt. In the reading of Ha-amek Davar, Moses has come to a clear understanding with Pharaoh; but, strangely, God has commanded this "borrowing" as one of the essential preambles to redemption. The result is a surreptitious quality, a sense of bad faith, as they leave Egypt, anxious, apprehensive of being found out. This *chipazon* consciousness permeates the Exodus, by day no less than by night; it informs the baking of *matza*, no less than the eating of the paschal lamb.

The effect of this *chipazon*-sense is to postpone, till after the Splitting of the Sea, any sense of complete freedom. Only after the Egyptians have been killed in the Red Sea are the Israelites released from the anxiety of *chipazon*, the fear of repercussions still to come.[82]

This emphasis on a kind of ungainly haste, which is inscribed in the text, even legislated ahead of time (in the case of the *chipazon* of the night), is highly enigmatic. Quoting Mechilta, Ha-amek Davar adds to the two focal points of *chipazon* (the Egyptian and the Israelite) a third:

> This is the *chipazon* of God's Presence. Even though there is no proof of this, there is a trace of this: "The voice of my Beloved! Here He comes! Leaping over the mountains, skipping over the hills . . . There He stands behind our wall, gazing through the window, peering through the lattice . . ." (Song of Songs 2:8–9). Will this be the same in the ultimate redemption? No; for the text says (Isa 52:12): "You shall not leave *be-chipazon* (in haste), nor go in flight, for God will walk before you."[83]

In the poetic narrative of Song of Songs, the redemption story is told: God came like the lover, "leaping over the mountains . . ." God acts in a mode of passionate syncopation, disregarding the conventions, overlooking the normal rhythms of history. For the people are not ready for redemption; some acceleration of events, some anticipation of ripeness must happen if they are to be redeemed. There is, therefore, a surreptitious quality, even as the lover peers through the window, the lattice. This is not a moment that can bear the full glare of the spotlight. It has in it the shyness of desire. Only when the Israelites reach Eitam can the Torah declare unequivocally: "And God walked before them" (13:21).[84]

The "trace" of evidence for this reading, according to Mechilta, is in Song of Songs. God's "leaping" there is finally set against the ultimate redemption, where there will be no haste, no panic, no leaping; and where God will walk, by full right, before them. Mechilta aligns the passionate haste of the Divine Presence with the human haste of the Exodus. The effect is to place the Exodus, even as it takes place in full daylight and before the eyes of all Egypt, in a mode of instability, of anticipation, even of shame. This "leap" of God, as it appears in Song of Songs, evades the daylight work-world. What peeps in at the window is the face of desire.

God's essential "leap," during the night of redemption, is a response to the people's panic haste, as they eat the paschal sacrifice. Something of this nighttime mode infiltrates the day; the lover springing over the hills and mountains defies the structures of time,[85] ignores the inevitability of process. In a sense, the Lover makes himself invisible, unaccountable, through His leaping. For to leap is to leap over time and space, as though they did not exist. It is to contract reality to the shape of desire. And there is a shame that accompanies such expressions of desire, whether they are Egyptian, Israelite, or those of the Divine Presence.

The Inspired Gaze of God

The *mysterium tremendum* of the night of redemption, therefore, has elements of the inscrutable. God's power is manifest; but the quality, the passion of that night evades the eye, the public testimony of observers. There is a confusion of blind haste in this "other night," that transmutes redemption from the public arena to an intensely private one. "Woe to the house whose window (*chalon*) opens out into darkness," said the midrash.[86] And another midrash answered, quoting Song of Songs: It is the Lover who comes leaping, "peering through the windows . . ." (*chalonoth*).

The window, the empty space (*chalal*) in the structure of the house, invites light, but is vulnerable to the darkness of the "*other* night." The house offers shelter from that void; but its windows hollow out a deepened sense of the void itself (*chalal-chalon*). It is by these windows that the Lover places Himself; His glance is not brazen, it has a shyness like the glance of one who approaches a future that is not yet expressible.

The same window, the familiar house window, faces out into what is beyond seeing. God's desire to look, is a displaced expression of human desire. It is the mysterious, fatal desire of Orpheus, as Maurice Blanchot describes it:

> That alone is what Orpheus came to seek in the Underworld. All the glory of his work, all the power of his art, and even the desire for a happy life in the lovely, clear light of day are sacrificed to this sole aim: to look in the night at what night hides, the *other* night, the dissimulation that appears . . . To look at Euridice, without regard for the song, in the impatience and imprudence of desire which forgets the law: *that is inspiration.*[87]

Inspiration is the critical moment, the midnight moment that never comes at midnight. It takes Orpheus toward the future, pronounces his ruin, and compromises even his work.

This inspired and forbidden gaze marks the movement of the leap, the *chipazon*, confused, precipitate, that lies at the very heart of the narrative. This gaze expresses impatience, insouciance, unconcern, inspiration, the leap—these are Blanchot's words for what lies at "the core of profound patience."[88] They provide a translation for the Hebrew words, *chipazon*, *medaleg*, *u-fasachti*, as they are embedded in a text that legislates extreme attention, profound patience. For the night of redemption is called *leil shimurim* (12:42)—a night of mindful waiting—God waiting for the end of exile, the Israelites waiting on God's word. The relation between the "infinite waiting" and the "brilliant point which has escaped" it is the pure flash of redemption.[89]

4. *Negatives, Questions, Borrowing: Destabilizing the Narrative*

THE AMBIGUITY OF EXODUS: *MYSTERIUM TREMENDUM* AND LAW

We have been exploring a radical instability—the nighttime/daytime ambiguity of the Exodus: on the one hand, a public, demonstrative event, declaring before the eyes of all the truth of God's narrative and the totality of His power; and, on the other, a moment of darkness, fear, ungainly haste, frozen immobility, resonant with the sounds of havoc beyond the blood-stained doorposts. This experience of the night is the first collective experience of the *mysterium tremendum*, of a power that cannot be caught in a net of words. And yet, it is precisely words, in the form of law and predictive narrative, that guide them through that *other* night, that "night within the night."[90] The impatience and the mindful waiting: both are inscribed in the Torah; both are already spoken, have taken on the form of words, of prescription, as the people enter the night.

Indeed, the ambiguities of the Exodus narrative are articulated in law. For instance, the fundamental directive to "remember the day of your departure from the land of Egypt all the days of your life," (Deut 16:3) is discussed in the Talmud,[91] and, on one reading, becomes the basis for the law that one should remember—that is, tell of—the Exodus *by night*, as well as *by day* ("*All* the days of your life—this includes the nights"). This discussion is quoted in the Haggadah, which is read on the Passover night; it not only institutionalizes the memory of the Exodus by night, but affirms a dialectical view of the very nature of the Exodus. Indeed, every night and every morning, we remember by night and by day, when we read the *Shema* prayer, with its chapter focusing on the Exodus; in this way, we daily encounter the nighttime dimensions of the narrative.

We have noticed how central to the narrative and to the laws of the original Exodus night is the *chipazon*, the deliberate panic in which the paschal sacrifice was to be consumed. It is this *chipazon*, in the logic of the verse we have just quoted, which will generate memory ("For it was in haste that you departed from the land of Egypt—so that you may remember . . ."). Disordered, uneasy, this condition defies words.[92] And yet it is striking that precisely during that night of *chipazon*, a newly stringent form of language begins.

In a brilliant comment, Meshech Chochma points out that the *lo* form of the negative command ("Thou shalt not . . .") is first used to the people during the Exodus night, signifying a new form of relationship between God and Israel:

> "Do not [*al*] eat any of it raw . . . You shall not [*lo*] leave any of it over until morning . . ." (Exod 12:9–10)

Al signifies a plea; *lo*, a command. The commentator illustrates his argument by quotations, showing, for instance, that the word, *al*, alone, is often qualified by *na*—"please."[93] Prayers to God are always in the form of *al*: ("Do not [*al*] hide Your face from me!" [Ps 27:9].) His claim is that only after the manifest clarity of the plague of the firstborn, when God has demonstrated His power and involvement in the particulars of each family,[94] does He come with specific and detailed demands of the people—holding them responsible for minute and apparently invisible infractions of the Law. The gaze of God becomes microscopic and critical, precisely after midnight of the Exodus night, when His providential power has been demonstrated. What had been a request before midnight ("Do not [*al*] eat any of it raw . . .") becomes a royal command after midnight: "Do not (*lo*) leave any of it over until morning." Before the plague of the firstborn, He had asked them to have faith in Him, to enact the hasty meal of free men; after midnight, they have become His servants, survivors of the general havoc.

In the context of our discussion of the night of the Exodus, this notion of the new stringency of law is highly evocative. It is precisely in the terror of the "*other* night," that the human relation to God takes on a new hardness. God no longer requests but demands. He has saved their lives: they owe Him total obedience; and He becomes responsible to and for them. A new awareness springs up among the Israelites of God's involvement in the minutiae of human action. This is the breeding-ground of law: acts of language whose impulse is always, at root, negative.

Kenneth Burke provides a provocative discussion of the function of the negative in human language. His definition of the human, in fact, includes the clause, "Inventor of the negative"; this he then inverts: "So far as sheerly empirical development is concerned, it might be more accurate to say that language and the negative 'invented' man." The negative does not exist in nature: this is the idea he draws from Bergson's *Creative Evolution* ("The Idea of Nothing"):

> To look for negatives in nature would be as absurd as though you were to go out hunting for the square root of minus-one. The negative is a function peculiar to symbol systems, quite as the square root of minus-one is an implication of a certain mathematical symbol system.[95]

The negative begins, he claims, as a command, as "Don't": its descriptive, informational uses develop later. "Laws are essentially negative; 'mine' equals 'not thine'; insofar as property is not protected by the thou-shalt-not's of either moral or civil law, it is not protected at all."[96] Burke goes further, claiming that the ability to use words, at all, implies negativity:

> For to use them properly, we must know that they are *not* the things they stand for. Next, since language is extended by metaphor which gradually

> becomes the kind of dead metaphor we call abstraction, we must know that metaphor is *not* literal. Further, we cannot use language maturely until we are spontaneously at home in irony.[97]

The strongly imperative connotations of God's language takes on the negative form immediately after midnight—that is, in the context of our discussion of the *"other* night," when all language is threatened. A firm, hard form of negative language for the first time appears in God's addresses to the Israelites. In Meshech Chochma's reading, this is a token of a new clarity, a new mutual responsibility. But, we may add, the context of the *mysterium tremendum* of that night gives such commands the force of antidote. Paradoxically, the negative gives the one who has entered the night-world, with its uncertainty, its anguish, its menace, as well as its impatient desire, a possibility of making distinctions, of acting against expectation.

The sense of God's scrutiny in the Exodus narrative is not, as in A. A. Mason's description of the superego, of eyes "cruel, penetrating, inhuman and untiring";[98] but of a Lover, passionately ignoring the limitations of time and space, and making similar demands of the beloved.

The negative commands of the Exodus have the unexpected effect of infiltrating even the positive commands. Once the word has been spoken, a newly critical consciousness attends the positive description: "You shall not leave any of it over until morning . . . This is how you shall eat it . . ." (12:10–11). The reader becomes aware of what is being excluded from the positive description: how are the Israelites *not* to eat, if this is how they are to eat? The word, *lo*, generates a new consciousness; no longer innocent, but questioning at every point, aware of metaphor and irony, as Burke claims. Aware, most of all, of the symbolic meanings affirmed, or excluded, in each of the detailed instructions for the night of redemption.

God's promises, too, are infused with a sense of the negative, of what might have been: "No plague will destroy you" (12:13), retroactively affects our understanding of "That night I will pass through the land of Egypt and strike down every first-born. . . and I shall see the blood . . . I will pass over you" (12:12–13). The *leap*, that is God's response to the Israelite engagement with the Law, is, of course, an essentially negative act: God *omits* the Israelite houses from the sinister course of destruction. The laws about the unleavened bread are also a "Thou shalt not," though the word that governs them, *tashbitu*—"you shall remove leaven" (12:15)—is what Burke calls a "quasi-positive."

The Imperative of the Question

The "hard-edged" sense of language that comes with the negative form generates questions.[99] The Talmudic word for the question, indeed, as we have noticed, is *kushiya*. At its heart is the idea of the hard, *kasheh*, the difficult, the resistant. For R. Hutner, the ability to question must now govern the relationship between God and man, as between parents and growing children. The aim of the relationship is to create, in R. Hutner's imagery, the "face of one who can receive," who actively generates meaning by asking questions. Now, the dialogue is the model for evoking narratives. Without the capacity to ask, to open up the closed issues, to break through the obvious, the self-understood, there *can* be no meaningful narrative.

In terms of R. Hutner's analysis, the Four Sons in the Haggadah, whose questions and answers are derived primarily from this Parsha, represent an essential dynamic in the transmission of memory. *Someone must ask a question;* someone must become aware of a difficulty, a blank, a dissonance. The worst case, in this view, is the son "who does not know how to ask." In such a case, *ath petach lo*—"You open up for him": but this opening is, by default, an act of *haggadah*, of telling—an unsolicited narrative, which represents a failure in the dynamic of the narrative that is engendered by questions.[100]

If the son who does not know how to ask questions is in the worst case, the "simple" son, who asks, in two words: *Mah zoth?*—"What is this?" (13:14)—is, in some readings, in not much better case. Rashi is scathing: "This is a stupid child, who does not know how to deepen his question, but *blocks* it, by asking, 'What is this?' " While most commentators regard the simple son as somewhere between the wise son and the wicked son, Rashi is more critical. The very form of this question "blocks" a penetrating answer; what he receives is the simplest version of the narrative: "It was with a mighty hand that God brought us out from Egypt, the house of bondage . . ." (13:14). Rashi's comment here is, in fact, a comment about narratives, and about the questions that engender or stifle narratives.

Narratives, then, are engendered by questions of a particular type. The first question cited in the Torah—the question later attributed by the Rabbis to the "wicked son"—occurs, as we have already noticed, in Moses' words to the people, preparing them, even before the historical reality of redemption has been played out, for a future of memory and forgetting: "And when your children ask you, 'What do you mean by this rite?' you shall say, It is the

Passover sacrifice to God, because He passed over the houses of the Israelites in Egypt . . ." (12:26–27).

The paradox underlying all questions about history is indicated in Mechilta:

> At that moment, bad news was brought to the Israelites: that the Torah would be forgotten. Some say that good news was brought to them: that they would have children and children's children!

The good news arises if we read *ki* as "*when* your children ask you," not as "*if* your children ask you": there is an assurance of generations to come. The bittersweet nature of questions has to do with forgetting and the desire to know. Without forgetting, there would be no questions. Is this—the inevitability of forgetting—bad news? Or is it good news, implying the constant rebirth of narratives, responses to the questions of those in whom distance and forgetting create desire?[101]

The issue is not decided, as so many true questions are not decided. It does, however, evoke yet again the ambiguity that, in rabbinic commentary, haunts the notion of narrative. How do we understand the questions of the future? Are they tragic, deplorable? Or a manifestation of life? For questions do destabilize: they find difficulty and distance, where one might have dreamt of ease and continuity.

Questioning and Borrowing

At the heart of the Exodus, there is, indeed, a drama of "questioning," of "*she'eilah*" (the biblical word for the question): "The Israelites had done Moses' bidding and borrowed (*va-yish'alu*) from the Egyptians objects of silver and gold, and clothing. And God had disposed the Egyptians favorably toward the people, and they let them have their request (*va-yash'ilum*)" (12:35–36).

Here, the word *va-yish'alu* is, of course, translated rather differently. This is the "borrowing" that God had commanded in His final prediction of the denouement of the story: "Please speak in the ears of the people, that they may borrow (*ve'yish'alu*) . . ." (11:2). This act of borrowing, Ha-amek Davar suggested, was the cause of the *chipazon*, the confused haste of the Exodus. Because they asked the Egyptians for silver and gold, the redemption took place in a certain anxiety—a nighttime flurry, lest the Egyptians realize that they had no intention of returning.

This *chipazon* is an essential aspect of Exodus: a loss of control, an experience of passionate feeling that brings them to taste angst, with the *matza* in their mouths. This taste, the sense of being driven out before they are ready to go, is their confrontation with the "strong hand" of God. The experience of anticipation, of the "missed beat," is almost a sense of contingency. At the same time, the narrative of redemption, told *before the fact*, removes the sense of contingency.[102] The effect is an ambiguous one: an experience of being driven out by forces that include the Egyptian haste in expelling them, their own internal anxieties, and, possibly, the "leap" that is the *chipazon* of God's presence; and at the same time of enacting the narrative that God has already told them.

At this moment of ambiguous consciousness, of loss of human control and of awareness of God's presence, the act of "borrowing" is central. It is this, according to Ha-amek Davar, that generates the tension in the people's experience of the Exodus. It is striking, on the other hand, that the expression, *she'eilah me* . . . invariably means to ask for an outright gift.[103] In other words, the concept of *she'eilah*—question, or request—introduces notions of instability. To ask is, in itself, to raise questions of meaning: is this a gift or a loan? Often only the context will help in interpretation. In the reading of Ha-amek Davar, the *she'eilah* is assumed by the Egyptians to be a loan, while the narrative—and God in commanding the *she'eilah*—couches it in the form of an outright gift.

I am suggesting that if, in the same narrative, questions and gifts/loans are referred to by the same word, this is not without significance. In both cases, the Torah speaks of desire: the commanded desire for silver and gold articles, and the desire of those who have forgotten for what they no longer know.

The Hard Question

A radical thesis on questions is described by Slavoj Zizek:

> . . . there is something obscene in the very act of asking a question, without regard to its content. It is the form of the question as such which is obscene: the question lays open, exposes, denudes its addressee, it invades his sphere of intimacy; this is why the basic, elementary reaction to a question is shame on the bodily level, blushing and lowering our eyes, like a child whom we ask "What were you doing?" It is clear in our every-

> day experience, that such a questioning of children is a priori incriminating, provoking a sensation of guilt . . . The basic indecency of the question consists in its drive to put into words what should be left unspoken, as in the well-known dialogue: "What were you doing?" "You know what!" "Yes, but I want *you* to tell me" . . . It aims at a point at which the answer is not possible, where the word is lacking, where the subject is exposed in his impotence.[104]

Conversely, children question their parents: "Father, why is the sky blue?"—"The child is not really interested in the sky as such; the real stake of the question is to expose father's impotence, his helplessness in the face of the hard fact that the sky is blue . . ."[105]

In Zizek's deliberately provocative rhetoric, shame and guilt are always engendered by questions. Interestingly enough, Zizek's model is the relation of child and father; the "obscenity" of the question applies in both directions, since there is an "innermost, intimate kernel" (the *kasheh*, the resistant core) to the self, that refuses to yield to words. This is a "leftover of every signifying operation, a hard core . . . which simultaneously attracts and repels us—which *divides* our desire and thus provokes shame."

Zizek's perspective, sweepingly and even violently articulated as it may be, fleshes out a challenging sense of the transgressive dimension of questions. If guilt and shame inform the obscenity of questions, their attack on the "inner residue that cannot be spoken of, and cannot be dominated," this sheds a new light on, for instance, R. Simlai's students and their insistence on posing the *hardest* possible question ["Rabbi, you fobbed *them* off easily . . ." they declared, contemptuously, of the "soft" question of the heretics.] The shocking dimension of this drama—and of all the Talmudic literature that privileges questioning—lies in the reader's sense that Zizek is right: questions *are* transgressive, tactless; and yet R. Simlai responds to his students as they drive him hard with their questions, close to the very brink of the unspeakable.

The "hardness" of the question is, then, precisely its brazen drive to put into words what should be left unspoken: that hard core that resists language. The question, indecent as it may be, creates the subject, makes the self aware of its own hard kernel, of its inner division.

Here, we might suggest, is the criterion by which questions can be evaluated. Three of the four sons ask questions; the fourth does not know how. This structure seems to imply that there is an art, or at least a skill, to the question. Rashi's harsh criticism of the simple son, who does not know how to "deepen" his question, who "blocks," stops up the gap where a good question would have created an opening, is thus a negative description of what a question should be. To block—*sotem*—in Talmudic rhetoric is the movement to hide, to leave implicit what might have become explicit. The good question, we might then say, is the one that strives to put something into words, that presses against the boundaries of the unsaid. The simple son, with his too-general question, skates over the surface: he is given an equally superficial, though correct answer.

The wicked son does ask a real question: "What is this *avoda* to you?" The word *avoda* is capable of a wide range of nuances: "worship, devoted service, ritual, hard work, slavery." It is important to notice that later commentaries on the Torah take it as a serious question, without disqualifying it as issuing from a "wicked" son. In other words, the rabbinic typology does not prevent later commentaries from engaging with the challenge of the question—usually understanding *avoda* as "ritual."

Its success as a question can be seen most readily in the response of the Haggadist. He recommends to the father: "Blunt his teeth!" (*Hakheh et shinav*). The emotion that the father is to express is clearly anger; he is to retaliate for the injury caused him by his son's question. The question has indeed been obscene. It has pressed him to "put into words what should be left unspoken." It "aims at a point at which the answer is not possible, where the word is lacking, where the subject is exposed in his impotence." As with Zizek's model question, "Father, why is the sky blue?" and in face of the hard fact of the relationship between God and Israel, the "real stake" of the question is to expose the father's impotence. At this point the word fails; because of the enormous demand of that relationship, and in face of the divided response of the father, the question creates shame.

"To question is to break with something; it is to establish an *inside* and an *outside*."[106] The Haggadah diagnoses the problem of the wicked son's question: "he has excluded himself from society." By not simply asking, "What is this *avoda*?" *but* "What is it *to you*?" he has placed himself *outside* the order of things: he is not involved in the *avoda*, in the relationship with God, in all its historical meanings. In this sense, his is a true question: it arises to disturb the sense of obviousness in which all is implicit. It arouses shame and anger.[107]

The father's answer is cryptic: " 'For the sake of this did God *to me*, when I came out of Egypt'—to *me*, not to *him*. If he had been there, he would not have been redeemed." The clearest fact is his marking of the son's "outside-ness." But the hypothetical aspect of this answer is rather strange:

"If he had been there . . ." And how are we to read the biblical part of the answer: "For the sake of this . . ." This is not, in fact, the answer that the Torah prescribes for the son who asks: "What is this ritual to you?"[108] In fact, it occurs later, in the section of laws relating to the Exodus, in the passage addressing the son who does not know how to ask (13:8).

Rashi identifies this as a reply to the "wicked" son, and comments: ". . . in order that I may fulfill His commandments, such as the passover sacrifice, the unleavened bread, the bitter herbs" ("For the sake of *this* . . ."). The father's answer seems inverted: where we might have expected, "Because of all that God did for me in releasing me from Egypt, I do this service," we read, "Because of this—my acts of service—God acted for me when I left Egypt." Ibn Ezra, like Rashi, reads in this paradoxical way: God's redemption had as its purpose my fulfilling His commandments.

The answer that the father gives the "wicked" son thus emphasizes the son's exclusion, and defines the ritual acts as God's desire of those He redeems. Since the questioner has already excluded himself, we wonder why this answer should hurt him, why this "blunts his teeth"? An original notion is proposed by Ritva: this "blunting of the teeth" is the frustration of one who sees everyone eating, while he is excluded. He cannot participate in the paschal meal, his father tells him, because of the prohibition: "No stranger may eat of it" (12:43). He has denied the principal beliefs of Israel, effectively alienating himself. Again, we might ask, why should this exclusion trouble the questioner who has already excluded himself?

Eating a meal with others, however, is an experience that, in a primary way, is a fulfillment of desire. Not merely the sensual aspects of the meal—the smell, the sounds, the sights, the textures, the tastes—but also the sense of community felt by those who eat together—these constitute a moment from which it is hard to be excluded. Socially and culturally, the questioner is made to feel his "outside-ness" as an untenable attitude. The cost of the question is borne in upon him, making him aware that a facile "outside-ness" is an illusion. He discovers his desire to participate, to be part of the story. There is, in fact, no answer to the alienated violence of his question.

The wise son's question is the most interesting. For it, too, is a real question. On one level, it asks for information, it questions the meanings of a detailed list of laws. And the answer apparently addresses this technical level: "Tell him all the laws, ending with the end of the Seder, the Afikoman." Again, however, this is not the answer written in the Torah, to the question: "What are the statutes and decrees and laws which God our God commanded you?" (Deut 6:20–25). There, the answer is a long narrative that begins with Egyptian slavery, covers the redemption, the gift of the Holy Land, and God's commandments "for our good." This benign history of goodness and life has as its frame the fulfillment of God's commandments. In effect, the answer given in the Haggada is a kind of foreshortened version of the same response. Narrative and law nurture one another—the redemption-narrative explaining the gratitude and responsibility of the people, the laws evoking wonder at the continuing narrative of goodness and life.

This is the classic understanding of the wise son's question. What makes it a real question, however, is not its encyclopaedist categories of laws, but precisely the awkward word, *etchem*—". . . commanded *you.*" This is awkward because it seems akin to the wicked son's terminology—"What is this ritual *to you?*" The wise son, too, asks a disturbing question, in which he opens up a distance between his father and himself. The father and his generation were there; he was not. This distinction between generations is always true. From his situation outside, the questioner, by the very word *Mah*—What?—asks for words to describe what is beyond words.

The wise son, however, articulates his question with exquisite care: ". . . which *our* God commanded *you.*" He speaks of "*our* God"; as Rashi says, "He does not exclude himself by the word, 'you,' because he says, 'our God.'" "Our God" is the expression of relationship, of responsibility to the Other.[109] This is a given in the wise son's question. He is both inside and outside, committed to God and His commandments, but not directly present at the original site of commandment. This is the eternal distance between child and parent, questioner and answerer. The wise son's question, therefore, does not merely demand information; it disturbs in its distance, even as it articulates a basic commitment.

Unlike the narcissistic alienation of the "wicked" son, the effect of the wise son's question is to touch on deeper levels of the father's knowledge. His answer has to do, again, with eating. It tells of the negative: "We do not eat anything after the passover offering, except the Afikoman." Implicitly, however, it indicates a positive situation: the lingering taste of the Passover offering (and the *matza*) in the mouth of the Israelite.[110] It is this sense-experience, the taste in the mouth, that generates the narratives that will fill the night. The taste—*ta'am*—of the Passover offering is transmuted into the *ta'amim*—the interpretations of God's commandments.[111]

5. *The Quest for a True Narrative*

The Taste of Freedom

The key to the wise son's question, therefore, lies in the words, ". . . *our* God . . . commanded *you*": the dialectic of distance and involvement. The key to the father's answer, in our reading, lies in the intimate experience of the "taste of the commandment." There is something beyond argument about a shared taste [*de gustibus non disputandum est*]. Beyond the level on which the wise son simply asks for information, is the level of the *Mah*, the question "What?" Here, he challenges his father to articulate that which should not be spoken. And, because he has voiced his basic commitment to God and to his people, his father answers him by articulating a law that governs the world of the mouth.

This is the level on which the wicked son has excluded himself: he may not eat the Passover offering together with his family. He may not eat, because of the Torah's ban: "No stranger may eat of it." "The stranger" is defined by the Rabbis as, "Whoever is alien to the words of Torah . . ." (Mechilta). The Ishbitzer[112] shifts the weight of meaning: he may not eat, because he *cannot* eat, because he is insensitive to the taste of the Passover offering, to the taste of freedom: "The meaning / taste—*ta'am*—of the passover offering is that one should feel the taste / meaning of freedom." Not everyone regards leaving Egypt as a good thing. As we have seen, there is a strong counter-narrative, an undertow carrying the people back to Egypt ("It is *good* for us to return to Egypt"), which the Torah itself describes as "the garden of God" (Gen 13:10). One who has spiritually left the world of Egypt and accepted the Torah can realize the "goodness of leaving Egypt." One who is "alien to the words of Torah," however, even if apparently performing the rituals of Passover, will feel no pleasure, no meaning (*ta'am*) in them. The Ishbitzer ends with a homely image: a father feels unforced, spontaneous pleasure on hearing his son praised, as compared with a stranger, who takes no pleasure in this praise.

In this reading there are no imperatives, no prohibitions, no punishments. One who is alien, unaffected by the redemption history, by the words of the Torah, will *obviously* not be capable of eating—that is, of truly tasting—the Passover offering. This taste is, as it were, a gourmet pleasure, not accessible to those whose pleasures lead them in different directions.

The difficulty that the Ishbitzer is addressing is related to the wise and wicked sons. The father's answer comes from an inexpressible dimension of personal experience. He speaks of the taste of the Passover offering, responding to the alienation of the wicked son and to the dialectical challenge of the wise son. What he intimates, essentially, is his own desire, which he challenges the son to recognize in himself.

The wicked son's error is simply his perspective: he imagines himself uninvolved in the passionate experience he is provoking in his father. The wise son recognizes his own desire, even as he stands "outside," and interrogates his father.

Something of this structure can be found in Kafka's story, "The Door of the Law," in *The Trial*.[113] The man from the country, who has spent his life at the door of the Law, unsuccessfully trying to gain admission from the doorkeeper, asks a last question before dying:

> "Everyone strives to attain the law, how does it come about, then, that in all these years no one has come seeking admittance but me?" The doorkeeper perceives that the man is at the end of his strength and his hearing is failing, so he bellows in his ear: "No one but you could gain admittance through this door, since the door was intended only for you. I am now going to shut it."

This final twist is described in this way by Zizek: the man "experiences how he (his desire) was part of the game from the very beginning." The point of the door never was some secret hidden beyond the door, but rather, "the door is intended only for me, to capture my desire." At first, the secret from which he was excluded seemed to be "the inaccessible heart of the Law, beyond the infinite series of doors." By the end, he realizes that the real secret is his own desire: his sense of exclusion is already part of the game.[114]

This is the difference between the questions of the wicked and the wise son. The wicked son will never realize the "taste" of the Passover offering, will interrogate the father, knowing that there is no possible answer to his question. The wise son will appropriate his own desire, and will, therefore, hear his father's answer as including him in the laws of the mouth.

> *To ask the hard question is simple:*
> . . . .
> *But the answer*
> *Is hard and hard to remember . . .*[115]

Narrative Precedes Redemption

We have explored subversive aspects of the Exodus which reveal a dimension of human experience not totally translatable into the public, demonstrative, empirical language of signs and proofs. The narrative of the night which is generated by destabilizing questions tells of an original *chipazon*, an unmodulated passion on the part of the Israelites, as well as of a leap, a *pesicha*, an undignified, "syncopated" movement on the part of God. The truth of this narrative never was transparent; and never will be. To some extent, each generation and each individual will always have to testify to this truth, which will always be on trial, in crisis. Such testimony will always contain something of the idiosyncratic and the personal; ultimately, the imperative to tell the story of the Exodus was and will be the imperative to find a way to give birth to its truth.

The narrative of darkness will recall a panic moment, a passionate, unformulated moment. The *she'eilah*, the question, provokes the narrative: before the reality of redemption comes the narrative of questioning. Moses transmits to his people laws governing the night of redemption, laws that will extend into the future the memory of that night. But this future narrative culminates in the questions of the future son, the one who is distant, who has forgotten. His question generates an answer, the narrative of God's leap. "And the people bowed low in homage" (12:27). Only after this imagined dialogue has been put into words is the actual narrative of the Exodus played out. The words come first, the questions, the laws, the explanations . . . In bowing down as they hear the narrative, the Israelites acknowledge the "tidings"[116] they have heard: of redemption, of the entry into the Holy Land, and of the future children. They are acknowledging their desire for a particular kind of narrative, one in which they will be involved in tasting the Passover offering. They are acknowledging the questioning that will follow an event that is yet to happen. This is the "bad news," according to Mechilta; it is also another face of the "good news," of children yet to be born.

Their acceptance of the *she'eilah*, in all its subversive potential, precedes the empirical certainties of redemption. Similarly, the *she'eilah* that was the "asking" for Egyptian silver and gold articles must precede redemption. This *she'eilah*, according to Ha-amek Davar, engendered *chipazon*, instability, a disturbance of the calm order of things. Without this "lurching" motion, it seems, there can be no redemption. Or at least not until the end of days, when, as Isaiah describes it, "You shall not leave in haste, nor go in flight. But God shall walk before you" (Isa 52:12).

Language and Silence

The *she'eilah* disturbs the world and, potentially, creates a new one. In its Talmudic guise, the *kushiya* is grounded in the *kasheh*, in the opaque, the resistant. In an important passage,[117] R. Nachman of Bratzlav writes of the uncanny, the unknowable world of the *kushiya*. Basing himself on the Lurianic idea of *tzimtzum*, R. Nachman describes the contraction of a God who permeates the universe, so as to allow for a hollow space, free of His Presence. Within this space, the *chalal panui*, a world can be created, a world of limits and measures, of time and space, of not-God. In this void, *kushiyot* are bred, unanswerable questions. Here, God is absent, therefore doubts and errors can proliferate unchecked. But this void is created by God: that is the paradox of the *chalal panui*. Subversive questions denying God Himself are generated by the void that God Himself has created. Without it, there can be no world, nothing that is not-God.

This paradox can be resolved only by faith, which realizes that God's reality encompasses even this void of His absence. Another paradox: those who enter that space are engulfed by irresistible doubts and subversive questions; but the great *tzaddik*, the righteous man, *should* enter that space, should explore those questions, and, through his own grappling with them, deliver those already lost in the maze. This type of the great *tzaddik* R. Nachman characterizes as "like Moses," following the Moses archetype. What marks this type is *shetikah*, silence, the capacity to contain the formless silence of that evacuated space.

Another paradox: all worlds, all forms, language itself, with its clear, definable articulations, emerge from a vacuous space, where there are no clear concepts, not even letters that can begin to ground, to pin down the slippage of ideas. Into this swarming silence, the *tzaddik* like Moses must enter: Moses who was "heavy of mouth," Moses of whom the midrash[118] relates that when he was shown the future martyrdom of R. Akiva, he cried out: "Is this Torah? Is this its reward?"—and was answered, "Silence! So it has risen up in My thought!" This type of *tzaddik* can absorb the unanswerable questions, accept a realm of thought that is higher than the realm of words (a play on God's answer—the realm of thought is "higher," "risen up" over the realm of words).

Moses has a quality akin to the "Negative Capability" of which Keats wrote: "that is when a man is capable of being in uncertainties, Mysteries, doubts, without any irritable reaching after fact and reason."[119] His capacity for "silence" can be redemptive for those engulfed in the dissonant silence of the evacuated space.

This final paradox is compelling: Moses' silence encompasses the inarticulate questions of that space; and at the same time, out of the silence emerges language, which crystallizes thought and creates all the structures of the human world. Most strikingly, R. Nachman writes of *machloketh*—disputes between scholars, who, through their very differences, create the world. In their disagreements they create a space between them, a *chalal panui*. Their difference is the basis for all creativity.

R. Nachman seems to suggest, on the one hand, that the void, teeming with questions, doubts, uncertainties, should be avoided; but, on the other, that the Moses-type should seek it out. On the one hand, the void proclaims the absence of God; but, on the other, that God Himself created it. On the one hand, the void is inchoate, lacking even the elements of human language (the "letters"); but, on the other, this void is the birthplace of language and of all the structures of human life.

At the heart of his paradoxes is the problem of the question, the unanswerable question. It is the measure of the great *tzaddik* to be capable of asking questions, "without irritably reaching after fact and reason." R. Nachman says elsewhere:[120] "This is the way that the human being is like God: God, too, has unanswerable questions." In asking questions of God, against God, without answers, the human being enacts his likeness to God. In this mode of the question, the *tzaddik* expresses his understanding that, because God is beyond human understanding, "it is necessary that there be questions of Him, against Him." Again, the paradox: the question against God is appropriate to a God who cannot be articulated, or "gentrified," to use Zizek's expression.

> The real question does not expect an answer. And if there is an answer, the latter does not satisfy the question . . . Any answer should bear in it the essence of the question, which is not extinguished by the one who answers.[121]

The space out of which questions emerge tells of separation—separation from God and from other human beings. Bridging this gap, which is taut with potential relationship, comes language; but the "distance is not abolished, it is not even diminished. On the contrary, it is preserved and pure by the rigor of the speech that sustains the absoluteness of the difference."[122]

Returning to the model question of the wise son, we notice that both poles are held in tension: ". . . *our* God commanded *you* . . ." The distance between son and father is not diminished by the shared commitment to the commands of God; nor by the father's answer, which addresses, impersonally, the intimate experience of desire. "Language does not abolish the distance between human beings, but brings that distance to life."[123] Because of the distance, room is left for each person to create his own world.

Redemption as "Syncope"

The kabbalistic term for the "evacuated space" is *chalal panui*. Through this expression, we return to the instability, the "*other* darkness" of the night of the Exodus. We remember the window, the *chalon*, that space in the walls of the home, that allows contact between inside and outside. "Woe to the house whose window opens out into the darkness!" Contact with the "darkness within the darkness" is mediated by a *chalal*—a void, which destabilizes the house. This is the source of Freud's expression for the uncanny—*unheimlich*, the unhomely—which arises in the midst of the familiar, the known. And yet, as we noticed, it is God, the Lover, who "peeps through the windows" of the beloved; shyly affirming His Presence, far from the noontime glare of the sun.

The modality of redemption is ecstatic, troubled, hurried, unripe. It is the leap, rather than the walk; question rather than answer; syncopated rather than orderly rhythm.[124] This modality belongs to the night; to dissonance; to blank spaces. "The night of Egypt" refers not only to the sufferings before redemption, but to an intrinsic dimension of redemption itself. "There is an angel in charge of conception, and his name is Night."[125]

There is a fertility peculiar to the time of the "cerebral eclipse,"[126] when limits, identities are banished. What was conceived during the night of the Exodus was the desire for freedom. Not an easy conception, it is engendered by terror, immobility, the leap, the fugitive glance through a window. This is desire for something unknown, unseen. As Paul Ricoeur puts it:

> . . . the slave who rebels against the master not only repudiates the master, but he also affirms that he is right; as Camus so rightly expressed it, without perceiving all the metaphysical implications of it: "In every act of rebellion, man experiences not only a feeling of revulsion at the infringement of his rights, but also a complete and spontaneous adhesion to a certain part of himself." And he adds: "Not every value leads to a rebel-

lion, but every rebellion tacitly invokes a value." Adhesion, invocation—words which are supremely positive. Shall we say that the object of adhesion is precisely what does not exist, since that part of himself which the slave raises before the master has no place in this world?[127]

The Birth-Drama of Israel

The idea of freedom has as yet no place in this world: it testifies to that part of the self that is an " 'I am,' beyond factual being." To adhere to it is to say, "I have worth."

The desire, the "taste," that is engendered during the night is symbolized, said the Ishbitzer, by the Passover offering. Focusing on the authenticity of desire, he sets up an unequivocal criterion for "inside" and "outside": those who are alien to the words of Torah simply have no taste for the gourmet delights of the Passover offering, in all its symbolism. His existential mediation on "No stranger shall eat of it" seems to divide the people into "haves" and "have-nots," in a spiritual sense.

But one may press the matter further, question this absolute division. For, as Ricoeur says, to rebel against slavery is to adhere to a part of oneself that "does not exist." The taste for freedom may appear in full energy on the Exodus night; or it may develop over forty years; or it may never be realized. The complexities inherent in "eating the passover offering," emerge powerfully in the following midrash:[128]

> "This is the statute of the passover sacrifice": R. Shimeon ben Chalafta said, When the Israelites left Egypt, God said to Moses: "Caution Israel about the commandment of the Passover sacrifice—'No stranger may eat of it. But any slave a man has bought may eat of it once he has been circumcised' (12:43–44)." When Israel saw that God had rejected the uncircumcised from eating of the Passover offering, the whole people instantaneously rose up and circumcised their servants and their children and all who left Egypt with them; as it is said, "And all the Israelites did so . . ." (12:50)
>
> This is comparable to a king who made a banquet for his friends. The king said, "Refuse entry to any guest who is not wearing my insignia." So God made them a banquet, with roast meat and unleavened bread and bitter herbs, since He had redeemed them from anguish. And he said to

> them, "If the seal of Abraham is not upon your flesh, you shall not taste of it." Instantly, all those who had been born in Egypt were circumcised. About them, it is said, "Bring in My devotees, who made a covenant with Me over sacrifice!" (Ps 50:5)

> Our Sages said, Israel did not want to be circumcised in Egypt; indeed, they all neglected circumcision in Egypt, except for the tribe of Levi, of whom it is said: "Let Your *Thumim* and *Urim* (the priestly breastplate with its twelve precious stones) be with your faithful one . . ." Why? Because "they observed Your precepts and kept Your covenant" (Deut 33:8, 9)—in Egypt. When God wanted to redeem them, they did not merit it. So what did God do? He called Moses and said, "Go circumcise them . . ." And many of them did not agree to be circumcised. So God said that they should make the passover sacrifice; and when Moses made the passover sacrifice, God decreed that the four winds which blow in Paradise should go and carry the aroma of that passover sacrifice, as it is said, "Awake, O North Wind! And come, O South Wind!" (Song of Songs 4:16) And its aroma spread forty days' journey. Then all Israel gathered in Moses' presence, and said: "We beg you, let us eat of your passover offering!" For they were weary (faint) of the aroma. And God said, "If you are not circumcised, you cannot eat—as it is said, '. . . This is the statute of the passover offering . . .' " Immediately, they presented themselves for circumcision; and the blood of the passover sacrifice mingled with the blood of circumcision. And God passed through them and took each one and kissed him and blessed him; as it is said, "I saw you wallowing in your blood" (*be-damayich*—literally, your *two* bloods). And I said to you, "Live in your (two) bloods" (Ezek 16:6)—"Live in the blood of the passover sacrifice; live in the blood of circumcision."

There are two different scenarios here: both relate to the central problem of circumcision, which God declares to be a prerequisite for eating the Passover offering. This is the "statute," the law which resists rationalization, and which the proof-text mentions; for the law of circumcision in a radical sense defies reason. This becomes, in a way that the midrash will explain, inextricably connected with the Passover offering.

The first scenario is one of spontaneous obedience, as supported by a verse in the Torah: "And all the Israelites did so." The imagery of the king who demands that all guests at his banquet wear his insignia conveys the impression that it is loyalty or solidarity that is being demanded of those who would share the delights of freedom. The Rabbis then depict the contrary situation: a complete neglect of the family tradition of circumcision, a people "denuded" of any right to redemption, and massive resistance to God's attempt to give them this commandment which would declare their commitment to God and to a certain idea of freedom.

If this first scenario deals with the absolute situations of immediate obedience and large-scale resistance, the second brings the people to a point of *retroactive* satisfaction as the blood of desire mingles with the blood of repugnance. The winds arising from Paradise, transporting the scents of the Passover offering, bring the people a quintessence of desire: the word for "wind," *ruach,* also means "spirit," implying a spiritual yearning, and punning with the word for "aroma," *rei'ach*, which traditionally is regarded as the most spiritual of the senses. Transcending reasonable limits of space and time, the aroma pervades over an expanse of forty days' travel. This time-period has an archetypal value as the period over which the embryo takes on full human shape. This rarified desire for the Passover sacrifice will engender the full humanity of each member of the people—at least in rudimentary form. The verse quoted from Song of Songs is the charge of the Lover, urging the winds to blow within the garden of the beloved, so as to bring forth her scent, her essential beauty.[129] In our midrash, it is the aroma of the Passover offering that is wafted by winds from paradise, blowing from four opposite directions—north, south, east, and west.

The image of the winds bearing yearning suggests to the Rabbis the idea of contrary, irreconcilable desires:

> Said R. Yehoshua . . . : In this world, when the south wind blows, the north wind does not blow; and when the north wind blows, the south wind does not. But in the time of the ingathering of the exiles, God will bring peaceful winds to the world and both winds will work together without suppression.[130]

In the light of this midrash, one can read the four winds bringing the aroma of the Passover offering as a complex and impossible desire, incompatible with the nature of this world, in which only one wind blows at a time. The contrary winds, harmonizing opposite principles, are summoned for the exceptional purpose of generating a complex, unspeakable desire, of intimating a potential wholeness beyond normal experience.[131]

The people, filled with a transcendent desire, are described as "weary of the aroma": an expression of the ambiguity of desire. The difficult secret of passion is intimated in this word: what they desire also repels them; almost fatally, it encompasses *too much* for the limits of this world.[132] More simply, they already know that it carries a price: the more intimate blood of circumcision. They are tired because they have struggled against the desire for an unspeakable wholeness—in vain. Their last attempt to fulfill desire without making the personal sacrifice is answered unequivocally by God: "this is the statute of the passover offering . . ." This is the mystery of spiritual desire—that it carries with it the demand for "the seal of Abraham," the mutilation that engenders wholeness.

Ironically, the tension of the ending of the midrash is greatly increased by the proof-text from Ezekiel. All the traditional commentaries understand the situation of God's beloved as still soiled by birth-blood [the word *mitboseseth*, here translated, "wallowing," holds resonances of defeat, degradation, soiling]; and translate *be-damayich chayi*: "*in spite* of your blood, you shall live!" Mobilizing these nuances, we can say that the two commandments—the Passover sacrifice and circumcision—which are to "birth" the Israelites, to bring them into a world of significant selfhood—have a repugnant dimension, implicit in the double bloodletting.[133] God's kiss and blessing has, then, a wrenchingly paradoxical quality: "in spite of your two bloods (with all their fatal intimations), you shall live." But also, "*because* of your bloods, you shall live."[134]

The "mingling" of the two bloods is the absolute confusion of desire and repugnance. God's kiss is the kiss of death and life. In this second scenario, a resistant people, unwilling to enter into the perilous ambiguities of circumcision, are "seduced" by the aroma of the Passover sacrifice. The mysterious fusion of the two *mitzvoth* involves them in a situation where, without conscious will, they find themselves *already desiring*. If this desire, relentless, brings them to circumcise themselves, to accept the unacceptable, it clearly represents more than a physical lust. It is a spiritual intimation of the complexities of freedom, an appreciation of the "goodness of leaving Egypt," in all its sacrificial dimensions.

This midrash, then, limns out a process, by which even those who have no taste for the Passover sacrifice are seduced by a difficult desire. One might call this, "the desire to be born, or to be transformed." Or, in Ricoeur's language, the desire to adhere to a part of the self that does not exist, that has as yet "no place in the world." Languishing in the tension of such a desire, each individual man accepts the paradoxical blood that births him, makes him redeemable.

The birth-drama of Israel, however, is suffused with the sadness of

God's account, in Ezekiel 16, of the future development of the child, cleansed, blessed, loved by God. Grown to full beauty, she plays the harlot, violates her covenant with God. It is from the vantage point of this violation that Ezekiel addresses the people, remembers its birth, God's love, its betrayal. Perhaps something of the whole chapter in Ezekiel permeates our midrash, lending it a tragic resonance. Freedom will always remain a notion fraught with ambiguities: haunted by different voices, questioning, mocking, insisting on a retelling of the story that will accommodate new forms of desire; and at the same time, challenging immediate perceptions, teasing us out of thought.

The narratives and counter-narratives that will divide the people until they enter the Holy Land forty years later will be attempts to make meaning of the tension of the night of the Exodus; to compose a response to the imperatives of freedom. These narratives will play out all that is hidden, ambiguous, and unresolved in the experience of redemption. Through these narratives, which constitute the very process of freedom, fathers and sons will confront the unspeakable kernel of desire and shame.

Two passages from the Chasidic master, Sefath Emeth, articulate a challenging notion of the redemptive power of narrative itself. In one passage,[135] he focuses on the "four versions (*leshonoth*—languages) of redemption": the four verbs used by God in His early announcement to Moses—"I shall deliver, I shall save, I shall redeem, I shall take . . ." (6:6–7). These are to be reported to the people, whose reaction is immediately described: "They would not listen because of shortness of breath, impatience . . ." (6:9). It is because of this spastic reaction, he writes, because of the "shortness of breath," the panic haste of the Exodus, that we must create narratives, constantly modulating and changing (the four "languages" that are versions of redemption). Because of the disorder of historical experience, there is a need for the ordering modalities of narrative, for the evolving understandings of generations of retelling. The command to narrate the Exodus, then, indicates the convulsive, unintegrated nature of the historical experience, and the compensatory power of language to redeem that *chipazon*, that raw factuality.

The groping for a true narrative is the very purpose of the Exodus. As Sefath Emeth puts it, in another passage:[136] the redemption from Egypt (*mitzrayim*) is a freeing from the "narrow places," the *meitzarim*, the straits of the soul, into an expansiveness in which all potential is realized. This release was intimated in the mystery, the unconsciousness of a people just born. It will become real in the narratives of memory that the people will tell, as they grow to adulthood. Some of these narratives will be subversive, even demonic. But the project will be "to utter true words," to re-evoke in a later time the power of redemption that is incarnate in language.

All the complex events of the Exodus are *le-ma'an te-saper*, "in order that you may relate the story" (10:2). More pointedly, the practices that will commemorate them are "in order that the Torah of God may be in your mouth" (13:9); in order to utter these true words, a continual process of engaging with the multiform "narrow places" of Egypt, of engaging with the ambiguities of desire, will be necessary. The narrow places are, on the most intimate plane, the straits of the throat passage, constricted with these ambiguities.[137] All the sliding meanings of the Exodus will require continual "re-fixing," to accommodate the claims of the human mouth and of the Torah of God.

4 *Beshallach*

SONGLINE THROUGH THE WILDERNESS

(13:17–17:16)

1. *"What?" Subversion in the Wilderness*

Preventing Subversive Thoughts

A remarkable feature of the liberation experience is the negative tonality that informs the narrative. At the moment of crossing the border, we might have imagined high elation, the intoxication of freedom; in so many literary accounts of breaking across borders to freedom, even in dangerous situations, a giddy symbolic joy is the main response to arriving on the "other side." In the Exodus narrative, however, we find a spate of negative statements. On the one hand, there is the baking of the *matza*, the unleavened bread, "for it had *not* risen, for they were driven out of Egypt and could *not* delay; moreover, even provisions for the journey they did *not* prepare for themselves" (12:39). On the other hand, "God did *not* lead them by way of the land of the Philistines, *because* it was close; for God said, *Lest* the people change their minds when they see battle, and return to Egypt"[1] (13:17).

The first of these negative descriptions we shall take up later. The second description, however, of God's choice of travel-route for the liberated people—or, rather, of "the road not taken," of the rejected itinerary—is given prominence by being placed at the beginning of the Parsha. To describe God's thinking process, as it were, and to reveal the rejected alternatives, together with an opaque rationalization for the chosen route, is certainly an unusual narrative strategy.[2] For what purpose are we told of the road not taken? And how are we to understand God's explanation of His choice?

Rashi's comment seems to clarify the issue:

> ". . . because it was close": and therefore it was easy to return to Egypt by the same road.
>
> ". . . when they see battle": If they had traveled by the direct route, they would have returned to Egypt. If even when He led them round by an indirect route [*me'ukam*—a crooked, zigzag road], they said, 'Let us appoint a leader and return to Egypt . . .' (Num 14:4), how much more so if He had led them by a direct route [*peshuta*—a simple, predictable route]!
>
> "lest they change their minds": They will *think a thought* about the fact that they have left Egypt; and will set their minds on returning.

Rashi explains: the logic of God's thinking is about the people's desire to return to Egypt. If the journey back is too easy (direct, straight), they will think the forbidden desire and act upon it. So God leads them by a crooked route, hoping that the complication will prevent their having such subversive thoughts. By being admitted into God's thought process, the reader learns one essential fact: the central importance of the people's desire to return to Egypt, even in the first elation of freedom.

The opposition of the road not taken (the "straight" road) to the route chosen (the "crooked" route) carries its own paradoxical resonance. Obviously, the straight road is preferable to the "crooked"; strategically, physically, and ethically; indeed, the metaphorical use of these expressions—the straight and the crooked paths—is a commonplace in ethical writings.[3]

Yet, here, the Torah makes a point of God's not taking the obvious route. Instead, a dubious, unmarked route[4] is chosen, for reasons that are related to a repressed desire. So far, we have had no evidence of such a desire; it is the omniscient God who first speaks of it, as though it were self-evident. Through this opening speech at the moment of redemption, we understand that the Israelites, even at this moment, are ambivalent about the movement to freedom. There are potential thoughts about the Exodus that they are primed to think. As proof of this, Rashi points to the later moments of regression, when the people explicitly plan to return to Egypt, even with the practical handicap of God's strategy—the circuitous, zigzag route.

On this reading, we perceive the strength of God's resolve that the people should not "think thoughts," should not "return to Egypt." But the problem, of course, is that, in spite of all God's precautions, the people do think those thoughts—not just in the case of the narrative of the Spies, which Rashi quotes, but several times before that culminating narrative. Indeed, in this very Parsha, before we have time to draw breath, we hear the people expressing such thoughts, several times. God, then, is represented as changing their itinerary, in order to prevent what, in fact, happens.

Gur Arye raises this problem and, in essence, makes the following suggestion: God's concern is that, if the people do, in fact, think such thoughts, they will surely act on them and try to return to Egypt. What He aims to prevent is the *ease* of such a return. He cannot prevent them from thinking thoughts; He can make it harder for them to act on them.

God, then, sees redemption in a mirror mode, as it were—the way out is also, potentially, the way back; and the people become players in a drama of burned bridges. The fact that they cannot easily return does not, however, prevent them from "thinking thoughts." The words for these thoughts are scattered throughout this Parsha, in episodes of fear and anxiety, in which the people's language "about the fact that they have left Egypt," tells of radical doubt.[5] It is not simply that they cry out in fright at the sight of the pursuing Egyptians: it is the sarcasm of the words they use, a sarcasm about God's intentions, about His relationship with them, about the meaning of this Exodus:

> "Was it for want of graves in Egypt that you brought us to die in the wilderness? What have you done to us, taking us out of Egypt? Is this not the very thing we told you in Egypt, saying, 'Let us be, and we will serve the Egyptians, for it is *better* [*tov*] for us to serve the Egyptians than to die in the wilderness?' " (14:11–12)

The radical nature of their doubt is revealed perhaps most abrasively in their use of the word "good" (*tov*) to describe Egyptian slavery, and to embed it in a fatalistic view of the narrative, which, already, hardly begun, is to end in the desert sands. Their thought represents a serious attempt to make sense of events. When they say, for instance, "Is this not the very thing we told you in Egypt. . . ?" we wonder: When did they ever say this? There is no record of such a protest in earlier chapters.[6] We may deduce the missing passage out of silence, perhaps at 4:31, or 5:21, or 6:9; in this case, their fear harks back to Moses' complaints, which we noticed in the previous chapter, that the people would not believe his message. The people's sarcasm at the Sea, then, seems to justify Moses' earlier skepticism about them. Alternatively, however, we may detect here a fabrication: a retroactive interpretation of the past, aligning it with the perceptions of the present. In other words, this is a moment of serious thinking, one in which the Israelites find it all too plausible that they have been seduced from a place of relative security to a place of sure death. They reread their story as a tragedy, a story about death: "Is it because there were no graves. . . ?" "What is this (*Mah zoth*) that you have done to us. . . ?" is the radical question of meaning. Is this a story of redemption; or of diabolical hatred;[7] or even—the most unnerving possibility of all—of the personal megalomania of Moses? In this last case, the people's question is addressed most personally to Moses: "*You* brought us to die . . . What have *you* done to us, taking us out of Egypt. . . ?"

Moses promises the frightened people, trapped between the Egyptians and the Sea, that they will never see the Egyptians the same way again. And, indeed, after the miraculous events of that night and morning, the people do see differently: "Israel *saw* the Egyptians dead on the shore of the Sea. And when Israel *saw* the great Hand that God had wielded against the Egyptians, the people *feared* God; they had faith in God and His servant Moses" (14:30–31). The difference is etched against a background of similarity: once again, it seems, vision leads to fear. Indeed, the two words form an assonance in Hebrew (*va-yar/va-yire'u*). Before, "the Israelites *lifted up their eyes and saw* Egypt was travelling after them. And they were *afraid* and cried out to God" (14:10). Now, they see Egypt dead—a very different vision—and fear God. What they see and what they fear has changed. But is the experience of fear changed? Is this new "fear of God" different from the primary fear of death?

The earlier fear led them to cry out to God, in the sarcastic terms we have already noticed. ("Is it for lack of graves in Egypt. . . ? What is this you have done to us?") The word *va-yitzaku*—"they cried out"—is traditionally associated with prayer,[8] so that the sarcastic speech jars against it. Ramban suggests that the narrative covers two phases: at first, the people pray to God to turn back the ominous march of Pharaoh's army; then, when they see Pharaoh continue his advance, they realize bitterly: "Our prayers have not been accepted," and "the evil thought entered their minds to doubt Moses' authenticity."

In this reading, the same word, *va-yitzaku*, modulates from a prayer to a nihilistic sarcasm. Ramban's text describes the effect of frustration, of the unanswered prayer, not only on the heart, but on the *tone of voice.* He compares the souring effect of time passing to "yeast in the dough," a metaphor for the working of the "evil inclination." A moment of faith easily breaks down into the pathologies of bitterness and rejection.[9]

When God silences Moses, "Why (*Mah*) are you crying out to Me?" He makes clear that what is needed is not prayer but action: "Let them travel on . . ." (14:15). One movement of faith is better than a thousand words of prayer. As an aphorism, this has a fine ring to it; but, of course, for God to silence Moses and the people is an enigmatic response to human prayer. As we shall suggest, the function of the word *Mah* is often to frame an apparently rhetorical question—only to reveal the unexpected complexity of the situation. Why, indeed, is Moses to stop praying? Why, similarly, does Moses instruct the people: "You be silent" (14:14)?

Perhaps the emphasis on silence as the people enter the Red Sea is a necessary part of the perception of the miracle. Listening to the sounds of the Israelite camp yields first prayers, then rebellious taunts, Moses' perhaps ambivalent tonalities,[10] silence—and song. The predictable emotions of the song would presumably be triumph, gratitude, faith. And yet, as we have noticed, the people's response to the miracle centers on fear: "When Israel saw the great Hand which God had wielded against the Egyptians, they feared God . . ." The people see the "great Hand," the destructive power of God wielded against their enemies, and, instead of rejoicing, they fear and they have faith. It is almost by a kind of afterthought, according to the classic midrashic reading, that Moses bursts into song: " '*Then* Moses sang': When he saw the miracle, it occurred to him ('It rose up in his heart . . .') to sing a song . . . His heart told him to sing, and he did so."[11]

Indeed, immediately after the miracle of the Splitting of the Red Sea and after the jubilant song of praise that follows it, the people again complain, this time about the lack of drinking water. Again, they use the interrogative *Mah* ("*What*") to introduce their complaint: "What shall we drink?" (15:24). Rashi comments that the word, *Va-yillonu* ("They complained . . .") is always in the passive form, since it reflects on the complainer. We might say that it expresses a certain sense of self rather than of objective reality.

A month exactly after leaving Egypt, the people again complain, this time of hunger (16:1). Here, they escalate the absurdity of their narrative: "If only we had died by the hand of God in the land of Egypt, when we sat by the fleshpots, when we ate our fill of bread! For you have brought us out into this wilderness to starve this whole congregation to death" (16:3).

It would have been better, apparently, to die with full stomachs in Egypt than to starve in the wilderness. Whatever else can be said about their Egyptian experience, one thing is clear: not to leave Egypt would have been better than to leave. God responds by sending the "bread from heaven," the manna. And the people "test" Him by disobeying His laws regarding its collection.

Immediately after this, the people again lack water; and again "think thoughts" about leaving Egypt: "Why (*Lamah*) did you bring us up from Egypt, to kill us and our children and livestock with thirst?" (17:3). They are given water, and the place is named (Massa and Meriva) to memorialize the "testing" (*massah*), the "dispute" (*riv*) of the Israelites with God: ". . . as though to say: Is God within us or not?" (17:7). This, again, is a grave question: it emerges from the narrative as the unspoken core of the dispute that the people have with God. Some of its implications we will explore later; here, I would like simply to point to the word *riv* ("dispute"), which expresses not merely a "complaint" but a real argument, a difference of opinion. (On one level, it is a legal expression for the opposing sides in a court of law.) Here, then, the people confront God, not simply with an immediate grievance—a need for water—but with a radical question about the nature of His relationship with them. At this point, Amalek appears and threatens the newly liberated people. He is defeated in war. This time, the Israelites are, significantly, silent.

Each of these points of tension deserves discussion. However, although God's design to prevent a return to Egypt has clearly been effective, all these moments of rebellion are, indeed, moments when the Israelites "think their thoughts" about the issue of the Exodus. Moreover, they express their thoughts in words. And all with impunity; God does not seem to be angered by this kind of thinking, of speaking.

Indeed, we might say that God has set aside for them a kind of "academic space" in which, precisely, to do their thinking. For this activity to be innocuous, they need the protection of a vast wilderness, so that acting on their thoughts becomes too complicated to be realistic. Their "crooked road" into the wilderness gives them, paradoxically, a freedom to think, to ask their subversive, sarcastic questions. It gives them, also, the outrageous freedom to "zigzag," not only geographically but intellectually, emotionally.[12] The road that is *akuma* ("crooked," "devious") threads through places of vision and faith and, adjacently, places of doubt and revision. It makes possible a journey that is like a graph curve (a modern Hebrew meaning for the word, *akuma*), zigzag lines joining highs and lows, discontinuities that are intellectually baffling to the reader, but that are presented by the narrator in a matter-of-fact, empirical spirit: this is the way it was; this is the way it is. These discontinuities cannot be avoided, or dispelled.

The Private Realities

At the conclusion of *The Varieties of Religious Experience*, William James emphasizes the concrete, individual experience, the "private realities," that may be narrow but always remain "infinitely less hollow and abstract than a science which prides itself on taking no account of anything private at all": "The axis of reality runs solely through the egoistic places—they are strung upon it like so many beads."[13]

These private realities, issues of momentum and energy, stagnation and lassitude—most of all, issues of personal narrative and the construction of meaning—assume physical form: in the realities of food, water, existential danger. Unflinchingly, the Torah traces the abrupt metabolic changes in the narrative of a people for whom, in the most obvious way, the body is a reality; the stomach, the innards, the heart, remain a continual reminder of dependence, risk, relationship. Both peril and ecstasy are grounded in the needs of the body[14]; and suffuse religious narrative with shifting, kaleidoscopic colors.

In view of this emphasis on the "particulars of rapture," what is *said* acquires new importance. The drama of the Exodus is invested in verbal responses, querulous, suspicious, as well as in the outburst of song—words and melody—that greets the miraculous act of God. At this stage, the graph curve of the people's progress through the wilderness is drawn through their volatile language—not through their acts. If the midrash praises them for their loving faith in following God, unprovisioned, into the desert, that praise focuses not on a heroic act, but on what they *did not say*:

> "Even provisions they did not prepare for themselves" (12:39): This tells the praise of Israel, that they *did not say*, "How can we go out into the wilderness without provisions;" but they believed and went, as we find clearly in Jeremiah 2:2: "I remember to your credit the devotion of your youth, your love as a bride, how you went after Me into the wilderness, into a land not sown."[15]

Similarly, when they obey God and, instead of proceeding to travel away from Egypt, they turn around toward the Red Sea, the midrash lingers, not on the act but on what they avoid saying:

> "And they did so": To tell their praise, that they obeyed Moses and *did not say*, "How can we go back in the direction of our pursuers—we need to flee from them." But they said, "We have only the words of the son of Amram!"[16]

The essential point here seems to be that they are praised for avoiding the hackneyed responses of a tired common sense. What they do not say is what anyone normally would say: they display a freshness of response, a capacity for transcending the obvious that expresses a newborn sensibility. At other points, of course, they say precisely what might have been expected; and God's disappointment is a kind of tolerant acceptance of a banal utterance.

"What?"—The Corrosive Moral Challenge

In a saga about body states, thinking and speaking, then, it is remarkable that the key word is *Mah*. The "What" question recurs constantly in the mouth of the people, of Pharaoh, of Moses, of God Himself. The thinking of thoughts, to which God allocates desert space, follows a trajectory that begins in physical experience and explores meanings, of past, present, and future. It also elicits from Moses answers that are themselves couched in the *Mah* form.

To list some of these *Mah* questions: Pharaoh pursues the Israelites, thinking, saying: "*What* is this we have done, releasing Israel from our service?" (14:5). The Israelites, for their part, attack Moses in their panic: "*What* is this you have done to us. . . ?" (14:2). They "cry out" to God and He answers Moses: "*What* (why) are you crying out to Me?" (14:15). Later, when they lack water: "*What* shall we drink?" (15:24). Responding to their complaints about hunger, Moses and Aaron twice say, "*What* are we (that you should grumble against us)?" (16:7, 8). The manna falls from the sky, and the people ask one another, " '*Man hu?*—What is it?' For they did not know *mah hu*—*what* it was" (16:15). To their second complaint about thirst, Moses responds, "*What* (why) are you in contest with me? And *what* (why) are you testing God?" (17:2). The people complain, "*Why* (*Lamah*) did you bring us up from Egypt?" (17:3). And Moses, in his turn, cries to God, "*What* shall I do with this people?" (17:4).

These questions can be divided into simple "What" questions and more sophisticated, effectively "Why" questions. "*What* shall we drink?" is a simple cry for water. However, as Cassuto remarks, *Mah* carries with it, as in Arabic, a strong sense of the negative: "*What* (why) are you crying out to Me?" is God's way of telling Moses *not* to cry to Him.[17] Addressed to another, the *Mah* question holds reproach, repudiation. Even the simple question, "*What* shall we drink?" is therefore clearly ironic: it challenges Moses to provide what is lacking. It is also unanswerable; instead, Moses cries out to God for help. Similarly, Moses and Aaron's "*What* are we. . . ?" is not as simple as it appears. Obviously, they are denying responsibility for the whole project of the Exodus: it is not their idea, but God's. Since they are angry at the people's suspicions that the whole story was of their engineering, their rhetorical question also expresses, however, a radical humility that the Talmud reads as a desirable human stance before God.[18] "*What* are we?" is compared to Abraham's "I am just dust and ashes!" (Gen 18:27); it even transcends Abraham's humility, in the tendency of the word *Mah* to evaporate into nothingness—*What* are we?—a mere wisp, a hollow question?

I am suggesting that even the "simple" *Mah* questions veil corrosive moral challenges. The *Mah* questions that demand a "Why" translation are more manifestly reflective, subversive, restless. "*What* is this that we have done?" Pharaoh asks himself, after releasing the Hebrew slaves: "*What* is this that you have done to us, in taking us out of Egypt?" the Israelites ask Moses: "*Why* are you crying to Me?" God asks Moses: "*Why* are you quarreling with me, *why* are you testing God?" Moses asks the people: "*Why*, then, have you brought us up from Egypt?" the people ask Moses. These questions interrogate the narrative of redemption: on Moses' side, they speak of the senselessness of the people's chafing against themselves and God; on God's side, they reject Moses' prayer, in a way that cries out for interpretation; on the people's side, they expose the countervoices that invert the narrative at every point. The *Mah* tries to push to the limit of the known, the obvious. To ask "What" or "Why" is not to ask for scientific definitions (in the vein of Mr. Gradgrind's "Definition of a horse"[19]), but to probe the unknown, to insist on depths yet to be plumbed.

One example is the Egyptians' apparently unremarkable question: "*What* is this that we have done?" As an idiomatic, rhetorical gesture, this simply indicates a change of heart on the part of the Egyptians, as the Torah itself comments (14:5)—equivalent to the sudden sense of "I must have been mad . . ." Such changes of heart, however, only seem inexplicable; the question may be rhetorical, but it invites a closer look at what in fact has changed. Midrashic narratives elaborate on this question of the change in the Egyptians' sensibility. One narrative is particularly compelling: after he has released the Israelites from Egypt, Pharaoh and his subjects realize what they have lost:

> "And (*vayehi*) when Pharaoh released the people . . ." (13:17) Who cried *Vai*—"Woe!"—Pharaoh! This is like a king whose son went abroad and was hosted by a wealthy man; the king sent frequent letters to the man, asking him to send his son home, till finally he went himself and brought his son home. Then, the wealthy man began to cry about losing the prince. His neighbors asked him, "Why are you crying?" He answered, "It was an honor for me while the prince stayed with me, because the king sent me letters and needed me and I was distinctive in his eyes . . ." That is what Pharaoh said, "When the Israelites were with me, God had need of me and I was distinctive in His eyes—He constantly sent me letters, saying, 'Thus says God, God of the Hebrews: Release My people!' " So when God came down and released His people . . . Pharaoh began to cry, "Woe (*Vai*) that I released the Israelites!"[20]

What Pharaoh has lost is a sense of *gravitas*, of *kavod* ("honor," "importance," "weight"). In all his resistance to God ("I shall *not* release the Israelites!"), he was involved in the high drama of being *needed* by God. Now, in obeying God, he subsides in a kind of spiritual breakdown: "Woe is me that I let them go!"

The irony is sharp: Pharaoh has finally done God's will in letting the Israelites go; but he has lost the vitality generated by God's challenges to his resistant heart. He needs to hold Israel captive, to draw on himself all the fire of God's plagues, in order to sense himself as in some sort of relationship—even an adversarial one—with the unknown God of Israel. With all the pain, and however indirectly, God was speaking to him. It is to recapture that ultimately suicidal sense of drama that he pursues the Israelites.

Such a reading, unusually, explores the changed world of Pharaoh's sensibility, without any reference to external changes.[21] In modern terms, we might speak of a sadomasochistic pathology, in which the tormentor requires the excitement of breaking taboos, the battle with conscience to give substance to his life.

If we couple this process of self-knowledge with the parallel *Mah?* question asked by the Israelites—"What is this that you have done to us. . . ?"—a similar pathology appears. Retrospectively, the people realize the drama, strangely satisfying, of being the victims, the desired ones, in a battle between God and Pharaoh. Now, released from the perverse fascination of the Egypt situation, they face a cruel death in the wilderness—the end of the story. In asking, "What is this that you have done. . . ?" they are really reproaching Moses, "Why on earth did you do it?"—emphasizing the losses entailed in a redemption that, on the face of it, seemed entirely benign.

We may fruitfully compare this question with the question God asks Eve, after the Sin: "What is this that you have done?" (Gen 3:13). This is, in fact, the second question in the Torah: first, He asked Adam a cluster of questions, "Where are you? Who told you you were naked? Did you eat of the Tree. . . ?" "What is this you have done?" by contrast, does not ask for the facts of the case; almost incredulously, God asks Eve, "Why on earth did you do this?"—referring to Adam's blaming her for seducing him. Her answer is, in rational terms, something of a *non sequitur*: "The serpent seduced me, and I ate." But it answers the hidden question, the rhetorical bafflement of God: "How could you. . . ?" As Rashi points out—on God's question of Adam, "Where are you?"—God knows where Adam is; He asks only in order to enter into relationship, into dialogue with the human being. The question drives Eve to an emotional truth that takes account of the mystery in human experience. Now, dialogue can begin.

Similarly, when the Egyptians ask themselves, "What is this that we have done?" or when the Israelites challenge Moses, "What is this that you have done?" the effect is to move beyond the world of facile rationalizations, to become aware of incongruities, gaps between the "public narrative" and the inner debate. In this sense, the people's challenge, ugly, ungrateful, and misdirected as it may be, represents a necessary truthfulness, a way of opening up a new depth of dialogue with Moses and with God.

At the very least, the people cry out of primal fear—"And they were very afraid . . . And Moses said, 'Do not be afraid . . .' " (14:10, 13). Moses responds by speaking of vision: ". . . see the deliverance which God will work for you today; for the way you see the Egyptians today you will never see them again." Instead of reassuring them about the objective outcome of the present crisis, he speaks of their personal perspective. Fear is born of a way of seeing; a changed way of seeing will change their feeling and thinking. It is this level of experience that the word *Mah* addresses: Pharaoh recognizes an unspeakable loss; Eve admits to her embarrassing gullibility; Moses responds to the challenge of adversary narratives by speaking of fear and personal vision.

The Enigma of Manna: Blank Misgivings

In all these cases, *Mah* expresses an unexpected challenge to the "normal" account of events. The central case of the *Mah* question, however, is, of course, the issue of the Manna, the miraculous "bread from heaven." Plausibly, the manna is named *man*, "because they did not know *what* it was" (16:15). Moses answers their question, now preserved in the name, by saying, "That is the bread that God has given you for eating." Nevertheless, the people's question of one another adheres to the food forever—despite Moses' explanation.

There is another reading of the name *man*, as meaning "a food preparation" (Rashi): for lack of any specific knowledge, they name the substance by this generic term. In both cases, the main feature of the *man* is its unknown identity. In one case, it is named for the mystery, which remains essential; in the other, its name evokes the sense of providence, of God's concern, which, precisely because of their bafflement, becomes its essential feature. Certainly after Moses' explanation, the people are confirmed in their sense of God's loving care for them; there is no need to change the simplicity of their first naming.

According to the first reading, however, there is a kind of absurdity in retaining the name—"What is it?" after Moses has explained its proper function. What is encrypted in the name manna, it seems, is the "un-knowing" of the first response: the awareness, perhaps, of an enduring mystery, beyond all the explanations. Bewildered, the Israelites turn to one another, seeking enlightenment. The absolute naïveté of their question, irreducible, childlike, evokes Wordsworth's lines, celebrating

those obstinate questionings
of sense and outward things,
Fallings from us, vanishings;
Blank misgivings of a Creature
Moving about in worlds not realized.[22]

Indeed, the meaning of the manna as intimating "worlds not realized," is the subject of Chasidic discourses by Sefath Emeth and Mei HaShiloach:

> The very fact that they *did not know* what it was is, in itself, the "bread that God commanded." For the purpose of knowing is to realize that we

> do not know . . . God remembers "how you followed Me into the wilderness, into a land not sown" (Jer 2:2), on which the Sages commented: "We were drawn after You, like cattle. 'Human beings and cattle You save . . .' (Ps 36:7)—those who are sagacious like human beings, yet see themselves as unknowing as cattle." (Chullin 5b)[23]

The paradox of the *Mah* question, then, lies in its sagaciousness, its penetrating, human cunning, and, at the same time, its eternal sense of otherness, of unanswerability. Without a real question, there can be no real answer and, at the same time, no real delimitation of what can be known. The greatness of the questioner is measured both by his astuteness and by his willingness to know that he cannot know. His understanding of the limits of his knowledge is fired by his sense of another world of knowledge, intimated but never penetrated.

The manna gift, therefore, is the gift, simultaneously, of knowledge and of "attraction": "We were drawn after you . . ." The "capacity to be drawn after someone or something," as Adam Phillips puts it, is quite different from the act of knowing:

> There is life before knowledge, and somebody before words. And every life is constituted through the generations that precede it, like an obscured inheritance ("Our simple childhood," Wordsworth writes in Book V of *The Prelude*, "sits upon a throne / That hath more power than all the elements").[24]

To be obsessed with acts of knowing, with becoming *expert*, is to ignore the primal reality of "being absorbed" in a given world.

Mei HaShiloach carries the idea further. He notices that the order of the narrative is reversed: first, we should have been told that "they did not know what it was," and then, "therefore, they called it *man.*" He suggests that, in fact, they saw clearly *what* it was, but could not fathom how this ethereal frosty substance could sustain them. This very bafflement, the sense of dissonance between the physical world and this barely embodied stuff—this is what Moses then defines as the "bread that God has given you for eating, to sustain your lives." That is the existence of Israel, the knowledge that "Not on bread alone does the human live, but on anything that God decrees" (Deut 8:3).[25]

Here, again, the manna sustains in as far as it baffles the banal definitions of the knowing mind. "Not on bread alone"—the sense of manna as *not* what was expected, the sense of human understanding as dependent on mysterious gifts, in itself nurtures the spiritual life of the people.

Manna as unknown, messenger from "worlds not realized," expresses the further reaches of the *Mah* question. "Thinking their thoughts," everyone involved in the Exodus asks this question: Pharaoh, the Israelites, Moses, and God. It is the motif of the Exodus, performed in different tonalities by each of the protagonists.

Its resonances go back, clearly, to the "four questions" of the children of the redeemed. As we have seen,[26] they range from the naive *Mah zoth?*—*What* is this?—of the "simple" son, to the embarrassing, unanswerable *Mah ha'avoda ha-zoth*—"*What* is this labor?" of the wicked son, and to the request, not only for factual information but for a sense of the father's subjective "taste" of the wise son. The failure among the sons, on our reading, is the son who does not know how to ask. There is not a hint of a *Mah* to be found in his mouth—so he is told the official version of the story—perhaps the words will "open" something in his mind (*ath petach lo*—"You open for him!").

In this book of revelation, knowledge is the purpose of all the signs and wonders and plagues of the Exodus.[27] The purpose of the Exodus is "to *know* that I am God." The revelation at Mount Sinai provides transcendent knowledge. But, at the same time, the motif of "not knowing" pervades the book, indeed, the whole Torah. From Pharaoh's "I do *not know* God," mirroring his original description as "*not knowing* Joseph," to the final description of Moses' death ("*No one knew* the place he was buried" [Deut 34:6]), the consciousness persists of a "cloud of unknowing": of another world, perhaps adjacent to this one, partially intimated, not mastered.

Pharaoh's tone is, of course, at polar distance from the narrative description of Moses, who "*did not know* that his face radiated light" (Exod 34:29). For the people, Moses is always one whose essence remains hidden from them: as they begin pressing Aaron to make them an idol, they say, "This man Moses—we *do not know* what has happened to him" (32:1). On one level, they are backing up their demand of Aaron to make a "god who will walk in front of us": Moses has unaccountably failed to return from Mount Sinai. On another level, however, as the midrash recognizes, they see Moses as "dead on a bier": Satan shows them an image of Moses gone away from them to another world, his dead body supine in the ether, essentially out of reach.[28] They respond with their constant sense of "not knowing" what Moses is about. This distance between Moses and the people represents the encounter both with the Other who is God, and with the other who is one's fellow human being. Levinas describes the "infinity" of the face of the other as its "open impenetrability." In this sense, not knowing comes to express one face of knowing. We shall return to this theme later.

2. *Song from Silence: The Terror in the Sea*

Vision and Terror

In considering the nature of the epiphany at the Sea, the order of events is important. The Israelites enter into the midst of the Sea, on dry land, pursued by the Egyptians. At daybreak, *Va-yahom* (14:24)—God sows confusion among the Egyptians, chariot wheels are lost, and they decide to turn back. At that point, God tells Moses to stretch out his hand over the Sea, and the waters fall back into place, submerging the retreating Egyptian armies.

In this description, the middle section, in which the Egyptians sense that God is fighting against them, is introduced by the word *Va-yahom*: God "sowed confusion among them." Here, Seforno picks up on a complex midrashic tradition and reads *Va-yahom* differently:

> *Va-yahom:* God confused them with all kinds of illnesses—as we find with the Philistines ("The hand of God was against the city, in very great confusion [*mehuma*]: they were all stricken with hemorrhoids" [1 Sam 5:9]). These illnesses are behind the reference in Deuteronomy 7:15 to the "evil diseases of Egypt." They explain the reference to the "great Hand of God that He wielded against the Egyptians" (Exod 14:31), which Israel *saw and feared.* This fear of God's great Hand is the *fear of the Egyptian diseases*, of which we read in Deuteronomy: ". . . of which you were terrified . . ." (28:60). The ten plagues contained no such diseases, except for the boils; while the Deuteronomy passage refers to *both* boils and diseases.

Seforno here resolves a textual problem: What and where were these diseases experienced? However, he also engages with a midrashic tradition that we narrate on the Seder night: that there were fifty plagues at the Red Sea, five times as many as in Egypt itself.[29]

What does this claim achieve? It seems that one main effect of this scenario—the Egyptians are painfully contorted with disease, even as they plow their way through the mud of the sea bottom—is to convey the fear that the Israelites feel, *for themselves*, at the sight of their enemies' pain. Rather than rejoice at their enemies' pain, they see themselves mirrored in it—"There, but for the grace of God . . ." This is the meaning of the verses toward the end of Deuteronomy, in which Moses warns the people of the costs of disobeying "this honored and fearsome" God: the punishment will be persistent and horrifying diseases, a reliving of "all the Egyptian diseases, of which you were terrified . . ." (28:58–60).

Their fear is based on the knowledge that they are not different from the Egyptians, that they are flesh and blood, vulnerable to punishment. Rashi emphasizes the personal nature of this fear:

> ". . . of which you were terrified" (28:60): This refers to the "plagues," when Israel saw the grotesque plagues that befell the Egyptians, they feared that they might befall them, too. One can see this clearly in God's warning after the Red Sea is split: "And it will be if you listen intently to God . . . all the diseases I have inflicted upon Egypt I shall not inflict upon you." (Exod 15:26)

A threat is useful only when it refers to what is truly feared. The fear with which the Israelites witness the massacre of the Egyptians rises from a recognition that they, too, are not exempt from the human condition. The Song, therefore, is no conventional outburst of triumph. It arises as an intention from Moses' heart, perhaps an unexpected response to the awed silence with which his people view the havoc of Egyptian bodies.

The most general description of the condition of the Israelites in the Red Sea is quoted by Rashi: the divine angel who walks in front of the Israelite camp is a figure of God's harsh justice, of that dimension of God's persona that threatens them with harsh and precise judgments:

> "An angel of God (*elohim*)" (14:19): *Elohim* invariably refers to "harsh justice." This teaches that Israel was placed in the scale of justice, at that time, whether to be saved or to be destroyed together with the Egyptians.

With this quotation from Mechilta, Rashi introduces the resonance of terror in the experience of the Israelites as well. Their fate hangs in the balance. As they run along the miraculous corridors between the surging waters, they sense the pursuit of the Egyptians, and also the plagues of disease from which they are assured of no immunity.

In an extraordinary version of a famous midrash,[30] the angels refrain from celebrating the Egyptian defeat because they see the anguish of the *Israelites* all night long.[31] In the better-known version of the midrash, it is the drowning Egyptians, "the work of My hands," that God pities and prevents the angels from celebrating. That version of the midrash is, of course, beloved of humanists for its universalist vision of God's concern. In the version we are now considering, however, there is an assertion about the Israelites' experience of that night. Terror, anguish, the knowledge that their lives tremble on the verge—these are the modes in which the Sages convey the experience of those ominous corridors.[32]

In some real way, the Egyptians and the Israelites are not clearly differentiated. The Israelites were redeemed from slavery, but were not, in fact, ripe for redemption. God, as it were, took out a mortgage on the future. The women played with their mirrors so as to achieve an *anticipatory* vision of their potential selves. This fantasy may be sufficient to release them from bondage. But in the moment of narrow scrutiny, pressed between the protective-menacing walls of water, their destiny is not assured. Fear accompanies them, each dry step is a miracle of salvation. Even when they sing their Song, the last part expresses their prayer about the future perils of historical process.[33]

We might ask: What is this fear good for? Why is this motif introduced into the miraculous saga of the Red Sea? The text replies: They saw, they feared God, they had faith, they sang. The procession of clauses allows us to say: Fear engendered faith and song. On the face of it, this is not a promising sequence. But as we explore further, the connection between fear of God and the Song will become clearer.

The Timing of the Song

To this end, it is rewarding to consider the *timing* of the Song. The mode in which the Israelites entered the Sea is widely celebrated as a paradigm of the "leap of faith." On the verse: "The Israelites entered into the midst of the Sea, on dry land . . ." (14:22), the midrash asks, "Did they enter 'in the midst of the Sea,' or 'on dry land'?" And answers: "From here you learn that the Sea was not split for them until they came right into it, up to their noses—only then, it became dry land."[34] The miracle, that is, happened only after the people had committed themselves entirely to God. On the threshold of death, they experience, most viscerally, the restoration to life, as the waters surge apart to either side of them.

Less known is the passage in the Talmud that discusses the praise-response to miracles:

> One who sees the corridors of the Sea should give praise and gratitude to God, as it is written: "And the Israelites came into the midst of the Sea, on dry land."[35]

Ha-amek Davar comments that the later verse—"And the Israelites went on dry land into the midst of the Sea" (14:29)—would be a more appropriate text to make the point about gratitude; for it describes the *end* of the walk through the Sea—they have already traversed the dry corridors ("they *went*"). This conveys the idea that the right moment to praise and thank God is at the *end* of the story of salvation: when one has emerged from the protective but menacing corridor of massed waters, one blesses and sings in gratitude. The point of entry into the Sea, however, is not yet the moment for song: the power of mighty waters, restrained into walls, is not yet an environment for relief and praise.[36]

The nephew of R. Naftali Zvi Berlin (author of the "Ha-amek Davar"), R. Baruch Halevi Epstein, quotes his uncle's opinion and disagrees. He notices Rashi's comment on the "corridors of the Sea": "the place through which they traversed the Red Sea." He reads Rashi as referring to the whole length of the corridor. That is, the Talmud is urging praise and thanksgiving while one is *in the midst* of the narrative. Before the tension is resolved, before one has emerged from the undetermined, ominous passage—that is the time for gratitude and song.

The implication of this reading is that the people sang while they were crossing, not after emerging, as most readers assume. The timing, of course, makes a difference. Do they sing their song of praise after salvation is complete? (The text does seem to suggest this: only after the conclusion of the narrative [14:31], when the Israelites see the dead Egyptian army, are we told, "*Then*, Moses and the Israelites sang this Song . . ." [15:1].) Or do they sing while still in the unresolved course of the miracle? The difference is related to the motif of fear that we have been exploring. If they do indeed sing while still in the process of crossing, the fear and anxiety which are part of that process, the sense of their fate hanging in the balance, must be imagined as informing that Song.

Both Ramban and Seforno, among the leading commentators on the Torah, affirm that this was, in fact, the scenario. "When Pharaoh's cavalry, chariots and riders, entered the sea" (15:19). . . "*Then*, Moses and the Israelites sang . . ." (15:1). The two verses frame the Song and set it in time: the people sang *while* the Egyptians followed them into the Sea, while they walked on dry land in its midst.

The Song: Terror and Joy

In view of our discussion of the terror and suspense of the Israelite experience, then, the Song is not simply an explosion of jubilant gratitude. In the course of traversing that corridor—and as we contemplate that space of crossing—singing breaks in as an unexpected response. As we have noticed, Rashi detects a moment of choice, of hesitation, as the idea of singing rises up in Moses' mind. ("*Then*, Moses would sing . . ." [15:1].) The reality that the Song comes to express is fraught with tension: massacre, overwhelming physical suffering, on the one hand, and the joy of God's salvation on the other. Complicating this reality further, is the intimation of doom hanging over the Israelites' heads, too: they know that they are in no way exempt from the human torment suffered by the Egyptians. In a time of harsh justice, no one is safe: "use every man after his desert, and who shall 'scape whipping'?"[37]

How is it possible to sing, to praise God for acting both cruelly and kindly? Indeed, this problem (of the relation between *din* and *rachamim*, rigorous, "hard" justice and mercy) is a central theme of the Song. Here is Rashi's comment, for instance, on 15:3:

> "God is a man of war, God (Hashem—the divine name that connotes mercy) is His name": even at the time He fights and takes revenge on His enemies, He still holds to His compassion for His creatures, nurturing all living beings—unlike a human king, who turns away from all other activities when he makes war, and lacks the strength to engage in both war and love.[38]

The complex reality that is celebrated in the Song—death and life, suffering and joy, justice and mercy—transcends a simple split between "us" and "them": the suffering and fear as the enemies' portion, the joy and elation as the Israelites'. Particularly in midrashic and Chasidic writings, both extremes of response are the poles of the Red Sea experience. Here, for instance, is Mei HaShiloach:

> "If there is no wisdom, there is no fear; but if there is no fear, there is no wisdom" (Avoth). By wisdom, we understand the confidence of the wise

man; if one has no fear of God, if one does not understand that in one instant, God can take from one all the wisdom and confidence, then one's wisdom counts for nothing; one's complacency is sheer folly. Equally, however, if there is no wisdom, there is no fear: that is, one who has no confidence in God, but always reacts with nervous fear—this is a compulsive reflex, and not a true fear of God. For one who truly fears God has strength and confidence in God.

That is the meaning of the two texts: "The Israelites walked *on dry land* in the *midst of the Sea*" (14:29), and "The Israelites entered *into the midst of the Sea* on *dry land*" (14:22). The Sea symbolizes fear and prayer; the dry land indicates strength and confidence, as in the mastery of Torah, which is Israel's strength. One knows one's prayer is answered if one can move out of prayer and into the study of Torah. Likewise, one knows that one's study of Torah is true if, together with the Torah one studies, there is a cry of prayer in the heart. For one must connect the two, prayer and Torah, fear and confidence.[39]

The dialectic proposed here emerges into song. In the reading that we have been exploring, it is while in the suspense and anxiety of the crossing that Moses suddenly finds it in his heart to sing. The meeting of terror and joy, destruction and birth, takes the people beyond the normal places of speech. It takes them, we have suggested, into silence. Moses silences the people's cries, God silences Moses' cries.

The *mysterium tremendum* that is the entry into the Sea, the tearing apart of the Sea, the birth of fearful energies held in tension as Israel crosses—this reduces the people to speechlessness. And it is from the heart of that silence that Moses conceives of a Song. What is uncontainable and inexpressible, he puts to words that are written in the Torah. What remains unwritten, of course, is the melody that gives voice to the mystery.

3. *The Women's Song: Attraction and Faith*

The Song: Attraction and Narcissism

The unwritten melody that gives life to the words on the page represents a new response in the people. Sefath Emeth names this response: it is an *attraction* that the people for the first time sense in themselves, when they see God's miracles. Till now, with all the miracles of Egypt, they have lacked this "capacity to be absorbed."[40] They have known, but they have not felt themselves held, entranced by the mystery of God's presence. For the first time, that is, they experience *emuna*, "faith," which Sefath Emeth defines as just this sense of "attraction."[41] Through their own act of commitment—the leap into the sea—they are caught up in the miracle; they have earned a vital place within it.[42]

This "attraction" represents a new stage in the people's relation to God. For the transcendent moment of the Song, at least, they express an ecstatic commitment that fuses justice and love, terror and elation.

It is, however, the distinct voice of women that most poignantly isolates this new moment of "attraction." At the end of the Song sung by "Moses and the Israelites" (15:1), the women enigmatically enact their own celebration: "Miriam the prophetess, Aaron's sister, took a drum in her hand, and all the women went out after her with drums and dancing. And Miriam chanted for them, 'Sing to God, for He has triumphed gloriously . . .'" (15:20–21).

Indeed, the women's separate song casts a shadow of ambiguity back over the first song, sung by "the Israelites." On first reading, we assumed that this refers to the whole people; when we encounter the women's dancing and drumming, however, we wonder at its timing, at their previous silence. The general song of the people is revealed as, possibly, not at all general: an absence of women becomes one meaning of *benei Yisrael*—"the *sons* of Israel." A cryptic passion of women is intimated.[43]

I would like to suggest that this women's song, in particular, expresses what Stanley Cavell calls

> an encompassing sense of another realm *flush with this one*, into which there is no good reason we do not or cannot step . . . Such a view will take singing . . . to express the sense of being pressed or stretched between worlds—one in which to be seen, the roughly familiar world of the philosophers, and one from which to be heard, one to which one releases or abandons one's spirit . . . and which recedes when the breath of the song ends.[44]

The movement to this "other realm," for Cavell, is a "leap," which is the singular attribute of operatic arias—particularly women's arias—and which ends when "the breath of the song ends." The dangerous aspect of being "stretched between worlds" is expressed in the common fate of the heroine in tragic opera: invariably, she dies. "Women's singing exposes them to death, the use of the voice to the stopping of the voice." For the singing voice exposes her "power of desire." More, it exposes her as thinking, as autonomously existing.[45]

The idea of "attraction," then, as Cavell notes, is perilously close to the idea of narcissism. Referring to Emerson, he writes:

> the moral constraint upon the human . . . can be expressed as an attraction . . . Attraction as the basis of commitment—as paradoxical as taking narcissism as the basis of altruism . . .[46]

The paradox of narcissism as the basis of altruism re-evokes for us the redemptive women's work with mirrors.[47] The words that the women speak to their husbands, as they are framed together in the mirror ("I am more beautiful than you") swing the men to another place.[48] This, in itself, is the "secret of redemption."[49] The mirror drama enacts the "capacity to be absorbed," to transcend the sterile literalism and limitations of Pharaoh's decrees, of that which must be.

Fundamental to this process, however, is the ability to speak the word "I." Dynamically, this is the core of the mirror scene: she says, "I am more beautiful than you;" and "swings" her husband to answer, "*I* am more beautiful than you." This is the narcissism that lies at the base of redemption. As Franz Rosenzweig puts it:

> "I" is always a Nay become audible. "I" always involves a contradiction, it is always underlined, always emphasized, always an "I, however."[50]

> . . . Only in the discovery of a Thou is it possible to hear an actual I, an I that is not self-evident but emphatic and underlined . . .[51]

The discovery of the "Thou," whether human or divine, makes narcissism the basis of commitment. The ability to say, "I, however" is the very ground from which the leap begins.

Perhaps the most powerful biblical expression of this moment of "attraction," arising out of the encounter of Lover and Beloved, is the cry of the woman in Song of Songs: *"Draw me after you, let us run!"* (1:4). She opens herself to the "other realm" of an attraction that will take her out of all conformities, out of the realm of the known. On the basis of a mere intimation from her lover, she proclaims her readiness to be united with him. And, immediately, "The king has brought me into his inner chambers"; there is a marriage—"Let us rejoice and delight in you"—and even today the woman still celebrates her original instinct to unite with her lover.[52]

This blissful narrative of attraction and faith that is retroactively vindicated does not, however, represent the whole narrative of Song of Songs. Traditionally read as an allegory on the history of redemption from Egypt, the narrative reaches a point where Rashi's reading introduces the painful complexity of reality:

> "Hark! the beloved! There He comes, leaping over mountains, bounding over hills" (2:8). [After describing in the most ardent way the love of the couple,] the poet returns to the beginning of the story—like one who condensed his tale and then returns to the beginning, saying, "I did not tell you the beginning of the story." He had narrated that "the king brought me into his inner rooms," but not *how* this happened—the full process of *how* God came to them with loving words in Egypt. Now, the poet returns and says: "This attraction, the *meshicha*, that I narrated, when my lover drew me and I ran after Him, this is how it was: I had lost all claim to redemption [literally, I spoke despair of redemption] till the four-hundred year period foretold to Abraham was over. But my Lover came, before the prescribed time, like one who leaps over mountains, bounds over hills . . ."

In Rashi's version, what has been left out of the passionate original narrative, where attraction is followed immediately by consummation, is the anguish of despair, the sense of distance that God overleaps with deerlike swiftness (2:9). Only in retrospect, after the marriage has been in place for a long time, can the poet realize the brokenness of the people before the Lover leapt into their world. As with Lacan's *"corps morcelé,"* the fragmented body-image of the child before the "mirror-stage," the construction of the past-before-redemption becomes possible only *after* redemption. Only after there is a knowledge of wholeness, of an "orthopedic totality," can the "disintegrated self," the "corps morcelé" be imagined.[53]

In this process, where imagination constructs both future and past, "attraction" is the first stage. In our discussion of the crossing of the Red Sea, the "attraction" is expressed in the Song, in which, "pressed or stretched between worlds," the people abandon themselves to the future, to a transcendence of the "roughly familiar world of the philosophers."

Song: The Undoing of Women

Cavell claims that the woman's voice in opera expresses the extremes of pain and pleasure, and the desire for a realm of transcendence. Breaking beyond the limits of the world, the heroine must die.[54] Cavell's inspiration in this discussion is Catherine Clément's book on the woman's voice in opera. She writes: "Opera comes to me from the womb. . . They will tell you that hysteria is a sickness . . . Do not believe it. Hysteria is woman's principal resource."[55] Provocative in style and content, this sentence enacts its own claim: "Hysteria is woman's principal resource." Song comes most naturally from the womb, from a relation to music and its desires, its "thinking," that is found most undisguisedly in the female.

From the transcendent yearnings of the woman's voice in song we return to the situation of the whole people at the Sea, or in the Sea. For Sefath Emeth,[56] this is a crucial moment. Since the Exodus, they have been in "great danger." They have been redeemed, but God has taken them "beyond themselves." They have not underwritten the miracles of Egypt with an "attraction" of their own. At the Red Sea, however, they come to a point, the very brink of song, where they see the power of God and have faith. If they see the miracle, then what kind of faith do they experience? If God's power has become empirical fact, what would faith mean? Sefath Emeth answers: "This time they saw the miracle and *were drawn after it.*" For the first time, they know what it is to be absorbed in the relationship with the Other. They have escaped the "great danger" that is inherent in a love where one side is without "attraction."

At this point, Moses is inspired to song. After the Song is over, the women's movement into song is described separately: "Then Miriam the prophetess, Aaron's sister, took a drum in her hand, and all the women went out after her with drums and dancing. And Miriam chanted for them . . ." (15:20–21). Led by Miriam, they sing a song, of which the first line, at least, is different from the men's song: "Sing to God, for He has triumphed gloriously."

This focus on the women's song, separating it from the men's, leads us to reconsider Cavell's description of women and song, in the context of the midrashic material. Perhaps the most ecstatic line in the Song, attributed generally to Moses and the Israelites, is "This (*zeh*) is my God and I will glorify Him" (15:2). This line, expressing a most immediate awareness of God—*Zeh*, in midrashic code language, signifies the "pointing finger," the visual, concrete apprehension of the object—is attributed, in the most important midrashim, to the women and infants among the people. Here are two examples:

> "This is my God": He revealed Himself in His glory to them, and they pointed their fingers at Him: a maid-servant at the Red Sea saw what even the prophets did not see.[57]

> When the Israelite women came to give birth (in Egypt), they did so in the fields, and God sent one from the highest heavens to clean and tend to them, like a midwife. So when God appeared to them at the Sea, they recognized Him first, as it is said, "*This* is my God . . ."[58]

In the first midrash, the "maid-servant" is not specifically a description of female experience: rather, it is a mode of logical inference, the maidservant marking the *least* visionary, the bottom rung of the ladder of spiritual sensitivity. The point is clear: *even* the maidservant saw more at the Sea than the greatest visionary in his prophetic moments.

In the second midrash, however, we find quite a different role for the women, who cry out, in instant recognition, "*This* is my God!" These are women who have given birth in Egypt—"in the fields"—that is, in fear of discovery and of the immediate killing of their boy babies. Shuddering in travail, these women have felt the shadow of death—both the "normal" shadow that hovers over all births, and the extraordinary circumstance of the Egyptian terror, which has set itself against babies and birth.

In this situation, God sends "one" to act as midwife, guiding mother and child into the world after birth. Clean and ready for the new world, both mother and child trail clouds of glory, dormant memories of the chasm that lay between that world and this. God's messenger is called in one source "an angel";[59] but, in another, we read that "God, in his own glory, descended . . ."[60] And this latter reading is clearly more appropriate to the theme of the midrash. For the women *recognize* their midwife when God appears over the Red Sea: what they have experienced of love and care in their own moment of crossing—at the breaking of their own waters—becomes a key to understanding the miracle at the Sea. From their most intimate knowledge of the verge, the seam joining life and death, they are "first" to know the God who splits the waters and brings life through to another shore.

In this reading, God Himself is the midwife, physically cleaning and soothing the rawness of birth. With Him are associated the fear, the pain and also the "encompassing sense of another realm flush with this one." These women are "naturally pitched at the brink"; they have the sense of "being pressed or stretched between worlds."[61] In response, they sing, communicating their knowledge of both worlds: again, in Cavell's terms: "one in which to be seen, the roughly familiar world of the philosophers, and one from which to be heard, one to which one releases or abandons one's spirit."

Unlike Cavell's singers, however, these women do not die—or, at least, not in any simple sense. But they encompass death in their Song. As we shall see, at least one Chasidic commentary goes very far in description of the "pitch" of the women's Song.

At this point, however, perhaps the clearest thing we can say is that, in their intimate vision of God—"*This* is my God . . ."—there is no vestige of the *Mah*, the "*What*" question, which belongs to this world, the one "in which to be seen, the roughly familiar world of the philosophers." The *Mah* has been entirely subsumed into the clear energy of "*This* is my God . . ." About this kind of experience, there can be no doubt: such a face at such a time cannot become blurred in memory. God's appearance at the Sea makes the women leap into song—". . . and I will glorify Him." A visual experience has become an oral one, as God's beauty moves from an external impression to the very surge of human desire. The Song, at its climax, cries out not "*What*" but "*Who*"—*Mi* not *Mah*: "*Who* is like You, O God, among the mighty!" (15:11). This is personal ecstasy, the pure sense of being entranced by an Other, a Person, inexpressible but intimate.

In this midrash, women sing but do not die. And yet, on another level, as Franz Rosenzweig perceives, it is always women who die of love: "Initially it is for the beloved that love is strong as death, even as nature has decreed that woman alone, not man, may die of love."[62] The voice of women singing of love, or of the birth-knowledge of God, expresses the inexpressible: "for the soul, revelation means the experience of a present which rests on the presence of a past, nevertheless does not make its home in it but walks in the light of the divine countenance."[63]

Such a Song of revelation indicates another world, another Face. In midrashic language, it conveys the idea of the "revival of the dead."[64] This Song, initiated by Moses, is headed by the future verb: in fact, a literal rendering of 15:1 begins, "Then Moses *will* sing . . ." The whole Song walks in the light of the divine countenance; encompassing death and love, past and present, in an awareness of what is "not yet." The birth imagery, focusing on women's recognition of God, most precisely conveys the sense of transformation. For the midwife's role is exactly this: with practical skill and knowledge to clarify ("clean," "beautify") what may be, to make it viable.[65]

The Women's Song

At the end of the Song,[66] Miriam (the prophetess,[67] as the Torah emphasizes) leads the women responsively in another Song. She is, indeed, named for the first time, as she sings and dances; though she figured prominently in chapter 2 (bringing the infant Moses to his mother to nurse), she has remained anonymous, simply "Moses' sister," until now. Essentially, she plays the role of Moses among the men; she sings and the women answer.

Strangely, however, the Torah describes Miriam as responding to the *men*: "And Miriam responded to them—*la-hem*," whereas a response to women only would be indicated by the exclusive feminine pronoun, *la-hen*. The clearest contrast to the men is that the women play musical instruments—"drums"—and dance during their Song; also that the opening words of their Song—"Sing to God . . ." are not identical with those of the men's Song—"Let me sing to God . . ."

The musical instruments are the focus of Rashi's comment which, I would suggest, engages with the difference between the two Songs:

> "With drums and dancing": the righteous women of that generation were confident that God would do miracles for them; so they brought drums with them from Egypt.

The "confidence of the women"[68] is their first and main response to the men's Song. All the difference of what the women bring to their Song is crystallized in these drums, expressive of faith in what is not yet. In all the anxiety of the redemption, when, as Sefath Emeth termed it, the Israelites are not really "attracted" by the miracles, the women have a quasi-physical assurance of future miracles to consummate those already experienced. They *prepare for miracles*: almost a contradiction in terms. They are set for wonder, carrying the instruments of song with them through the corridors of fear. They have always known—at least since the mirror work with their husbands, or since their encounter with God as midwife—that the future is incipient in the present.

The drums, then, express their faith in a world touching this one, "from which to be heard." What the women add to the men's Song relates to the theme of "the future in the present." For the women, as we have seen, this is no theoretical notion, but one lived in the flesh. The fact that "Miriam, the prophetess," leads the women reminds us of her prophetic function in the dark days of Egypt.[69] But, more poignantly, her very name is connected with the bitterness (*Marah*) of those days. The midrash links her, unlike the other redeemers, Moses and Aaron, back to the beginnings of Egyptian persecution:

> "I had no peace" (Job 3:26): from the first decree that Pharaoh laid upon me—"And they *embittered* (*va-yimareru*) their lives" (Exod 1:13) . . . But then God raised up a redeemer for me—that is, Miriam, *named for bitterness.*[70]

The very origin of the story of the Exodus is signified by "bitterness." Still nameless, and with this bitterness of her people's suffering in her veins, Miriam rises as a prophetess. She redeems it, but not in a magical sense. She does not make it disappear: rather, she re-deems it, she re-thinks it, she sings it into a different place. Forever, her name will speak of it. Her Song will arise from it, anticipating the future without denying present and past.

The Song: Women in the Middle

The singular position of Miriam and the women who "go out after her," is caught in a haunting midrash that begins with the classic desire of the angels to sing a song of trimph:

> When Israel came out of the Sea, the angels came to sing first, in the presence of God. God said, "Let My children sing first"—as it is said, "Then [God said], Let Moses sing!" (a play on "Then, Moses *will sing*"—in the future tense). So David the Psalmist said: "First come singers . . ." (Ps 68:26)—these were the Israelites who stood by the Sea—". . . then musicians . . ."—those were the angels. Why? God said to the angels: "It is not because I want to humiliate you that I say, Let *them* sing first. But because flesh and blood should sing first, before one of them dies. But you, as long as you desire, you remain alive."
>
> This is like a king who saved his son from captivity. The palace servants wanted to praise the king, and his son also wanted to praise him. They said to the king, "Our lord, who shall praise You first?" He answered them: "My children, from now on, whoever wants to praise Me, shall praise Me." So when the Israelites came out of Egypt and God split the Sea for them, the angels wanted to sing a Song, and God said, "Let

> Moses and the Israelites sing first—and after that, you shall sing: 'First come singers'—that is, Israel; 'and then musicians'—that is, the angels."
>
> ". . . among maidens playing drums:" these are the women, who gave praise *in the middle*, as it is written: "Then Miriam took the drum in her hand . . ."[71]

God halts the angels in their desire to sing. Human beings, "My children," must sing first. The reason that God gives relates precisely to the "inferiority" of human beings to angels: because they are flesh and blood, because they are mortal, singing is urgent for them, it cannot be postponed—"before one of them dies." Unlike the angels, who preserve their being eternally, human beings live under the shadow of death. It is this that gives bitterness, an essential melancholy, to song. "The individual pinch of destiny,"[72] as William James called it, requires the redemption of song, as song requires that "private" reality to give it a place to leap from. The king decides the issue of priority by asserting his relationship with the weak and powerless. The Song that cannot be delayed is that of the "children of God," mortal, flesh and blood, with time's winged chariot audible behind them.

The midrash plays, of course, with the reader's expectations. Where the naïve reader might have expected the angels, close to God, immortal, unembodied, to be given priority, (s)he finds that it is, paradoxically, the human being, time-bound, mortal, embodied, who sings first. It is only, however, when the midrash passes beyond this rather predictable reversal,[73] and engages with the ending of the verse from Psalms, that a claim of greater stringency is made. The strange phrase "*amidst* (*be-toch*) maidens playing drums," is turned around in the midrash: "*in the middle* (between human and angelic), are the maidens playing drums"; and these maidens are associated with Miriam and the singing women.

Placing the women in the middle, in time and space, breaks up the binary simplicity of the pattern. It compels us to question the urgency of the Song, as it relates to human beings; or, conversely, to confront the separate status of women, "between" the human and the angelic. It seems that this is no glib, courtly compliment to the female. Quite precisely, the narrative says something about women as different from men, in relation to song. If men have priority, it is, we have suggested, because of the urgent mutual need of music and the mortal. For women, it seems, this need is not as urgent; for angels, there is no pinch of destiny whatsoever.

Why are song, music, voice, and drum less urgent requirements for women? We may suggest that it is because women come to the miracle of the Sea already prepared. They recognize God, after their own travails, at the verge of death. They come set for transcendence, miracle, and song. They have been attuned to bitterness and death and to a realm beyond them. Rosenzweig articulates the link between women's experiences of love and death:

> Already in the tremors of love her heart has become firm. It no longer needs the tremor of death. A young woman can be as ready for eternity as a man only becomes when his threshold is crossed by Thanatos . . . Once touched by Eros, a woman is what man only becomes at the Faustian age of a hundred: ready for the final encounter—strong as death.[74]

In her Song, the woman has the strength of experience. This makes her song less poignant, less sharply necessary. In the midrash, the women who play drums "in the middle," between human beings and angels, are, in Hebrew, *alamoth*—young girls. The word evokes youth, speed, and passion, the leap of the young girl seeking transcendence.[75] It is also a midrashic code word for Miriam, who is called *ha'alma*—in the early narrative of her finding a wet nurse for Moses (2:8). Rashi's comment there treats this word almost as an adverb: she goes off on her quest, vigorously, buoyantly, like a young *alma*.

Our midrash, then, in quoting Ps 68:26, evokes this buoyancy of Miriam that removes her, with her timbrels, from the existential anguish of "flesh and blood." If we summon up another association with the strange word, *alamoth*, we find an earlier verse in Psalms: "For God—He is our God for ever; He will lead us beyond death (*al-muth*)" (48:15). *Al muth*, as two words, indicates immortality—"beyond death." God, eternal guide, is pointed out—*zeh elokim*—" '*This* is our God . . .' " Connecting the two verses, we have a richly evocative concept: Miriam in her buoyancy, with her timbrels, her ardor, expecting miracles and song to develop out of bitterness, becomes a paradigm of faith in a God who will lead human beings beyond death.[76] With the women who "go out after her," her Song is heard at the brink of eternity.

From here, we may take one more step. This is one of the midrashic descriptions of the world to come:

> In future, God will lead the dance of the righteous, as it is written: "Set your hearts upon the walls of Jerusalem" (Ps 48:14): *Le-chelah*—"walls,"

> is read, but the written text has *le-cholah*—"upon the dance." They, the righteous, will rise up with *almuth*, with agility, buoyancy, total energy, and point at Him, as it were, with their fingers, and each will say: " 'For this is God, our God for ever'—in *al-muth*—like those young girls of whom it is written: '. . . amidst maidens playing timbrels' " (Ps 68:15). Aquillas translates: in the world beyond death (*athanassia*). *Olamoth*—that is, God will guide us in both worlds: in this world and in the next.[77]

The word *alamoth* introduces two jarring concepts: of youth and love,[78] and of death.[79] *Al muth*, however, introduces death, *thanatos*, only in order to transcend it. Eternity now becomes part of the complex resonance of the word. The vision of the future places God at the center of a circle dance (*cholah*): eternally wheeling around God, pointing fingers with passionate immediacy at the heart of the circle, the righteous transcend death. In this image "beyond death," the righteous are compared to "young girls," specifically to Miriam and her women drummers—both because of the association with timbrels and because of the reference to the dance (*bi-mecholoth*).

Such a reading would claim a place for Miriam's ecstatic Song at the Sea that vies with that of Moses. The question of difference in the women's Song focuses on two things: the timbrels and the actually changed text: "Sing to God . . ." instead of "I will sing to God . . ." A provocative interpretation of these differences is offered by R. Kalonymos Kalman Epstein, author of *Ma'or Va-Shemesh*.[80] This is, in fact, the third of three different interpretations offered by him: the previous two place Miriam and the women, quite conventionally, in a position inferior to that of Moses. In them, by virtue of her femininity, the spirituality expressed in Miriam's Song remains incomplete.

Miriam's Circle Dance

In his third discourse, however, R. Epstein focuses on the midrash about the ultimate dancing circle of the righteous: he reads the women's dance at the Sea as the type of this ultimate choreography of the human relationship to God. The circle is a kabbalistic image for equality: all points on the circumference are equidistant from the center, hierarchies (figured by a straight line) disappear. The basic hierarchy, in kabbalistic thought, is the relation between masculine and feminine, the one who bestows and the one who accepts. All classical notions of teacher and student, higher and lower are modeled on this linear, hierarchical relation. By contrast, the circle expresses the eschatological future, where all will see God's light equally, and all categories, including the division of masculine and feminine, will become irrelevant.

Miriam leads the women in such a circle dance, intimating that supreme condition of spiritual consciousness. Moses, still bound by the categories of masculine/feminine, could sing only of a future circle song: "I *will* sing to God . . ." But Miriam, with her circle-dance, *drew down* (*mashcha*—"to attract") the transcendent light, achieved the highest possible awareness, and therefore could sing, in the present tense: "Sing to God!" There is a striking theurgic motif here: a suggestion that her circle of women constructs a new reality. In this circular modality, in all its feminine imagery, she transcends hierarchies, differences between masculine and feminine.

Most unconventionally, R. Epstein attributes to Miriam and her dance a more sublime consciousness than that of Moses. She transcends all categories and brings into the world of the present what Moses can only anticipate in the future. It is striking that, in this interpretation, it is the dance that generates the light: the women produce an energy in the light of which all participate equally in the presence of God. R. Epstein quotes Jeremiah: "A woman shall encircle a man" (31:22); and "No longer will they need to teach one another, for all of them, from the least of them to the greatest, shall know Me, says God" (31:34).

The Song of Miriam here becomes a dimension of the ultimate circle dance, with its ability to transcend this-worldly polarities: male and female, giver and receiver. Perhaps, we can suggest, her dance song also encompasses the other great polarity: birth and death. Unlike the men, the women already know God. The revelation at the Sea is for them something of a confirmation, since God's appearance in a place of danger and fear is their own intimate awareness writ large. Bitterness is the basis of Miriam's being. She has learned, in the private, spontaneous sphere, the leap into Song. She is practiced in miracles, and expectant of them. Attraction, the ability to draw God's light down into the world, is grounded in an already instinctive bodily sense of "being attracted" to the "other realm."

For this reason, perhaps, she does not sing first. Her relation to song is knowing, physical; her fear of death less clamorous. Her Song is realized in the present, rising up with assurance from the bitterness that is its origin. At the same time, she is *betoch*—in between men and angels—"pressed or stretched between worlds." Attracted to the "other realm," the "one from which to be heard," she sings, she releases her spirit. For R. Epstein, by force of her desire, she "draws down" the supreme light. For Cavell, the moment of stopping is the end of the singer's being: "women's singing exposes them to death, the use of the voice to the stopping of the voice."[81] In the Torah narrative, there are no deaths, as first the men and then the women end their Song. Instead, there is a triumphant final line: "God shall reign for ever" (15:18). A claim is made on eternity,[82] even as, according to our reading, the people still tread the precarious floor of the sea. "God shall reign": an inspired challenge to time? Or a prayer that what has been known in the course of the Song may continue throughout history?[83]

4. *Miriam's Well: A Songline in the Desert*

Adjacency: Ecstasy and Bitterness

As the Song ends, the people emerge on the opposite shore. It is then that they see "the Egyptians dead on the shore of the sea. And when Israel saw the mighty Hand that God had wielded against the Egyptians, the people feared God; they had faith in God and his servant Moses" (14:31). At this juncture, after the Song, there is a baffling midrashic tradition that asserts that the people revert to skepticism, to counter-narratives, and say, "Just as we have emerged on this side of the Sea, the Egyptians are coming up on the other shore, and will be pursuing us. Only when God actually showed them the dead bodies of the Egyptians, did they 'have faith in God and his servant Moses.' "[84]

This disenchanting midrash shows the Israelites as returning instantly to their previous mode, their worst fears overpowering narratives of faith and hope. This, in itself, the instantaneous backlash after the visions at the Sea, is a dismal comment on the durability of ecstasy. All too immediately after the ecstasy at the Sea, it seems, quotidian reality returns. What they do not see with their own eyes, they do not believe. They revert to the empirical, the this-worldly, the "roughly familiar world of the philosophers," the world "in which to be seen."[85] Till they see the Egyptian corpses, all theories are possible; and a congenital anxiety about the master-narrative of redemption resumes its sway.

The tension of "adjacency," of the skepticism immediately following the ecstasy of the Song, is exacerbated by the language used in the verse that the midrash quotes to prove its point: "Then they rebelled about the Sea, at the Red Sea" (Ps 106:7). The word for "rebellion"—*meri*—may not immediately draw our attention; but the Israelites then travel for three days, without finding water, and arrive at a place called *Marah* ("bitterness"), where they complain about the undrinkable, bitter water. At this point, we cannot avoid noticing the *mar*-root: it occurs four times in one verse (15:23). We remember that Miriam is named for that bitterness, for her capacity to redeem undrinkable water. The sound *mar* resonates with the *meri*, the rebellion on the shores of the Sea; and—of course—with the bitterness in which the redemption story began: "They embittered their lives" (1:14). Miriam has seemed to recede from the narrative after her Song; but now she is uncannily evoked in these words of bitterness and rebellion. On an unconscious level, her presence is intimated throughout the people's reversion to skepticism, to the *What* questions ("What shall we drink?" [16:24]).[86]

The connection between Miriam and Marah is confirmed by a classic midrash: in recognition of Miriam's Song,[87] a well springs up in the desert. This well, the gift for Miriam, miraculously accompanies the people on their travels through the wilderness. When Miriam dies, it disappears.[88]

Clearly, Miriam's Song brings the gift of spontaneous water, gushing freely from the depths of the desert itself. (It is actually a *rock* that accompanies them and flows on demand.) Something of the woman's mode of singing is reflected in this "natural" miracle of the well. At the same time, this well begins in a bitter place, the very rock that Moses will strike in a wasteland. For Rephidim evokes Marah, the second thirst is inevitably associated with the first. The bitterness of Marah seeps through. Miriam's name and sensibility will always accompany the Israelites, with their paradoxical play on opposite poles: bitterness and sweetness, rock and water.

The connection between opposites is Miriam's gift to the people. For this problem of "adjacency," of what might vulgarly be called "mood swings," will describe the history of the Israelites, throughout the wilderness. Transcendent vision, followed by drought and skepticism: this will become a pattern that Miriam's well, essential but almost totally effaced in the Torah text, quietly addresses.

"The best feelings of our nature," Wordsworth says, are those which "though they seem opposite to each other, have another and a finer connection than that of contrast." The connection is "formed through the subtle progress by which, both in the natural and the moral world, *qualities pass insensibly into their contraries*, and *things revolve upon each other*."[89] The "crooked route" that God sets for the people may become an emblem for their spiritual and intellectual route through the desert. They are detached from civilization, not merely geographically—"as the crow flies"—but in terms of the convolutions of their inner lives. The zigzag course of their experiences requires the drawing of lines to join the jagged points. Instead of a map to guide them, they have their own history to contemplate, a graph curve (*akuma*) to draw, if they are to detect how "qualities pass insensibly into their contraries."

5. *After the Song: Bitter Water and the Gift of the Sabbath*

Marah: The Post-Ecstatic Mode

The moments of profound experience—at the Red Sea and at Mount Sinai—occur in wastelands, where water is not all that is lacking. In the reading of Mei HaShiloach, for instance, the three days without water become a hiatus of spiritual aridity:

> After their great preoccupation (*esek*, involvement, busy-ness) at the Red Sea, where they sang the Song, and after the great revelation in which "a maidservant saw more than the prophet Ezekiel," they travelled for three days, without God bestowing upon them any further revelation (literally, any experience of renewal). That is the meaning of, "They did not find water:" they did not find any desire or delight, and they became very dejected. Then, God "showed him a tree" (16:25); Onkelos translates, "God *taught* him counsel:" that is, that this low-ebb time, without any "busyness," also contains the light and goodness of God. Since it is God's will, it too constitutes a profound goodness—as we have learned in the midrash: "He made the bitter sweet."[90]

The "bitterness," in this account of "post-ecstasy," is precisely the loss of ecstasy. Now, there is a period of ennui, almost, one might say, of boredom. Adam Phillips describes boredom as a "diffuse restlessness . . . the wish for a desire." In children, this is an ordinary experience: "the bored child is waiting, unconsciously, for an experience of anticipation"; his boredom is "akin to free-floating attention." In this sense, with all his irritable confusion, "the child is reaching to a recurrent sense of *emptiness*, out of which his real desire can crystallize." In his customary mode of paradox, Phillips celebrates the virtues of boredom. The adult should not try to distract or interest the child, for boredom offers an opportunity—to confront emptiness, and to take one's time to find one's desire.[91]

Phillips's epigraphs are illuminating:

> "Life, friends, is boring. We must not say so."
> —JOHN BERRYMAN, "DREAM SONG 14."

Phillips's point is precisely that the essential boredom of life *should* be admitted and confronted. Again:

> "Inability to tolerate empty space limits the amount of space available."
> —W. R. BION, COGITATIONS

"Empty space" is one way of describing a wilderness. In this sense, the heart of the wilderness experience for the Israelites will have to do with the encounter with emptiness, with boredom. Like Phillips's child, who is "a sprawl of absent possibilities,"[92] the Israelites are looking, undistracted by ready-made objects of desire, for something to hold their attention.

THE ENCOUNTER WITH EMPTINESS

Phillips quotes a passage by D. W. Winnicott, in which he describes how the baby, after a period of hesitation—ignoring at first the shining tongue depressor placed near him—will accept the reality of his desire, and place the spatula in his mouth, chewing or "smoking" it. No one tries to resolve the baby's hesitation. "Instead of expectancy and stillness there now develops self-confidence."[93] The period of hesitation is a necessary stage in the organic discovery of desire; any attempt to force the infant is violently resisted.

Boredom, Winnicott suggests, is the stage before there is a spatula to be found. The child needs to have "the full course of the experience": boredom, expectancy, unforced desire. This scene becomes for Winnicott a paradigm of the analytic process. The child is "only able to find his desire again in so far as his testing of the environment affords satisfactory results."[94] After this testing period the child, the patient, is "ready to use" the object—the spatula, the "good" interpretation.

This model becomes, I suggest, a powerful key to reading the "boredom," the restlessness, the hesitation of the Israelites after the preoccupation, the total absorption, of the Red Sea. "They could not find water"; an arid time ensues, without passion or desire. And God "teaches" the "profound goodness" of the vacant time, that it offers an opportunity for them to find their own desire. They must find, in the dry, unmiraculous wilderness, something that makes sense for them to use.

To this end, God lets them walk in the endless emptiness, which is the essence of the desert. The prophet Hosea calls it "a thirsty land" (*taluvoth*) (13:5). Rashi comments: "a place where one desires all good things and does not find them." This experience of the "sprawl of absent possibilities," is a part of the full course of what they are to encounter. When they are arrested by a desire—thirst or hunger—then hesitation ceases. This is a difficult time, as Winnicott and Phillips note: it is the time in which the people test God, repeatedly.[95]

Shabbat: The Paradoxical Gift

The simple question for the bored adult, Phillips suggests, is "What does one want to do with one's time?"[96] This question is, ultimately, the focus of the passage in Mei HaShiloach. The emptiness, the lack of passionate preoccupation is bitter—and then sweet. God teaches its "sweetness," homeopathically, as it were: by giving them, at Marah, the place of the bitter water turned sweet, the laws of Shabbat, the day of rest. This is a traditional reading[97] of the words: "There, He made for them statutes and laws" (15:25)—"There, God gave them a few sections of the Torah to *preoccupy* them: Shabbat . . ." (Rashi).

Effectively, the gift of Shabbat is, like the spatula, an offer of a *preoccupation*, an object of passionate desire. It is given early in the journey, before Mount Sinai, even before the empirical Shabbat experience of the manna, which does not fall on Shabbat and requires human involvement to engage with its absence. Now, it is given in the form of a *law*: structured to hold the attention of the people. In itself, however, Shabbat is the very enactment of "vacancy"—of "not-doing," of an apparent lethargy. In the "empty time" of Shabbat, the question of the wilderness comes to its sharpest expression: "What does one want to do with one's time?" In its earliest form, therefore, Shabbat is a paradoxical gift—bitter-sweet, curing the bitterness with bitterness.

Before the people can decide that they can "make use" of this gift, time must elapse. The natural course of things will move from the sheer articulation of the law of Shabbat to the tangible experience of the absent manna, the "gift" of Shabbat: "See! God *has given* you the Shabbat . . ." (16:29). One might say that this time, as it develops into the "period of hesitation," of which Winnicott writes, is similar to Keats's "diligent indolence."[98] Out of this apparent lethargy, blankness, there arise for the artist the images and words that will preoccupy him. This is the fertile gap that Mei HaShiloach describes, and that the gift of Shabbat enacts.

When Shabbat becomes an object of desire, it is associated with the manna, which falls as food (satisfaction of desire) and as mystery ("What is it?"). Recognizing their desire, the people name it as essentially unappeasable. The ongoing *Mah* question, empirical, skeptical, modulates from restlessness and boredom to "expectancy and stillness." They acknowledge the essential mystery of desire: "The soul cannot be filled" (Eccl 6:7). Even as they eat, a deeper expectation awakens.

In all the complaints and quarrels of the Israelites, the problematic process of discovering desire is significant. As they recount their bitter narratives of a vengeful, malign deity who births them only for death, they search for something to hold their attention. In reality, for something to love, to become absorbed in, in full conviction of being loved. God, like the mother in Winnicott's experiment, must absent Himself, recede from the mode of miracles, in order to allow the people to discover their own desire.

6. *A Center of Gravity? "Remusicking" the People*

Ecstasy and Boredom: Only Connect?

The problem for the Israelites becomes, we have suggested, the problem of connecting opposite experiences. How is the ecstatic revelation of the Red Sea to be connected with the arid, uninspired waiting that follows? The people thirst for water, for intimations of transcendence, and find its absence bitter indeed.

After thirst comes water; after hunger, quails and manna. And again, there is thirst—"There was *no-water* (*ayn mayim*) for the people to drink" (17:1). The word *ayn* connotes "nothingness," a fearful vacuum of all that gives human beings a sense of a "local habitation and a name" (*Hamlet*). Here, explicitly, as the *ayin* sense engenders counter-narratives—"*Why* have you brought us up from Egypt?"—Moses responds by naming their condition: "*Why* (*Mah*) are you disputing with me? And *why* are you testing God?" The people's agitation, their *Mah* fictions, are turned against Moses, and he again cries out, "*What* shall I do with this people?" The rock, in full view, is split apart by Moses' staff and the water flows. This is the rock, the well, that will accompany them through the desert.

But the problem remains: how to connect the "boredom" with the ecstasy, the wilderness with the gift of water. Miracles are isolated events; in some real sense, they do not meet the needs of the people. If, as Winnicott suggests, the essential project of growth is the discovery of desire, of what Sefath Emeth calls "attraction," this must pervade the inner world at all times—the empty times as well as the ecstatic times. Miracles, in a sense, only cause the people dejection, as they sense their own helplessness to continue the work of desire.

"Is God in Our Midst?"

In a most powerful sentence, the Torah condenses the essential problem of the Israelites. The place where the people complain about water is named for their complaint and for their testing of God. This in itself is strange, since the story was apparently about their testing *Moses* (17:2): it was only Moses who, in his response, spoke of their testing *God* (17:3). But the sentence continues: ". . . for their testing God, *saying*: *Is God* (*ha-yesh*) *in our midst, or not* (*ayin*)?" (17:7). The fact is that the people were never, in the course of the narrative, heard to say this. It is as though the Torah is revealing repressed meanings, indicated by the word *leimor*—"saying, as if to say": this testing, apparently a political suspicion of Moses' authenticity, *really meant to say*, "Is God in our midst, or not?"

In other words, the apparent rebellion against Moses is a screen for a much more radical question. This question, which brings to an end a section of the Torah that focuses on the *Mah* question, is, at its core, a question about *Yesh* and *Ayin*: Is there . . . or is there not? The either/or alternatives engage with the problem of being—to be or not to be. Against the backdrop of *Ayin*, of non-being, of a wilderness in which miracles, even the daily miracle of the manna, cannot affect the spaces in between, the people ask, not about the existence of God or about His power—they have had ample evidence of that; but about His being "*in our midst*"—or else, *ayin*—there is nothingness.

Most graphically, Rashi quotes a midrash on this radical question (17:8):

> "Then Amalek came": The people's question is immediately followed by the menace of Amalek, as if God said, "I am always among you, and ready to provide all your needs; and yet, you say, 'Is God among us, or not?' As you live, the dog will come and bite you, and you will cry out to Me, and then you will know where I am!" This is like a man who set his child on his shoulders and went off on a journey. Whatever delicacy the son saw, he would ask, "Father, get me that!" and his father would do so. This happened several times, till they met someone and the son asked him: "Have you seen father?" His father then said, "You don't know where I am?" And threw him off him, and a dog came and bit him.

The relationship of child and father is carefully delineated. The child is set on his father's shoulders: that is, he cannot see his father, but only the gifts his father constantly hands up to him. These gifts are a response to need; as the child demands, so the father provides. The basic relation between them, then, is one in which the child, quite plausibly, feels omnipotent. As in early infancy, before separation, the child senses no gap between self and other. To want is to have.

Therefore, the shock of the child's question—"Have you seen father?"—is more apparent than real. At first, the reader assents to the father's outrage, even perhaps to his punitive anger. But on second thought, the child's question seems not so outrageous. For the child cannot see his father, only his gifts. The question itself implies a new stage of development: an awareness of separateness. As he rides his father's shoulders, he originally feels his father to be an extension of himself, part of his "oceanic" consciousness. Now, he is assailed by a new awareness, and requires to see his father.

The father's reaction, excessive and harsh as it seems, also has psychological purpose. By throwing the child off his shoulders, he gives the child, for the first time, a sense of separateness. Now, helpless on the ground, with the dog approaching, the child can *see* his father. The world of reality, of differentiation and alienation, opens up: this is Amalek, representing the bite of the disenchanted world. The paradox, of course, is that precisely from out of this hard reality, it becomes possible to see God, or to see, at least, where He is not.

This parable is intended to explain the people's question: "Is God in our midst, or not?" Quite exactly, their question relates to what is "in their midst," at their core. Straddling his father's shoulders, the child wonders about what lives at his center. He may sense his father, but only as an extension of himself. He requires the distanced perspective of a differentiated other to attest to his father's place. His question is, therefore, a question of "Where"—not "What" or "Who" or "Why" but "Where." That is, "How do I relate to him in my newly sensed identity and complexity?"

The people's question: "Is He in our midst?" similarly expresses an almost impossible desire: to see Him as located in the most intimate center of the self. In the parable, the child first asks another person, trying to appropriate an external perspective on his own reality. But the father will not allow this strategy—the child must find his own answers: "From my flesh, I shall see God" (Job 19:26). For the people, the question is a matter of life and death: ". . . or not"—literally, "or else, *ayin*, nothingness." If God is not at the center, then—nothingness.

We remember Jeremiah's accusation, defining a later devolution of God's people: "*They never asked themselves, 'Where is God*, Who brought us up from the land of Egypt, Who led us through the wilderness, a land of deserts and pits, a land of drought and darkness, a land *no man had traversed, where no human being had dwelt*?' " (2:6). An essential question has fallen out of use; but here, sensitive to the wasteland into which they are precipitated, they ask the intimate question of relationship—or, at the least, as the Torah implies (". . . *as if to say*, 'Is God in our midst?' "), they have a repressed awareness that this question underlies their "testings" of God.

A Center of Gravity?

What can the people mean by requiring God to be situated "in their midst"? The Torah itself articulates the people's question as an unspoken, even repressed, but essential demand. Behind all the screens, the demands for water and food, this is the real need. They have quarreled with Moses, and Moses has asked them, "Why do you dispute with me, why do you test God?" There is something enigmatic about the people's "testing" work: Moses is baffled and the Torah formulates the real question that is the solution to Moses' bafflement, a formula that the people themselves could not, at this point, have articulated. Moses can now name the place for the vital testing work that the people have been approaching: ". . . for their testing God, *as if to say*: *'Is God in our midst, or not?'* " What is the felt experience behind this either/or demand?

I suggest that the profound need of the people is for a center of gravity to contain the zigzags: their volatile reactions to redemption. There have been gifts, miracles, revelations, responses to their desires and fears. Equally, there have been times when "they could not find water": times of "boredom," waiting for something to happen. Knowing God only as bestower of gifts, worker of wonders, the people have seen miracles, and they have believed. They have known the "attraction" to the other realm that has momentarily appeared accessible. But they have also known the *ayin*: the days of walking without desire or fascination.

It is this experience of "separating" from God that makes them discover their own desire: to have God as a core of stability in the world of *ayin*. That is, not only "to know that I am God *in the midst of the earth*" (8:18), but to sense Him as the connecting line[99] that joins the points on the graph, the inner "songline" that maps the human world of ecstasy and disenchantment.[100] The midrash expresses the idea quite clearly: "Is God in our midst or not?"—the child needs to sense the father as part of himself, in all his vicissitudes, even in alienation and absence; most critically, in the absence of miracles. To have God at the center is to be involved with Him, sensing Him no longer as the object of a "What" question, on the one hand, or as automatic dispenser of miracles, on the other.

The midrash expresses the possible nuances of the people's demand:

> "Is God in our midst, or not?" What was their dispute? R. Yehuda said: "If He is master[101] over all reality, as He is over us, then we will serve Him. If not, we will rebel."
>
> R. Nehemiah said: "If He provides us with nourishment, like a King who resides at the center of the State, and his people do not have to ask him continually for food,[102] then we will serve Him. If not, we will rebel."
>
> The Sages said: "If we have doubts in our hearts, and He knows how we are questioning, then we will serve Him. If not, we will rebel." God replied: "If you seek to interrogate Me, let the wicked one (Amalek) come, and interrogate you!" Instantly, "Amalek arrived . . ."[103]

In the first reading, the people ask simply about God's *power* in the world. In the second, they demand a God who is not known through His gifts: that is, they stipulate a situation in which they have independence, are freed of the pressure of constant desire. In effect, they are dissatisfied with the daily dispensation of manna, the chronic dependence on miracles that the manna represents. They now imagine a condition in which they have sufficient resources to develop and provide their own sustenance, and in which God is known as the ultimate provider only. This would mean liberation from desire, and, intimately, from the daily consciousness of need that leads to God.

The third reading is the most sophisticated one. What the people want is a God who knows not only what is in their stomachs but what is in their hearts, their minds. They imagine a God who not only provides food and water, in miraculous response to their needs, but knows their inner oscillations, their stream of narratives and counter-narratives. In other words, who remains at their heart even as they detach themselves from Him. This is a need for a God who can hold the restlessness of heart and mind; who "knows," in the sense of intimacy and acceptance, that which does not know Him.

This version of the people's question speaks of God's "knowing" the uneasy fluctuation of the human heart, lovingly fathoming their discontinuities. This desire encompasses all the complaints and interrogations of God's power, or of His disinterested benevolence. God at the center now becomes a "meta-question": about that which gives stability to the volatile, the changing, the unstable. God answers: if you interrogate Me, know that that will mean painful interrogations of yourselves, in your chosen separateness.

Miriam's Well: A Songline through the Wilderness

It is against this background that Miriam's well becomes expressive: a rock that "rolls" with them (*megalgel*) through the desert, a potential object that responds to desire. In always being with them, it evokes connection, the line that joins the disjointed experiences of transcendence. In being a rock, it partakes of the unyielding reality of the desert. This is the gift given in recognition of Miriam's song which, *Ma'or Va-Shemesh* suggested, intimated a condition where all categories dissolve. It is a song that must come to an end in this world. But after it, there does not have to be death. The desire that inspires it can make use even of the differences of high and low, transcendence and limitation, boredom and fascination, to make a more continuous melody.

Miriam's itinerant well, I suggest, constitutes a kind of songline[104] through the wilderness. Wherever it rolls, it sings with an unheard music. When Miriam dies, it disappears. Its motion suggests both instability and stability (*megalgel*—"rolling"—is the movement through vicissitudes, *gilgulim*, but achieves a kind of calm sameness in difference); it appears wherever human beings are, between life and death.

At Miriam's death, it disappears; and there is one last song, the only other recorded song in the Exodus saga.[105] Once more, at Meriva, at the end of forty years in the desert, the people complain about lack of water. And Moses is angry and strikes the rock instead of speaking to it—and is banned from leading his people into the Holy Land. Despite the complexity of this narrative, I would suggest simply that the constant problem of the people has been one of "constancy," of *emuna*, faith. Moses is blamed for giving up the struggle to ignite "belief" in the people: "Because you have not made them *trust* Me enough to sanctify Me in the sight of the Israelite people, you shall not lead this people into the land . . ." (Num 20:12).

Belief, faith, trust, as Maharal articulates it, has to do with this capacity to discover in oneself an organic, "natural," and continuing "attraction" to God. Such an *emuna* can be nurtured only by words, not by blows or by anger.[106] Forty years in the desert have not sufficed fully to attune the people to the hidden melody of Miriam's song. In a tragic coda to the narrative of the desert, Moses is found wanting in the essential project of the wilderness: of helping the people discover their "natural" resources of desire.[107]

The wilderness journey is to be an exercise in stabilizing the sense of God through vicissitudes, as, gradually, He withdraws His miracles. The capacity to be "attracted" is associated, in Hebrew, with the notion of continuity (*nimshach-hemshech*). This is attraction, not as an explosion of ecstasy, but as a rhythm that links the jagged edges of experience.

For singing is more than beauty, or unsatisfied desire. In his third Sonnet to Orpheus, Rilke writes: "song is reality":

A god can do it. But will you tell me how
a man can penetrate through the lyre's strings?
Our mind is split. And at the shadowed crossing
of heart-roads, there is no temple for Apollo.

Song, as you have taught it, is not desire,
not wooing any grace that can be achieved;
song is reality. Simple, for a god.
But when can we be real? When does he pour

the earth, the stars, into us? Young man,
it is not your loving, even if your mouth
was forced wide open by your own voice—learn

to forget that passionate music. It will end.
True singing is a different breath, about
nothing. A gust inside the god. A wind.[108]

If "song is reality," the anguish for the human being lies in "Our mind is split": most sharply, in the question "But when can *we* be real?" Confronting death, nothingness, the "shadowed crossing," Rilke searches for something beyond "that passionate music." "True singing is a different breath . . ." On the difference between kinds of singing, he writes:

> It is not only the *hearable* in music that is important (something can be pleasant to hear without being *true*). What is decisive for me, in all the arts, is not their outward appearance, not what is called the "beautiful"; but rather their deepest, most inner origin, the buried reality that calls forth this appearance.[109]

The Healing Song of Redemption

The fundamental problem is one that R. Nahman addresses most poignantly, in a teaching[110] that he himself regarded as critically important for the spiritual life. Most destructive, he declares, is the problem of dejection. When one enters this wasteland a sense of worthlessness vitiates all capacity to live and to approach God. The objective facts may well be depressing; introspection may lead to a realistic sense of inadequacy and guilt. But this then generates a pathological paralysis, in which desire becomes impossible.

His solution is a kind of spiritual generosity—to oneself as well as to others. One should search in oneself for the one healthy spot, among the guilt and self-recrimination. This one spot, which remains recognizable, *must* exist. If one reclaims it, one then has a point of leverage for transforming one's whole life.

R. Nahman creatively interprets a verse from Psalms (37:10): "A little longer and there will be no wicked man; you will look at where he was, and he will be gone." "A little longer" can be read as referring to space, instead of time: one microscopic "spot" of health still to be found (*od*—that which survives and links one to one's "real self") becomes a way of banishing all wickedness. Finding the "spot" in oneself (as well as in others) becomes a therapeutic measure: one changes one's sense of oneself, and makes it possible, in reality, to be transformed.

The essential attribute for spiritual health, R. Nahman characteristically declares, is "joy." Enveloped in sadness, the human being is easy prey for Satan. Finding some basis, however tenuous, for joy, becomes a religious duty. R. Nahman is clearly familiar with sadness and the microscopic, destructive intelligence it brings into play. That way lie madness and death; and he seeks life, *in spite of* . . .

To this end, he develops a striking theory of spiritual healing as *melody*. Having found one good spot, one should continue the search for another, and yet another. Drawing those fragmentary, disjointed moments into connection with one another, one creates a *niggun*, a song: a way of drawing a line through the wasteland and recovering more and more places of holiness.

Music arises from joy, but the power of a "true singing" comes from sadness. In every *niggun*, there is the tension of the struggle between life and death, between falling and rising: the tremolo that marks the human voice. This means the affirmation of a line (*shira* [song]/*shura* [line]) that threads through the waste places. The revelation of a good place, of inspiration and attraction, is not sufficient, since "It will end." It is the continuum, the vibrating thread that generates "true singing." The thin line of a melody selects for goodness and beauty but is given gravity by melancholy, the "different breath, about/nothing. . ."

Melody, continues R. Nahman, opens the heart to prayer: "I will sing to my God while I exist (*be'odi*)" (Ps 146:2)—with my *od*, with that surviving, pure consciousness of being alive. For R. Nahman, the work of the *niggun*, the redemptive melody that vibrates between high and low, is the work of self-healing, which then qualifies one to lead others in prayer. Moses is the prototype of the leader who can inspire others to the song of redemption. The sense of dejection, of being divided from God, is the sickness from which all seek healing. Only in melody can the dislocated spots of holiness become part of a living songline, making the fragments whole.

Moses' Hands: Oscillations of Faith

In this teaching, song is the key to the gates of prayer. We return now to our zigzag narrative of complaint and ecstasy. It reaches its climax as Amalek attacks and Moses stands on the mountaintop, in this place of "weak hands" (Rephidim), and, enigmatically, directs the course of battle with his hands:

> Then, whenever Moses held up his hand, Israel prevailed; but whenever he let down his hand, Amalek prevailed. But Moses' hands grew heavy; so

> they took a stone and put it under him and he sat on it, while Aaron and Hur, one on each side, supported his hands; thus his hands remained steady until the sun set.[111]

The tension concentrated in Moses' hands is palpable. The fortunes of war depend on them; but they are heavy, gravity-bound human hands. What we witness is not an icon of the eternally inspiring leader, hands static in elevation, ecstasy shining from the gold leaf. But human hands, weary with the effort of aspiration.

In what sense can the Torah mean that victory and defeat depend on Moses' hands? Is this a magical effect of the charismatic leader who can manipulate destiny? Famously, the midrash comments:

> Did Moses' hands make or break the fortunes of war? No! But as long as Moses raised his hands, the Israelites would *look at him*, and have faith in the One who had commanded him to do so. As a result, God did miracles for them . . .[112]

The role of Moses' hands is to model for the people the attraction upward that is faith. His hands rise in the age-old position of prayer. One might say that, like a conductor of an orchestra, he stands in full view of the people craning their necks to look upward.

But the music that he generates is the complex music—joyful and sad—of the human heart. For his hands are heavy; and we hear in some detail about the technical arrangements—the stone, the human support—to keep them high in the air. What is the purpose of this rather ponderous description?

On one reading, the most usual one, "his hands *remained steady* until the sun set" (*emuna*, meaning, "firm," "unwavering"), so that the people might produce the inner music that is life and strength. Rashi, for instance, translates, "Moses' hands were held in faith, spread out to heaven, in a firm and faithful prayer."

As against this, there is the "true singing" of the split mind. Ha-amek Davar reads simply, "Moses' hands—*in their high position and in their low*—created faith in the hearts of Israel." Even after all the technical supports are in place, the meaning of Moses' figure, set on a mountaintop against the sky, is not static. This is a human body, straining to defeat gravity and being defeated by it. To have one's hands upstretched in prayer, to be "stretched between worlds" (Cavell), may produce a visual illusion of motionless aspiration. But if Moses, like Miriam and her singing women, is to be *heard* rather than seen, then his song-prayer will have risings and fallings, minute oscillations that are the very breath of faith.

The Work of "Remusicking"

The Parsha portion that we have been discussing is, on one level, the preamble to the giving of the Torah at Mount Sinai. Before the Torah, however, comes prayer; which means song; which engages with the problem of inconsistency and the search for inner stability. Confronting the *ayin* of the wilderness, with the gifts of ecstasy sharp in memory, the people must begin to develop the even tone that contains the extremes of high and low. To sing is to enter a fully human world in which these extremes are held in tension.

No longer miracles—but song and prayer. As he models prayer, Moses' hands no longer hold the staff, imperiously outstretched over sky, land, and sea. His hands are empty, they quiver beseechingly with the weight of flesh; they create faith in the hearts of the people.

"Every disease is a musical problem, every cure a musical solution" (Novalis). Oliver Sacks frequently writes of the healing and freeing power of music. In *Awakenings*, for instance, a former music teacher, suffering from Parkinson's disease, is given motion, power, restored personality by music. "As I am unmusicked," she says, "I must be remusicked."[113]

On the way to Mount Sinai, it seems that the Israelites, too, must be remusicked. Their music is to be, like Miriam's well, a continuous accompaniment, rolling through vicissitudes, connecting the disjointed moments of joy. "You are the music/while the music lasts" (T. S. Eliot). The work of Miriam's well is to trace a songline through the forty-year-long indirection that is the wilderness narrative.

God takes the indirect route, says the midrash with a startling simplicity, so that they may traverse the wilderness, eat manna, drink of this well—"and the Torah will settle in their bodies."[114] It is their bodies that are to house the Torah. Day after day, they are to become attuned to the inner music that will allow them to move spontaneously, from a newly powerful center. This is the work of "remusicking": thoughts and questions, fears and fantasies are to be given free play, while the habit of a pure desire takes hold of their bodies. Given world enough and time, the vibrations of a new music may liberate them from the decrees of Egypt.

5 Yithro

"IF A LION ROARS . . ."

[18:1–20:23]

1. *Jethro and the Trauma of Revelation: A Paradigm*

JETHRO JOINS THE ISRAELITES: A NEW STRUCTURE OF IDENTITY?

The experience of Revelation is attended by conflicting emotions. For the people standing at Sinai at the highest point of their national history, fear vies with love, repulsion with attraction. In the biblical text, they recoil, yield place to Moses. In the midrashic narratives, the tension of desire and terror becomes central and overwhelming. The nature of this tension is the subject of our exploration: Why do the people recoil, resign their prophetic role to Moses? And how is one to relate to such a retreat?

In a characteristic juxtaposition of narratives from different registers of experience, the Torah prefaces the terror and glory of the giving of the Torah with the story of a family reunion. Moses' father-in-law, Jethro (*Yithro*), arrives in the Israelite camp, bringing Moses' wife and two sons. Chapter 18 tells in a matter-of-fact way of this family reunion, of a meal shared with Aaron and the elders, and of Jethro's suggestions for improving the Israelite legal administrative systems: essentially, he proposes a judicial hierarchy, with Moses dealing only with the problems of greatest complexity.

Although it is narrated before the Israelites' great encounter with God at Mount Sinai, this episode contains elements that lead the rabbinic sages to place it, historically, *after* Sinai. There is, for instance, the reference to Moses' work as "teaching the statutes of God and His laws" (18:16); these, obviously, could only have been administered after the Law was given. Why, then, if it happened after, is the Jethro episode narrated before Sinai?

The midrashic reading opens up thematic analogies between the Jethro narrative and the giving of the Torah. It endows the very first word of the Parsha with profound resonance:

> "And Jethro, priest of Midian, father-in-law of Moses *heard* all that God had done to Moses and to Israel his people, that God had taken Israel out of Egypt" (18:1): What report did Jethro hear that made him come and accept Israel's religion? R. Joshua said: "He heard of the war against Amalek." R. Eliezer said: "He heard of the Giving of the Torah and came . . ." R. Eliezer ben Yaacov said: "He heard of the splitting of the Red Sea and came . . ."[1]

This midrash makes a radical assumption: Jethro's "coming" is no longer a simple family affair, but rather it represents a spiritual crisis in his life, a recognition of the power of God and a desire to unite his fate, in some sense, with that of the Israelites. Read in this way, the first part of the chapter culminates in an actual ritual of proselytization. Jethro proclaims: "Now I know that God is greater than all the gods . . ." (18:11), and then: "Jethro, Moses' father-in-law, took a burnt offering and sacrifices for God, and Aaron and all the elders of Israel came to eat bread with Moses' father-in-law in the presence of God" (18:12). These are the sacrifices of the proselyte, of the one who commits himself to a full acceptance of the Torah. Indeed, they parallel the sacrifices that the Israelites bring in token of their commitment to the Covenant (24:5).[2]

In this midrashic reading, the central question, therefore, is "What did Jethro hear that made him commit himself to God and His Torah?" The word *va-yishma*—"he heard"—becomes vital: what one hears has power to move one to heroic transformations. However, the question that the Rabbis ask—and answer in three different ways—is already plainly answered in the text: "Jethro . . . heard *all that God had done* to Moses and to Israel, his people, that God had taken Israel out of Egypt." The Rabbis' discussion therefore seems redundant: Jethro heard the whole story of redemption and was inspired to join the people who experienced such wonders.

But the Rabbis are, it seems, asking a more acute question: What was the *specific* narrative that had such power to move Jethro? Behind this compelling question lies a radical understanding of the power of narrative to address the privacies of individual experience. The story that has generative power is more than a chronicle of events: it is a way of rendering a moment, a drama, that seems to resonate with the listener's inner idiom. Registering such a narrative, Jethro is drawn to hear more.

This kind of hearing, therefore, is not passive. According to Rashi, a report of one among the many miracles of the Exodus draws Jethro away from the substantial realities of his world, into the desert:3

> *Into the desert* (18:5): We also know that this happened in the desert! But the text sings Jethro's praise: that he was settled in the honor of the world, when his heart prompted him to go out to the wilderness, a place of emptiness, in order to hear words of Torah.

Jethro chooses desert nothingness over the "honor of the world." His choice is, on the face of it, absurd: that is the thrust of the midrashic reading of the words, "into the desert." The high seriousness of Jethro's intent emerges from that absurdity. Only in the wilderness can he "hear words of Torah," only a "place of nothingness" can yield him his desire.

Connecting this comment by Rashi (based on the Mechilta) with the opening of the Parsha, therefore, we decipher the core-narrative of Jethro: "He heard a story that moved him to leave all the honor of the world . . . in order to hear words of Torah." *Hearing* the story generates in him a desire to *hear* words of Torah. Clearly a different genre, "words of Torah" are made accessible to him, desirable to him, by means of a narrative.

The words "the honor of the world" (*kevodo shel olam*) bear a resonance that I would like to explore. If Jethro is presented in Rashi's version of the text as a hero of spiritual curiosity, inflamed by a story to leave all the glory of the world, then we seem to have a paradigm for the situation of the whole people of Israel, receiving the Torah in the wilderness. If such an analogy exists, indeed, it seems to be to the advantage of Jethro: unlike the Israelites, he has everything to lose in this venture. What he has to lose is crystallized in Rashi's expression, "the honor of the world." The word *kavod*—"honor"—suggests *weight* (*kaved*), a sense of position in the world, of substantial being. This he abandons in his desire to hear. And, as we read on in Rashi's commentary, we discover a continuing use of the word *kavod*, "honor," in relation to Jethro. A theme emerges that will raise questions about the inner world of one who approaches Sinai. In this extended narrative, the word *kavod* becomes a key to the paradoxes of the Sinai experience.

In rabbinic typology, Jethro is characterized as the *pethi*—the naïf, the seeker after truth, who is open to all forms of worship.[4] When, for instance, he makes his declaration: "Now I know that God is greater than all the gods" (18:11), Rashi comments:

> This teaches that he was acquainted with all the idols in the world, for there was not one that he had not worshipped.

This kind of uncalculating openness, the readiness to worship, is expressed by the word *pethi*, perhaps best translated, "gullible, seducible." In Rashi's text, Jethro's willingness to worship is conveyed in terms of his relation to *kavod*. If, for instance, he is immediately described as "father-in-law of Moses," Rashi comments (18:1):

> Here, Jethro defined his honour as being in relation to Moses—"I am father-in-law of the king!" Previously, Moses had seen his father-in-law as the source of prestige, as it is said, "He returned to Jether, his father-in-law" (4:18).

Jethro abandons all the honor of the world, the sense of a substantial identity, and now finds prestige in his relation to his son-in-law, Moses. In the next verse, indeed, he is described *only* as "father-in-law of Moses," his personal honorific, "priest of Midian," being dropped. And in 18:17, even his name, Jethro, is omitted: his identity is now totally absorbed into his relation with Moses.

The honor that Jethro has left behind has been replaced, therefore, by a new structure of identity. The vital importance to Jethro of such a structure emerges in Rashi's reading of his opening message to Moses:

> *"I, your father-in-law, Jethro, am coming to you . . ."* (18:6): "If you don't come out to greet me for my own sake, come out for the sake of your wife; and if not for her, come for the sake of her two children."

Jethro's plea here is for a demonstration of *kavod*: that the prestige in which he is held be staged by Moses. He asks for formal recognition. And indeed, "Moses went out to greet his father-in-law" (18:7):

> Great honor was done to Jethro at that time: since Moses went out to greet him, Aaron came out too with Nadav and Avihu—and who could see these leaders come out to greet him without coming out too?

This demonstration of honor for Jethro expresses a sensitivity to the situation of one who has abandoned his past, his social identity. The subtle indication in the text, however, is that Jethro actively lays claim to such validation. Rashi's commentary makes this quite clear; and produces a complex portrait of a genuine spiritual enthusiast, who hears an inspiring story that makes him abandon all the honor of the world; but who at the same time expresses a naïve concern with his *kavod*, his social prestige, even in the "place of nothingness."

Rashi's text continues:

> *"And Moses narrated to his father-in-law everything that God had done"*: in order to attract his heart, to bring him close to the Torah (18:8).

The narrative that Moses tells is one of suffering and salvation: its aim is to "attract his heart," to involve him emotionally in the Israelite adventure. The rhetoric of Moses' story subtly flatters Jethro, giving him a sense of his own importance. On the face of it, indeed, his reaction is naïvely wholehearted: "Jethro rejoiced at all the goodness that God had done for Israel, in saving them from the hand of Egypt" (18:9):

> *"Jethro rejoiced . . ." (va-yichad)*—that is the plain reading. But the midrash reads: "his flesh became *chidudin chidudin*—pins and needles [a play on the word *va-yichad*—"he rejoiced"/*chad*—"sharp"], for he was pained by the destruction of Egypt—as in the popular saying, "Even to the tenth generation, do not denigrate the proselyte's people of origin."

In this midrashic comment, Rashi intimates the complexity of Jethro's situation. On the one hand, he is drawn to the Israelite faith, he responds joyfully to the history of God's love for His people; on the other, the weight of the past still hangs heavy upon him. His involuntary nervous reaction betrays his visceral loyalties. Against his conscious intent, which has led him to abandon those loyalties, his flesh expresses his involvement with that "honor of the world," which had till now constituted his sense of specific gravity within it. Rashi may even be punning on the word *meitzar*—*mitzrayim*: "Jethro was *pained* by the destruction of *Egypt*": his pain is an Egyptian pain and arises out of Jethro's Egyptian past.[5]

In this portrait, Jethro carries the imprint of past identity, even as he is drawn to strip himself of that *kavod* and engage with the "nothingness" of Sinai. The pressure of his history makes his skin prickle; joy and pain coexist within him.

It is out of a sensitivity to the position of the one who has sacrificed his past to the demands of a future dominated by Sinai that Moses gives Jethro every compensatory sign of honor. In Rashi's narrative, Moses personally waits on Jethro at the festive meal he eats with the Israelite leaders "in the presence of God" (18:12).

The issue of honor is, then, close to the heart of Jethro's concerns. In Rashi's reading, even in his advice to Moses about the necessity for a hierarchical system to deal with the people's legal questions, Jethro's concern is focused on the honor problem:

> *"Moses was seated to judge the people, while the people stood from morning to evening"*: Moses sat like a king, while they all stood. This was hard for Jethro, that Moses was taking the *honor* of the people lightly. So he rebuked him, as it is said: "Why are you alone seated, while they are all standing?" (18:14)

Rashi interprets the text to say that Jethro is perturbed at the offense to the *kavod*, the dignity of the people. In the Torah text, however, it seems at least as plausible to read his concern as being for Moses, worn out by the overwhelming demands of the people. Before he makes his administrative proposals for a pyramid structure of small-claims courts, he specifically warns Moses: "You will wither up, as will this people who are with you . . ." (18:18). Nevertheless, Rashi, obeying a profound intuition about Jethro, places the question of *kavod* at the center. Even the idiom for Moses' exhaustion expresses the sense of weight: ". . . for the thing is too heavy (kaved) for you . . ." Rashi's comment is: "Its weight is too great for your strength." By insisting on the palpable experience of strength taxed by a burden, Rashi conveys Jethro's anxiety about *overloading*, about the possibility that a human identity may be fractured, disintegrated, eroded. His warning, "You will wither up," too, tells of erosion of the fibers of being. His concern is obviously for Moses' health, but his imagery remains preoccupied with the hazards of identity.

Jethro's advice, therefore, is to delegate the work of legal administration, as a way of lightening his burden, which others will now bear with him (18:22). The ultimate effect of this reform will be, "You will be able to stand,

and all this people too will come to its place in peace" (18:23). These expressions will resound with new power, when we come to read of the people's "standing at Sinai." In paradigm form, Jethro is staging the essential problem of the Sinai experience: Can one hold one's standing-ground there? Can one bear the burden without implosion? Can one's *kavod*, one's recognizable identity, remain intact in the encounter with the transcendent God who speaks from the wilderness? In abandoning the honor of the world, Jethro's urgent need is for the reaffirmation of the human measure.

The Trauma of Sinai: The Therapeutic Narrative

Jethro's case is the more interesting in that, according to the midrashic view, he has not personally experienced the revelation at Sinai: he comes, we remember, *after* the giving of the Torah. That is, the overwhelming scene of thunder and lightning, the endless *crescendo* of the ram's horn, and the smoking mountain have been registered by him merely in the form of a narrative. But, even in that form, it has had the power to draw him out of his *kavod* and into a place of nothingness. The power of words, of imagination, is both prodigious and unnerving. And Jethro's anxiety, revealed even in his pragmatic advice, hovers around a core awareness of the problem of *kavod*, of continued being in a recognizable self.

In this midrashic perspective, therefore, the Sinai experience is communicated to the reader *first* through the medium of one who was not there, one who came *after*. By indirection, the reader has a first intimation of the potentially destructive or humiliating power of the moment of Sinai. To some extent, indeed, the Revelation can be called a trauma. We shall consider this dimension of the Israelite experience at some length. In Jethro's case, however, the transformation that threatens to undermine his familiar reality is mediated by words, by reports ("Jethro heard . . ."); and is made bearable to him, I suggest, by the therapeutic narrative told him by Moses.

We have noticed Rashi's comment that Moses' intention was to "attract his heart, to bring him close to the Torah." One implication of this is that if Jethro is to be brought close, his emotional condition *requires* words of sweetness and meaning. His situation is volatile, with repulsion and attraction in tension with one another. Therefore, Moses tells a salvation story, which addresses the most basic anxieties and desires of the listener: "And Jethro rejoiced at all the goodness that God had done for Israel . . ." (18:9).

The therapeutic narrative, however, has larger and more penetrating power than this. We noticed Rashi's disconcerting "double reading" of *va-yichad yithro*: "he rejoiced," but also, "his flesh broke out in pins and needles." Moses' narrative engages on a visceral level with the ambivalence of a Jethro both drawn toward the Israelites and their God and fearful of the impact of Sinai upon his selfhood. His body bears within it the imprint of his past: the "pins and needles" are the symptom of subconscious conflict. It is this conflict, between the objective, "hard-edged" facts of his life, his "case-history," and the subjective yearning of his soul, that the therapeutic narrative must address.[6]

The idea of such a narrative, indeed, of a healing through story, is the subject of Rabbenu Bahya's introduction to this Parsha. Basing his discussion on the verse from Psalms: "The tongue's healing is the Tree of Life . . ." (9:7), Bahya defines the power of the tongue precisely as the power "to heal the sick-souled." This psychotherapeutic power is more effective, he claims, than that of drugs or medicines, notably in that it not only "removes the illness," but "augments human life": it is the Tree of Life. Ultimately, the reference is to the language of the Torah. By the same token, language has an equivalent destructive potential to sicken the spirit.

In Bahya's discussion, the "sick soul" is the soul that is far from God; the language of the healer can bring him to the spiritual wholeness that is closeness to God. In a classic midrash, Abraham wore at his throat a jewel-pendant that had the power to heal the sick.[7] This, writes Bahya, represents the healing virtue of language in Abraham's throat: his narratives brought people close to God. Moses, likewise, told Jethro a story of God's power and goodness that moved him to adhere to the Israelite faith. This is the man, Bahya reminds us, who left the stabilities of civilization and went into the wilderness, in order to "enter under the wings of the Shechina (the Presence of God)."

This passage speaks of the power of language from a moral rather than a psychological perspective. The therapeutic narrative is, in fact, an evangelical narrative, unequivocally guiding, by its rhetorical force, the lost soul to God. This conflation of the therapeutic and the didactic, however, does not entirely confine the healing power of the tongue to the rhetorical. For even in Bahya's own discourse, there is an instructive ambiguity about the effect of Moses' narrative: it causes Jethro to convert, but Jethro is described as the man who has already made all the necessary spiritual movements away from civilization and into the wilderness, "as soon as he heard of the Exodus." Moses' narrative works not to bring near one who was far, but to bring near one who has already come close. The virtue of the narrative, therefore, is that it engages with the ambivalences, the attraction and the repulsion, of one who, against all odds, approaches Sinai. If therapeutic language is to give life, it must address a real trauma, a wound inflicted, in a sense, by the very encounter with God.[8]

2. *Standing at Sinai: The Instability of Love and Fear*

Seeing and Hearing: Mystical Experience and Verbal Interpretation

It is with this paradigm in mind that we turn to the Israelite experience of Revelation. The contrast is clearest in the direct, unmediated quality of their narrative. Unlike Jethro who "hears" about events of the past, they themselves "see." Indeed, their awareness of this personal "seeing" is the object of God's first message to Moses at Sinai: "Thus you shall say to the house of Jacob and tell the children of Israel: '*You have seen* what I did to Egypt, how I bore you on eagles' wings and brought you to Me' " (19:3–4). Rashi comments:

> "*You have seen*": "It is not merely a tradition in your hands; it is not in language that I transmit to you, nor through witnesses that I testify to you. But you yourselves have seen what I did to Egypt. How many wrongs they had committed before they fastened onto you! Yet I never punished them till it was you they tormented."

In this reading, the approach to Sinai is through the people's consciousness of their own experience. By triple negatives, God eliminates the most normal transactions that, through time and space, communicate His involvement in the world: by cultural traditions passed from generation to generation; by the language of a messenger; or by testimony of a witness to those who have not seen. These common dislocations of experience are extraordinarily absent in this Revelation: "You yourselves have seen": the emphasis is present in the Hebrew text, but resounds with a singular force after reading Rashi.

This self-consciousness of an unmediated, personal relation with God, moreover, is, in Rashi's reading, of a particular kind. In God's punishment of the Egyptians, the people have seen a manifestation of His love for themselves. The Egyptians' civil rights record had been far from impeccable before the Israelite persecution; but it was Israelite suffering that brought God to intervene. It is, therefore, love and not hate that is the burden of this first message at Sinai. God wants them to become aware of His singular love for them. This personal knowledge then becomes the basis of a demand: "Now, if you will *listen* faithfully to Me and keep My covenant, you shall be My treasured possession among all the peoples . . ." (19:5). The sequence is clear: because you have *seen*, unmediated, events that speak of your belovedness, therefore *listen*, obey My covenant, so that your special status is underwritten by your own acts.

However, even in this unique instance in history, the unmediated vision of God's acts of love is not quite as transparent as a naïve reading might convey. For it is God's words, His interpretation, his focusing on the meaning of the Egyptian story, that constructs that awareness of direct vision. There is a quiet irony, it seems, in the rhetoric of "You have seen . . ." For ultimately, vision depends on words, on shapings, imaginings of experience. Perception depends on conception.

This irony becomes more dramatic when, directly after the Revelation at Sinai, God again says, "*You have seen* . . ." Here, with no time-elapse, no possible blurring of memory, God still finds it essential, it seems, to frame in words the epiphany that has just been enacted: "*You yourselves saw* that I spoke to you from the heavens" (20:19). Rashi again comments:

> There is a difference between what one sees and what others tell one—which one is sometimes ambivalent about believing.

Again, the emphasis is on the unequivocal certainty of personal experience. But again, I suggest the more complex "second thought": God is insistent on words mediating even this most overwhelming of visual experiences. Rashi in fact emphasizes the verbal medium: " 'Thus you shall say': in this form of words . . ."

This paradox of vision and hearing, of personal experience informed by language, irradiates the whole account of Revelation. In the most general sense, it is clear that the "Standing at Sinai," *ma'amad har sinai*, as it is traditionally called, was a visual, as well as an auditory experience: the mountain burns in fire, there is smoke and lightning. There is, also, the mysterious reference to "*seeing* the Voices" (20:15). And yet, forty years later, Moses will tell his people: "God spoke to you from the midst of the fire: 'The sound of words you hear, but no image do you see—nothing but a voice' " (Deut 4:12).

The simplest explanation of this verse is that God is focusing the people's awareness on the fact that the Revelation contained no visual representation *of God*. The fire, intense darkness, and other visual experiences are not denied. Again, however, we notice that this is an interpretation of experience—albeit a privileged one! Essentially, God is impressing on the people the true form of their perception: you heard, you did not see. And this informing of perception can only be conveyed in words—in words that privilege words and voices over visions. The fact that it is Moses who conveys God's words to the people, after the elapse of forty years, naturally increases the sense of alienation from the primary experience.

It seems, then, that in traditional readings, the most direct and transparent moment of Revelation is shot through, made iridescent, by interpretation. This raises questions about the meanings of seeing and hearing, about the relative status of mystical experience and of the world-making activity of the mind. As we explore the midrashic accounts of the Revelation, we shall attempt to catch the flashes and shadows of these questions.

"On Eagles' Wings": A Metaphor for Transcendence

Within God's opening interpretation of the Exodus history is contained a powerful image: "*You have seen* . . . how I bore you on eagles' wings and brought you to Me" (Exod 19:4). The fact that a metaphor is used at this most significant and *serious* moment, theologically considered, in world history, is in itself surprising.[9] Indeed, except for the poetic text of the Song of the Sea, this is the only metaphor in the Exodus narrative. When, in 19:18, the smoke on the mountain is compared to the smoke of a furnace, the feebleness of all imagery to express the transcendent reality of Revelation is the subject of Rashi's commentary. There is, obviously, an inadequacy about metaphor or simile that is sensed as embarrassing:

> *Merely* like a simple furnace? Not more? But the text says: "The mountains flamed in fire to the very heart of the heavens" (Deut 4:11)! But the simile is to convey to the ear what it is capable of hearing . . .

Rashi contrasts the embarrassingly weak simile with a more "adequate" factual description of the burning mountain. But the simile is justified, he claims, because of its very homeliness, its attunement to the human ear, to the need of the mind to "domesticate" the uncanny, to figure it back into the world of normal experience.

Perhaps, then, we may say that imagery is avoided when the aim of the narrative is to convey transcendence, phenomena that baffle and rupture the human mind. When, however, the aim is to have the reader search for a niche in experience to house the uncanny, an image will be used.[10] Such images are rare, and the more conspicuous for their rarity.

It is in this context that God's metaphoric flight about the Exodus strikes the reader with an exotic force: "I bore you on eagles' wings, and I brought you to Me." The effect of the image is, of course, to convey intimacy, protection, love, speed; but also, I suggest, the enormous power of the adult eagle, effortlessly carrying its young through the air. In other words, it engenders in the people a sense of their own *lightness*. It deflates their grandiosity, and evokes a relation to God, in which their *kavod*, their weightiness, becomes insignificant.

The image itself thus achieves the uncanny: it evokes past experience, the physical sensations of carrying and being carried, the imagined empathy with eagle and young, to convey a spiritual modality in which the weight, the substantiality of self are neutralized. Past identities are swept up in a rush of God's wings. History is driven entirely by God's motion. The human reality, the gravity of personal experience, is absorbed into that surge.

Such a consciousness of the unbearable lightness of being, however, is bearable only for short periods and only within the world of imagination. The metaphor is deployed, therefore, to induce in the people a momentary and partial sense of a transcendent perspective—attuned to "what the ear is capable of hearing."

The Desire for Vision

The narrative continues with Moses bringing God's message to the people:

> And all the people answered as one, saying, "All that God has spoken we will do!" And Moses brought back the people's words to God. And God said to Moses, "I will come to you in a thick cloud, in order that the people may hear when I speak with you and trust you for ever." Then, Moses reported the people's words back to God (19:8–9).

It seems that Moses reports the people's response *twice* to God (He "brought back" and he "reported" the people's words). Ha-amek Davar suggests the following scenario: first, Moses reports the fact of the people's commitment to obey God's word. Only after God has promised to allow the people to "overhear" His communications with Moses, however, does Moses respond with the fuller meaning of the people's original answer: "all that *God has spoken*—all that we personally *hear Him speak*, that we can understand for ourselves—we shall do." Their cryptic response contains within it both a simple commitment and a deeper desire for personal hearing and understanding.

Rashi opens up the issue, in his commentary:

> *"The people's words"*: I have already heard the people's response, that their wish is to *hear from You*—for one who hears from a messenger is not the same as one who *hears directly* from the King. "Our wish is to *see* our King."

Seeing and hearing are conflated in this response. The people wish to hear God's words directly; they wish to see God. In the Mechilta, which is Rashi's source, however, there are two separate issues: first they speak of direct, as opposed to indirect communication; then, they speak of seeing, as opposed to hearing. And God accedes to *both* requests: the first, in His promise that the people "will *hear* when I speak to you . . ." and the second in the later statement: "On the third day, God will come down, *before the eyes of the whole people*, on Mount Sinai" (19:11).

These two dimensions of experience, seeing and hearing, are, in the Mechilta, separated, and presumably not synonymous. Rashi, however, conflates them, conveying the impression that the desire to see God is identical to the desire to hear directly.

In Ramban's commentary on this verse, hearing from God becomes equivalent to prophetic experience:

> The people shall hear when I speak with you—and *they themselves will become prophets, when I speak*—they will not simply believe on the authority of others, as it is said, "God said to me: Gather the people for Me, so that I may have them hear My words, in order that they may learn to fear Me all the days." (Deut 4:10) Moreover, they will believe in you eternally, through all generations: And if there should arise in their midst a prophet or a dreamer of dreams, who opposes your words, they will repu-

diate him immediately. For they have already seen with their eyes and heard with their ears that you have reached the highest level of prophecy. For that reason, God said, "The people will hear when I speak with you:" they will hear My words from out of the fire, and they will know that I, God, am speaking with you, and they will believe My words and also believe in you for ever. That is what the people say: "This day *we have seen* that God will speak with a human being and he may live" (Deut 5:20)—meaning, "The possibility of hearing God speak has been *realized* by us, in the seeing of our eyes, as God desired." So, from now on, "you (Moses) go close to God"—for we know that you have attained greatness—"and listen to all that God, our God says, and we will hear from your mouth, and obey"—for your prophecy has now been validated, that it is the highest of all.

In this important passage, Ramban wants to demonstrate that the purpose of the people's "overhearing" God speaking to Moses is not simply to bolster their belief in the possibility of such communication:[11] that has been amply affirmed by them in the course of the Exodus saga. More subtly and more radically, the purpose is to give them *personal experience* of prophecy: hearing God's voice themselves, "they themselves will become prophets." For Ramban, this is the inner meaning of the Revelation at Sinai. For a certain period of time, the whole people know what it is to be a prophet. But—and this is the paradox—the effect of their knowledge is to give them a finer appreciation of Moses' superiority; ultimately, it will make them withdraw from their own pretensions, in face of his excellence. Like an amateur musician, whose appreciation of the virtuoso is sharpened by his own practice of his instrument, the people, "practicing prophecy," will have their ears more keenly attuned to Moses' virtuosity than is possible for any nonparticipant.

To convey this personal experience of prophecy, Ramban uses the visual image—"they *have seen with their eyes*"—even though the text speaks of the people *hearing* God's words. And the text he quotes from Deuteronomy: "This day we have *seen* . . ." he translates: "Prophecy has been *realized by us, with the seeing of our eyes* . . ." It seems clear that the visual expression is to convey a primary, indubitable experience. It is this that will equip them to value Moses' excellence and, indeed, to surrender their own desire in the face of his superiority.

For Ramban, therefore, the people fulfill the real will of God in desiring immediate experience, in being granted it, and—perhaps most importantly—in recognizing their limitations and passing the baton of prophecy to

Moses. This is the meaning of the enigmatic sequence of their speech in Deuteronomy: "For what mortal ever heard the voice of the living God speak out of the fire, as we did, and lived? You go close and hear all that God our God says, and then you tell us everything that God our God tells you . . ." (Deut 5:23–24). One might ask: If they have heard God's voice and survived, why do they surrender that experience? If they have emerged unscathed, that would seem to be an argument for maintaining their prophetic stature. For Ramban, however, they are now sufficiently enlightened to know their own limits. Now, they are capable of a vital appreciation of Moses' virtuosity, and they retreat from their recent desire. And God acclaims their decision: "They did well to speak in this way . . ." (5:25). The gift of prophecy was rightly given to them, so that it might be rightly surrendered.

Rashi's narrative moves in a rather different course. The people's desire to hear directly from the mouth of the King modulates into a desire to "see our King." Seeing is presented as an intensification of immediate experience. We remember, however, that in Rashi's midrashic source, the Mechilta, seeing represented a separate desire, separately granted.

Immediately following this come God's insistent instructions about limits, about cordoning off the mountain. These are given both before the descent of God upon the fiery mountain and after: God summons Moses to the top of the mountain, only to send him down again with reiterated warnings to the people: "Let not the priests or the people break through to come up to God . . ." (19:24). Rashi comments:

> *"Let them not break through"*: let them not break through their lines, out of their desire to see God, and approach the mountain slope.

The desire to see God (or, more literally, "their desire to God, to see . . .") is a transgressive force that may lead them to break their lines. "Breaking through," as Rashi goes on to explain, indicates the disintegration of a structure: "those who separate themselves from a structure of people break that structure." The "structure of people" (*matzav anashim*) most obviously refers to the lines of Israelites drawn up at the foot of the mountain. But it also carries existential connotations: the warning is against separating from the human condition. Optical desire—and as yet we have not discussed the nature of that desire—threatens ruin to self and to approved modes of constructing the human situation. Therefore, repeated with slight variations, the injunction to set bounds for the people: the importance of limits, distances, curbs on an infinite desire.

One way of understanding the danger of Sinai emerges from Seforno's commentary:

> *"Let them not break through . . ."*: when I speak with them. Lest they think that—since they have achieved the level of a face-to-face prophecy, just like you—they can ascend to your position.

Here, Seforno identifies the danger of a heightened consciousness. The intoxication that may sweep the people away is related to the prophetic experience itself. Face to face with God, they may lose all contact with the reality principle, with a sense of the distinctions and distances that characterize the human world.

The Reverse Stampede

God's concern must, of course, by definition be valid. His knowledge of human nature is privileged. But the striking paradox here is the fact that, after all these elaborate precautions against the practice of desire, the people, so far from rushing forwards, recoil from their position and, in what might be called a reverse stampede, withdraw from the mountain-base. And, in an equivalent move of regression, they surrender the immediacy of their prophetic mode to Moses:

> All the people saw the voices and lightning, the sound of the shofar and the mountain smoking; and when the people saw it, they moved and stood at a distance. They said to Moses, "You speak with us, and we will listen; but let God not speak with us, lest we die."
> (20:15–16)

Mysteriously, the Torah relates that they "saw the voices." This literal translation has inspired a range of mystical discussions in midrashic sources. It is, of course, quite possible to avoid this register of interpretation by translating figuratively, as do many of the medieval commentaries, and even some of the midrashic sources: "they *witnessed* the thunder and lightning . . ." It is the effect of this moment of perception, however, to make them move, or "shudder" (Rashi's midrashic translation of the word *va-yanu'u*) and fall back from the mountain. Is this recoil the effect, simply, of the rolling thunder and lightning and other sensory impressions? Or is there a moment in which the senses fuse, the moment of ecstasy that mystics have attempted to register, or that the symbolist poets called synesthesia?

In Ramban's view, we remember, this regressive movement is precisely the right one: their enlightenment has brought them to recognize Moses as the prophet beyond compare. But for Rashi, the situation is more ambiguous. He has emphasized the force of the people's desire; now, he must account for their retreat from desire. Quoting the Mechilta, he comments:

> *They saw the voices:* They *saw the audible*, which is impossible to see anywhere else
>
> . . . *the voices:* which were uttered by the mouth of God
>
> *and they moved: va-yanu'u* means "they shuddered"
>
> *and stood at a distance:* they recoiled twelve miles to the rear—the whole length of their camp—and the ministering angels came and helped to restore them to their place.

Rashi emphasizes the enigma of seeing voices: essentially, he says, this is inconceivable, untranslatable into other terms. It indicates an experience of God's voice without precedent or explanatory context. And in his description of the people's recoil from Revelation, a powerful and unexpected dialectic is introduced. A shudder runs through the people at each of the Ten Commandments, a wave of fear that carries them backwards the full length of their camp. Essentially, this means that the fear, the trauma inflicted by the experience of hearing God's voice, makes them, as a group, *lose their footing*: they yield the ground they have so much desired. And then, the angels help them to move forward again, to regain their former position. In other words, the people travel twenty-four miles in response to each of God's ten utterances: all in all, the Ten Commandments provoke them to two hundred and forty miles of motion![12] This is the hidden, kinetic dimension of what is traditionally known as the "Standing at Sinai."

With this powerful midrash, Rashi intimates an intensity of inner motion, an ebb and tide of response to God's voice. In order to hold their *human* position, angelic energies must counteract the long shudder that possesses them at each of God's utterances. It seems clear that it is not the *content* of the Commandments that so undermines their stability, but the very fact of hearing God's voice. And although, in the midrashic scenario, they regain their original position, their fear represents an existential reality that is expressed both in the repeated statement: "The people stood at a distance . . ." (20:18) and in their delegating Moses to act as go-between (20:16).

The Volatile Standing at Sinai

A certain human standing (*ma'amad*), an existential posture is disrupted at the very moment that is called *ma'amad har sinai*: the Standing at Sinai. This becomes stance as oscillation, a motion that rocks them to the very roots of being.[13] The Torah was given, says the Talmud (Berachoth 22a) "in dread and fear and trembling and shuddering": this was the foundational experience of their encounter with the Torah and, since these emotions can be experienced at all times, the Torah may be learnt at all times, even in periods of impurity.[14] This terror, however, which is registered in the spontaneous recoil of a nation which had recently been avid with desire, becomes, in Rashi's account, part of a vital dialectic. Like the systolic and diastolic rhythm of the heart, the people oscillate: angels are at work, perhaps God Himself assists in the reconstitution of the human position.

The extreme polarities of their response to Revelation are seen by Ha-amek Davar as expressing a moment of immense growth. The people are stretched to the limits of their strength. The effect is to release a new sense of their own capacities, a new awareness of their ability to contain previously unknown extremes. On this reading, when Moses reassures the people in this vein: "Do not be afraid, for in order to test (*le-nasoth*) you, God has come to you . . ." (20:17) and when the word *le-nasoth* is translated by Rashi, "to exalt you," Ha-amek Davar develops the idea: it is human spiritual greatness that is God's purpose in revealing Himself—the ability to endure suffering, in the immense amplification of inner resources that is the heritage of the ordeal of Sinai.

The implications of this reading are quite radical: the purpose of Revelation is to develop *human* qualities. What is enacted at Sinai is the revelation of the *human* being in larger range and strength. A new consciousness is born in this revelation; the Israelites endure an initiation that ensures them against the extremities of history. God comes at Sinai, so that the human may come fully into its own.

The Terror of Sinai

The source of the people's terror is, to a great extent, undescribed; or, rather, it is indicated in such a way as to evoke bafflement: "The people saw the voices . . ." The simplest reading, as we have seen, is that it is the thunder and lightning, the fire and the smoking darkness, the sensory trauma that precipitates the people into a new consciousness of the world. However, in the narrative in Deuteronomy, as well as in innumerable midrashic accounts, it is specifically the "voices" that provoke the traumatic response in the people. Here is the Deuteronomy version of the narrative:

> When you *heard the voice out of the darkness*, while the mountain was burning in fire, you came close to me, all the heads of your tribes and elders, and said, "God our God has shown us His glory and we have heard His voice out of the fire; we have seen this day that though God speaks with man, he may live. Now, why should we die, if this great fire consumes us; if *we hear the voice of God* our God any longer, we shall die. For who that is all-flesh *has heard the voice of the living God* speak out of the fire, as we have, and lived? You go close and hear all that God our God says, and then you tell us everything God our God tells you, and we will listen and obey." (Deut 5:20–24)

Although fire and cloud and thick darkness—the visual character of Sinai—are described, it is clearly "the voice out of the darkness" that prompts the people to surrender the immediacy of their relation to God. At first, Moses defines this as the central experience: "When you heard the voice out of the darkness . . ." The fiery mountain is secondary, background to the voice. In their speech, the people do refer to both seeing and hearing, bringing both together in "we have *seen* this day that though *God speaks* with man, he may live" (v. 21). But we remember Ramban's translation of "we have seen": "we have realized, it has become immediate to us."

The logic of their speech, however, remains enigmatic: if they have seen that it is possible to survive the strain of revelation, why do they fear death—death, specifically, from hearing the voice of God? For it is the revelation of the voice that can be fatal, and that is made equivalent to being consumed by the great fire. The mysterious question in v. 23: "Who that is all-flesh has heard the voice of the living God speak out of the fire, as we have, and lived?" elaborates on their extraordinary survival, after such revelation. But, again, we may ask: even if this survival is exceptional, nevertheless they are alive! Why, therefore, do they entreat Moses to hear in their place? Why do they limit their role to hearing Moses' words, rather than God's?

To be consumed by fire is the desire and the dread of those who hear voices. When Moses refused God's mission at the Burning Bush—according to the midrash, a seven-day resistance—the emblem of a bush that burns and is not consumed is deployed to reassure him.[15] To hear God and to speak with His voice is to burn with an inner fire. To have the voice of God speak from one's own throat is to know oneself invaded, unfamiliar, consumed. The possibility of burning, like the bush, without being entirely consumed is what compels Moses' attention in the first place. He resists, in the real and instinctive terror of the human being who both desires the fire and fears extinction.

An equivalent terror, I suggest, is experienced by the whole people, on hearing God's voice. If they, too, have become prophets, this must mean that the fire has invaded their inner being. The trauma is one of violation; they no longer know themselves.

The enigma of the Sinai moment, however, can be registered in the fact that this threatening voice is "the voice of the *living* God"; and that they are alive to speak of it. It is almost as if it is life, and not death, that they fear; as though the oscillation of their response expresses a visceral ambivalence about the life-gift that is offered at Sinai.

The historic effect of their terror is that Moses hears and speaks in their place. Moreover, the effect on future generations is that specific people, prophets, will be chosen to fulfill this role that the people now recognize is beyond their capacity. In Deuteronomy 18:15–17, the connection with the future is made explicitly:

> God your God will raise up for you a prophet from among your own people, like myself; to him you shall listen. This is just what you asked of God your God at Chorev, on the day of the assembly, saying, "Let me not hear the voice of God my God any longer or see this great fire any more, lest I die." And God said to me, "They have done well in speaking like this."

Here, as in the earlier Deuteronomy passage, God approves of their delegating prophecy. They are reclaiming an appropriate, modest human posture. Ramban, we remember, reads their short-lived prophetic experience as of merely instrumental value: it generates in them a new belief in the excellence of Moses' prophecy. Their fear is a right fear; God Himself validates it.

And yet, there is more ambiguity in the Torah text itself, and certainly in the midrashic narratives, than this account allows for. If it is the voice of the living God that terrifies them, even as they know themselves alive, then the healthy-mindedness, to use William James's expression, of Ramban's position, may seem not entirely satisfactory. The recoil of the people, for instance, is described in many midrashic sources as a kind of death:

> R. Levi said: Two things Israel requested from God—to see His glory and to hear His voice. And they did see His glory and hear His voice, as it is said, "See, God our God has shown us His glory and His greatness," and it is written, "His voice we have heard from out of the fire." (Deut 5:21) But *they did not have strength to stand*, for when they came to Sinai and He was revealed to them, they fainted (lit. their souls flew away), when He spoke with them, as it is said, "I was faint (lit. My soul left me) when he spoke" (Song of Songs 5:6). But the Torah asked God for mercy: "Does a king marry off his daughter and kill his household? The whole world is rejoicing, and Your children die!" Immediately, they revived, as it is written, "God's Torah is perfect, restoring life" (Ps 19:8).[16]

The people have no strength to stand the experience of God's glory, as expressed in "hearing His voice from out of the fire." They swoon; effectively, they die. And are restored to life, strangely by the Torah, God's daughter, who is to be given in marriage to the Israelites. The Torah gives life; while the Revelation of God, His voice, perilously ravishes the soul. Two orders of experience are delineated in this and many other midrashic sources. The Torah, the Commandments, the ethical and ritual structures given at Sinai, are distinguished from the overwhelming, potentially fatal voice of God, which is beyond human strength to bear. The nations of the world, not directly involved in this encounter, rejoice: the world's survival depends on the success of this marriage, on the Israelite capacity to accept the Torah.

In a similar vein, one of the midrashic commentators[17] suggests, we can read the expression of the people's fear as the reaction of those who have died and been resurrected: "Who that is all-flesh has ever heard the voice of the living God speak out of the fire, as we did, *and lived*—i.e., and *returned to life*?" (Deut 5:23). This reading connects this verse with the end of the previous one: ". . . we shall die" is read "we have died . . . and returned to life." In some versions, a dew falls from heaven to revive them.[18] In this context, having known death and resurrection, their desire to delegate to Moses becomes more comprehensible.

In these midrashic narratives, the people experience the extremes of death and life at each of the Ten Commandments. To hear the voice of God is to suffer the unbearable; to receive the Torah is to return to life, to one's recognizable self.[19] To stand at Sinai is to achieve some equilibrium, some possible standing-ground, where God's voice may bearably inform the Torah.

Sinai: The Encounter with the Unbearable

We return to our questions: what is the terror of God's voice? What is the nature of the trauma that it inflicts? And what is its relation to death and life? A cluster of midrashic sources describes the experience of God's voice as being registered at the very margin of the bearable:

> "I am God your God . . ." (20:2). It is written, "Has a people ever heard the voice of God. . . ?" (Deut 4:33). Heretics asked R. Simlai: "Are there many gods in the world?" He asked, "Why?" They answered: "Because it is written, 'Has a people heard the voice of *elohim*,' in the plural!" He told them, "But it does not say, 'God *speaking—medabrim*'—in the plural, but *medaber*—in the singular!" His students then said to him: "You have fobbed them off with a reed (i.e., easily): what do you answer us?" So R. Levi explained again: "Has a people ever heard the voice of God. . . ?" If it had said, "The voice of God is in *His* strength," the world would not have been able to stand. But the text says: "The voice of God is in *strength*" (Ps 29:4)—that is, *according to the strength of each individual*—young men, according to their strength, and the old, according to their strength, and children, according to their strength. God said to Israel: "Just because you heard many voices, do not think that there are many gods in heaven, but be aware that I am God your God, as it is said, 'I am God your God . . .' "[20]

The plural dimension of God's voice indicates an exquisite compatibility with the "strength of each individual," with the specific world in time and space that is a human being. If God had spoken with a single voice, it would have shattered the world: "the world would not have been able to bear it." In other midrashim, indeed, earthquakes and volcanic eruptions threaten to return the world to chaos. But here, the wonder of Revelation consists of six hundred thousand different qualities of voice that are registered by each listener. God allows his unequivocal voice, the magisterial soul of *anochi*, the

"I am God . . ." which opens the Ten Commandments, to be refracted into myriads of subjective voices. One paradoxical implication is that Revelation is both objective and yet fully subjective, attuned to the consciousness of each individual. But another implication—significantly different—is that the voice of God places a strain on the strength of each individual: what is registered lies at the very limit of the bearable.

These two facets of Revelation become clearer in the following midrash:

> "All the people saw the voices . . ." (20:15): not ". . . the voice," but ". . . the voices." R. Yohanan said: when the voice came forth it did so only according to the strength of each individual Israelite, according to what he could bear. So, it says, "The voice of God is in strength" (Ps 29:4)—according to the strength of each individual. Said R. Yossi bar Hanina: If this surprises you, learn from the manna which fell for the Israelites in the wilderness: its taste was adapted to each individual taste, *so that they should be able to bear it;* if this was so with the manna, how much more so with the voice of God—that *it should not cause injury.*[21]

Here, the phrase, "as much as he could bear," is added to "according to the strength of each individual." And the analogy with the manna, which varies its taste according to the individual palate—a congenially hedonistic notion—is similarly qualified by the unexpected phrase, "so that they should be able to bear it." If even the manna, dropped from heaven, has an *unbearable* dimension that requires tempering, individuation—then, certainly, the voice of God requires modulation if it is not to injure the listener.

What is endangered by the heavenly manna is an earthly integrity, the familiar world of taste, sensitivity, sensibility. The word *ta'am*—"taste"—also connotes "meaning": what is varied according to each individual, then, is the subjective experience, the construction of significance attaching to the manna—and to the voice of God. This is the dimension of *kavod* that Jethro abandoned in his journey into the wilderness. The encounter with the *kavod* of God is experienced as an invasion, an annihilation. For that reason, it is tempered to the limit of the bearable, so that a world of meaning can survive the transformations of encountering God.

The traumatic effect of God's voice on creation is the subject of Psalm 29, where God's voice kindles flames of fire, convulses the wilderness, strips forests bare (v. 7). In view of this prodigious cosmic effect, Jethro's expectation that his *kavod* will be reconstituted, that he will be compensated in the same coin for his losses, emerges as rather naïve. Similarly naïve, perhaps, is his confidence that administrative restructurings of society will make it possible for Moses to stand, to withstand the burden that threatens to crush him. What Jethro experiences with paradigmatic clarity, however, is the real human anxiety about the erosion of *kavod*, of a stable, recognizable identity. The experience of the unbearable, of that which tests and stretches the limits of consciousness, is the essential ordeal of Sinai.

A famous midrash makes the point about the ponderous weight of Sinai:

> "They took their places at the foot of the mountain" (19:17): . . . This teaches that God suspended the mountain over them, like a barrel, and told them, "If you accept the Torah, all is well; if not, here will be your grave."[22]

The crushing weight of the mountain will be alleviated, "all will be well," only if they accept the Torah. Once more, we register the opposition between the terrors of Sinai and the ethical and ritual Torah, between Revelation and the Commandments that are its content, between the voice and the words.[23] The mythic posture of a people beneath such a mountain is one of *courage*—a courage commensurate with their fear.

A Scene of Madness

God's voice is again the subject of the following midrash, where it assumes a further dimension of traumatic power:

> God said to Aaron, "Go to meet Moses, towards the wilderness" (4:27). It is written, "God thunders marvelously with His voice." (Job 37:5). What is "thunders"? When God gave the Torah at Sinai, He manifested unimaginable wonders to Israel with His voice. He would speak, and the voice would go forth and resound throughout the world. Israel heard the voice approaching them from the South and ran towards the South to receive the voice. From the South, it veered to the North, so they ran to the North. From the North to the East, and they ran to the East; and from the East to the West, and they ran to the West. From the West, it moved, so they heard it from heaven, and cast their eyes upwards; and from there, it shifted to the earth, so they looked down, as it is said: *"From the*

> *heavens*, God let you hear His voice, to afflict you; *on earth*, He showed you His great fire; and from the midst of that fire you heard His words" (Deut 4:36). And Israel said to one another, "Wisdom—where can it be found?" (Job 28:12). They said, "Where does God come from—East, or South?" as it is said, "God came from Sinai and shone upon from Seir" (Deut 33:2) and "God is coming from the South." (Hab 3:3) It says, "All the people saw the voices"—not "the voice," but "the voices."[24]

Again, the focus is on the proliferating voices. But this time, the voices are not comfortingly attuned to the energies of each individual. In a hallucinatory sequence, the people run in all directions, seeking the elusive voice of God. The vertigo of such a search is registered in the quotation from Job: "Wisdom—where can it be found?" (Wisdom, Rashi comments, refers to the Torah.) Wisdom, says Job, is not to be found in any physical place, neither in the land of the living nor in the depths of the sea. It cannot be bought for any price, nor valued against any precious substance—gold, silver, onyx, sapphire.

This is the enigma that the midrash evokes: wisdom, or Torah, can, essentially, be found *nowhere*. Job's question, "Where—*me-ayin*—can it be found?" translates literally, "From *nothing*, *nowhere*—*ayin*—it is to be found." The people's search for the origin of God's voice is a fruitless quest for an equivalent—for a context in which to understand it. But it comes from nowhere, not even from the heavens, though there are proof-texts for each of the six directions they try. All the comforting formulations that locate God's voice are deliberately undermined by the experience of vertigo which ultimately yields *ayin*, nothing.

It is this *ayin*, however, the incommensurability of the voice of God with any other experience, that constitutes the singularity of the human desire. In a famous play on the word *ayin*, R. Yosef Albo reads the verse: "Man has no (*ayin*) superiority over the beast," (Eccl 3:19) as "The superiority of man over the beast is *ayin*"—the awareness of nothingness, the vertigo of an unpalliated desire.

In this disturbing midrash, the voice of God generates a radical instability in the people. As in the Mechilta about the people traveling two hundred and forty miles in order to "stand at Sinai," God's voice provokes movement. This time, however, it is not an oscillation, but a fruitless quest, in which the six compass points of empirical reality are explored in vain. This is, in fact, a scene of madness; the rational need to find a source for the voice provokes a crazed stampede, with the voice willfully eluding them.

In kabbalistic imagery, the classic mapping of the world yields six compass points: the four directions, up and down; the seventh point represents the heart of the matter, the nub of the world.[25] As in the relation of the Shabbath to the six days of the week, or of the Shemitta (Sabbatical) year to the six years of agricultural labor, the seventh of the series is the hidden meaning, the truth that cannot be translated into other terms. The elusive origin of God's voice represents this seventh point. Where is it to be found, if not at the heart of the vortex? After all the explorations of desire, there is a return to a still point: "the still point of the turning world."

3. *The Site of Transcendence: Retreat and Reclamation* 

The Flight from Life

This is the point addressed in the next midrash:

> "Who shall not fear You, King of the nations!" (Jer 10:7) This can be compared to a money-lender who filled his pocket with gold coins and stood calling out, "Whoever wishes may come and borrow!" Everyone heard him and fled—thinking, "When he comes to reclaim his debt, *who will be able to stand, to bear it?*" So, God came down to Sinai to give the Commandments and prevent the world from falling apart, as it is said: "The earth trembled, the sky rained because of God" (Ps 68:9); and "The mountains quaked" (Judg 5:5); and "The pillars of heaven tremble" (Job 26:11). And Israel shuddered, as it is said, "The whole people shuddered" (Exod [19:16]); and the mountain shuddered, as it is said, "The whole mountain shuddered violently" (19:18). Why all these tremors? *Because He spoke words of life!* And the prophet cried out: "If a lion roars, who shall not fear?" (Amos 3:8)[26]

The paradoxical response to God's voice is fear—fear, strangely, of life. The parable of the moneylender apparently neutralizes the paradox: the gold coins send everyone running in the opposite direction, simply because they do not come free. They will have to be repaid; and the flight-response expresses a vivid imagination of that future moment of repayment. Likewise, the parable suggests, the gold of God's words makes a stringent demand of the people. And they shudder in apprehension of failure to fulfill that demand.

Read in this way, God's offer of words of life clearly has its terrifying aspect. The people shudder at the responsibility entailed by those words. This is a realistic apprehension about their own possible inadequacies. However, the imagery invites a closer scrutiny. In the parable, for instance, the people's reaction is surprisingly unequivocal. One might have imagined a more ambivalent response to the offer of gold. Also, to accept the gold coins would mean, obviously, to *use* them, to engage in transactions—buying, selling, consuming, trading. The anxiety inheres in the outcome of these transactions: will they yield the equivalent of the original coins to repay the moneylender? Simply to retain the gold coins, unused, would certainly ensure repayment, but would also be pointless.

Similarly, in the people's response to God's words of life, there is little ambivalence. And something of the paradox survives, after all, in the rhetoric: "Why all these tremors? Because He spoke words of life!" There is an enigmatic ellipsis here: the implications of "repayment" are deliberately not spelled out. And, indeed, the reader must ask: What is it to "repay" words of life? Is it simply, as the commentaries suggest, to fulfill the Commandments? Is this the "transaction" that will leave the borrower solvent and able to repay the creditor? Is this the anxiety that makes people and mountain tremble? But these "words of life" are benign, they are to save the world from implosion, from a return to chaos: if so, what is the demand they make that engenders such unambiguous terror?

God's gift of the Torah is no gift, according to this midrash, but a loan. That means responsibility: who will be able to stand at the time of repayment? But, without the Torah, the whole world shudders and collapses. The midrash depicts a kind of "double bind" situation. The people have no choice but to accept the Torah; but the shudder betrays a profound recoil. Unlike the would-be borrowers, they cannot flee: they must accept, for the sake of life. But it is life itself that makes them tremble, that holds them responsible.

"Who?"—Prophecy Lays Claim

Here, I suggest, is the heart of the matter. The midrash begins with a verse from Jeremiah: "*Who—Mi*—shall not fear You, King of the nations. . . ?" And ends with a verse from Amos: "If a lion roars, *who—mi*—shall not fear? . . ." The nature of this fear is not the primitive *frisson*, on hearing a lion's roar. It is, as the end of the prophet's question makes clear, the fear of having to respond: "If God speaks, *who shall not prophesy?*" Beyond the fulfillment of specific commandments, lies a more radical terror. For what God's voice demands is not, simply, listening, but that responsive speech that is *prophecy.* The unbearable burden is, primarily, an individual one: "*Who* shall not fear You? *Who* shall not prophesy?" "*Who?*" is the penetrating, inescapable claim on each person, according to his strength—as much as he can bear, to the very limits of the bearable. Here, a mass commitment to the Covenant offers no shelter: "All that God has spoken we will do" (19:8). "Who?" challenges each individual with the impossibility of silence.

The singular mode, indeed, emerges in the final version of the Sinai narrative, which we have already studied:

> God your God will raise up for you a prophet from among your own people, like myself, to him you shall listen. Just as you asked of God your God at Chorev, on the day of the assembly, saying, "Let me not hear the voice of God my God any longer or see this great fire any more, lest I die." And God said to me, "They have done well in speaking like this" (Deut 18:15–17).

The issue here is prophecy: the people surrender their prophetic role to the "professional" prophets of the future. But the emphasis is on the individual, and on a most personal response to the voice that is like fire. All the verbs are in the singular form: "Let me not hear . . . lest I die," resounds with a primal truth, that evokes Franz Rosenzweig: "Only the singular can die and everything mortal is solitary."[27] God's response refers to the people in the plural form, clearly projecting the nation as an aggregation of individuals, whose profound responses achieve a general consensus. Even here, however, God reverts to the singular, in considering potential problems in the acceptance of the prophets of the future (vv. 19–22).

In the earlier, central, Deuteronomy version of the Sinai narrative, although the verbs are plural the question that the people ask focuses on the word, *mi—Who?*: "*Who* that is all-flesh has heard the voice of the living God speak from out of the fire, as we have, and lived?" (5:23). The question is about the power of the individual to bear the radical demand of the *living* God. Perhaps—we remember the midrashic theme—this requires a willingness to die and be reborn, to touch extremes that pre-Sinai existence has never addressed?

> Just as a furnace tests barrels, which are suitable for wine, which for oil, and which are cracked, so the words of Torah test human beings.[28]

The furnace image derives from the fiery mountain with its smoke rising like the smoke of a furnace (20:18). This is the place in which human beings are proven, their mettle tested. The Hebrew for "testing," here, is *bodek*, the term for inquiring after the true nature of a person or object. At root, it means to split, to break into, to penetrate. It involves an invasive act, to sound out an inner reality. This is the effect of the words of Torah: it penetrates, generates keener knowledge of the capacity of the individual to resound to the voice of God.

Franz Rosenzweig writes of this sounding and re-sounding:

> The word as heard and as spoken is one and the same. The ways of God are different from the ways of man, but the word of God and the word of man are the same. What man hears in his heart as his own human speech is the very word which comes out of God's mouth.[29]

The terror of Revelation, in this sense, is the recognition of what springs forth from the only place where the voice of God can originate. This is the place of "nowhere," of *ayin*, that all the external searches fail to locate: the seventh place, within the *mi*, the interrogated self. Only from that interior can there spring forth something both known and unknown, something at the limit of the bearable that declares that it must be born. Artists, like prophets, must bear the impingement of the new, which originates both outside and inside. Tchaikovsky describes the state in which "a new idea awakens in me and begins to assume a definite form. I forget everything and behave like a madman. Everything within me starts pulsing and quivering . . . If that condition of mind and soul, which we call inspiration, lasted long without intermission, no artist could survive it. The strings would break and the instruments be shattered into fragments."[30] Abraham Heschel writes: "Would one expect a human being of flesh and blood to remain robust, smug, and calm when overwhelmed by the presence of God?"[31]

Revelation: A Tiger Lashing His Tail

Those who are called on to respond to God's voice are most shaken by what is revealed *within themselves*. Czeslaw Milosz reflects on the experience of writing poetry:

> *In the very essence of poetry, there is something indecent:*
> *A thing is brought forth that we didn't know we had in us,*

So we blink our eyes, as a tiger had sprung out
And stood in the light lashing his tail.[32]

This is a birth of a kind; a revelation of a kind. The poem has come at us from outside, but its terror is what it has generated within us. The tiger lashing his tail is strange and familiar: uncanny, *unheimlich*, in Freud's sense. It emerges from an intimate place, known forever, but suppressed till this moment. Every significant revelation has this quality: it is brought forth from us, but we did not bring it forth. We didn't know we had it in us, but it stands, larger than life, indecent, recognized. 'Forth the particulars of rapture come.' (Stevens)

Each tiger is unique, and uniquely fearful. "If a lion roars, who shall not fear? If God speaks, who shall not prophesy?" William Blake's tiger spans the gap between the real tiger and the metaphorical:

Tyger! Tyger! burning bright
In the forests of the night,
What immortal hand or eye
Could frame thy fearful symmetry?

In what distant deeps of skies
Burnt the fire of thine eyes?
On what wings dare he aspire?
What the hand dare seize the fire?[33]

Essentially singular, the tiger fractures all the competencies and knowingness of the past. All *kevodo shel olam*, the "honor of the world" vanishes. Blake's incantatory questions about the origin of the tiger proclaim *ayin*, the *nowhere*, the scorching luminousness of a revelation that defies language and context. For the poet, this is the heart of the paradox, since if he is to net the tiger in words, he must recognize, appropriate the transcendent.

For the prophet, there is one requirement: to *listen* to God's voice. To listen means to speak, to bear the tiger that springs forth. One may, however, refuse; the possibility is there. One may cringe and deafen oneself to the penetrating voice. This possibility is treated as a vital failure and categorized in legal terms:

> One who suppresses his prophecy . . . his death is at the hands of heaven, as it is written: "It shall be that the man who does not *listen* to My words that he speaks in My name, I Myself will call him to

account." (Deut 18:19)—"Listen" can be read, "cause others to listen," or "obey."[34]

The verse in Deuteronomy, which follows directly on the passage we have studied about the people delegating prophecy, clearly speaks of one who refuses to listen to (obey) the voice of the prophet. In the Talmudic reading, this injunction is extended to the prophet himself. The prophet may "not listen": may suppress the prophetic voice, which is his own voice, but which comes from nowhere and strives to be born within him. The punishment is death "at the hands of heaven," since no human being can frame his offense, only God: "shall call him to account." The language of the Talmud suggests the intimacy of the failure and of the extinction that comes in its wake.

In a similar vein, the Talmud continues: "Two prophets do not prophesy in the same style."[35] The true prophet has a unique voice; he conveys what he has heard, according to his own strength, as fully as he can bear it. To speak with the voice of another is to commit the subtle plagiarism that betrays the false prophet.

The Site of Transcendence: Cracking Up

If the terrible beauty that is born at Sinai is to be of more than historic interest, it must, the Rabbis insist, be continuously reexperienced. The midrashic principle is *limuda ke-netinata*: every time the Torah is studied, something of that unnerving revelation must happen. Christopher Bollas describes the human predisposition for such revelations. He quotes Schiller: "Only inasmuch as he changes, does man exist; only inasmuch as he remains unchangeable does he exist." Personality is "merely the predisposition to a possible expression of his infinite nature." There is, Bollas writes, a "specific urge to give form to one's lived experiences, in Schiller's view, a form drive (*Formtrieb*)."[36]

For this to be achieved, on any level, a certain grandiosity must be deflated. Or, in the language of the midrash, the "honor of the world" must be abandoned. There must be a "cracking up," an experience of incoherence, of the dissemination of meanings, a "meditation full of questions."[37]

Emmanuel Levinas gives an account of the "ontological status, or *regime* of the Revelation [which] is . . . a primordial concern for Jewish thought":

> . . . its word comes from elsewhere, from outside, and, at the same time, lives within the person receiving it. The only "terrain" where exteriority

> can appear is in the human being, who does far more than listen. Which means, surely, that the person, the uniqueness of the "self," is the necessary condition of the breach and the manifestation which enter from outside? Surely it is the human, fracturing the identity of substance, which can, "by itself", enable a message to come from outside? . . . the uniqueness of each act of listening carries the secret of the text; the voice of Revelation, in precisely the inflection lent by each person's ear, is necessary for the truth of the Whole.[38]

"The inflection lent by each person's ear" is essential to the fullness of Revelation. "The witness testifies to what has been said through him."[39] "If one had been missing, the people could not have received the Torah."[40]

Levinas continues:

> The Talmud affirms the prophetic and verbal origin of the Revelation, but lays more emphasis on the voice of the person listening . . . Man is not . . . a mere receiver of sublime messages. He is, at the same time, the person to whom the word is said, and the one through whom there *is* a Revelation. *Man is the site of transcendence.*[41] (*emphasis added*). . . Does the spirit reach its limit in self-possession? Are there not grounds for imagining a relation with an Other (*Autre*) that would be "better" than self-possession? . . . Perhaps . . . seeking, desire and questioning are therefore better than possession, satisfaction and answers.[42]

The willingness of the human being to be the site of transcendence is the central issue. For this means a willingness to hear the question that awakens one from stupor and petrifaction. It is a disruption, an openness to the Other, to an "incessant questioning . . . like an inextinguishable flame which burns yet consumes nothing."

The position of the Israelites at the base of the mountain graphically evokes the "site of transcendence." What Rashi calls the "human position" is the line of people that should hold firm in all the tumult of Revelation. The command that God gives Moses is, "You shall set bounds for the people round about . . ." (Exod 19:12). On this, Meshech Chochma comments: it is the people, not some point on the mountain, that is the border of transcendence. God's glory reaches down to the place where the human being stands: "Face to face, God spoke with you at the mountain" (Deut 5:4). The people form the outer structure of God's presence, dividing His glory from the uninspired world. For this reason, even the mountain base may not be touched, for as long as God's presence remains: it is holy ground. The revelation extends right down to the people themselves. Like the courtyard of the Temple, the people represent a transitional space, through which Moses must pass, if he is fully to realize the holiness of the mountain. Before the Ten Commandments are uttered, indeed, he is told to descend and reascend (19:24): on this reading, he is required to ascend the mountain, by traversing the "human position" held by the Israelites at the very limit of transcendence.

This liminal space, which is the people's standing-ground, is the site of transcendence. We remember the midrash that describes how it becomes a base for oscillation. The people "see the voices": they vibrate and dislocate themselves with each utterance of God's voice. Angels, God Himself, assist them to find their standing-ground again. This oscillation, repeated ten times, lies at the very heart of the "Standing at Sinai." For in this movement, in which coherence and stability are fractured and reconstituted, the people flee the tiger that has sprung forth from them; it requires all the energies of the living God to move them back into the position of meeting. They run from an intensity of life, from the words of the living God, and from the transactions, the uses of those gold coins that are demanded of them. These words are, in essence, questions about the unique transactions that each individual can make with them. It is the uniqueness of use that marks the true prophet, who, through the intensity of the fracturing, through what Bollas calls "disseminations," develops a personal idiom.

The terror of all this is palpable. Like Jethro, the people suffer the loss of dignity, of identity. Something demands to be born. But this motion, back and forth, systole and diastole, is the very motion of life. It is the flicker of the flame, the ebb and flow of the ocean. Without it, there can be no Standing at Sinai. It means bearing the tension of the tiger's ambiguous origin: within and without.

The Site of Transcendence: A Space for Play?

To see the voices, says the Mechilta, is to *hear* the Word, and to *interpret* it. This represents the transitional space, where, in Winnicott's mapping of human development, the child, benignly nurtured by the mother, loses an old illusion of omnipotence. Separating from that *kavod*, from the subjective fantasy that one has created the breast that one always finds at the moment of desire, the child plays alone, in the presence of the mother. That aloneness, I suggest, is the moment of Sinai. There, the people separate from an illusion of self-sufficiency. There, at the base of the mountain, is the "location of cultural experience." "The use of an object symbolizes the union of two now separate things, baby and mother, *at the point in time and space of the initiation of their state of separateness.*"[43]

At this most critical juncture of their history, when an illusion of God's relationship to them is disrupted, and a new consciousness of His otherness is born, the transitional space at Sinai is the site of transcendence where a new human possibility develops: that otherness may be recognized and a different kind of union achieved. The object that the Israelites "use," the transitional *phenomenon*,[44] that helps them live in the space of loneliness out of which tigers may spring, is the Torah. It is the "use" of the words of Torah, the human transactions, the interpretations, the play on those words, that saves them from the terrors of God's voice.

The relation, indeed, between the words and the voice, the Giving of the Torah and the Standing at Sinai, is one mediated by the human space, and the possibility of "playing" within it. "If Your Torah had not been my *plaything*, I should have perished in my poverty!" cried the Psalmist,[45] in a moment of burning vision. Winnicott quotes Tagore: "On the seashore of endless worlds, children play."[46] It is precisely the play mode that generates the unique and variable idioms of relationship—to other human beings and to God. Between the purely inward and the purely outward lives the sense of Revelation that is flickering, perilous, able to tolerate the risks of interplay. The play experience has, Winnicott notes, no climax; it has infinite variability; it is "the separation that is not a separation but a form of union."[47]

For the people standing at Sinai, the fear that sets them shuddering backwards seems far-removed from the idea of play. And, indeed, as we have seen, for Ramban and some midrashic sources, this is a serious and purposeful fear, a right fear, that represents the climax of the drama at Sinai. Physically, they vacate their original standing-ground; existentially, they delegate to Moses the perilous revelations involved in hearing the voice of God. Quite unambiguously, God approves the people's surrender of their prophetic stance:

> "God heard the *voice of your words*, when you spoke to me; and God said to me, 'I have heard *the voice of the words* of the people, that they have spoken to you. They have done well, in speaking like this. Would that (lit. "Who would grant that") this heart of theirs would remain always, to fear Me, and to keep all My Commandments.' " (Deut 5:25–26)

Unequivocally validating the people's withdrawal, this passage is the basis for Ramban's view: the prophetic experience was granted them only in order that they should achieve this moment of humility and acknowledgment of Moses' transcendent spiritual power. This was a consummation devoutly to be wished. "I have heard the voice of their words," is God's authentication of the salutary terror behind the words.[48]

Ingratitude: The Poverty of Sanity

At the same time, however, that expression, "the voice of the words," repeated within one verse, is so ponderous, in a sense so redundant, that a certain skepticism arises in the reader. The relation of voice to words has been central to our discussion of God's voice. It was not, we have suggested, the words, the content of the Ten Commandments that made the people shudder. It was the voice of God that constituted the essential Revelation that created a new knowledge within the people. It is because of His voice that, in the most radical midrashim, their souls fly away, they swoon, they die. And it is the Torah, the words, the possibility of interpretation, of play, that revives them: "Shall the whole world rejoice, while Your children die?" the Torah intercedes with God. Now, God hears the "voice of their words." And, in a similar vein, the text conveys a sense of inner significance, of an irreducible presence, a personal idiom that underlies the rhetorical intent of the words. What God hears is not "the words which they have spoken to you." It is the *voice* of the words that God registers: the work of the subconscious, the latent ideas and images that are the people's inner life. Of this, God says nothing but "I have heard . . . They have done well, in speaking like this."

But after He has apparently approved the people's fear, He says, enigmatically, wishfully: "*Who—mi*—would grant that this heart of theirs would remain always . . ." (5:26). Again, the penetrating, interrogative *mi* that probes for an individual response. But here God speaks with a poignancy rarely paralleled in the Torah. God is *wishing;* not commanding, or recommending, or promising. This most human mode of speech sounds strangely in His voice. It evokes a world of human sensibility beyond His government, unmanageable, object of His desire.

The Talmud registers God's appeal in a slightly different tonality:

> "*Who* (*Mi*) would grant that this heart of theirs . . ." Moses said to the people: "You ingrates, children of ingrates! When God said to Israel, '*Who*

would grant. . . ?' they should have replied, '*You* grant it!' " "Ingrates," as it is written, "We are sick of this flimsy bread!" "Children of ingrates," as it is written, "The woman whom You gave me, she gave me of the Tree and I ate . . ." (Gen 3:12). Moses gave them these hints about ingratitude only after forty years had passed, when it is written, "God did not give you a heart to know and eyes to see and ears to hear till this very day" (Deut 29:3). Rava said: "We learn from this that a student comes to understand his teacher only after forty years."[49]

When God says, "*Who* would grant. . . ?" He is implicitly asking for a response: "God, You grant it!" In other words, the people have missed an opportunity to answer to God's wish. A certain literal-mindedness makes them deaf to the harmonics of God's only apparently rhetorical question. This obtuseness is called by Moses "ingratitude." It is traced to the original words of ingratitude: Adam blaming Eve, God's gift to him, for the sin of eating the fruit of the Tree. This primal human response to God's goodness is then again registered in the people's rejection of the manna in the wilderness.

"Ingratitude" seems not quite the appropriate term, in both these cases. Obviously, Adam had reason to blame Eve for seducing him to eat the forbidden fruit, for regarding her as a not entirely benign element in his world. And the people clearly did not find the manna a totally satisfying food. "Ingratitude," likewise, is the name given to their subtle failure of response to God's wish: "*Who* would grant. . . ?" Tosefot comments: "This is why they are called ingrates, because they did not want to say, '*You* grant . . .'—because they did not want to be grateful to Him (lit. to recognize His goodness).' " In this definition, ingratitude becomes a matter of will. It implies a willful repudiation of goodness, an intolerance of a relationship in which goodness has been bestowed. If they *refuse* to say, "God, You grant it . . ." it is because the receiving of goodness is, in some real sense, unbearable to them. Subtly, the Talmud indicates a radical human refusal. Finding the origin of that refusal in Adam means that a universal problem is being addressed: a gift is maligned, its goodness denied—whether the gift is Eve, "whom You have *given* to be with me" (Gen 3:12), or the manna, which, as we have seen, needs adapting to each person's taste, to make it *bearable*.

In the case of God's wish, "*Who* would grant. . . ?" He paradoxically asks for a gift, while His real wish is that the people ask Him to grant the gift. In other words, God is represented as offering them the gift of maintaining the condition of Sinai forever. Since the offer is not explicit, since it is couched in the idiom of a rhetorical question, the people can quite simply ignore it. This act of repression is diagnosed by the Talmud as ingratitude; and by Tosefot as a willful rejection of God's unbearable goodness. What is unbearable about goodness? Why is ingratitude so primordial a human response?

The people's enigmatic failure at Sinai is the subject of a comment by Rashi:

> *"You speak to us"* (Deut 5:24): [Moses said:] "You have weakened me like a female (a reference to the feminine form of the pronoun, 'You'—*at*). For I have sorrowed over you and you have demoralized me; when I saw that you are not anxious to come close to Him in love, and that you did not find it beautiful (lit.) to learn from the mouth of God, and not from me."

Moses, it seems, is unhappy with the people's retreat from the immediate encounter with God. In their reaction to God's voice, one element is tragically missing: love. Only love would have made them able to tolerate the oscillations of Standing at Sinai. Love, expressed by a sense of God's goodness and a willingness to accept that goodness. At root, this is the meaning of gratitude: *hakarath tova*—acknowledging the goodness of the Other, allowing it to enter. Ingratitude—*kefiyath tova*—on the other hand, is the sense of being forced, or violated, by goodness, of being compelled into a relationship that threatens one's autonomy.[50]

When the people refuse to hear more from God, Moses experiences disappointment. Fear, not love, has dominated the people's response. They retreat, and God supports their words, but nevertheless addresses their inner world, as He appeals, "*Who* would grant. . . ?" Essentially, he asks for a wholehearted acknowledgment of His goodness, of the gift that is His offer of relationship. But again, the people retreat. The moment of failure is registered in silence. They do not *want* to acknowledge goodness, to risk the obligations of acceptance. To have said, "God, You grant it!" would have been to desire transcendence, or that form of transcendence that has leapt out of themselves, like the tiger lashing his tail.

Such a desire would have been a prodigy, a marvel in the history of human desire. There is nothing more ordinary, closer to a rudimentary human nature than the fear of goodness, the retreat from the risks of relationship. The space at the foot of the mountain where the people stand is, potentially, the play-area of which Winnicott writes. Here, the challenge is to discover the possibilities of play, of eventual integration, so that the ebb and flow of response to each of God's utterances yields to a form of delight.

Before such an integration can become possible, however, the experience of "unintegration," the shudder of Sinai, must be tolerated.

But the people choose sanity; an appropriate fear governs them. And Rashi has Moses express radical dismay: "You have weakened me, demoralized me . . ." In Winnicott's words: ". . . much sanity . . . has a symptomatic quality being charged with fear or denial of madness, fear or denial of the innate capacity of every human being to become unintegrated, depersonalized, and to feel that the world is unreal." And, in a footnote, "Through artistic expression we can hope to keep in touch with our primitive selves whence the most intense feelings and even fearfully acute sensations derive, and we are poor indeed if we are only sane."[51]

"We are poor indeed if we are only sane": the people's choice to retreat from the site of transcendence, with its risks, its threat of incoherence, condemns them to a kind of poverty. The Talmud calls this failure "ingratitude": the allergic response to the demands of goodness.

The Evolution of Love

Strikingly, the loving response that God waited for in vain at Sinai takes forty years to develop; and appears, in mature form, in Moses' praise of the people, just before his death: "God has not *given* you a heart to know, eyes to see, and ears to hear, till this very day" (Deut 29:3). Rashi's comment is significant:

> *"God has not given you a heart to know"*: to recognize the loving acts of God and to cling lovingly to Him.
>
> *"Till this very day"*: I have heard that that was the day that Moses gave the Scroll of the Torah to the Levites—as it is written, "And he gave it to the priests, the sons of Levi" (31:9). The whole people then came into his presence and said, "Moses, our teacher, we too stood at Sinai and received the Torah. It was given to us! Why, then, are you giving your tribe control over it? One day, they will tell us, 'It was never given to you, only to us!' " Then, Moses rejoiced at their words, and replied, "This day, you have become a people! (27:9)—this day, I realize that you cling lovingly to God and desire Him."

Moses' joy is paradoxical. For the first time, he celebrates a popular outburst of rancor! This time, however, their complaint is desirous, possessive.

What Moses hears in the "voice of their words"—and never heard before—is the love that acknowledges and invites the gift of goodness. After forty years of desert wandering, they are finally ready to enter into a mature covenant with God—"besides the covenant that He had made with them at Chorev" (28:69). This moment, we may say, is a "fictional" moment. The genre of their narrative suddenly changes: from an episodic narrative of epiphanies and failures, it has become a "comic" narrative, a divine comedy. Finally, after forty years of trials and rebellions, there is a moment of illumination that transforms the reading of the past.

This moment of transformation, however, is the end of a process that began at Sinai, a journey in the course of which the people were to become capable of loving and being loved by God. Before he dies, Moses hears in their voices a tone that he can celebrate: "This day, you have become a people!" To have a heart and eyes and ears is to be able to relate to the other, without being paralyzed by fear for one's own autonomy.

It has taken forty years to understand the desire of God that was veiled in the idiom, *"Who* would *grant. . . ?"* Subtly, the text now provides a kind of closure: "God did not *grant* you a heart . . . till this very day" (Deut 29:3). The same verb, *natan*, indicates that the people have grown towards an acknowledgment, a desire for God's gift of a knowing heart. This means a capacity to live in the interplay of the human and the divine. If it has taken forty years to glimpse such a possibility, that, says the Talmud,[52] is normal: fully to understand one's teacher's mind takes quite as long. And so conveys the very nature of relationship: the slow development, the conscious and unconscious processes that cannot be accelerated. To come retroactively at an understanding of God's wish—"Who would grant. . . ?"—is to come at an interpretation that belongs organically to its own time.[53]

The Therapeutic Narrative: Hearing the Un-heard

In the midrashic literature we have been exploring, the people's primary reaction to God's revelation was a shudder at the threat to a stable identity, to a recognizable self. For Jethro, too, the issue of *kavod* was central and required immediate consideration by the Israelite leaders. Like a prologue to a play, his story tells of the sensitivities of one who has abandoned the density of a familiar identity, in order to "hear words of Torah." Arriving after the Torah is given, however, he has missed the essential disintegration of self that Sinai has provoked in those who stood at its base.

In an attempt to attract his father-in-law, Moses told him a story. It was a story, we remember, that made him rejoice and—at the same time—that made his flesh prickle. The power of narrative to heal trauma is related to its effect on the body where subconscious loves and loyalties are inscribed. Jethro has already heard the story of God's redemption of Israel, but now Moses tells it again, so that Jethro's deepest ambivalences are involuntarily engaged. This is the catharsis that, at least for the moment, brings healing.

In the telling of a story, something new is engendered. What was left raw, unripe, not understood in the past can suddenly engage with the unprecedented time and space of a new telling. In a powerful and characteristic passage, Sefath Emeth[54] places language at the very heart of the story of redemption. The Exodus, as history, happened "in haste" (*chipazon*),[55] its meanings not fully assimilated. Explicitly, the text narrates that God's four promises of redemption—the four different terms used are "I shall take you out . . . and I shall save you . . . and I shall redeem you . . . and I shall take you to be My people . . ." (Exod 6:6–7)—are "not heard" by the Israelites, "because of impatience and hard labor" (6:9). By drawing attention to the redundant play of language—the four synonyms for redemption—and by having the people, at the moment of their own salvation, unable to attest to it, even to recognize it, Sefath Emeth constructs the *narrative* of the Exodus as the imperative of the future. "In every generation, there is a new revelation of the expressions for redemption."

The Passover night, called the Seder night, is the primary time of narratives: the time orders (*seder* means "order") the details in such a way as to generate new understandings. This is a work, he writes, for all the generations. The unripeness, the haste of the Exodus is an invitation to posterity to find new meanings in the encounter between the narrative and the flesh and nerves of a new time. In this sense, narrative can compensate for the shortcomings of an original moment.

In an obvious sense, nothing can equal the primary moment, the moment of witness. Those who were there at Sinai heard and saw, as no one can after them. "You yourselves have seen—not through words or texts or testimony." No delegation or substitution is possible. "No one," writes Paul Celan, "bears witness for the witness."[56] No one can replace the one who "stood at Sinai," who heard God's voice and ultimately refused to hear. The burden of the unbearable Revelation is unique. Yet, paradoxically, its most eloquent testimony is the people's delegation of it to Moses. And all future generations are said to have stood at Sinai. The responsibility falls on them, therefore, to bear witness for the original witnesses: to rehear God's voice and, with the flesh and nerves of a new sensibility, to fill the gaps of the past.

The imperative of narrative, the commandment to "tell the story of the Exodus," comes to its climax at Mount Sinai. It is here that narrative, when it comes to heal, becomes most essential. As with the narrative to Jethro, this healing must engage with the ambivalences, the oscillations, that are the human response to revelation. Such a narrative is, inevitably, individual: "If a lion roars, who shall not fear? If God speaks, who shall not prophesy?"

6 *Mishpatim*

BEFORE REVELATION:
THE HEARING HEART

[21:1–24:18]

1. Before Revelation: The Book of the Covenant

The Ratification of the Covenant

The section of the Torah covered by chapters 21–24 contains social rules, moral imperatives, civil and criminal laws, ritual prescriptions, and an affirmation of God's promises to Israel. The whole section is connected to the preceding section (the Ten Commandments): "*And* these are the laws . . ." (21:1). These many rules and injunctions emanate from God at Sinai, in the same way as the Ten Commandments.[1]

The organic continuity of the Decalogue and the following laws constitute a narrative that reaches its climax in chapter 24. This chapter relates the ratification of the Covenant. Nahum Sarna writes: "The climactic scene in the historic covenant drama is about to be enacted. An elaborate rite of ratification takes place, after which Moses is called upon to ascend Mount Sinai in order to receive the tangible, permanent symbol of the covenant: the two stone tablets into which the Decalogue is incised."[2]

Sarna points out the literary markings of a complex unit that began with chapter 19. Chapter 24 "frames the unit by the sevenfold use of the key stem *d-b-r*, 'to speak, word,' in both the opening and closing chapters, and by the sevenfold employment of the stem *y-r-d*, 'to go down,' in chapter 19 and of its antonym *'-l-h*, 'to go up,' in this chapter."[3]

This ratification of the Covenant is narrated in the first eight verses:

> Then to Moses He said, "Come up to God, you and Aaron, Nadav and Avihu, and seventy elders of Israel, and bow low from afar. Moses alone shall come near God; but the others shall not come near, nor shall the people come up with him." Moses came and narrated to the people all the words of God and all the laws; and all the people answered with one voice, saying, "All the things that God has spoken we shall do!" Moses then wrote down all the words of God. And he rose up early in the morning and set up an altar at the foot of the mountain, with twelve pillars for the twelve tribes of Israel. He sent young men among the Israelites and they offered burnt offerings and sacrificed bulls as wholeness-offerings to God. Moses took half of the blood and placed it in basins, and the other half he sprinkled on the altar. Then he took the book of the covenant and read it aloud to the people. And they said, "All that God has spoken we will do and we will hear!" Then Moses took the blood and dashed it on the people and said, "This is the blood of the covenant that God now makes with you concerning all these words!"

The opening phrase, "Then to Moses he said," inverts the usual syntactical order, emphasizing that Moses is the focus of the commandment. Moses is singled out in 24:2, as well: he alone is to come near God, although other leaders are to accompany him in the first stages of the ascent. It is Moses, too, who then narrates (*va-yisaper*) to the people "all the words of God and all the laws."

At this stage, Moses is obeying God's earlier injunction: "This is what you shall say to the Israelites . . . And these are the laws that you shall place before them . . ." (20:19; 21:1). He is communicating to the people all the divine instructions he has received since the Ten Commandments. And the people, having been informed of the basic categories of the Covenant, repeat the words of their earlier commitment, using the same formula as in the days before the Torah was given and later expanding it ["All that God has spoken we shall do *and we shall hear!*" (24:7).] The blood-sprinkling ritual frames the reading of the Book: a visual transaction completes the enactment of the Covenant.

Central to this ratification of the Covenant is the writing and reading of a "book." Sarna points out that the commitment to writing was an essential part of the ratification process of treaties in the ancient Near East; and that a similar public reading, with popular assent, took place in the days of King Josiah: these "were necessary elements of the ratification process. Interestingly, some Hittite treaty texts require periodic public recital of the terms of the pact before the vassal and his people."[4]

Sarna also plausibly suggests that the people's original formula of consent is expanded (from "We shall do," to "We shall do and we shall hear"), since this is their last act of public participation in the Covenant.

Abarbanel adds a nuance to the people's assent. After committing themselves the previous day ("We shall do"), they have had the night to consider the implications of their assent. Despite the many laws and rulings they have now been taught, they do not renege on their original commitment. On the contrary, they declare themselves willing to *hear more*, if God has further instructions for them.

The narrative continues with Moses fulfilling the divine command and ascending the mountain once again, this time to receive the Tablets of Stone (24:12). His prolonged stay at the summit will then precipitate the people's betrayal of the Covenant, the crisis of the Golden Calf.

Rashi's Version: Chronology Recast

This narrative of events following the Ten Commandments is the subject of a radical rereading by Rashi. Basing his commentary on Mechilta, Rashi recasts the chronology of events.[5] His claim is essentially that 24:1–12 (the section that Sarna calls the ratification of the Covenant) is an account of events *preceding* the Ten Commandments:

> *Now to Moses He said:* This section was given before the Ten Commandments. On the fourth of Sivan, he was told, "Come up to God." (24:1).
>
> *Then God said, "Come up to Me on the mountain:"* after the Ten Commandments. (24:12).

In Rashi's midrashic narrative, therefore, this section begins with a flashback to the fourth of Sivan, three days before the Ten Commandments were uttered. God informs Moses that *after* the Ten Commandments, he will ascend to the summit. First, however, he fulfills God's commands, comes down the mountain, and initiates a Covenant, sealed in the sacrificial blood.

Only after this are the Ten Commandments given; and Moses then reascends the mountain.

Strikingly, in this version of the narrative, the Ten Commandments are obscured. As Rashi frames events, they are the invisible pivot that gives order to the "before" and "after" of time. The words of Revelation that had been the explicit center of the narrative in chapters 19–20 are absent in Rashi's flashback. Now, it is the Book of the Covenant that is the focus of the days preceding the Ten Commandments.

Moses first narrates God's words; then writes them down, and then reads them aloud to the people. The problematic aspects of Rashi's narrative are conspicuous and troublesome. In general, one might object—and Ramban, in fact, does object—to the "scrambling" of the chronological order of the text. Implicitly, Rashi introduces here, as in several places in his commentary, the principle that "there is no necessary chronological sequence in the Torah." One might assume, then, on the principle of Occam's Razor, that Ramban who, in contrast, tends to favor ordering events in the historical sequence in which they are narrated, is both more elegant and more intelligible. What is to be gained by Rashi's interpretive move, the flashback segment of 24:1–12?

In terms of the details of the passage, too, Rashi's reading seems cumbersome. What is the burden of the message that Moses "narrates" to the people? "The words of God," he explains, refers to the instructions about separating the sexes and cordoning off the mountain, in preparation for the Revelation. In other words, this verse (24:3) overlaps the account in 19:15. But, in this flashback narrative, what could be the meaning of the "laws" that Moses relates? The obvious reference—to the laws of Sinai that followed the Ten Commandments—is ruled out by Rashi's chronology: clearly, *before* Revelation, these laws cannot have been communicated to the people. Rashi explains:

> This refers to the seven Noachide laws and to Shabbat, and the honoring of father and mother, and the Red Heifer, and other laws that were given them at Marah. (24:3)

The obvious—and elegant—reference to *mishpatim*, the laws of Sinai, is set aside in favor of laws read by tradition into fissures in the text. That is, the seven Noachide laws and the laws given at Marah are not even explicit: they are the subject of oral interpretations of nuances in the text. The laws of Marah, for instance, arise from an enigmatic expression in 15:25: "There

He made for them statutes and laws . . ." This becomes the basis for a Talmudic reference to laws given the people before Sinai.[6]

Rashi thus makes these pre-Sinaitic laws the subject of Moses' "narrative" to the people. It is to these that they respond: "We shall do!" At this point, too, Ramban objects: Surely the word *va-yisaper*—"he narrated"—suggests *new* data? Is the word appropriate for material that has long been familiar to them? The question about the innovative force of narrative has implications that we shall explore later.

But at this point we remember Moses' narrative to Jethro: "Moses *narrated* to his father-in-law all that God had done to Pharaoh and to Egypt for the sake of Israel" (18:8). Since Jethro had already heard "all that God had done for Moses and Israel His people" (18:1), Moses' narrative seemed redundant. But the power of an *old* story cannot be lightly dismissed. In Jethro's case, Moses' narrative evoked joy and nervous agitation.[7] In Moses' narrative to the people, similarly, his subject matter may be familiar, without losing its compelling power.

In Rashi's commentary, however, the plot thickens. Dating the events of our section on the fourth and fifth of Sivan, he spells out the contents of the text that Moses writes, the Book of the Covenant:

> *And Moses wrote:* from the Creation to the Giving of the Torah. He also wrote down the commandments they were given at Marah. (24:4)

Moses' text, which he reads aloud to the people, is a narrative that covers the history of the world from Creation to the present moment. Effectively, he reads out the whole of the Torah till the date of writing. It is to this text—with the addition of the laws of Marah—that the people respond, "All that God has spoken we shall do and we shall hear!" This is the basis of the Covenant, with the expanded commitment of the people. The oral narrative—of laws both primordial and recent—elicited "We shall do!" But the written narrative—the early history of the world that constitutes the first segment of the Torah—evokes an added promise: "and we shall hear!"

The reading aloud of this text is placed firmly at the center of the ritual enactment of the Covenant. Before it, there are sacrifices (24:5) and the division of the blood (24:6): half is "taken" and sprinkled on the altar walls; the Book of the Covenant is then "taken" and read "into the ears of the people, who respond, 'We shall do and we shall hear!' " (24:7); and the other half of the blood is "taken" and sprinkled on the people (24:8). The three uses of the word, *va-yikach*—"he took"—marking the sprinkling of the blood, the reading of the Book, and sprinkling of the blood—signify the nexus, the tissue of connection between God and Israel. At its center, where the divine and the human meet, is the Book. For Rashi, this Book is the Torah itself.

In this reading, therefore, the people are exposed to the text of the Torah—the narrative and some laws—before the Ten Commandments are given, before the Revelation moment. Their classic response, "We shall do and we shall hear!" is, specifically, a response to the narrative "from Creation to the Giving of the Torah."

In treating this section as a flashback, Rashi is inviting the reader to share a difficult perspective. He is apparently on the track of something elusive that cannot be articulated in any other way. What is the strength of the flashback technique, that would justify such a cumbersome strategy? If the events of 24:1–12 indeed occurred before the Torah was given, they might more lucidly have been interleaved into the primary narrative in chapter 19.

Moreover, what is suggested by Rashi's narrative of the preamble to Revelation? Before the people can receive the Ten Commandments, they must affirm the Covenant—a Covenant that emerges as consisting of seven principles of "natural law" (the "Noachide laws") various laws given a few weeks previously, and the story of the world as narrated in the Torah. This Covenant is not the "ratification" of a treaty whose terms are spelled out in some detail, but a commitment to something beyond obedience ("and we shall hear!") that Moses invites as he reads an enigmatic text "into their ears." In other words, his reading asks for a "hearing" response that is to transcend the pragmatic. "Into the ears of the people," suggests an intimacy of reading:[8] Moses is reading to touch them, to join reader and listener in a union that is not a merging. "We shall hear!" is their acknowledgment of the demand of the moment.

2. *Reading the Book: The Desire for Metamorphosis*

The Rupture at Sinai

Implicit in Rashi's reading is a moment of existential meeting with God that is a precondition of Revelation. This is an experience of rupture: all previous history comes to an end, is written down and, in an unprecedented register of consciousness, is read aloud and affirmed. We notice, indeed, that chapter 19, narrating the people's arrival at Sinai, begins without the customary connective: "On the third new moon after the Israelites had gone forth from the land of Egypt" (19:1). The usual form would be, "*And it was* in the third new moon." Meshech Chochma points out that this is an unparalleled mode of introducing a new historical event. "Nowhere in the whole Torah is there another case" of such a missing *vav*, or connective. He suggests that this disjunction reflects the end of the book, as Moses writes it down and reads it out.[9] From the words, "On the third new moon," a new text begins, to be written after the Ten Commandments, and beginning, like the Creation story, without the usual connectives.

In this way, Meshech Chochma is offering literary support for Rashi's reading. The text of the Torah retains a trace of the break between the pre-Sinai and the post-Sinai segments. There is a fissure—the missing *vav*—that indicates a moment *before* Revelation when the people assented to a Covenant based on a narrative of the world. Some unthinking continuum is ruptured as the people approach Sinai. They are exposed to a narrative that frames the past in a new way, in a way that bears some integral relation to law.

The *newness* of the Sinai moment is, indeed, Rashi's subject. He emphasizes, for example, the idea that the sprinkling of blood is a ritual feature of the Covenant that is universally connected with the ritual of immersion (*tevila*): "there is no blood-sprinkling without immersion" (24:6). Immersion in water most vividly evokes the symbolism of rebirth, of emergence to a new life. Both immersion and blood (circumcision) characterize the entry of the proselyte into the Jewish faith. It is in this vein that Rashi focuses on the period leading up to the Revelation, as the crucial period of the Covenant.

A possible approach to Rashi's reading is indicated by Maor VaShemesh, a nineteenth-century Chasidic commentator.[10] He points out that the people's formula of commitment, "All that God *has spoken*, we shall do and we shall hear!" issues strangely from the lips of those who, according to Rashi's thesis, have *not yet heard* God speak. What they mean, he suggests, is the seven Noachide laws, the laws given at Marah—all the laws that are styled "natural law," which form the basis of civilization. The category of "natural law" includes the injunctions against murder, sexual disorder, and theft, as well as honoring one's father and mother, and even keeping the Shabbath as a day of rest: all these are prudential institutions by which all human societies protect and preserve themselves. In committing themselves to the Covenant, the people recognize that the force of these laws lies not in their pragmatic, conventional nature, but in the fact that they are the will of God—given "by the command of the Creator." Before the Torah is given, Moses renarrates to them the "old laws," the "old story" from Creation to the present—but in a newly sacralized form. Natural law is newly infused with a sense of relationship to God, the Creator, who desires these modes of behavior.

According to this reading, the shift experienced by the people is from an unvarying performance of natural duties as the basis of a civilized life to a performance of the same duties in a way that changes from day to day. This shift is characterized by a new sense of time, as the fulfillment of the requirements of the law becomes a prism in which an evolving, ever-changing sense of relationship to God is mirrored. Every day brings a new and richer consciousness of those actions that, in the mode of natural law, would become automatic.

This new spiritual sensibility is partly brought to bear on the laws that have been part of human culture before Sinai. If the people can commit themselves to a new relation even with these "rational" laws, then they are qualified to receive the specific Revelation of Sinai.

Transformation of Old Meanings

Moses' narrative of the old laws, in effect, precipitates the people into a kind of blankness, in which the modalities of the past are exposed in a newly perceived spiritual sterility. They respond: "All that God *has spoken*—all the old laws—we now commit ourselves to fulfilling in a new way." In this view, the Covenant involves the people in a newly modulated relation to the world—a revisiting of familiar cultural vistas. This requires the consecration of sacrifice, the sprinkling of blood, the total immersion in water—and the reading of the history of the world from the beginning, so that the old meanings may be transformed, in the Light of a face.[11] On hearing this reading, they respond, "We shall do and we shall hear!"—committing themselves to a rearticulated relationship with the world of the past, and declaring themselves ready for the new laws of Sinai.

Maor VaShemesh adds a fine reading of a famous midrash, quoted by Rashi (19:1):

> "On this day, they came to the wilderness of Sinai:" on *this* day, not on *that* day? To teach you that the words of Torah should be new in your eyes each day.

The midrash bases the idea of the eternal newness of the Torah on the word, "this"—indicating the immediacy of the Gift of the Torah to the experience of each reader through the generations. Maor VaShemesh raises an objection: when the Israelites arrived at Mount Sinai, they had not yet been exposed to any words of Torah. How, then, can the moment of arrival, *before* the Torah is given, serve as a paradigm of the eternal freshness of the words of Torah? His answer is radical in its implications: before the process of Revelation begins, there is a *spontaneous* understanding that their relation to law has been inadequate; and a spontaneous resolution to imbue the old forms with new meanings, as the expression of God's will. The sense of "newness each day" derives from this new conception of law as the reflection of a relationship with God.

The intriguing aspect of this reading is the idea that a heteronomous concept of law is said to originate in a spontaneous or autonomous human recognition. At base, it is the desire for an existential, transformative experience of law—of culture—that opens the human being to a restructuring of the past and to the new dimensions of the future. The paradox, of course, is striking. The achievements of human reason, the social and ethical arrangements of civilization, now become the "commandment of the Creator," and are to be enacted in that spirit; while this shift in sensibility is generated by no irruption of the divine into the natural world, since it *precedes* any such irruption. Human beings, of their own accord, realize that in all their previous obedience to moral law they "have done nothing, for all was habit and convention . . ."

Revisioning Culture

The new era dawns, therefore, *before* the Torah is given. The Torah comes to answer a human readiness for a revisioning of culture. Moses "narrates" the old laws and receives the people's commitment to "re-do" the cultural field of the past. The face of the Other has been absent; before the new can come into being, a sense of absence must be recognized. In the psychoanalytic situation, the narratives of the past are revisited, restructured, in the transformative presence of the analyst. Through the dynamic of transference, the analyst provokes the patient to engage anew with the sterile old stories. It is the desire for such a redemptive Presence within culture, I suggest, that leads the people to Mount Sinai.

God as transformative Presence comes, commanding, from outside. But the desire for Him comes from within human consciousness, as do the forms in which that Presence is clothed. Christopher Bollas writes of the "quest for the transformational object," which arises out of the primary transformations of the mother-child relation. The presence of the mother achieves the resolution of infant discomforts: "emptiness, agony, and rage become fullness and content. The aesthetic of this experience is the particular way the mother meets the infant's need and transforms his internal and external realities."[12] The child incorporates not only the milk, but the *form* of the mother's handling. At a later stage, the maternal aesthetic includes language: "With the word, the child has found a new transformational object." This is "the second human aesthetic, the finding of the word to speak the self."[13]

For Bollas, the adult bears within him the structure of the maternal aesthetic. He will seek aesthetic moments with transformational others; and the quest will be shaped by the idioms of an internal world informed by the "thematics of mother's discourse": "In a sense, we learn the grammar of our being before we grasp the rules of our language."[14]

Bollas quotes from Kenneth Grahame's children's novel, *The Wind in the Willows*, where the rat hears what he feels is an ethereal sound: "Rapt, transported, trembling, he was possessed in all his senses by this new divine thing that caught up his helpless soul and swung and dandled it, a powerless but happy infant in a strong sustaining grasp."[15]

The desire for transformation is, likewise, I suggest, the subject of the passage from Maor VaShemesh. In his reading, it is this desire that brings the people to Sinai. And it is specifically Moses' reading of the Torah, the narrative from Creation to the present, that acts as a transformational object. In hearing this written text read aloud, the people rethink, redescribe the historical past. This experience, preceding Revelation and making it possible, has an uncanny quality, evoking early, unremembered metamorphoses of being.

The Power of the Text

Reading from a written text "into their ears," Moses evokes an intimate desire. As a result, they commit themselves to a reconstituted past, as well as to the Revelation ahead of them: ". . . and we shall hear!" It seems that the reading of a text has power to engage with the future in a way that oral narrative cannot achieve.

In midrashic sources, indeed, this theme of the transformative effect of a text read aloud is to be found in other contexts. Two examples come to mind, one portraying the early history of Israelite redemption, the other dealing with issues of closure—Aaron's acceptance of his own death.

In the first midrash, from Shemoth Rabba, texts appear as the authors of redemption:

> *"Let heavier work be laid upon the men"* (5:9). This teaches that they had in their possession scrolls with which they would play (*yishta'ash'u*) from Shabbat to Shabbat, saying that God would redeem them, because they rested on Shabbat. Pharaoh told them, "Let heavier work be laid upon the men and let them keep at it and not pay attention (*yish'u*) to false words."—Let them not play (*yishta'ash'u*) and let them not rest (*nefishin*—lit., "breathe") on Shabbat.[16]

The idea of Shabbat is suffused with the play activity around the Scrolls. The power of reading, of the refreshing play of the mind in relation to a text, is the significant privilege of Shabbat. The lightness of this play is correctly identified by Pharaoh as dangerous: "Let heavier work be laid upon them." As the king of heaviness, with a heart that is constantly growing heavier, harder, more impermeable, Pharaoh recognizes the threat of lightness. The reader of these scrolls is benefiting from the leisure-time of Shabbat to escape into a world of redemption. Quite aptly, therefore, Pharaoh bans Shabbat, the time of rest, or more literally, the time for air, for taking a deep breath (*nefishin*).

What Pharaoh has recognized as his greatest enemy is the human capacity to *read*—which means to reread, to reinterpret, to reappropriate the words of the past. Such reading is redemptive and dangerous to the totality of Pharaoh's empire. It suggests an "alternity," to use George Steiner's expression; it gives voice to the human capacity to create counterworlds, to posit otherness, as against the gravity and repose of nature:

> *Language is the main instrument of man's refusal to accept the world as it is.* Without that refusal, without the unceasing generation by the mind of "counter-worlds"—a generation which cannot be divorced from the grammar of counter-factual and optative forms—we should turn forever on the treadmill of the present . . . Ours is the ability, the need, to gainsay or "un-say" the world, to image and speak it otherwise.[17]

The activity of language, Steiner ingeniously argues, has much to do with saying "the Thing which was not," in Jonathan Swift's contemptuous phrase about lying. In *Gulliver's Travels*, the Houyhnhnms condemn the unclear, the ambiguous, on ethical, pragmatic, and philosophical grounds: "The Use of Speech was to make us understand one another, and to receive Information of Facts; now if anyone said *the Thing which was not*, these Ends were defeated."[18] As against this, Steiner proceeds to expound the "creativity of falsehood," as he traces it in various aspects of Greek mythology, ethics, and poetics.

"We invent for ourselves the major part of experience," says Nietzsche. I suggest that the power of speech to "alternate" on reality, to "say otherwise," is the play activity that Pharaoh must crush. To suffocate the lambent flame of imagination and language, "let heavier work be laid upon the men." The Shabbat idea offers an escape from necessity, from the realm of the pragmatic: it is a rest time that offers breathing space, language space. In the playful activity of reading, reality is redescribed, reinvented.

Steiner quotes Velimir Khlebnikov, the Russian futurist—"Words are the living eyes of secrecy"—and comments: "They encode, preserve, and transmit the knowledge, the shared memories, the metaphorical and pragmatic conjectures on life of a small group—a family, a clan, a tribe."[19] Such an experience of shared secrecy is the Shabbat play with texts that makes redemption thinkable. "If Your Torah had not been my *plaything* (*sha'ashu'a*), I should have perished in my poverty," said the Psalmist.[20] The Torah is for reading, study, narration, and interpretation: but, most vitally, it is for play.

Begetting the Truth

A second example of the transformative effect of reading is found in a poignant midrash on the death of Aaron: Here, in an act to set beside Moses' reading of Genesis to the people before the Revelation at Sinai, he reads Genesis together with his brother Aaron:

> God said to Moses, "Do Me a favor and tell Aaron about his death, for I am ashamed to tell him." Said R. Huna in the name of R. Tanhum bar Hiyya: What did Moses do? He rose early in the morning and went over to Aaron's place. He began calling out (*korei*), "Aaron, my brother!" Aaron came down to him and asked, "How is it that you have come here so early today?" Moses answered, "There is a *davar*, a thing/word, a problem from the Torah that I was mulling over (*meharher*) during the night, and it

> gave me great difficulty. That is why I have come over to visit you so early in the morning." Aaron asked, "What is the problem?" Moses answered, "I don't know what it was—but I do know that it is in the book of Genesis. Bring it, and let us read (*nikra*) in it." They took the book of Genesis and read in it, story by story, and at each one, Aaron said, "God did well, He created well." But when they came to the creation of Adam, Moses said, "What shall I say about Adam who brought death to the world?" Aaron replied, "My brother Moses, you surely would not say that in this we do not accept the decree of God? We have read how Adam and Eve were created and how they merited thirteen wedding canopies, as it is said, 'You were in Eden, the garden of God' (Ezek 28:13), and how Adam ate of the Tree, and was told, 'For dust you are, and to dust you shall return' (Gen 3:19)—and after all this glory, that they should come to this . . ." Then Moses said, "What about me—who had control over the ministering angels? And what about you—who halted the spread of death? Is our end not the same? We have another few years to live—perhaps twenty years?" Aaron said, "That is only a few years." Then Moses brought the number down more and more, until he spoke of the very day of death. Immediately, Aaron's bones felt as if they were quaking. He said, "Perhaps the *davar*, the word, the thing, was for me?" Moses answered, "Yes." Immediately, the Israelites saw that his stature had shrunk, as it is said, "The whole community saw that Aaron was about to die" (lit., had died) (Num 20:29). Then Aaron said, "My heart is dead within me, and the terror of death has fallen upon me." Moses asked him, "Do you accept death?" And he answered, "Yes . . ."[21]

As in Rashi's interpretation of the Book of the Covenant, Moses' reading matter is, specifically, the book of Genesis. Reading now becomes a shared act of recovery: it involves an active calling out (*kriya*), a summoning of the hidden meanings of the text. Aaron is moved to the roots of his being by the beauty of God's creation, as described in Genesis. It is Moses who raises the problem of death, and who presses the discussion from the literary to the personal level. When Aaron's bones start quaking and he surmises, "Perhaps the word is *for me*?" the midrash evokes the terror of a moment of recovery. Philosophical resignation is disrupted in a shattering recognition of physical disintegration and diminution. If resignation returns, it is the acquiescence that comes after terror, and retains its trace. Only the shared reading of the text could have achieved such a complex moment.

The most enigmatic aspect of the midrash is Moses' declaration that he does not remember what the word of Torah was. Presumably, this represents Moses' strategy in fulfilling his mission: he claims to have forgotten the troubling matter of the night, so as to institute a shared search through the text of Genesis. But possibly, Moses' forgetting is genuine. Particularly in view of the almost Oedipal tension of Moses' relation to his elder brother from the beginning of the narrative, his mission is indeed unbearable to him. A spasm of oblivion grips him. The dark word of the night, repressed, is to be sought out in the infinite Word of God—the text that, in this midrash, too, already exists.

The reading quest becomes not merely a fictional search, with a foregone conclusion—the tidings of death—but, quite genuinely, an attempt to recover a lost truth. Writing about the psychoanalytic project, Shoshana Felman makes a similar point:

> Psychoanalysis . . . profoundly rethinks and radically renews the very concept of the testimony, by submitting, and by recognizing for the first time in the history of culture, that one does not have to *possess* or *own* the truth, in order to effectively *bear witness* to it; that speech as such is unwittingly testimonial, and that the speaking subject constantly bears witness to a truth that nonetheless continues to escape him, a truth that is, essentially, *not available* to its own speaker.[22]

In this "underground of language," testimony becomes a mode of access to truth. The one who witnesses is also "the one who *begets* the truth, through the speech process of the testimony."[23] Felman describes how Freud, through his own testimony to his dream about his only partially successful treatment of his patient, Irma, *"give[s] birth* to the entire theory of dreams, and to its undreamt of implications."

"What is begotten by the unconscious testimony of the dream" might be a description of the process by which Moses and Aaron "give birth" to the forgotten "word of Torah." "One does not have to possess . . . the truth in order effectively to bear witness to it": conveying such a dark message to his brother, Moses forgets it and enters a kind of psychoanalytic dialogue with his brother, an unpredictable journey through the text of the Torah.

In this sense, reading is a summoning, a "calling" to the Torah text. It requires a disruption of prior knowledge. Mallarmé, the French symbolist poet, writes about writing: "One does not write luminously, on an obscure field. . . ; man pursues black on white."[24] The writing of the words of the Torah was, in the haunting midrashic description, "black fire on white fire." To read such a text is to engage with at least a residue of that darkness.

Moses' invitation to his brother to read the book of Genesis would be, in this case, an invitation to participate in the unforeseeable. The well-known text will generate in those willing to risk its obscurities a truth not possessed ahead of time. "Perhaps the word is *for me*?"

3. *"We Shall Do and We Shall Hear"*

The Virtuosity of the Angels

I return, now, to Moses' other reading of Genesis, as the Book of the Covenant. This, Rashi claims, was the preamble to the Revelation: the dimension of the days leading up to the sixth of Sivan that is not described in the original narrative in chapter 19. For Rashi, chapter 24 (1–11) is a flashback, illuminating an undisclosed theme of those days of expectation. In the very nature of the flashback, there is a sense of exposing dark corners of the past; there is the sudden revelation, too late to be in any objective sense effective, of the essence of the past. For the subject of the flashback is usually the repressed heart of the matter. All that has been narrated is exposed in its inadequacy, as well as simply illumined.

The essential preparation for the giving of the Torah is an act of rereading the texts of the past. Such a rereading testifies to a sensibility never before known; it brings to birth the new, precisely insofar as it yields up its grasp of truth. For, in this area, to possess is to be possessed. Or, as Maor VaShemesh put it, to reread the old laws is to realize that, in obeying them, one has "done nothing." This encounter with "nothing," with the staleness of old possessions, provides difficult access to the new.

The response of the people is "We shall do and we shall hear!" In a classic discussion, the Talmud interrogates the apparent reversal of order:

> When the Israelites said, "We shall do," before "We shall hear," six hundred thousand angels came down and attached two crowns to each Israelite, one for the *doing*, the other for the *hearing* . . .
>
> When the Israelites said, "We shall do," before "We shall hear," there came forth a heavenly voice: "Who revealed to My children this secret

> that the ministering angels use?—as it is written, 'Bless God, His angels, who are mighty of strength, and *do* His word, to *hear* the voice of His word.' (Ps 103:20)—first they *do*, then they *hear*."[25]

At first sight, the idea of doing before hearing implies a kind of rashness, a lack of circumspection. Rashi, in fact, directly addresses this, when he observes that the Israelite response is different from that "of other servants, who first listen to the command, to find out whether they are able to accept it, or not." And, in the same Talmudic passage, the Sadducees criticize the Jewish people as *ama paziza*—"a rash people, for whom the mouth passes before the ears. . . You should have listened in order to know whether you were able to accept."

This very rashness, however, is called by God "the secret of the angels." Implicit in this description is the idea of a modality generally inaccessible to the human. Rather archly, God chides the people for making use of an esoteric order of things: "Who revealed this to you?" is, of course, a covert compliment to the angelic virtue within an apparent irrationality.

In saying, "We shall do, and we shall hear!" the Talmud implies, the people assume some of the virtuosity of the angels, who are capable precisely of such a brilliant power of action. Like the virtuoso musician, whose skill makes movement seem to happen before thought ("hearing") can intervene, the people discover a genius for generous and decisive commitment. All the hesitations that beset the amateur have long been resolved: the fingers fly faster than the eye or the ear can observe. In the case of the musician, however, this angelic condition is the fruit of much practice and years of experience. In the case of the people's response, it is spontaneous, unpracticed, a "beyond-freedom," to use Levinas's expression, a "lucidity without tentativeness."[26]

The Temptation of Temptation

In his essay, "The Temptation of Temptation," Levinas depicts his conception of the "perfectly adult effort" of the people at Sinai. He writes on this Talmudic passage:

> They do before hearing. It is a secret of angels which is in question here, not the consciousness of children. Israel would thus have been another Prometheus. It would have seized upon the secret of pure, unmixed intelligences.[27]

"Another Prometheus": Israel, acting contrary to logic, is not, strangely, acting in childish faith. If one accepts the Torah before one knows it, this is "what underlies any inspired act, even artistic, for the act only brings out the form in which it only now recognizes its model, never glimpsed before."[28] To act in this way is to go beyond knowledge, to go beyond the "temptation of temptation."

The people, "mighty of strength," like the angels, are able to contain the "non-knowing with which philosophical knowing begins."[29] This "non-knowing" is set against the "temptation of temptation," the condition of Western man. Sardonically, Levinas describes this condition:

> He is for an open life, eager to try everything, to experience everything, "in a hurry to live. Impatient to feel." . . . Ulysses' life, despite its misfortunes, seems to us marvelous, and that of Don Juan enviable, despite its tragic end. One must be rich and a spendthrift and multiple before being essential and one.[30]

In Levinas's discussion, Plato and Christianity share the prejudice that lies at the basis of Western civilization: "All temptations must be possible."

The alternative to this is not a mere innocence, "defined purely negatively as a lack, associated with naïveté and childhood, marking it as a provisional state."[31] The integrity of the people's commitment precedes the choice between good and evil. It is an adherence to the good that is expressed in "a way of *actualizing without beginning with the possible*, of knowing without examining . . ." This "pact with the good" is prior to any particular choice; and is incompatible with "all that moral extraterritoriality opened up by the temptation of temptation."[32]

Such a direct relation with the true, Levinas claims,

> can only be the relation with a person, with another. The Torah is given in the Light of a face. The epiphany of the other person is *ipso facto* my responsibility toward him: seeing the other is already an obligation toward him. A direct optics—without the mediation of any idea—can only be accomplished as ethics . . . Such a knowledge is one in which its messenger is simultaneously the very message.[33]

The confrontation at Sinai is essentially "face to face"—an encounter with the Face of the Other. This is the experience that underwrites "We shall do and we shall hear!"—a response to the "gleam of exteriority" in the face of the Other.[34] This is the place where totality breaks up. It is a "relation with what always overflows thought":[35] the "astonishing feat of containing more than it is possible to contain."[36]

In Levinas's discussion, the new consciousness of Sinai becomes a paradigm for all relationships with the Other. A primordial solipsism is challenged, called into question:

> To approach the Other in conversation is to welcome his expression, in which at each instant he overflows the idea a thought would carry away from it. It is therefore to *receive* from the Other beyond the capacity of the I, which means exactly: to have the idea of infinity. But this also means: to be taught. The relation with the Other, or Conversation, is a non-allergic relation, an ethical relation: but inasmuch as it is welcomed this conversation is a teaching.[37]

The emphasis on learning and teaching renders the situation of encounter with the Other as *unbearable*—"beyond the capacity of the I"—and yet, strangely, *welcome*. This is the paradoxical force of the "non-allergic" relation, of the *receiving* of the Other. Its foundational narrative is the *receiving* of the Torah, face to face, with the welcoming words, "We shall do and we shall hear!"

The people greet the "indiscreet face of the Other that calls [them] into question. The Other—the absolutely other—paralyzes possession." Their response, in this act of hospitality, is to an experience of teaching: "This voice coming from another shore teaches transcendence itself. Teaching signifies the whole infinity of exteriority. And the whole infinity of exteriority is not first produced, to then teach: teaching is its very production."[38]

For Levinas, therefore, Sinai is the site where transcendence is first "taught" to human beings, in the form of the ethical relation to the "face" of the other. This new awareness now infuses culture, the laws and practices of civilization, with an absolute and personal urgency, the sense of "the command of the Creator." The infinity encountered at Sinai is also the infinity encountered in the face of *any* other. It requires action, response, that comes before any calculation or choice.

"We Shall Do": Realizing the Hands

A model for the problematic nature of such a response is suggested in the midrashic notion that, in approaching the mountain, all crippled limbs were healed—including the hands, "for they said: 'We shall *do* and we shall hear!' "[39] The power of action is signified by healthy hands; without the imaginative experience of "having hands," the people could not have committed themselves to the Other at Sinai.

In an essay entitled, simply, "Hands,"[40] Oliver Sacks describes a congenitally blind victim of cerebral palsy. Highly intelligent and literate, she is inexplicably incapable of using her hands. Since the hands are not usually affected by cerebral palsy, Sacks finds her declaration that they are useless as "lumps of dough" startling. He speculates that she has been overprotected and has therefore never developed a normal use of her hands. Quoting the professional literature, he tells of cases where the gnostic systems that allow perceptive use of the hands were "dissociated" as a consequence of injury.

Sacks's patient has a complete "developmental agnosia," with no "memory" whatsoever of her hands. With some emotion, he describes her "birth as a 'motor individual' " and, indeed, as a complete "perceptual individual." Her imagination helps her to achieve a literary kind of recognition of objects she has never before seen or felt. In the fullest sense, she acquires hands. The doughy hands come to interrogate reality, to "taste" the faces of others, until she achieves local fame as a sculptress.

The core of Sacks's essay is the question of *praxis*, the need for *use* of limbs that have become de-realized. Sacks quotes Goethe: "In the beginning is the deed." The sudden re-realization of the hands that are tricked into action reverses the physiological data. The wonder that inspires this and many of Sacks's case histories is the possibility of rebirth, the sudden leap back into subjective reality and "life."[41]

If the midrash tells of limbs crippled in Egypt and cured at Sinai, it seems concerned with the rebirth of complete "perceptual individuals." The damage done in Egypt is not only a violation of muscles and bones: but of an inner self-mapping of power and coherence. The ordeal at Sinai, at one level, is a way of bringing back into use the imaginary equivalents of the broken limbs. "It is not right," says God, "that I should give My Torah to the crippled."[42] The problem is not, primarily, physical health. Rather, to have healthy hands is to be able to *say*: "We shall do." At this moment, there is a conscious wonder at a power lost beyond living memory and recovered in the Light of a face.

We remember Jacob's hands, as he blesses his grandsons, Ephraim and Manasseh (Gen chapter 48). He crosses his hands (*sikel et yadav*), in order to give Ephraim priority over the elder son, Manasseh. Joseph protests: Manasseh is the firstborn. And Jacob answers: "I know, my son, I know."[43] Clearly, the blind Jacob knows what he is about. Some of the commentaries[44] translate *sikel* (here, "he crossed"), in accordance with the root meaning "intelligence": "He moved his hands with conscious knowledge." Jacob is quite aware of who stands at his right, who is the firstborn, and whom he wishes to place under his right hand. Other commentaries,[45] however, translate *sikel*: His blind hands have their own cunning: caressing, they find their way to the heads of the children, in a kind of bodily knowledge, in which the hands are more than implements of the intellect. "I know, my son; I know," says Jacob, expressing an intelligence in which the hands are not mastered but integrated into a trusting wholeness.

The Offense against the Ear

Returning to the people's declaration, "We shall do and we shall hear!" we notice that we have celebrated the power of *na'aseh*—"We shall do!"—of an unhesitant action that responds in reborn vitality to the face of the Other. The awareness of the Presence of the Other now infuses all acts with a new energy, which changes, increases from day to day. In this awareness, "We shall do!" is the response to Moses' oral narrative of the history of the world, to the old laws. However, after Moses has written the Book of the Covenant and read it out to them, they add *Nishma*—"We shall hear!" And in the Talmudic narrative of Sinai, we remember, there were *two* crowns bestowed on the head of each Israelite. "Hearing" may in that narrative be overshadowed by "doing"; but it can clearly not be entirely effaced. And, indeed, for the Chasidic writers, it becomes climactic, the form of commitment that in the reversed order of Doing/Hearing piques imagination.

By adding the word *ve-nishma*—"and we shall hear!"—Maor Va-Shemesh suggested, the people declare their openness to the future, to the new laws of the Torah. Another Chasidic writer, Sefath Emeth, registers the harmonics of *na'aseh ve-nishma* with closer attention to the "hearing" dimension.[46] He begins his homily by quoting the law given earlier in the Parsha about the slave who refuses to accept freedom after six years of slavery:

> If the slave declares, "I love my master and my wife and children: I do not wish to go free," his master shall take him before God. He shall be brought to the door or the doorpost, and his master shall pierce his ear with an awl; and he shall remain his slave for life. (21:5–6)

The Sages comment:

> "Why is the ear singled out of all limbs of the body? God said: The ear that heard on Sinai: 'the children of Israel are My slaves' (Lev 25:55), and not slaves of slaves—and yet he went and acquired a master for himself—let that ear be pierced!"[47]

Sefath Emeth asks: Why should the ear be mutilated, since the sin is basically one of *action*, not of *hearing?* His answer places the faculty of *hearing* at the center of the Jewish spiritual enterprise. When the Israelites committed themselves to the Covenant, saying, "We shall do and we shall hear!" they expressed a desire to go beyond the *doing* mode, beyond the basic requirements of the Commandments. "We shall hear!" means that they hold themselves alert to further and finer intimations of God's will. This attitude of alertness to the extralegal dimensions of the Torah signifies an aspiration to respond at any moment to God's will. In the case of the slave, quite possibly he feels comfortable with his master; he has achieved an equilibrium that allows him to maintain his religious life in slavery. But, insists Sefath Emeth, it was not for this that Israel was created: their destiny is not a slavish, robotlike performance of prescribed acts, but a life of continuous, passionate "listening" to God. A slave, or, for that matter, an exiled people, cannot achieve this condition. For this reason, a slave who loves his master, who has abdicated the difficult freedom that transcends rote-living, has offended primarily against his *hearing*. In token of a failure in the work of transcendence, his ear is marked.

Sefath Emeth adds a comment on the slave's words: "I love my master." He sets this against the Commandment, "You shall love God." Effectively, the slave is proclaiming an easier way of loving God, through love of the master and of all the provisions of his slave-status. He *prefers* this indirect form of religious life. This, however, represents a regressive mode, a failure, essentially, of the *ear*.

In this passage, the Chasidic writer attaches the largest value to the faculty of hearing. The destiny of the Jewish people, he claims, lies precisely in their openness to the continual revelation of the not-yet-revealed. The already-revealed is to be obeyed; but beyond that, and closer to the heart of the spiritual life, is the constant quest indicated by *nishma*—"We shall hear!" The slave becomes the prototype of a stupefied existence, which confines itself to correct behavior. In such an existence, what is loved is the "master," not God.

In this analysis, freedom becomes essential to loving God and doing His will. A static obedience misses the point, since it is the desire to be more than one is, to lay oneself open to intimations beyond one's experience, that marks the spirituality of *na'aseh ve-nishma*, "We shall do and we shall hear!"

". . . We Shall Hear": Welcoming the Expression of the Other

This understanding of the hearing-mode is, of course, very different from that of the Talmud. There, hearing meant the rational understanding that normally precedes commitment; and the reversal of order in *doing* before *hearing* signified an uncalculating readiness to obey. But in Levinas's analysis of the Talmudic passage, this readiness is engendered only in relationship to the face of the Other. As we have seen, Levinas characterizes the Face, the way in which the Other presents himself, as *expression*: "To approach the Other in conversation is to welcome his expression, in which at each instant he overflows the idea a thought would carry away from it."[48] This encounter "at each moment destroys and overflows the plastic image," left by the static image of the face. By focusing on the mode of *welcoming the expression* of the Other, Levinas indicates the sensitivity of the moment-to-moment reality of relationship. It is this quality that suffuses the *na'aseh ve-nishma* commitment: "We shall do and we shall hear!" is the readiness to entertain the "idea of infinity."

Here, Levinas comes close to the concept of spiritual "hearing" in Sefath Emeth. His ethic of aspiration is a movement toward the Other: "To hear a voice speaking to you is *ipso facto* to accept obligation towards the one speaking."[49] And this sensitivity to the voice, to the "expression" of the Other, is the essential work of Sinai.

The slave in love with slavery has offended against the ear, in a way that no specific violation of the law can match. He has "deafened" himself to the voice that speaks each day and makes Revelation a daily affair. Indeed, the words that the slave uses, "I do not wish to go free"—*lo etze*—jars against the primary theme of Exodus. In a book where "going out of Egypt" is the thematic premise, "I shall not go out" resonates demonically. This is, of course, a private, even a domestic mode of refusal; but perhaps it is precisely in the domestic arena, in the attitude toward the masters, the habitual, the already known, that freedom is affirmed or repudiated.

> The ear that heard at Sinai, "You shall have no other gods in My presence"—and yet he went and broke off the yoke of the Kingdom of

> Heaven and accepted the yoke of human beings—may that ear be pierced![50]

In this version of the midrash, the sin of the slave is idolatry. A direct, vital welcome of God is replaced by the fetishisms, the fixities of a world of "masters." In this apostasy, the first victim is the human ear.

4. *The Flashback at Sinai: Reading as Self-Creation* 

Before Revelation: The Human Quest

When Moses writes the Book of the Covenant and reads it aloud "into the *ears* of the people," this is a moment of pure freedom. Before the Torah is given, they are asked to restructure the apparent order and meaning of the past. Both narrative and law present themselves and are recognized as valueless without the presence of the Other, without the welcome expression of His face.

Beyond the objective realities of maintaining a civilization, there is the dimension of transcendence, the constant undoing of a self-possessed knowledge. The reversal of hearing and doing suggests a breakdown in the linear logic of knowingness. In the discussion by Maor VaShemesh, this moment of blankness precedes Revelation. In its wake comes a fully *human* quest for the face of the Other, a welcoming of His expression that transforms all that is already known. Only after human awareness has been extended, and after the people have declared themselves ready for further encounters with transcendence, can the Torah be given.

In the Talmudic passage, *doing* and *hearing* are rewarded by two crowns on each head. Levinas beautifully comments:

> But is it certain that the crowns were rewards? Weren't they the very splendor that doing and hearing take on when they follow each other in the inverse order to that of logic?[51]

The people wear the crowns of *doing* and *hearing* to celebrate a new order. Both acts become splendid within a new organic structure. Perhaps a talent for inverting the order of verbs is precisely the active hearing that narratives invite. When Moses reads the history of the world, they hear it not as a linear chronicle, but as a familiar story, familiar laws, to be reconsecrated.

That is, they hear with a sense of flashback, illuminating the now-banal with the light that can only shine today. To say, "We shall do and we shall hear!" is to commit oneself to invert the order of things forever. It means to adopt a posture of "un-knowingness," that constantly "destroys and overflows" plastic images of all kinds.

THE HEARING HEART

R. Nahman, too, writes about knowing and un-knowing.[52] In his discussion, *na'aseh* and *nishma* represent the revealed and the hidden dimensions of reality:

> *Na'aseh*—"We shall do"—refers to the revealed—that is, to the commandments that one can fulfill, on one's own level. *Nishma*—"We shall hear"—refers to the hidden—that is, to things that one cannot grasp. For *around* each commandment, there are other things, which belong to the class of the hidden. The commandment itself one can fulfill; but the spiritual work that surrounds the commandment is largely unknown, hidden. This, too, is the relation of the Torah and prayer: the Torah can be known and fulfilled; while prayer is generated in that area that surrounds each commandment, which is enigmatic. For *hearing* is a function of the heart, as in Solomon's prayer: "Give Your servant a *hearing heart*." And the heart expresses itself to God in prayer.

These two dimensions of *na'aseh* and *nishma* are to be found at every level and in all worlds. Moving from one level to another, one's previous *nishma*, area of hiddenness, becomes one's new *na'aseh*, area of fulfillment; and one acquires a new area of *nishma*, of hiddenness.

In this difficult passage, R. Nahman maps the world as consisting of nuclei of commandments, of required acts, surrounded by aureoles of words that "tease us out of thought." These aureoles—the language is explicitly circular—pass one's understanding; yet clearly they are part of the field of consciousness. They form a kind of horizon, a sense of presence, of the not-yet-known.

Arthur Green writes of this figure in R. Nahman's account of the spiritual journey:

> At any given point where the seeker stands in his religious life, his mind is filled with some particular content of understanding: he conceives of God in some specific way. This conception is the *penimi*, that which is

> "within" the mind at that moment. This *penimi*, however, is inevitably attached to a *maqqif*, a conception beyond the mind's present grasp, one which at the same time both challenges the *penimi* and offers a conception on a higher level. Man's task is to seek out this *maqqif*, to bring it into his mind as a new *penimi*, and thus to seek a still-higher challenge and resolution. This is the theoretical expression of Nahman's call for constant growth.[53]

A sense of "not-knowing" is constantly engendered by the presence of an "aura" surrounding the known. Walter Benjamin defines the "aura" of natural objects:

> We define the aura . . . as the unique phenomenon of a distance, however close it may be. If, while resting on a summer afternoon, you follow with your eyes a mountain range on the horizon or a branch which casts its shadow over you, you experience the aura of those mountains, of that branch . . . To pry an object from its shell, to destroy its aura, is the mark of a perception whose "sense of the universal equality of things" has increased to such a degree that it extracts it even from a unique object by means of reproduction.[54]

The uniqueness of a natural object, or of a work of art, is its aura. In order to perceive this, one must allow a "distance" to intervene. The contrary urge—to get hold of an object at very close range—is to obliterate that uniqueness. Benjamin describes the ritualistic basis of the aura of the work of art, which has been in decline since the Renaissance. The *cult* value of the picture, he claims, finds a last refuge in photography: "For the last time the aura emanates from the early photographs in the fleeting expression of a human face. This is what constitutes their melancholy, incomparable beauty."[55]

In Benjamin's discussion, the elusive phenomenon of "aura" is last seen in these early photographs, which evoke in the viewer a "free-floating contemplation." It is the human face that is the last survivor in a historical transformation in the function of art—the photographed face that evokes a sense of uniqueness, of distance.

In R. Nahman's poetic text, as in Benjamin's, spiritual power emanates from the uniqueness, the distance of the object. R. Nahman appropriates Solomon's prayer: "Give Your servant a *hearing heart*"[56] to evoke the desire for the aura. When the people say, "We shall do and we shall *hear*," therefore, they express a commitment to the difficult dialectic of the known and the hidden. This commitment, or desire, becomes poignant in the context of Benjamin's elegiac analysis of the "decay of the aura."

In relation to the Torah, however, R. Nahman, Sefath Emeth, Maor VaShemesh, and Levinas all take their stand on an eternity of revelation. Welcoming the human face, its presence, its "expression," remains the metaphor that informs and transforms the giving of the Torah.

The Flashback: "Perhaps the Word Is for Me?"

If we return to our starting point, and reconsider Rashi's anachronistic reading, we can now suggest that the flashback technique—which seems to yield such a labored, unnatural reading of the text—affords a unique, even an ethical advantage. It gives the reader the transformative moment of a remystified past: the same moment as Moses gave the people when he read them a familiar book, familiar laws, suddenly strange. For them, the past is transfused by a new Presence, and they declare themselves ready for more such transfusions in the future: "We shall do *and we shall hear*!" For the reader of the Torah, a narrative that told of the terror of God's Revelation, of boundary lines drawn round the mountain, and of Moses summoned upward and sent downward at the command of God, is now reread as the project of a Covenant. Here, Moses is central, the agent of relationship between God and the people.

This flashback, like the people's revisiting of the past, confronts the reader with the presence of the Other. A rigidity, a knowingness of possessing truth, is disrupted as, with difficulty, we superimpose the imagery of covenant, of blood halved and sprinkled, of a book written and read and received, over the old narrative. We experience a "spot of time," a double-exposure effect. What led up to the Revelation at Sinai acquires a rich undecidability, an aura to which the reader may well respond with *na'aseh ve-nishma*, "We shall do and we shall hear."

In our reading, Rashi has been engaged in a "flashback within a flashback": he has drawn us back in time, to illuminate a shadow, an absence, of which we were not even aware. In that sudden pool of light, the people are discovered, as they are drawn back to the time of Creation and onward through time, till the present day. And they, too, like Moses reading with his brother, encounter God and themselves in unsuspected corners. "Perhaps the word is *for me*?"

In this way, the present moment of the people is transformed, as it transforms. And the reader of the Torah, too, experiences the jolt, the disorientation of a revised reading. Suddenly, the aura appears. Perhaps it must be there, if one is to receive the Torah at all.

> "This day, God has commanded you to do all these statutes" (Deut 27:16). Why "*this* day"? Did God never give commandments to Israel till now? But this was the fortieth year!—as it is said, "And it was in the fortieth year in the eleventh month" (1:3). But Moses told the Israelites, Let the Torah be precious to you each day as though on this very day you received it at Mount Sinai!
>
> Said R. Yochanan: Anyone who makes true meaning of Torah, it is as though he *made himself*—as it is said, "God commanded me at that time to teach you the statutes and laws, to do them (*la'asothchem otham*)" (4:14). It does not say *la'asoth otham* ("to do them") but *la'asothchem athem* ("to make *yourselves*"—reading *otham* without the *vav*). From here, we learn that it is as though he made and created himself.[57]

The activity of reading the Torah is the activity of self-creation. Because the unseizable Presence of God surrounds the letters, the words, the graspable and the performable, the human being "gives birth" to a truth never before known. Ultimately, the purpose of the Revelation at Sinai is the creation of a human being. "Only in the discovery of a Thou is it possible to hear an actual I, an I that is not self-evident but emphatic and underlined."[58] A new consciousness is born, in which object and aura, rationality and mysticism, fusion and distance, daily seek equilibrium.

7 *Teruma*

THE SANCTUARY IN FIRE: COMEDY AND TRAGEDY

[25:1–27:19]

1. The Mishkan and the Golden Calf: A Question of Order

The Mishkan: Retaining Revelation

Before the eyes of the Israelites, Moses recedes toward the summit of the fiery mountain: "Now the vision of the glory of God was like a consuming fire at the top of the mountain, before the eyes of the Israelites. Moses went inside the cloud and ascended the mountain; and Moses was on the mountain forty days and forty nights" (24:17–18).

So ends the previous Parsha, with an image of consuming fire, cloud, and an enigmatic intimation of Moses' forty-day encounter with God. A human being ascends into consuming fire: the image is imprinted on the vision of the Israelites massed at the foot of the mountain.

Then, without transition or preamble, we read the beginning of the new Parsha:

> God spoke to Moses, saying: "Tell the children of Israel to bring Me gifts; you shall accept gifts for Me from every person whose heart so moves him. And these are the gifts that you shall accept from them: gold, silver,

> and copper; blue, purple, and crimson yarns, fine linen, goats' hair, rams' skins dyed red, tahash skins, and acacia wood; oil for lighting, spices for the anointing oil and for the aromatic incense; onyx stones and other stones for setting, for the ephod and for the breast-plate. And let them make for Me a sanctuary that I may dwell among them. Exactly as I show you—the pattern of the Tabernacle and the pattern of all its furnishings—so shall you make it. (25:1–9)

After the terror of mystic encounter comes the shock of material—an inventory of metals, wools, woods, skins, oils, spices, and stones, culminating in the simple divine demand, "Let them make for Me a sanctuary that I may dwell among them." The jar of dissonance is palpable. Moses dares the consuming fire to obey God's call, and *this* is the burden of His will!—a list of banal objects with which to construct a home for Him to live in! The seamless flow of the narrative intensifies the reader's wonder.

Traditionally, there have been two kinds of response to this sense of wonder. One is represented by Ramban, the other by Rashi and a large body of midrashic sources. In Ramban's reading, the Israelites have been transformed by their encounter "face-to-face" with God; they have received the basic commandments and committed themselves to fulfilling them; to affirm this, they have entered into a Covenant with God. In essence, they are like proselytes. They have fulfilled God's first stipulation before the Revelation at Sinai: "Now, if you will listen faithfully to My voice and keep My covenant, you shall be My treasured possession among all the peoples. Indeed, all the earth is Mine, but you shall be to Me a kingdom of priests and a holy nation" (19:5–6). In view of all this, Ramban writes: "Behold, they are holy, fit for a sanctuary for God's Presence to dwell among them. And so, the first thing God commanded was the Tabernacle (Mishkan), that there should be among them a house dedicated to His name . . ."[1]

In Ramban's reading, the idea of a sanctuary for God in their midst is a token of transformation: after the Revelation and the Covenant, they have become fit vessels for the Presence of God. He continues to describe the "secret of the Mishkan (Tabernacle)": it is to be a version of Mount Sinai that they can carry with them on their travels.[2] There are many linguistic resonances linking Sinai with the Tabernacle, including references to God's "glory,"[3] and to His voice[4] emerging "from the midst of the fire,"[5] and "from between the cherubim"[6] (the gold of the cherubim representing fire). The Mishkan is to provide a solution to the problem of retaining Revelation—how is Sinai to remain with them, part of them, central to them? How is the possibility of linking the sublime and the mundane realms to become a bearable reality? How is the fire of Sinai to be tolerated in ordinary life? Is there an imaginable version of an intersection between these two realms, a portable fiery nexus, that will not consume its vehicle? Otherwise, Sinai will become a remembrance of things past.[7] For Ramban, this possibility is realized in the people's transformation at Sinai. They are now worthy to carry a version of Sinai with them on their travels through the wilderness, a medium for God to continue revealing Himself.

A modern version of this notion of the significance and purpose of the Mishkan is offered by Cassuto:

> we must realize that the children of Israel, after they had been privileged to witness the Revelation of God on Mount Sinai, were about to journey from there and thus draw away from the site of the theophany. So long as they were encamped in the place, they were conscious of God's nearness; but once they set out on their journey, it seemed to them as though the link had been broken, unless there were in their midst a tangible symbol of God's presence among them. It was the function of the Tabernacle [literally, "Dwelling" in Hebrew] to serve as such a symbol. Not without reason, therefore, does this section come immediately after the section that describes the making of the Covenant at Mount Sinai. The nexus between Israel and the Tabernacle is a perpetual extension of the bond that was forged at Sinai between the people and their God . . . This is . . . the significance of the clear parallelism between the last sentences of the preceding section, describing how the Divine Presence dwelt upon Mount Sinai, and the closing passage of our Book, which depicts, in like terms, how the Divine Presence abode in the Tabernacle . . . [The] very design of the Tabernacle was able to inspire the people with the confident feeling that the Lord was present in their midst.[8]

In both of these readings, the narrative of Sinai runs seamlessly and cogently into the instructions for the Mishkan.

The Golden Calf and the Mishkan: An Alternative Chronology

By contrast, the other major traditional view of the narrative structure—that of Rashi and his midrashic sources—emphasizes rupture, disjunction. Here, for example, is Midrash Tanchuma:

> "Let them make for Me a sanctuary that I may dwell among them." When was this passage about the Mishkan said to Moses? On Yom Kippur (the Day of Atonement) itself [when the people were finally forgiven for the sin of the Golden Calf], even though the Mishkan-instructions are written before the narrative of the Golden Calf. Said R. Judah in the name of R. Shalom, "The order of the Torah narrative is not necessarily chronological, as it is said, 'Her course meanders for lack of knowledge.' (Prov 5:6) So do the paths of the Torah and its narratives meander. On Yom Kippur, Moses was told, 'Let them make Me a sanctuary . . .' How do we know? Because Moses ascended the mountain on the 6th of Sivan and spent forty days and nights there. And then, another forty days, and another forty days—altogether, a hundred and twenty days. So you find that atonement was achieved on Yom Kippur [the tenth of Tishrei]. And on that very day, God told him, 'Let them make for Me a sanctuary . . .'—so that all the nations may know that the Golden Calf has been atoned. That is why the Mishkan is called the Tabernacle of Testimony (38:21), for it is testimony to the whole world that God resides in your sanctuary. Said God, 'Let the gold of the Mishkan come and atone for the gold of the Golden Calf, of which it is written, "All the people broke off their gold jewelry": (32:3) therefore, the atonement is through gold. "And these are the gifts that you shall accept from them: gold . . ." (25:3).' God said, 'I will bring healing to you and cure you of your wounds.' " (Jer 30:17)[9]

On this account, there is a radical omission in the Torah narrative. Soundlessly intervening between Sinai and the Mishkan is the catastrophe of the Golden Calf. The text may seem to read seamlessly, but it holds a fissure at its heart. The Golden Calf narrative, which we find in Exodus 32–34, is written out of chronological order. In historical sequence, it preceded the instructions for the Mishkan. The Golden Calf was made on the sixteenth of Sivan, forty days after Moses' first ascent on the mountain; while the

Mishkan instructions were given eighty days later, on Yom Kippur, the tenth of Tishrei, and only as a token of full atonement for the sin.

This tortuous reading, which is rather prevalent in the midrashic literature,[10] and which Rashi adopts,[11] has a radically disorienting effect on the reader. The principle which the midrash cites—"The Torah narrative is not necessarily in chronological order"—offends some basic reading instinct of narrative decorum. It alienates with its implicit warning: "Not all is as it seems! The Tabernacle may be described before the Golden Calf but, in fact, it was commanded after."

In this midrash, in fact, the sense of discomfort becomes quite palpable in the quotation from Proverbs 5:6: "She does not chart a path of life; her course meanders for lack of knowledge." The subject of this description in Proverbs is the "strange woman," whose seductions are to be evaded. In the very expression, "*strange* woman," the Proverbist conveys alienation; the author of the midrash imports this resonance into his text, even as he describes the oblique strategies of Torah narrative. If, indeed, the order of the narrative is not necessarily chronological, this evokes discomfort, alienation in the reader, and the midrash takes account of this response.

Why, in that case, does such a large body of midrashic literature—as well as several of the classical commentaries—adopt this reading? In what way is the more straightforward reading of Ramban and Cassuto unsatisfactory? What is the specific and necessary insight to be gained from the tortuous reading? If the Golden Calf episode preceded the instructions for building the Mishkan, why is it narrated after them? This seems a far from elegant solution to the problems of historical narrative. A highly artificial structure is superimposed upon the chronology of events: to what end?

The Mishkan: A Therapeutic Project

Taking up the question from the reader's perspective, we notice the ambiguity of such a reading. We read with an *arrière-pensée*; at each point, we remind ourselves of a repressed narrative which sheds uneasy light on the clarities and objectivities of the Mishkan—materials, measurements, structure, and furnishings. For if, on Ramban's reading, these are simply an expression of the intimate presence of God, or, on Cassuto's, of the "perpetual extension of the bond that was forged at Sinai," they have now become an afterthought, a reaction to the Golden Calf debacle, perhaps a concession to the need for concrete representation so disastrously manifested in that episode.

Even the inventory of materials is saturated with a history of failure: "Let the gold of the Mishkan come and atone for the gold of the Calf." The atonement function of the Mishkan evokes the idea of a therapeutic project, as, indeed, our midrash clearly implies, in its closing quotation from Jeremiah: "I will bring healing to you and cure you of your wounds." There is an intimate, repressed sense of the Mishkan's function that has everything to do with the Golden Calf. Viewed psychoanalytically, the Golden Calf is a disaster that was always waiting to happen. The Mishkan comes to engage with a profound pathology that finally comes to crisis in the Golden Calf. So unbearable is this sense of what the Mishkan portends that it cannot yet be brought to consciousness. The daytime reality of the building instructions is therefore invested with a secretive, compelling meaning that arises from the story not (yet) told. In some literal sense, the gold splendor of the Mishkan *covers for* (the literal meaning of *kapper*—"atone") a network of associations not yet explicit in the text.

This idiosyncratic field of associations is constructed into a world, the lineaments of which are largely unconscious. Jonathan Lear calls this world an *idiopolis*: in it, powerful fantasies seek reenactment, the aim of which is to endow the world with comprehensible meaning.[12] He asks a provocative question: "Might transference, as it emerges in analysis, be an attempt to turn the analyst into an artifact, a *covering* [my italics] . . . Just as the superego serves as a 'covering' for a powerful unconscious phantasy, so it seems that the analysand attempts to make the analyst into the statue of the Commendatore."[13]

If we elaborate on Lear's question, we may ask: might the intersection of Mishkan and Golden Calf, as it eventually emerges in the text, be an attempt to turn the Mishkan into an artifact, a "covering"? By "covering," Lear refers to a conscious idea that is used as a representative of unconscious wishes or fantasies and that is linked to them by a web of associations. What is transferred, essentially, is an intensity:

> The conscious idea now has a new meaning as a result of its links to the unconscious. It has been endowed with unconscious significance, both in the sense that it now expresses unconscious ideas and in the sense that this very fact must remain hidden.[14]

One implication of this notion of covering is that a "one-to-one relation between a covering and a covered idea is only a first approximation."[15] The meaning of such a conscious idea, as of a dream, cannot be given by a simple decoding of symbols and meanings. Lear refers to *The Interpretation of Dreams*, where Freud "insists we do not really understand the meaning of a dream until we understand its location in an entire network of wishes, prohibitions, and associations."

In a similar vein, I suggest, the Mishkan, in its specific and "conscious" detail, is in the midrashic, nonchronological reading embedded in a web of associations, of which the reader is at first unconscious. It serves as a "covering" for unspeakable wishes and fantasies. And—following Lear's analogy—it may also serve as a transference object: on the one hand, yielding to the idiosyncratic imagery of unconscious desire, it is permeated with the patterns of meaning habitual to the people; on the other, it interrogates those meanings. This transference process, with its two aspects, is in fact a single process. In the analytic situation, "the analyst is being drawn inside an idiopolis"; in Freud's words, the transference provides "new editions of old conflicts." Lear adds: "By that he does not mean that it is just the *latest* edition, but that it is to be a *revised* edition."[16] If, for instance, the analysand has made the analyst into a maternal "covering," the analyst has been learning "the deeper resonances of the 'mother tongue' and gaining a view of the dynamic, conflicted structure of psyche and world." The result is that the analyst's interpretations no longer come from the outside: "it is, for the analysand, as though the ritual itself is speaking. *But 'mother' has somehow changed her tune* [emphasis added]. In speaking the 'mother tongue,' the analyst tries also to reflect back to the psyche an image of itself as a conflicted whole."[17]

I suggest that the Mishkan, in similar vein, speaks a "mother language" to the desires and fantasies of the people. Embedded at their very center, it "covers" a network of unconscious wishes. But, in Lear's phrase, " 'mother' has somehow changed her tune." A new transference meaning emerges from the old symptoms, rituals, and emotions. "Let the gold of the Mishkan come and *cover* (*ye-chapper*—atone) for the gold of the Calf." At first, the gold of the Mishkan seems solid, objective, external. Gradually, its "representative" function looms larger: it begins to glimmer and flare with a fire[18] that makes it a true material of the Israelite *idiopolis*. This is the gold of the calf, emerging from a fire that is the very stuff of fantasy, destroying categories, boundaries between self and other, inside and outside. It "cooks," "melts," dissolves all that is hard, stony, external. Eventually, this "covering" function evolves into new transference meanings. "Mother" somehow changes her tune; and the people become aware of a transmuted world of values and passions.

I have delineated this model of the relation between Mishkan and Calf in the barest schematic form. My project is to flesh out this scheme and to limn some of its dynamic workings. In the broadest sense, this project will carry us to the end of Exodus, with the final construction of the Mishkan.

Thematically, the subject is indicated in God's initiating words: "Let them make Me a sanctuary that I may dwell among them" (25:8). These words, heard against the moaning and spitting of calf-fire, raise the central question: what kind of world can be constructed, such that God can dwell in it, dwell in them? By "world," I mean something akin to Lear's idiosyncratic world, the *idiopolis* of unconscious wishes and fantasies that permeate objective reality. The problem posed by God's demand will be, quite simply, one of changing the world. This is, ultimately, the meaning of redemption. The aim of Exodus is to help its participants to take apart a private world that has held them captive. In the end, after their physical release from slavery, a new recognition of inner conflict, even of potentially tragic inner conflict, will be the key to experiencing themselves as active "makers" of the world.

In this process, the Golden Calf, adumbrated in the Mishkan instructions, will emerge into consciousness. It will be narrated as though it happened later. But, as a particularly poignant midrash has it, "Till I performed that act [the Golden Calf], You did not bring Your presence to dwell in our midst. But when I did perform that act, You said, 'Make Me a sanctuary so that I may dwell among them.' "[19] Clearly, there is an ironic dimension to the linkage of Sanctuary and Calf. In some real sense, the Golden Calf necessarily precedes the Mishkan; it is "covered" by it; and new meanings emerge from the dynamic complexity of the intersection.

2. *Disparity: The Vision of Fire and the Earthly Model*

The Fiery Model

On several occasions, God adds to His instructions a phrase referring to a vision of a model of the Mishkan, which was shown to Moses on Mount Sinai. In the initiating sequence, for example, we find: "Let them make Me a sanctuary . . . *Exactly as I show you*—the pattern of the Mishkan and the pattern of all its furnishings—so shall you make it" (25:8–9). In similar vein, at the end of the chapter, we find: "*Look*, and make them according to the patterns for them *that are being shown you* on the mountain" (25:40). This visual resource is found, as Cassuto points out, "in the very passages where the lack of details is most noticeable." "Much of what is essential [for the purpose of fashioning the Tabernacle] is not in the Book."[20]

The text does not provide a completely detailed manual for the construction of the Mishkan. The midrash explores some unexpected implications of this realization:

> R. Joshua of Sichnin in the name of R. Levi said: When God told Moses, "Make Me a Mishkan . . ." should he not have erected four pegs and stretched the Mishkan-tent over them? But it teaches you that God showed Moses up above a red fire, a green fire, a black fire, a white fire; and told him, "Make it according to the pattern that you are being shown on the mountain." (25:40) R. Berechya in the name of R. Batzla said: This is like a king who had a splendid garment made of jewels. He said to his personal friend, "Make me one just like it!" He answered, "My lord the king, can I make one like it?" The king replied, "I remain in my glory, but you have your materials." Similarly, Moses said to God, "My God, can I make anything like these fires?!" God replied, "Blue, purple and crimson yarns, fine linen . . ." God said, "If you make what is above below, I shall leave My palace above and descend and condense My Presence among them below."[21]

The paradoxical perspective begins with the description of what Moses "should have done": simply set up four pegs and stretch a tent over them. In other words, making a sanctuary for God is so blatantly absurd that the most authentic response would have been a minimalistic one—not to gild the lily, as it were. Here, in God's proposal of a building project, resonances of the past are heard: of Egyptian building projects, in which the individual was subsumed, submerged; of those "store cities" (*arei miskenoth*) of which the Talmud delineated two possibilities—either they endanger (*mesaknoth*) their builders, or they impoverish them (*memaskenoth*).[22] In either case, one might imagine a visceral Israelite revulsion to the idea of an elaborate construction project. But God then shows Moses a model of the Mishkan made of four fires. Whatever the particular symbolic significances of the four colors may be, it is remarkable that what God has done, effectively, is to complicate Moses' task. Showing him a model has not helped him to comprehend the project better. On the contrary, it makes him recoil: "My God, can I make anything like these?" As in the analogy with the king and his jeweled robe, Moses is paralyzed by the incommensurate grandeur of the model. Even its materials far transcend his resources.

God's demand, to make a replica of the fiery model, is *existentially* beyond his means. How to use fire, which destroys boundaries and categories, in order to create a distinct structure in which God may dwell? God's answer is apparently simple: like the king who says, "I remain in my glory, while you work with your materials," God lists yarns and linens and declares them the human materials for "making what is above below"—in other words, for replicating the fires. Not only will He not be insulted by the travesty of the reproduction, He will descend from His fiery habitation and dwell in the human structure.

In what sense, one may ask, is this structure of "cheap materials" *like* the fiery original? What is the condition for God's descent, for the *tzimtzum*, the condensation of His presence? To offer another analogy, is this not like an attempt to translate Shakespeare into pidgin English? One understands Moses' recoil. Why has God complicated matters by showing the vision of fires? And what would it mean to make a copy of those fires in wools and woods?

Vision Complicates

The vision serves an ambiguous purpose: in some sense, it furthers the building project, but, at the same time, it deconstructs the very possibility of such a project. Whatever guidance it provides, it is clearly not of the construction manual–type, illustrating for practical clarity. It is, virtually, an anti-Mishkan vision, exacerbating Moses' original skepticism.

Dynamically, the midrash has followed an unusual course, beginning with a relatively unproblematic solution (the minimalist "tent")[23] and progressing to a sense of "quandary," which is not entirely resolved in God's final gnomic utterance: "If you will make what is above below . . ." Vision does not clarify; it complicates.[24]

Another midrash, in a similar vein, deals with the fashioning of the menora (candelabrum):

> Three things *gave Moses difficulty:* the fashioning of the menora, the laws of the new moon, and of insects. What was the problem in fashioning the menora? When Moses ascended the mountain, God showed him how to

> fashion the Mishkan. When He showed him the construction of the menora, *Moses had difficulty.* So God said, "Look, I am fashioning it in front of you!" What did God do? He showed him white fire, red fire, black fire, green fire, and of them fashioned the menora, with its cups and knobs, its blossoms and six branches, and said to him, "*This* is the work of menora." (Num 8:4)—showing him with His finger. Nevertheless, *Moses had difficulty* with it. What did God do? He engraved it upon his hand and told him, "Descend and fashion it as I have engraved it upon your hand, as it is said, 'Look and fashion them according to their patterns . . .' " (Exod 25:40)[25]

Here, the ironies of vision proliferate. At first, God shows Moses how to make the menora; Moses has difficulty and God models the process for him. He demonstrates the whole complex dynamic of making, stage by stage, in four fires. The reference to God's finger is clearly didactic: the demonstrator points to significant details, as he works—"*This* is the work of the menora." "Nevertheless, Moses had difficulty!" "Nevertheless!" It is perhaps genuinely surprising that Moses finds the learning process so hard, since God is such an understanding and lucid teacher—even using different colors for the model. But surely that "nevertheless" has an ironic undertone, for those four fires again evoke the sense that the human being is being asked to live beyond his means. The clarity of the demonstration is, after all, specious; the project is out of Moses' reach.

Indeed, we notice that even before God shows Moses the fiery prototype, the menora always was "difficult" to fashion. Its difficulty stems most obviously from its complexity: it is an artifact of baroque detail and elaboration. But, perhaps, in addition the difficulty lies in the association with *fire*. Not only the fashioning of the menora but its function will engage with fire. In some radical sense, this element must always be *kasheh*, difficult, dense though fluid, expressive of contrary powers. In Gaston Bachelard's words,

> fire is . . . a privileged phenomenon which can explain anything . . . all that changes quickly is explained by fire. Fire is the ultra-living element. It is intimate and it is universal. It lives in our heart. It lives in the sky. It rises from the depths of the substance and offers itself with the warmth of love. Or it can go back down into the substance and hide there, latent and pent-up, like hate and vengeance. Among all phenomena, it is really the only one to which there can be so definitely attributed the opposing values of good and evil.[26]

In the Mishkan, fire's continual presence is represented by the menora. Moses' initial difficulty is therefore not surprising. What is arresting is God's modeling in fires, with its dubious alleviation of the original difficulty.

The Solution: Palm-Knowledge

God's solution is compelling: He engraves a model of the menora on Moses' hand and tells him to copy it: "See it and make it!" The transcendent fires are, essentially, tattooed onto his hand. The image is haunting. If we try to tease out some of its implications, we may say, first, that Moses' hands are now engraved with a vision. The connection between hand and eye is made taut; seeing and making become intimates, secretly linked. For it is not simply a drawing *on* Moses' hand, though even that would focus attention on the hand as that part of the body that can be "consulted," that is part of oneself and yet external to oneself. But the description of "engraving" is a tactile one: it is an invasive procedure, whose scars will leave Moses with a personal "manual," in the true sense, of the Mishkan. Inscribed deep within his flesh, he will carry with him a version of the fiery model. In a modest, intimate place, on the palm of the hand, he will bear the mark of transcendence.

This *chakika*, this engraving, evokes that other intimate mark, the inscription of circumcision. That mark is described by Derrida as "that singular and immemorial archive . . . which, though never leaving you, nonetheless has come about, and is no less exterior, *exterior right on* your body proper."[27] As with circumcision, Moses' hand-inscription involves an incision into the skin which "never leaves," but is not innate, which is interior and exterior at the same time. Like circumcision, it becomes a tactile "archive," making oblivion impossible.

We find an illuminating use of this imagery in Isaiah 49:14–16: "Zion says, 'God has forsaken me, God has forgotten me.' Can a woman forget her baby, or disown the child of her womb? Though she might forget, I never could forget you. See, *I have engraved you on the palms of My hands* . . ." The absurdity of a woman's forgetting her baby, who is the child of her womb—part of her proper body, though now external to it—is marshaled to illustrate the impossibility of God's forgetting His people. " 'I have engraved you on the palms of My hands'—to see you and remember you constantly" (Rashi). This is Derrida's "immemorial archive," a stored awareness, imprinted, palpable as well as visible.

In a simple sense, God's strategy with Moses is that of a teacher, whose pupil has a learning problem: he adds the sense of touch to the register of sense stimuli. Moses will know the fiery model and be able to reproduce it, through the palm-knowledge that is a private sensation. An imprinted form is known by a sensitive caress of the skin:

> The caress, like contact, is sensibility. But the caress transcends the sensible . . . The caress consists in seizing upon nothing, in soliciting what ceaselessly escapes its form towards a future never future enough, in soliciting what slips away as though it *were not yet.* It *searches*, it forages. It is not an intentionality of disclosure but of search: a movement unto the invisible . . .[28]

This caress represents an entirely different order of imagination than the one that sees the hand as grasping, mastering, powerful. This is the order of the *tender*, which "designates a *way*, the way of remaining in the *no man's land* between being and not-yet-being."[29]

Approaching the caress from an anthropological perspective, Elias Canetti writes of the pleasure of the fingers, as the basis of the grooming instinct as a social procedure. Even mobile, restless animals like monkeys, display endless patience in grooming: "Through it the fingers become more and more sensitive. The feeling of many hair tips simultaneously engenders a particular sense of touch which is entirely different from the crude sensation of snatching or grasping."[30] From this sensitivity grows the ability to shape objects, to sew, to stroke. This is quite different from the "hardening exercises" of hands and fingers, the "ceaseless confrontation with hardness," which leads to the use of the stick, "the earliest weapon," the "first in the long series of *hard* instruments."[31] Here, the hand is the "first vessel": "The fingers of both hands intertwined are the first basket."[32] The intimate experience of the hand enacting shapes precedes the making of these shapes, precedes even the perception of those shapes in nature. "It was the fingers forming a hollow to scoop up water which made the cup real . . . What man, with the help of his hands, enacted, was only *made* long afterwards, when it had been enacted often enough. *Words* and *objects* are accordingly the emanations and products of a single unified experience: *representation by means of the hands.*" This transformation of the hand is the earliest incorporation into himself of all that represents human culture.

This is the modality of the hands as the site of the caress, of tenderness, of the tentative as opposed to the tenacious, of groping as opposed to grasping, and of intimate formings and transformations that will generate culture. It is this motif that is introduced by the midrash as God engraves the fiery model of the menora into Moses' hand.

Moses' Hands: A New Modality

This is a moment that gains significance from the central role Moses' hand has played in the history of the Exodus. It is his hand, for instance, grasping the staff, that has brought plagues down upon the Egyptians, that has charged the Red Sea to split apart. But a new modality of the hand begins, I suggest, when Moses holds his hands in the air and mysteriously conducts the fortunes of war in the battle against Amalek. In that enigmatic scene, Moses instructs Joshua to lead the Israelite force, for "tomorrow I shall station myself on the top of the hill, with the staff of God *in my hand*" (17:9). When, however, Moses is described at the top of the hill, there is no mention of the staff:

> whenever Moses held up his hand, Israel prevailed; but whenever he let down his hand, Amalek prevailed. But Moses' hands grew heavy; so they took a stone and put it under him and he sat on it, while Aaron and Hur, one on each side, supported his hands; thus his hands remained steady until the sun set. (17:11–12)

Strangely, the physical, human weight of Moses' hands need support if they are to remain "steady" (*emuna*); and yet, in the previous verse, there is clearly no "steadiness": his hands rise and fall, and with them the fortunes of war. Where, indeed, is the staff? Obviously not in his hand, asserts Ramban; for his hand-gesture is *nesiath kapayim*, *perisath kapayim*, the classic gesture of the hands *outspread* in prayer. Open, defenseless, groping upward, not clenched around a weapon, this is the hand that brings victory on this occasion.

In this gesture, according to one midrash, Moses models prayer to his people fighting below. In a surrealistic description, their involvement in battle is refigured as a miming of Moses' prayerful gestures: "they saw Moses kneeling down, and they knelt down, falling upon his face and they fell upon their faces, spreading their hands to heaven."[33]

An existential stance is demonstrated by Moses. The hand expresses the heart, as we find in the classic midrashic comment on the scene:

> "Whenever Moses held up his hand, Israel prevailed . . ." (17:11) Did Moses' hand make or break the fortunes of war? But this teaches you that as long as the Israelites gazed upwards and *submitted their hearts* to their Father in heaven, they would prevail; and if not, they would fail.[34]

An invisible line is drawn between Moses' hands and the people's hearts. A subtle influence moves in both directions, directing a quest, seizing upon nothing, fed by its own hunger, a movement unto the invisible.[35] To achieve this connection, the staff has to be dropped, the fingers must grope, caress, create a new form.

This "new hand" is both delicate and heavy. It is the natural human hand, not the agent of miraculous power and destruction. If the Talmud asks with apparent naïveté, "Did Moses' hands make or break the fortunes of war?" the question acquires its force only here, in this new modality. Before this, Moses' hands did indeed transform the destiny of the human and natural world, as he repeatedly wielded his staff to bring plagues of horror down upon the Egyptians. At this moment, however, the only power of the hands is as an extension of the heart, as a potent sign of yearning that affects the hearts of his people.[36] It is this hand-heart connection that determines the fate of war. Expressive of this connection is the Targum's translation of the description of victory: "his hands remained steady (*emuna*) until the sun set—his hands were *spread in prayer* until the sun set." The word *emuna*, signifying firmness, steadiness, also expresses "faith." Moses' hands become the conduits of prayer, their steadiness no longer a simple physical immobility.

Moses' posture at the top of the mountain is poignantly described by Ha-amek Davar. His hands *generate faith* in his people, precisely by their rising and falling. It is the oscillation, the natural vibration of hands of flesh and blood that creates faith in those who watch and imitate. This gesture, tentative, delicate and heavy at the same time, is the gesture of real human hands, not the static, iconic image of prayer in Byzantine art, for example. These hands need support, they are subject to the laws of gravity. In their sensitivity, they suggest an alternative model to that of the triumphal miraculous staff.

Here is the intentionality that solicits "what slips away as though it were not yet."[37] This hand will have four fires engraved upon its palm. "It grasps nothing, issues in no concept."[38] Moses' final enigmatic failure—the narrative of the waters of Meriva that condemns him to die in the desert (Num 20)—is clearly focused on a regressive return to the staff modality. When he hits the rock instead of speaking to it, his hand returns to grasping, to the conceptual. At issue there is the problem of faith, of *emuna;* of the caressing, questioning modality that consists in seizing upon nothing, and that learns its own complex stability: "God said to Moses and Aaron, 'Because you did not have faith in Me (*he'emantem*) to sanctify Me before the eyes of the Israelites, therefore you shall not lead this congregation into the land that I have given them' " (Num 20:12).

If God engraves the menora on Moses' palm, therefore, this is to initiate a new way of knowing the fiery prototype. God tells Moses, "See it and make it, according to the pattern that you were shown on the mountain" (Exod 25:40). Imprinted in his flesh, he carries an impression of the menora in four fires. It is known by touch and by sight, and yet, as with Levinas's caress, it represents a quest for that which eludes touch. It is a space left within his skin that marks his memory with an absence, something precisely not grasped.

Perhaps this is one of the associations that will sign him as the *mechokek*—the engraver, the lawgiver. In Deuteronomy 33:21, Moses blesses the tribe of Gad: "There the portion of the *mechokek* is hidden." The Talmud comments: "From here we learn that Moses is called the *mechokek*, the Lawgiver."[39] Moses' grave is hidden, unknown: "No one knows his burial place to this day" (34:6). This is the source of his power as *mechokek*, as Lawgiver: the one who can make a profound impression on the hearts of others has lived with an intimate knowledge of *chakika*, of being imprinted, of a hollowness traced in the flesh.

3. *Inner Space: God Inside and Outside*

Fiery Gold: The Invisible Space at the Center

The model of the Mishkan and, specifically, of the menora is presented by God in a vision of fire. We have noticed that this model is, initially, distinctly unhelpful, that it seems to create a difficulty where none had previously existed. We noticed, too, that fire is an unlikely substance as a building material: fluid, destructive, the essence of instability. It is, moreover, the element out of which the Golden Calf emerges. Again, the ambiguity about timing comes to the fore. If the Golden Calf has already been made, Moses and the people know on their pulses what fire can breed. But, so far, in the daylight realm of the text, there is no conscious reference to the Calf; it remains a repressed awareness, a sense of anguish around the image of fire. And, in some form, it must haunt Moses in fashioning the sanctuary.

A desire that has found instantaneous gratification in the Golden Calf remains intense, although repressed, *because* repressed. This is a desire that is associated with fire and with the gold that is the static representation of fire. The question that animates the Mishkan, therefore, is that evoked by God's command: "Let them make Me a sanctuary that I may dwell among them." How to use the gold, how to represent the fires in such a way as to create a *habitable* world, habitable by God and therefore by human beings?

In such a building, the gold will be shaped to different ends from the gold so resplendent in Byzantine art and architecture. There, gold serves the "politics of bedazzlement";[40] it represents a blinding power. One looks and is amazed. In the Mishkan, however, the gold remains, in an important way, *invisible.* It is donated by the people in the most homely, familiar forms—personal jewelry, for instance. But the interior of the Mishkan is never seen by them, never grasped by their eyes. It is, strictly—and for all but those who serve in the Mishkan, the priests and the Levites—the stuff of imagination. The fire is represented at its most intense in the gold-covered Ark at the heart of the Mishkan, with its pure-gold Cover (*kapporeth*) and the pure-gold Cherubim at either end. And this, of course, is seen by no human eye. Only on Yom Kippur, on the Day of Atonement, the Day of Covering, the High Priest alone penetrates to that inner sanctum, the Holy of Holies—and then only when surrounded by a fog of incense.

The invisible gold at the heart of the Mishkan teases the imagination. "Let them make Me a sanctuary . . ." The substantial object, the sanctuary—what is it, in essence? Rashi comments: " 'Let them make Me a *house for holiness*'—that is, not a sacred *object*, but a space in which holiness is potential."[41] Siftei Chachamim, a commentary on Rashi, articulates the idea: "So that I may dwell *in their midst* (*betocham*)—in a house, a structure that has a *midst*"—that is, a hollow core where God may dwell.

The definition of a sanctuary, therefore, is the space at its center. From this point of view, the architectural project is concerned primarily with the use of space. A structure is not the walls but the habitable space defined by the walls. The nature of this habitation is the crucial question. What is to happen in this *middest*,[42] at the heart of the mystery? Like the hollow traced out in Moses' palm, there is to be an emptiness, an absence which will define the sacred space. "Only if we are capable of dwelling, only then can we build."[43]

The Space for Holiness

The need to free space for holiness is the basic problem. This is true of inner space, as well as of outer space. For outer space, with its objective structures, is permeated with inner space. The Mishkan is permeated with human desire and fantasy. If God's command is, "Let them make Me a sanctuary that I may dwell *in their midst,"* this refers, most obviously, to the *middest* of human beings as God's dwelling place. That is, He will live not "in it," but *"in them."*[44] The essential space is the space within the human heart.

Bachelard writes of space in daydream:

> Topoanalysis . . . would be the systematic psychological study of the sites of our intimate lives. In the theatre of the past that is constituted by memory, the stage setting maintains the characters in their dominant roles. At times we think we know ourselves in time, when all we know is a sequence of fixations in the spaces of the being's stability—a being who does not want to melt away, and who, even in the past, when he sets out in search of things past, wants time to "suspend" its flight. *In its countless alveoli space contains compressed time. That is what space is for.* (My italics.)[45]

From this standpoint, it "makes sense . . . to say that we 'write a room,' 'read a room,' or 'read a house.' "[46] To read the Mishkan is to seek the sites of "compressed time," where memories are motionless, achieve a saturated inwardness. In the very structure of the building, there are fissures, spaces, where what cannot be grasped abides. Here, for example, is one account of the function of the Mishkan space:

> "Let them make Me a sanctuary that I may dwell in their midst." It does not say, "in its midst," to convey that the place they shall sanctify to His presence shall be "in the midst of the Israelites," that they shall embrace the Mishkan with four banners [i.e., in all four directions, marked by tribal banners]. Possibly, this is God's response to the desire of the people when they saw at Mount Sinai how God was surrounded by the banners of the angels, while He was a Sign in their midst. Then, they desired yearningly that it should be so in their midst. And so the One who plumbs the heart's depths replied, "Let them make Me a sanctuary and I will dwell *in the same way* in their hearts."[47]

The space that opens up to contain God is the space of desire. It is in response to a deep, perhaps subconscious yearning (God is "the One who plumbs the heart's depths") that the apparently abrupt command comes from God: "Let them make me a Sanctuary that I may dwell in their midst." In this inspired reading, God satisfies a human longing, an awareness of unfilled space. The origin of this longing is "possibly" a vision at Mount Sinai, of God held, contained on all four sides by the hosts of angels. Instantly, the people conceive a female desire to embrace, to surround (*lèhakif*), to hold God as a Sign among their banners.

The Desire to Contain God

God plumbs the heart's depths, finds what is stable, steadfast but hidden, not obvious. For the obvious desire is, surely, to *be held*: in erotic terms, and in terms of religious experience, the desire to be contained in the Other, to be led by Him, to be covered, protected by Him, is primary. In biblical imagery, such wishes are gratified in the narrative of being led by the pillars of cloud and of fire; in midrashic imagery, of being protected by the Clouds of Glory above their heads. The desire to *contain* God at the center of one's being, however, as the hosts of angels hold God at their center, registers a more mature fantasy. Here, one wishes not to be guided, guarded, but to *have significance*—to bear the Sign at the core of being.

This is the desire for density, which is proper to one who feels fragmented. A poignant, because ambivalent expression of this desire is the people's rebellious cry at Massah, "Is there (*yesh*) God in our midst or not?" (literally, "or else nothingness [*ayin*]") (17:17). The alternatives are stark—*yesh* or *ayin;* being or nothingness. Beneath all the fluctuations, the myriad shapes of desire, this is the radical question. And if we consider that the Golden Calf narrative has already happened, the people's desire for density becomes more complex. It becomes a desire for constancy, for memory, for a sign, an inscription deep within the flesh. But it becomes, in essence, a conflicted desire, the wistful fantasy of a people who know themselves inconstant, who, on some level, must have desired inconstancy. Or HaChaim describes the yearning for "God at the center" as the "true" desire: God who plumbs the heart's depths discerns this and brings it to realization. But the wish to hold God at the center is passionate in proportion to the strength of the counter-desire that would place God outside and leave the inner space unoccupied.

God Inside and Outside

The question of God inside or outside gives a paradoxical force to the following midrash:

> "They shall bring Me gifts." (25:2) This refers to the verse, "I am asleep but my heart is awake." (Song of Songs 5:2) The community of Israel said, "I have fallen asleep in relation to the End, but God is awake, as it is said, 'The rock of my heart and my portion is God eternally.' (Ps 73:26) I am asleep in relation to the commandments, but the merit of my fathers stands up for me and my heart is awake. I am asleep to the fashioning of the Golden Calf, but my heart is awake—God knocks upon me: 'They shall bring Me gifts—Open for Me, My sister, My friend! How long shall I roam about homeless? For My head is drenched with dew . . . (Song 5:2) But make Me a sanctuary, so that I should not be outside.' "[48]

In three images, the midrash fleshes out the paradox of stupor and alertness in the same person: "I am asleep but my heart is awake." In each, a general insensibility is counteracted by a mysterious force within the heart that vividly represents God. The *internality* of this force is clear in the first example ("The Rock of my heart is God eternally"); less clear in the second (Where is "the merit of my fathers" situated?) In the third example, the ambiguity about inside and outside becomes dreamlike: the people are stupefied by and about the Golden Calf and God "knocks" at their heart, pleading for admission. In other words, God is outside, trying to wake the beloved from her stupor; but the proof-text simultaneously calls Him, "my heart": "my heart is awake." God is external, excluded from the human heart by an insensibility; but, impossibly, He is also the inner essence of the heart, that inwardness that secretly colludes with the divine lover. The heart is sensitive, it throbs deep within the sleeping self, colluding, identifying with the "knock" of God.

The image of the divided heart is found in medieval emblem books in the form of a sleeping woman, with a throbbing heart *outside* her body, pulsing demonstratively. The heart knocks, begs for entry into its proper place. It is outrageously exiled, sodden with dew. So God asks to be admitted to the sanctuary "in their midst." This would restore Him to His rightful place; His knock is an attempt to wake the people stupefied by the Golden Calf to a sense of their own hollowness.

This knock of the Lover, however, which is also the heartbeat of the beloved, is the focus of a powerful tension. The Hebrew word *hirtik* refers to a knuckle-knock.[49] Its root *ratak* encompasses opposite meanings: to join, to weld; to be emptied out, dry, crooked, to snap (as in Ecclesiastes 12:6: "Before the silver cord snaps and the golden bowl crashes.")[50] The Lover's knock thus expresses both the desire for union, for a restored density of immanence, the Lover reinstated at the human center, and a dry separateness, an unassuageable yearning. His pathos is imagined by the human being who is aware of a double response: an answering desire and a fascination with the situation of desire. The *ratak* root, indeed, comes also to mean, "to fascinate," or, in the passive mode, "to be spell-bound." "How long," the Lover in the midrash cries, "How long shall I be outside?" Timing is all. There is a time for separateness and longing, and a time for union. On both sides, there are perils. One peril is of losing the moment and remaining alone, hollow. In the Song of Songs, the beloved delays opening the door till it is too late. Fascinated by his passion and hers, she finally opens, and he is gone:

> I was asleep but my heart was awake. Hark, my beloved knocks! "Open for me, my sister, my wife, my faultless dove! For my head is drenched with dew, my locks with the damp of the night." "I have taken off my robe—how shall I put it on again? I have bathed my feet—how shall I soil them again?" My beloved put his hand through the aperture, and my heart was stirred for him. I rose to let in my beloved; my hands dripped myrrh—my fingers, flowing myrrh—upon the handles of the bolt. I opened the door for my beloved, but my beloved had slipped away, he had gone. I was faint because of what he said. I sought him, but I could not find him; I called, but he did not answer. (Song of Songs 5:2–6)

On the other hand, to admit him too soon is to overlook otherness, not to allow fascination its own history. This is the delight and the dilemma of the erotic situation in Song of Songs: most powerfully, too, it evokes the delight and dilemma of the relationship between God and the human being. God's knock both asserts the right of entry and preserves distance. The human being resists and yearns, aware of the double peril: on the one hand, hollowness, loss; on the other, idolatry, a rigidity, a specious density that would put an end to fascination. The space that God claims must retain the imagination of otherness, of "the need to empty oneself in order to fill oneself by creating difference."[51] What is needed is an exquisitely tuned play between the two poles: "The cosmos teeters uncertainly on its axes and will cease to exist if one stops imagining it, stops playing with it—for then the cosmos returns to its densest, homogeneous innerness. Yet the cosmos imagined and played with also will cease to exist if it is emptied utterly, and innerness turns wholly into otherness."[52]

The tension between God-inside and God-outside is associated in the midrash with the sin of the Golden Calf. To be asleep is to be stupefied by the fantasy of density, of rigidly containing God. To be awake, pulses beating, is to be aware of distance, difference, to yearn to open at the right moment. That is, God cannot be inside if He is not outside, if the heart cannot imagine its emptiness.

Gaston Bachelard expresses the paradoxical relation between inside and outside in terms of warmth and cold:

> . . . we feel warm *because* it is cold out-of-doors . . . Baudelaire declares that dreamers like a severe winter. "Every year they ask the sky to send down as much snow, hail and frost as it can contain. What they really need are Canadian or Russian winters. Their own nests will be all the warmer, all the downier, all the better beloved . . ." Like Edgar Allan Poe, a great dreamer of curtains, Baudelaire, in order to protect the winter-girt house from cold added "heavy draperies that hung down to the floor." Behind dark curtains, snow seems to be whiter. Indeed, everything comes alive when contradictions accumulate.[53]

"Everything comes alive when contradictions accumulate." In terms of the dream imagery of Song of Songs, Bachelard's epigram seems just. Since the midrash associates the erotic fascination of lovers with God outside/inside the human being, we may carry some of the vitality of contradictions into our exploration of the concept of the Mishkan.

A Chasidic story tells of the Rebbe who approaches one of his followers during the confession on Yom Kippur. The worshiper is ritually striking his chest as he confesses his sins, and the Rebbe gently but devastatingly tells him, "Don't knock so hard—there's no one home!" Ruefully, the story gestures at the human stupor, at the manic effort to come awake that is vehement in proportion to that stupor. The image of God knocking at the heart, asking for sanctuary, evokes the sterile ironies of this situation, even as it affirms a more hopeful possibility. If there is in reality "someone home," if there is a wakeful heart, then the hollow knocking is not absurd.

The very word *mishkan* hovers over the contradictions of inside and outside: it is the noun derived from the original verb of God's demand: *ve-*

shachanti—". . . that I may dwell among them." It means, not permanent dwelling, settling, but a nomadic, "flickering" modality, in which the fire is and is not contained.

The Hollow of Holiness

The space "in their midst," then, that God desires is, precisely, the space of desire. God desires human desire. Sefath Emeth quotes a midrash on the words, "Let them bring Me gifts" (25:2). The Torah text literally reads, "Let them *take* Me gifts," which leads the midrash to describe the people as acquiring the Torah and, with it, "taking Me":

> Does it happen that the seller is sold along with his goods? God said to Israel, "I have 'sold' you My Torah and, as it were, I have been 'sold' along with it." This is like a king who had an only daughter. A king came and married her. He wanted to depart for his own country with his wife. The father said to him, "My daughter whom I have given you is my only daughter: I cannot part from her, but neither can I tell you not to take her, for she is your wife. But do me this kindness: wherever you go, make me a little hut to stay in with you, for I cannot let my daughter go." So said God to Israel: "I have given you the Torah. I cannot part from it, but neither can I tell you not to take it. But everywhere you go, make Me a house to stay in—as it is said, 'Let them make Me a sanctuary that I may dwell among them.' "[54]

Sefat Emet comments: God asks for a "hut" which will express an absolute passion in the heart of the people—a passion for the Torah, God's "daughter." Only if the people are inseparable from the Torah, God will set aside His majesty and set up house in the "hut," the Mishkan. For God to reside in a hut, essentially in a *shack*, is beyond human comprehension. It becomes imaginable only if the Torah is "your wife": that is, if, in all one's activities, "one leaves a space for God." This is the space of desire, the hollow of holiness.[55]

Holding such a space free for potential habitation by God requires great energy. Inertia breeds a consoling sense of density. Hans Leowald writes of the difficulty of eros as compared to the obvious appeal of the death-drive:

> It remained an insoluble problem for Freud to fit his life drive [or eros] into his new definition of drive . . . The inertia or constancy or unpleasure

> or Nirvana principle . . . fits in perfectly with the death drive, insofar as the latter is "the expression of the inertia inherent in organic life." In this sense, the death drive is really nothing new, not a conception that should have taken psychoanalysts by surprise . . . What is new, and this does not seem to fit with the inertia principle . . . is the concept of Eros, the life or love drive.[56]

This irreducible erotic principle lies, I suggest, at the very heart of the Mishkan project. It represents the quest for wholeness, which inhabits the gap between the transcendent and the immanent realms; it creates that transitional space which "initially both joins and separates the baby and the mother."[57] Here, objects begin to symbolize the union of two now separate beings, "at the point in time and space of the initiation of their state of separateness."[58] In this space, messages are transmitted between worlds, and eros[59] carries words, prayers, and sacrifices between those who, separate, must reinvent ways of love.

The question posed by the Mishkan is a question about space, about the center, the heart of the matter—that which is *betocham*, "in their midst": what is the Mishkan, in the fullest sense, *about*? This is, on one level, the question of Bachelard's "topoanalysis," that "auxiliary of psychoanalysis" which is concerned with "the sites of our intimate lives."[60] The question in fact arises immediately on Moses' first encounter with God at the Burning Bush. The angel appears to him in a blaze which is the very heart of fire (*be-labath esh*), in the midst of the bush. Here, there is a burning without consumption: a mystery that makes Moses swerve from his path. Commenting on this unusual word, *be-labath*, Rashi reminds us of the fire of Sinai which will burn on this same site "to the *heart* (*lev*) of the heavens."[61] Rashi associates the words *lehava*, *shalhevet* (flame), and *lev* (heart), evoking questions about the relation between fire and the human heart. For the angel appears by means of the heart's fire; he cannot exist without it.

The effect of this opening scene is to initiate a central theme in the narrative of the Exodus: about the nature of fire as an image for the heart. One midrash, indeed, reads "in the heart of the fire": "to give Moses heart (i.e., encourage him), so that when he arrives at Mount Sinai and sees those fires, he will not be afraid."[62] In other words, we are concerned not with the physics or the chemistry of fire but with its relation to human fear and desire.

There is clearly a connection between the fire of the Burning Bush and the fire of Sinai which, however, explicitly, does consume: "The vision of the glory of God was like a consuming fire at the top of the mountain" (24:17). Most significantly, from the heart of both fires comes the voice of God conveying messages to the people. From the heart of the Mishkan, too, comes the voice of God. Indeed, we may say that that is the heart of the matter, the very nub of what the Mishkan, like the Burning Bush and the fiery Sinai peak, is "about." It is about language emerging from fire.

The structure of the Mishkan represents this very clearly: at its center is the Holy of Holies, at the center of which is the Holy Ark, with the two golden, fiery cherubim facing one another:

> Make two cherubim of gold—make them of hammered work—at the two ends of the Cover. Make one cherub at one end and the other cherub at the other end; of one piece with the Cover shall you make the cherubim at its two ends. The cherubim shall have their wings spread out above, shielding the Cover with their wings. They shall confront each other, the faces of the cherubim being turned towards the Cover. Place the Cover on top of the Ark, after placing inside the Ark the Testimony that I shall give you. There I will meet with you, and I will speak with you—from above the Cover, from between the two cherubim that are on top of the Ark of Testimony—all that I will command you to convey to the children of Israel. (25:18–22)

At first reading, this description generates a certain shock: human figures inhabit the Holy of Holies, figures fashioned of gold. This seems embarrassingly close to the language of paganism. At every point, indeed, the gold of the Mishkan and the gold of the Calf play off against each other, in an evocative shimmering that rides the very verge of travesty. "Let the gold of the Mishkan come and *cover* for, atone for the gold of the Calf."

But in the Mishkan the gold, representing fire, motion, infinite transformation, is not the sacred object. Rather, it *frames* the sacred space, the hollow out of which God will speak. The heart of the Mishkan is the *space between* the wings of the cherubim which, from an unbridgeable distance, at opposite ends of the golden Kapporeth (the Cover of the Ark), gaze towards each other, even as they gaze downwards at the Ark. That oblique gaze frames the space between the cherub figures. The faces, half-turned towards each other, half-turned downwards, suggest an intensity, a fear and love of fire. The "shy, oblique gaze" is of two who must "tame" each other. We remember the Little Prince and the Fox who learn to fan the fire, without being consumed, in an intimacy that grows with time.[63]

The Heart of the Mystery

At the heart of the Mishkan, then, is an emptiness set in fiery gold. From this electric space, framed by the two cherubim and the Ark Cover, God will speak. "Make two (*shenayim*) cherubim." Rabbenu Bahya comments on the unusual usage of *shenayim*, rather than *shenei*, for "two." *Shenei* would have expressed identity, sameness; *shenayim* expresses difference. The two cherubim, therefore, are to be imagined as male and female. Later, the word *shenei* will be used (25:22), to emphasize that they are alike in their gold material and in their union. But the essential modality of the cherubim is *difference*, separateness. Indeed, an important Talmudic passage bears witness to the erotic relationship that will be set at the heart of the Temple:

> Said R. Kattina: When the Israelites came up to Jerusalem during the pilgrim festivals, the *parocheth* (the curtain veiling the Holy of Holies) would be removed for them and they would be shown the Cherubim, which were intertwined with one another. They would be told, "Look! You are beloved before God as the love of male and female."[64]

This description of the erotic embrace as the heart of the mystery of the Temple is vulnerable to satiric mockery. The Talmud, indeed, continues to narrate how the Romans, on conquering the Temple, invaded the Holy of Holies, eager to discover its secret, to pluck out the heart of its mystery:

> They emerged bearing the cherubim and mockingly paraded them through the streets of Jerusalem: "These Israelites, whose blessing meant blessing, and whose curse meant curse, are preoccupied with such things!" They proceeded to denigrate them, as it is said, "All those who had honored her now denigrated her, for they had seen her nakedness." (Lam 1:8)

But there is a paradox that the Romans, in their glee at the apparent erotic cliche at the heart of the Israelite Temple, have vulgarly overlooked. For the cherubim are described in Exodus 25:18–19 as *separate*, fixed at opposite ends of the Ark Cover. It is their glances that are intertwined. What unites the separate beings in all their radical difference is a possibility of *dibbur*, of language—"I will speak with you there" (25:22). There, *sham*, between the two, is the site of language. This is the event, the moment of encounter, that the space is all "about": "I will meet with you there."

"In its countless alveoli space contains compressed time. That is what space is for."[65] The encounter will not be continual, a fixity. It will partake of the flickering, ever-changing, unpredictable quality of fire. Rashi's comment on, "I will meet with you," is "When I arrange a time to speak with you, that is the place I will fix for the meeting . . ." (25:22). The space between the cherubim will be the potential site for the moments of meeting.

It is Hamlet, we remember, who presses Guildenstern to recognize the heart of his mystery: "You would seem to know my stops, you would pluck out the heart of my mystery, you would sound me from my lowest note to the top of my compass—and there is much music, excellent voice, in this little organ, yet cannot you make it speak."[66] The problem with music, with *dibbur*, with language, in the largest sense, is that one cannot force it. Against the knowingness that *already knows*, Hamlet sets the "much music, excellent voice," potential within his little organ. This can be produced only by play, not by violation.

The music, the language that is to issue from "between the cherubim," ultimately defies human control. The cherubim, representing fire, or wind,[67] represent a dynamism that no medium can figure forth. In the words of Rabbenu Bahya, the erotic imagery is of an unmediated passion (*ha-devekuth . . . b'lo shum emtza'i*). That is, at the heart of the Mishkan, *sham*, there—is an absence of forms that, directly from the heart of the fire, addresses the problem of the Golden Calf. The golden figures, with the yearning curve of their wings, frame a distance that only language can bridge. We remember Walter Benjamin on friendship: "It does not abolish the distance between human beings but brings that distance to life."[68] And Blanchot: "The relationship with the other, who is the others, is a transcendent relationship, which means that there is an infinite and, in one way, insurmountable distance between me and the other who belongs to the other shore . . ."[69]

"There Is No There There": The Absence of Sinai

In thinking of what the Mishkan is "about," then, one thinks of absence, of potential space. "There is no there there" (Gertrude Stein). Between the cherubim and beneath them there is, of course, an object: the Holy Ark, with its golden *kapporeth* (Cover). In the Ark is placed the "Testimony that I shall give you" (Rashi to 25:16). Rashi comments: "This refers to the Torah which serves as testimony between Me and you that I have given you the commandments that are written in it." By "the Torah," he presumably means the Stone Tablets.[70] His main emphasis is on the role of the Tablets as testimony to an event—the Revelation at Mount Sinai. In other words, at the heart of the Mishkan, there is merely a *sign* of a past encounter, written words recording in engraved form an oral event. "There is no there there."

Pressing the point, we may say that to have an engraved text—letters creating an empty space in the heart of stone—at the center of the Mishkan is to create an absence. "Le rose est l'absence de toute rose" (Mallarmé). "The written word, rose, is the absence of all rose." All rose, the full, sensuous experience of the rose, is lost when one writes about it. It is because of the loss, because of the passage of time, that one writes. This is what George Steiner calls the "disjunction of language from external reference," which has splintered "the foundations of the Hebraic-Hellenic–Cartesian edifice."[71] Mallarmé's move is to deprive words of all correspondence to "things out there": "to see and use them as somehow representational of 'reality' in the world is not only a vulgar illusion. It makes of language a lie." Here, Steiner argues, is the critical "breakpoint with the *Logos*-order": Mallarmé's repudiation of the covenant of reference, and his insistence that nonreference constitutes the true genius and purity of language, entail a central supposition of "real absence . . . The truth of the word is the absence of the world."[72]

In the heart of the Mishkan, then, there is an engraved text that speaks of the absence of Sinai. According to one tradition, indeed, the Ark contained also the shattered Tablets that evoke the Golden Calf—that is, the repudiation of Sinai in the most figurative form. *Nothing* is represented there. There is a deconstruction of "insured content, of cognitive ballast. . . The idolatry, the theological-philosophic animism in any pretence to meaningfulness must be laid bare. Signs do not transport presences."[73]

The absence at the center evokes Mallarmé's experiments with *les blancs,* which Steiner cites as "emblems of absence": "the blanks on the page, the white abysses of silent nothingness between the lines . . . They fissure, they disseminate any naively cosmological sense of a meaningful continuum, of a legible 'text of the world . . .' "[74] In terms of the text that inhabits the Ark, its letters engraved in stone are described as "black fire on white fire."[75] As with the fiery menora model engraved on Moses' hands, fire leaves the trace of an uncanny absence.

In the architectural language of the Mishkan, therefore, this uncanny absence constitutes its center, whether as an engraved text of testimony or as the space of language and silence that joins and separates the two cherubim. The oblique gaze of desire embracing Ark and Other flickers in the invisible, never-to-be-seen heart of fire. In Ezekiel's vision, the Chayoth, the fiery angels, emerge from a gleam "like *chashmal*" (Ezek 1:4). This mysterious term—used in modern Hebrew for "electricity"—is translated midrashically as "now speaking, now silent" (a combination of *chashoth*—silent; *memalleloth*—speaking).[76] The electric tension of speech and silence, of expression and listening to the Other, is what animates the vacant core of the Mishkan, in the midst of the fire. Such dialogue between two who are irrevocably different requires sacrifice, an ability to live without the total consummation of desire. But how else is it possible to live at all, without being consumed?

Ultimately, then, it is the oblique encounter between faces, between transcendencies, that animates the Mishkan. There, it seems, God dwells. The flickering heart of fire, a voice, a presence, an absence, language and silence. In its darkest form, this is Celan's "No One's-Rose." In his "Psalm," the Jewish people, reduced to dust in the ovens of Auschwitz, have become the Bush burned to a Nothing rose, a No-one rose. Celan "un-names" God as the Shoah erased millionfold the names, the identities of its victims.[77]

No one kneads us again out of earth and clay,
no one incants our dust.
No one.

No one even "speaks about" this; *bespricht*—the word Felstiner translates as "incants"can also mean "speak about."[78] No one, not God, will speak about this reversion to dust. In this darkest Psalm, the fire has consumed all, even language itself.

In counterpoint to "No One's-Rose," the absence of all rose, comes God's assurance, "I will dwell in their midst." Out of this central space there will issue a voice, which will speak *with* Moses. ("I will speak with you there" [25:22].) A dialogue between God and the human being is what the Mishkan is "about." For such a dialogue to become imaginable, the people must grow beyond the fantasy of merging. In Winnicott's words, the interplay between separateness and union must find its potential space. This interplay generates a new language to replace the lost oneness.

4. Learning the Mishkan: A Possible Nexus?

The Erotic Possibility

In an important sense, the Mishkan comes to offer a new response to a radical problem. The problem is the possibility of a nexus between the sublime and mundane realms. "In the absence of eros, we have tragedy: the sublime and mundane realms may intersect, sometimes with horrible consequences, but the meaning of that intersection remains humanly incomprehensible."[79] In the Mishkan, the erotic possibility is intimated in the space between the cherubim, which will be animated by language and silence. There, God will dwell, as a nomad dwells, not as a fixity, but as One who speaks and falls silent before the face of the other. The Mishkan remains a site for the visiting Shechina, not a settled habitation. When David is fired with enthusiasm to build a house for God, God answers him, "From the day that I brought the people of Israel out of Egypt to this day I have not dwelt (*yashavti*) in a house, but have moved about in Tent and Tabernacle."[80] Volatile, beyond human comprehension, God's presence yet expresses itself in language that Moses can comprehend—"I will speak with you." The nexus between the heavenly and mundane realms is "face to face"—in the nexus of language and silence.

On the midrashic reading, this solution is embedded in a fraught narrative context. It is offered to a people who have tried to find their own solution and been badly burned. This narrative context is not explicit in the text. But as we read of God's instructions to build the Mishkan, the shadow of the Golden Calf looms, implicit, repressed. The effect is to give an uncanny intensity to the technical objectivity of the building specifications. And the disparity that the midrash notices between physical materials and the fire of the vision is exacerbated by the afterimage of the Golden Calf, grotesque, absurd.

The Afterimage of the Golden Calf

The power that invests the Mishkan instructions, then, derives partly from a sense of *incomprehension* about the Golden Calf. The reader returns to a kind of innocence: what could that golden animal have represented that its gold should be mirrored so shamelessly in the sacred space? Teasing us out of thought, these instructions address a private world, at this point only dimly envisaged, of fear and desire.

If we look more closely at the midrashic literature, we can discover a clearer idea of the time-scheme within this inverted narrative. A sense of possible chronology will sharpen some of the implications of the Golden Calf–Mishkan sequence. For instance, let us look at the mysterious and powerful passage in 33:7–11. The narrative moment is after Moses has successfully interceded for the people and God's original intention to destroy them totally has been rescinded. Moses has shattered the Tablets of Stone and then ground the Golden Calf into dust. Three thousand of the people have been killed and innumerable others have died in a plague. God has declared that He will now send an angel to lead the people into the Holy Land: He Himself will *"not go up in your midst"* (33:4). "The people heard this evil thing and they mourned": in token of mourning, they "stripped off their ornaments from the mountain of Chorev" (33:6).

It is after this narrative of divestment and loss, of a sense of self now eviscerated, emptied of God, that there follows an enigmatic scene:

> Now Moses would take the Tent and pitch it outside the camp, at some distance from the camp. It was called the Tent of Meeting, and whoever sought God would go out to the Tent of Meeting that was outside the camp. Whenever Moses went out to the Tent, all the people would rise and stand, each at the entrance of his tent, and gaze after Moses until he had entered the Tent. And when Moses entered the tent, the pillar of cloud would descend and stand at the entrance of the Tent, while He spoke with Moses. When all the people saw the pillar of cloud erect at the entrance of the Tent, all the people would rise and bow low, each at the entrance of his tent. God would speak to Moses face to face, as one man speaks to another. And he would return to the camp . . . (33:7–11)

Moses pitches his personal tent, now strangely called the Tent of Meeting, outside the camp. The language of externality is remorselessly pressed home: "outside the camp . . . far from the camp . . . would go out . . . which was outside the camp . . . and when Moses would go out . . ." Then, there is a switch from this insistence on externality to Moses' entrance into his interior. Significantly, this emphasis on Moses' inwardness is mediated by the people's imagination; it is they who gaze after him as he enters his tent, they who see the cloud descend and speak with Moses, they who respond by falling on their faces at their own tent-entrances.

The externality of Moses' tent clearly expresses God's displeasure. If God is angry with the people, if he has left "their midst," leaving them empty at the core, Moses too enacts the divine anger and alienation by pitching his tent outside the camp. His thinking is described epigrammatically in several midrashic sources: "If they are banished by the Teacher, surely they should be banished by the student!"[81] Moses thus mimes God's anger and his Tent of Meeting pitched outside the camp travesties the desired meeting of God and the human "in their midst"; the word for "meeting" is used five times in the instructions for the Mishkan. This demonstrative tableau of loss results in the people's seeking God *outside* the camp and in the fraught silent scene where they contemplate Moses' back as he recedes into his own private Tent of Meeting.

When does this take place? One view quite plausibly maintains that, since this is a scene of alienation and anger, it must have happened during the middle forty-day period, the period of anger after the Golden Calf—that is, from the seventeenth of Tammuz till the beginning of Elul. This is the period before God accedes to Moses' later prayers and agrees to return to the midst of the people (33:12–17). That Moses spent this middle period of anger among the people but demonstratively alienated from them is the view of a number of midrashic sources.[82] On this reading, God ends this period by telling Moses, "If you remain angry and I remain angry, who will bring them closer?" This leads to an unexpected translation of 33:11: *Ve-shav el ha-machaneh*—"Then Moses returned to the camp." That is, Moses restores his Tent to the body of the people, is reincorporated among them, in token of forgiveness.

However, a different view is taken by Rashi.[83] Surprisingly, and against the midrashic view, he translates *ve-shav el ha-machaneh* as part of a continuing dynamic: "He would go out of the camp to his tent *and he would return to the camp*." In Rashi's reading, this repeated journey, inwards and outwards, takes place after Yom Kippur, after the people's sin has been forgiven. Moses would move back and forth between camp and private Tent of Meeting during the period from Yom Kippur (tenth of Tishrei) till the Mishkan was erected (first of Nisan). In his Tent, he receives God's instructions for the Mishkan and then returns to the camp to teach them to the elders. In Rashi's narrative, there was no time before this for such a scenario: Moses had returned to the top of the mountain immediately after the Golden Calf episode. Only after Yom Kippur, when full forgiveness was granted, was the Mishkan commanded in token of atonement. Till the Mishkan is completed, this externalized Tent of Meeting is the medium for God to speak "face to face" with Moses. This continues until the first of Nisan, when the Mishkan is completed; from then on, all communication with God takes place from there. Interestingly, Rashi quotes the Midrash that treats the "return to the camp" as the resolution of this tableau of alienation, but clearly regards his own reading as the *peshat*, the historically cogent reading.

Rashi's scenario is puzzling in at least one important way. If this scene takes place after the people are forgiven, why does Moses keep his tent outside the camp? Why are the instructions for the Mishkan, that symbol of the desire for inwardness, for the density of a condition replete with God, given from an alienated site, outside the camp? Surely such a scenario expresses God's anger, His refusal "to go up in their midst" of an earlier period?

After Forgiveness: God and Moses Outside

Maharal[84] discusses the question: why is the private Tent of Meeting still outside the camp, if the people are forgiven? He answers that "even though God is reconciled with them, they are still, as it were, banished, alienated." Their full atonement still awaits the sacrifices in the Mishkan—the bullock of the sin offering, the young calf, the red heifer—all evoking the Golden Calf and expurgating that sin. Maharal here makes a subtle discrimination, between *God's being reconciled with them* on Yom Kippur and *their being reconciled with Him*. Some intimate schism remains. They are still "as it were, alienated, banished."

On this reading, an intermediate region is set up between anger and reconciliation. After Yom Kippur, God has forgiven them, but they are still restive, they lack the full ability to atone, to become at-one with God. In this intermediate period, they learn about the Mishkan; this learning takes the form of language, language between God and Moses, outside the camp, and language between Moses and the people, inside the camp.

This period is passed in passages outwards and inwards, with the people intently gazing after Moses as he leaves the camp. That is, after Yom Kippur and until the Mishkan becomes a physical reality, capable of consummating atonement, the people have their most intimate religious experience in contemplating the externality of God and of Moses. They stand at the entrance to their own tents watching Moses as he recedes into the entrance to his tent. Here, the language of the Torah conveys the imaginative movement in the people's hearts, as they follow Moses into his interior.

The midrash wonders, What can they be thinking? What does a people think as it becomes aware of its own hollowness? Rashi quotes: "Happy is the man woman-born who is so assured that the presence of God will enter behind him into his tent entrance!"[85] This is a hypothesis about the contents of a fantasy. The people are possessed by a wistful yearning: Moses, receding from their midst, represents a personal possibility of connection with God. They imagine him entering his interior space: not finding God there, but with God *behind* him. Expressive of a confidence that does not need visual validation, the image complements the fantasy of God at the heart. This image will be picked up and reversed in the passage describing how Moses sees God only *from the back:* "You shall see My back, but My face shall not be seen" (33:23)[86]—the scene that follows this one in the Torah narrative, but that, in Rashi's reading, transpired before this one.

This scene culminates in a dialogue "face to face, as one man speaks to another." This is not an image of fusion, of God at the center. The work of inward reconciliation that the people still have to consummate focuses largely on their maturing fantasies of inside and outside. On Yom Kippur, they are formally forgiven, but they are still in a false position, they are guilty of *mauvaise foi*, of an essential inauthenticity. The following period is a time of language about the Mishkan, of a spiritual and imaginative confrontation with distance, alienation, emptiness.

A Secret Repentance: Intimate Transformations

This is the critical time of *teshuva*, of penitence, of inner work to reconstruct the *idiopolis* of fantasy and desire. In this process, Moses is the "transference-figure," receding and entering his interior, returning to their midst. A link is established between Moses' tent and the Mishkan; both are Tents of Meeting, both represent the role of imagination in the encounter with God. Both represent a subtle counterpoint to the fixity, the fetishized centering of the Golden Calf.[87]

> When the Israelites were in the desert, they acted offensively. Then, they did *teshuva*, they repented in secret, as it is said, "Whenever Moses went out to the Tent . . . and when Moses entered the Tent . . . when all the people saw the cloud . . ." This teaches that their *teshuva*, their repentance, was in secret. Therefore, God's compassion was stirred and He gave them Yom Kippur for forgiveness, to them and their children and their children's children till the end of all generations.[88]

The moment of "secret *teshuva*" is the moment when the people prostrate themselves, each in the privacy of his tent-flap. At that liminal place, at the *petach*, the tent entrance (referred to four times in three verses), which is both inside and outside, the people imagine Moses entering his liminal place, with God at his back. The midrash focuses on the shift from "Whenever Moses went out . . ." to "when Moses entered . . ." This complex reverie works profoundly within them, so that, in an existential sense, it is they who create the dynamic of Yom Kippur. The essential work of Yom Kippur, the intimate repentance, has been invented by them: God responds by giving them the formal resource to all posterity.

This "secret" moment, viewed as a national phenomenon, is a significant break point in the spiritual history of the people. Contrasting with the public Sinai moment ("*We* shall do and *we* shall hear!") is the private work with fantasy and desire, "each at the entrance of his tent."[89] Where the people had first spoken of "doing" (*na'aseh*), fulfilling God's commandments, they had regressed to the point of pressing Aaron: "Make (*asseh*) us gods who will walk before us" (32:1). Now, God gives them a therapeutic instruction: "Let them make (*ve-assu*) Me a sanctuary . . ." In Rashi's reading, this therapeutic making/doing lives first in the transitional space between inside and outside, in the months of Moses' passage between the two worlds, and in the private reverie that imagines it.

At base, this is what it is to build a Mishkan: it requires a new awareness of hollowness that is not neutralized by stable Presence. This is the double creation of the people: in the spatial realm, a sanctuary for God to live in their midst; in the temporal realm, Yom Kippur, the real possibility of inward transformation through time. The two will converge in the physical Mishkan, where atonement will be enacted. But the phase of spiritual reverie, when the heart creates its own space for God, is the crucial one.

Comedy and Tragedy

God demands/promises, "I shall dwell in their midst." Does this describe an imaginable reality? The answer must be ambiguous. Essentially, there must be two narratives, a comedy and a tragedy.[90] The comedy is represented by God's perspective, from which the Mishkan is inevitable. The desires and longings of the patriarchs and matriarchs, of generations of spiritual aspiration, make such a meeting between God and the human a necessity. The nexus between realms is situated in the space at their center and is mediated by language; it is given in the Torah without any explicit reference to contingencies, to the sin of the Golden Calf. In this "comic" reading, the Golden Calf is an episode, an incidental problem; after which the original concept of the Mishkan is restored.

But the other interpretation of the narrative is as a tragedy. This is represented by the human perspective. From this perspective, the possibility of such a meeting is bizarre, subject to travesty. Either a fetish will occupy the "middest," or the lover will simply elude them. ("My beloved slipped away, he was gone" [Song of Songs 5:6].) This is the narrative of indirection, of alienation and complexity, that is repressed in the Torah. But this tragic narrative, too, is essential. Without the Golden Calf, God will not bring His presence to rest in their midst. A new awareness of the complexity of inside and outside, of density and hollowness, must precede the construction of a Mishkan that will have stability in its mobility. The people require the "words of Torah," the dialogues of Torah, that draw energy precisely from error, from memory and experience. "No one can comprehend [*omed al*—lit. 'stand upon, be stable upon'] the words of Torah till one has stumbled over them."[91]

In this "tragic" reading, the experience of sin is the very means by which the transcendent and the human realms can find a potential space for interplay. When the Mishkan is commanded, it is more than a mere concession to human weakness; more, even, than a homeopathic, therapeutic gesture. It represents an *impossible idea*, a project that has already been proven disastrous. It arises out of a fire that would be unknown to the people if they had not been singed by it.

For the reader of the Torah, however, there remains the "double reading," the comic and the tragic interpretations of the same drama. As in an Escher engraving, the text of the Torah flickers with ambiguity. And the reader experiences that inner shift that destabilizes the idolatrous security of meaning. Perhaps only a text that flickers in this way can maintain its power through time.

8 Tetzaveh

LOSS AND GAIN

[27:20–30:10]

1. *Moses and Aaron: Fraternal Idyll or Narrative of Anger?*

"And as for You . . ."—Moses at the Focus

> "And as for you, you shall instruct the Israelites to bring you pure olive oil of beaten olives for lighting, for kindling the Eternal Lamp." (27:20)

With unusual emphasis, God turns to Moses: *Ve-atta tetzaveh*—"*And as for you*, you shall instruct . . ." The redundant pronoun in *ve-atta*, "and as for you," substitutes for the more usual imperative form, *tzav*—"Instruct . . ." or the simple future form, *tetzaveh*—"You shall instruct . . ." Such an insistent, abrupt focus on Moses has aroused much discussion among the traditional commentators on the Torah. He has surely all along been God's agent for instructing the people in all the details of the building of the Mishkan. Normally, the "and as for you" mode would be used to point a contrast with the preceding material. But here, even the verbs in the previous chapters place Moses squarely at the center of the action: "And you shall make the courtyard of the Mishkan" (27:9); "And you shall make the altar" (27:1); "And you shall make its horns" (27:2); "And you shall make a curtain of blue . . ."

(26:31). Indeed, the direct instructions to Moses—"You shall make . . . you shall place . . . you shall join . . ." is a leitmotiv of the previous Parsha, without the emphatic pronoun, *ve-atta*. What shift in focus requires the sudden use of *ve-atta*, in a context where Moses is everywhere the subject of God's address?

One possible answer is suggested by Ramban: in the case of the pure olive oil for the Eternal Lamp, Moses is to play a personal role, not simply to instruct others to fashion the sacred objects; he *personally* is to scrutinize the oil for purity. Ramban's reading, however, leaves much unexplained. *Why* the personal focus on Moses in relation to the oil for the menora? What is to happen after Moses dies? Who will then take over this particular function?[1]

The unusual form, *ve-atta*, "and as for you . . ." becomes more insistent—and perhaps more challenging—when we notice that it recurs twice within the first five verses of the Portion: "*And as for you*, you shall bring forward your brother Aaron, with his sons, from among the Israelites, to serve Me as priests" (28:1); "*And as for you*, you shall speak to all who are wise of heart, whom I have filled with the spirit of wisdom, to make Aaron's vestments for consecrating him to serve Me as priest" (28:3). In relation to two more instructions, Moses is placed at the epicenter of God's address: initiating his brother, Aaron, into his dynastic role as High Priest, and instructing the craftsmen who will fashion the priestly robes. In all three cases, Moses is singled out as the vehicle of God's will: "And you . . . and you . . . and you . . ." In all three cases, paradoxically, Moses is to assume a direct responsibility in an area that is specifically not his own: it is his brother Aaron who will tend the Eternal Lamp, who will function as High Priest, who will wear the priestly robes. A tension, therefore, accumulates around God's address to Moses: some mysterious train of thought is continued, running against the grain of assigned function. Implicitly, enigmatically, it is Moses who represents the dynamic out of which the priestly function takes its vital force.

The larger context of the enigma reveals an additional complication. This Parsha, which is concerned with the priesthood, its function, and inaugural processes, contains not one mention of Moses' name. This is, in fact, the only Parsha in the last four books of the Torah that does not explicitly mention Moses or include Moses as narrator. Most exceptional is the absence even of the formula, "And God said to Moses . . ."

Ba'al HaTurim connects this absence of Moses' name with his own self-sacrificing offer to God, "Erase me from Your book that You have written!"

(32:32). This suggestion clearly assumes the midrashic chronology we have discussed in chapter 7:[2] *before* the instructions for the Mishkan were given, the people sinned with the Golden Calf and Moses was moved to plead for their survival by offering his own life. If the people are to be destroyed, Moses asks for all record of his own name to be deleted from God's book.

It is this Moses-free text, then, that is introduced by three occurrences of the emphatic address to Moses: "And as for you . . ." The paradox is compelling: absence and presence, anonymity and insistent naming. Moses' role becomes both conspicuous and problematic. Another way of focusing the paradox is to notice that the Parsha is almost always[3] read during the week in which the date traditionally associated with Moses' birth and death occurs: the seventh of Adar. The tension set up between absence and presence is reflected in a liturgical dimension which evokes the mystery of a life that ends on the same day it begins.

Birth and death, gain and loss, are figured in the reassuring intonation of *ve-atta*—"And as for you . . ."[4] in a context where his name is absent and Aaron's name dominates. Aaron's name, indeed, occurs seven times within this passage (27:20–28:5).[5]

Moses and Aaron: Reversion to Typology?

The subliminal tension in the relationship of Moses and Aaron is the subject of a penetrating midrash:[6]

> "And as for you, you shall bring forward your brother Aaron . . ." (28:1). It is written, "If Your Torah had not been my plaything, I should have perished in my poverty" (Ps 119:92). When God told Moses, "As for you, you shall bring forward your brother Aaron . . ." He did him an injury. God said, "I had possession of the Torah, and I gave it to you: if it were not for the Torah I should have lost My world!" This is like a wise man who married his relative and after ten years together, when she had not borne children, he said to her, "Seek me a wife!" He said to her, "I could marry without your permission, but I seek your cooperation." So said God to Moses, "I could have made your brother High Priest without informing you, but I wish you to be great over him."

The analogy invoked in the midrash is startling. Telling Moses to appoint his brother High Priest is like a husband telling his wife to look for another, more fertile wife for him. The meaning of *heira lo*, "God did Moses an injury," is harshly illuminated by this analogy. An outrageous, even indecorous demand is made on Moses' *invetanuth*, his cooperation, his compliance in a project that frustrates his own aspirations. The midrashic term *invetanuth*, "humility," derives from the word *anav*, "humble," which the Torah, in a rare moment of explicit character-portrayal, describes as Moses' dominant characteristic: "Moses was a very humble man, more so than any other man on earth" (Num 12:3).

Significantly, the term *invetanuth* is used in the parable of the wise man and his wife, while in the narrative of God and Moses it is translated into the demand that "you be great over him." The obvious dissonance between humility and greatness, then, becomes the central tension of the midrash: what God wants of Moses is a forebearance, a compliance that will be renamed as greatness.

In terms of the relation between Moses and Aaron, the irony of God's desire is exacerbated. Of the two brothers, Aaron is the older—the "greater," therefore, in age. He is to be Kohen Gadol, literally, the *Great* Priest. And yet, Moses' sense of injury is justified; he had some right to expect that the High Priest's role would be his. On the basis of the paradigms of Genesis, the notion of primogeniture overturned has become a new convention: the younger brother proves himself to be the child of destiny and supersedes the older, the *gadol*, the "greater." Abel, Isaac, Jacob, and Joseph are the most prominent examples. Moreover, as the recipient of all God's instructions about the Mishkan, Moses is justified in expecting to be the prime actor within its precincts. The shock of exclusion, therefore, represents a reversion to the original typology, to the domination of the elder brother. The irony is intensified by God's cryptic demand that in this situation of demotion, Moses show himself "great over him."

Humility and Greatness

The axis of humility/greatness is first introduced and tested in a classic midrashic comment on Moses' first encounter with God at the Burning Bush. There, God's opening words were, "Moses! Moses! . . . Do not come closer . . ." (Exod 3:4–5). This is the midrashic reading:

> And he said, "Here I am!" . . . "Here I am, ready for priesthood and for kingship!" . . . God replied, "Do not approach closer—that is, your chil-

> dren will not offer sacrifices (lit., bring close to Me), because the priesthood is reserved for Aaron your brother . . . and the kingship for King David." And yet, Moses attained both: the priesthood, when he officiated during the seven days of Inauguration of the Mishkan, and the kingship, as it is written, "Then he became King in Jeshurun." (Deut 33:5)[7]

In this important midrash, Moses makes an instinctive claim to both priesthood and kingship. God repudiates his claim, on both scores: these are dynastic roles and his children will not inherit either function. But, during his own lifetime, the basic justice of his instinct is acknowledged in some form: in a provisional or cryptic manner, he becomes both priest and king.

The complexity of Moses' relation to "greatness" is thus indicated at the foundational moment at the Burning Bush. His famed "humility" is not a lack of aspiration or of conscious genius: he is attuned to the two possible modalities of greatness, priestly and kingly, sacred and political. But God inhibits him: "Do not come *closer*!"—*Al tikrav halom*—and later confronts him with the shock of *ve-atta hakrev*—"Bring Aaron your brother *close*—initiate him into the priestly role that I have denied you from the beginning."

In the midrashic parable, the husband asks his wife to find him a new wife, "because she had not borne children." In terms of Moses' situation, the notion of infertility both invites and resists translation. Some core function has not found expression in Moses' relation to God; because of this failure, Aaron is to replace him. The notion of a "sterility" that is represented by Moses' loss of the priesthood evokes a poignant sense of his "dys-dynastic" fate: his biological children are not his spiritual heirs. In a biological sense, Moses does not "propagate" his connection to God; he does not duplicate himself, effectively, his "marriage" to God is sterile. This implication in the midrash is given a paradoxical force by the fact that the wife is her husband's "close relative"—*kerovato*. That is, Moses is "close" to God, he has a natural affinity to Him, in His wisdom, but he is unable to bear fruit. Therefore, God says to him, "Do not come *closer*" and "Bring your brother, Aaron, *into closeness* to Me . . ." The intimacy with God that is the High Priesthood is not for Moses. And yet, in some dimension, he is apt for it, naturally attuned to it. His problem is connected with fertility, with the dynastic function of priesthood that he is incapable of fulfilling.

Sefath Emeth[8] probes the paradox of sterility and closeness to God. Perhaps an extraordinary encounter of the human with the divine is, by the nature of things, inimitable? The priestly or the kingly role can be passed down through the generations; but Moses as the "man of God," (Deut 33:1)—read in mystical literature as referring to an intimate erotic relation with God—transcends the world of propagation. A unique passion defies comprehension or duplication. There is a tension between the erotic and the procreative that is reflected most evocatively in biblical narratives of infertile marriages.[9]

Attempting to make these concepts imaginable, we may ask: What is the nature of the defeat that God asks Moses to cooperate in enacting? In what sense is compliance greatness? And what is the compensation for his forbearance, his *invetanuth*? In the midrash, his compensation is called Torah, which preserves the world from extinction. In an audacious move, the midrash puts the Psalmist's words in God's mouth: "If it were not for the Torah, which I have given to you, I should have lost My world!"[10] It is the Torah as a "plaything" that God gives Moses; his role therefore is of vital, incomparable significance. God asks him to comply with His reallocation of the priesthood as a gesture of voluntary greatness; somehow, this is related to the primacy of the Torah, which is now entrusted to Moses in a playful mode that radically differs from the original "gift" at Mount Sinai. It is Moses, therefore, who is virtually charged with the survival of the world.

The Fraternal Idyll: Moses Loses the Priesthood

The complex situation of loss and gain that is sketched in this midrash unfolds in a further midrash on the relation between Moses and Aaron:

> All seven days while Moses was at the Burning Bush, God urged him, "Go on My mission," and Moses answered, "Send by the hand of someone else!" (4:13). This was repeated every day. Then God said to him, "I am telling you, 'Go!' and you tell Me, 'Send by the hand of someone else!' As you live, tomorrow I will pay you back! When the Mishkan is constructed, you will expect to become High Priest, and I will tell you, 'Call Aaron to be appointed High Priest!' " That is why it is said, "Moses called Aaron and his sons . . ." (Lev 9:1) . . .
>
> Moses told Aaron, "God has instructed me to appoint you High Priest." Aaron replied, "You have labored so hard on the Mishkan and I am made High Priest!" Moses replied, "As you live, even though you have become

> High Priest, it is as though I had become High Priest! Just as you rejoiced when I rose to greatness, so I rejoice in your greatness."
>
> When had Aaron rejoiced for Moses? When God had told Moses, "Now go, I shall send you to Pharaoh (3:10)—this role is assigned to you," Moses had answered, "Please, my lord, send by the hand of someone else!"—that is, "You will cause my brother to resent me, since he is the elder, and yet you send me on this mission!" Then God had said, "As you live, you are right that he is older than you—nevertheless, he will see you and rejoice in his heart." (3:14)
>
> Said R. Shimeon bar Yochai: "That same heart that rejoiced in the greatness of his brother, let precious stones be set upon it, as it is said, 'And Aaron shall bear the names of the Israelites on the breastplate *upon his heart.*' " (28:29)
>
> So, all seven days that Moses was preoccupied with the Mishkan, he sprinkled the blood, and turned the fat parts to smoke. Then God said, "What do you think, that you are to be High Priest? Call Aaron and his sons to become priests."[11]

Here, Moses' loss of the priestly role takes on the coloration of punishment. For seven days, he resisted God's mission at the Burning Bush; and with an ironic equivalence, God allows him to serve for seven days as High Priest in the inauguration of the Mishkan, before disabusing him of his expectation of retaining that role forever. Moses' loss is unequivocal, as is the pain of disappointment—he will *expect* to be High Priest—that answers to God's "disappointment" with Moses' resistance to His call. Indeed, God's reproach to Moses—"I say, 'Go—*lech!*' and you say, 'Send by someone else!' "—evokes the paradigm of Abraham's classic movement of obedience to God's call, "Go—*lech lecha*!" God's expectation is frustrated by Moses' avoidance. In addition, the midrash exacerbates this refusal ("Send by the hand of someone else!"): instead of being Moses' last response at the end of a complex dialogue, as it appears in the biblical text, this becomes his ongoing blunt repudiation—"all seven days at the Burning Bush."

In this midrashic version of the narrative, God surprises Moses with His selection of Aaron as High Priest. But here, clearly, the midrash seems to double back in its tracks. For that "surprise" decision is foretold to Moses at the Burning Bush—"You will *expect* to become High Priest." In other words, there is no surprise, since Moses is forewarned from the earliest period of his life.

This inconsistency invites a closer examination of the complex dynamics of the brotherly relationship. The midrash portrays the relationship as an idyll of selfless joy in the "greatness" of the other. We learn that Moses' reluctance to accept God's call is rooted in a reluctance to anger his elder brother; God acknowledges the justice of Moses' reservation but attests to Aaron's noble altruism: "He will rejoice in his heart." For this sincere and selfless joy, Aaron is rewarded by the priestly breastplate as emblem of the pure heart that beats beneath it. This is the narrative of the fraternal idyll which culminates in Moses' equivalent selflessness in rejoicing at Aaron's appointment as High Priest.

The Other Narrative: Anger and Loss

Counterpointed to this, however, is the theme of Moses' resistance, God's anger and punishment, and Moses' disappointment at losing the High Priesthood. Rashi meshes both narratives in his commentary:

> (4:13) *"Send by the hand of whomever You will send:"* By the hand of the one You are accustomed to send, that is, Aaron. Another explanation: by the hand of someone else whom You will choose to send. It is not my destiny to lead the people into the Holy Land and to be their future redeemer. You have many redeemers!
>
> (4:14) *"And God's anger burned . . ."* R. Yehoshua ben Korha said, Every burning anger recorded in the Torah leaves a trace. Here, there is no trace recorded, and we have never found that any punishment was the result of that anger. R. Yossi answered him: Here, too, there is a trace. "There is Aaron your brother, *the Levite*" (4:14)—who was destined to be a Levite, not a priest, while the priesthood I had determined would issue from you. From now, this will not be so, but he will be priest and you Levite, as it is said, "And Moses, man of God, his sons were named *as Levites*." (1 Chr 23:14)
>
> *"Even now he is setting out to meet you:"* when you go to Egypt *"and he will see you with joy in his heart:"* He will not, as you think, resent your rise to greatness. For this, Aaron came to merit the breastplate which is set over the heart.

Rashi focuses on the textual link between God's anger and the following sentence about Aaron. God expresses His anger by reallocating the priesthood: from merely Levite, Aaron will now become priest, while Moses, who had been destined to have priesthood "descend" from him, is demoted to simple Levite status. At the same time, Rashi quotes the midrash about Aaron's altruistic joy at Moses' leadership.

In this double narrative of resistance and punishment, on the one hand, and of mutual fraternal love, on the other, neither the midrash nor Rashi comments on God's description of Aaron: "I know that he speaks readily" (4:14) (*dabber ye-dabber*—lit. "speak, he will speak"). On the *peshat*, the primary reading of the passage, this characterization of Aaron's eloquence is quite intelligible: God is partially acceding to Moses' refusal to convey His message; since Aaron is a natural speaker, he will convey Moses' communications from God to the people. In terms of the midrashic reading, however, the subject of the verse is the transferred priesthood; Aaron's condition as a speaker, as a man of language, contrasted with Moses' avowed condition as "not a man of words" (3:10), must, then, be in some sense relevant to his destiny as High Priest. Moses has refused to speak in God's name; now, God takes him at his word and strips him of a role that apparently has a radical connection with language.

We notice, indeed, how the introduction of the midrashic narrative[12] about the High Priesthood complicates a lucid plot. Without this strand, the story is quite clear: even the midrashic motif about Aaron's altruism blends unobtrusively into the main narrative. What does the theme of the lost priesthood contribute to the reader's understanding? On the textual level, there is, of course, the problem of God's anger, which seems to make no impact on the plot. But, in addition, we may suggest that the theme of the lost priesthood is pushed back to this earliest period to evoke the complexity of loss and gain in Moses' life.

He begins his prophetic career by resisting the prophetic role: he is not a speaker, he says in many different ways. By insisting on his language problem, he makes God angry. The fact of God's anger, we may say, must indicate a serious position taken by Moses. Anger reflects a choice that Moses has made and that must leave its mark on his life. He has chosen not to speak, perhaps he is gravely incapable of speech; and at the same time, he loses the priestly role. In the future, the Tanchuma source adds, he will experience disappointment at his loss and, ultimately, will accept an apparently diminished role. Then, his joy for his brother will mirror his brother's heartfelt present joy for him.

Interleaving the two midrashic narratives, the reader registers profound ambiguity: Moses takes one role from his brother (prophecy? leadership?) and yields him another (priesthood); on the one hand, he is admirably reluctant to trespass on his brother's territory and selflessly glad at his assumption of the priesthood, and on the other, he is resisting God's call and disappointed at his own loss.

Revisioning Loss and Gain

The complication of the midrashic narrative of loss and gain is partly a function of the passage of time. We have noticed the apparent confusion in God's punishment of Moses: if he is alerted at the very beginning of the narrative to the fact that he will not become High Priest, how can he *expect* that he will become High Priest, as he inaugurates the Mishkan? If he expects disappointment, how can he be disappointed?

I suggest, therefore, that when he is first told that the hereditary role of priesthood will not be his, his realization of the meaning of that role is still limited. On some visceral level, in harping on his speech impediment, he has rejected it for himself. God's anger expresses the seriousness with which He takes him. It is only at a much later juncture, however, that Moses will realize more fully the implications of his loss. At that point, he will construct the meaning of the priesthood in such a way as to "rewrite" his own relationship to it; he will think of himself as appropriate for the role and God will disappoint him.

This scenario, then, represents not simply a "punishment" for refusing God's mission but a radical perspective on subconscious issues of Moses' history. This is the process that Freud describes as "Nachtraglichkeit": "memory traces being subjected, from time to time to a re-arrangement in accordance with fresh circumstances—to a retranscription." Sexual development is a classic area in which "memory traces can only be understood with the emergence of sexual feelings." Essential to the process is forgetting, which gives rise to a continual "remaking something that to all intents and purposes never existed . . . memory is a way of inventing the past."[13]

Rashi's text focuses the issue by offering a second interpretation of "Send by the hand of someone else!":

> "Send by the hand of someone else whom You will choose to send. It is not my destiny to lead the people into the Holy Land and to be their future redeemer. You have many messengers."

Moses displays an intuitive knowledge that he will not consummate the mission of redemption. And the same mechanism of repressed memory comes into play. At the end of his life, he will plead with God to let him lead the people into the Holy Land; his plea will be a newly urgent response to a deferred action which he now redescribes in his consciousness. But by affirming an early stratum of knowledge of his ultimate rejection—whether as natural leader or as High Priest—Rashi gives us a Moses whose life is a continual quest for echoes of loss.

In psychoanalytic terms, it is the loss of the mother that forms the primal stratum, forgotten and retranscribed, of experience. In Moses' history, it is difficult not to notice the double loss of the mother, in his infant separation from his biological mother, Jochebed, and in his separation from his nurturing mother, the Egyptian princess. Indeed, the theme of double identity is clearly significant in considering Moses' life; he loses an Israelite identity to gain an Egyptian one, and then loses that in a voluntary resumption of his Israelite identity. His primal experience, as a son, of loss and gain is then played out in the midrashic narrative of loss and gain in relation to his own "sons": his spiritual power splits into separate nonbiological lines, to Aaron and to Joshua.

"We are compulsive revisionists with an unknowable vision," writes Adam Phillips.[14] The vision of loss that Moses is given at the Burning Bush is to be reviewed or revised in the course of his life. It will evoke themes of responsibility and guilt, on the one hand, and of obscure privilege, on the other. And in this drama of redescription, the axis of humility and greatness will be tested and retested.

2. *Loss and Gain: Aaron's Garments and the Ambiguities of Representation*

Power and Forbearance: The Priestly Robes

We return to our original midrash in which Moses' appointment of his brother as High Priest is compared to a wife's quest for a rival wife. Here, the axis of humility and greatness is central. God demands of Moses a compliance, a forbearance in his own diminishment, that is then translated as "Be great over him!" The two notions of power and forbearance are classically associated in the Talmudic description of God:

> Wherever you find power (*gevura*) of God, there you find His humility (*invetanuth*). This principle is written in the Torah, in the Prophets, and in the Scriptures. In the Torah it is written: "For the Lord your God is the supreme God and the supreme Lord," which is followed by, "He does justice to the orphan and the widow." (Deut 10:17–18) This is repeated in the Prophets: "So says the exalted One, the sublime One who lives eternally . . ." which is followed by "Yet with the contrite and the lowly in spirit. . ." (Isa 57:15) And again in the Scriptures: "Extol Him who rides the clouds, the Lord is His name . . ." which is followed by "the father of orphans, champion of widows . . . " (Ps 68:5–6)[15]

The Talmud traces biblical passages where God's power is juxtaposed to His forbearance. More accurately, *invetanuth* emerges as God's association with the depressed members of society, the widow, the orphan, the demoralized. This divine proclivity informs the demand God makes of Moses in our midrash. Essentially, in requiring a humility that is another face of greatness, God looks to Moses for a genetic marker of the *tzelem elokim* (the image of God), the godlike play of the lion and the lamb in one face. The humility or forbearance that Moses is to express in appointing Aaron to his own role is, at base, a matter of relationship. As God displays a magnanimous imagination in nurturing the less impressive members of society, so Moses is to realize in himself an empathy for those who are stripped of power. It is loss, divestment of the priestly robes, that is to open up for him an alternative sensibility.

In this process, language plays a powerful if enigmatic role. Aaron, not Moses, is the speaker, the man of words; Aaron, not Moses, will be High Priest. On the face of it, the priestly function does not require much eloquence; it does, however, require the wearing of robes, of a priestly costume:

> "You shall wind turbans upon them and gird both Aaron and his sons with sashes. And so they shall have priesthood as their right for all time." (29:9) If one serves as a priest without the full priestly raiment, one's service is disqualified. At the time their raiment is upon them their priesthood is upon them. If their raiment is not upon them, their priesthood is not upon them.[16]

The clothing makes the priest. Not to be attired in exactly the right clothes is sufficient to disqualify the priest from the ritual. This uncompromising association of the priest with his raiment invites exploration. To be a priest is to be born to the function, and to wear the clothes of a priest.

What, in fact, is the definition of the word, *kohen* (priest)? Rashi indicates an unexpected ambiguity in the concept. Commenting on 28:3, where the word *kohen* is used as a verb ("You shall make Aaron the priestly raiment to sanctify him, to *make him a kohen* to Me."), Rashi writes:

> To sanctify him, to initiate him into the priesthood through his raiment, so that he may be a *kohen* to Me. The expression, *kohen*, means "to serve."

Kohen indicates "one who serves." It is a function within a system, a verb rather than a noun. When, for instance, the text refers to Aaron's son, "who is *kohen* in his place," this should be translated, "who *serves* in his place" (29:30). This function can be fulfilled only in the proper robes.

On the other hand, Rashi comments on 19:6:

> "You shall be to Me a kingdom of priests (*Kohanim*)": *princes*, as we find, "And the sons of David were *kohanim."* (2 Sam 8:18) [Clearly, the Davidic line could not have been priests; Rashi resolves this problem by translating *kohen* as *prince.*]

On Rashi's second translation, *kohen* is not a role, a function of service, but a status, a noun, an indication of power. Between Rashi's two translations runs an axis similar to the one we have noticed between the terms "greatness," and "forbearance." The virtues of the lion and the lamb are linked to one another in a necessary tension; to be a *kohen* is both to act out a role of service, to submit to a superior force, and to be an aristocrat, aware of power in oneself.

This tension between Rashi's two translations represents, I suggest, a real complexity in the meaning of priesthood. To wear the regalia of the Kohen is to express an innate grandeur, on the one hand, and to fit oneself out for work, on the other. These two poles are only apparently in opposition, however. For the prince in all his essential splendor functions within a hierarchy of power, while the service role reflects some of the majesty of the power who is served. At the same time, the range of possible points of balance between the two poles remains undetermined and the axis between them remains a site of tension.

A similar tension is described by Ramban in his comment on the purpose of the priestly raiment. The Torah affirms that the raiment is *le-chavod u-le-tiffareth*—"for glory and beauty" (28:2); and Ramban writes:

> He should be dignified and glorious in dignified, glorious garments, as the text says, "Like a bridegroom adorned with glory" (Isa 61:10). For these garments are royal raiment; kings were clothed in such garments at the time of the Torah . . . The clothes should be made for Aaron to serve in them for the glory of God who dwells among them and for the beauty of their strength—"For You are the beauty of their strength." (Ps 89:18) It is also written, "The house of our holiness and our beauty where our fathers praised You." (Isa 64:10)—"holiness" refers to His glory, and "beauty" to the beauty of Israel. . . And the clothes must be fashioned with full intentionality (awareness of their sacred purpose) and possibly even require *kavvana* (awareness of the complex meanings expressed in them). That is why God said, "And you shall speak to all who are wise in heart whom I have filled with the spirit of wisdom" (28:3)—that they should *understand* what they are making.

The purpose of the clothes is for glory and beauty; they represent the grandeur of God, in serving Whom the priest, too, becomes glorious. They constitute a language of prestige and power. Ramban emphasizes the aesthetic, representational function of the priest's vestments, in all their majesty and humility; the High Priest is arrayed like God's ministering angels, expressive of total attention, of a being so irradiated with an awareness of God that *even* its vestments dazzle. If the vestments are to have this authentically expressive power, inside and outside must match; therefore, Ramban emphasizes the consciousness and intentionality even of the craftsmen who fashion them.

Here, we approach the problematic heart of the issue. The position of the High Priest as representing God's glory is reflected in the aesthetics of his regalia. In a sense, the body and the soul of the man within the clothes become irrelevant: his *appearance* is all-important. The ecstatic intensity with which the High Priest was *seen* at the most exalted moment of his service is described in lyrical verses recited on Yom Kippur. Triumphant with joy, he emerges from the Holy of Holies; the only human being ever to experience that space, which is ordeal and intimacy, he has achieved atonement for himself and for all his people:

> *Like a tent stretched over the supreme beings—was the appearance of the Priest*

Like thunderbolts issuing from the brilliance of the angels—was the appearance of the Priest . . .

Like the image of the rainbow in the cloud—was the appearance of the Priest . . .

Like a rose in a pleasure garden—was the appearance of the Priest

Like a garland set on the king's brow—was the appearance of the Priest

Like the glow on the bridegroom's face—was the appearance of the Priest

Like the purity of a pure diadem—was the appearance of the Priest . . .

The changing conceits evoke the indescribable: in the priest's face is reflected an inner beauty that does not shame the purity of the priestly raiment. As the following refrain has it, "*Happy was the eye that saw all these;* but the hearing of the ear makes us sad." Since the destruction of the Temple, we mourn the loss of that aesthetic moment; what survives is merely *mashma ozneinu*, oral report, indirect hearing about what once was seen.

The High Priest, then, offered the people a visual intimation of the majesty and humility of one who has come close to God. Beyond the personal contingencies of his human situation, he comes to represent the intersection of the human and the divine. Ideally, his vestments clothe and cover his body in such a way that he is transmuted into a vision of God's glory that registers no dissonance between inner and outer worlds.

The Representation of Self: Possible Dissonance?

However, the possibility of such dissonance cannot be ignored. Beyond the obvious possibility that the priestly position may be abused—the possibility of hypocrisy and opportunism[17]—there is the more fundamental tension between the ceremonial and the personal. This awareness, of course, has developed in Western sensibility since the Renaissance; a skepticism about "clothes making the man." When we look at Velasquez's *Infanta* studies, for example, it is impossible not to register the pallid, overburdened child's face and body within the ponderous panoply of royalty—impossible, that is, not to register dissonance of body and costume. Such a sense of dissonance focuses on social roles, representations of self in the world, the language by which power expresses itself.

If Ramban, therefore, emphasizes the priest's clothing as representative of royalty, it is not surprising that he will also emphasize integrity, not only in the wearing of the clothes but even in their making. Since the possibilities of dissonance are so clear to the historical, satirical imagination, there is a corresponding need to require a high order of consonance between inner and outer, intention and display. The more prestige is expressed in the garments, the more demanding is the requirement of an authenticity that is traced back to their very origins.

We remember Hamlet, who is obsessed with the issue of self-representation: "Seems, madam! nay, it is, I know not 'seems' . . . I have that within which passes show, These but the trappings and the suits of woe,"[18] he cries to his mother, in protest against the ease with which the court has cast off both the show and the reality of mourning. The treachery of a sanctimonious court makes "all forms, modes, shapes of grief" untrustworthy indications of inner truth. Hamlet scorns the world of representation; his characteristic tone on the subject is a kind of bemused disgust—"Now get you to my lady's chamber, and tell her, let her paint an inch thick, to this favor she must come."[19] The perilous relation between play and reality dominates the rhetoric of the play, from the appearance of the Ghost to Hamlet but not to his mother to the "play within the play" and to the Dumb-Show within the play within the play.

In a moment of almost mystical awareness, King Lear expresses an equally tortured sensibility when, seeing Edgar naked in the storm, he cries:

> "Is man no more than this? Consider him well. Thou ow'st the worm no silk, the beast no hide, the sheep no wool, the cat no perfume . . . Thou art the thing itself; unaccommodated man is no more but such a poor, bare, forked animal as thou art. Off, off, you lendings! Come, unbutton here."[20]

Lear is overwhelmed by the animal strangeness and pathos of the human body; but, most of all, by its *reality.* Nothing can compare with the *truth* of the "poor, bare, forked animal." "Thou art the thing itself." He is compelled to strip himself, too: nakedness has a contagious power. Strikingly, he characterizes clothing, too, as animal-based: silk, leather, wool, perfume have bestial origins, and their constructed dignity comes to seem officious by contrast with the pitiable, heroic vulnerability of the body wincing in the storm. As

Lear strips himself, vehement to attain that "nothing" that is the rudimentary human reality ("In nothing am I changed but in my garments . . ."), the Fool restores us to the sane equilibrium of worldly judgment: "Prithee, Nuncle, be contented, 'tis a naughty night to swim in . . ."

Through Lear's mad eyes, we have glimpsed a world of skeletal truth. All clothes crumple in the storm, when they are most needed. Not all the Fool's sagacity can cure us of what we have seen. If there is to be salvation, it must be by following the clue of "nothing," wherever it leads.

Representation and Reality: The Importance of Intentionality

The tension between Lear and the Fool around the question of clothing is not, I suggest, entirely absent in any representation of the question. Clothing is indispensable, physically, culturally, even in terms of the soul's needs; but clothing obscures the honest, flinching truth—"the thing itself." It is perhaps because of this tension that the medieval commentaries stress the continuity of inner and outer, in connection with the priestly vestments: even the tailors and seamstresses must be pure of heart and aware of the symbolic meanings of their art. Only so can the potential inauthenticity of costume, of the trappings of civilization, be redeemed.

We have noticed Ramban's emphasis on intentionality. Seforno, too, recurs constantly to this theme, in his commentary:

> "And they shall take the gold" (28:5): Just as they should have full intentionality at the time of working with the gold, so they should even when they first take it in hand . . .
>
> "And the stones shall be . . ." (28:21) The verb "to be" indicates that from the very beginning of their existence, they shall be dedicated to the purpose of having the names of the tribes written upon them.

The craftsmen are to bridge the gap between representation and reality by the exercise of *kavvana*, of contemplative power, in their work. In the Talmud, a vivid example is given of the extent of such intentionality: if a thread was used to test the color in a pot of purple-blue dye (*techeleth*—the dye used for certain elements in the High Priest's vestments), then the thread becomes invalid for sacred use, as does the pot of dye.[21] This is because pot and dye were used in a merely technical, "unintentional" process. The dyeing must be performed specifically for the purpose of fashioning the sacred garments.

Implicit in these demands is an awareness of the treachery, the "insincerity" of the material world. Heroically, the priests, the craftsmen, all who are involved in the world of surface, of display, of the aesthetic, the expressive, work to bring outer and inner into harmony. Indeed, the radical "treachery" of garments becomes transparent in the Hebrew word for clothing, *begadim*, with its similarity to the root meaning treason, deception. The priestly vestments engender an ambivalent awareness of both the majesty, the transforming power of clothing, and of its "insincerity."

At issue is the difficult question of authenticity in the larger world of representation, the world of language itself. The problem of translation presents a particular case of the radical issue and of the ambivalence that surrounds it. On the one hand, *il traduttore e traditore*—"To translate is to betray." On the other, there is Walter Benjamin's compelling claim:

> Translation . . . ultimately serves the purpose of expressing the central reciprocal relationship between languages. It cannot possibly reveal or establish this hidden relationship itself; but it can represent it by realizing it in embryonic or intensive form.[22]

Beset with potential inauthenticity, translation yet has the potential of representing a hidden significance, "through an embryonic attempt at making it visible." Benjamin's claim about the secret interrelation of languages in translation can be applied to the use of language itself. In George Steiner's words, the problem "inside or between languages" is basically the same: "A study of translation is a study of language."[23] Cultural representations of all kinds, the "transfer of meaning in space,"[24] the use of the symbolic resources of clothing—in all these human modes of communication, the stakes are set high, as are the risks of treachery and inauthenticity.

The Anxiety of Representation

It is, therefore, with an awareness of this ambiguous value of the priest's vestments that the medieval commentaries interpret the technical descriptions of these vestments with an extreme alertness to symbolic meaning. Each measurement, each material, each color translates in the mind of the craftsmen and of the priests into elements in a more rarefied, alternative, spiritual structure. The High Priest cannot be considered as an idiosyncratic individual wearing the vestments: he is a pure consciousness that allows the vestments to mean fully and purely what they mean.

In describing the priestly diadem, for instance, the Torah says, "It shall be upon his brow continually to bring them favor before God" (28:38). The Talmud comments: " 'Continually' implies that he should never let his mind be distracted from it."[25] The diadem, with God's name engraved on it ("Holy to God") is to be unremittingly present to consciousness; the High Priest is to caress it with his hand so as to retain that continuity of awareness that gives his vestments their legitimate power.

In these examples of the demand for intense consciousness, the problem of embodiment is evoked. The High Priest's vestments invest him in anxiety, no less than in glory. Ultimately, it is not only the diadem that is to be "Holy to God," but its wearer. If the dissonance between vestment and wearer is palpable, if there is not "that within which passes show," the trappings become hollow.

The Cult of Nudism

We have registered the Scylla of the situation of clothing; the Charybdis is represented by the converse dilemma. If the intense preoccupation of the wearer *totally* underwrites the statement of the vestments, have they not become, in a different sense, a hollow suit of clothes, representing values that bear little relation to the *personal* identity of the wearer? A sensibility totally subdued to the meanings of a costume arouses a certain uneasiness, which the midrashic narratives express with a subtlety that transcends time.

These narratives tell, for example, of the satirical voices that question the very concept of God dwelling in a human structure. These voices, called the *leitzanei ha-dor*, the scoffers of the generation, ask sardonically, "Is it possible that the Divine Presence should come to dwell through the son of Amram (i.e., Moses)?"[26] The question has lost none of its ironic force; wherever there is an attempt to construct the human experience as a vessel for godliness, these sardonic voices are heard: "How is such an embodiment of the godly possible?" The question rises to sharper pitch when the focus is an individual, a priest, who wears the costume of holiness.

The question is an important one and its critical force is often salutary. Indeed, one implicit answer involves what Kenneth Burke calls "the cult of nudism in . . . thought." He describes the periodic quest in the history of thought for a "fresh basis of simplification":

> Thinkers "went nudist"—and it may be no accident that, in simpler souls today, we find the tendency bluntly symbolized by the literal doffing of clothes . . . Surely, at every point in history when an orientation has been radically brought into question, we may look for a nudist sect—and we may look for a parallel cult of nudism in the remoter areas of thought. Nudism represents an attempt to return to essentials, to get at the *humanistic* as the sound basis above which any scheme of values must be constructed.[27]

This "nudist" tendency is one possible response to those historical moments when the sacred vestments have lost their full and unquestioned meaning. "Off, you lendings!" is one reaction to a bewilderingly complex and privileged wardrobe of human constructions. In Burke's analysis, modern efforts at simplification have led many thinkers to find the key to human relationship in the sphere of the brutal and to a new quest for "some immovable 'rock' upon which a new structure of certainties can be erected."[28] Themes of conquest and surrender were privileged, militaristic images dominated the economic and the cultural fields, and extreme statements, freakishness, universal specialization became symptomatic of a culture of simplification. The need to break with the past became compulsive: "the race distrusted its parentage, and children distrusted their parents. In this respect the era was one long record of symbolic parricide: no wonder many came to consider the 'Oedipus complex' as the basis of human motivation."[29]

Such an analysis of late-nineteenth-century thought relates implicitly to the problem of hereditary vestments, of dynastic privilege. Philosophical nudism represents one response to the cultural accretions, the traditional coatings that have lost their organic relation to the body of the human wearer. This is the response that rejects complex, ideal constructions, in the quest for "the thing itself." This is, also, perhaps, the urge that brings Thoreau to Walden: the urge to "drive life into a corner, and reduce it to its lowest terms, and, if it proved to be mean, why then to get the whole and genuine meanness of it."[30] It is the urge to live economically, without waste, within "a perfect ecology of the spirit."[31]

The Non-Existent Knight

Italo Calvino provides a haunting version of the problem in his novella, *The Non-Existent Knight.* He posits a situation in which personal human existence ceases altogether. His hero is a knight in the wars of Charlemagne who simply does not exist within his suit of armor. The empty suit of armor functions with immaculate purposefulness, inhabited by a consciousness that regards the phenomenon of bodies, appetites, and personality with a blank incomprehension.

The theme of anxiety in relation to costume, to role and duty, representation and ritual is examined in the dialogues that Sir Agilulf, the "non-existent knight," holds with uncomprehending others—with the king, with Raimbaud, an enthusiastic young knight whose personal passion to avenge his father inspires his militarism, and with Gurduloo the gluttonous, cabbage-smeared squire. Through these encounters, the ferocious and sterile clarity of the non-existent knight is hauntingly sketched. The priestly role, all clothes, sleepless and lucid, is essentially the subject of Calvino's novella:

> "I'm talking to you, paladin!" insisted Charlemagne. "How come you don't show your face to your king?"
>
> A voice came clearly through the gorge-piece, "Sire, because I do not exist!"
>
> "This is too much!" exclaimed the emperor. "We've even on strength a knight who doesn't exist! Let's just have a look now."
>
> Agilulf seemed to hesitate a moment, then raised his visor with a slow but firm hand. The helmet was empty. No one was inside the white armour with its iridescent crest.
>
> "Well, well! Who'd have thought it!" exclaimed Charlemagne. "How d'you do your job, then, if you don't exist?"
>
> "By will power," said Agilulf, "and faith in our holy cause!"
>
> "Oh yes, yes, well said, that is how one does one's duty. Well, for someone who doesn't exist you seem in fine form!" . . .[32]

Agilulf meets the young Raimbaud, who is fascinated and appalled by his compulsive ritualism, his inability to sleep, and his total identification with his suit of armor:

> "For me there's no doffing. *Doff or dress has no sense to me.*" (Emphasis added)
>
> Raimbaud had raised his head and was looking into the cracks of the visor, as if searching in that darkness for the glimmer of a glance.
>
> "How's that?"
>
> "How d'you mean how's that?"[33]

"Not even a glimmer of a glance" responds from the darkness within the visor: no expression of tension between person and persona, appetite and will. The sight of the non-existent knight battling the shadowy wraiths of the dawn by solving geometric problems causes Raimbaud anguish, especially when he realizes that he too has his rituals to "avoid plunging into the void." To be totally invested in these rituals is to disappear as an anguished, ambivalent, sensuous being. Indeed, as Agilulf's last question implies, it is not even to understand the bizarre character of the disappearance.

The problem of the relation of person and role is complicated by the caricature figure of Gurduloo, all appetite and amorphousness, the negative exposure of Agilulf's disembodied white armor:

> "All is soup!" resounded his voice from inside the vat, which tipped over at his onslaught . . . Then the vat moved like a tortoise, turned over again, and Gurduloo reappeared.
>
> He had cabbage soup spattered, smeared, all over him from head to toe, and was stained with blacking. With liquid sticking up his eyes he felt blind and came on crying, "All is soup!" . . .
>
> Raimbaud found this so worrying it made his head go round; not so much with disgust though, as doubt at the possibility of that man in front of him being right and the world being nothing but a vast shapeless mass of soup in which all things dissolved and tinged all else in itself . . . Agilulf

> was standing impassively near him with arms crossed, as if quite remote and untouched by the squalid scene; and Raimbaud felt that he could never understand his apprehension.[34]

Raimbaud finds a moment of balance in contemplating the untenable extremes represented by the non-existent knight and the soup-spattered squire. Calvino seizes on a central axis of European sensibility: the collaboration of Don Quixote and Sancho Panza, which offers a solution to the problem of the armored body. By pairing the ideal, geometric, ceremonial type with the empirical, shapeless, instinctive type, the real anguish of the human situation may be ignored. A narrative of domination seems to resolve the issue; the non-existent knight dominates and regulates the soup-smeared squire. However, as Cervantes shows in his satire on the theme, domination-relationships are prone to subtle reversals, especially in historical moments of crisis.

Kenneth Burke discusses the role of dominating groups in terms of what he names the "priesthood function":

> The members of a group specifically charged with upholding a given orientation may be said to perform a *priesthood function.* If we define a priesthood in this technical sense, we find that in the priesthood of today the clergy take a minor part: The function is mainly performed by our college professors, journalists, public relations counselors, sales promoters . . . The decay of a priesthood (when they more or less definitely resent the work that is asked of them) leads to a division between *priests* and *prophets.* The priests devote their efforts to maintaining the vestigial structure; the prophets seek new perspectives whereby this vestigial structure may be criticized and a new one established in its place.[35]

Extending the notion of the priesthood far beyond its technical sense, Burke delineates a tension that is not confined to religious societies. His focus is the time of "decay of a priesthood," when the dissonance involved in maintaining the structure is acute. Our subject, on the other hand, is the time of initiation of a priesthood, when spiritual energies run high and the vestments seem a glorious transcendence of the merely personal. At such a time, as Calvino reminds us, there is a different hazard: of vestments that walk empty, eviscerated of personal life, of "the glimmer of a glance." Eviscerated, precisely, of tension, or imagination.[36]

"Coats of Skin": The First Essay in Self-Representation

The problem we have delineated represents an axis, with two directions. The High Priest and his vestments can be read in opposite ways: either the problem is one of emptiness—the role has taken over, leaving no personal perspective whatever—or it is one of dissonant density—the idiosyncratic human being who wears the vestments experiences tension, or frustration, or hypocritical vainglory.

These two possibilities are alternatives: they cannot be experienced simultaneously. And yet, we remember Wittgenstein's model for ambiguity: the duck/rabbit figure; even though we cannot perceive the figure as both duck and rabbit simultaneously, we can know that it is also the other while it is being experienced as the one. This "perceptual or philosophical flick or trick," in Christopher Ricks's words,[37] can be applied to the ambiguity of the situation of the High Priest and his vestments. In the midrashic and Chasidic literature on the priestly garments, such an awareness of the ambiguities of clothing pervades discourse. We recall T. S. Eliot's definition of wit, as a "recognition, implicit in the expression of every experience, of other kinds of experience which are possible."[38]

The ambiguity can be traced back to a provocative midrash on the first clothing of Adam and Eve after their sin:

> R. Eliezer said, "Of the skin that the serpent sloughed off God made coats of glory for Adam and his helpmeet; as it is said, 'And God made for Adam and his wife coats of skin and He clothed them.' (Gen 3:21)"[39]

The problem that the midrash intends to resolve is the origin of the first clothes. Described as "coats of skin," they seem to depend on death: some animal has been killed and flayed to make these first human garments. Since death has not yet entered the world, the midrash solves the problem with the figure of the sloughed skin of the serpent. That is, the skin foreshadows death, represents the serpent's consciousness of death-in-life. In effect, the facade of the serpent goes to make dignified coverings for human beings. The paradox is striking: the serpent, all deception, representation, plausible language, verbal display, is reconstructed into an attribute of human dignity.

A classic midrash on the expression, "coats of skin, *or* (in Hebrew)," concentrates the paradox in one word, one deliberate misreading: Rabbi

Meir reads the word *or*, "skin," as *or*, "light":[40] these are spelled differently but are virtually homophonous. The play of *or/or*, "skin/light," the disposable, treacherous surface and the luminous quality of integrated being, makes an evocative claim. The symbolic resonances of *or*, "skin," range from the deathly to the vital, from the disposable skin cells that are shed daily, to the acute sensitivity of nerve endings. This, too, is an axis that leads in two directions: the very word *or* (in the form of *er*) conveys "alertness," the capacity to respond to stimuli; but if the serpent sloughs its skin every seven years, as the midrash earlier recounts,[41] the organic skin becomes a husk, and the serpent undergoes violent rebirth, complete with labor pains.[42] The axis of nudity and encrusted surface now becomes a site for possible experience. Ideally, the midrash construes *or* as *kavod*, as dignity for the human being. Some point of creative tension, it affirms, is potentially attainable.

The midrashic symbolism penetrates deep. The serpent skin, brilliant and disposable, comes to represent representation itself. Its origins are suspect: the serpent's gift of rhetoric, its ability to mobilize weighted words, poetic language, has altered the destiny of the human race. Yet, God Himself then clothes human beings in this macabre garment, serpent skin, *to their glory.*

If God is the One who clothes human beings in serpentine garments, who helps human beings to don and doff clothing (we remember that the fig-leaf girdles[43] would have to be removed, presumably, as the serpentine coats are donned), our attention is drawn to the human function of dressing and undressing. Banal as it appears, this activity is initiated into the world by God, and clearly evokes the tension of inner and outer.

We remember Sir Agilulf, who is innocent of this ritual and its meanings: "For me there's no doffing. Doff or dress has no sense to me."[44] For the non-existent knight, there is not even a "glimmer" of a sense of mystery about this lacuna in experience: "How d'you mean how's that?" That is, Calvino implies that it is precisely the ambiguity, the donning and doffing of robes and representations, that characterizes human beings. And, in the Torah narrative, it is God Himself who aids Adam and Eve in their first essay in self-representation.

Moses the Dresser

In the relation between Moses and Aaron, clearly it is Aaron who wears the vestments, the given forms of a hereditary role. Moses' role is less defined. But, significantly, he has the task of dressing Aaron as he is initiated into his priestly role. In this task, then, he imitates God, who dresses the first couple: "Dress Aaron and his sons in these garments; anoint them, and ordain them and consecrate them to serve Me as priests" (Exod 28:41). It is Moses who invests Aaron into his priesthood.

In our original midrash, it was the wife who was to select a new wife for her husband: this describes the fraught moment when Moses clothes Aaron in priesthood. Moses is thus the "dresser" of others, while clothing seems entirely irrelevant to himself. The only reference to Moses' clothing is to the shoes he removes at the Burning Bush.[45]

In dressing Aaron, however, Moses serves in a not merely pragmatic fashion. This becomes hauntingly evident in God's commanding Moses to take Aaron up the mountain to his death: "And strip Aaron of his vestments and put them on Eleazar, his son. Then, Aaron will be gathered in and die there" (Num 20:26). This deathbed doffing and donning of priestly robes signifies Aaron's shedding the husk of his role, which is identical with his life. In this process of divestment, Moses is the essential agent; in effect, this act of stripping Aaron and dressing his son is the sole purpose of Moses' presence on the mountain. And the word *le-hafshit*, "to strip," is, of course, the same word as the midrash uses of the serpent when it sloughs its skin. That is, a radical ambiguity about skin and clothing, personhood and role, is intimated here. What is Moses' place in this terminal scene?

Rashi offers a poignant midrashic reading:

> "His clothing": this refers to the High Priest's vestments in which Moses had clothed him; he now divested him to put them on his son, in his presence. Moses said to Aaron, "Enter the cave"—and he entered. He saw a bed spread and a candle lit. Moses said, "Ascend into the bed"—and he ascended; "Spread your hands"—and he spread them; "Close your mouth"—and he closed it; "Close your eyes"—and he closed them. At that moment, Moses coveted that death of Aaron. That is why God later told him, "You shall die on the mountain that you are about to ascend . . . as your brother Aaron died . . ." (Deut 32:50)—that death that you desired.[46]

Moses' role is one of guidance to his brother in his death passage: stage by stage, he moves him through the choreography of a model death. He also offers Aaron the last consolation of seeing his son inherit his greatness, literally invested in his garments.[47] At the same time, however, the midrash obliquely comments on Moses' own experience. The implicit contrast between the brothers is spelled out in Rashi's earlier comment:

"Take Aaron your brother": Take him with words of consolation: "Happy are you that you see your crown passed on to your son, which I shall not merit."[48]

Moses defines for Aaron the privilege of his situation: "What you have I do not have." What Aaron has is the serenity of a role that can be transferred to his children, of meanings that can be conveyed through time and space. His personal death can be accepted with an extraordinary equanimity because he possesses a vocabulary that can be transmitted. Aaron is not alone in his death; he can be helped by Moses to experience his own virtual survival in his son.

Moses, on the other hand, "covets that death," for it is alien and fascinating to his spirit. If he is not High Priest, that is because forms and formulas, ceremonies and rituals, the treacheries and seductions of language were always inimical to him. Therefore, he has no heirs of his spirit and he dies alone: "And Moses, servant of God, died there . . . and he buried him in the valley . . ." (Deut 34:5–6). Who buried him? "God in His glory . . . R. Ishmael said, 'He buried himself . . .' "[49]

The uncanny image of Moses burying himself is not radically different from that of God burying him. These are, I suggest, two modes of expressing the same notion: that Moses' death is unique, unmediated by any ceremonies of clothing, unattended by the kindness of human language. Strangely, Rashi implies in his passage on Aaron's death that God does grant Moses the death he envied in Aaron. This is difficult to integrate into Rashi's own reading of Moses' death, alone with God. Perhaps, Rashi implies that the real desire of Moses is for a death accomplished in serenity like Aaron's; and that that desire is met, in the quite different tonality of Moses' death.

Moses—Without Vestments, Language, Dynasty

From his first protests at the Burning Bush, Moses had said, "I am not a man of words; I am heavy of mouth and heavy of tongue; I am of uncircumcised lips . . ." We remember the midrashic narrative in which Moses resists God's call for seven days, God becomes angry, and the High Priesthood is transferred to Aaron. Moses thus loses the modality of the formal, the aesthetic, the hereditary, of that use of language which is "specifically charged with upholding a given orientation."[50] He loses it, but, in a sense, on his own admission, he never had it. His attachment to the world of silence, of the unarticulated, is expressed by Schoenberg in his opera, *Moses und Aron*, as greatness and pain: "None can, none may give Him utterance! O Word, Word, Word, That I lack!"

The harmonious integrity of Aaron, totally invested in his garments and capable of seeing his son invested in them, in his turn, is also a linguistic posture. In transferring the priesthood to him, God says, "I know that he is a ready speaker" (4:14). Aaron is at peace with his position on the axis of language and silence. He is happily embodied in his role, he wears his garments without either vanishing entirely or suffering the dissonance of inner and outer.

Moses' destiny is written in a different language. He will not wear vestments of any kind; but he will be essential to helping Aaron don and doff his garments. He never was a man of words, of fixed roles and representations; and yet the midrash repeatedly harps on the injury God does him in denying him the priesthood. In some enigmatic sense, Moses will *expect* to be High Priest. Almost vindictively, it appears, God tells him: "What do you think? That you will become High Priest!" Or, in the first midrash, the wise man tells his wife: "Seek me a wife!" Moses desires a greatness that is plausibly but not properly his.

The reason for the husband's bizarre request of his wife, we remember, is that she "has not borne children." In the case of Moses, not giving birth means that, unlike Aaron, he is not invested in the world of procreativeness, of inherited orientations. If this is a limitation, it is also expressive of an inner world that simply evades reproduction. Sefath Emeth emphasizes the starkly nondynastic character of Moses' greatness.[51] At the same time, such a "sterile" situation clearly causes Moses some anguish and does, in some measure, reflect a limitation in his relation to the world.

Aaron, on the other hand, is progenitive; his spiritual and physical procreation move in harmony. His inner world is communicable to his children. For this to be possible, a difficult tension must be maintained between the man and his vestments.

3. *Aaron: Finitude and Infinitude*

Pomegranates and Bells: Full and Empty

An illuminating teaching by R. Yaacov Leiner of Ishbitz[52] examines the elements of this tension. Among the vestments of the High Priest is the robe, with its hem ornamented with seventy-two bells interspersed with seventy-two pomegranates. These extraordinary details are recounted in the biblical text in the following way:

> On its hem make pomegranates of blue, purple, and crimson yarns, all around the hem, with bells of gold between them all around: a golden bell and a pomegranate, a golden bell and a pomegranate, all around the hem of the robe. Aaron shall wear it while officiating, so that the sound of it is heard when he comes into the sanctuary before God and when he goes out—that he may not die. (Exod 28:33–35)

The High Priest is described as moving to the sound of bells as he enters and as he leaves the sanctuary. "And its voice shall be heard": (lit.) that is, the voice, the sound of the robe. What is the purpose of this resonance of the robe? Is it, as Ramban suggests, a kind of courtesy in the presence of the King, a signal of approach and departure? This would suggest the real boundary that is crossed by the High Priest as he enters and leaves the Mishkan. Transfigured by his vestments, he penetrates some humanly impenetrable area. Ramban, in fact, quotes a Talmudic passage on the High Priest's entry into the Mishkan:

> "And no human being shall be in the Tent of Assembly . . ." (Lev 16:17) Even those [that is, the angels] of whom it is written: "And their faces resembled human faces." (Ezek 1:10)—even they were to be absent from the Tent of Assembly. Therefore, He commanded that the High Priest make a noise like one who calls out: "Remove all human presence from before me!"[53]

Rabbi Yaacov Leiner, in his commentary, *Beit Yaacov*, builds on Ramban's reading. The bells, clappers jangling from a hollow center, symbolize a mode of spiritual ecstasy: literally, a standing outside oneself, an overwhelming consciousness of the nothingness of the human person within the priestly robes. The High Priest as he enters the sanctuary loses all sense of his own density, of the contingencies, the idiosyncrasies of his own existence. The bell becomes an image for a hollowness that resounds almost unbearably with God's presence. "My heart is hollow within me," cries the Psalmist (109:22).[54] If this is the symbolic burden of the bell, expelling all vestiges of the human from its sacred clangor, then the pomegranate, by contrast, is dense, full of seeds, of a sense of substance and power. "Even the sinners of Israel are full of Mitzvoth as the pomegranate is full of seeds—

even the empty ones."[55] In R. Yaacov's teaching, this becomes the fundamental confidence that human life is full of meaning, that it is dense with a self-possessed reality.

In R. Yaacov's teaching, both these modalities, of the bell and of the pomegranate, are needed. The bell resounds with the wild clangor of transcendence; the human being loses himself in the presence of God; the human image is entirely effaced; one is absorbed into the fire of the divine. "The High Priest was not a human being . . . when he was possessed by the Holy Spirit, his face flamed like torches."[56]

However, continues R. Yaacov, such ecstasy can be overpowering: who would want to return to himself, from out of such rapture? Therefore, the robe resounds with its double message. In an exquisite paradox, it is the pomegranate that the High Priest "hears" as he enters the intoxicating space of holiness; it reminds him throughout his service not to surrender entirely to the fire. Even in the midst of his fervor, he must retain the desire to return to his individuality, to his dense humanity. "God desires the being of the body, just as He desires the being of the soul." When he leaves the sanctuary, however, it is the bell sound that he should hear: as he begins to become real again, returning to his defined sense of self, he should retain some vestige of "other kinds of experience which are possible."[57]

Emptiness and fullness are the ambiguous "voice of the robe." In this teaching, it is not God who will hear this "voice," but the High Priest himself. If he is to survive the fire in which all forms are transformed, he must retain some enclave of desire for the human form; without ecstasy, however, there is only a specious empiricism. The High Priest, moving to the counterpoint of pomegranates and bells, must negotiate a path between the perils of "nudism," of a reductivism that sees the humanistic as the "sound basis on which any scheme of values must be constructed,"[58] and those of spiritual intoxication.

On the one side is Charles Dickens's Mr. Gradgrind (in *Hard Times*), with his obsessive insistence on objective perception: "Now, what I want is Facts. Teach these boys and girls nothing but Facts . . ." on the other, Shakespeare's Owen Glendower (in *Henry the Fifth*), who boasts, "I can call spirits from the vasty deep," only to be mocked by Hotspur, "Why, so can I, or so can any man. But will they come when you do call for them?"[59] This is the tension between a frosty stoicism and a mysticism in which self-consciousness and moral responsibility are lost.

It is the latter risk that more keenly concerns R. Yaacov Leiner. And, indeed, in terms of the biblical narrative, it will be merely a few months before Aaron's sons are consumed in "strange fire," on the very day the Mishkan is consecrated (Lev 10:1–2). This enigmatic narrative is followed by a ban on intoxication: "And God spoke to Aaron, saying, 'Drink no wine or other intoxicant, you or your sons, when you enter the Tent of Meeting, that you may not die'" (10:8–9). Rashi connects this law with the preceding episode: the young men died because they entered the sanctuary in a state of intoxication.[60] And Emmanuel Levinas inscribes the ban on drunkenness as the epigraph to the first section of *Difficult Freedom*—"Beyond Pathos."

Among the many midrashic comments on the episode, one diagnoses the failing of the young men as one of "excessive joy"; the strange fire is the fire of an obliterating ecstasy, a spiritual intoxication, in which the forms of human responsibility are melted down: "When they saw the new fire descended from the highest heaven . . . they rose up to add love to love; as it is said, 'They *took* strange fire'—'taking' refers to joy."[61] And the theme of fire becomes central in this midrash, a fervor that blinds and ultimately issues in acts of suicide and violence. In Levinas's text, the "emptiness" of such ecstatic joy is hazardous to an adult encounter with the human face of the other. Because there is nothing human within the Holy of Holies, a seductive escape from responsibility may transform the bell-sound into a siren-song. When the human face begins to flame like a torch, some essential boundary between self and other is endangered.

In other midrashic sources, Aaron's sons are indicted of bizarre sins of omission and commission, that manifest the narcissistic violence that is the peril of spiritual "emptiness": they would not marry, they had no children, they wish for the death of Moses and Aaron, so that they can realize their own greatness.[62] Emptied of the human, his face aflame, the priest may devolve into the inhuman.

This is one possible danger, the danger of the bell. On the other hand, one who is totally self-possessed, who is dense, with clearly marked boundaries, is also endangered. "One who does not feel himself lost is without remission; that is to say, he never finds himself, never comes up against his own reality."[63] The existentialist vision of the danger of fullness, of the pomegranate, represents the other message of the priest's robe.

The tension between the messages is expressed in an *aural* image—the sound of the robe is to be heard by the priest—which is more subtle than the visual impression of the unequivocal "glory and beauty" of the vestments. The priest's ear is to register the inner ambiguity of his position, of the bell and pomegranate.

Two Kinds of Despair

Beside this reading from *Beit Yaacov*, we can set Kierkegaard's analysis of two kinds of despair:

> while one sort of despair plunges wildly into the infinite and loses itself, a second sort permits itself as it were to be defrauded by "the others." By seeing the multitude of men about it, by getting engaged in all sorts of worldly affairs, by becoming wise about how things go in this world, such a man forgets himself . . . If one will compare the tendency to run wild in possibility with the efforts of a child to enunciate words, the lack of possibility is like being dumb . . . for without possibility a man cannot, as it were, draw breath.[64]

"Without possibility a man cannot, as it were, draw breath": this is Kierkegaard's description of a choked plenitude, in which the reality of "the others" embeds one in necessity. His words evoke the original diagnosis of the Israelites, before redemption: "They could not listen to Moses, because of *shortness of breath* (lit.) and harsh labor" (6:9). Embedded in the power structure of Egypt, ciphers in the crowd, the people were without breath, dispirited, without possibility.[65]

The opposite condition in which one "plunges wildly into the infinite," lacks the "power to . . . submit to the necessary in oneself, to what may be called one's limit."[66] This is "infinitude's despair," the fantastical, the limitless:

> The fantastical is that which so carries a man out into the infinite that it merely carries him away from himself and therewith prevents him from returning to himself . . . Now if possibility outruns necessity, the self runs away from itself, so that it has no necessity whereto it is bound to return—then this is the despair of possibility. The self becomes an abstract possibility which tires itself out with floundering in the possible, but does not budge from the spot; to become oneself is precisely a movement at the spot.[67]

Kierkegaard analyzes the dual psychological hazards of possibility and impossibility, emptiness and fullness. Between the *mysterium tremendum et fascinosum*, on the one hand, and the need to live decisively and confidently, the human being is caught in an eddy of anxieties. R. Yaacov of Ishbitz reads the priestly robe as resonant with a sustainable tension between these polarities. Again, an axis is constructed, joining and separating finitude and infinitude. The priest's ear is attuned to his particular "spot" on that axis, so that he can move without floundering.

4. *Moses and the Culture of Playfulness: A Surprising Centrality*

Moses: Recalled to Himself

If the High Priest's role involves a kind of tightrope balance, Moses' relationship to his brother and to the lost priesthood now reclaims our attention. Moses wears no robe, his ear registers neither the bell nor the pomegranate. As we have seen, the midrashic sources focus a profound ambivalence that animates his responses to his loss. On the one hand, he is not a speaker, a player in the world of representations, while, on the other, he expects to become High Priest. On the one hand, God is angry at Moses' resistance to His mission, and deprives him of a role he had appropriated for himself, while, on the other, He asks for his active cooperation, his "greatness." On the one hand, Moses wholeheartedly rejoices in Aaron's appointment, while, on the other, like the wife in the midrash, he has clearly suffered an injury.

In the relationship of Moses and Aaron, mutual recognition, called "rejoicing for the other," is achieved. In Moses' case, recognition of Aaron involves disillusion about himself. In the Tanchuma midrash, God tells him, "What do you think? That you are going to become High Priest?" The tone of God's rejection of Moses' aspirations is difficult to define. Apparently, Moses is totally absorbed in his priestly role during the consecration period of the Mishkan. God jars him awake, as it were: for him, the priesthood is a fantasy, a misreading of his own identity and destiny. He is asked to emerge from the fantasy in which he is absorbed and to "call" Aaron to this role: the "calling" is the summons of disenchantment, the end of a silent merging. To call Aaron is to be recalled to himself.

"And as for You . . ."—Language as Play

"*Ve-atta*—And as for you, you shall command. . . *Ve-atta*—and as for you, you shall bring Aaron close . . . *Ve-atta*—and as for you, you shall speak . . ." (27:20–28:3). We return to the question with which we began, about the triple, emphatic address to Moses, in a Parsha in which his name does not appear. What is the force of *Ve-atta*—the intimate second-person, contrasting in some sense with the previous text? We have noticed that the contrast is not obvious, since Moses has been the subject of most of the preceding chapters.

Here, we turn to Midrash Tanchuma,[68] which will offer us an unexpected tonality in reading the word *Ve-atta*—"and as for you":

> How old is the infant when he is circumcised? Our Rabbis taught: an infant is circumcised at eight days. Why? That was Isaac's age when he was circumcised. Said R. Shimeon bar Yochai: "Come and see—there is nothing dearer to a person than his son, yet he circumcises him! Why?" Said R. Nachman ben Shmuel: "In order to do the will of his Creator. He sees his son pouring blood from his circumcision and yet accepts it in joy." Said R. Chanina: "Furthermore, he even incurs expense and makes that day a day of rejoicing—which was *not* commanded. That is the meaning of the text in Psalms (71:14): '*As for me*, I will hope always, and add to the many praises of You.' Furthermore, a person will go and mortgage himself, take out loans, in order to make that a day of rejoicing . . ."
>
> Said R. Yudan: "When does a child become precious to his father? When he begins to speak. That is the meaning of the text: 'Truly, Ephraim is a dear son to Me, a child that is dandled (*yeled sha'ashuim*—a child of play)' (Jer 31:20) What is a child that is dandled? Around the age of three or four, when he begins to speak and is playful in the presence of his father."

The father who circumcises his baby is, in the most obvious way, sacrificing natural human feeling to God's will. Like Abraham, he is obeying a divine command. He does more than this, however: he "augments" the commandment, by making the circumcision day a time of joy. He goes beyond himself, he transcends the letter of the law, he "incurs expense," existentially as well as economically, and he enacts "what was not commanded."

In effect, he improvises, transforming the sacrifice into a feast. In the context of a commandment of dread, where only the desire to do God's will can justify the act, such an improvisation becomes all the more compelling. The proof-text crystallizes the theme: "*As for me*, I will hope always, and add to the many praises of You." Hope is an act of magnanimous imagination, constantly amplifying the bare resources of reality.

In the second part of the passage, the topic seems to change abruptly. The child's early speech development seems connected with circumcision only by the theme of childhood. But the underlying theme of the passage is the theme of play: the joyful creativity of the child beginning to use and love language becomes a mirror for the imaginative generosity of the father who circumcises his child. Language and circumcision are often held together in Chasidic texts by a pun on the word, *milah*: which in biblical Hebrew means "circumcision," and in Rabbinic Hebrew, "word." The child plundering the resources of language is asserting separateness, his mastery of the resources of his culture. He is both participant and solitary.

In Winnicott's terms, the child is alone only in the presence of someone. He quotes Tagore: "On the seashore of endless worlds, children play"; and interprets:[69] babies come up out of the sea of union with the mother and discover the endless worlds of play, of power and danger in the margin that is neither sea nor land. The child in the midrash is most loved, paradoxically, at the point where he asserts separateness. The tension of union and separation, continuity and contiguity,[70] is focused in the two words *mishta'ashea le'aviv*—"he is playful *by himself* in the presence of his father."[71]

The paradigm of circumcision recreated into festivity focuses on the theme of emptiness and fullness that we have discussed in connection with the High Priest. In the relation between human will and God's will, self-possession and possession, the midrash intimates a third "potential" area, to use Winnicott's term, in which the human being grows in his capacity to remake the world through language. This creative power is different from the balance of opposites that Aaron and the High Priesthood represents. Here, there is play, in a separation that sustains relationship. From this space, something new is born, something strictly unpredictable. The playful act can happen only in the nurturing presence and difference of the father, but it expresses an energy that is not a balance of forces, but a freedom, a responsiveness to hints that generates an imaginative language.

Indeed, we may say that there is an essential imbalance, a joyful instability in the child's first experiments with language. It is not competence that is displayed by the child and loved by the father; rather an uncertainty, an incompetence, that does not impede fluency. And the adult capacity to "play," to transform the tone of reality, likewise is born not of stasis but of an inspired insufficiency. There is, Wordsworth writes in his note to "The Thorn," "a consciousness of the inadequateness of our own powers, or the deficiencies of language," in any attempt to "communicate impassioned feelings . . . During such efforts there will be a craving in the mind, and as long as it is unsatisfied the Speaker will cling to the same words . . ."[72] Even such a blatant "incompetence" as the repetition of words is not necessarily tautology; it may represent an inadequacy which is the very register of passion.

"And as for You . . ."—The Unthought Possibility

This midrash is found at the very beginning of Tanchuma on our Parsha; however, there is no explicit link with the text of the Parsha. I would suggest that an implicit link exists, in the reference to the circumcision of Isaac. In Genesis 17:1–8, God makes a covenant with Abram. He promises that Abram shall be father of many nations, that his name will be changed to Abraham, that he will be exceedingly fertile, that he will be given the Holy Land, and that God will sustain this covenant, with Abraham's descendants eternally. It is then that God turns to Abraham with the word *ve-atta*—"And as for you . . .":

> Then God said to Abraham, "*And as for you*, you and your offspring to come throughout the ages shall keep My covenant. Such shall be the covenant between Me and you and your offspring after you, which you shall keep: every male among you shall be circumcised . . ." (17:9–10)

"And as for you," introduces Abraham's side of the covenant, paralleling God's opening pronoun, *ani*—"As for Me, here is My covenant with you . . ." (17:4). The effect of *ve-atta*, as Rashi puts it, is to "augment" (*mossif*) the material of the previous passage. That is, there is a sense of the unexpected about the sudden turn to Abraham, under his new name, and about the demand of circumcision.

Since a covenant usually has two partners, the turn to Abraham may seem quite predictable. However, Rashi's comment, with its sensitivity to the tonality of *ve-atta*, is supported by historical findings on the nature of treaties in the Ancient Near East. Typically, these were formulated between a suzerain and a vassal state. In the case of God and Abraham, their relative status is clearly unequal. God makes magnanimous promises; and then places Abraham in a role of almost embarrassing symmetry—"And as for you . . ." Circumcision, surprisingly, will even the balance between the human and the divine. Essential to the first articulation of circumcision, therefore, is the pronoun *ve-atta*, which shifts expectation and provokes imagination.

Earlier cases of *ve-atta* confirm the "surprise" function of the structure.[73] The first occurrence is in the context of God's words to the serpent after the Sin: speaking of its future relation with the human, God says: "He will strike at your head, *and as for you*, you shall strike at his heel" (Gen 3:15). The force of *ve-atta* is caught by Rashi: "*Even though* you have no stature, you will bite his heel, and *even from that spot*, you will kill him." Against logical expectation, the serpent will discover his power even from his newly diminished vantage point ("On your belly shall you crawl and dust shall you eat all the days of your life" [3:14].) "And as for you" registers the surprising effectiveness of the serpent's bite. What is conveyed is not symmetry ("He will . . . and as for you, you shall . . ."), but asymmetry (". . . your head . . . his heel."). *Ve-atta* opens up an unthought possibility.

The second case of *ve-atta* occurs in God's message to Cain: ". . . Sin crouches at the door; its urge is toward you, *and as for you*, you shall be its master" (4:7). Rashi reads this as referring to the desire of sin to subdue Cain; "but if you wish, you will prevail over it." Again, *ve-atta* is read almost as a non sequitur addition to the thrust of the sentence. The general tendency of God's words is negative, a warning about the dangers of sin, but meaning pivots on *ve-atta*: after all, Cain retains the power to transform an ominous situation.

"And as for You . . ."—Unexpected Power

When, therefore, God addresses Moses three times in a relentless ground bass of *ve-atta . . . ve-atta . . . ve-atta. . .* , the effect is triply transformative. Essentially, in announcing the new dispensation of priesthood, He has cut the ground from under Moses' feet. In the new world that is represented by the Mishkan, God's Presence is to be centered in the space created by Moses and his craftsmen. Moses has been at the imaginative heart of the enterprise. Yet, without warning, God has shifted the center from Moses to Aaron. The betrayal cannot be exaggerated: "He did him an injury," says the midrash, with conscious restraint. The midrash about the wife who was asked to seek out another wife for her husband unequivocally conveys the outrage; indeed, in the Hebrew text, he asks her starkly, "Seek me a wife," without the palliative, "*another* wife." In the kind of relationship of which marriage is a paradigm an exclusive intimacy is violated at this moment. This sense of outrage is clearly present even in biblical descriptions of polygamous marriages and despite the historically conventional nature of such arrangements.

In the story of Moses, there is, similarly, a moment when God shifts the center of stability away from Moses, as Aaron, his vestments, his functions, becomes the unequivocal focus of the Mishkan commands. Precisely at this juncture of loss, Moses is addressed by God: "And as for you . . . And as for you . . . And as for you . . ." The effect is uncanny. On the face of it, he is being placed in a merely instrumental position: he is to charge the people to prepare pure olive oil for the Eternal Lamp, he is to initiate Aaron into his central role, he is to instruct the craftsmen about the priestly vestments. But the undertow of the expression *ve-atta*, as we have seen, compels a contrary reading: implicitly focusing attention on the unexpected power of Moses' role. As in the earliest usages of the word that we have studied—in Abraham's role in the Covenant, or in the power of the serpent's bite, or in Cain's ability to control his evil instincts—*ve-atta* carries a revelation of subtle re-centering. An apparently clear balance of forces begins to shift.

Here, the Tanchuma passage on circumcision and the "playful" freedom of father and newly verbal child becomes significant. The two proof-texts in the midrash shed light on one another. The first explains the father's ability to make the day joyous, "which he was not commanded": "*And as for me*, I will hope always, and add to the many praises of You" (Ps 71:14). The effect of *va-ani*—"And as for me . . ."—is similar to that of *ve-atta*—"And as for you . . ."—in our narrative: unpredictably, the Psalmist discovers in himself resources of hope, treasures of language with which to praise God. Ibn Ezra reads: "*Even though the day of my salvation be far off*, I shall continue to hope and to praise You."[74] This is hope "in spite of . . .": a virtuoso creativity of augmentation.

Elaboration, Play, Hope

The capacity for *hossafa*, for elaborating, augmenting, without support from the world, is precisely the theme of the midrash. The father of the newborn infant has little objective basis for his festive invention; this is an act of generous imagination. Similarly, the child who begins to play with language is defined in the second proof-text: "Truly, Ephraim is a dear son to Me, a playful child" (31:20). Again, there is a loneliness about the child who begins to "*play by himself* in the presence of his father."

Both proof-texts are deployed to illuminate a "lonely" situation, in which an energy and fertility of imagination is revealed. The father who can "augment" a sacrificial posture into a joyful one, the child who begins to experiment with language, once he has disengaged from the maternal breast—both express the privileged value of freedom.

In Winnicott's depiction, the infant needs a "potential space," a site of separation from the mother, in which union can be reenacted with a difference. That space, indeed, means difference. Knowing his difference from the mother, the child begins the interplay which is possible between two separate selves. This interplay need not take the form of explicit interactions: it can, as Marion Milner puts it, be like the interplay of the edges of two curtains, or of a jug placed in front of another jug.[75] This is the child's first experience of relationship to objects. Essential is the ability to keep inner and outer reality separate, yet interrelated.

The freedom of the play-space has its melancholy dimension. This is intimated in the Psalmist's use of the word for hope—*ayachel*—which contains the root for "space" (*chalal*) within it. Hope becomes necessary, even intelligible, only where there is a break in continuity. While two are merged, God and the human being, the mother and the child, hope has no meaning. It is in separation, as a space widens between self and other, that hope, the interrelation of two selves, like the mute interplay of the edges of two curtains, becomes possible. When this space widens, something new must be born, or it spells isolation and death.

In just this way, Job speaks of hope, when he cries, "Even though He slay me, I will hope for Him—*lo ayyachel*" (13:15). *Lo ayyachel* is written, "I will *not* hope"; it is read, however, "*to* Him I will hope" (a play on two spellings of *lo*, indistinguishable to the ear). André Neher writes beautifully:

> the Bible in this verse effects one of those encounters which, thanks to the interpretational system of the *keri-ketib*, allow the human ear to hear what should be read and the human eye to read what should be heard, thus compelling the human spirit to take its stand upon the limits of the intelligible, the very frontier-situation of Job's existence . . . Job says two words, *lo ayahel*, simultaneously denoting hope and despair . . . these simultaneous but contradictory cries being the matrix of a new world.[76]

Hope and hopelessness meet here; in the space, the *chalal* at the heart of hope, there is a hollowness, a loss of substance that should extinguish all hope. Indeed, the word *chalal* is the word for a corpse, a husk emptied of life: "He may well slay me; I will have no hope." But at this rupture, as the umbilical cord breaks, the child emerges into life: "[he] says 'Yes' to silence, *hen*—the first word of Job's exclamation in this verse, acknowledgment and acceptance of the genesis, the birth . . ."[77]

Hope and despair, likewise, underwrite the Psalmist's declaration, "*And as for me*, I will hope always and add to the many praises of You." This is a hope without objective stimulus, as the subtle modulation of "And as for me . . ." resounds against God's silence. Precisely this hope/despair, too, underwrites the second midrashic proof-text, about the playful child who has moved into his "potential space." A fluid movement of the spirit engenders relationship.

Moses: Language that Recreates the World

Moses, too, I suggest, is situated at this "seashore of endless worlds," in Tagore's phrase. It is God who places him there: in all his despair at losing the center ("Seek me a wife!"), he is asked for a compliance that is a greatness. Like the child, he begins to play in the widening space that opens up between himself and God. Here is the greatness, the power of growth that he is to discover.

In our midrash, God clarifies the high seriousness of the issues. "If Your Torah had not been my plaything, I should have perished in my poverty" (Ps 119:92). These words are put into God's mouth: "If it were not for My Torah, which I have given to you, I should have lost My world." Or, perhaps, the world would have lost Him. The Torah, so enigmatically essential to the life of the world, is given to Moses: it is to be a "plaything" to him. This is the point on which hope and despair pivot. In losing one kind of connection with God, Moses is thrown into empty space. God asks him to *play* with the words of the Torah: that is, to accept distance and loneliness, and to recreate union in the fluid and changing interactions with His Torah. In this sense, play is entirely untrivial. God's world depends upon it.

The play mode generates a different relation to language from that suggested by Aaron's garments. The priestly garments are a language of representation, public, functional, at best incarnating an aesthetic vision of the transcendent. This is language in its ceremonious, relatively static mode—

explanatory, factual, in principle reproducible. Nothing may be changed in these vestments; though a new set is made each year, after Yom Kippur, it is identical to the previous one. The beauty of classicism imbues these garments; the perils of rigidity (the nonexistent wearer) and irrelevance ("All is soup!") haunt them. They pass from father to son, newly fashioned for each wearer but bearing the patina of tradition.

Moses' language, on the other hand, is born of instability, of a rude exile. Thrust out, he is reminded of the self who had said, "I am not a man of words," and who was taken at his word. That role, of public, representational language, is now Aaron's: "I know that he is a ready speaker"—*dabber ye-dabber* onomatopoeically conveys the automatic quality of such speech. And Moses is left with the task of "dresser": he will aid Aaron in donning and doffing the priestly garments. As Aaron assumes his role and is divested of it, he moves between fullness and emptiness. He must achieve a kind of cybernetic skill in accommodating these poles of experience. How are we to understand Moses' role as "dresser," as agent of Aaron's transformations, as the one who plays with the Torah and holds God and the world in interplay?

Playful language is, essentially, poetic language. It arises at moments of transition, even of fracture of received narratives; old ways of combining words recede to the margins. The poet plays in the space that Keats named *negative capability*: "where a man is capable of being in uncertainties, Mysteries, doubts, without any irritable reaching after fact and reason."[78] In this space, one moves into and out of many forms, many roles. One can even, in Keats's self-description, become a sparrow pecking at the gravel: ". . . if a Sparrow come before my Window I take part in its existence and pick about the Gravel."[79]

Infinite variability is a characteristic of Winnicott's play-space, "contrasting with the relative stereotypy of phenomena that relate either to personal body functioning or to environmental actuality." "One can think of the "electricity" that seems to generate in meaningful or intimate contact . . ."[80]

In delivering the Torah to Moses as a "plaything," therefore, God is invoking the poet's genius for continual reinvention of reality. This is language, not as fitting the world, but as strongly recreating it. It involves a self-consciousness about vocabularies and their effect in creating and destroying worlds.

Richard Rorty writes of the playfulness of poets:

> [It] is the product of their shared ability to appreciate the power of redescribing, the power of language to make new and different things possi-

ble and important—an appreciation which becomes possible only when one's aim becomes an expanding repertoire of alternative descriptions rather than The One Right Description.[81]

Such a playfulness is essential to the survival of God's world. Here, I deviate from Rorty, who, in his next sentence, asserts: "Such a shift in aim is possible only to the extent that both the world and the self have been dedivinized." In terms of our midrash, the opposite is true. Both the world and the self discover God revealed in the play of the Torah, in the "expanding repertoire of alternative descriptions." It is "*My* world" and "*My* Torah" that are given over to Moses' play.

The Culture of Playfulness

This is the modality that is created by Moses' forbearance, his compliance in loss. In the space that has opened up between himself and God, a new "electricity" is generated. Strikingly, at the very point in the history of the Israelite relationship with God where law is crystallized, transmitted in written or engraved form, where the creative surge seems frozen in place, a new culture of playfulness arises. The formalism and ceremoniousness of the priesthood is given to Aaron, the postures and images of holiness and service. Moses, however, is to discover a different valence of spirituality that is called the Oral Torah, the Torah of the Mouth. This is the Torah of infinite redescription, of a thickening web of relationship constantly rewoven.

Moses will generate complex, irreducible interpretations: "The meaning of a poem can only be another poem."[82] His special responsibility will be the olive oil for the Menorah. R. Naftali Zvi Yehuda Berlin[83] discusses the symbolic import of this: it represents the light of the Torah and its power to renew itself and to generate infinite light. This "wondrous power," which he identifies with "the power of *pilpul*, of creative ingenuity," is figured in the seven branches of wisdom and the elaborate knobs and blossoms of the Menora design. He reminds us that R. Tarphon used to celebrate a brilliant interpretation with the words, *kaftor va-ferach*—"A knob and a blossom!"[84] That is, all creativity draws inspiration from the fantastic beauty of the Menora. "One who sees olive oil in a dream should expect the illumination of Torah."[85]

In this creative modality, Moses is supreme. "Let them bring the pure olive oil for illumination *to you*" (27:20).[86] Though he is the younger of the brothers, Moses is addressed reverentially by Aaron: "Please, my lord . . ." (Num 12:11). Their intellectual powers are radically different. Aaron is fully capable of conceptualizing and teaching the text; but Moses is gifted with the genius for luminous redescription. Without Aaron, there can be no tradition, no stability of meaning. But without Moses, there can be no light.

The interrelation of the two brothers, in their difference, is the intimated meaning of the repeated *ve-atta*, in the context of the practices and vestments of priesthood. Moses' genius, and that of all who resemble him in future generations, is for *pilpul*, for *silsul*—for sublime surges of creativity. The crown of Torah, unlike the crown of priesthood, or the crown of royalty, is not hereditary: it is, according to Maimonides, potentially accessible to every Jew: "Whoever wishes may come and take."[87] Democratic in essence, it is yet the most important of the crowns, as the kingmaker is greater than the king,[88] or the "dresser" than the one dressed. "The real virtue of these crowns, the crown of priesthood and the crown of royalty, is drawn only from the crown of Torah."[89] At root, even the hereditary castes arise from an act of willful creativity, from the abrupt, unpredictable decision of God. In that God-like space, Moses-figures in each generation[90] may, with an idiosyncratic urgency, resume the sacred play.

This space can generate worlds, just as, in the kabbalistic cosmology, God's world was generated by an act of *tzimtzum*, of self-retraction. A space, a *chalal panui*, was evacuated of the divine, and a world became possible. In our opening midrash, God pivots the continued existence of "My world" on the continued self-retraction and creativity of those who play in the spaces separating the letters of the Torah.

R. Nahman[91] modulates the kabbalistic notion of the *chalal panui*, the evacuated space, into a psychological key. He quotes *Ethics of the Fathers*: "All my days, I have grown up *among* the sages."[92] In his reading, this becomes: ". . . I have grown *in the space vacated between* the Sages." Because of the differences of opinion and sensibility, of role and "costume," that characterize the Sages, new worlds can be created. If a dense unanimity existed among thinkers, there would be no intellectual space for new perceptions. The growth of the individual, his idiosyncratic forms of conceiving the world, make him, effectively, a creator of worlds. In this, he resembles his Creator, who also used unprecedented language to create the world out of silence.

That is, the Moses-type must find enclaves of silence in the pandemonium of discourses. The evacuated space becomes Winnicott's "potential space," out of which new ways of relationship are engendered.[93] In infant experience, Jessica Benjamin proposes, the newness arises from a new balance between "inside" and "outside." Separation from the mother allows for an aloneness in the presence of the other that makes authentic impulse possible. "Here begins the sense of authorship, the conviction that one's act originates *inside* and reflects one's own intention. Here too begins the capacity for full reciprocity and attention to what is outside, freedom to be interested in the object independent of the presence of need or anxiety . . ."[94]

The space provided for authentic interaction between self and other thus avoids the dual peril, the Scylla and the Charybdis, of impinging and being impinged upon. The aim of the transitional experience in the infant's development is not simply to soothe himself, thus internalizing the mother's function, but to develop his own capacities in a "holding environment."[95]

In R. Nahman's description of the *chalal panui*, the space in which the self can grow to "separate connectedness" with reality, the stakes are set high. The issue is the God-like ability of human beings to create worlds. Quoting the Zohar, R. Nahman reads Isaiah 51:16: "I have said to Zion, You are My people—*ammi atta*": "Do not read *ammi*, but *immi*—You are *with Me*."—"Collaborate with Me in creating worlds." Ultimately, the fluent silence out of which new language can emerge becomes thick with new voices.

Aaron and Moses: Tension and Protean Creativity

Aaron's cloak with its skirt swaying with bells and pomegranates, became, in the teaching of R. Yaacov Leiner, a figure for the continuing tension between emptiness and fullness. One mode of that tension lies on the axis between playfulness and formalism, the free play of mind and sensibility and the ceremonious investment in hereditary values. A schematic contrast between Moses and Aaron would place them at opposite ends of the axis, Moses representing the magnanimous imagination, the negative capability that creates worlds, while Aaron represents the functionalism of a fixed and ritualized incarnation. Such a schematic approach, however, as we have seen, would not do justice to either Moses or Aaron. The tension of polarities exists for both.

Aaron is the wearer of vestments that evoke the dialectic in its visual, even tactile form: between the empty vestments and the dense particularity of personal experience, between the donning and the doffing of armor. In the teaching of Beit Yaacov, this dialectic involves a constant corrective process, rebalancing the extremes by contemplating the complementary values of bell and pomegranate. This is the spiritual complexity of the work of priesthood. Predicated upon commitment to a given role, it is ambushed by pathologies on both sides. In a sense, the sterile polarities become ultimately indistinguishable. The High Priest, in the moment of his triumph, emerged intact from the Holy of Holies, becomes an image of resplendent and aesthetic harmony: "Happy is the eye that saw these things!" The human face in its pure white setting is beauty itself. On Yom Kippur, the bells and pomegranates have been wholly integrated into his being; he no longer wears the resonant robe, just the simplicity of the four basic priestly garments, for his face is eloquent with the harmony of bell and pomegranate. The beauty is as intense as it is momentary; the imagery of the Piyyut (the liturgical poem read on the Day of Atonement), largely drawn from organic life, evokes an exquisite equilibrium.

The figure of Aaron, therefore, in all its statuesque panoply, conveys the poignancy of a tension resolved for an instant. Life and form, self and world, originality and tradition find an instant of equipoise. The priestly role, incarnated in the hereditary caste will move through all possible positions on the axis, from the sons of Aaron, who are consumed by fire, to the sons of Eli, who consume the sacrifices dedicated to God. In the end, after the destruction of the Temples, Aaron's role will become a mythic moment in history, to be recounted but no longer witnessed: "Woe to us that we have only the hearing of the ears!" In effect, the tension of bell and pomegranate will prove untenable.

Moses, too, knows this tension. But, in a context devoted to the priesthood, to garments and functions of holiness, God singles him out and addresses him, "And as for you, you . . ." Nameless, in a sense childless, in a sense parentless, child of two cultures, Hebrew and Egyptian, Moses is absorbed into no single role. He is the prince of Egypt whose brothers are slaves. A protean figure, he wears many crowns. Neither priest nor king, he yet will play both roles, wear both crowns. He is absent from the Parsha; and yet he is pervasive from the beginning: "And as for you. . . And as for you. . . And as for you . . ."

Perhaps most significantly, Moses is the man of silence; but out of his silence emerges a voice thick with many harmonics. Abstaining from language—"I am not a man of words!"—he arouses God's anger. What is God's anger but a way of signaling a recognition of Moses' seriousness, of the large stake that he has in his silence? The transfer of the priesthood from Moses to Aaron rebalances the relationship of the brothers, challenging Moses to acknowledge the trace of otherness that his silence engraves within him.[96] And in the end, the midrash affirms the paradoxical nature of his silence: he speaks not one language, but seventy:

> "These are the words that Moses spoke:" Israel said, "Yesterday you said, 'I am not a man of words!' and now you have so much to say!" Said R. Yitzhak, "If you are inarticulate, study Torah and you will be healed.

Moses had already learned the whole Torah, in the wilderness facing the Red Sea. That is the meaning of, 'Then the lame shall leap like a deer, and the tongue of the dumb shall shout aloud.' (Isa 35:6) Come and see—when God told Moses, 'Go, I shall send you to Pharaoh,' Moses answered, 'This is an outrageous mission, for I am not a man of words. Seventy languages are spoken in Pharaoh's palace, so that every foreigner can be addressed in his own language. If I go on Your mission and they examine my claim to be the messenger of God and they find out that I cannot speak with them, will they not mock me: "Look at the messenger of the Creator, who does not know all the languages fluently!" It will be scandalous, for I am not a man of words, I am of uncircumcised lips (6:12)!' God answered: 'But Adam was not instructed by any teacher—how did he know seventy languages, as it is said, "And he called them names." (Gen 2:20)? It does not say, "a name for each animal," but "names." And yet you say, "I am not a man of words!" ' Forty years after Israel had left Egypt, Moses began to translate the Torah into seventy languages: 'He began to expound this Torah' (Deut 1:5). The mouth that had said, 'I am not a man of words!' now said, 'These are the words . . .' And the prophet proclaimed, 'Then the lame shall leap like a deer and the tongue of the dumb shall shout aloud.' Why? 'For waters shall burst forth in the desert, streams in the wilderness' (Isa 35:6). That is why it is said, 'These are the words . . .' "[97]

All meanings are intimated in that silence, as all living water shimmers within the arid spaces of the desert. Unable to speak any language, Moses is compelled to draw from the resources of his silence, an infinite, protean energy that gives life to all vocabularies. It is Moses' energy, the crown of Torah, says R. Zaddok HaCohen, that gives energy to all other crowns, the crown of priesthood, the crown of royalty.[98]

"And as for you . . ." God intimates to Moses, in barely audible invitation. The second person connection, challenging and always surprising, is of the largest significance. André Neher writes, "Man is always a second person, who is called upon and who is never alone in his self."[99]

Moses: The Magnanimous Imagination

The problem of basing a dogma and an institutionalized practice on a protean creativity is a serious and perennial one. "It is very hard," writes

Mark Edmundson, "to consolidate and administer a dogma on the basis of a practice that, in certain phases, enjoins the undoing of all stabilities and holds everything 'titular and ephemeral,' including the self."[100]

If a Romantic ethos of self-recreation may endanger the social order, if polymorphous energy, invention and boldness tend to make violence into a method, then God's call to Moses, three times repeated, "And as for you . . ." becomes weighted with a moral imperative of its own. Moses' midrashic response to his brother at the moment when the difference between them has been most acutely crystallized is a paradigm of the positive force of the protean sensibility: "As you live, even though you have become High Priest, *it is as though* I had become High Priest."

"As you live . . .": with this idiom, Moses transcends the predictable operations of power and violence. "It is as though I had become High Priest": the greatness of *invetanuth*, of the God-like humility of the one who plays and creates worlds, resounds in these words of deepened relationship. His embodied ethical response to God's challenge ("I seek your forbearance/greatness") is a movement of magnanimous imagination: since I and you, inside and outside, are to play distinct roles, a relationship of empathy becomes safe, and the world of fantasy can be acknowledged.

The relationship will not be one of complementary dual unity, in which activity and passivity are internalized and reversed, and which, Jessica Benjamin argues, is the basic structure of domination, but one of intersubjectivity.[101] In this mode, the struggle for omnipotent control which has dogged the brothers of Genesis can be set aside. Not without sacrifice, Moses relinquishes his claim to absoluteness; the brothers recognize each other in their difference and sameness. If Moses has a superiority over Aaron, that is because of his imaginative magnanimity and his readiness to lose the hard casing of selfhood in an empathy with the other.

It is in this sense, perhaps, that Moses is compared in the midrash to the wise man's "close relative" (*krovatho*). The protean power of the Torah that he represents is the closest to God. At the same time, he cannot "give birth"; he cannot reproduce his protean self. Self-replication is the essence of the hereditary castes, royalty and priesthood. But his genes will not transmit his form of genius; for that transmission, some other form of communication will have to be invented. The influence of Moses on the future generations will be oblique, in a sense impalpable: a kind of subtle contagion will spread from face to face, from teacher to student: a light, not a priestly robe; a crown paradoxically available to all.

9 *Ki Tissa*

THE GOLDEN CALF:
FIRE IN THE BONES

[30:11–34:35]

1. The Golden Calf: Fickleness or Intransigence?

Moses Is Gifted with Torah

The pivotal experience of the Exodus is surely the Revelation at Mount Sinai, twinned with the Golden Calf that so rapidly follows it. Indeed, if we adopt the midrashic flashback perspective on the narrative,[1] the Golden Calf is deceptively separated in the biblical text from the moment of Revelation: narrated twelve chapters later, it actually preceded all the data of the Mishkan. Essentially, it is inseparable from the encounter with God at Sinai.

By the time the reader of the Torah reaches this narrative, however, it has been long "repressed," during the externalized legal passages relating to the Mishkan. The Golden Calf is a disaster that has been waiting to happen. Inconceivable treachery, it is also an inevitable reaction to Revelation. Indeed, the paradox of the Golden Calf centers on the work of memory: it is both forgetting and remembering, in a complex sense that we shall explore. Forgetting the glory of Sinai, the people also fix themselves in a posture of rigid loyalty to memory that is no less relevant to the idolatrous passion.

Forty days on Mount Sinai culminate in a gift from God to Moses:

> When He finished speaking with him on Mount Sinai, He gave Moses the two tablets of the Covenant, stone tablets inscribed with the finger of God. (31:18)

The gift is narrated with succinct force: it occurs at the end of a process of language, "when He finished speaking with him." After such speech, a silence falls; and stones are given, accepted. These stones are engraved with letters, words. They, too, are language, but they represent the permanent residue of a dialogue between God and man.

The relation between the many words of Mount Sinai and the scripted stones is questioned by the Talmud:

> At first, Moses would learn Torah and forget it—until it was given him as a gift, as it is said, "He *gave* Moses . . ."[2]

In this midrash, the Torah is experienced first as material to be mastered, susceptible to all the slippages of memory. Moses plays the role of the human being eroded by failures of retention: to be a "learner and forgetter," is to represent the pathos of the human situation in time. These forty days of strenuous encounter with God culminate in an act of total gift: "and He gave . . ." is God's fulfillment of His original promise to Moses: "Come up to Me on the mountain and wait there, and I will give you the stone tablets with the teachings and commandments which I have inscribed to instruct them" (24:12).

Here, all Moses' strenuous efforts to retain the Torah in memory are superseded by an act of divine generosity: the bestowal of total recall. Effectively, Moses becomes supernaturally *gifted.* Or, to frame the idea differently, the nature of God's gift is that He gives Moses relief from the approximations and frustrations of the learning process.[3] These stones, inscribed by the finger of God, offer a formalized resolution of all the struggles of speech *with* God. That original study partnership,[4] the *chevrutha* of God and Moses, each speaking with the other, has come to its climax in a gift that will make further dialogue irrelevant. Embracing the stones traced by God's finger, Moses has reached a moment of apotheosis, of total mastery. "Great things are done when men and mountains meet" (William Blake).

This moment, however, is the last moment of an old world. As it is narrated in this single verse that prefaces the story of the Golden Calf, we half notice that God's gift has not registered its weight in Moses' arms. That weight will be sensed only after the crisis, as Moses descends the mountain "with the two tablets of testimony *in his hand*" (32:15). Then, the Torah will linger over the tablets, the writing, as objects *in Moses' hand;* their divine origin, the supernatural script will be pressed home at the very moment that Moses will smash them. Now, however, in the last tableau at the top of the mountain, before the Golden Calf narrative, God's gift remains strangely impalpable.

The Golden Calf: The Time Factor

From the image of Moses, supremely gifted at the top of the mountain, then, the narrative cuts to the Israelites, at the base of the mountain:

> And the people saw that Moses was delayed in coming down from the mountain, and they gathered against Aaron and said to him, "Come, make us a god who shall go before us, for that man Moses, who brought us up from the land of Egypt—we do not know what has happened to him." (32:1)

The contrast between above and below is subtly suggested. Between the solitary grandeur of Moses in the presence of God and the panicked abandonment of the people, the narrative mediates by the use of the word *boshesh*: "he was delayed." In itself exotic—never found elsewhere in the Torah[5]—the word conveys the quality of the people's rebellion. "The people saw that Moses was delayed": the people perceive a *lateness*, an absence that is measured by time. The reader knows that Moses is sublimely present at the top of the mountain, while the people at the base are almost comically provoked by lateness.[6] The peculiar anxiety of this sense of the missed moment is fleshed out by Rashi:

> ". . . Moses was delayed . . ." an expression of lateness . . . When Moses ascended the mountain, he told them: In forty days' time, I shall be back, in the first six hours of day (i.e. before midday). They thought that the day of his ascent was included in the count, while he meant forty complete days, which began with the night. Since he ascended on the seventh of Sivan, the count began the following night and ended on the seventeenth of Tammuz. But on the sixteenth of Tammuz, Satan came and threw the world into chaos: he showed them an image of darkness and deep fog and chaos, as if to say, "Surely Moses is dead—that is why chaos is come to the world."[7]

Implicit in this reading is a pun on the word *boshesh—Ba shesh!*—"The sixth hour has come!" The people's nervous perception of lateness is graphically plotted in a scenario of temporal misunderstanding. Rashi amplifies the text with a narrative of specific disappointment: "*Ba shesh!*—the promised time has come—and that man Moses . . . we do not know what has happened to him." The speech conveys the people's pervasive anxiety about Moses: "We have *never* known exactly how to define him,[8] and now he has disappeared into the fire, and the sixth hour of the fortieth day has come . . ." Moses' elusive quality is confirmed when a time schedule is betrayed. A latent anxiety about Moses' nature, about his essential affiliations, is activated in an apparently trivial moment of lateness.

Rashi, citing the Talmud,[9] explains the rational basis for the misunderstanding. The calculation of the forty-day period is distorted by a full twenty-four hours, if the count begins by day instead of at night. The idolatrous project of the Golden Calf, in effect, is predicated on an *ambiguity*, for which Moses is at least partially responsible. This ambiguity, apparently technical in nature, produces a time lag in the people's expectations and the residue of that time lag is the Golden Calf.

If we explore the midrashic narrative further, we find that its mythic imagery largely serves to exonerate the people. Not content with the scenario of a misunderstood time frame, the midrash has Satan show the people an "image of darkness, deep fog and chaos, *as if to say*, Surely Moses is dead . . ." That is, a mass hallucination affects the people. Indeed, in Rashi's Talmudic source, the satanic fantasy is of Moses dead on a bier. In response to this hallucination the people cry: "*this* man Moses, who brought us up from the land of Egypt—we do not know what has happened to him."

A specific image of Moses, satanically generated, is responsible for the people's faithlessness. The world becomes a phantasmagoric blur; chaos is come again. Imagination spawns icons of meaninglessness. In Rashi's Talmudic source, Satan moves from insidious speech to visual fantasy; only then, afflicted by a vision of horrifying intimacy, the people make their demand of Aaron. Manipulated by Satan, their panic response seems almost plausible.[10]

The weight of the time factor in the people's betrayal is reminiscent of infant experience as described by D. W. Winnicott in *Playing and Reality.* He writes of the trauma suffered by the infant if the mother is absent for a period that exceeds the infant's capacity to retain her in imagination:

> The feeling of the mother's existence lasts x minutes. If the mother is away more than x minutes, then the imago fades, and along with this the

> baby's capacity to use the symbol of the union ceases. The baby is distressed, but this distress is soon *mended* because the mother returns in x+y minutes. In x+y minutes the baby has not become altered. But in x+y+z minutes the baby has become *traumatized* . . . We must assume that the vast majority of babies never experience the x+y+z quantity of deprivation. This means that the majority of children do not carry around with them for life the knowledge from experience of having been mad. Madness here simply means a *break-up* of whatever may exist at the time of *a personal continuity of existence.*[11]

The condition that Winnicott simply terms, "madness," is, I suggest, the condition of the people experiencing an x+y+z quantity of deprivation. Some essential root of continuity with the personal beginning has, for them, been snapped. That this is a question of time, of lateness, is only apparently a trivial circumstance. For time is of the essence in questions of attachment and separation, trust and trauma.

The Golden Calf Substitutes for Moses

The analogy with that infant experience that cannot tolerate unpunctuality in the love-object leads us further afield. The midrashic pun on *Ba shesh*—"It's six o'clock!"—intimates the infantile, compulsive quality of the people's dependence on Moses. In one of Rashi's sources, the satanic motif is narrated thus:

> The Rabbis said: Satan was effective (lit., "he found his hands") at that time: Moses was seen *suspended between heaven and earth*, and the people pointed him out with their fingers saying, "This man Moses . . ."[12]

The mass hallucination has Moses suspended between heaven and earth, removed from them, neither among them nor in front of them; his image hovers, with a mythic ambiguity, between the upper and lower realms. And that ambiguity about the God-man Moses is Satan's strongest suit. Compelling their imagination, elusive to rational understanding, child of two cultures and speaker of no language, Moses torments the people by his absence. Like Gracchus the Hunter, in Kafka's story, the Moses-figure in their imagination needs to be released from a limbo that is neither life nor death. The hold that his figure has on their fantasy means, on the one hand, a madness of deprivation, and, on the other, an astonishing ease of substitution.

This, indeed, is one of the mysteries of the Golden Calf episode. For Moses—or the icon of him to which he is satanically reducible—is both essential and exchangeable. This, of course, is the way of all fetishes: they evoke a visceral need, withdraw all power into themselves, and yet are susceptible to cruel destruction, if they betray the adoration of their worshipers.

If a few hours' absence beyond Winnicott's x-period can lead the people to "madness," this must raise questions about the nature of the connection between people and leader. If what is at stake is life's continuity, then the ruthlessness with which a grotesque substitution is effected both is and is not astonishing.

The people's view of Moses is most lucidly limned in their words of abandonment: "This man Moses who brought us up from the land of Egypt . . ." Meshech Chochma[13] reads powerfully: for them, Moses has become the source of supernatural power—it is he who has brought them out of the land of Egypt. Just here, at root, is their pathology: as God diagnoses it to Moses a few verses later, "Go down, for your people *whom you brought up from the land of Egypt*, have acted corruptly" (32:7). Implicitly, God tells Moses: The people's corruption consists in their projecting all power onto *you*. In other words, Meshech Chochma implies, idolatry has begun long before the Golden Calf emerges from the fire. Moses himself has become a fetish in the sensibility of the people. In Winnicott's terms, a madness of discontinuity has afflicted them, in which they are unable to "use" Moses in his absence, unable to sustain the "personal psychic reality" of his image.[14]

Responsibility for this "idolatrous" state of affairs is, however, not easily determined. If the infant-mother analogy is accepted, the issue of responsibility becomes difficult, perhaps even irrelevant. A disruption has occurred between the two protagonists, and out of this disruption emerges, with a bizarre naturalness, the Golden Calf. The relation between Moses and the people is exposed, at a moment of strain, as one of pathological dependence: pathological, clearly, in its grotesque progeny. The scorn of the Psalmist places the narrative in satirical perspective: "They have exchanged their glory for an image of a bull that feeds on grass!"[15] Between God and the Calf, Moses emerges, unexpectedly, as a problematic transitional figure.

To see the genesis of the Golden Calf—of fetishisms and idolatries—in a projection of divine power onto the image of Moses is to remember the people's plea, in the very heart of Revelation: "You speak with us and we will listen; but let not God speak with us, lest we die" (20:16). Later, Moses detects in that moment a profound betrayal of a potential relationship between themselves and God. In Rashi's words, Moses later describes the crisis:

> "[And you said] . . . 'And you [*at*—the female pronoun] speak to us . . .': You weakened my strength like a female, you demoralized me, for I saw that you were not anxious to draw close to Him in love, and that you were not attracted to learning from Him rather than from me."[16]

The paradox is palpable: Moses is begged by his people to substitute for God's voice and complains of "weakening." That is, standing in for God unnerves him, diminishes his human power. This key moment at Sinai, therefore, informs a subtle shift in the understanding of power. Moses gains in charismatic force, as godly power is invested in him; but the midrashic decoding of the feminine form *at* intimates that, in barely acknowledged ways, he has lost. The end of the drama is not at all subtle, as the grotesque image of alienated power that is the Calf leaps into the space evacuated by Moses.

The problem of idolatry, then, becomes a problem of dependence, in which both divine power and human power are travestied. The terror of Sinai, the consuming fire on the mountain, was the terror of the face-to-face relation of God and the human ("Face to face, God spoke with you" [Deut 5:4].) In order to sustain such a relation, it is, as C. S. Lewis suggests, necessary to *have a face.*[17] The implications of this will be the subject of our exploration of the Golden Calf episode.

At this point, however, we may say both that the face is the most exposed, public portion of the self and that it bears a unique trace of inwardness. The ordeal of the face is that it must meet the gaze of other faces, without betraying the truth of its own gaze. The Golden Calf narrative begins with an act of seeing ("And the people saw that Moses was delayed . . .") and ends with an act of seeing ("The Israelites saw that the skin of Moses' face was radiant" [34:30]). Between these two moments, the potential of faces meeting, of seeing and not seeing, is the complex theme of the narrative of idolatry.

Idolatry: A Dialectical Definition

The biblical ban on idolatry is susceptible to very different definitions. A radical suggestion is made by Beit Yaacov:[18] he reads, "You shall not make for yourself any graven figure nor any image . . ." as including even God's Commandments, if the form becomes more important than the vitality it expresses. The relation to all objects, even the ritual forms of the spiritual life, can become fossilized and therefore idolatrous. There are two possible indications of pathology: one is the *pessel*, the graven figure, when an object is cut and shaped into autonomous form; the other is the *temuna*, the image, when an object is eviscerated of all meaning apart from human use. Both these relationships with objects, Beit Yaacov insists, are idolatrous, since the object is perceived as distinct from God.

Beit Yaacov here adumbrates an arresting complexity in the notion of idolatry. As we continue our discussion of the Golden Calf narrative, this ambiguity will remain with us and will inform much of the discussion. At this point, however, I should like to emphasize a radical ambiguity in relation to the fetish: the relation may be one of fixation on form, of adoration of the object; or it may be one of contempt for the object as *mere* form. One excess may be termed the mythic perspective, the other the rational perspective. The fascination of objects makes them seem indispensable, while a disenchanted gaze strips them entirely of grace. Both excesses are idolatrous, in that both detach the world from God.

The dangers of adoration—not least, the "feet of clay" syndrome—are obvious. Less obvious are the perils of contempt, which rejects the authority of all forms. Emerson expresses the passion of that contempt:

> There are no fixtures in nature. The universe is fluid and volatile . . . The Greek sculpture is all melted away, as if it had been statues of ice; here and there, a solitary figure or fragment remaining, as we see flecks and scraps of snow left in cold dells and mountain clefts in June and July. For the genius that created it now creates somewhat else . . . Everything looks permanent until its secret is known. A rich estate appears to women a firm and lasting fact; to a merchant, one easily created of any materials, and easily lost.[19]

The ephemeral nature of all forms evokes in Emerson an exhilaration about genius, thought, motion. On the other hand, Freud describes the complementary need to "loosen the fixation of the libido to the object by disparaging it, denigrating it and even as it were killing it."[20] Between Emerson's exhilarating contempt and Freud's recognition of the cruelty of detachment a tension exists that Emerson himself articulates in an eloquent image:

> The life of man is a self-evolving circle, which, from a ring imperceptibly small, rushes on all sides outwards to new and larger circles, and that without end. The extent to which this generation of circles, wheel without wheel, will go, depends on the force or truth of the individual soul. For it is the inert effort of each thought, having formed itself into a circular wave of circumstance,—as for instance an empire, rules of an art, a local usage, a religious rite,—to heap itself on that ridge and to solidify and hem in the life. But if the soul is quick and strong it bursts over that boundary on all sides and expands another orbit on the great deep, which also runs up into a high wave, with attempt again to stop and to bind. But the heart refuses to be imprisoned; in its first and narrowest pulses it already tends outward with a vast force and to immense and innumerable expansions.[21]

An inevitable repetition of wave and ridge, expansiveness and inertia, can be acknowledged and its deadening effect yet transcended. To affirm vitality is Emerson's response to the recurrent rigors of the boundary. The relation between "Thought's perilous, whirling pool," and "the zone that girds the incarnate mind,"[22] however, raises disturbing questions about the process by which the self gives up an erotic object. If the erotic object is the Golden Calf, and if idolatry is fixation on that object, what is to be done to achieve detachment, to release the wave to a new orbit? The forms of the ridge, whether religious rites or the rules of an art, deserve a more complex attention than simple disparagement; for, as Beit Yaacov implies, they, too, hold something of God.

The Master Narrative of Infidelity

In the midrashic treatment of the Golden Calf narrative, the ambiguous relation to the erotic object mirrors the complexity of Beit Yaacov's double definition of idolatry. On the mountaintop, for instance, God reveals to Moses the catastrophe of the people's betrayal: "Go down, for your people have acted corruptly . . ." (32:7). What is the corruption of which God speaks? Ramban comments: this means the destruction of a fabric of meaning, and describes an inner attitude detectable only to God. Even though the Golden Calf was actually worshiped by a limited number of the people—those punished in massacre and plague—God's anger is aroused by an almost universal syndrome. The vast majority of the people are caught up in the "abnormality" of the Golden Calf. In Kenneth Burke's terms, "it was normal to be abnormal."[23]

The normal abnormality of idolatry is described by God: "They have been quick to turn aside from the way that I commanded them. They have made themselves a molten calf and bowed low to it and sacrificed to it, saying: 'This is your god, O Israel, who brought you out of the land of Egypt!'" (32:8). "They have been quick to turn aside . . ." In God's mournful rhetoric, the time frame, again, is essential. Like the word *boshesh* ("delayed"), the word *maher* ("quick") implies an irony and a pathos: there the people, and here God, marvel at the ease of abandonment, at how a way of constructing identity can, in an instant, be ruptured.

The Talmud fleshes out the irony of the time frame, figuring the people's betrayal as erotic treachery:

> Said Ulla: Shameless is the bride who plays the harlot while still under her wedding canopy. Said R. Mari the son of Samuel's daughter: What verse refers to this? "While the king still sat at his banquet, my spikenard gave forth its fragrance" (Song of Songs 1:12). Said Rav: Yet His love was still with us, for "gave forth" is written, not "made offensive."[24]

The outrage of infidelity is limned in a grotesque fantasy of synchronicity. The bride is *still under her wedding canopy*: morally, the midrashist's voice rises to a scream. The spatial image of the wedding canopy conveys an even more bizarre temporal image. At the very moment of commitment to her husband, she surrealistically "plays the harlot" with her lover. The image puts the reader under great strain: the inconceivable scenario conveys the inconceivable secret of the Golden Calf.

The quotation from the Song of Songs presses home the sense of emotional violation: while the king is still at his wedding banquet, his bride is stirred by desire for her lover. An intimate, mistimed reality is framed by the husband's sexual rage. By a double-exposure effect, wedding canopy and site of harlotry are telescoped in time and space. What rage could be more justifiable? And yet, as Rav points out, there is an unexpected delicacy even in the violent imagery of the midrashic narrative: the language shows a paradoxical tenderness for the bride, even as her offense is intimated.

The midrash has indicated an ambivalence in God's accusation of the people: "They have been quick to turn aside . . ." The synchronicity of betrayal elicits violent anger and strange tenderness. So far from minimizing the people's infidelity,[25] this midrash excruciatingly raises the pitch of the rhetoric and compels the reader to interrogate the reality represented by adultery-under-the-canopy.

The theater of betrayal is in the heart. There, more painfully than in objective, observable behaviors, the people have turned away from God: "They have made themselves a molten calf, and they have bowed low to it and sacrificed to it, saying: 'This is your god, O Israel, who brought you out of the land of Egypt!' " Such a series of accusations normally intensifies toward a climax. Here, the worst outrages of active idolatry occur first in the sentence, ending rather weakly with an act of speech: ". . . and they have said . . ." However, as Meshech Chochma and Ha-amek Davar both point out, this act of speech is the true climax of the series. Here is the heart of idolatry: "if one says to an object, 'You are my god,' one is subject to capital punishment and divine punishment."[26]

In the Second Commandment, indeed, this radical relation to the idol underlies all the external forms of worship: "*You shall not have any gods before Me* . . . You shall not make . . . You shall not bow down . . . You shall not worship them" (20:3). The four stages: inner orientation, making, bowing, and worshiping, are echoed in God's account of the Golden Calf—with the rhetorical climax reserved for inner orientation, "And they said: 'This is your god, O Israel . . .' "

The order of God's charges indicates His pain and anger, which culminates in the people's emotional betrayal. *Acts* of idolatry are dwarfed by the intimate reality of erotic attraction. This is the reality that is conveyed by the images of synchronicity in the midrash, and by the language of speed in the biblical text. The Psalmist, too, emphasizes this temporal outrage in his account of the wilderness rebellions: "They *soon forgot* His deeds; they *would not wait* to learn His plan" (Ps 106:13). Erotically fickle, the people are said to have forgotten. Their sin is a failure of memory.

"A Stiff-Necked People": Perverse Fidelity?

Against this master-narrative of infidelity, God now introduces a description of the people that will acquire classic status: "I see that this is a stiff-necked people" (32:9). Paradoxically, the expression, coined for this occasion, implies an unexpected *fidelity* to old ideas. In Rashi's words: "They turn the stiff back of their necks toward those who would rebuke them and refuse to listen." To be stiff-necked, then, is to be intransigent, loyal to a fault. This is, effectively, the opposite of fickleness, inconstancy. Far from forgetting, the people are described as remembering too well; the bony back of the neck conveys a paradoxical insusceptibility to the words of a new Lover.

If the implications of the "stiff neck" are taken seriously, then, they disturb a primary notion of idolatry as infidelity. Perhaps, after all, the people are all too pious in their attachments? Perhaps they have never, in fact, left Egypt, that place of the deaf and the dumb and the callous-hearted?[27] Perhaps there is a pathology of Egypt that can be healed only by a capacity to *listen*? "And He said, 'If you will listen attentively to the voice of God, your God . . . giving ear to His commandments and keeping all His laws, then I will not bring upon you any of the diseases that I brought upon the Egyptians, for I am God, your healer' " (15:26).

Piety and Impiety: A Counter-Narrative

Such an emphasis on the stiff neck, on insusceptibility, as the core of idolatry would, however, entail a switch of perception. Kenneth Burke deploys a similar switch when he discusses psychoanalysis as a technique of nonreligious conversion:

> It effects its cure by providing a new perspective that dissolves the *system of pieties* (emphasis added) lying at the roots of the patient's sorrows or bewilderments. It is an *impious* rationalization, offering a fresh terminology of motives to replace the patient's painful terminology of motives. Its scientific terms are wholly incongruous with the unscientific nature of the distress. By approaching the altar of the patient's unhappiness with deliberate irreverence, by selecting a vocabulary which specifically violates the dictates of style and taboo, it changes the entire nature of his problem, rephrasing it in a form for which there is a solution.[28]

Burke reverses the conventional meanings of piety and impiety. Neurotic unhappiness constitutes a system of pieties. In the simplest mode, he claims, piety is present, "when the potter moulds the clay to exactly that form which completely gratifies his sense of how it ought to be."[29] Such a sense of piety shows "a marked affinity with childhood experiences," and it "can be painful, requiring a set of symbolic expiations."[30] Psychoanalysis, healing, conversion, work by imposing "impious" new meanings on the patient's "sorrowful poem."

In effect, then, if we import Burke's terminology, we can read the "stiff-necked" charge against the people to imply that they have resisted the new meanings of Sinai, for the good reason that these are deliberately incongruous with the pieties of past experience. The Torah rephrases the old vocabulary of unhappiness in a "form for which there is a solution." Therapists who perpetrate such impieties must expect resistance, even, according to Adler, physical blows as reward for their pains.

> For we must expect to meet with fury, when desecrating the altar of a patient's misery, to which he has brought the most pious offerings, weaving about it the very texture of his self-respect, developing an entire schema of motivations above this central orientating concern, profoundly stressing certain values and rejecting others according to their fitness for this integrative work, and clinging to the structure all the more passionately since, if it began as the *cause* of his distress, by the time the patient has finished building, it has become his only bulwark against distress.[31]

In this masterly rendering of the ambiguities of piety, Burke provides us with a counter-narrative of the Golden Calf. Where one version of the idolatry phenomenon will emphasize fickleness, changeability, polymorphous instability, another will emphasize rigidity, insensibility, pious fury. These are the two faces of idolatry—infatuation with the object, rejection of the object. In one narrative, God's antagonist is everything that is received from culture and from others; indeed, this may include large parts of the self that have been formed by the residues of the past. In the other narrative, idolatry is represented by a restless mania which constantly seeks "like a hungry man for new object-cathexes."[32]

In Mark Edmundson's analysis, Emerson typifies the first narrative, in which the spirit of God is expressed in energy, in transformational moments, in "the shooting of the gulf, in the darting to an aim."[33] The other narrative is characterized by Freud; here, the internalization of the past, the "setting up of the object inside the ego," becomes a "therapeutic goal" (19:29). For Freud, the process of relinquishing erotic objects leaves its trace within the ego, which becomes a "precipitation of abandoned object-cathexes." This is the work of mourning, which constitutes the therapeutic project: to remake the ego "in a form that resembles the image of the lost object . . . Mourning is a way of sustaining and consolidating authority, of sacrificing whatever there might be of originality to the urge to maintain some continuity with one's past self, and of conforming to a revised standard biography."[34]

Resistance to this process can be seen as the necessary movement of the soul, which must continually quit "its whole system of things, its friends, and home, and laws, and faith, as the shell-fish crawls out of its beautiful but stony case, because it no longer admits of its growth, and slowly forms a new house."[35] To resist that resistance is, on this view, to impede growth: ". . . to us, in our lapsed estate, resting, not advancing, resisting, not cooperating with the divine expansion, this growth comes by shocks."

Alternatively, resistance to the mourning process can be seen as "melancholic" self-undoing, which offers a temporary illusion of freedom: "The manic subject plainly demonstrates his liberation from the object which was the cause of his suffering, by seeking like a ravenously hungry man for new object-cathexes."[36]

Essentially, the same circular process is being viewed from opposing perspectives. One reading of the Golden Calf narrative, in effect, emphasizes the betrayal of a revelation, the inexplicable lightness with which erotic objects are exchanged; while the other focuses on the paralysis that preserves the deadened forms of the past and of the self.

In this second reading, the revelation on Sinai represents an "impious affront" to the received ideas of the Egyptian past. The Golden Calf is a reaffirmation of the already known, a regression from the disruptive vocabulary of Sinai. In this narrative, a lightness, a capacity for transition and transformation, is tragically missing from the spiritual repertoire of the people.

In God's first accusation of the people, then, nuances of both charges appear. On the one hand, the people have changed "too quickly" from the erotic commitments of Sinai; on the other, they are stiff-necked, sclerotic, invested in the outward forms of the past. The issue of time is central to both versions of idolatry. If fickleness is the charge, then time is not sufficiently internalized, it slips away without leaving its trace; but if conformity to dead usages is the pathology, then that, too, generates, in a different sense, a *loss of time*:

> The objection to conforming to usages that have become dead to you is, that it scatters your force. It loses your time and blurs the impression of your character. If you maintain a dead church, contribute to a dead Bible society . . . I have difficulty to detect the precise man you are.[37]

In the first scenario, the Golden Calf represents the obliteration of Sinai; in the second, a regression beyond a Sinai that never really happened.

Decoding God's account of the people's sin, therefore, leads in two apparently contrary directions: inconstancy and rigidity. One of Freud's central axioms—that full satisfaction in erotic life is unattainable—seems relevant to the problem of the Golden Calf. The people are, I suggest, trapped in a "double bind" situation, in which pathological responses shade off into one another. Their spiritual dilemma is the Freudian perplexity writ large:

> Far from being a champion of unbridled sensuality, Freud acutely understood the intimate connection between libertine and ascetic behavior. Both are excesses, derived from an imperfect emancipation from childhood's insatiable love of authority-figures . . . If from Freud we may infer that monogamy is not a very satisfactory arrangement, the results of his science may also be taken to show that man is a naturally faithful creature: the most inconstant sexual athlete is in motivation still a toddler, searching for the original maternal object.[38]

Since for Freud the "original object" is represented by an endless series of substitution objects, none of which, however, brings full satisfaction, the doomed quest of eros will generate either the libertine or the ascetic excess—or both. In the Golden Calf narrative, a relentless drive from object to object and a fixation on received forms are both expressions of a debilitating "standard biography." If the Talmudic image of the bride's compulsive infidelity suggests erotic babble, it also reflects an erotic dumbness. For this reason, the tone of sexual fury that informs the imagery of the midrash (the reference to the "fragrance" of the bride) is, as Rav suggests, poignantly tempered by tenderness.

2. *Moses: Intercession as Radical Solidarity*

The Question of the Future

The question that emerges with overwhelming force is the question of the future. Are such compulsive reenactments of a primal ambivalence the inevitable pattern of the future? Clearly, in the midrashic versions of the Golden Calf episode a pockmarked future history of infidelity and intransigence has left its traces. The essential question, then, is of the possibility of *teshuva*, of change. If "love of authority" is the underlying perplexity of human experience, is an authentic relation to the other at all conceivable?

This is the question as Seforno frames it, and as it relates to the "stiff-necked" imagery of God's charge: "They have an iron sinew in their neck, so that they cannot *turn to listen* to the words of any moral teacher. The result is that *there is no hope that they can change.*"[39] In such a situation of moral despair, God issues his dire decree: "Now, let Me be, that My anger may blaze against them and that I may destroy them. And I shall make you into a great people" (32:10).

If the people are incapable of hearing, they are incapable of transformation. Essentially, there has been no exodus from Egypt. Lemming-like, human beings swim toward extinction, with occasional orgiastic outbursts. God's anger has a cold and radical logic: "I shall make *you* into a great nation," evokes God's original promise to Abraham and implies that that pact has been violated. Implicitly, God tells Moses: It is time for a new beginning.

However, in the very words with which God depicts rupture with His people—who are now coldly termed "*this* people"—He virtually undercuts His own decision. "Now, let Me be . . ." God, as it were, asks Moses for permission to destroy. By this tonal modulation, the music of His declaration is profoundly affected. Rashi crystallizes the midrashic reading:

> *"Now, let Me be . . ."* We have not yet heard that Moses prayed for them, and yet God says: "Let Me be . . ." But here, God opened an opening [lit.] for him, and informed him that the issue depended on him: if he would pray for them, He would not destroy them.

Rashi's midrashic source continues:

> "I shall make you into a great nation." Moses replied: Does the merit of Abraham, Isaac, and Jacob not stand against Your anger? How, then, shall my merit stand?[40]

Evoking the merit of the Patriarchs in his prayer of intercession, Moses also rereads God's foundational promise to Abraham: "I shall make you into a great nation" (Gen 12:2). The midrash implies that this is precisely the "opening" that God had made for him, in referring to the promise to Abraham. The manifest meaning of God's invitation to Moses is rupture, discontinuity with the past: "Let us begin the world over again." But by asking for Moses' complicity, in that disturbing phrase, "Now, let Me be . . . Give Me freedom . . ." God has intimated a subversive meaning: "*Do not* let me be . . . Help Me to net the echoes of My original promise to Abraham . . ."

Moses Decodes God's Subconscious Meaning

In terms of the midrashic imagery of adultery, the husband cries for revenge, in a tone of self-evident moral outrage. In tension with that morality, however, God asks Moses to articulate for him a kind of unofficial, idiosyncratic morality: "Why, O God, should Your anger blaze against Your people. . . ?" (32:11). The audacity of the question is inexplicable, unless some alternative moral universe is being indicated.[41]

"Now, let Me be . . ." releases its most radical implications in the Talmudic version:

> R. Abbahu said: If this were not written in the text, it would be impossible to say such a thing. This teaches that Moses seized hold of the Holy One blessed be He, like a man who seizes his fellow by his garment and said before Him: Sovereign of the Universe, I will not let You go until You forgive and pardon them.[42]

"If this were not written in the text, it would be impossible to say such a thing": with this midrashic idiom, we are alerted to an audacious and profound perception. In commonsense terms, it is obvious that the text does not explicitly state that Moses seized hold of God. The midrashic project, however, reaches far beyond such banal observations: it invites us to read again, to open our ears to the complex tonalities of God's speech. If we can hear, we too can be changed. And, once the midrash has alerted us, how can we not hear God's ambivalent plea: "Now just let Me be . . . and I will destroy them. . ."?

The midrashic rhetoric attributes to God a subconscious, an alternative narrative. God responds to an unvoiced protest on the part of Moses. Implicitly, He invites him to persist in his Ancient Mariner narrative passion: "Do not let Me be . . . Only your version of the narrative can save them, can save our shared history . . ." Unconscious speaks to unconscious, as a certain kind of forgetting—Freud's "evenly suspended attention"—supersedes the attempt to fix specific things in memory.

God's covert invitation to Moses can, indeed, be read back into His speech of accusation: "And God spoke to Moses, 'Go, descend . . . They have been quick to turn aside . . .' *And God said to Moses*, 'I have seen that this is a stiff-necked people . . . Now, let Me be . . .' " This speech clearly falls into two parts, separated by the repeated, "And God said to Moses . . ." Nehama

Leibowitz has shown that the structure of the repeated formula, "And He said . . ." indicates a pause, in which the interlocutor fails to respond. First, God accuses the people of infidelity; Moses has no defense. Then, God changes tack, moves to the opposite charge, of rigid attachment to a primary authority figure, and then *proceeds to declare His own rigidity of intent*: "Now, let Me be . . ." That is, if the people are fixated on some indispensable primary object, then God declares His equivalent fixation on revenge. In this context of stiff-necked relentlessness, the only intimation of relief is God's veiled call to Moses to display a responsive obduracy of his own.

In this scenario, Moses is pitched into a war of the Titans: human mythic fixations conflict with the divine will. The clash is absolute and irresoluble: the human must be consumed in divine fire. God's manifest proposal is that Moses cross over, join the God with whom he has become so intimate, and reconstruct, from his own body and spirit, the narrative of the godly in the world: "Now, just let Me be . . . And I shall make you into a great nation . . ." But in the interstices of this official project, God asks Moses to "stand in the breach,"[43] to create a narrative that will bridge between the opposing fixations of man and God.

Adam Phillips writes powerfully on "Just Rage":

> There is no anger . . . that is not revenge; no rage without the betrayal of an ideal, however unconscious, however exorbitant that ideal might be. In my bad temper I expose . . . *my furtive utopianism:* my horrifying, passionate ideal of, and for, myself.[44] (My italics.)

If God's rage expresses a "furtive utopianism," the Zohar seizes that covert divine idealism as it figures God, "unconsciously" urging Moses to disable His anger by revisioning the world:

> When God said to Moses, "Now, let Me be . . . And I shall make you into a great nation . . ." immediately, Moses replied, "For the sake of my own success, should I abandon the cause of Israel? Now, all the nations of the world will say that *I have killed the Israelites, as Noah* [killed the people of his generation]. . . It is better that I should die and Israel not be destroyed!" Immediately, "Moses entreated God . . ."—he sought mercy for them and God's mercy on the world was aroused.[45]

In this startling passage, the Zohar rereads Noah's obedience to God's commands—to build the ark and save his own family as a genetic basis for a future humanity: what looks like normative obedience is in fact collusion in the destruction of the world. Moses perceives the analogy with his own situation and prefers to die, rather than incur such a charge. The moral intuition that Moses articulates constitutes a momentous advance in ethical sensibility: to accept God's offer to found a new nation on Moses, reconstructing history with Moses as patriarch of a revised world, would mean in effect to conspire, like Noah, in destroying the sinful world.

Indeed, the contrast between Moses and Noah may be deciphered from a possible wordplay on *Hanicha li* ("Let Me be . . .") and *Noach* (Noah): God signals to Moses to respond not on the conscious level of His apparent desire to destroy, but on the unconscious level of His desire to save the people; and Moses, unlike Noah, catches the drift of God's intention, rather than unimaginatively obeying His explicit words. Noah becomes the paradigm, then, of an unimaginative literalism, which is harshly judged as murder. This moral vision is Moses' creation, making sense of God's implicit communications. To achieve this order of sensitivity to the *unexpressed* desire, a kind of self-forgetful attention is necessary.

Fire in the Bones

When Moses, in the passage from the Zohar, prefers to die rather commit genocide, he, in effect, makes a judgment on the kind of narcissism that underlies Noah's obedience. Where, one wonders, does the Zohar find any hint of such a readiness on Moses' part? In a later speech, he will explicitly offer, "Erase me from Your book that You have written!" (32:32). "Your book" may indeed refer to the "book of life"; but that sacrificial offer of Moses' life lies in the future. In this first prayer, beginning with the words, "And Moses entreated God . . ." (32:11), there seems to be no basis for such a notion of self-sacrifice: Moses simply refers to God's historical pact with the Israelites and pleads for reprieve from the full extent of God's anger. In the content of this prayer, there is no offer to give his life for his people.

However, the unusual word for Moses' entreaty—*va-yechal*—"And Moses entreated God"—suggests a basis for the Zohar's reading. A classic midrash presses hard on this rare expression for prayer:

> This teaches that Moses stood in prayer until fever (*achilu*—"sickness"—a pun on *va-yechal*—"entreaty") seized him. What is *achilu?* Said R. Eliezer: a fire in the bones.[46]

Va-yechal is decoded to register a fiery intensity that affects Moses' very bones: he becomes "ill with prayer." This intimate fever is Moses' response to the fever of God's anger. Moses answers the implicit invitation of God's unspoken desire; he satisfies the "furtive utopianism" of a blatant rage.[47] In this reversed narrative, in which God speaks to interrogate Moses' moral truth, Moses offers himself, his very bones. *Atzamoth/atzmuth*, bones/the self: the site of this fire is some hard, essential place of identity.

An imaginative reading by Meshech Chochma explores the nature of the "fire in the bones" that inflames Moses' prayer:

> Moses extended his prayer about the Golden Calf until he felt that in his very bones, as well, the same pathology existed. For the father's contribution to the son is the bones;[48] and Moses' grandson was Jonathan, the priest to the idol of Micah. Moses was therefore motivated to pray against God's decree ("I shall destroy them and make you into a great nation"), for in his sons, too, the same defect would be found.[49]

The basis of this imaginative reconstruction is a verse in Judg 18:30, which describes the idolatrous priest, "Jonathan, son of Gershon, son of Me*na*sheh" (with the letter *nun* written small). The Talmud decodes this strange orthography to refer to Moses' grandson, reading "son of *Mosheh*" (the three letters other than the *nun* are the same consonants as in "Moses"). This covert connection between Moses and a priest of idolatry becomes the basis of a psychoanalytic restructuring of Moses' self-awareness. When he "entreats" God, he brings into play the fire that burns in his core of life, in that part of him that will transmit to his heirs. A mere two generations will bring that genetic potential to full bloom: the identity of Moses' grandson will have to be disguised in the biblical text.

In this reading, the fire in Moses' bones proclaims his humanity, his sense of identity with his people. He is no freak of nature; neither is he a divine foundling. Invited to contribute a pure genetic strain for a newly chosen people, he responds by radically identifying with the Golden Calf perplexity. If the licentiousness and frigidity of the bride are to engender inevitable destruction, then he, too, knows himself capable of that same perverse fire.

Such a view of Moses' prayer takes us far beyond the notion of intercession. It implies a sacrifice of the narcissistic myth of difference. Here, Moses makes a clear commitment to one side of his ambiguous identity. For the history of his birth and early life contains elements of uncertainty that, we have suggested, have always fascinated and troubled the people: "this man, Moses, we do not know, never have known, what he is" (32:1). Suspended between heaven and earth, as Satan evokes him in mass hallucination, Moses must decide between death and life, upper world and lower world. The ease with which he relates to the upper world, and with which he converses with God, has been, from the beginning of the narrative, painfully contrasted with his "heaviness of mouth," in speaking with human beings. On the axis joining the divine and the human, he is poised at a point of maximum strain; some natural proclivity makes him tend toward God.

Now, God invites him to abandon the human world in which the erotic life is bound to failure: he is to found a new dynasty. In terms of the midrashic material and of Meshech Chochma's reworking of it, Moses responds by affirming his human identity. The words of his prayer are, in a sense, less important than the fire that informs it, a fire of self-knowledge that brands him as fully human.

The profound paradox of this sacrificial act of self-knowledge is that he redeems not only his people but his own role in their history. In acknowledging a human fire, his own susceptibility to the very evil that threatens his people, he is enabled to place the full weight of his selfhood in the scale of judgment. The first act of this drama of sin and transformation ends with the words, "And God repented of the evil He had intended to do to His people" (32:14).

If, as the Talmud suggests, Moses' prayer is informed by a "fever," a "sickness," we may remember the "sickness of Egypt" that we have already discussed.[50] That sickness was related to a catastrophic deafness; and "exodus from Egypt" is the project of release from that deafness and from the hazards of libertinism and asceticism of which Freud speaks. The ability to hear becomes the key to *teshuva*, to repentance; it involves an erotic quest in which the object can affirm human continuity without deadening human vitality. If Moses, too, has a sickness of fire in his bones, his solidarity with the predicament of his people is affirmed, even as it offers hope for transformation.

The Evil Counter-Narrative: Hated by God?

Indeed, in his first prayer, he refers satirically to the doctrine of inevitable evil: "Why should the Egyptians say: 'In *evil*, He brought them out, in order to kill them in the mountains and to destroy them from off the face of the earth.' . . . And God repented of the *evil* He had intended to do to His people" (32:12, 14). The evil of which Moses speaks is the lowest common denominator of human destiny: the inevitability of death and suffering, the mocking laughter of the gods who offer delusions of release only to "kill them in the mountains." This is the Egyptian counter-narrative, the narrative of necessity.

This narrative, first announced by Pharaoh to Moses in Egypt—"See, *evil* is before your faces" (10:10)[51]—will accompany the Israelites as phantasmagoric possibility throughout their journeys in the desert. At base, the evil of such a narrative is the perception not of the love of God but of His hatred. Indeed, at the end of the desert years, Moses reminds his people of a later, crucial sin—the sin of the Spies—with these words: "You sulked in your tents and said, '*It is because God hates us* that He brought us out of the land of Egypt, to hand us over to the Amorites to obliterate us' " (Deut 1:27).

That is, approximately thirty-nine years after the event, Moses will make an unnerving diagnosis of the national pathology underlying all the rebellions: "You said, 'God hates us and therefore brought us out of Egypt.' " This demonic counter-narrative, of course, gathers plausibility with each massacre and punishment in the wilderness. Its power lies in its intimation of an organic evil informing the whole narrative, and in its radical despair about human "lovability."

The psychological issue—"Are we loved or hated by God?"—is compellingly reworked by Rashi (1:27): what the people are in fact describing is their own hatred for God. This is the repressed evil that Moses finally articulates, a resentment that they project onto God. What other emotion can a human being have for a God who lures one into hope, into the illusion that redemption is possible? Radically, this hatred is focused on Sinai and on the *impiety*, in Burke's sense, of the Sinai project. Uncannily, indeed, the midrash intimates the nexus of Sinai/Sin'ah ("hatred"). In the next section, we shall explore the people's ambivalence at Sinai, and the Golden Calf that is engendered by that failure in love.

At this point, however, I suggest that Moses' achievement in averting the "evil" of God's intention is to deploy his own "sickness" as part of the redemptive narrative. A sinister fire burns in his bones: related to the fire from which the Golden Calf has emerged. A fantasy vision of reality has, for the people, constructed a world in which God's fire is a "consuming fire": in one way or the other, they will inevitably be destroyed. This world of hatred Moses recognizes as, potentially, his own. This recognition is his redemptive gesture. Acknowledging his own complicity in creating such a world, Moses presents to God—and, later, to his people—a possibility of revisioning. Emotional worlds are not, after all, irremediable; they can, over time and with the help of one who speaks the language—the idiolect, in Jonathan Lear's psychoanalytic application of the linguistic term[52]—of that world, be taken apart. This, at any rate, is the project of Moses' intercessions: to intimate the possibility of transformation.

Smashing the Tablets: A People beyond Transformation?

As the narrative continues, we wonder at the sustained energy of these intercessions. In a sense, the story might have ended at this point: God has acceded to Moses' empathic prayer. Yet the narrative continues, circling round and round the same question of the possibility of transformation. In successive encounters, Moses confronts the people, Aaron, God, and again the people, until finally his enigmatically shining face offers a cryptic resolution. The narrative advances and eddies back, repeats and contradicts itself: God forgives, He does not forgive; He will not destroy, He does destroy; He will not personally lead the people to the Holy Land, He does lead them there; His face cannot be seen by a human being, Moses' face is seen by all Israel as a fearful reflection of his encounter with God.

And through all the episodes and encounters runs the question of Moses' identity, of an elusiveness that the "fire in the bones" only partially resolves. "We *do not know* what he is," say the people in frustration, and abandon him to the heavens. "Moses *did not know* that the skin of his face radiated light," says the Torah at the end of the story, without narrating any crisis of knowledge.

The first episode that follows Moses' prayer violently ruptures any illusion of closure: Moses comes down from the mountain and discovers the people dancing around the Golden Calf. In great anger, he smashes the tablets of stone, inscribed with the finger of God. That is, although God has revealed the people's sin to him at the top of the mountain, a traumatic revelation yet awaits him at the base: "As soon as Moses came near the camp and saw the calf and the dancing, he became enraged; and he hurled the tablets from his hands and shattered them at the foot of the mountain" (32:19).

The issue of sin and forgiveness is apparently not at all closed: for Moses, it represents a wound that continually gapes anew. What is it that so outrages him that the closure at the top of the mountain avails him so little at the base? Seforno points to the new element in the narrative, the knot of an unbearable revelation:

> "When he saw the calf *and the dancing*, he became enraged . . .": When he saw how they rejoiced at their own ruin—as we find in Jeremiah 11:15: "You exult while performing your evil deeds." At this, Moses became infuriated and he despaired of any possible repair for such distortion or of any possible return to their integrity, when they might be capable of receiving the tablets of the Law.

Seforno takes the pulse of the Golden Calf event: it is this pulse, the life-beat of the dance, which enrages Moses and hurls him into a new despair. Of this orgiastic joy he had received no hint at the top of the mountain. In this new perception lies the difference between the two perspectives—from above and from below. From above, the Golden Calf is farce and fickleness, or tragedy and impotence; from below, it is comedy, in the real sense—that is, order, vitality, fertility. It is precisely this jubilation, this rediscovered harmony of old pieties, that reveals to Moses the true, empirical dimensions of the moment.

The Calf-Dance: An Ecstasy beyond Prayer

These dimensions are related to the problem of living within time. Having just experienced the terror of Moses' "lateness"—the discontinuity of identity effected by the loss of the object, the sense of self thrown up on some alien shore—the people now have recourse to a profound consolation: the oceanic sense of merging with the other in an ultimate harmony—the pulse of the dance. Selfhood, difference, is lost in an eternal present, without either memory or desire, shame or disappointment. The circle-dance is a figure for eternal recurrence, for oceanic wholeness; the people dance round the Calf in grotesque parody of such wholeness.[53]

Unprepared, Moses witnesses the *shamelessness* of the Golden Calf moment. Here, indeed, is the source of his despair—the absence of conflict, of any apparent basis for revisioning the event. Indeed, the proof-text quoted by Seforno has Jeremiah similarly deploring the joy-in-evil of his people; on which Radak comments: "They feel no *shame* in their evil." Shameless, the people's nerve ends are cauterized; they dance in a timeless ecstasy in relation to which reflection and re-creation are foreign modalities.

On this reading, Moses breaks the Tablets of Stone because he senses the irresoluble situation of the people. Their joy and shamelessness undermine all possibility of change; they articulate a version of reality, a "piety," in Kenneth Burke's terminology, that finds unalloyed exhilaration in regressing to a world before time. Moses' anger, then, is one in which the "furtive utopianism" of God's anger no longer seems to have a basis. Without conflict or reservation, the people's "piety" places them beyond transformation.[54] In all the blatant vitality of the dance, there is a hypnotic, fixed quality that makes alternative visions of reality unimaginable.

This unconflicted state, indeed, is the very essence of the Golden Calf moment. The Ishbitzer,[55] for instance, defines this moment as the desire for a total vision, without history, without development, without—significantly—*prayer.* In such an aesthetic mode, all is seen simultaneously, structurally, architecturally. Life within history, the waves moving toward culmination and ruin, the history of obsolescence, is avoided. The disintegration of the flesh, the instabilities of desire, the knowledge of reality as "ruins-in-the-making"—these humiliations are obscured in an ecstatic vision.

Strikingly, the Ishbitzer sets the Golden Calf in the context of the theme that immediately precedes it: Shabbath (31:12–17). For Shabbath represents an intimation of that oceanic reality, of the ultimate "day that is entirely Shabbath," when an ultimate harmony will become manifest. This consummation devoutly to be wished will make prayer irrelevant, since prayer is the expression of those who live within time and must implore God for glimpses of meaning. To be obliged to pray every day, three times every day, is to be a volatile creature, barred from total and timeless revelations. However, such a consummation uncannily evokes the totality of death, which, as Hamlet ruefully acknowledges, may, like sleep, have its own bad dreams:

To die, to sleep—
No more, and by a sleep to say we end
The heart-ache, and the thousand natural shocks
That flesh is heir to; 'tis a consummation
Devoutly to be wished to die to sleep!
To sleep, perchance to dream, ay there's the rub,
For in that sleep of death what dreams may come
When we have shuffled off this mortal coil
Must give us pause . . .[56]

It is possible that behind the Ishbitzer's meditation on the Golden Calf lies a pun on the word *egel*, Calf. In Aramaic, *be-agala* means "very soon, immediately, swiftly."[57] The predicament of the people is focused, therefore, on the desire to consummate the turbulence of time; they are guilty of a spiritual arrogance that violates the modesties of human perception. They cannot sustain a kind of existential patience in vicissitude, in "delay." In Winnicott's expression, a "madness" of loss leads them into an ecstasy that unnerves Moses with its hunger.

In this ecstasy of full possession, the people, essentially, deny loss and the need for symbolic substitutions. If time has no meaning, the conscious separateness of self, the distance between self and all that is "not-me," ceases to exist. Precisely here, in this timeless, unmediated totality, is the site of Moses' despair. It is this modality that Seforno identifies with the "dancing" round the Calf that constitutes the "great sin" of the people.[58] This expression Moses reiterates several times in his reproaches to the people and to Aaron and in his prayers to God. In Seforno's radical reading, the "great sin" is not the mere fact of making the idol; rather, it is the unequivocal joy that seals the soul against transformation.

The "crooked timber of humanity"[59] is, then, the subject of Moses' revelation at the bottom of the mountain. From the perspective of "below," he witnesses the orgiastic release of their dancing; and smashes the God-inscribed tablets.

This moment is one of absolute loneliness for Moses. Above, at the mountaintop, he had identified with the human, had acknowledged the intimate "fire in the bones," the predicament of idol-desire that unites him with his people. But now, below, he sees that the people are *paru'a*—"out of control" (32:25). Seforno translates: "He saw them *exposed*, their secret joy revealed." There is no conflict, no one to speak with a different voice. And Moses is isolated, in a way that was unimaginable "above," at the mountaintop.

Perhaps, the anguish of his situation can be read in the biblical play on words: *va-yechal*—"he entreated" (32:11) and *mecholoth*—"dancing." That is, the Moses who, "above," implored God for forgiveness out of a profound solidarity with his people, out of a knowledge of the fire in his own bones, recognizes with a new shock, "below," the force of that fire when he witnesses the sheer passion of the dance at the mountain base. At this moment, nothing remains for him but to smash the divinely written tablets.

Solidarity and Loneliness

Why does he smash these tablets? A classic midrash narrates that the "letters flew away into the air"; and the tablets became crushingly heavy.[60] It is the structures of symbolic meaning that Sinai had yielded him that "fly away." Without these structures, deeply engraved into the human heart, there is only stony residue. This is the reading of Sefath Emeth:[61] Moses witnesses the failure of God's words to find a real place within the hearts of the people. As they dance, he sees the words of Sinai flicker and vanish. In smashing the tablets, then, he enacts the unbearable heaviness of their hearts, of his heart.

Breaking the tablets is, in a sense, Moses' supreme act of identification with his people. Rather than separate from them, sustaining his own deeply engraved awareness of God's words, of the lightness-within-heaviness that is the revelation of Sinai, he enacts an ultimate personal solidarity with them. The meaning of this solidarity becomes problematic when we explore the real and apparently impassable distance that opens up at this juncture between Moses and his people. This is the distance that I have called his "loneliness." It is in full awareness of loneliness that Moses smashes the tablets. The nexus of loneliness and solidarity is the theme I should like to explore at this point.

Tragic Realization: The Tablets as Fetish?

Moses' loneliness is, I suggest, one facet of the secret that is revealed to him with unprecedented force at the base of the mountain. The dazzled joy of the dancing exposes a hidden truth. One way of expressing that truth, as we have seen, is articulated by Sefath Emeth: the letters, the words of God, have left no deep imprint in their hearts. A deeper desire possesses them: for any object, any fetish, with which they can lose their self-consciousness, their entrapment in time. If Moses, as idealized object, has failed them, they turn to the Golden Calf in a reflexive motion towards an idiom of their time.[62]

For Moses, this moment is one of traumatic, retroactive understanding. The orgiastic release of the people's dancing tells him what his own role has been for them. This is the profound loneliness that leads him to smash the tablets. For he realizes that the fetishism he is witnessing represents a fantasy in which he too had figured. His loneliness is born of the distance between the person and the uses to which the persona is put.

Moses, therefore, smashes the tablets, not in pique, but in a tragic realization that a people so hungry for absolute possession may make a fetish of the tablets as well.[63] The whole narrative of redemption has now been pathologically restructured for him: the tablets of revelation take on the macabre lineaments of another idol.

3. *The Murdered Prophet: Repressed Memory and the Power of Religious Tradition*

Resisting Sinai: Killing the Prophet

We have traced a number of related themes—the ambivalence about time and human timefulness, the two faces of idolatry, the counter-narrative of hatred that endangers the future, the mutual mirroring of Moses' processes and those of the people. These interwoven themes become intolerably—explosively—congested at the moment of the Golden Calf. This is the moment when the people strain most painfully under the weight of Sinai. In their fantasy, fetishes of all kinds give form to experience. At Sinai, God forbids the most radical desires of the human heart. If, as the midrash asserts, Sinai means *Sin'ah*—hatred—for the nations of the world,[64] the midrashic narratives around the Golden Calf ponder the implications of that hatred. Here, the hatred of the nations for the newly mapped world of Sinai, for the heroic demands that world makes of them, is introjected inward, into the hatred of God's people for the messages and messengers of Sinai.

This hatred is expressed most violently in the midrashic notion that it engenders not only idolatry but murder. The victim is Hur, Moses' nephew, son of Miriam, his sister. Rashi cites this midrash in his commentary:

> "And Aaron saw . . ." In the midrash:[65] he saw many things. He saw Hur, his nephew, who had rebuked the people and was killed by them.
>
> "And he built an altar . . ." He understood (a pun on *va-yiven*—building/understanding) from the one who was sacrificed in his presence (a pun on *mizbeach*—altar/from the sacrificed one).[66]

In this provocative midrash, Aaron collaborates with the idolators because he realizes the murderous intensity of their need. They have found a scapegoat for their own fury of abandonment. Representing Moses and the Sinai revelation, Hur, who was left with Aaron as substitute for Moses when he ascended the mountain,[67] quietly disappears from the text. The midrash notes this disappearance and decodes it as a repressed sacrifice: the people have acted out their love/hatred in a scene of horror that is then repressed in the text of the Torah. In other words, this murder is the most significant element in the history of the Golden Calf, significant precisely because it has been masked. And Aaron's collaboration with the people is, at root, a movement of fear in the face of their passion.

One expression of the people's love/hate ambivalence is to construct symbols and prophets into idols; another is to destroy them: ". . . each single struggle of ambivalence loosen[s] the fixation of the libido to the object by disparaging it, denigrating it and even as it were killing it."[68] Resisting the object, the authoritative narrative, the subject, however, then renews the idolatrous cycle: "The manic subject plainly demonstrates his liberation from the object which was the cause of his suffering, by seeking like a ravenously hungry man for new object-cathexes."[69]

The Nations of the World: Hatred, Murder, Suicide

In the case of the "nations of the world," the hatred of Sinai is relatively uncomplicated. It is the subject, for instance, of George Steiner's meditations on anti-Semitism in *In Bluebeard's Castle*. The argument is simple: the "invention" of monotheism is responsible for the world's hatred of the people who perpetuated it: "The abruptness of the Mosaic revelation, the finality of the creed at Sinai, tore up the human psyche by its most ancient roots. The break has never really knit."[70] "Hitler's jibe that 'conscience is a Jewish invention' provides a clue," writes Steiner.[71] The strangeness of the monotheistic idea, the sense that the Mosaic revelation, perhaps all revelation, comes as an "interruption" to normality—these exerted unbearable pressure on the human spirit. Image-making imagination itself was banned; an unimaginable abstraction replaced them.

Under such intolerable pressure, humanity took revenge, on one level, by "murdering God." Steiner quotes Nietzsche at length:

> "Whereto has God gone," he cried. I shall tell you! "We have slain him—you and I! All of us are his murderers! . . . How shall we comfort ourselves, who are killers above all killers? The holiest and mightiest that the world had hitherto possessed has bled to death under our knives—who shall wipe that blood off us?"[72]

Resentful of centuries of suffering under the unattainable ideal of the one God, Western culture has murdered Him. More concretely, they have murdered the Jews who conveyed His strenuous message to the world. "The holocaust . . . speaks for a world both older than Sinai and newer than Nietzsche."[73] In making Moses an Egyptian in his last work, *Moses and Monotheism*, Freud was making a sacrificial move: too late, he was "trying to wrench the lightning rod" out of the hands of the Jewish people.

> The demands of Judaism, of Christianity, of messianic socialism, all presented Western culture with what Ibsen called, "the claims of the ideal." All originated with the Jews and, ultimately, produced hatred, the hatred for the unattainable. "The Jew became, as it were, the 'bad conscience' of Western history."[74]

Steiner's case is passionately felt and worded: the Holocaust is the final solution to an unrest introduced into the world at Sinai. In "The Defence of A. H," Steiner has Hitler himself make the case against the Jews: "You are not Godkillers, but *Godmakers*. And that is infinitely worse. The Jews invented conscience and left man a guilty serf."[75] The Holocaust is European civilization's revenge against the high ideals of Sinai.

The simplicity of Steiner's case is, however, only apparent. Clearly the hatred of the Jews is hatred of inextricable elements within the European identity. Steiner quotes Kafka: " 'He who strikes a Jew strikes down man/mankind' (den Menschen)." For the European, the Jew represents the residue of his own idealism; his destruction is a "self-mutilation."[76] The Holocaust is, at its heart, an act of suicide.

The Israelites: A Repressed Murder

The area that Steiner does not confront, however, is that of Jewish ambivalence. In the midrashic narratives of the Golden Calf, we find this ambivalence, the love and the hatred for the Sinai demand, writ large. Under the wedding canopy, the bride plays the harlot. Moses is barely a day late in descending the mountain, and he is replaced by a calf. And, masked in the narrative, the people murder the prophet: Moses realizes that his own people have, in absentia, as it were, murdered him. Hur's murder is repressed in the text of the Torah; it returns, with greater power, to haunt the future history of the people.

In terms of our discussion, this theme of prophet-murder, "Moses-murder," is crucial. It forms the core of Moses' experience, of the "loneliness" of his return to the world "below." In this experience, he realizes not simply the inconstancy of the people ("How could they forget so fast?") but their inner deadening, their stiff-neckedness, that closes them off from vital experience. ("Perhaps they are incapable of hearing, of knowing anything at all?") The "insatiable love of authority-figures"[77] breeds both excesses: libertinism and asceticism. It isolates Moses; in fantasy, it kills him.

The killing of the prophet, of the charismatic leader is, of course, the central motif of Freud's *Moses and Monotheism.* Here, Freud speculates about the uncanny survival of Jewishness, in the most radical sense, about the phenomenology of religious tradition:

> There is an element of grandeur about everything to do with the origin of a religion, certainly including the Jewish one, and this is not matched by the explanations we have hitherto given. Some other factor must be involved to which there is little that is analogous and nothing that is of the same kind, something unique and something of the same order of magnitude as what has come out of it, as religion itself.[78]

The power of a religion to hold the loyalty and imagination of its followers over many generations requires some explanation that transcends conscious transmission. For Freud, the explanation lies in repressed collective memory: the original murder of the primal father is reenacted in the murder of Moses, an Egyptian monotheistic teacher and leader, by the Israelites. Yosef Hayim Yerushalmi writes of the "shock of recognition,"[79] through which the Israelites are reunited with their long lost Father in the teachings of Moses. However, it is only when the primal parricide is repeated, when Moses is slain and his teachings forgotten, that the power of Jewish tradition becomes a "trilling wire in the blood,"[80] a compelling force in the life of the people. The repressed returns to grip the imagination of the people:

> Fate had brought the great deed and misdeed of primeval days, the killing of the father, closer to the Jewish people by causing them to repeat it on the figure of Moses, an outstanding father-figure. It was a case of "acting out" instead of remembering . . .[81]

When the repressed memory of Moses' murder returns, it has invaded, in incalculable ways, the blood and nerves of the people.

In a felicitous turn of phrase, Yerushalmi terms Freud's theory, "psycho-Lamarckism." He criticizes Freud's transition from individual to group psychology, and his use of the notion of the transmission of acquired characteristics which makes such a transition possible. At the same time, Yerushalmi focuses on the "essential drama" of *Moses and Monotheism*, the enigma of religious tradition, of an allegiance that survives the centuries, lies not in conscious teachings and practices but in the unconscious force of a repressed knowledge.

In his final chapter, "Monologue with Freud," Yerushalmi engages Freud in a Talmudic debate, deploying arguments on both sides. He dismisses Freud's "phylogenetic fantasy," on the grounds that biblical and rabbinic traditions are extraordinarily honest in condemning the violence and rebellions of the people: so traumatic an event as the murder of Moses could hardly be concealed in such an ethical climate. To flesh out his point, Yerushalmi cites several examples of such narratives of rebellion and murder. If Moses had indeed been murdered, this too would have been recorded, "eagerly and implacably, in the most vivid detail, the quintessential and ultimate exemplum of the sin of Israel's disobedience."[82]

Within such a tradition of explicit vilification of the people, therefore, Yerushalmi argues, the notion of repression is simply not to the point. The significance of *Moses and Monotheism* lies in Freud's "uniquely powerful formulation" of the question of the phenomenology of Jewish religious tradition. To speak of the "memory of a people" is to engage in a "psychological metaphor, useful, but not to be literalized."[83]

This criticism of Freud raises important issues. But perhaps Freud's solution to the mystery of religious memory merits another reading. Yerushalmi dismisses rather airily Freud's hypothetical response to his list of overt rebellions and murders:

> You may also try to turn the tables on me and even welcome the texts I have brought forward, regarding them as "screen memories" that merely mask the original origin and fate of Moses. That, of course, is your prerogative. But in so doing you would be ignoring the essential character of Jewish tradition . . .[84]

To evoke the essential character of Jewish tradition in rebuttal of such a notion is perhaps to beg the question. For while I hold no brief for the historical solution, the "phylogenetic fantasy" proposed by Freud, it does seem that Jewish tradition has included suggestive margins around the recorded acts of rebellion, margins of evocation that would indeed shift the balance between the written and the unwritten, open up intimations of Moses-murder, figured on a surface that exposes profound movements of spiritual tension.

The Return of the Repressed

Before turning to these midrashic indications, I would like to notice some important work on Freud's *Moses and Monotheism*, published since Yerushalmi's analysis. Jacques Derrida,[85] Jan Assmann,[86] and Richard Bernstein[87] have all written of the significance of unconscious memory traces in the transmission of *suppressed* oral traditions. Bernstein summarizes the findings of Derrida and Assmann. Freud's problem is to explain "the discontinuity and reversal of a tradition (as well as its continuity)." Equally, he must explain "the power and intensity with which a long-dormant religious tradition can re-assert itself." Conscious mental processes are insufficient to account for "the *unconscious* dynamics involved in reception and resistance to tradition."[88] Besides conscious oral traditions and rituals, on the one hand, and biological genetic coding, on the other, there exists a third possibility: the survival of unconscious memory traces.

> Freud maintains that communication that takes place between human beings is *never* exhausted by what is conscious and explicitly communicated. This is not only true among contemporaries but also in the transgenerational communication that constitutes a living tradition.[89]

He quotes Assmann on the cultural significance of the concept of latency and the return of the repressed: "Since Freud, no theory of culture can afford not to take these concepts into consideration. The old concept of tradition has proved insufficient."[90]

The murder of the prophet as a powerful memory trace affecting the reception of and resistance to religious tradition is precisely what we find in the midrashic narratives to which we now turn. The killing of Hur, narrated in Midrash Rabba and enshrined in Rashi's text, is, of course, an example of the "return of the repressed": it is veiled, unreadable, in the text of the Torah, marked only by an enigmatic absence. On three significant occasions, Hur was mentioned together with Aaron;[91] from now on, Aaron figures alone. The midrash about prophet-murder, that is, serves as a repressed memory; it is susceptible to the disavowals of the reader, as well as to the shock of recognition.

A primal image of the dead prophet hovers in midair, "suspended between heaven and earth."[92] Fear and fascination gather round it; as do other conscious, semiconscious, and unconscious memories. Some are explicit: Jeremiah is almost lynched in the Temple (Jer 2:26); Zechariah, son of Yehoyada, the priest, is stoned by order of King Josaiah (2 Chr 24:21). The midrash also tells of more actual killings, not explicitly given in biblical sources: Jeremiah was, in fact, murdered and buried; Shemaiah the prophet and Ahijah the Shilonite were killed by their kings; and even Isaiah was "sawed apart with a saw" by King Hezekiah, son of Menasseh.[93]

Such midrashic material touches on the unacknowledged strata of violence in the national memory. What reads in the biblical texts as thwarted intention is consummated in the midrashic texts; a macabre excess of hatred for God's messengers is, time and time again, surrealistically acted out. Suppressed in the texts, this excess signals the intense fascination of God's word; such indescribable passion can be generated only by a fraught relationship between the human being and the divine.

The murder of Hur is, effectively, a double "screen memory"; that is, it is concealed, and it itself conceals the real desire of the people: to kill Moses. The murder is illustrated in the midrash by a proof-text from Jeremiah (2:34): "Even on your skirts is human blood to be found." One commentary, Or HaChaim, explicitly connects this bloodstain with a desire to kill *Aaron;* and reads: " 'The people gathered *against* Aaron' (32:1)—to kill him." A bloodstain on the skirt: the trace of a repressed history. "It is not hinted at in the Torah, so that its imprint should not sully the future honor of the people." But it is intimated in Hur's sudden disappearance and in the bloodstained verse from Jeremiah.

Or HaChaim virtually foreshadows Freud in his play on the notion of repression and recovery. The full shame of the Golden Calf story is concealed, he suggests, since it serves no purpose other than as an exemplum for collective transformation. For this purpose, a minimal version of the story is revealed, screening the violence and shame for which no words can be found.

Perhaps the most powerful example of the idolatrous and iconoclastic vortex that issues in prophet-murder is that narrated in Numbers 14:10, during the incident of the Spies: "And the entire community threatened to stone them with stones, when the glory of God appeared . . ." On the conscious level, the narrative tells of Caleb and Joshua, rescued at the last moment by the fire of God's presence.

However, Yerushalmi himself quotes a midrash in which the repressed implications of this biblical story are spelled out:

> And who were they? Moses and Aaron. [But the verse continues] *when the glory of God appeared [in the tent of meeting to all the children of Israel].* This teaches us that they [the Israelites] were throwing stones and the Cloud [of God's glory] would intercept them.[94]

A serious attempt is made on the lives of Moses and Aaron. This is not a mere intention[95] and its victims are not secondary figures, Joshua and Caleb, as in the biblical story of the Spies. The murder is prevented, or rather it is absorbed by the Cloud. More than this, however, the midrash hints at the veiled fantasy of the people, reading the sentence as a run-on statement: ". . . And the people threatened to stone *them and the glory of God.*" The object of the people's anger is only apparently Joshua and Caleb; even Moses and Aaron are only manifestations of the hidden object of their hatred. It is the glory of God that is the target of their stones and it is the glory of God that absorbs them, so that no trace is left on the surface of the narrative.[96]

In this sense, Freud's notion of repressed strata of national memory has an expressive power that Yerushalmi does not sufficiently recognize. While it is true that Jewish tradition takes an almost masochistic interest in self-excoriation, the most potent material in that tradition is precisely the unwritten material, the midrashic material. It is this that has created the trilling wire in the blood, the compelling power of a repressed and recovered passion.

Moses as Traumatized Prophet: The Elijah Syndrome

Such midrashic retrievals of unconscious memory open up opaque or ambiguous texts. The stoning is ambiguous in two senses: in the identity of the victims and in the structure of the sentence; while the ghost of Hur emerges unexpectedly from a perfectly satisfactory "conscious" reading of the text. In terms of the experience of the reviled prophet himself, a similar "doubleness" can be imagined. Moses confronts the people who have just murdered his *alter ego*, his displaced self. The moment is one of intimate destruction: a narrative of meaning and hope has been violated by the sensed realities of dependence and resentment. Moses learns, unmistakably, that for his people he has been divine, adored, and disparaged, that he represents that charismatic otherness to which his people would surrender their own power and then, at the first hint of disillusion, would stone it in petulant betrayal.[97]

The loneliness of such a knowledge is Moses' situation as he reenters the world "below." But his response to that loneliness—or, rather, his refusal of obvious responses—compels wonder. The reflexive reaction of the traumatized prophet does not need to be imagined. We find it written out in full pathos, in the narrative of Elijah, who, in a companion piece to the Golden Calf betrayal, flees into the desert and bemoans his fate:

> He arose and ate and drank; and with the strength from that meal he walked forty days and forty nights as far as the mountain of God at Horev. There he went into a cave, and there he spent the night.
>
> Then the word of God came to him. He said to him, "Why are you here, Elijah?" He replied, "I am moved by zeal for God, the God of Hosts; for the Israelites have forsaken Your covenant, torn down Your altars, and have put Your prophets to the sword. I alone am left, and they are out to take my life." "Come out," He called, "and stand on the mountain before God."
>
> And lo, God passed by. There was a great and mighty wind, splitting mountains and shattering rocks by the power of God; but God was not in the wind. After the wind—an earthquake; but God was not in the earthquake. After the earthquake—fire; but God was not in the fire. And after the fire—a sound of thin silence. When Elijah heard it, he wrapped his mantle about his face and went and stood at the entrance of the cave. Then a voice addressed him: "Why are you here, Elijah?" He answered, "I am moved by zeal for God, the God of Hosts; for the Israelites have forsaken Your covenant, torn down Your altars, and have put Your prophets to the sword. I alone am left, and they are out to take my life."
>
> God said to him, "Go back by the way you came, and on to the wilderness of Damascus. When you get there, anoint Hazael as king of Aram. Also anoint Jehu son of Nimshi as king of Israel, and anoint Elisha, son of Shaphat of Avel-meholah, to succeed you as prophet."[98]

Sole survivor of the massacre of God's prophets, Elijah cries with self-conscious pathos to God: "I alone am left—and they are out to take my life!" God's answer is indirect, enigmatic. Like Moses, Elijah has withdrawn from human society for forty days and forty nights; like Moses, too, he has entered a cave—indeed, "*the* cave on the mountain of God at Horev." Now, God tells him to go out and receive divine revelation: like Moses, he is to stand on the mountain in God's presence. Again like Moses, he experiences the raging tempest, the shattering wind, the quaking earth, the consuming fire; in none of these phenomena, however, does he find God. Finally, after the fire; he hears "a sound of thin silence." Significantly, however, God does not explicitly say, "There is God."

The end of the scene has Elijah at the mouth of the cave, with God interrogating him about his experience: "Why are you here, Elijah?" And Elijah woodenly repeats, word for word, his previous incantation of self-pity and resentment. As in Sartre's notion of *mauvaise foi*, Elijah is *acting himself*, he has not *heard* God's answer, he has not heard the voice in the thin silence. And God tells him to anoint Elisha as prophet in his place. In the words of Rashi's commentary: "I cannot deal with your kind of prophecy, since you act the prosecutor against My children."[99]

In this powerful scene, Elijah disqualifies himself from the role of prophet: he responds to the loneliness of his position with a reflexive paranoia and anger. He enacts the murdered prophet, vilifying his murderers. Worse, he *repeats* the act after God has intimated to him an alternative response. If God is to be found, Elijah must abandon the high drama of prophetic anger, the posture of the rejected messenger of God. Wind, earthquake, fire—all the symbols of the first revelation at Sinai—"God is not there." If God is to be found in the "sound of thin silence," then Elijah must find Him. This is no banal discovery, buttressed by conventions of Revelation: God manifested in fire, earthquake, and tempest. This is a subtle God, silent, modest, who needs a prophet to discover Him. Elijah fails to be that prophet, as he mouths truisms about the people's evil and his own pathos.

Most compelling in the narrative are the implicit references to Moses' similar situation: forty days, the mountain of God at Horev, the cave,[100] the wind-quake-fire epiphany. Yet Moses' spiritual inventiveness emerges with greater force for the comparison: his response to the "murdered prophet" situation avoids all the postures of self-pity, self-aggrandizement, fear, and vilification. Elijah's robot response at first seems entirely plausible. It is only after he has repeated it that its calcified, deadened character becomes obvious. Like the people, he is exposed as "stiff-necked," deaf to the voice of the thin silence.

Elijah has abandoned the one essential role of the true prophet: to be, in Yochanan Muffs's expression, His Majesty's Loyal Opposition. That is, to free himself of reflex reactions, to transcend the standard vocabularies of hatred and fear, and invent a narrative of transformation for his people. In his failure, he evokes the paradigm of Moses, who was confronted with the same despair, the same grotesquely deadened reality as Elijah. Radically isolated by the people's hatred and love,[101] Moses, however, had discovered a visionary, redemptive response. Because of this response, he had become *the* prophet of God.

4. *The Renewed Covenant: Vision and Effacement* 

Moses' Response: A Summary

What, then, is Moses' response? Or—to phrase the question differently—what is the purpose of extending the narrative of prayer, punishment, and forgiveness, over so many scenes, beyond the core narrative at the top of the mountain? If we outline the events ensuing on the smashing of the tablets, we produce the following summary: Moses burns the Golden Calf and forces people to drink its dissolved powder; he interrogates Aaron, who weakly replies; he invites the Levites, who proclaim themselves "for God," to kill the guilty Israelites—three thousand of them; he accuses the people of their "great sin" and returns to the mountaintop to intercede again for them; God threatens punishment of the guilty, withdraws His presence from the people, and sends a plague against the guilty; God repeats that an angel will now replace Him in leading the people; the people mourn their loss; Moses withdraws from the camp and sets up his Tent of Assembly outside the camp, the people watching from the rear as he recedes to his tent to speak with God; Moses intercedes again; God accedes to his prayer; Moses asks to see God's glory; God refuses to show His face, but agrees to let Moses see His "back" from the crevice in the rock; Moses is told to hew out a new set of stone tablets, on which God will again inscribe the words of the Covenant; as he gives Moses these second tablets, God speaks His Thirteen Attributes; Moses again prays for God to lead the people and God renews His Covenant; finally, Moses descends from the mountain with the second set of tablets, unaware of the light irradiating his face. He speaks to the people and then covers his face with a veil; this becomes a pattern of veiling and unveiling in Moses' future encounters with God and with the people.

Even in this brief summary, Moses clearly emerges as the one constant figure in the multiple dialogues of the narrative. Repeatedly, he prays to God, presses for his desire: "May God go in our midst," and minimizes God's partial concessions. He offers to sacrifice his own personal destiny, his narcissistic interest in his own narrative: "Erase me from Your book . . ." In effect, he sacrifices the conventional, narratively gratifying pose of martyred prophet, the Sturm und Drang of an epic role.

He refuses to play such a role because it casts the people into the corresponding role of villain. Instead, he volunteers to be entirely effaced from the narrative. Or, when that offer is rejected, he enters a dance with God and the people: a dance in which his back, not his face, is seen by the people, and in which God's back, not His face, is seen by Moses. Ultimately, in the second version of the Covenant, and as sign of God's renewed Presence, he brings another set of tablets and a face radiating light, which is sometimes seen and sometimes effaced.

The Pivotal Moment: "Please Show Me Your Glory!"

The center of gravity in the narrative is the moment when Moses apparently interrupts his project of intercession and asks God for a personal revelation: "Please show me Your glory!" (33:18). In fact, this is not an interruption but a coda to a successful prayer: God has acceded to his desire that He "go with us": "Even this thing that you have spoken I shall do, for you have found favor in My eyes" (33:17). Essentially, the Golden Calf narrative might have ended at this point. But inspired by his success, Moses continues: "Please show me Your glory!" and God replies enigmatically:

> "I will make all My goodness pass before you, and I will proclaim before you the name God, and the grace that I grant and the compassion that I show." And He said, "You cannot see My face, for man may not see Me and live." And God said, "See, there is a place near Me. Station yourself on the rock and, as My glory passes by, I will put you in a cleft of the rock and shield you with My hand until I have passed by. Then I will take away My hand and you will see My back; but My face must not be seen." (33:19–23)

This is the point where the narrative digresses, apparently, from the agenda of national forgiveness and renewal to the private, mystical concerns of Moses. God's face, and His back, become literalized in a way that even the Revelation at Mount Sinai has not approached: God's hand will cover Moses' face and will uncover it; he will see one part of God but not the other.

A specific sense of body is deployed to suggest a mystical vocabulary that alone can convey the ineffable. This is Moses' most personal prayer; God's fullest response is to pass by his face and call out His Thirteen Attributes.

Immediately, Moses falls to the ground in obeisance and presses his last prayer on God: "If I have gained Your favor, O God, please let God go in our midst, even though this is a stiff-necked people. Pardon our iniquity and our sin, and take us for Your own!" (34:8–9). Here, Moses resumes his role as intercessor, apparently repeating his previous petition (33:15–16). To this last prayer, God responds by renewing the Covenant and teaching Moses its laws.

The question of structure emerges with compelling force: how does Moses' desire for personal mystical revelation mesh with the narrative of sin and forgiveness? It is remarkable that while he speaks in the first person singular when he asks for the vision of God's glory, he modulates to the first person *plural* in v. 9: "If *I* have gained your favor . . . let God go in *our* midst . . . pardon *our* iniquity and *our* sin, and take *us* for Your own!" At the culmination of Moses' work of prayer, he identifies with the sin of the people; quietly, undramatically, the pronouns change. The fire in his bones is, by this point, so thoroughly integrated that it sparks out unself-consciously in his syntax. Apparently minor inflections of his voice manifest his solidarity with his people and his transcendence of paranoid and narcissistic postures. Moses has found his *own* "voice in the thin silence": he speaks with a quiet normalcy that seems to emerge seamlessly from the vision he has just experienced.

His reference to "*our* sin" is set in high relief against his earlier pronouns. Reproaching the people, he used the rhetoric of "*You* . . . *I*" "*You* have sinned—*I* shall go up. . . *I* shall atone for *your* sin." Pleading with God, he spoke of "*this* people . . . *their* sin . . . Erase *me* . . ." (32:30–33). It is only in the prayer that leads to the vision of the cave and to God's final forgiveness that Moses begins to modulate from *I* to *we*: "For how shall it be known that Your people have gained Your favor unless You go with *us*, so that *we* may be distinguished, *Your people and I*, from every people on the face of the earth?" (33:16). God's reply still focuses on Moses' personal grace as the reason for His favor. Only after the revelation of the cave does Moses make the last movement to full solidarity with the people: "Pardon *our* iniquity and *our* sin . . ."

The Time of Favor: Knowing How to Lose

The narrative, then, pivots on the uncanny moment of Moses' request to "see Your glory" (33:18). Rashi conveys this as a crucial moment: "Moses saw that it was a time of favor, that his words were acceptable. He therefore made a further request to show him the vision of His glory." Moses intuits this as a "time of favor": there is a tide in the affairs of men and Moses senses the flow of love. The very expression, "a time of favor," is, of course, deeply anthropomorphic: it speaks from the experience of the human being that lives within the ebbs and flows of time. To adopt a geological metaphor, what shift has affected the plates, the strata of human experience, so that a unique moment of transformation becomes possible?

The two episodes just narrated provide a clue. In the first, the people heard God's decree, removing Himself from among them, "for it is a stiff-necked people": an angel is to substitute for the divine Presence. "And the people heard this evil thing and they mourned, and no one put on his finery" (33:3–4). This is the moment when unseen geological strata are perceived to have shifted: in kabbalistic terminology, God moves from anger to love.

This is the first allusion to the people's mysterious "finery," which appears for the first time in the text, just as it is relinquished. Much interpretive ink has been spilled in the attempt to decode this "finery." Let us simply suggest that some accessory virtue "from the mountain of Horev" (33:6) had attached itself to them in the first Revelation: some splendid immunity or power,[102] a sense of oceanic merging. But a ridge had formed on the wave and had left them stranded from God. In stripping themselves of this "finery," of a factitious omnipotence, the people initiate the "work of mourning": they acknowledge their loss, and begin to move into the world of desire and of language.

This theme, of loss, mourning, and melancholy, is Julia Kristeva's subject in *Black Sun*: "My depression points to my not knowing how to lose—I have perhaps been unable to find a valid compensation for the loss?"[103] Knowing how to lose means "going through mourning for an archaic and indispensable object," separating from it, transposing it into the realm of language. Evidence for this can be found in the child's acquisition of language, when "that intrepid wanderer leaves the crib to meet the mother in the realm of representations . . . If I did not agree to leave mother, I could neither imagine nor name her."[104] To imagine, to name, to speak to another, these are the rewards of a successful act of mourning.

This linguistic process, however, begins with "knowing how to lose." In Kristeva's discussion, depression is the condition of those who are "painfully riveted" to the object of their loss; fascinated by that object, they disavow its loss. The cost is not only a "fundamental sadness," but an "artificial, unbelievable language."[105] Connection between people becomes calcified, as does the connection between people and God: "The depressed person is a radical, sullen atheist."

Without language and without the avowal of loss, there is no desire and no creativity. Even a sense of tragedy is absent: "Within depression, if my existence is on the verge of collapsing, its lack of meaning is not tragic—it appears obvious to me, glaring and inescapable."[106]

The Israelites who mourn and lay aside their "finery" are, I suggest, Kristeva's victims of depression, of an illusory omnipotence. Silent, stiff-necked, they experience that impalpable turn of the spirit that cries out with a sense of evil, of tragedy: "They heard this evil thing . . ." God is not in their midst. And they begin the work of mourning, of loss, which may restore them to desire, to "interest in words, actions, and even life itself."[107]

Beit Yaakov[108] describes the shift from a specious omnipotence to "humility and prayer." In the move, the people find a nexus with God. Prayer, after all, is desire and language. In their worship of the Golden Calf, they had rejected the realm of prayer, and the acknowledgment of the erosions of time. Now, in this shift, they discover the "time of favor," a mysterious modulation of human experience that attunes them with God. Since they have chosen relationship over omnipotence, God, too, is moved to mercy and for the first time in the course of this catastrophic episode calls them, "the children of Israel." The music is once again in tune.

This moment, then, is the effect of *mourning*. The people relinquish a fantasy. The entire episode of the Golden Calf may be called a "mourning piece," for the narrowing of possibilities, for the passing of time. The world of remembering and forgetting replaces the world of total possession. The Golden Calf was a defense against the possibility of irreparable harm. To attach oneself to an idol is to absorb, at least in fantasy, some of its divinity. To obey God's ban on idols is to expose oneself to all that erodes the self—to time, and death, and chance.

The Time of Favor: The People See Moses' Back

If the "time of favor," then, is the effect of mourning, of avowed loss, it is marked, firstly, by the people's stripping off their "finery," and, secondly, by the enactment of that loss in the haunting scene of Moses' withdrawal from the camp. Each person stands at the entrance to his own tent, and watches as Moses recedes from them to his own personal "Tent of Meeting" where he speaks with God, "face to face, as one speaks to one's fellow" (33:11).

This enigmatic scene directly precedes the "time of favor." Here, as I have suggested in chapter 7,[109] the people experience Moses' back, his withdrawal, as a figure for God's withdrawal. "Whoever sought God would go out to the Tent of Meeting" (33:7). As they gaze after him, they imagine, according to the midrash, his experience of "speaking face to face with God": "Happy is the man born of woman who is so assured that God's Presence will enter his tent-entrance after him."[110]

At this moment, repeated many times,[111] the hungry gaze of the people is not hypnotized by a presence but provoked by an absence. In two words, Seder Eliyahu Rabba defines the quality of the moment: this is *teshuva beseter*, a private repentance.[112] Each person, in existential solitude, goes through a process of revision. The image of the camp as a constellation of tent-flaps, each holding its occupant, its gaze, compellingly conveys inwardness as a general experience.

Moses Sees God's Back

Again, the incommunicable experience is primarily of loss, of mourning. It is at this point that the strata, the residues of the past, manifest the subtle shift that is called the "time of favor." Here, the deadened objects of old fascinations are relinquished and an impalpable attunement with God is known, and now, Moses desires to see God's glory. That is, in the loss of all forms, Moses desires an experience that God Himself translates as "seeing My face." And God denies him this, but instead shows him His "back." As the narrative continues, this oblique revelation merges into an auditory experience: God proclaims His Thirteen Attributes—"God! God! a God compassionate and gracious, slow to anger, abounding in kindness and faithfulness . . ." (34:6). To hear these is, in a sense, to see God's back.

This passage is one of the most opaque in the Torah. The question is unrelenting: What is it to see God's back? Rashi offers a cryptic midrashic translation: "He showed him the knot of His *tefillin*, His phylacteries."[113] This extraordinary midrash seems to aggravate the anthropomorphism of the biblical text. The *tefillin* knot, however, is a phenomenon of the *back of the head*: what Moses is to see after God removes His obscuring hand is that part of the *tefillin* that signifies that one is *not seeing the tefillin itself*. Through this daring image, the midrash conveys the experience of *not seeing* the heart of the mystery. That total knowledge, in which time and change are blindingly effaced, literally "passes him by": in the darkness of the cave, his gaze is protectively covered by God's hand. What he sees is the *aftermath* of

God's presence, its effects, what it leaves in its wake. The *tefillin* knot is the trace left by His presence. As a knot, a *kesher*, too, it binds, it forms a link between the divine and the human. Only this "knot" of relationship, separating and uniting, is presented to Moses' gaze.

Another attempt to translate the notion of "God's back" focuses on the mode of revelation called prayer. In the time of favor, God offers Moses a partial fulfillment of his desire:

> "The time has come for you to see My glory, as much as I permit you to see. For I want and will to teach you the order of prayer . . . of mercy pleas, so that even if the merit of the patriarchs is exhausted, teach Israel to do as you now see Me doing, wrapped in a *tallith* [prayer shawl] and proclaiming the Thirteen Attributes . . ."[114]

The vision of God as he teaches Moses the art of prayer is of One praying, enveloped in a *tallith*. God, that is, models prayer to God: "I shall call on the name of God in your presence" (33:19). Moses thus sees the enveloped figure of God—he does not see His face—and hears the voice of a human prayer: the voice out of the thin silence.

The Gift of Prayer

If, then, in the "time of favor" which is the people's mourning for the loss of the idol, Moses desired full mystical experience, God grants him something very different. The gift of prayer entails a submission to time, to the limits of human perception. Prayer is an avowal of loss, of gazing on the knot, on the nexus, merely.

But it is also to find words, to "concatenate" them, in Kristeva's expression: "God! God! a God compassionate and gracious, slow to anger . . ." It is to revive desire and compassion; and to relinquish total possession. The eye yields its claim, is covered when God's face passes, is uncovered only when it has passed. This erotic play of veiling and revealing replaces the public Revelation at Mount Sinai.

The desire to see God's face is at the same time the desire to be seen, to be transformed by His gaze. The mystical desire is "not only to see the face of God *but to become that very face* in the visual confrontation"[115] (emphasis added). By contrast, Moses is evidently denied that very transformation of his face. Since he experiences God only by indirection, from the darkness of the cave, from the language of prayer, he must accept a distance, a difference.

This is the distance between "speaking to God, face to face, as one speaks with one's fellow" (33:11), and "seeing God's face" (33:20). To encounter God's face is possible only within language, in a "speaking with" Him that respects difference. The difficulty of this encounter is in its humbling effect: the only union possible is in relationship, which means separateness.

It is, therefore, significant that this qualified encounter with God leads Moses to a full solidarity with his people: "Pardon *our* iniquity." This is the moment when he makes his profound choice, to speak out from the side of the human. The fire in his bones, now, affects his language, so that *I* and *we* shade off into one another. At this moment, God renews His covenant.

Learning and Forgetting: The Work of the Night

If Moses has seen the invisibility of God and accepted a loneliness that places him squarely within the human situation, he has essentially reverted to being, in the words of the midrash, one who "learns and forgets." This condition now becomes an essential dimension of revelation:

> "And he was there forty days and forty nights": (34:28) How did Moses know how many days he spent on the mountain? Above there is no night. . . How did he know? Because in one place it is written: "And I *stood* on the mountain, as I did the first time . . ." (Deut 10:10); while in another it is written: "And I *sat* on the mountain forty days and forty nights . . ." (9:9) You learn from this that while God spoke with him, he would stand, and when God departed from him, he would sit and revise what he had learned. That is, he both *stood* and *sat*. When God spoke with him, he knew it was day, and when God told him, "Study your Torah," he knew it was night, as David wrote: "Day to day makes utterance, night to night speaks out." (Ps 19:3)[116]

The relationship between Moses and God now has two faces, a daytime face and a nighttime face. Two dimensions of the teacher-student relation are intimated in this midrash: when God is present, speaks, the student stands, receives the luminous teaching. But when God is absent, in the silence of the night, the student sits and appropriates "his" Torah. The night mode is, therefore, the mode of loss and reconstruction. In the rhetoric of this midrash and of many others in a similar vein, the new covenant introduces the world of the Oral Law, in which Moses labors in language to reconstitute a forgotten source.

"It was good for me that I was humbled, so that I might learn Your Torah" (Ps 119:71). With the second Tablets of Stone, Moses acquires the creative strength that produces "midrash and aggadoth and talmud"—all the resources of the Oral Law.[117] This new world of language opens up for him only when a certain "humbling"—an acceptance of God's absence and of the necessity for the work of the night—marks him. In order to acquire *his* Torah, he must sit alone in the dark, with a different kind of attention from that of one who receives illumination from his teacher. This kind of creativity comes to him with the second set of stone tablets; now Written Law and Oral Law leave on him the traces of a dual revelation: an explicit daylight revelation and a nocturnal revelation that demands of him the labor of interpretation.

Moses' Face Radiates Light

When Moses, then, descends the mountain with the second tablets, a new regime begins. This is signaled by the light that radiates off his face: after all, his desire to be transformed has been enigmatically, unwittingly realized. The fascination of this light fills the last verses of the narrative. Questions abound: what is the nature of the light? Why does it appear just at this juncture? What is its origin? Why does Moses at first "not know" about it? (34:29). If the people are at first afraid of his luminous face, so that they recoil from him, what overcomes their fear? What is the role of language in this description, if we notice that the root *d-b-r* ("speak") is used seven times? And what is the function of the veil with which Moses sometimes covers his face? Most intriguingly, why does it seem that Moses is *unveiled* when he speaks with the people, as well as when he speaks with God? One might have expected that when he interacts with an overawed people he would veil himself.

Indeed, an ambiguity about veiling and unveiling is inscribed in the text: "Whenever Moses went in before God to speak with Him, he would leave the veil off *until he came out;* and when he came out and told the Israelites what he had been commanded, the Israelites would see how radiant the skin of Moses' face was. Moses would then put the veil back over his face until he went in to speak with Him" (34:34–35). In v. 34, it seems that Moses is unveiled only when speaking with God—*"until he came out"*; when he emerges from God's presence and speaks with the people, he presumably veils himself. However, in v. 35, it becomes clear that the people do see his radiant face, and that he veils himself again only after speaking with them.

The basic question is the origin and nature of Moses' "rays of light." Rashi poses the question and offers one of several possible midrashic answers:

> What was the origin of the rays of Beauty? Our Sages said: "They were from the cave, when God placed His hand over his face, as it is said, 'And I shall cover you with My hand.' (33:22)"[118]

Revelation by Veiling

The origin of Moses' rays of light is "from the cave": a cryptic answer that teases the midrashic reader out of thought. "From the cave": from the darkness deepened by God's obscuring hand, from not seeing God's face, Moses' face was imprinted with light. From the nighttime "making of his own Torah," alone in a fissure in the rock, after God has turned His back; from his longing gaze after God's *tefillin* knot, after the nexus that signifies an invisible Face; from the "time of favor," when loss and mourning engendered a new humility of prayer: from all these, Moses' face is scarred with radiance. A new source of revelation opens for him, this time not one of effortless "gift," but of struggle; a vein of language, of Oral Torah, of a new and arduous partnership with God. The revelation-by-veiling is, in a real sense, a *wounding* experience: it leaves a mark, a brand, the stigma of fire. Revelation, in this intimate sense, always leaves such a trace: like the writing of a great poem, it is a "sudden fusion, a falling together of many things formerly apart," as Kenneth Burke phrases it.[119]

Why is it only now that Moses radiates light? Perhaps because this light indicates a history of indirection, of loss and compensation. Or, as Beit Yaacov[120] puts it, even if the first Revelation was more direct than the second, its light was merely *seen* by Moses: it was not *absorbed* by him, not appropriated to his own narrative of desire. With the second Revelation, Moses' heart accepted a deep imprint, precisely because, in the aftermath of the Golden Calf, God had been lost and found. In the dazzle of God's presence, the human face cannot radiate its own light; only as He withdraws, He leaves sparks, fragments of fire.

Moses as a conductor of light re-evokes the imagery of fire in the bones, in a new modality. The fire of idolatrous passion, of erotic desire for and repulsion from the object, has been subsumed into the more modest phenomenon of light. This, indeed, is implied in an alternative answer offered in Midrash Tanchuma to the question of the origin of the light rays: "From where did Moses merit the rays of Beauty?" asks the midrash: implicitly asking, *Why* did his face shine? "Some said that when God taught him Torah, he absorbed the rays of Beauty *from the sparks* that issued from the mouth of God's Presence." Moses appropriates the elusive, caustic sparks of God's mouth, so that they leave their brand on his face.

The midrash continues:

> R. Samuel bar Nahman said: The tablets measured six handbreadths in length and three in breadth. Moses held two handbreadths, God held two, and there was space of two between them: from there, Moses took the rays of Beauty. R. Samuel said: When Moses finished writing the Torah, there remained in his pen a little ink, which he wiped over his head: from there, the rays of Beauty were formed, as it is said, "Moses did not know that the skin of his face was radiating light."

In these narratives of origin, the light is explained by a motif of indirection: in the sparks, in the elusive, central section of the tablets, in the vestiges of ink left over from the explicit text of the Torah—in all these, what cannot be proclaimed, or formed into manifest characters, nevertheless makes its subtle mark. Such intimations affect Moses' heart and being, like Eliot's "trilling wire in the blood." This most personal revelation, intuitive, at the very margins of language, glimmers out of Moses' face.

However, the answer selected by Rashi—"from the cave"—contains the most compressed poetic force. Rays are the expression of a narrowing and intensifying of light, piercing through a crack, for instance. In the crevice in the rock, with God's hand shielding his eyes, he achieves a moment of oblique vision. The nature of such a ray-like perception emerges most powerfully from the proof-text quoted in the midrash: "It is a brilliant light which gives off rays from His hand; and there His glory is hidden" (Hab 3:4). God's light is hidden, and that obstruction creates brilliant rays. Indeed, quite prosaically, human vision becomes possible only by a limiting of vision: too close, too bright, too total a light simply dazzles and blinds. A fissure in the rock yields piercing fragments of illumination which are not merely seen, but absorbed into the very fabric of Moses' being.[121]

Fire in the Bones and Light in the Face

In describing Moses' radiant descent from the mountain, the Torah emphasizes, not his light, but his *unawareness* of that light: "And as Moses came down the mountain . . . Moses did not know that the skin of his face was radiant, since he had spoken with Him" (34:29). "Moses did not know": this is the principal clause of the sentence. *Not knowing* the light takes precedence over the existence or the origin of the light.

It is, of course, significant that the text describes that origin as being simply, "since he had spoken with Him."[122] The light is generated by language, by a dialogue between Moses and God. The most important aspect of that dialogue is that it leaves its mark on Moses' face, *unknown to him.* Because he is so intimately involved in the Revelation, he is quite unself-conscious. An intense inwardness, a kind of perceptual modesty, focuses Moses' attention on the work of interpretation and obscures from him all awareness of how he is seen by others.

In Chasidic teachings, this unself-conscious absorption becomes an ideal condition for holiness. In one such source,[123] for instance, the repeated reference in the text to "coming down"—"Moses *came down* from Mount Sinai. And as Moses *came down* from the mountain . . . Moses did not know . . ." (34:29)—suggests that the condition for such a light is humility. Moreover, the strange anonymity in referring to God—"his face was radiant, since he had spoken *with Him*"—evokes an almost impersonal exhilaration at speaking the sacred words *with Anyone.* That is, the light comes from the unself-conscious joy of *dibbur*, of articulating the sacred words; the fact that God is his interlocutor is secondary to the passion of his involvement. A fire of enthusiasm burns in him.

In such a reading, the raw fire in the bones has become sublimated into the light in the face. Not knowing comes to mean a kind of forgetfulness of his own consuming fire. Indeed, Rashi makes the connection between the consuming fire and Moses' rays of light:

> "And they feared to come close to him": Come and see how great is the power of sin: before they sinned, it says, "The vision of God's glory was like a consuming fire at the top of the mountain before the eyes of the Israelites" (24:17) yet they were not afraid or unnerved. But once they had made the Calf, even the rays of Beauty terrified and unnerved them.[124]

From consuming fire to Moses' radiant face: a transition effected by the Golden Calf and Moses' transformed energy. If the people are now afraid even of these rays, it is because they are now sensitized to fire: the Golden Calf leapt out of fire, prancing with demonic vitality;[125] and finally Moses burned it in fire (32:20). They do not underestimate the light that radiates from Moses' face: its origin, too, is fire.

Moses Our Teacher: The Nexus of Language

What allows them, after all, to come close to Moses is the fact that he *speaks* to them. Seven times the word *dabber*—speak—is used in this short narrative. As they look in his face, he speaks to them all that God has spoken to him on Mount Sinai (34:32). Only after he has finished speaking with them does he place a veil over his face. And, thereafter, this becomes a pattern: the shining face is characterized by language, either with God or with human beings; at all other times, "unspeaking" times, the face is veiled.

The light rays, then, are significantly related to the act of language. They are generated by speaking with God: what role do they play in the human encounter? As we have noticed, there is a perplexing ambiguity to the veiled/unveiled alternation: one might have expected Moses to *cover* his face, that intimidating evidence of Revelation, in speaking to the people. And, indeed, as we have also noticed, v. 34 does seem to suggest such a pattern.

However, if Moses' face is uncovered as he speaks to the people, this may suggest something about the nature of the dialogue. At this moment, in the fullest sense, Moses acquires his central identity as *teacher.* The fire in his bones is transformed into the light in the face; and Moses allows his people to see that most private light, generated by God's absence and much lonely labor—allows them to see it, deliberately, as an aid in their learning process.

This is the reading of Ha-amek Davar, emerging from the Lithuanian, anti-Chasidic tradition. At the center of Moses' destiny is his teaching role; and, as with any teacher, the face is a potent learning aid. Expressive, ironic, intimating a hinterland of meaning, it is part of the teaching. Once it is the "Oral Law" that is being transmitted, the teacher's face becomes quite indispensable. "And your eyes shall see your teacher."[126]

In this foundational encounter between Moses and his people, then, a pedagogical pattern is set in place. Moses deliberately exposes his face, "traumatized" by rays of vision through a fissure in the rock. In tension with each other, the mystical and the pedagogical impulses find a resolution in the play of the veil. In fact, Ha-amek Davar resolves the ambiguity about the veil (is it up or down when Moses speaks with the people?) by suggesting a third possibility: the veil is removed when Moses speaks with God, *until* he emerges from the Tent of Meeting. Then he replaces it, but folds it up in a deliberate move of exposure, so that the people may see his face while he speaks to them. Then, he draws the veil down over his face till his next "speaking with Him."

This third position of the veil, like Winnicott's "potential space," allows for subject and object to relate in a "play space" that belongs to neither. This is the space of language, neither inside nor outside. Ingeniously, Ha-amek Davar reads the difficult last sentence: "And the Israelites saw the face of Moses *because* (*ki*) the skin of Moses' face radiated . . ." He folds back the veil, knowing now the charismatic effect of his own light and willing to inform his teaching with that charisma.

Ha-amek Davar here touches on the very core of the problem of idolatry. "Charisma" can enslave both object and subject. The need to withdraw the energies of the self from the "bankrupt object"[127] can, as we have seen, result in melancholy and murder. But light can be perceived only through an irradiated medium; and without light, there can be no revelation. This is the dilemma of the Golden Calf.

To escape the oppression of the past, its dead usages, to "shoot the gulf," means to carry some version of the past with one. For Moses, the trace of the past is imprinted in his face: the light of nocturnal struggle. This dark light[128] transforms him from charismatic prophet to charismatic teacher. The difference lies in the nexus of language that joins teacher and student: *speaking* to each other, a light is transmitted. It neither consumes nor is consumed. The student glimpses the power of the teacher's wound: the work of the cave, of the sparks, of the vestiges of ink.

If this encounter is to succeed, the teacher must transmit a sense of continuous transition, continuous revelation. This is the work of the Oral Law, rooted in remembering and forgetting. "You find nothing more beautiful than modesty," says Midrash Tanchuma.[129] The first Revelation took place in the glare of the public gaze; the second Revelation excluded any human gaze.[130] This unwitnessed, unself-conscious encounter represents the most radical liberation from idolatry. Moses has no image to serve, not even the image of his own past words. For here, too, in the received vocabulary, in the written text, is a potential form of idolatrous fixation. Against such mesmerism, Moses lives the reality of the cave, of an oblique and fragmentary vision. Instead of being the inert reflection of God's face, his own face gleams with the light of a constant becoming.[131]

Generous Desire: The Student Receives the Teacher's Face

The effect of such a face on the student is, in a complex sense, mimetic. If, as R. Nahman of Bratzlav avers, "Anyone who has eyes to see can recognize in the face of the student who is his teacher," this is not a matter of slavish imitation. Delicate and largely unconscious forces are at work to "remodel" the student's face. This is the process that Freud described as "transference." And the Golden Calf stands as a monumental warning against the abuse of this process. For R. Nahman, however, what is "transferred" is not the totality of the teacher's image. The student is not shaped according to the mold of the teacher. That would be to fix the student's world and to prevent his development. Rather, the student receives that light of his teacher's face which is his *wisdom* ("The wisdom of a person illuminates his face."):[132]

> When the student receives his teacher's wisdom, he "receives his face." For this reason, he should look into his teacher's face as he receives his wisdom, as it is written: "And your eyes shall see your teacher."[133]

The student, in a movement of will, opens himself up to the teacher's wisdom. In doing so, he "receives his face": an act of encounter, even of hospitality. (*Kabbalath panim*—the receiving of the face—is the traditional Hebrew idiom for the host-guest relation.) Paradoxically, it is the student who becomes host to his teacher's light.

In such a case, then, what is transferred is no fixed image, but an energy, a trace of the work of the cave. Indeed, we may say that a kind of generous desire must impel the student to house such a perilous light. This notion of wisdom leaves the face wounded in its radiance.

A powerful Chasidic comment conveys a sense of the relation between the light of the face and all that is unexpressed:

> It was said of Jonathan ben Uzziel that when he was sitting preoccupied in Torah, any bird who flew overhead was instantly burned.[134] My grand-

father, Sefath Emeth, used to say: Now, let us imagine how great was Hillel, the teacher of Jonathan ben Uzziel: the bird who flew overhead was not even singed, for his fire blazed inwardly, leaving no sign on his face![135]

The veiled face of Moses expresses nothing of the fire within; the revealed face, however, conveys a glimmering impression of that fire. No birds burn in that fire; its power is in its concentrated inwardness. It intimates what cannot be said, and thus avoids both infatuation with the "already said," with the object, and disparagement of that object. In its loneliness, it is with God; its wisdom is of and in God, even as He turns His back. It arouses fear, not an immediate empathy; and, in the act of speaking, it communicates that subtle contagion that overcomes fear.

The Oral Law: A Sense of "Baffled Intensities"

The seven-times repeated word *dabber* (speak) becomes, then, the ground bass of this passage. In language, face to face, Moses transmits his wisdom which, in language, is also face to face with God. The forms of a language that flourish in the half light are essentially what Moses has to teach his people: how *not* to see, how *not* to know. Perhaps such a language—called the Oral Law—is most appropriately learned from Moses who began in silence: "I am heavy of mouth and heavy of tongue" (4:10).

The child who learns to speak knows the difficulty of relinquishing what Adam Phillips terms "her inarticulate self, the self before language (what the poet Seamus Heaney refers to as 'pre-reflective lived experience')."[136] Moses is the archetype of the human being who never quite accommodates to the competencies, the efficiencies of language, which always remains something of an enigma to him, sensed in his mouth and tongue and lips. He relinquishes his original silence, emerges into language, but not into glibness. Between these two modalities, his words are fraught with "baffled intensities."[137] They initiate a long tradition of rereading, reinvention, that is rooted in a conscious ignorance.

5. *Imaginative Reconstruction: The Imperative of Forgetting*

Forgetting and Remembering: A Critique of Language

At this point, we return to our opening theme of forgetting and remembering. We began with this theme and we will end with it. We have explored other related themes: the anxiety of the human beings about living in time, the ambivalence that constitutes the moment of the Golden Calf; the hatred and love that issue in murder; repression and the return of the repressed; the role of the unconscious, of memory traces, in the transmission of culture. These themes, each with its own dynamic, cluster around the Golden Calf moment. At their heart, I suggest, is a sustained concern with time and memory, a fascination with both the timeless moment of full presence and the subtle gifts of temporality and process. In Jewish tradition, particularly in midrashic and Chasidic texts, this tension is figured in the relation between *torah she-bi chtav* (the Written Torah) and *torah she-baal-peh* (the Oral Torah), between the Revelation engraved in stone and the enduring process of interpretation.

At first, we remember, before God made Moses "gifted," with total mastery of the Torah, he was one who "learned and forgot." As soon as he became totally competent "above," at the top of the mountain, the people made the Golden Calf "below," at its base. The desire for mastery is related to the idolatrous impulse. By the end of the narrative, Moses has reverted, "regressed," back to not-knowing, to the cave and its rays of light piercing the dark.

If any image or form can become an idol, adored and disparaged, then one's own knowledge, one's own words, offer no immunity. Nietzsche writes against language: "That which we can find words for is something already dead in our hearts; there is always a kind of contempt in the act of speaking."[138] The contempt of the speaker for his own words is palpable in Hamlet's disgusted cry, as he bemoans himself that he "Must like a whore unpack my heart with words."[139] Even God's word from above can become "dead in our hearts," unless the language of competence and mastery is tempered with that of silence.

The Golden Calf is the compelling symbol of the power and the powerlessness of the object. At base, we have noticed, it is born of a *lateness*, of a time gap. How long does it take to lose faith? A mere forty days, answers the biblical narrative. In this diagnosis, the pathology is one of forgetting:

". . . That it should come to this, But two months dead, nay not so much, not two . . . O most wicked speed . . . to post With such dexterity to incestuous sheets!"[140]

Another midrash on the time gap, however, inflates this notion of inconstancy to a pitch of absurdity that makes us question whether forgetting is, in fact, the problem:

> It does not say *avru*—"they have transgressed . . ."—but *saru*—"they have turned aside quickly out of the way . . ." (32:8) When they were at Sinai, they were like lilies and roses, but now they have become refuse (*serayoth*), they have become thorns. They did not delay even an hour or two but immediately turned aside.
>
> R. Simeon ben Yohai said: "They were with God only eleven days, for they were devising how to make the Calf the remaining twenty-nine days that Moses was on the mountain, as it is written, 'Eleven days from Horev' (Deut 1:2), and after that they came to the ways of Esau [i.e. idolatry, which is the meaning of] 'By the way of Mount Seir.' "
>
> R. Eleazar ben Jacob said that for twenty-nine days they were with God and schemed for the remaining eleven days how to make the Calf, for it is written, "Eleven days from Horev . . . by the way of Mount Seir," that is, it was for eleven days that they copied the deeds of Seir.
>
> Another explanation of "By the way of Mount Seir:" Just as Esau reproached and blasphemed God, so did they reproach and blaspheme before their idols; just as Esau was an idolator, so were they.
>
> R. Judah ben Ila'i said: "They were only one day with God, for Micah explicitly states, 'But since yesterday My people is risen up as an enemy' (Micah 2:8). God said, 'Yesterday only did you exclaim: "All that God has spoken, we will do and obey," (Exodus 24:7) and today you say, "This is your god, O Israel." ' "
>
> R. Simeon ben Halafta said: "They were only two days with God, for it says, 'Yet my people have forgotten Me days without number.' (Jeremiah 2:32) How many are implied by 'days'? Two. R. Jonah proved this number from another source, because it says, 'Me they seek only a day a day.' (Isaiah 58:2)"

Another explanation of "They have turned aside quickly . . ." R. Simeon ben Halafta said, "You have taken the wrong path from the very outset. A man on a journey after walking two or three miles may begin to wander from his path in the third mile, but surely it is not usual for him to stray in the very first mile? This is what God said, 'When you intended to sin, could you not have waited until the second or third day, that you had to start on the very first day?' "

R. Meir said, "It was not even one complete day before they sinned, for while they were yet standing at Sinai, proclaiming, 'We will do and we will obey,' their hearts were already concentrated on idolatry, for it says, 'But they beguiled Him with their mouth, and lied to Him with their tongue.' (Psalms 78:36)"[141]

In a sense, this midrash elaborates the harlotry-under-the-wedding-canopy motif. It is a series of fascinated variations on the same outrage: if a mere forty days' fidelity was contemptible, an almost unimaginably cursory essay in memory, then the Sages, in this midrash, condense that brief period of "being with God" even further. Not even an hour; eleven days; twenty-nine days; one day; two days; not even one day: the order of these hypotheses of fickleness has no apparent logic or direction. The passage conveys a kind of unruly anguish around the core notion that is articulated in the last hypothesis by R. Meir: Not even one day: they stood at Sinai and *mouthed the words*, "We will do and we will obey," while their hearts were focused on idolatry.

It is not difficult to hear Nietzsche's critique of language as undertone to this passage: "That which we can find words for is something already dead in our hearts . . ." As they speak their commitment, their hearts are already distracted. All the other speculations—one day, eleven, forty—are an illusion about the people's vestigal loyalty to God. For, in essence, it is not a question of *forgetting* God and the Revelation at Sinai, as we might have thought. Their pathology is not a feebleness of memory. Rather, it is the unrecognized *survival* of memory: the repressed desire for the Golden Calf that remains strong in their hearts, even as they intone the formulae of a new faith.

Such a reading—and all the hypotheses in the midrash approximate toward this diagnosis—represents the people as in the grip of an involuntary and disguised memory. Consciously, they accept the Revelation of Sinai; unconsciously, they stubbornly retain the "pieties" of the past. Indeed, the provocative proof-text from Psalms implies an element of pretense in the Sinai commitment: in Adam Phillips's terms, repression involves areas of life about which one can "pretend to lose" one's memory.[142]

The opening image in the midrash, of the rose that reveals its thorns, establishes this core idea of a memory that only pretends to be lost. This is the view of the Golden Calf pathology that indicts the people as "stiff-necked": not changeable, but relentlessly unchanging. Some residue of the past refuses to give way, to shift: that is the Golden Calf. On the one hand, the idiom of the midrash contrasts "yesterday" and "today," implying an incomprehensible forgetfulness. Indeed, the proof-text from Jeremiah explicitly makes the charge of forgetfulness: "And My people *have forgotten Me* days without number." However, it is striking that the verse is deployed to prove that the people *were with God* two days: to describe the period of remembering, not of forgetting. To be with God may, paradoxically, involve fruitful acts of forgetting.

A Forgetting Which Is a Way of Remembering

The paradox of remembering and forgetting can be expressed in many ways. Adam Phillips writes of Freud, for instance: ". . . there is a forgetting, which is a way of remembering."[143] In this mode, the people "forget" the idols of desire at Sinai; they bury them, only to preserve them the more securely. Freud uses the antiques in his room as an exemplum for this work of the unconscious:

> everything conscious was subject to a process of wearing away, while what was unconscious was relatively unchangeable; and I illustrated my remarks by pointing to the antiques standing about in my room. They were, in fact, I said, only objects found in a tomb, and their burial had been their preservation; the destruction of Pompeii was only beginning now that it had been dug up.[144]

To make the unconscious conscious, Freud argues, is to make it disappear. Unconscious memory is imprinted in the body and in the emotional habits; only by an act of retrieval, of reconstruction, can it lose its power. Psychoanalysis, then, is a "cure by means of the kind of remembering that makes forgetting possible."[145]

If the Golden Calf, then, represents a repressed desire, the people "forget" it at Sinai, as a strategy for more potently remembering it. Forgetting the forbidden desire invests it with tenacity. If a cure is to be achieved, it must be by way of consciousness, interpretation, memory.

In this Freudian mode, God's command to the people: "Remember, do not forget, how you angered God, your God, in the wilderness . . ." (Deut 9:7) resounds with a blatant redundancy that is not, after all, redundant. Moses urges on the people a kind of memory that will not collude with forgetting. The forgetting of repressed desire may be masked, protected by "screen memories" of all kinds. Moses advocates tapping these screen memories, which, in Christopher Bollas's image, have become "underground wells in the deserts of time."[146]

Tapping these sources means narrative: the continual retelling of the sagas of anger: "how you angered God . . ." "Remember, do not forget . . ." presents a strategy for overcoming the evasions of forgetting: " 'Remember'—keep repeating them in your mouth" (Sifrei). The purpose of verbal repetition is to make the past available for transformation: otherwise it remains inert and compels repetition in action.

Images: Drinking the Calf

If narrating the Golden Calf is the central strategy for overcoming the oblivion that engenders repetition—if a helpless acting out of the idolatrous predicament is to be foiled by conscious memory—then the physical fate of the Golden Calf becomes a vivid figure for this paradox. Moses burns it, grinds it to dust, throws it into the river that descends from Mount Sinai, and *makes the people drink it*. To speak of eating or drinking is to use "the language of the oldest—the oral instinctual impulses":

> [T]he judgement is, "I should like to eat this", or "I should like to spit it out"; and, put more generally: "I should like to take this into myself and to keep that out." That is to say, "It shall be inside me" or "it shall be outside me."[147]

What is taken inside is remembered, what is kept out is forgotten. So much seems obvious; but, as Adam Phillips perceptively asks: "is forgetting . . . more like eating something or like spitting it out? Just as you can only repress something once you have acknowledged it, similarly you can only spit something out once you have tasted it."[148]

In making the people drink the water silted with Calf grit, Moses is apparently making them acknowledge, "digest," the Golden Calf: "it will be metabolized by your body, and fuel your future," says Phillips of one possible form of forgetting. "The question becomes not: what do I want to forget and what do I want to remember?, but: which form of forgetting do I want to use?"

In the midrashic amplifications of this drinking ordeal, the most guilty of the people die of this digestive moment. The analogy with the wife suspected of adultery who is made to drink the "bitter waters" (Num 5:11–31), is a midrashic commonplace:[149] an intimate testing takes place, as memory either kills or transforms.

The alternative to such a reconstruction of memory is "acting out": that is, eternal repetition of the idolatrous syndrome: "the compulsion to repeat . . . now replaces the impulsion to remember" (Freud). Phillips paraphrases: "In our repetitions we have found a way of remembering something by never knowing what it is; and by not knowing we make it unforgettable."[150]

The Golden Calf is to be disposed of by remembering it; in this way, it can be "forgotten" as a compelling image of desire. In Freud's words on the work of meaning and interpretation: "The destruction of Pompeii was only beginning now that it had been dug up. . ." By digesting the past, rather than pretending to lose it, one can transform it.

Images: Smashing the Tablets

However, the Golden Calf narrative contains another cryptic image for forgetting: the tragic moment when Moses shatters the tablets. The Torah does not tell of the fate of the fragments; unlike the Calf powder, they seem to disappear from the text and thus from memory. But one midrashic tradition places them in the Ark of the Covenant in the Holy of Holies, together with the second set of tablets. A mysterious preservation is enacted here: a preservation of a most potent symbol for "forgetting."

The Talmud articulates the paradox: "If the tablets had not been shattered, the Torah would not have been forgotten in Israel."[151] Breaking the tablets symbolizes the undoing of memory, the lugubrious hazard of oblivion. And yet, mysteriously, Moses' initiative in this act of rupture is applauded by God: "There are times when the undoing of Torah is its fulfillment, as it is said: '. . . the tablets which (*asher*) you broke' (Deut 10:2)—'More strength (*Yishar kochacha*) to you for breaking them!' "[152] In this unexpected midrash,

God congratulates Moses for introducing the phenomenon of rupture, of forgetting, into the tradition. If the Torah is forgotten, the effect is not, after all, unmitigatedly tragic. For out of oblivion comes interpretation, reconstruction, the act of memory that re-creates the past.

In an important essay on the "uses of forgetting,"[153] R. Hutner traces the vitality of the Oral Law to this phenomenon. He cites a midrash that narrates the first major Israelite cultural amnesia and its fortunate effects: "During the mourning period for Moses, three hundred laws were forgotten; Othniel ben Kenaz reconstructed them through his *pilpul*, his ingenious interpretations."[154] That is, forgetting, loss, mourning engender a surge of creativity, as the fixed forms of the "already said" give way to the dynamic transformations of "saying."

As R. Hutner emphasizes, a central dimension of this forgetting is the growth of *machloketh*, of controversy. As the Torah is forgotten, the first *machloketh*, the first recorded controversy, arises.[155] Multiple perspectives proliferate when memory loses its mastery. This development itself can be viewed in opposite ways: for R. Hutner, oblivion becomes something of a *felix culpa*, yielding a residue of creativity that has enriched the Jewish mind. It becomes possible for God to congratulate Moses for breaking the tablets, for initiating "forgetting" in the cultural world of the people.

The ultimate effect of this act of iconoclasm is to generate vitality. In Torah discourse, *torah she-baal-peh*, the Oral Law, literally the Torah of the Mouth, disagreement nurtures a respect for the other in his difference:

> The relationship with the other, who is the others, is a transcendent relationship, which means that there is an infinite and, in one way, unsurmountable distance between me and the other who belongs to the other shore . . .[156]

The Uses of Forgetting

The forgetting that makes this kind of creativity possible is, I suggest, the central problem of the Golden Calf narrative. If a first reading of the narrative yields a sense that the people's pathology is one of inconstancy, of forgetfulness—"Quickly they have turned aside from the way . . ." (32:8)—further consideration of the text and of the midrashic material suggests the contrary perspective: the people suffer not from too much forgetting but from too much memory. The Golden Calf represents an "atrophy of experience," in Walter Benjamin's phrase, that reflects the "replacement of narrative by information."[157]

At the very moment that they stand at Sinai, mouthing "We will do and we will obey," "their hearts were not solidly with Him."[158] They are incapable of "being with God," even for one day. This harsh glare on the hearts of Calf-worshipers reveals an unexpected pathology. It is not that they cannot retain an impression, a memory, but that they are too much in the grip of successive impressions, of the successive shocks of information. Frenetically registering the images of the moment, a necessary process of assimilation never takes place. Narrative never happens—that narrative that "embeds [a happening] in the life of the storyteller in order to pass it on as experience to those listening."[159]

On this reading, the very quality of the encounter at Sinai is questioned. Even as they stand there, the people are incapable of remembering Sinai. What do the Sages achieve in tracing infidelity back to the very inception of the marriage? Such a reading sacrifices a great deal; what does it gain?

It seems that such a radical reading probes the paradoxes of memory and forgetting. Instead of deploring the brevity of memory, it engenders reflections on the virtues of forgetting. That is, what the people can be seen to lack is a capacity for that free-floating attention, the psychoanalytic forgetting, that leads one to wear one's memory with a difference. In the analyst, the art of forgetting involves an "act of faith. It implies a belief that there is a process . . . that gets to work by not trying to remember; and for which conscious, as opposed to pre-conscious or unconscious, memory is a saboteur."[160] The patient in analysis also "forgets": that is, in free-associating, forgets himself, his received version of himself. Indeed, as Adam Phillips arrestingly puts it: "it is only when two people forget themselves in each other's presence, that they can recognize each other."[161]

It is precisely this kind of free-floating or "evenly suspended attention" that is lacking in the history leading up to the Golden Calf. The people who retreated from Revelation, and interposed Moses between themselves and a "being with God," were retreating from the profound and personal encounter that might result in dreams, in art. This evaded encounter is called "listening." As in the psychoanalytic model, this implies a kind of attention that the people resist: instead, they delegate Moses to assume the risks of listening: "If we hear the voice of God, our God, any longer, we shall die . . . You go closer and hear all that God our God says, and you tell us all that God your God tells you, and we will listen to you and obey." (Deut 5:22, 24) Against the work of the unconscious, they deploy fixities, conscious memories, the "stiff neck" that prevents listening.

Forgetting, in this sense, is essential to communication, to symbolization, to Revelation. The ironic possibility thus arises that the "time lag" of Moses' absence, Moses' "lateness" in returning from the mountaintop, was potentially a resource for creating meaning. One cannot remember without having forgotten: Sinai becomes available for transformation into experience only if there is a space of deferral, an interval in which all fixities are withdrawn. Even Moses, even the tablets of stone, as we have seen, are capable of blocking that process of transformation. The people, however, are unable to forget in the right way. Instead, they repeat the patterns of the past.

Involuntary Memory: A Way of Being with God

When, therefore, forty years later, Moses urges the people to remember and not to forget the narrative of anger, and especially the narrative of the Golden Calf, one understanding of this is as an act of exorcism. Only by remembering, by processing the potent unconscious patterns of the past can one dispose of them. The other therapeutic possibility, however, is that healing memory works in a different way: by weaving new connections, dream connections, in which forgetting is at least as significant as remembering.

Walter Benjamin writes about this "involuntary memory":

> the important thing for the remembering author is not what he experienced, but the weaving of his memory, the Penelope work of recollection. Or should one call it, rather, a Penelope work of forgetting? Is not the involuntary recollection, Proust's *memoire involontaire*, much closer to forgetting than what is usually called memory? And is not this work of spontaneous recollection, in which remembrance is the woof and forgetting the warf, a counterpart to Penelope's work rather than its likeness? For here the day unravels what the night has woven . . . an experienced event is finite—at any rate, confined to one sphere of experience; a remembered event is infinite, because it is only a key to everything that happened before it and after it.[162]

It is in this sense that the narrative of the Golden Calf becomes not merely a national trauma but a "key to everything that happened before it and after it." If on one level the Golden Calf is to be remembered in order to be forgotten, on the other, the tablets are smashed, are "forgotten," in order to make them available for transformation, for imaginative reconstruction. Between the two models, the perplexities of idolatry are intimated. Both remembering and forgetting are essential; both are catastrophic in the wrong context.[163]

"Being with God," ultimately, is the challenge of Sinai. The midrash raises many hypotheses: *how long* were they with God? and how soon did they begin to devise the Golden Calf? Was it eleven days, or twenty-nine days, one day or two, or were they not even one day with God? Perhaps, the midrash dares to speculate, they never were with God, because a fatal atrophy in the heart of experience would not let them relinquish memory?

Against such a poignant record of overconsciousness, the Torah sets the radiant face of Moses. Imprinted with the cave, with not-seeing, Moses' face brings an afterimage of transcendence to the people. Their response is an initial awe. But beyond that there is language, narratives of the past that are nurtured by both memory and forgetting. Here, a relationship, a "being with God," comes to mean speaking and listening. Here, the text, the *textum*, the web of lived life, is constantly unraveled and rewoven.

10 Va-Yakhel— Pekudei

THE FIERY IMAGINATION

[35:1–40:38]

1. *Mishkan and Shabbat: Alternative Modalities*

MISHKAN AND SHABBAT: TWO PRINCIPLES

In the last section of Exodus, Moses transmits to the people God's instructions about building the Mishkan. In overwhelming detail, these instructions, already spelled out in chapters 25–31, move into the public domain: where previously they had been the burden and promise of God's dialogue with Moses, they are now conveyed to the people and translated into forms and materials. Finally, the elements are assembled and the Mishkan arises, a complex, integrated space for God to dwell in "Let them make Me a sanctuary that I may dwell among them" (25:8).

Before Moses embarks on the repeated inventory of objects and materials, however, he urges on the people the sanctity of Shabbat, the Sabbath day:

> "These are the things that God has commanded you to do: On six days, work may be done, but on the seventh day you shall have a sabbath of complete rest, holy to God; whoever does any work on it shall be put to death. You shall kindle no fire throughout your settlements on the sabbath day." (35:1–3)

Rashi's comment is classic:

> "Six days": He prefaced the instructions about the Mishkan work with the warning about Shabbat, to tell them that the Mishkan does not supersede Shabbat.

An intimate tension is set up between Shabbat and the Mishkan: before even beginning to speak of the building work, it is necessary to articulate a kind of *anti-Mishkan* principle. One might indeed have thought that the Mishkan does displace Shabbat, that the crafts that go to create the holy space would continue through the weekly day of sacred time. Since the word *kadosh* ("holy") appears in both contexts, ("... *holy [kodesh]* to God"; "Let them make Me a *sanctuary [Mikdash]*"), the imperative of the Mishkan work might well have overridden the weekly pause of Shabbat. Not so; and therefore Moses speaks of Shabbat before the Mishkan work, to counteract a perhaps natural hypothesis.

In this matching of the Mishkan principle against the Shabbat principle, the tension is articulated most vividly through the midrashic play on the words, "These are the things": *Eileh ha-devarim.* "These," as opposed to the singular form of the command to build the Mishkan, "*This* is the thing ..." (35:4), indicates a mode of plurality, a sense of the complexity of the work-categories forbidden on Shabbat. So, a numerological count of the letters of *Eileh ha-devarim* ("And these are the things ...") produces thirty-nine;[1] this is a coded reference to the thirty-nine types of work that are needed to build the Mishkan, and these are banned on Shabbat. In the Mishkan, all these kinds of labor are required, admired, integrated into an organic space; *but*—and the limitation is so stringent that it must preface the detailed specifications of the Mishkan work—on Shabbat, just these kinds of work, in all their variety, are forbidden. Indeed, the Sages deduce that violation of each prohibition is punishable separately. That is, a range of work that in the Mishkan becomes unified by its sacred purpose, is diffused on Shabbat into thirty-nine separate taboos.

The point emerges clearly from the word *melacha*—"work, craft"—which is characteristically used for the creative activity invested in the Mishkan.[2] This same *melacha* is forbidden on Shabbat: "On six days *melacha* may be done, but on the seventh day you shall have a sabbath of complete rest, holy to God; *whoever does any* melacha *on it shall be put to death.*" The Talmud sharpens the point by asserting that *only creative acts* are forbidden on Shabbat, not destructive ones.[3]

In conveying to the people this paradoxical pairing of Shabbat and Mishkan modalities, Moses in fact fulfills God's specific command. His last words before the Golden Calf narrative had been a similar pairing of Mishkan and Shabbat instructions: after concluding the building specifications, God had added a passage about Shabbat and about the ban on *melacha*, which He had prefaced with an emphatic address to Moses: "God said to Moses: '*And you speak* to the Israelites saying, "Nevertheless, you must keep My sabbaths . . ."' " (31:12–13). Evidently, it is important that Moses personally convey the Shabbat message to the people. This he does immediately after his final descent from the mountain, after the Golden Calf drama of sin and pardon has been played out. On the day after Yom Kippur,[4] he assembles the people, so that all, young and old, women and men, will hear of the Shabbat-Mishkan nexus directly from his lips.[5]

Most striking, of course, is the fact that, in conveying God's message, Moses reverses the order of the Mishkan and Shabbat instructions from chapter 31. Here, in chapter 35, he relays Shabbat before the Mishkan, completing a chiastic structure with the Golden Calf narrative at its heart: Mishkan—Shabbat—Golden Calf—Shabbat—Mishkan. Thus the crisis that separates God's instructions to Moses from Moses' transmission to the people is the sin of the Golden Calf. I will return to the significance of this pattern toward the end of my discussion.

Alternative Sensibilities?

The sense that the Shabbat sanctity overrides that of the Mishkan is conveyed in God's speech to Moses by the unusual expression *ach*—"nevertheless." Strongly limiting the Mishkan principle, God now introduces a counterprinciple. Creative work, *assiyah*, which is the very process of the Mishkan (*Ve-assu*—"Let them *make* Me a sanctuary"; the building instructions employ eighty uses of some form of the word *assiyah*)[6] is now included as a subsidiary clause, in the Shabbat prohibition (31:15). This non-*assiyah* is now the condition for a different creativity, a different *assiyah*: "*to make* (*la'assoth*) the Shabbat" (31:16).

The absolute tension between Shabbat and Mishkan, doing and not doing, is registered by Seforno:

> "And on the seventh day . . ."—you shall do no work on it, *even* the work of the Mishkan.

> "Whoever does any work. . . ."—*even though* it is the work of God's commandment.[7]

"Even though" expresses the paradox: one divine commandment—to work, to do—is overridden by another—not to work, not to do. The need to emphasize this arises from its intuitive difficulty.

Rashi, too, conveys the depth of the "prejudice" that the Shabbat prohibition must overcome:

> "And you speak . . ."—*even though* I have appointed you to command them about the work of the Mishkan, let it not be light in your eyes to suspend Shabbat because of that work.
>
> "*Ach*—nevertheless . . ."—*even though* you are compelled by enthusiasm for the work, let Shabbat not be suspended by it.[8]

Moses is addressed personally at this juncture, because he is at the very fulcrum of a passion for the Mishkan that might plausibly have swept away the Shabbat consciousness. Bearer of so many commandments to do, to make, he might have lost that contrasting sensibility that is associated with Shabbat. Even the people, not so directly involved in hearing God's voice, are described as *ridufin*—"pursued, compelled, obsessed"—by the Mishkan work. Rashi's idiom is intense; he describes a state in which the people have become fascinated by this work, in a sense passively caught up by a force ("pursued") that requires an equally forceful counterpoint: "Let Shabbat not be suspended by it."

The nature of this compulsion will be the subject of our exploration in this chapter. Moses is entirely implicated in this inflamed state: even more than the people, he carries the many words of God that frame the imperative of work. Rashi's comment powerfully shifts the focus away from the objective area ("Nevertheless, keep My Sabbaths"—stop the creative work of the six-day week) to the subjective area ("Nevertheless, keep My Sabbaths"—do not allow your obsession with creative work to displace an alternative sensibility.) Evidently, the Mishkan work holds such an obsessive power that emphatic limits have to be placed on it.

2. *Bezalel: A Reverie on Gold and Fire*

"You Shall Kindle No Fire . . ."

In transmitting the Shabbat-Mishkan nexus to the people, Moses introduces a new theme, never before explicitly articulated: "You shall kindle no fire throughout your settlements on the sabbath day" (35:3).[9] That is, instead of conveying God's words: "it shall be a sign for all time between me and the people of Israel. For in six days God made heaven and earth, and on the seventh day He ceased from work and was refreshed" (31:17), Moses speaks of the Shabbat ban on kindling fire. How does this ban relate to the thirty-nine specific work-categories?

Seforno reads the function of fire as precondition to all forms of creative work: "Even though kindling fire is on the whole destructive, nevertheless, since it makes all, or most, forms of work possible, it is forbidden on Shabbat" (35:3).

The paradox is arresting. Fire is destructive: *therefore* it should be permitted on Shabbat. But fire is necessary for many forms of creative work: *therefore* it is forbidden. The ambiguity of fire—destructive and creative—is intimated here. But it is the creative role of fire that is problematic. A purely destructive fire, apparently, would pose no problem on Shabbat.[10]

This fire, capable of opposite effects, lies at the heart of the Mishkan project—technically because so many of the crafts require its use, and conceptually in senses that we have yet to explore. In spite of that central role, or because of it, it is banned on Shabbat. In our text, indeed, the prohibition of fire symbolizes all the specific forms of work only hinted at in the midrashic numerology.

Metaphorical Fire

Indeed, we may say that, in a metaphoric sense, "fire" appears in the people's avid enthusiasm when Moses appeals to them for donations to the Mishkan. This is the fire in the heart, which is the subject of Moses' first address: "Take from among you gifts to God; everyone *whose heart moves him* shall bring them . . ." (35:5). In a play on words, a Chasidic reading suggests that it is the heart that is to be brought to the Mishkan.[11]

The people respond with overwhelming passion:

> And everyone who excelled in ability and everyone whose spirit moved him came, bringing [*va-yavo-u . . . va-yavi-u*] to God his offering for the work . . . All the artisans who were engaged in the tasks of the sanctuary came, each from the task upon which he was engaged, and said to Moses, "The people are bringing more than is needed for the tasks entailed in the work that God has commanded to be done." Moses immediately had this proclamation made throughout the camp: "Let no man or woman make further effort toward gifts for the sanctuary!" So the people stopped bringing: their efforts had been more than enough for all the tasks to be done. (35:21; 36:4–7)

An excess of gift has, in the end, to be restrained. The word *hevi-u*—"they brought"—is used in one form or another nine times in this passage. Moses' words have never before been so successful: they have precipitated an avalanche of giving that, on the purely practical plane, must be stemmed. Conceptually, however, why must the fire in the heart be prevented from its full expression? The fear of "too much" seems an ungenerous response to such an ebullient moment in the history of the people.

Stemming the Flood of Generosity: The Inverted Parable

A midrashic reflection on ebullience suggests an unexpected frame of reference:

> Aaron said to them: "Break off the golden rings . . ." (32:2). And the people broke off their golden rings and showered them upon him until he was compelled to exclaim: "Enough!" This was the point of Moses' rebuke: "And Laban, and Hazeroth, and Dizahab." (Deut 1:1)[12] This can be compared to a young man who came to a city and found the people collecting money for charity, and when they asked him also to subscribe, he went on giving until they had to tell him that he had already given enough. Further on his travels, he came to a place where they were collecting for a theater, and when asked to contribute toward it, he was also so generous that he had to be told, "Enough!" Israel, likewise, contributed so much toward the Golden Calf that they had to be told, "Enough!" And they contributed so much gold to the Mishkan that they had to be told, "Enough!" as it is said, "For their efforts had been more than enough for

all the tasks to be done." (37:7) The Holy One Blessed be He then said: "Let the gold of the Mishkan atone for the gold they brought toward the making of the Golden Calf."[13]

The people's relation to the Golden Calf and to the Mishkan are set into a single matrix: in both cases, they are spontaneously generous with their gifts of gold; in both cases, they have to be restrained, so overwhelming is the flood of gift. It is striking that the only evidence for such an irrepressible generosity in the case of the Golden Calf is found in a midrashic reading of *Dizahav*: a place name on their desert itinerary becomes a reference to "enough gold!" That is, as with the Mishkan, the people have to be told "Enough!" to stem the flood of giving.[14]

To make the point, we are offered the parable of the young man and his gifts to theater and charity. He, too, has to be restrained from a kind of obsessive drive to give. Ultimately, it is God who cryptically links the two events: "Let the gold of the Mishkan atone [lit. 'cover for'] the gold of the Calf." This process of atonement[15] becomes mysterious when we notice that, in the parable, the order of events is reversed: first, the young man gives money to charity, and then to the theater. In the framing midrashic narrative, however, the people first give gold for the Golden Calf and then for the Mishkan. It is this narrative that is plausibly described as "atonement"; the Mishkan is the redemptive project that gains them forgiveness for their earlier sin.

In this case, the parable, with its inverted order of events, seems to do the midrash a disservice. If the young man first gives to charity and then to the theater, the normal sequence of repentance is absurdly inverted. Instead of progressing, the young man is regressing. So as to make the moral point cogently, the order in the parable might easily have been reversed—theater first, then charity.

In effect, however, the inverted parable sets up a tension between narrative and parable, between *mashal* and *nimshal*. The sequence is confused, so that a simple optimism about right objects replacing wrong objects becomes impossible. The story of the young man, with his compulsive, morally opaque generosity, seeps into the midrashic narrative of the people. A linear progression from evil to good forms of energy is undermined in the parable structure, where the time sequence cannot objectively indicate redemption or atonement. It is only God's words that retroactively restructure the events of the past, expressing a "wish" that *this* should cover *that*.

God's words are in the jussive form: "Let it be . . ." Without His words, the facts carry no unequivocal meaning. Essentially, God suggests a possible world, imposing order on the promiscuous generosity of His undiscriminating people. Unnervingly, the midrash leads the reader to question the difference between Golden Calf and Mishkan, charity and theater. For the young man, such difference is not at all blatant. Both activities are signified by gold, by the giving of gold. In a subjective sense, are these activities similar or different?

From God's perspective, of course, a wishful world emerges in words: "Let the Mishkan cover for the Calf." To superimpose one image over the other is God's project: the wishful mode implies that God asks for human collaboration, a human vision of this gold and that, of this passion and that. A psychoanalytic retranscription of reality is invited: in effect, a remaking of the world.

As in Nelson Goodman's account of the use of symbol systems, the issue is the construction of a world from previous versions. Giving different weights and emphases to features of received worlds, human beings "condemn to nonreality," for instance, in Jerome Bruner's phrase, "everything that exists between C and C#."[16] In both art and science, this "world-making consists in the processing of symbols"; in place of a naïve realism, Goodman emphasizes the structural importance of human intentionality. Bruner articulates the basic notion of a cognitive philosophy:

> The moment one abandons the idea that "the world" is there once for all and immutably, and substitutes for it the idea that what we take as the world is itself no more nor less than a stipulation couched in a symbol system, then the shape of the discipline alters radically.[17]

"The world" constantly asks to be remade, reformed, by the human being. In this midrash, God suggests a possible recuperative re-forming of the stipulations of "reality." At the same time, other worlds, less redemptive, remain potentially makeable. The undiscriminating generosity of the people, the gold-fire[18] of their giving, can construct alternative worlds, with different emphases and deletions.

The unnerving power of this midrash, however, lies in the apparent equivalence of objects of generosity. The young man is in the throes of a passion that recks little of differences. Is the desire for the Golden Calf entirely symmetrical with that for the Mishkan? Both objects are constructed of gold, and both emerge from fire: materials and processes are then identical. Is this fire indistinguishable from that fire? Is this generosity a kind of nervous tic? And, if so, what is the terror that it would want to obscure?

Working in Fire: The Therapeutic Image

Another midrash in Shemoth Rabba also takes up the question of the relation between the Golden Calf and the Mishkan. Here, the emphasis is on the work of the master-craftsman, Bezalel, who was the primary artisan of the Mishkan:

> "See, God has called by name Bezalel." (35:30) It is written, "Behold, I have created the smith" (Isa 54:16): this refers to Bezalel; "that blows the fire of coals:" when Israel sinned with fire, as it says, "And I cast it into the fire, and there came out this calf" (32:24), Bezalel came and healed the wound. It is like the case of a doctor's disciple who applied a plaster to a wound and healed it. When people began to praise him, his teacher said, "Praise me, for I taught him!" Likewise, when everybody was saying that Bezalel had constructed the Mishkan through his knowledge and understanding, the Holy One, blessed be He, said, "It was I who created and taught him, as it says, 'Behold, I have created the smith.' " Hence, Moses said: "See, God has called by name Bezalel."[19]

In both verses—"*Behold*, I have created a smith . . ." and "*See*, God has called by name Bezalel . . ."—the reader is summoned to wonder. There is a mystery in the fire-work of the smith and of Bezalel. This rhetoric of wonder is amplified in the midrashic parable. The medical student achieves an unexpected cure; the professor claims that praise rightfully belongs to him, "for I taught him." In a bizarre analogy, God deflects praise for Bezalel's "fire-work" therapy in the Mishkan: "It was I who created him and taught him!"

The analogy with the jealous professor is a rather uneasy one. But we notice that in the frame-narrative, God does not say, "Praise Me!" but simply, "It was I who created and taught him." This He says in response to the universal acclaim of Bezalel's "wisdom and understanding," which are responsible for the "fire-work" of the Mishkan. What would be implied by God's insistence on taking credit for His student's achievement?

Bezalel's Gift: The Divine Source

To work in fire is to de-form and to re-form objects. Indeed, the proof-text from Isaiah continues: "Behold, I have created the smith to fan the charcoal and produce the tools for his work; so it is I who create the instruments of havoc" (Isa 54:16). The forms that emerge from fire can wreak havoc; but they too can be destroyed in fire. The skill of the fire-worker, who can undo and redo is, God asserts, a wonder that no apprenticeship to a human teacher could teach.

In the description of popular acclaim, Bezalel's "wisdom and understanding" are praised; but to an ear attuned to the biblical text the final term of praise is missing: "See, God has called by name Bezalel . . . And He has filled him with the spirit of God, with wisdom, with understanding, *and with knowledge*" (Exod 35:30–31). These three characteristics of Bezalel, repeated from 31:3, have become a formula for completeness of wisdom. There are different interpretations of the precise scope of each, but *da'at*—"knowledge"—is clearly climactic, the consummation of spiritual-intellectual achievement.

It is, therefore, significant that popular praise of Bezalel stops short of this highest term; and that God essentially translates it into his own terms: "It is I who have created him and taught him!" In other words, God indicates the divine source of a gift that others regard as the product of learning ("wisdom"), or of natural acuity ("understanding").[20] The missing term—*da'at*—alludes to the mystery of a gift that can be explained in no other way than as "taught by God."

Working in fire, curing fire with fire, is such a gift. Unaccountable in empirical terms, Bezalel's work is both aesthetic and therapeutic. "See, *I* have called by name Bezalel . . ." says God, not in jealousy or even pride; but to elicit wonder, a sense of the uncanny. In this midrashic reading, Bezalel's power is no mere skill, no familiar virtuosity; but an activity of *da'at*, in which materials from different worlds recombine to make new worlds.

The Golden Calf from Fire: An Uncanny Vitality

The Golden Calf emerged from gold and from fire; Bezalel uses the same materials, the same energy to make the Mishkan. In Aaron's account, indeed, there was a sense of the unpredictable, of a demonic force in the gold form that appeared out of the fire: "I cast it [the gold] into the fire and there emerged this calf!" (32:24), he explains to Moses, with a perhaps genuine astonishment. He is troubled by the event. In Rashi's words: "I did not know that the Calf would emerge, and it did!" Admittedly, it is not difficult to hear a comic undertone to this speech, as modern commentators have been quick to point out: Aaron is denying responsibility for the Golden Calf.[21] But at the same time, one can sympathize with Aaron, for whom the world has suddenly become incomprehensible: a monster has formed itself from the gold earrings he has just held in his hands. Beyond reason, beyond knowingness, an appalling power manifests itself from out of the fire.

This experience of the uncanny accompanies the birth of the Golden Calf:

> "Aaron saw"—that it had a spirit of life in it, as it is said: "They exchanged their glory for the image of a bull that feeds on grass;" (Ps 106:20) and he saw that the work of Satan had prospered, so he could not [lit. "did not have the mouth to"] push them away entirely.[22]

The mythic image of a calf *feeding on grass*, gleaming with animal life, effectively closes Aaron's mouth, clips his wings as a teacher of the One God.

The mythic theme is, however, the subject of much debate in midrashic sources. If the Calf indeed manifests vitality, then perhaps the idol is not without power? In a countermove, and in an ironic mode, another midrash presents the theologically correct position:

> "And Moses entreated God, saying, 'Why O God, should Your anger burn against Your people?' " (32:11) . . . R. Nehemiah said: When the Israelites committed that sin, Moses began to appease God. He said: "Master of the universe, they have provided You with help, and You are angry with them! This calf that they have made will help you: You will make the sun rise and it will take care of the moon; You will bring forth the stars and it the planets . . ." God answered: "Moses! Are you, too, misled like them! For there is nothing in the idol!" And Moses replied: "If so, why are you angry with Your children?"—as it is said: "Why, O God, should Your anger burn against Your people?"[23]

More than winning a debating point, Moses has touched a sensitive nerve: what, indeed, might justify God's anger? What ideal, utopian demand have the people failed to meet in making the idol, or at least in offering gold, fire, for transformation? Since "there is nothing in the idol!"

Another midrash treats Aaron's account of the vitality of the Golden Calf as a mere slip of the tongue:

A person should always be careful with his replies, for as a result of Aaron's reply to Moses (". . . and there emerged this Calf!"), the heretics broke away.[24]

Rashi comments:

The heretics could rationalize their heresy by saying, "There is reality to idolatry."

Even as a slip of the tongue, however, or as a less-than-cautious formulation, Aaron's description is fraught with subconscious meanings. One more midrash on the reality or unreality of the idol touches, even more intimately, on this nerve of subconscious life, on T. S. Eliot's "trilling wire in the blood." Here, the issue is the "reality" of the queen's adultery with a *dalpakei*, some kind of wooden object:

"Why, O God, should Your anger burn against Your people?" This can be compared to a king who entered his house and found his wife fondling a *dalpakei*, a wooden figure. He was furious, but his friend said to him, "If it could give birth, you would have a right to be furious. . . !" The king replied, "I know that this figure has no power at all, but this is to teach her that she should not behave like this."[25]

Adultery and Anger: Psychic Intensities

The suggestive and enigmatic behavior of the queen constitutes the core of the midrash. Whether or not there is any "reality" to the object of her passion, the reality of the passion itself is undeniable. The friend's logic brings a knowing view of reality into collision with a subjective world of unsatisfied desire, which glows the more luridly for its absurdity. The friend's advocacy is ultimately tendentious, since the king's anger responds to an emotional layer of experience that the friend will not confront. This anger, in the Hebrew idiom, "burns": it is fire and the queen's grotesque passion, also fire, provides the spark for a conflagration that the friend's sophistries cannot extinguish.

In terms of Moses' plea, therefore, the argument against anger is revealed, in this and other midrashim, as not only ineffective but even subtly provocative. In order to appease God, Moses will have to appeal to a density of relationship with His people that acknowledges and supersedes anger. For, subjectively, what has emerged from the fire has reality: it is a spontaneous formal expression of what Christopher Bollas calls a "psychic intensity."

By his own account, all Aaron has to do to trigger this intensity is to ask, "Who has gold?" (32:24).[26] Who has gold? Who has fire? In Aaron's mind, the story of the Golden Calf is one of a terrifying simplicity: a bare question electrifies the people; a hint is taken and the Golden Calf is spontaneously generated.

The Antidote

If Bezalel, therefore, has the power to create an antidote to this "psychic intensity," that power, the midrash affirms, must come from God. If he can work with the same fire to produce a therapeutic counter-form, his art cannot have been learned from a master, nor is it the product of the pragmatic strategies of the problem-solving mind: it is *da'at*—uncanny, godlike, transcending any given cognitive structure.

In Arthur Koestler's analysis, the creative modality represents the height of human genius—the ability to make combinations, to move beyond habitual frames of thought, and to integrate alien materials. He names it "bisociation": it "means combining two hitherto unrelated cognitive matrices in such a way that a new level is added to the hierarchy, which contains the previously separate structures as its members." The bisociative act "means combining two different sets of rules, to live on several planes at once."[27]

In this act of "mental self-repair," conventional frames of reference are combined, cross-fertilized.[28] Koestler includes scientific discovery, art, and humor in his spectrum of activities sparked by moments of bisociation. Such moments have something of the riddle about them: two frames of reference are brought into electric contact and a fiery energy is generated.

In the case of Bezalel, the nonrational gift for intuitive combinations is credited directly to God: it fits no preexisting set of rules. In his art, he can meet the imaginative needs of the people, those needs that led them to respond to a mere hint with unsuspected passion: "Who has gold?"

The Wonder of Bezalel: "Taking the Hint"

This enigmatic energy of the artist is the subject of an important comment by Ramban:

> "And they came, everyone whose heart exalted him . . ." (35:21) This is said about the wise ones who did the work, for we do not find this phrase, *nessa'o*, "the exaltation of the heart," about those who brought donations; rather, the expression, *nadav*, "their heart moved them," is used. The reason for using the expression "whose heart exalted him" is that they undertook to do the work, although there was no one among them who had learned these crafts from a teacher, or had trained his hands in any way to do them. Rather, a person who felt in his nature that he knew how to practice such skills, "[whose] heart was lifted up in the ways of God," (2 Chr 17:6), would come before Moses and say, I will do all that my lord describes . . . So the text says that there came before Moses "everyone whose heart exalted him" to undertake the work, and "everyone whose spirit moved him" brought the offering.[29]

Those whose hearts "exalted" them or "buoyed them up" are those who have never learned a craft, yet who know that their hands, untutored, can consummate the work. This sense of inspiration,[30] of unaccountable courage, is the experience of all the craftsmen, in Ramban's reading. Gratuitously, they sense an inner response to Moses' words, to the mere hint of names for skills that they have never practiced.

The wonder of this ability to "take a hint" becomes central to Ramban's understanding of the genius of Bezalel:

> "See, I have called by name Bezalel, the son of Uri, the son of Hur . . ." (31:2) God said to Moses, "See, I have called by name . . ." and Moses said to Israel, "See, God has called by name . . ." (35:30) The reason for this is that Israel in Egypt had been crushed under the work in mortar and in brick, and had acquired no knowledge of how to work with silver and gold, and the cutting of precious stones; they had never even seen them. It was thus a wonder that there was to be found amongst them such a great, wise-hearted man who knew how to work with silver and gold, and in cutting of stones, and in carving of wood, a craftsman, an embroiderer, and a weaver. For even among those who study from ex-

perts, you cannot find one who is proficient in all these crafts. And even those who know them and are skilled in practicing them, once their hands are continually at work in lime and mud, lose the ability to do delicate and fine art-work.

Moreover, Bezalel was a great sage in wisdom, in understanding, and in knowledge, to understand the secret of the Mishkan and all its furnishings, why they were commanded and at what they hinted. Therefore, God said to Moses that when he saw this wonder he should know that "I have filled him with the spirit of God," to know all these things in order that he would make the Mishkan . . . The Rabbis also said: "Bezalel knew how to combine the letters with which heaven and earth were created."[31] They meant by this that the Mishkan alludes to the structure of heaven and earth, and he knew and understood its secret.[32]

Ramban's analysis is, at base, historical. This is a people with no artistic tradition. The Egyptian slavery, the work with mortar and bricks, constitutes a kind of "anti-artistic" background; not only have they never worked with fine materials, they have never even seen them. In other words, they are a culturally, even a sensorily deprived nation. The wonder (Ramban repeats the word *pelle*—"wonder") of a multifaceted genius like Bezalel, therefore, is twofold: without training, he is expert in all fields of craftsmanship; and he is blessed with "wisdom, understanding, and knowledge," to fathom the esoteric meanings in God's instructions for building a structure that is a key to the mysteries of heaven and earth.

Bezalel masters the technical and the philosophical or mystical dimensions of the artist's work. The word "See!" expresses the prodigious nature of such an intuitive and profound knowledge. In language saturated with mystical residues, Ramban conveys the primordial, gratuitous energy that fills such an artist.

Contrasted with this enigmatic, polymorphous energy are the constructed forms of Egyptian brickwork. Not only do these constitute no cultural background for the artist; in their coarse, repetitive objectivity, they imperil that spark that is the wonder of Bezalel. Indeed, we notice that in the first part of Ramban's description, negatives abound: the people had not learned, had not seen, were not able. . . Against this background, Bezalel's gratuitous genius emerges with a childlike purity: in a sense, as Ramban himself goes on to suggest, he comes straight from Eden. One can hardly help, however, sensing in this marvelous birth a counterpart for the demonic birth of the Golden Calf, springing whole and vital from the flames. An association of Bezalel with the Golden Calf is strangely confirmed: it is not only that the artist works with fire; he too appears in the world unexplained, unaccountably potent, like the Calf.

Ramban ends by quoting a classic Talmudic account of Bezalel's gift: "He knew how to combine the letters with which heaven and earth were created." In combining the elements of the Mishkan, Bezalel is responding to hints from the cosmos. Intuitively, he grasps the "secrets" implicit in the work and, in Koestler's terms, "bisociates," combines matrices that were hitherto unrelated.

Ramban's claim for Bezalel, then, goes far beyond the depiction of a craftsman. To be Bezalel is to be the artist who works in fire: effectively, to be a mystic, a world-maker. Indeed, the Talmudic word for "combining," *tzaref*, carries the associations of "working-with-fire," "smith-work." Godlike, Bezalel creates new worlds from elements never before fused.

Bezalel: In the Shadow of God

This notion of the artist is further played out in the commentary of Ha-amek Davar. He questions the unusual expression for the artists: *chachmei lev*, "the wise of heart, into whose heart God has given wisdom" (36:2). And he defines the gift as the spontaneous knowledge, as in a child, of which art form will prove congenial. The moment of inspired choice is an "exaltation of the heart," in relation to a specific kind of work. Ha-amek Davar describes a sort of Montessori or Pestalozzi educational environment, in which the child freely and truly chooses his own materials.

In this "romantic" reading, the commentator places great faith in the myth of the informed heart. "The heart has its reasons which reason cannot know" (Pascal). The courage to listen to the prompting of the heart is the gift of God. Following this inspired moment of choice, many years of hard work may be required to master the chosen craft. Unlike Ramban, Ha-amek Davar does not speak of a miraculous and instantaneous mastery; the wonder is simply in the initial confidence of choice.

However, underlying the romantic element in these readings of the artist's work and providing a strong taproot to nurture them is a classic midrash that makes a still more startling claim:

> "And Bezalel, the son of Uri . . . made all that God had commanded Moses:" (38:22) "All that Moses had commanded him," is not written

> here, but, "all that God had commanded Moses"—even in matters that his master had not told him, Bezalel's opinion was attuned with what Moses had been told on Sinai.[33] For Moses told Bezalel to make the furnishings first and the Mishkan afterwards but Bezalel said to him, "Surely, it is the way of the world first to build a house and then to place the household utensils in it!" Moses replied, "So, indeed, did I hear from the mouth of the Holy One, blessed be He." Moses also said, "Bezalel, you must have been in the shadow of God (*be-tzel-el*), for absolutely so did God command me!" And Bezalel did make the Mishkan first and then he made the furnishings.[34]

The artist's intuition fills the gap between the verse "Bezalel made all that God had commanded Moses" and the unrealized "as Moses had commanded him." There are cases where Moses revised God's words and Bezalel simply knew God's will and consummated it. The play on Bezalel's name ("You must have been in the shadow of God . . .") expresses this unmediated knowledge that bypasses the deflections of the messenger.

In the shadow of God, Bezalel becomes an archetype for primary, inspired knowledge. One might even say that he most purely fulfills God's project in creating the human being: "Let us make man in our image [*be-tzalmenu*] . . ." (Gen 1:26). To be the "image of God," the *tzelem*, perhaps invokes a "shadowing" ability (*tzel*): a subtle, self-effacing sensibility that can pick up on hints, on intimations that are almost nonexistent. In a context in which blatant images of God emerge from fire, the midrash constructs Bezalel as the subtle knower of secrets, filled with the spirit of God.

The formulaic phrase, "He made all that God had commanded Moses," is, of course, repeated many times, particularly in the context of the fashioning of the priestly garments. In a daring passage, Ha-amek Davar explores the implications of the midrashic reading.

> "And Moses saw all the work and behold, they had done it as God had commanded Moses, so had the Israelites done all the work; and Moses blessed them." (39:43): Moses found it marvelous that "they had done it as God had commanded Moses," because he had not had time to teach them all the detailed instructions as God had taught him; and yet Bezalel, through his peculiar genius, had achieved perfect accuracy in his work. "In the shadow of God," he had intuited the precise forms of God's will.[35]

Ha-amek Davar cites another source to suggest that "as God had commanded Moses" refers to the original command: "Let them make Me a sanctuary, *such that I may* dwell among them" (25:8). In fulfilling this, Bezalel had made each object with perfect intuition, so that it is habitable by God.

In this reading, the Mishkan presents not just an architectural challenge, or a test of craftsmanship in many areas. It is a symbolic world that mirrors God's own creation of the world, a formal expression of a large imagining. Without learning all the details, Bezalel improvises and achieves a kind of affinity with God in his work.

The Mishkan: Replica of a Fiery Model

If the Mishkan represents God's creation of the world, the artist who constructs it truly—even with incomplete guidance—is indeed "taught by God." Such a view of the Mishkan is supported by many linguistic analogies between the account of the Mishkan and that of Creation.[36] But, one may ask, what is it to build *truly*? Is it to intuit some platonic reality, an image in God's mind, and to materialize it in gold, linen, and wood, exactly according to the model? Is there an ideal form that, as consummate craftsman, Bezalel simply knows, before and beyond words? Or is his intuition, as we have suggested, free to create entirely new combinations of elements, to think new thoughts whose fitness for God's presence is manifested not in the exactness of the replica but in the intensity of the vision?

That Bezalel's genius transcends a technical mastery of materials and forms, or even a kind of inspired common sense,[37] is suggested by the following midrash:

> When the Holy One, blessed be He, commanded Moses, "Make Me a Mishkan," he should have just put up four poles and spread out the Mishkan over them! We must therefore infer that the Holy One, blessed be He, showed Moses on high red fire, green fire, black fire, and white fire, and said to him: "Set it up according to the manner of it that you were shown on the mountain." (26:30) R. Berechyah in the name of R. Bezalah compared this to a king who, possessing an exquisite robe worked in precious stones, said to a member of his household, "Make me another like it!" The latter answered, "My lord the king! Am I capable of making one like that?" The king replied, "I remain in my glory and you use your materials!" In the same way, Moses said to the Holy One, blessed be He, "O God, am I capable of making such things?" God answered him, "Do it in the manner I am showing you . . ."—with blue,

with purple, with scarlet, and with fine linen. "If," said the Holy One, blessed be He, to Moses, "you will make in the world below what is in the world above, I shall leave my counselors on high. I will descend and condense My Presence among them below."[38]

To make the Mishkan "according to the model that you were shown on the mountain" (25:40) might have indicated pedantic, mechanical imitation; or else, a minimalist sketch of the original—"four poles." Instead, the midrash presents the problem of the Mishkan as, precisely, the problem of fire, of fires, of four fires.

Improvisation: Responding to Hints

One reading of this would abandon entirely the replica idea. Moses' materials that seem to fall so far short of the visionary fire are to create not a replica, but an earthly *version* of the fiery model. In such a version there is nothing given, nothing fixed: it is a human improvisation, a total response to hints, suggestions from the world of fire. In making such a structure, the artist ultimately is led back to *himself*, to the fire within, to his own capacity to be electrified.

The Mishkan as improvisation is clearly an eccentric notion, since the instructions are so detailed and quantitatively precise. However, an element—perhaps a crucial element—of improvisation is suggested by the differences between the original instructions and the executed work. For Ha-amek Davar, for instance, these become emblematic of the creative vitality of the artist "in the shadow of God." The Temple in Jerusalem, too, was not identical at every point with the Mishkan in the wilderness. These changes open up space for a notion of inspiration or of improvisation.

A radical view of this kind is taken by the Chasidic master R. Levi Yitzhak of Berditchev. He comments on the first mimetic instruction: "'. . . Exactly as I show you—the model of the Mishkan and the model of its furnishings—and so shall you make it' (25:9): Moses and his generation conceived of the sanctuary by their own light, their own prophetic vision—'and so you shall make it': through the generations,[39] you shall make God's sanctuary according to the visions of your own time and place."[40]

No single blueprint governs the forms of the Sanctuary. "So you shall make it—in accordance with the visions, the idioms of that time." In such a teaching, idiosyncratic elements may inform the sacred space. Entirely new combinations of letters, of forms, will manifest the imaginary fire.

In this Chasidic teaching, there is a conscious sanctification of the idiosyncratic. "No two prophets speak in the same style."[41] It is the personal light of the prophet that gives him unique access to God's will. The Chasidic master does not delimit the prophetic vision to past time. His teaching alludes to all times and their visions. And, we may add, texts in which fire figures as centrally as it does in these midrashic meditations on the Mishkan inevitably evoke the intimacies of the human soul. In the words of Gaston Bachelard, "Fire is more likely to smoulder within the soul than beneath ashes."[42]

The Imaginative Act: Deforming Images

It is here, in the smithy of human imagination, that we approach the images of the Mishkan and of the Calf, in all their similarity and their difference. Bachelard writes of the tension between imagination and images:

> We always think of the imagination as the faculty that *forms* images. On the contrary, it *deforms* what we perceive; it is, above all, the faculty that frees us from immediate images and *changes* them. If there is no change, or unexpected fusion of images, there is no imagination; there is no *imaginative act.* If the image that is *present* does not make us think of one that is *absent*, if an image does not determine an abundance—an explosion—of unusual images, then there is no imagination . . . Thanks to the *imaginary*, imagination is essentially *open* and *elusive.* It is the human psyche's experience of *openness* and *novelty.* More than any other power, it is what distinguishes the human psyche . . .[43]

Images, in all their presence and power, are constantly transcended by imagination. If we accept Bachelard's analysis, then, the work of Bezalel is to respond to the rigors of a questing imagination; it is the faculty of deforming the images offered by perception. It involves swarms, explosions, unexpected unions of images; but it pulls loose from the "all too stable background of our familiar memories."

The similarity of the Calf and the Mishkan is that both come from fire and are constituted from gold. But the difference has to do with imagination, with the transcending, even the repudiation of images. We remember that

Hur, Bezalel's grandfather, was martyred, in the midrashic narrative, for resisting the people's desire for a fetish.[44] God then chooses as the artist of the Mishkan one who genetically, as it were, knows the rigors of the iconoclastic imagination. He "knows how to work in every kind of thinking work" (35:33); even in thought, that is, he is to pull himself loose of the stable bedrock of images and perceptions.[45]

Thinking-Weaving Work: The Bisociative Imagination

"Thinking work"[46] characterizes Bezalel and the other master artists. This work is informed by imagination, in a sense that Rashi powerfully describes in his comment on the woven fabric of the curtains:

> "Thinking work": This is weaving work, not embroidery—with different figures on each side of the curtain—a lion's face on this side and an eagle's face on that side.[47]

Beyond the technical difficulties of this two-sided weaving work, the description provides an emblem for the "bisociative" work of the imagination. The mind of the artist is not allowed to rest on a stable image; it must shuttle back and forth, across the boundary, encompassing two images, two matrices, separating them, and integrating them.

This "homeospatial" dimension of the Mishkan work is entrusted to the best artists, the "wise of heart."[48] These are complex spirits who can respond to hints, who do not require exhaustive information. Their mode of seeing is modeled on God's complex vision, as it is portrayed in a powerful midrash:

> And God said, "I have indeed seen . . . (*ra'oh ra'ithi* [3:7])"—"You see only one sight, but I see two. You see only how they will come to Sinai and receive My Torah, but I see how after I come to Sinai to give them the Torah, on My way back in My chariot drawn by four animals, they will contemplate it and withdraw one of the animals in order to anger Me with it; as it says: 'Each of the four had the face of an ox on the left.' (Ezek 1:10) With that they will anger Me; as it says: 'They exchanged their glory for the image of a bull that feeds on grass.' (Ps 106:20)"[49]

In Koestler's terms, God's vision is "bisociative," fusing Sinai and Calf into a new reality. If God points this difference out to Moses, it is presumably to suggest that a godlike complexity of vision is within his capacity as well. In the midrash, God teaches Moses a direction for his imaginative development.

God's Vision: Beyond the Fetish

As in a hologram, however, the detail of the Golden Calf narrative also reflects the larger structure of atomistic as against complex vision. The people sin by *excerpting* a fragmentary reality—the ox—from the divine chariot empowered by four animals. In referring to Ezekiel 1:10, the midrash moves into a kabbalistic frame of reference. For our purposes, we may notice simply that the ox kabbalistically represents *din*, strict justice, the sinister side of reality (the ox is placed at the *left* of the chariot), desolation, an unredeemed realism—a whole spectrum of unenchanted associations. The people select this image, with its field of memories, to represent the psychic intensity of the wilderness experience.[50] Somewhat in the manner of Milton's "Evil, be thou my good," they select one facet of the rich, divine—and therefore human—prism.

By fixating on one image, they betray imagination. "If the image that is *present* does not make us think of one that is *absent*, if an image does not determine an abundance—an explosion—of unusual images, then there is no imagination . . . a stable and completely realized image *clips the wings* of the imagination."[51]

The Calf-Ox is such an inhibiting image, confining imaginative power to a stable form. This is the sin of the Golden Calf, a sclerosis of the imagination. In God's complex, "unstable" vision, however, this image of the people constitutes only one element. In a sense, then, God reproaches Moses for foreshadowing the human need for bedrock, for the stable form of a single cognitive frame.

The alternative, God-taught model for vision involves a doubleness, a desire for otherness. "The secret of the One cannot be seen except where there are two."[52] "Unity is plural and, at minimum, is two" (Buckminster Fuller). This paradox is played out in the Mishkan, in the "thinking work," two-sided, crafty, dynamic; in the central node of space between the wings of the cherubim, from which God speaks;[53] in Bezalel's genius for combining the letters with which heaven and earth were created.

Bezalel's therapeutic art, one may say, is to reintegrate the letters that, according to one classic midrash, flew off the Stone Tablets.[54] A ponderous mass of stone was left; the crushing weight of it dropped from Moses' arms and shattered. Fire was essential to that crisis: the fetish emerged from fire and the disenchanted residue of stone is also the residue of fire. And Bezalel recomposes the fragmented letters—*with fire;* he knows how to combine them—*le-tzaref*—melting in the heart of fire the congealed fragments of imagination.

Ambiguous Fire: Inwardness and Outwardness

This ambiguous fire, generating calves and cherubim, can be described by using the dynamic model articulated by Don Handelman and David Shulman, in *God Inside Out.* In a different, mythic context, they describe an imaginative voyage from an inner, heated, timeless state, in which all is connected, through an awareness of gaps in the red-hot texture of reality. Through these gaps, the self "devolves outward into time and bounded form, in a process of cooling and congealing. Externalization is the mode in which these discontinuities exist and have an effect."[55] This movement outward, toward petrified form, eventually turns inward, internalizing the energies that have been spent in the self-externalizing drive and through a transformative heating or melting rediscovering the preexisting totality within. And the cycle continues, with further discontinuities creating further ruptures in holistic being.[56]

I suggest that this process, from inwardness to outwardness to inwardness, constitutes the central paradox of fire. A "playful impulse" is involved: "what is inside simply must *play itself out.*"[57] Irresistible separations will devolve from a state of fluid, red-hot continuity: "all the coordinates of our inner worlds—time, space, name, identity—reflect the drive to objectify and thereby delimit and destroy . . . parts of ourselves keep going dead and dry."[58]

This voyage outward and inward is part of the fire reverie, as Bachelard describes it. "The *dreaming man* seated before his fireplace is the man concerned with inner depths, a man in the process of development . . . fire gives to the man concerned with inner depths the lesson of an inner essence which is in a process of development: the flame comes forth from the heart of the burning branches." Bachelard quotes Rodin: "Each thing is merely the limit of the *flame* to which it owes its existence."[59]

The inner, generative flame exerts a fascination that can lead to death, to extinction. Bachelard calls this the *Empedocles*[60] *complex*: "Fire is for the man who is contemplating it an example of a sudden change or development . . . [it] suggests the desire to change, to speed up the passage of time, to bring all of life to its conclusion, to its hereafter . . . The fascinated individual hears *the call of the funeral pyre.* For him destruction is more than a change, it is a renewal."[61]

The Primal Reverie: Fear and Fascination

This reverie unites "the love and the respect for fire, the instinct for living and instinct for dying." Indeed, the archetypal fire in Exodus, the "heart of flame" in the Burning Bush, similarly both lures Moses closer to see "this great vision," and warns him off ("Come no closer!" [3:5]). The "great vision" is a dream of a burning fire that does not consume: a reverie out of the very heart of fire, the inward place of transformation. This *heart/flame* (*labath/lehava*) arises in his reverie, "in order to hearten him (*le-labvo*), so that, when he comes to Sinai and sees *these fires,* he will not be afraid."[62]

The Burning Bush is to "immunize" Moses against the terrors of fire which will constitute a real dimension of his journey. This function of the primal reverie of fire is implicit in Rashi's comment:

> "And this shall be your sign": that I have sent you and that you will succeed in My mission: as you have seen the Bush fulfilling My mission without being consumed, so shall you go on My mission without being harmed.[63]

Fear of and fascination with fire, with what Bachelard calls the *pyremenon*—the product of fire, the "phenomenon through fire"—is Moses' most human characteristic. For fire changes everything: the phenomenon caused by fire "must be speeded up or slowed down; we must grasp the point (or extra degree) of fire which leaves a mark on a substance as we do the *instant* of love which leaves a mark on our existence."[64] He quotes Paul Valéry:

> there can be no giving up, no respite; no fluctuations in thought, courage or humor. These arts [of fire] prescribe, in its most dramatic aspect, the close combat between man and form . . . Any error is fatal: the piece is ruined. Whether the fire dies down or whether it blazes up, its caprice means disaster . . .[65]

This unforgiving quality of the work in fire, the need for a precise temperature, a rigorous attention to the turning point between "too-hot" and "too-cold," makes Moses hesitate more than once. "Caprice" means disaster; the consciousness of time is exquisite, excruciating. But the desire for what can be gained only at immense risk draws him, despite himself, into the heart of fire.

Indeed, the "great vision" that compels his gaze at the Burning Bush is a vision of just this kind. The Bush is aflame but it is not consumed: that is, a moment of exquisite awareness comes to him, when the fire is nurtured, "fed," without destroying its object. Impossibly, a radical desire is consummated without consuming or being itself extinguished. At such a moment, transformation without death becomes imaginable.

Bezalel's *Da'at:* Knowing the Moment

Bezalel, on the other hand, lives with a different consciousness of time. He "knows how to fuse the letters of creation": he has the *da'at*, the integrative knowledge, to heal with the very fire of disintegration. He seems to *play with fire*, with an intuitive knowledge of what must play itself out. He "knows," I suggest, not only "how" to combine the letters, but "when." In other words, he is able to bide his time, to consummate meanings only when the time is ripe, when the letters have had a chance to "breathe," as it were.

This exquisite sense of timing is an essential characteristic of *da'at*, of "bisociative" knowledge. Fusion with an other, like the work with fire, is a matter of an *instant*, of a *sha'at ratzon*, a moment of affinity. The paradox of such a knowledge is that it deals with the interaction of *separate* beings, whose successful meeting depends on mediating, in time, between separateness and union. "And Adam *knew* (*yada*) his wife Eve . . ."—clearly alludes to sexual union. But *da'at* is also differentiation, analysis: "If there is no *da'at*, where does the power of discrimination come from?"[66] Without the sense of an other, there can be no union.

Bezalel's godlike genius is, then, his sense of timing, his ability to resist the urge to make the facile images that will clip the wings of imagination. This possibly is the wonder at which the midrash gestures: "See, I have called by name Bezalel . . ." "Behold, I have created the smith . . ." The marvel is the consciousness of the artist who works in fire: vigilant, passionate, and cautious at once.

Taking the Hint: Negative Capability

Adam Phillips writes powerfully about the modality of the artist, or of "the artist inside us": he is "all the time on the look-out for material to make a dream with." Drawn to specific fragments of experience, the artist "secretly" transforms them into a personal idiom, a mode of self-fashioning. This unconscious project also constitutes the "unofficial education" of every student who wants to feel the reality of his material.

In the paradigm case of Bezalel, the wonder is just this capacity to be "taught of God"; in other words, to be susceptible to the hints, the sparks of all four fires, and, equally, to resist the blandishments of the stable, objectified form. Bezalel's work is the counterpart to the brute haste of the Golden Calf fetish. Keats has a wonderful phrase to describe this way of living in time: "diligent indolence." Or, in a now classic formulation, "negative capability": that state in which "man is capable of being in uncertainties, Mysteries, doubts, without any irritable reaching after fact and reason."[67]

The strength of such a capability can be grasped only if the fear of fire is no stranger to one's dream life. Marion Milner writes about her experiment with what she called "free-drawing": the useless doodles, she found, were "the kind in which a scribble turned into a recognizable object too soon."

> It seemed almost as if at these moments one could not bear the chaos and uncertainty about what was emerging long enough, as if one had to turn the scribble into some recognizable whole when in fact the thought or mood seeking expression had not yet reached that stage. And the result was a sense of false certainty, a compulsive and deceptive sanity, a tyrannical victory of the common-sense view which always sees objects as objects, but at the cost of something else which was seeking recognition, something that was more to do with imaginative than with common-sense reality.[68]

The hunger for recognizable objects, for a calf, for example, is related to what Milner calls "a sense of false certainty, a compulsive and deceptive sanity." What is sacrificed in the process she calls "imaginative reality": that energy of imagination that is stemmed by the reassuring image. The movement of a "compulsive and deceptive sanity" registers as a precipitate flight from the fire.

Adam Phillips calls one of Keats's letters a "small manifesto against conscientiousness":[69] "For Keats, inspiration means being able to take the hint."[70] Phillips discusses quotations from Keats, Henry James, and Wittgenstein, detecting the subtle pulse of a sensibility to hints: "Hints start things off; and we have no idea beforehand what might be a hint for us."[71] An anecdote at a dinner table or a trifling line from a mediocre play can provoke inner revelations. The imagination is fed without being force-fed; it is nurtured without destroying what feeds it. "It is not only a tuned responsiveness, it is also an unconscious radar for affinities; for what speaks to one by calling up one's own voice (that is how one knows that something or someone speaks to you, *it makes you speak*)."[72]

Phillips's understanding of the transformative power of hints largely precludes intention: "more often than not, the useful hint is not intended as such." In his work with fire, Bezalel, we have suggested, creates partially in response to hints. Orders, commands cannot account for what Bezalel achieves. Phillips dismisses the possibility of God's playing a role in this drama of inspired contingency, in the unknowable encodings of the unconscious: "Only a God—an all-knowing one—would be able to predict what a person might be able to use." The rhetorical flourish—Phillips is describing an outlandish fiction—provokes the reader to wonder: perhaps just such a God is present in the improvisations and transformations of Bezalel's work?

> "And I shall fill him with the spirit of God, with wisdom . . ." (31:3). This teaches you that God only fills with wisdom one who already has wisdom . . . The shopkeeper who is about to sell wine or honey or oil and brine—if he is intelligent, he will smell the jar: if it smells of wine, he will put in wine. Similarly, with oil or honey or brine. So God sees that a person has in him a spirit of wisdom and fills him with wisdom—as it is said: "I shall *fill* him with wisdom . . ." for he already had wisdom in him.[73]

In the logic of this midrash, filling Bezalel with wisdom implies a movement of *filling up*, of confirming the idiosyncratic character of the individual. This is no arbitrary selection of a craftsman. The source of Bezalel's wisdom is both internal and external. An aroma of wisdom is perceptible in him, a residue of inward development. God confirms this and helps him to disseminate his idiom; to fulfill the inner psychic intensity in worlds beyond the coherent place of origin:

It is essential to one's personal freedom to break up lucid unities of thought, lest consciousness become a form of ideational incarceration. Indeed, the more profound a psychic intensity, the less permanent its registration in consciousness, for the ideas deriving immediately from it soon give birth to a plenitude of further and divergent thoughts which disseminate in countless ways.[74]

The effects of disseminating the idiosyncratic aromas of the jar are incalculable. The uses to which the substance will be put can be neither fully imagined nor controlled. Wisdom, like perfume, or wine, or like language itself, circulates to unpredictable effect.[75]

Perfume: Disseminating Intensity

Perfume also circulates in the following midrash, to irresistible effect:

[The Mishkan] is a testimony to the whole world that Moses was appointed by God to erect the Mishkan. R. Isaac said: This can be compared to a king who took a wife whom he loved very dearly. In the course of time, he became angry with her and deserted her, and her neighbors taunted her, saying, "He will no longer return to you." Subsequently, the king sent her a message: "Prepare my palace and make the beds, for I am coming back to you such-and-such a day." When that day arrived, the king returned to her and became reconciled with her, entering her chamber and eating and drinking with her. At first, her neighbors would not believe all this; but when they *scented the fragrant spices*, they at once knew that the king had become reconciled with her.

Similarly, God loved Israel, bringing them before Mount Sinai, giving them the Torah, and calling them kings, as it says, "And you shall be to Me a kingdom of priests" (19:6), but after only forty days, they sinned. The heathen nations then said: "God will never be reconciled with them," as it is said, "Men said among the nations: 'They shall never again sojourn here.' " (Lam 4:15) But as soon as Moses pleaded for mercy for them, God forgave them, for it says, "And God said: I have pardoned according to your word." (Num 14:20) Moses then said: "Master of the World! I am quite satisfied that You have forgiven Israel, but do please make it known among all the nations that You have no more resentment against Israel in

> Your heart." God answered, "As you live, I will cause My Presence to dwell in their midst," for it says, "And let them make Me a sanctuary, that I may dwell among them." (25:8) "By this, all the nations will know that I have forgiven them." That is why it says, "The Mishkan of *the testimony*," because the Mishkan was a testimony to the Israelites that God had pardoned their sins.[76]

The parable of a mysteriously ruptured marriage and an equally mysterious reunion presents the skepticism of the neighbors as entirely plausible. A restored domesticity—the intimacy of the cleaned palace, the spread beds, the food and drink—has no power to convince those outside the palace. Only the fragrance of perfume circulating from the palace makes the reunion imaginable.

Similarly, the nations are skeptical about God's forgiveness of the Israelites after the Golden Calf. Here, however, there is little mystery. The moral framework of the narrative is firmly outlined: the people sin, the nations—representing the responses of natural justice—cannot conceive of forgiveness; Moses pleads, God forgives. The coda narrates Moses' dissatisfaction with an unpublicized reconciliation between God and the people, and God's declaration, "I shall come to dwell among them." This presence of God is, then, the equivalent of the perfume circulating from the palace. A kind of second honeymoon makes its intimate world manifest in uncontrollable ways: like perfume, the reunion of God and Israel is irresistibly disseminated in the larger world.

Perfume is expressive of all that is "undemonstrable" about the intimacy of a relationship. Private, idiosyncratic, it circulates to unpredictable effect. God's presence among the people has a similarly pervasive and enigmatic effect.[77] It is the expression of an "inordinate love," as the midrash describes the king's love for his wife (*chibva yoter mi-dai*—here translated, "loved her dearly"). The neighbors, the nations, are rationally justified in their skepticism. The privacies, the rituals of relationship, do not translate into terms that the public world can acknowledge. What would "returning" to her mean? The resumption of a previous model of marriage? Or an explosive dissemination of new intensities of experience? The perfume, God's presence within the people, suggests the latter: an order of intensity unprecedented in the time before rupture.

After the Golden Calf: A New Order of Intimacy

This question about the nature of God's forgiveness is evoked by both Ramban and Rashi, and affects their classic controversy about the order of the narrative.[78] For Ramban, God had commanded Moses about the Mishkan long before the people sinned with the Golden Calf. This, indeed, is the sequence of events as narrated in the Torah. They sinned, and then, "there was a return to the early time of nuptial love; and therefore Moses transmitted all the commandments about the Mishkan that he had been given before."[79] The "second honeymoon" allows the consummation of the marriage in the form that had always been God's design: the building of the Mishkan and God's presence among the people.

For Rashi, however, "the Mishkan is testimony that God had forgiven their sin—for behold, His presence had come to dwell among them!"[80] Rashi is here alluding to our midrash about the king and queen to whose reunion the "perfume" of God's presence serves as testimony. In Rashi's reading, a completely new situation is initiated after the Calf narrative, as God comes to dwell in their midst. This is not the fulfillment of an original design, but, in an important sense, a *consequence of the sin*, a new conception of the relationship.

In support of this idea that the Mishkan represents a new order of intimacy, R. Eliyahu Mizrahi, in his super-commentary to Rashi, makes an intriguing claim.[81] It is possible that God had commanded the Mishkan at the beginning of the narrative, as it is narrated in the Torah, and that Moses had simply not transmitted these instructions to the people till after God had forgiven them. On this view, however, what would have given Moses the confidence that he might now transmit those instructions to the people? Simply the fact that God had given him the second set of Tablets, for instance, would not be sufficient to justify his decision to reinstate the original intimacy of God's design. Forgiveness, even the continuation of the *status quo ante* of the covenant at Sinai, would not justify an assumption on Moses' part that the Mishkan idea—far transcending the *status quo ante*—was to be conveyed to the people. The confirmation of the religious structures of the Sinai revelation (*kiyyum ha-dat*, in Mizrahi's phrase) is one thing; but creating a place for God's presence among them would be an expression of *chiba yetera*, of an inordinate love.

On this hypothesis, Moses would have no license to initiate this newly intense phase of relationship. There remains, therefore, only the alternative view: that the Mishkan idea had never been broached before; that only after the people are forgiven for the Golden Calf, God says to Moses, "Let them make Me a sanctuary that I may dwell among them," and in that sentence transforms the relationship to one of unimagined intimacy.

This discussion, effectively, frames God's command, "Let them make Me a sanctuary, that I may dwell among them," as a performative utterance. God's words incalculably transform reality, create a new state of being. Like perfume, language circulates to unpredictable effect. Allusive, evoking images and memories, God's words hint at possibilities. What, rationally, do they mean? This evocativeness, even elusiveness, is the "testimony" that God has forgiven the people. A new, "inordinate love" is the undefinable condition, transcending the continuity of religious structures, of the world after the Golden Calf.

Inordinate Love: A Form of Knowledge

An "inordinate love," that can only be hinted in perfume, in language, must remain, to some extent, mysterious. The words *chiba yetera*, however, evoke the mishnaic aphorism: "Beloved is man, who is created in the image of God; *inordinate love* [*chiba yetera*] is in the fact that he has been informed [lit., given knowledge] that he is created in the image of God."[82] To be created in God's image is a fact; but to have been given knowledge of it is the affirmation of a project. When God first informs a human being—Noah (Gen 9:6)[83]—of his likeness to God, He makes a claim upon him, uses the language of imagination to provoke him to transcend the undifferentiated horror of the Flood. This hinting is a form of knowledge, of *da'at*, that offers to germinate in unpredictable ways.

After the Golden Calf narrative, a new sensibility, signified by the Mishkan, prevails. As opposed to the clear commands of Sinai, the Mishkan instructions contain germs of suggestion, invite the artists to weave idiosyncratic webs. Like perfume, this activity has incalculable effects; and hints at the "inordinate love," the extraordinary, redemptive grace that invests such a difficult freedom.

The Mishkan Completed and Devoured by Fire

At the end of Exodus, after all the details of the Mishkan have finally been composed into the integrated structure, an enigmatic coda describes how Moses cannot enter it:

> When Moses had finished the work, the cloud covered the Tent of Meeting, and the presence of God filled the Mishkan. Moses could not enter the Tent of Meeting, because the cloud had settled upon it and the Presence of God filled the Mishkan. When the cloud lifted from the Mishkan, the Israelites would travel on their various journeys. But if the cloud did not lift, they would not set out until such time as it did lift. For over the Mishkan a cloud of God rested by day, and fire would appear in it by night, before the eyes of all the house of Israel throughout their journeys.[84]

The problem of cloud that becomes fire by night bars Moses' access to the Mishkan.[85] This last mention of fire in Exodus generates a midrashic narrative about fire as part of the human reverie:

> "For over the Mishkan a cloud of God rested by day, and fire would appear in it by night . . ." (40:38) When the Israelites saw the pillar of cloud resting on the Mishkan, they rejoiced, saying: "Now God has been reconciled with us." But when night came, the pillar of fire descended and surrounded the Mishkan. Everyone saw it as one flame of fire and began to sorrow and weep, saying, "Woe to us! For nothing (lit., emptiness) we have laboured! All our great work has been burnt up in a moment!" They rose early next morning and saw the pillar of cloud encompassing the Mishkan. Immediately, they rejoiced *with an inordinate joy*, saying, "This is testimony to the world that if they wanted to make such a thing they could not. Why? Because of God's great love for Israel." That is why it says: "His shade I desired and sat in it, and his fruit was sweet to my palate." (Song of Songs 2:3)[86]

The fire at night is experienced as ultimate loss; in an instant, the work of months is consumed. This unforgiving power of the instant is the power of fire. It terrifies and fascinates. Bachelard's term, the *Empedocles complex*, comes to mind: the instant of love that leaves its brand on the erotic and spiritual life both compels and appalls:

> "To disappear, to be swallowed up, to leave no trace!" moaned the heart of the woman intoxicated with idea of destruction. "In a second this fire could devour me like a vine twig, like a wisp of straw."[87]

The people dream a dream of fire, of emptiness superseding the density and productivity which that fire had facilitated. They then wake to cloud and rejoice *exceedingly*: the language of the midrash moves into the superlative after the fire-dream of the night. Where previously they had simply "rejoiced" at the cloud that signifies God's Presence and forgiveness, they now "rejoice with an inordinate joy." Strangely, although the cloud encompasses the Mishkan in the same way as the fire, the fact that the Mishkan is, virtually, invisible does not inhibit their joy. Unlike the fire, the cloud allows for continuity: as an object of reverie, it can contain structures, even as it envelops them.

The Shade of the Apple-Tree: The Eccentric Movement of Desire

The inordinate or excessive joy of the people is articulated mysteriously: it is a response to the cloud which is testimony to the special love of God. In this context, the verse from Song of Songs is enigmatic: the desire of the beloved for the apple tree, for the sweet rapture of its shade and its fruit, does not seem to be related to the joy of the people at the death and resurrection of the Mishkan.

I suggest that the great love of God for his people is known by them as an experience of shade, of a taste in the mouth, of desire. After the night when all had been consumed in fire, they discover their own idiom of love: a personal "taste" for the apple tree which, according to the midrash, objectively offers no shade:

> This apple tree—everyone flees from it in the *hamsin* [the hot, dry season], because it has no shade. So all the nations fled from God when He gave them the Torah. But "I desired His shade and sat in it."[88]

Powerfully, the Israelites' choice to receive the Torah is portrayed as a personal, almost an eccentric movement of desire. Objectively, Sinai offers the human being little of what he naturally seeks in the spiritual life—little shade on a blistering day. There may even be an allusion here to the famous midrash in which God holds the mountain over the people's heads "like a barrel": "If you accept My Torah, good. If not, here shall be your grave." That is, the coercive aspect of Sinai is ironically described as protective shade: a perspective that the nations understandably find difficult.

Unaccountably, however, the Israelites are drawn to the imagination of Sinai which, to them, offers substantial shade and sweet fruit. Like Bezalel in the shadow of God, they sense an affinity, an unmediated and congenial reality that initiates an apprenticeship.

This idiosyncratic taste for the apple tree, the sense that they will know how to use the hints, almost impalpable, of what Sinai suggests, emerges as a kind of "gourmet" sensibility:

> "His fruit was sweet to my palate:" Said R. Isaac: These were the twelve months the Israelites spent facing Mount Sinai, *sweetening themselves* with the words of Torah. For what is the meaning of "His fruit was sweet to my palate"?—"To *my* palate it was sweet, but to the palate of the nations it was bitter as gall."[89]

The effect of twelve months facing Sinai is an educated palate; the sweetness of the Torah is not accessible to the uninformed palate. Only those who have experienced all the fiery vicissitudes of Sinai, of the Golden Calf and the Mishkan, will develop a connoisseur pleasure, perhaps even an arcane delight in an enriched consciousness. The sweet fruit of Sinai ultimately represents a people "sweetened," seasoned, pacified to a new self-awareness.

This idiosyncratic way of experiencing Sinai constitutes intimate "testimony" of God's love. It is only after the energies of fire have been fully played out—cloud and fire and cloud—that a new taste for the penetrating heat opens the people to an "excessive" joy that mirrors the "great love" of God. This is, perhaps, the measure of the "inordinate love" that comes of *knowing* that one is created in the image of God, of *knowing* that God's Presence is in one's midst. For this, both discontinuity and continuity are necessary: the destructive dimension of fire and the sense of the "inner essence which is in a process of development."[90]

3. *Shabbat and Mishkan: The Fiery Dialectic*

Shabbat: Diligent Indolence

We began with the counter-realities of Shabbat and Mishkan, of a condition in which fire, medium of the Mishkan achievement, may not be kindled on Shabbat. Perhaps we may now say that these two modalities represent two ways of living time. Fire represents the urgency of productive time, lived for its objective creations, for the forms of self-knowledge that devolve from the inner heat. The work of the Mishkan, then, stands as testimony to the creative power of the people, to the many ways, the thirty-nine ways, of relating to the world and transforming it,[91] in which fire is essential. This work is, at base, a manifestation not of the kinds of objects in space that are created, but of a way of using time: purposeful, productive, often ruthless.

As against this modality, there is Shabbat: "You shall kindle no fire throughout your settlements on the sabbath day." Shabbat is virtually defined as *non-fire*: that is, as time not used, unproductive, the shadow opposite of the making of the Mishkan.

What may be understood by such a notion of Shabbat as "fallow time"? The notion evokes Keats's "diligent indolence," his "negative capability," Marion Milner's "doodles." For the capacity to "doodle," undignified as that may sound, is an essential dimension of the creative life. This time of the "doodle" is the time that resists premature certainties; resists the hunger for recognizable objects, the sense of a "compulsive and deceptive sanity." This time of "diligent indolence" allows the "thought or mood seeking expression" to mature.[92]

In terms of ways of living time, then, the Shabbat modality is in a dialectical relation to the Mishkan modality. However, in terms of fire imagery, the two modalities seem in entire opposition: one banning fire, the other nurtured by it. Here, too, nevertheless, a dialectic is at work. For the creative work of the Mishkan can become a frenzy: as Rashi phrases it, "Even though you will be *obsessed* (*ridufin*) by it, let Shabbat not be superseded by it." In the interests of the fire itself, that is, for the sake of the fullness of the work, there must be Shabbat. In the combat between man and form, fire, or at least the informing reverie of fire, is essential; but if the counter-principle of Shabbat is not respected, it will consume that form and ultimately itself.

"Diligent indolence," as a premise for creativity finds expression in, for example, Yeats's "Long-legged fly":

Like a long-legged fly upon the stream
His mind moves upon silence.

Analogous with "the spirit of God hovering over the face of the deep" (Gen 1:2), the creative spirit is incarnated in history, in love, and in art. In all three stanzas, the refrain occurs, evoking the reverie that precedes creation. In the last stanza, the subject is Michelangelo reclining on the scaffolding of the Sistine Chapel:

With no more sound than the mice make
His hand moves to and fro.
Like a long-legged fly upon the stream
His mind moves upon silence.

Master artist, his work will haunt the dreams of "girls at puberty" and so transform fecund reality; but to achieve that, he must be abandoned to his own dreams.

In terms of Milner's "doodle," too, we remember Saint-Exupéry's Little Prince, who begins his narrative with his Drawing Number One, achieved after deeply pondering the adventures of the jungle. The drawing is of a boa constrictor in the act of swallowing an animal; but the grown-ups predictably see only a picture of a hat, and are not at all frightened. Whimsically, the Little Prince conveys the life of the imagination, a way of living time in play and in dream, as well as the horrified curiosity of a child contemplating the six sleeping months it takes the boa constrictor to digest its prey. This is a slow fire, indeed, an image of constricted consumption.

Shabbat: An Absolute Priority

Shabbat, as time for reverie, for contemplating the work of fire and internalizing it, counteracts the hunger for premature certainties, for completed images that deaden the imagination. More accurately, its effect is not simply "counteractive," but prophylactic: *before* the fire takes hold, the Shabbat reverie conditions the fever of the work. It is perhaps for this reason that, after the Golden Calf experience, Moses changes the order of God's commands and *prefaces* the Mishkan instructions with the Shabbat *caveat*. In some pristine universe, Shabbat may serve as a palliative to the productive frenzy of the six days; but in the world of more complex knowledge that follows the Golden Calf, Shabbat must come first. For now, lying fallow, not-doing, allowing hints and suggestions to be caught in the spider's web of the mind becomes the very condition of creativity: which, in Henry James's words, "takes to itself the faintest hints of life, [and] . . . converts the very pulses of the air into revelations."[93]

For this reverie to be possible, time has to be made for time. Shabbat is such time, as is the Shemittah year—the seventh, fallow year which normally is considered the end of a process, a time for regeneration. However, in describing the Shemittah year, the Torah gives it an absolute priority:

> *When you enter the land* that I give you, *the land shall observe a sabbath of God.* Six years you may sow your field and six years you may prune your vineyard and gather in the yield. But in the seventh year the land shall have a sabbath of complete rest, a sabbath of God . . . (Lev 25:2–4)

In this account, the *first* act of the people entering the Holy Land is to let it lie fallow.[94] This can be true only in a dream sense; legally, as the next verse makes clear, the Shemittah *follows* six years of sowing and reaping. But, conceptually, Shabbat is primary. Like Marion Milner's "doodles," or Winnicott's "squiggles," it initiates a freedom which, like free verse or free association, makes new combinations and connections possible.[95]

Making a World for Bezalel

Shabbat before the Mishkan, "rest" or "regeneration" before work: this is a human reversal of God's order in creation. Moses reverses the order because diligent indolence, a state of molten inwardness, is the very crucible of creation. Apparently unproductive, it eventually yields the *tzirufin*, the composite forms of imagination. In placing Shabbat first, Moses is, essentially, placing Bezalel in vital connection with God: he is not merely a virtuoso of his craft but educated by God Himself.

"See!" God says to Moses, "I have called by name Bezalel . . ." And rouses him to wonder at the Bezalel phenomenon, to value it, to enter into a nurturing relationship with it. For without a world that tacitly supports him, Bezalel cannot have his reveries; like Winnicott's infant, to grow and create, he needs to play alone in the presence of a loving other. Moses hears God's invocation and transmits it to the people: "See! God has called by name Bezalel . . ." Subtly, Moses has now created a world for Bezalel, where he can play-in-work.

An implicit symbiosis now links Moses and Bezalel: each in his own way knows the secret power of the fire. From his earliest days, Moses has learned to fear the fire and to be reassured by it. From the infant experience of coals and crown, with the impeded speech that it produces, to the great vision of the heart of fire at the Burning Bush, which is to hearten him to face the fires of Sinai, he learns a cautious audacity which leads him into the consuming fire of Mount Sinai—"burning to the very heart of the heavens" (Deut 4:11). For Moses, those vast spaces, empty, ferocious to some, hold an inner heat that will become his if he merits it.

For Bezalel, the fire is the divider and the transformer, the place and time of fusion. "In the shadow of God," he has an intuitive confidence in the moment, an ease with the empty time that awaits that moment. In the presence of Moses and the people, and in a world of orders and systems, he can tolerate the ruptures, consummate the unions offered by time.

An Intimate Dream

Ultimately, in speaking of Bezalel and of Moses, we are speaking of the intimate human dream of fire. It is in the language of dream that the midrash speaks when it evokes the desire for union and the fear of being consumed, when it meditates on the heart (the wise of heart, the wakeful heart) and on passionate young men who indiscriminately give gold. It is in the language of dreams, too, that Bahya speaks when, at the end of Exodus, he relates the fire over the Mishkan to the words *beit yisrael*, the house of Israel: ". . . and fire would appear in it by night, before the eyes of all the *house of Israel*" (40:48). The "house" is the place of sexuality, of momentary unions and abiding tension, a place where man and woman, fiery substance, are connected by the presence of God.[96] It is in the house of Israel, and before the eyes of those who live in it, that the fire appears in all its power.

The Book of Exodus, then, ends with the people contemplating that fire. They see it as the fire of the Shechina, of the Presence of God; a transmuted version of the consuming fire of Sinai. And in the intimacy of their lives together, each couple needs no candle; for the pillar of fire accompanies them in their exits and entrances.[97]

Notes

Introduction

1. See Gary Porten, "Defining Midrash," in *The Study of Ancient Judaism,* ed. J. Neusner (New York, 1981), 59–60.

2. Gerald Bruns, *Hermeneutics Ancient and Modern* (New Haven: Yale University Press, 1992), 115.

3. Elliot R. Wolfson, *Through a Speculum that Shines* (Princeton: Princeton University Press, 1994), 328.

4. See chapter 1, 57–58.

5. See Yalkut Shimeoni, 828.

6. These dialogues are found in Exod 12:26–27; 13:8; 13:14; and Deut 6:20–21.

7. Isaiah Berlin, *The Crooked Timber of Humanity* (New York: Knopf, 1991), 5–6.

8. See chapter 3.

9. Stephen Mitchell, *Hope and Dread in Psychoanalysis* (New York: Basic Books, 1993), 102.

10. Thomas Mann, *The Magic Mountain* (New York: Knopf, 1991), 541.

11. See chapter 9.

12. Mei HaShiloach I, 30a–b.

13. Daniel Boyarin, *Intertextuality and the Reading of Midrash* (Bloomington: Indiana University Press, 1990), 40.

14. Pirke Avoth 5:26.

15. See chapter 1.

16. Tanchuma Pinchas, 7.

17. I am grateful to Dina Kazhdan, Tali Stern, and Bracha Zornberg who pointed this out to me.

18. *Selected Poems* (London: Faber and Faber), 112.

19. See, e.g., Sefath Emeth, VaEra, 25.

20. R. Kook, *Olath Re'iyah,* 26–27.

21. Susan Sontag, " 'Thinking Against Oneself': Reflections on Cioran," in *Styles of Radical Will* (New York: Anchor Books, 1993), 74–75.

22. Sefath Emeth, Pesach, 72.

23. See chapter 3.

24. For a similar notion of transgenerational religious experience, in which the later experience completes and in a sense transcends the original, scriptural experience, see Sefath Emeth, Pesach, 55.

25. Meshech Chochma to 32:19.

26. Rashi to 38:8. See chapter 1.

27. Soren Kierkegaard, *The Sickness unto Death,* trans. by Howard V. Hong and Edna H. Hong (Princeton: Princeton University Press, 1980), 30.

28. Ibid., 31.

29. Ibid., 32.

30. Ibid., 33–34.

31. Ibid., 34.

32. See chapter 8 for a discussion of finitude and infinitude figured in the "bells and pomegranates" of Aaron's priestly robe (pp. 378–381).

33. Cf. the classic midrashic pun on Pesach—*Peh sach* ("the mouth speaks")

34. Kierkegaard, *Sickness,* 35. See chapter 2 for a discussion of speech as an expression of liberation from Egypt.

35. *Pachad Yitzhak, Pesach,* 77. It is interesting that it is *women's* desire that serves as a model for this inexpressible spiritual energy.

36. B. Pesachim 36a.

37. Shoshana Felman, "Education and Crisis, Or the Vicissitudes of Teaching," in *Testimony: Crises of Witnessing in Literature, Psychoanalysis, and History* (Routledge, Chapman, and Hall), 15.

38. See Mei HaShiloach II, 13b.

Shemoth: The Mirror of Redemption

1. Jan Assmann, *Moses in Egypt: the Memory of Egypt in Western Monotheism* (Cambridge, Mass.: Harvard University Press, 1997), 2.

2. This is Ramban's description of the theme of Exodus (Chavel [Hebrew], vol. 1, 279).

3. See Hizkuni on 1:7.

4. See Rashbam and Rashi on 1:7.

5. See Shemoth Rabba 1:7. The hypothesis about multiple birth is merely the basis for further speculation: perhaps each belly held twelve babies? Or sixty?

6. Shemoth Rabba 1:7.

7. Rashi bases the sextuple-birth idea on *vayishretzu,* presumably after the midrashic notion that *sheratzim* (reptiles) produce no fewer than six young at a time (see Pesikta d'Rav Kahana [10:85b]).

8. Compare the use of *shiretzu* in God's instructions to Noah after the flood (Gen 9:7), where it connotes both divine blessing and the compulsive drive to fill the denuded, post-flood world. Also, see my *The Beginning of Desire,* 10–17, for a discussion of the two axes of human experience—the horizontal, "swarming" axis, and the vertical, "dominating" axis—in the Creation narrative.

9. See B. Berakhot 28b: "I run, and they run—I run towards eternal life, while they run towards the abyss . . ." (This is part of the prayer of gratitude for the opportunity to redeem the mortal condition by learning Torah; it is to be said on entering the Beit Midrash [House of Study] each morning).

10. Shemoth Rabba 1:8.

11. See, e.g., Shemoth Rabba 1:32.

12. See Torah Shelemah 86: (Seder Eliyahu Rabba 21). In some sources, Pharaoh's decrees are primarily intended to undermine their practice of circumcision (e.g. Pirke d'Rabbi Eliezer 29).

13. Lawrence Weschler, *Calamities of Exile* (Chicago: University of Chicago Press, 1999), 37.

14. Shemoth Rabba 1:12.

15. Semprun, *Long Voyage,* 75–76.

16. Num 12:3.

17. See Ha-amek Davar on the difference between God's words (*veshame'u* le*kolecha*) and Moses' (*lo yishme'u* be*koli*): Moses doubts that the people will take him seriously, will pay attention to him as bearer of prophecy—a more radical doubt than one about the content of the prophecy.

18. B. Erchin 15b.

19. Indeed, he begins his comment on the verse with this midrash; only after it, does he return to the *peshat,* the more obvious contextual reading of the phrase.

20. Pirke d'Rabbi Eliezer 48.

21. Significantly, the period that the Israelites lived in Egypt is defined as "four hundred and thirty years," to the very day of the Exodus (12:40–41). This time frame is traditionally traced back to the birth of Isaac.

22. Shemoth, p. 18.

23. Mei HaShiloach, Shemoth 2.

24. See Elaine Scarry, *The Body in Pain: The Making and Unmaking of the World* (New York: Oxford University Press, 1987).

25. Charles Dickens, *Hard Times* (New York: Signet Classics, 1961), 198.

26. This is a frequent concern in Oliver Sacks's work, where the starting point is neurological—e.g. *Awakenings* (HarperPerennial, 1990), 284–285, on the question of posture in Parkinsonism: ". . . every posture is an "I" no less than an "It." . . . And it is precisely this which is missing in Parkinsonism—there is a loss of naturalness in posture and action . . . a loss of the living "I" . . . And this is the rationale of an "existence" therapy: . . . to inspire with the personal and living, and, in the directest

sense possible to awaken and quicken . . . "Where It was," writes Freud, "there I should be."

27. Midrash Lekach Tov in Torah Shelemah 3:126.

28. Nehama Leibowitz quotes Franz Rosenzweig on Luther's failure to reproduce the fourfold repetition of the word "God." The Vulgate and the Septuagint to different degrees also fail to translate this form. The King James and the NJB translations are faithful to the original Hebrew. (Leibowitz, *Studies in Shemot* [Jerusalem: World Zionist Organization, 1981], 22–23).

29. See Ramban 5:22.

30. 6:1.

31. Yalkut Shimeoni Shemoth 247.

32. B. Sukkah 11a.

33. "Be fruitful and multiply" (Gen 1:28) is traditionally considered the first commandment by God to human beings: in having children, fulfilling their instinctual nature, they are obeying the divine will.

34. Yalkut Shimeoni Shemoth 247.

35. The simplest explanation of this is that building work kept the workers in the fields overnight, thus effectively preventing marital relations and procreation.

36. Rashi: B. Sotah 11b. Rashi in fact quotes the Mechilta to the effect that the water of the Red Sea that ultimately drowned the Egyptians was turned into clay, in punishment for their persecution of the Israelites. Clay-torment of others leads to their own clay-death, in a simple, physical sense. The imagery of clay, however, raises questions about the conceptual equivalence of the Egyptian crime and punishment.

37. Pirke d'Rabbi Eliezer, 48.

38. Metzudath David: Ezek 37:11.

39. Franz Rosenzweig, *The Star of Redemption,* trans. William W. Hallo (Notre Dame: University of Notre Dame Press, 1985), 3.

40. Ibid., 4.

41. "It is the ultimate conclusion of this doctrine that death is—Nought. But in truth this is no ultimate conclusion, but a first beginning, and truthfully death is not what it seems, not Nought, but a something from which there is no appeal, which is not to be done with" (Rosenzweig, *Star,* 4).

42. John Berger, *Keeping a Rendezvous* (New York: Vintage International, 1992), 29–31.

43. Tanchuma Va'era, 5.

44. Moses can be understood as implying that *he,* of all people, will not be believed—a lifelong stranger to Israelite society and culture. Aaron, on the other hand, as the accepted "prophet" of the time, may have more credibility.

45. Christopher Bollas, *Cracking Up* (New York: Hill and Wang, 1996), 48–102.

46. Bollas, *Cracking Up,* 65, 69.

47. Shemoth Rabba 3:3.

48. Nadezhda Mandelstam, *Hope Against Hope* (New York: Atheneum, 1970), 48.

49. Vaclav Havel, *The Power of the Powerless* (New York: Palach Press, 1985), 27–34.

50. Rashi significantly describes the work on the store-cities as consolidating and strengthening already existing structures, making them "fit" for preservation (1:11).

51. Berger, *Keeping a Rendezvous,* 31.

52. Havel, *Power,* 37.

53. The word recalls Noah's *teva*—commonly translated "ark." Structurally, therefore, this is a device for survival, in this case suggested not directly by God's command, but by maternal counsel. Within the specific field of imagery of the midrashic Exodus narrative, however, the ironic associations of the clay-block, hollow, with the live baby within, compound and complicate the survival motif.

54. B. Sotah 12b.

55. See Malbim 2:6. Biblical examples are 1 Sam 15:15; Jer 50:14.

56. Mechilta d'Rabbi Shimeon bar Yochai, Shemoth, 4.

57. See Rashi 3:10.

58. Havel, *Power,* 29.

59. Thomas Mann, *Dr. Faustus* (Middlesex: Penguin, 1949), 361.

60. Max Raphael, *Prehistoric Pottery and Civilization in Egypt* (Pantheon, 1947), 76.

61. Herbert Read, *Icon and Idea* (New York: Schocken, 1965), 47.

62. Read, *Icon,* 42.

63. Rashi 15:4. See Charles Dickens, *Bleak House,* for similar imagery of mud, fog, filth, and lucre as symbols of a moribund world.

See also Norman O. Brown, *Life Against Death* (Middleton, Conn.: Wesleyan University, 1959), part 5, "Studies in Anality."

The important midrashic theme of God's creation of the human in a *manual* act of forming moistened earth is clearly related to our theme. God's design in molding the human is significantly described as *lenefesh chaya:* like the animals, the human becomes a "living being" (Gen 2:7). But Rashi emphasizes the intense vitality of the human, transcending that of the animals: this is expressed in the faculty of language (see also Targum Onkelos). In this way, God's creative act is paradoxical at its core: manipulative, controlling, on the one hand, but bestowing the gift of language, which frees the human from subjection.

64. Read, *Icon,* 4.

65. See, e.g., 7:22; 8:11; 8:15—"Pharaoh's heart became hardened."

66. Milan Kundera, *The Unbearable Lightness of Being* (London: Faber and Faber, 1985), 195.

67. See Richard Wollheim, *Art and Its Objects* (Cambridge: Cambridge University Press, 1980).

68. B. Sotah 11b.

69. Tanchuma Pikudei 9.

70. Rashi 38:8.

71. Compare the commentary of Ibn Ezra (38:8), which makes just this ascetic suggestion.

72. See, e.g., 1:6: "Don't stare at me because I am swarthy, because the sun has

gazed upon me." The aesthetics of blackness—and of tanned skin—here clearly appeal to convention, to the imagery of a laboring and sun-exposed slave class, and to a submerged association with moral taint.

73. Ramban 38:8.

74. The use of the ewer for the Sotah (the wife suspected of adultery who is put through a ritual involving water: see Num 5:11–31) ordeal is of central importance; it does not, however, enter my main area of discourse in this chapter. Thematically, of course, there are clear connections between the subject of this chapter and the problem of misarticulated sexuality, suggested by the Sotah.

75. See Torah Shelemah, Vayakhel-Pekudei, appendix 6.

76. The polished copper mirrors of Masada come to mind.

77. Kundera, *Unbearable Lightness,* 84.

78. Kundera, *Unbearable Lightness,* 86.

79. *Hamlet* III.ii.21.

80. *Hamlet* III.iv.19–20.

81. Lionel Trilling, *Sincerity and Authenticity* (Cambridge, Mass.: Harvard University Press, 1973), 25.

82. Jacques Lacan, "The Mirror Stage," in *Écrits* (New York: Norton, 1977), 1–2.

83. Lacan, *Écrits,* 4.

84. Jane Gallop, *Reading Lacan* (Ithaca: Cornell University Press, 1985).

85. Lacan, "Some Reflections on the Ego," quoted in Gallop, *Reading Lacan,* 84.

86. Berger, *Rendezvous,* 33–34.

87. Shemoth Rabba 1:20.

88. Ibn Ezra 1:15.

89. Shemoth Rabba 1:17.

90. Midrash HaGadol 4:13.

91. Berger, *Keeping a Rendezvous,* 32.

92. Rashi follows this minimalist reading: "He was separated from her because of Pharaoh's decree, and then he brought her back and remarried her" (2:1). He translates in accord with the requirements of the biblical text, without midrashic elaboration.

93. For example, B. Sotah 12a. The Talmud translates "A man *went* . . ." by ". . . *went after* his daughter's advice . . ."

94. B. Megilla 14a.

95. This is based on an alternative reading of "The king of Egypt died . . ." (2:23): he was stricken with leprosy, which is analogous to death, and would slaughter Israelite babies and bathe in their blood. . . This is Rashi's reading, based on Targum Jonathan, Shemoth Rabba etc; its virtue is that it directly explains the groaning of the people. Its implication then is that the same Pharaoh features as the villain of the whole narrative.

96. Quoted in Rashi 1:8.

97. It is striking that the midrash relates the Revelation at Mount Sinai as centering on a moment of radical anxiety: "God suspended the mountain over their heads, like a bucket, and said, 'If you accept the Torah, good; if not, there shall be

your grave.' . . . God made a condition with His creation: 'If Israel accepts the Torah, you shall exist; if not, I return you to emptiness and void' " (B. Shabbat 88a).

98. Ramban: Gen 37:15.

99. Rashi: Gen 37:35.

100. Indeed, some sources suggest that Jacob, on this basis, *realizes* that Joseph cannot be dead, since he has not forgotten him! See Bereshith Rabbati 221.

101. See Ramban 4:10.

102. Emmanuel Levinas, "Revelation in the Jewish Tradition," in *The Levinas Reader,* ed. Sean Hand (Oxford: Blackwell, 1989), 197.

103. Pachad Yitzhak, Pesach, 46 [3].

104. B. Berachoth 9b.

105. Gur Arye to 3:14.

106. Martin Buber, "Prophecy, Apocalyptic, and the Historical Hour," in *On the Bible* (New York: Schocken, 1982), 77–78.

107. Ramban 3:13.

108. Mei HaShiloach: Yithro.

109. Shemoth Rabba 1:18.

110. See 1:16 where the wordplay is explicit: "When you deliver the Hebrew women, you shall look at the birthstool (*ovnayim*—lit., the stone supports for childbirth): if it is a boy (*ben*), kill him . . ." (1:16).

111. See Tanchuma Tazria-Metzora 3.

112. Shemoth Rabba 42:9.

113. Sefath Emeth, 4.

114. See Emmanuel Levinas, "The Temptation of Temptation," in *Nine Talmudic Readings,* trans. Annette Aronowicz (Bloomington: Indiana University Press, 1990), 42–48.

115. Rashi 33:11. This is a deliberate misreading of the text: "And Moses *would return* to the camp . . ."

116. Berger, *Rendezvous,* 33.

117. Wallace Stevens, "Notes Toward a Supreme Fiction."

118. Tanchuma Shemoth 9.

Vaera: The Exile of the Word

1. See Ha-amek Davar.

2. See chapter 1, pp. 25–34.

3. This is Everett Fox's translation of *arel sefatayim.*

4. Sefath Emeth, 40.

5. Yalkut Shimeoni, 828.

6. I have largely followed the Fox translation here.

7. Rashi continues to affirm that Aaron is the prophet referred to in 1 Sam 2:27 and in Ezek 20:5. This is a classic midrashic tradition.

8. Robert M. Cover, "Nomos and Narrative," in *Harvard Law Review* (November 1983): 22.

9. Tanchuma Shemoth 27.

10. Tanchuma Shemini, 3.

11. B. Zevachim 102a.

12. I am adopting the midrashic view that the same Pharaoh is the subject throughout the narrative (Pharaoh's death [2:23–25] is read in many midrashic sources to refer to an attack of leprosy). Moses "killing" Pharaoh is emblematized in "Moses held out his arm over the sea, and at daybreak the sea returned to its previous state . . ." (14:27).

13. See Robert A. Paul, *Moses and Civilization* (New Haven: Yale University Press, 1996), 113–14, for a discussion of Moses' agency in accomplishing the destruction of the Egyptians at the Red Sea.

14. See Paul, *Moses,* 112, for a discussion of the possible incestuous complexities of the Egyptian dynastic family and of Moses' place within it.

15. The legend is found in Shemoth Rabba 1:26; it is recorded in Josephus, *Jewish Antiquities;* Freud refers to it in *Moses and Monotheism* (New York: Vintage, 1939), 13n2. [See Paul, *Moses,* 234n9].

16. See Paul, *Moses,* 79. My account of the legend is based on his.

17. Midrash HaGadol 6:2.

18. B. Sanhedrin 111a; quoted in Rashi on 6:1.

19. George Steiner, *No Passion Spent* (New Haven: Yale University Press, 1996), 358.

20. Ibid., 351.

21. Ibid., 352.

22. Ibid., 357–358.

23. Num 12:3. See Ramban 4:13.

24. Franz Kafka, *Parables and Paradoxes* (New York: Schocken, 1975), 43–44.

25. Walter Benjamin, *Illuminations* (London: Fontana, 1973), 129–30.

26. B. Nedarim 31b.

27. B. Nedarim 32a.

28. In a provocative interpretation, R. Yosef Kimchi reads God's message to Pharaoh, which directly precedes this narrative—"Israel is My firstborn son. I have said to you, 'Let my son go, that he may worship Me,' yet you refuse to let him go. Now I will slay your first-born son" (4:22–23)—as a veiled message to the messenger: that is, to Moses. It refers to *Moses'* resistance to God's word, to the processes of redemption that can be engendered only through language.

29. See 7:22; 8:11; 8:15; 9:12.

30. See, e.g., Shemoth Rabba 9:4.

31. It is interesting to note that God's previous warning about Pharaoh's refusal relates only to the factual level: "He will not send the people free" (4:21). That was followed by Pharaoh's verbal defiance of Moses and Aaron ("Who is God that I should listen to His voice. . . ?" [5:2]): that is, Pharaoh still responded actively, spoke about not-listening. After God foretells that he will not listen, however, Pharaoh essentially stops speaking his defiance.

32. Ernest Becker, *The Denial of Death* (New York: Free Press, 1973), 118.

33. Ibid., 31.

34. Tanchuma 14.

35. See Becker, 32: "We read that men of the Chagga tribe wear an anal plug all their lives, pretending to have sealed up the anus and not to need to defecate."

36. Ibid., 31.

37. Ibid., 36.

38. Michael Walzer, *Thick and Thin: Moral Argument at Home and Abroad* (Notre Dame: University of Notre Dame Press, 1994), 93.

39. Ibid., 96.

40. Ibid., 97.

41. The word is Lionel Trilling's—see *Sincerity and Authenticity,* 99.

42. Erich Neumann, *The Origins and History of Consciousness* (New Jersey: Princeton University Press, 1973), 16.

43. Herbert Fingarette, *The Self in Transformation* (New York: Harper Torchbooks, 1965), 58.

44. Quoted in Mary Douglas, *Purity and Danger* (London: Routledge, 1994), 163.

45. Shadal quotes 1Sam 1:5 ("God closed her womb"); and Deut 29:3 ("God has not given you a heart to know . . . till this very day") as examples of this rhetorical mode.

46. Hail, the seventh plague, reverts to the original form: "Pharaoh hardened his own heart" (9:34).

47. See Ramban 9:12.

48. See Ramban on 7:3 for a classic discussion of the moral implications of the loss of the possibility of repentance.

49. See Pirke d'Rabbi Eliezer, 48; and Yalkut Shimeoni, 184.

50. Leprosy plays a role, too, in Egyptian cultural memory of the Exodus. One Egyptian history, written by the priest Manetho in the time of Ptolemy II, for example, represents Moses as a rebellious leader who made himself leader of a colony of lepers. Jan Assmann argues that in this way, Egyptian idolators reacted with mutual loathing to the repudiators of idolatry (Assmann, *Moses,* 4–5).

51. B. Sanhedrin 101a.

52. Pirke d'Rabbi Eliezer, 48. The last sentence appears in some MSS of the midrash.

53. The theme of healing occurs even in the terms in which Rashi explains the first plague: "The Nile will stink so that the Egyptians will become weary of drinking the water of the Nile": They will become weary of seeking a remedy for the water of the Nile, to make it drinkable (7:18). In the first plague, as distinct from the later ones, the people react with a normal human attempt to "cure" the undrinkable water. The instinct to heal is fundamental. But after a week of fruitless efforts (Rashi cites the midrash to the effect that each plague lasts a week [7:25]), fatigue sets in. Thereafter, there is no reference to any therapeutic endeavor.

54. D. W. Winnicott, *Playing and Reality* (London: Routledge, 1997), 5.

55. Ibid., 6.

56. Sefath Emeth, 40.

57. Sefath Emeth, 36.

58. Seforno on 6:12.

59. Seforno goes as far as to claim that their inability to consider the message of God leads to the partial cancellation of that message. "I shall give it [the Land] to you" (6:8), is not fulfilled; instead, the Land is given to their children. The problem of the forty-year delay in the desert—which is attributed in the biblical text itself to the sin of the Spies—is here traced back to an underlying pathology. Counter-narratives neutralize the power of the divine narrative.

60. See Cassuto on 5:9.

61. See Kenneth Burke, *Language as Symbolic Action* (Berkeley: University of California Press, 1966), 471, for a discussion of the Greek usage *ascholein*—"to be engaged in business activity"—formed by prefixing a negative to the verb *scholazein*—"to occupy one's leisure." Work and leisure display the opposite values from the English, "with the Greeks, in an era of slavery, using a negative where we use a positive, and vice versa." Unemployment, "the ability to occupy leisure nobly," is, surprisingly, called in Aristotle's *Politics* "the first principle of all things," the *arche panton*. "Yet what is such a principle," exclaims Burke, "if not God!"

62. Tanchuma Vaera, 6.

63. Winnicott, *Playing*, 5.

64. Ibid., 6.

65. W. R. Bion, *Cogitations* (London: Karnac Books, 1992), 53–54.

66. Ibid., 54.

67. Gaston Bachelard, *L'Eau et les rêves*, 262, quoted in *On Poetic Imagination and Reverie* (Dallas: Spring Publications, 1987), lix.

68. George Steiner, *In Bluebeard's Castle* (New Haven: Yale University Press, 1971), 115.

69. Ha-amek Davar notes that *vayedaber mosheh el hashem*—"Moses spoke to God"—is used only once in the Torah: it is too forceful an expression. Here, the usage *lifnei hashem*—"in the presence of God"—is significant.

70. 7:7. The mention of his age is quite unusual in biblical style.

71. Shemoth Rabba 3:1.

72. B. Sanhedrin 89a.

73. In Hebrew, the Talmud plays on the word *yishma/yashmia*—the sin is refusing to listen/to make audible—even to himself—the word of God.

74. Ramban on 4:10.

75. B. Niddah 30b.

76. Bachelard, *L'Eau et les rêves*, 262.

77. Likkutei Moharan 60:8.

78. See Likkutei Moharan 60:6.

79. Devarim Rabba 1:1.

80. Bachelard, *L'Eau et les rêves*, 262.

81. See, e.g., 9:16, 10:12, etc. The general purpose of the plague-narrative is to teach all to "know the Lord"—an expression repeated ten times, and an elaborate narrative response to Pharaoh's original, arrogant, "I do not know the Lord" (5:2). See Leibowitz, *Studies in Shemot*, 170–171.

82. Ha-amek Davar on 6:7. He makes use of the tradition that understands the

four cups of wine, that are obligatory on the Passover night, to express the four stages of God's promise of redemption; and adds that the fifth cup, not obligatory, expresses the option of high spiritual evolution and self-transformation ("God-intoxication")—the acme of the redemptive experience.

83. The psychoanalytic analogy for the cabalistic idea of "the Exile of the Word" was first suggested to me in lectures by Rabbi Daniel Epstein.

84. Likkutei, 66:4.

85. Adam Phillips, *On Kissing, Tickling, and Being Bored* (Cambridge, Mass.: Harvard, 1993), 81–82.

86. Ibid., 83.

87. Sefath Emeth, 36–37. The difficulty of redemption emerges from the midrash he quotes: "It was hard for them—*kasheh*—to separate from idolatry."

88. Elias Canetti, *Crowds and Power* (Middlesex: Penguin, 1973), 338–339.

89. Sefath Emeth, 25.

90. Tanchuma Devarim 2.

91. Benjamin, *Illuminations*, 257.

92. Becker, *Denial*, 91.

93. Deut 32:13.

94. B. Sotah 11b.

Bo: The Narrative of the Night

1. Seforno introduces this nuance: taking account of "I know that you will still not fear God. . ." (9:30), he suggests that Moses has given up on Pharaoh's spiritual recognition of God's power, but still hopes that Pharaoh's confession, "God is in the right" at least means that Pharaoh has reached his limit of suffering. This general reading is also that of Rashbam and Hizkuni.

2. This is the view of Shadal. See chapter 2, 105.

3. Meir Sternberg, *The Poetics of Biblical Narrative* (Bloomington: Indiana University Press, 1985), 103.

4. Ibid., 105.

5. Ibid., 112–113.

6. Ibid., 114.

7. Survivors of the Spies narrative would have been under twenty at the time of the sin; by definition, not having reached the age of legal responsibility, their testimony is not acceptable.

8. J. Berachot 5:1.

9. Joseph's tears are his response to the "fabrication" by his brothers of a death-bed appeal from their father, Jacob ("Please forgive the sin of your brothers. . ."). The Talmud (Yevamoth 65b) is unequivocal about the invented status of their message to Joseph. This last encounter between Joseph and his brothers, then, takes place in an atmosphere of manipulation: the brothers' only moment of full contrition is veiled in falsehood and mediated by unknown messengers. His reply to them—apparently reassuring and harmonizing all jarring voices from the past—is a

merely pragmatic attempt to control a dangerous situation. Truthfulness is entirely absent from this final encounter. See Rashi to 50:21—" 'He spoke to their hearts': Words that are congenial to the heart." He spins narratives of apparent closure, which in reality have a destabilizing effect.

10. This is the reading of Ha-amek Davar.

11. B. Shabb. 97a.

12. Susan Handelman, "The 'Torah' of Criticism and the Criticism of Torah: Recuperating the Pedagogical Moment," in *Interpreting Judaism in a Postmodern Age,* ed. Steven Kepnes (New York: New York University Press, 1996), 231.

13. Ibid., 224.

14. See the commentary of Meshech Chochma on 32:19.

15. Sternberg, *Poetics,* 115.

16. See Maimonides' scathing dismissal of objective miracle as a basis for faith: *Hilchoth Yesodei HaTorah,* chapter 8.

17. A painting called *Impression Soleil Levant.*

18. John Berger, "The Eyes of Claude Monet," in *The Sense of Sight* (New York: Vintage International, 1985), 189.

19. Ibid., 191.

20. Ibid., 193.

21. Ibid., 194.

22. Ibid., 191.

23. Ibid., 194.

24. Ibid., 195.

25. Ibid., 196.

26. Shemoth Rabba 13:4.

27. Bereshith Rabba 8:7.

28. The phrase is taken from the title of an essay by Yochanan Muffs in *Conservative Judaism,* vol. xxxiii, no. 3 (Spring 1980): 25–37.

29. See the Etz Yosef commentary on the midrash.

30. Bereshith Rabba 8:8.

31. In the third case, the students do not insist on a better answer. But see the continuation of the dialogues in the Jerusalem Talmud, Berachoth 9:1.

32. See previous note, which suggests an endless sequence of such dramas.

33. One notices with sadness how often the word *kasheh* is used in modern Hebrew, when people speak of disaster. All intelligent discourse is reduced to this one word, helplessly repeated, and implying, it seems, both that it is "hard to bear," and that it resists language and explanation.

34. Slavoj Zizek, *The Sublime Object of Ideology* (London-New York: Verso, 1989), 69.

35. Ibid., 204.

36. Marc-Alain Ouaknine, *The Burnt Book,* trans. Llewellyn Brown (Princeton: Princeton University Press, 1995), 179.

37. See Gur Arye to 12:29.

38. Shemoth Rabba 18:1.

39. B. Berachoth 4a.

40. Rashbam 9:16.

41. Mechilta d'Rabbi Shimeon bar Yochai.

42. "There was not left of them *even one*" (14:28) is read, "There was not left of them *more than one*" (Mechilta 2:6; Midrash Tehillim 106).

43. Felman, "Education and Crisis," in *Testimony: Crises of Witnessing,* 5. I am grateful to Susan Handelman for drawing my attention to this article.

44. Ibid., 9.

45. Ibid., 15.

46. Ibid., 15–16.

47. Ibid., 16.

48. Ibid., 18.

49. Ibid., 19.

50. Ibid., 21.

51. Ibid., 24.

52. Ibid., 15.

53. Ramban 13:16.

54. J. Pesachim 5:5.

55. Mechilta Bo, chapter 13.

56. Midrash Shir Ha-Shirim 15a. See Torah Shelemah to Exod 10:10 [note 29].

57. One midrash notes that the question of endings is graphically inscribed in Pharaoh's words: the end-letters of *neged peneichem*—"facing you"—read the word, *dam*—"blood" (Chemdat Yamim 16a).

58. See chapter 2, 96–97.

59. Rashi, in his comment on Joshua 5:9, attributes the continuing power of the Egyptian "disgrace" to the *erev rav*—the rabble who disseminate dissonant narratives.

60. I am grateful to Rabbi Arye Strikowski, who pointed this out to me.

61. Seforno to Deut 1:27.

62. Yochanan Muffs, *Love and Joy: Law, Language and Religion in Ancient Israel* (New York: The Jewish Theological Seminary of America, 1992), 2.

63. Ramban's version is slightly different from the Mechilta text, and closer to the text in Midrash Tehillim 113:2.

64. See midrashim on the phrase *be'etzem ha-yom ha-zeh*—"on that very day"—which is read "in the fullness of daylight," and connotes a challenge to adversaries. E.g. Sifrei, Ha'azinu 32:48.

65. The irony of the Egyptian pressure is underlined by the use of the word *va-techezak*—"they applied force"—which contains the root *chazak*—"strong": one of the repeated words to describe the obduracy of Pharaoh's heart. Implied is a polar swing of the habits of force, from resistance to active pressure to leave.

66. See 12:29, 30, 31, 42.

67. See A. Alvarez, *Night* (New York: W. W. Norton and Company, 1996), 37. Alvarez cites Bruce Chatwin (*The Songlines* [London: Picador, 1988]), who in turn quotes Robert Brain's hypothesis that there was a "specialist killer of the primates" called *Dinofelis,* "the false sabre-tooth."

68. Ibid., 39.

69. In the Israelite narrative, this capacity to enter and see the contents of Egyptian interiors tells of moral restraint: nothing is taken during the darkness.

70. Rashi's two answers are: in order that the Israelite deaths during the darkness may remain unremarked by the Egyptians; and in order that the Israelites may enter the Egyptian houses and make an inventory of "borrowable" property.

71. Tanchuma 1.

72. The biblical source of the expression is in Ps 78:49.

73. Tanchuma reads this plague as retribution for the Egyptian plan to "imprison the Israelites." It is, essentially, an experience of *immobility.*

74. Maurice Blanchot, *The Space of Literature,* trans. Ann Smock (Lincoln: University of Nebraska Press, 1982), 163.

75. Ibid., 167.

76. Ibid., 168.

77. Ibid., 169.

78. Baba Kama 60a.

79. Cf. 1 Kings 18:21: "How long will you keep hopping between two opinions (lit. branches)."

80. See Zizek, *Sublime Object,* 87–88 for a description of the "quilting" effect of these points, which totalizes, halts, fixes the "free floating elements" in an ideological space.

81. B. Berachot 9a.

82. In this vein, Ha-amek Davar reads the midrash (b. Berachoth 9b) in which the Israelites resist God's command to ask the Egyptians for silver and gold: "This is like a man in prison who is told, 'You will be released tomorrow, with a lot of money.' The prisoner answers, 'Please let me out today, and I will ask for nothing.' " The issue of timing is central to this parable: the borrowing of the silver and gold has a *delaying* effect on the experience of full freedom.

83. See Ha-amek Davar 12:11 (in Harchev Davar).

84. See also Psalm 114, which describes the "skipping" of the mountains and the hills, at the time of the Exodus.

85. See Shir Ha-Shirim Rabba 2:19.

86. Tanchuma 2.

87. Blanchot, *Space* 172–173.

88. Ibid., 176.

89. See Pachad Yitzhak, Pesach 1, for a discussion of the concept of *zerizuth*—"alertness"—that in some measure parallels Blanchot's description.

90. John Cheever, *The Journals,* quoted in Alvarez, *Night,* 44.

91. B. Berachot 12b.

92. Cf. "I said in my *haste (chofzi),* All men are false . . ." (Ps 116:11). On one reading, the declaration of the Psalmist is belied by being described as *be-chofzi* "in haste, rashly"—we understand that not all men are false. But on another reading, "All men are false," is the Psalmist's comment on his way of using words: it amplifies the description, *be-chofzi,* condemning himself as false. Again, the effect is to undermine the relation of words to reality.

93. See, for instance, Gen 3:8; 18:3; 18:30.

94. See Baba Metzia 61b: "I am the One who discriminated in Egypt between Egyptian and Israelites first-born . . ."

95. Burke, *Language,* 9.

96. Ibid., 11.

97. Ibid., 12.

98. A. A. Mason, "The Suffocating SuperEgo: Psychotic Break and Claustrophobia." Quoted in Alvarez, *Night,* 39.

99. In Pachad Yitzhak, Pesach, 47, R. Hutner discusses the kabbalistic notion of the movement from the ten *ma'amoroth* ("sayings"), with which the world was created, to the ten *dibroth* ("speakings"—i.e. the Ten Commandments). The first is "soft," while the second is "hard": its aim is to have an impact on the other. A new era begins at Mount Sinai, therefore, that R. Hutner describes as one of *chesed shel emmet*—one in which God's love is expressed in demands for mature responses and growth on the part of human beings. An essential dimension of this "hard-edged" (*kasheh*) encounter is *questioning* (*kushiyoth*) by human beings.

100. See Meshech Chochma to 13:14–15. The two forms of narrative are compared within a short passage. "You shall *tell* (*ve-higadta*) your son" is addressed to an immature son, who—unquestioning—is not ready for responsibility. "And it will be when your son *asks* you," on the other hand, is the question that marks the son as sufficiently mature to receive not only an answer, but an act of commitment: the following commandment of *tefillin* (phylacteries), which this commentator reads as part of the father's answer.

See also Or HaChaim, who discusses the fact that the same answer is given to the wicked son as to the one who does not know how to ask. The latter is criticized for lacking not an intellectual but an essential moral attitude—a sense of wonder.

In the Haggadah, following on the "answer" given to the son who failed to ask, is an example of *derasha,* an exposition composed of questions and answers about the text of the father's answer. Perhaps a model to the reader who feels uncomfortably akin to the unquestioning son?

101. One may object that the questions and answers of the Four Sons, given in formulas, do not allow for the invention of new answers. However, the very structure of the Four Sons passage—a rabbinic construction, drawing on texts that are not composed as a single unit in the Torah—creates the sense of multiple possible relationships between father and son.

102. See Gur Arye to 12:34.

103. See Rashbam to 3:22.

104. Zizek, *Sublime Object,* 179. The thesis is from Aron Bodenheimer, *Why? On the Obscenity of Questioning* (Stuttgart: 1984).

105. Ibid., 180.

106. E. Jabes, *Du desert au livre,* quoted in Ouaknine, *Burnt Book,* 179.

107. "To put to the question," was a medieval expression for torture.

108. 12:26–27. Rashbam suggests that this change—not simply quoting the answer given in the Torah—indicates that the father should respond to the immediate situation. He is not restricted to the words of the Torah, but should meet the full

concreteness of the question, in all its nuances ("To me—and not to you.") [Haggadah Shelemah, p. 24, note 268].

109. See Hizkuni to Deut 6:20. He reads the very mention of God's name as signifying relationship.

110. See Abudraham, in Haggadah Shelemah, p. 21, note 226.

111. See Haggadah Shelemah, p. 22, note 228.

112. Mei HaShiloach, Bo, 2.

113. Franz Kafka, *The Trial* (Middlesex: Penguin, 1970), 236–237.

114. Zizek, *Sublime Object,* 65–66.

115. "The Question," in W. H. Auden, *Poems,* selected by Edward Mendelson (Everyman's Library, 1995), 14.

116. Rashi to 12:27.

117. Likkutei Moharan 64.

118. B. Menachoth 29.

119. *Letters of John Keats,* selected by Frederick Page (Oxford: Oxford University Press: 1965, 53.

120. Likkutei 2:52.

121. Maurice Blanchot, *L'Entretien infini* (Paris: Gallimard, 1969), quoted in Ouaknine, 281.

122. Ibid., 282.

123. W. Benjamin, *Understanding Brecht,* trans. Anna Bostock (London: 1977), 73.

124. Catherine Clement (*Syncope,* trans. Sally O'Driscoll [Minneapolis: University of Minnesota Press, 1994]) writes of syncopation: it "begins on a weak beat and carries over onto a strong beat . . . The first beat is that of hesitation, the second that of the dissonance that is born as if by surprise when the accent carries the weak beat over—unduly!—onto the strong beat" (pp. 4–5). The experience of syncope is "a cerebral eclipse," so similar to death that it is also called "apparent death" (p. 1). "There are artists whose work reproduces the scenario of syncope: a surprise, a delay of life, a violent anticipation, and a slow return to what one calls 'the self' " (p. 21).

125. Sanhedrin 99a.

126. See note 124.

127. Paul Ricoeur, *History and Truth* (Evanston: Northwestern University Press, 1965), 323.

128. Shemoth Rabba 19:6.

129. See Rashi to Song of Songs 4:16.

130. Shir Ha-Shirim Rabba 4:31.

131. The end of the midrash describes the winds bringing the scattered exiles from the four corners of the earth to their central place. A similar idea of the transcendent unity of incompatibles appears in Esther Rabba 2:14.

132. See Georges Bataille, *The Accursed Share,* trans. Robert Hurley (New York: Zone Books, 1993), vol. 2.

133. Even the banquet given by the king, in the first, idyllic scenario, is both a celebration of release from anguish, and composed of a bittersweet menu: roast meat, unleavened bread, and bitter herbs.

134. A similar sense of horror and fascination haunts the strange scene in which Moses (4:22–26), at the beginning of his mission, is attacked by God and saved by his wife's mysterious act of circumcision. The references to circumcision and to blood in the plural form, as well as the erotic implications of the references to "bridegroom" ("You are a bridegroom of bloods to me!") evoke a similar sense of resistance and desire in Moses' early response to God's call to that described in the midrash.

135. Sefath Emeth VaYikra, Pesach, p. 72.

136. Sefath Emeth, Bo, p. 47.

137. Likkutei Moharan 66, 4.

Beshallach: Songline Through the Wilderness

1. See Ha-amek Davar to 13:17. He argues against Ramban that "although it was," is not an appropriate translation for the word *ki* (it is not one of the four basic translations in rabbinic tradition). *Ki* means "because"—one of the four translations—without palliating the paradox of such a causal explanation.

2. Cf. Gen 18:17: God's "decision-process" to reveal to Abraham the impending destruction of Sodom is described in soliloquy, at a moment of rhetorical crisis.

3. Dante's *Divine Comedy* begins with the traveler "whose straight way was lost," as he entered the dark forest. In a striking reading, Robert Pogue Harrison suggests that "it is precisely because Dante is moving in a straight line that he loses himself in the 'selva oscura'." It is only in learning a more circuitous route that he finds his way out of the forest. (*Forests: The Shadow of Civilization* [Chicago: University of Chicago Press, 1992], 82).

4. See Nahum Sarna, *Exploring Exodus* (New York: Schocken Books, 1987), 103: "It is easier to delineate the route that the fleeing Israelites avoided than to chart the course they actually took to their destination . . ."

5. Adam Phillips writes of Winnicott's concept of the mind: "*the mind always seems to come in afterwards* (to repair, to reflect, to reconstruct, to formulate, to consider, to fetishize, etc.). All thoughts are afterthoughts . . ." (*Terrors and Experts* [Cambridge, Mass.: Harvard University Press, 1996], 102).

6. Rashi identifies this protest with the moment when the slave foremen defy Moses after the failure of his first approach to Pharaoh. They are so sure of their reading of reality that they summon God to adjudicate (5:21).

7. See chapter 3, 159–164.

8. Rashi to 14:10: "They seized hold of their fathers' craft . . ."—the "craft" of prayer which had been the peculiar genre developed by the Patriarchs.

9. Cf. "Drawn-out expectation (*tocheleth*) makes the heart sick (*machalah*)" (Prov 13:12).

10. See Ramban to 14:15.

11. Rashi to 15:1.

12. By contrast, the road not taken is called *peshuta* ("simple," "straightfor-

ward"). On another level, this term may also indicate the *peshat* meaning of the narrative: the clear, continuous line of God's narrative.

13. James, *The Varieties of Religious Experience* (London: Fontana Library, 1960), 477.

14. See Phillips, *Terrors,* 93.

15. Rashi to 12:39; quoting the Mechilta.

16. Rashi to 14:4.

17. U. Cassuto, *A Commentary on the Book of Exodus* (Jerusalem: Magnes Press, 1967), 165.

18. Chullin 89a.

19. Charles Dickens, *Hard Times* (New York: Signet Classics, 1963), *Book the First, Chapter II.*

20. Shemoth Rabba 20:5.

21. See, e.g., the several midrashim that tell of Pharaoh's belated realization of Israel's value—which was either intrinsic or developed *after* liberation.

22. "Ode: Intimations of Immortality from Recollections of Early Childhood," *Poetry @ Prose,* selected by W. M. Merchant (London: Rupert Hart-Davis, 1955), 576.

23. Sefath Emeth 84.

24. Phillips, *Terrors,* 11.

25. Mei HaShiloach 2, Beshallach.

26. See chapter 3, pp. 180–186.

27. See, e.g., 7:5; 7:17; 8:6; 8:18; 9:14; 9:29; 10:2; 11:7; 14:4; 14:18.

28. Rashi to 32:1.

29. Midrash Tehillim 78:15. The claim is made on the basis of a play on the expressions the "finger" and the "hand" of God, thus multiplying ten (the hand) by five (for each finger).

30. See Megilla 10b.

31. Pirke d'Rabbi Eliezer, 42.

32. There are, of course, many midrashim that depict luxurious, personal corridors within the Split Sea, lined with fruit and all manner of delights. Even those corridors, however, are a glass world, transparent, suggesting that even in their well-furbished tunnels, the Israelites remain aware of the Egyptian anguish.

33. See Seforno to 15:16–18.

34. Shemoth Rabba 21:9.

35. B. Berachoth 54a.

36. See Ha-amek She'eila on 26:2.

37. William Shakespeare, *Hamlet,* II.ii.533.

38. See also Rashi to 15:6, 12, 16. And Seforno and Ramban.

39. Mei HaShiloach 1, Beshallach.

40. Phillips, *Terrors,* 11.

41. Cf. Rashi to Deut 32:10: "Even there, in the howling wilderness, they were attracted by faith . . ." Cf. also Maharal, *Gevuroth Hashem,* chapter 7.

42. Sefath Emeth 69.

43. See Introduction, 7–9.

44. Stanley Cavell, *A Pitch of Philosophy* (Cambridge, Mass.: Harvard University Press, 1994), 144.

45. Ibid., 146.

46. Ibid., 143.

47. See chapter 1, 56–71.

48. "To swing" is a literal translation of Rashi's word, in his version of the midrash: "she seduces (*meshadalto*) him with words" (38:8). The physical sensation behind the word is kinetic: she moves him to another state of being.

49. See Pirke d'Rabbi Eliezer, 48.

50. Rosenzweig, *Star,* 173.

51. Ibid., 175.

52. See Rashi to Song of Songs 1:4.

53. Lacan, *Ecrits,* 4. See chapter 1 for a discussion of the "mirror stage" notion.

54. See the fate of the heroine in Kieslowski's *The Double Life of Veronique,* for a film exploration of this idea—"she who sings must die."

55. Catherine Clément, *Opera, or the Undoing of Women,* trans. Betsy Wing (Minneapolis: University of Minnesota Press, 1988), 176. Quoted in Cavell, *Pitch,* 169.

56. Sefath Emeth, 69.

57. Rashi to 15:2, from Shir Ha-Shirim Rabba 3:15 and Mechilta Shirah, chapter 3.

58. B. Sotah 11b.

59. Shemoth Rabba 1:16.

60. Shemoth Rabba 23:9.

61. Cavell, *Pitch,* 144.

62. Rosenzweig, *Star,* 156.

63. Ibid., 157.

64. See B. Sanhedrin 91b.

65. Cf. Socrates' description of himself as a midwife, using language to clarify and transform thinking.

66. See Ramban to 15:20.

67. Partially explaining also why she is identified as "Aaron's sister" (15:20), Mechilta amplifies by telling the story of how Miriam prophesied the birth of Moses, the future redeemer; and of how she persisted in her confidence of prophecy throughout the vicissitudes that followed: her father's acceptance of her prophecy, the baby born, only to be surrendered to the Nile, where she stationed herself in prophetic steadfastness, open to knowledge of the future (2:4). Now publicly acknowledged as a prophetess, she brings her prestige to bear on the distinctive Song of the women.

68. In Rashi's source, the Mechilta, it is "the righteous," who have the confidence—without gender determination. Rashi, it seems, is sharpening the midrashic language to engage with the Torah text, which speaks, of course, of women.

69. See note 65.

70. Shemoth Rabba 26:1. Job is the speaker in this midrash: the reference to his suffering Pharaoh's decrees is, presumably, linked to the midrashic tradition that

places him at the Egyptian court, silently accepting Pharaoh's anti-Israelite policy. See Shemoth Rabba 1:12 and 12:3.

71. Shemoth Rabba 23:8.

72. James, *Varieties,* 477.

73. There are many similar passages of what becomes a conventional surprise in the jostlings of angelic and human in the presence of God.

74. Rosenzweig, *Star,* 156.

75. See Clement, chapter 4, "The Girls Who Leap into Space," *Opera, or the Undoing of Women.*

76. See R. Hutner, *Pachad Yitzhak, Pesach* (New York: Gur Aryeh, 1988), 1:11–12.

77. VaYikra Rabba 11:9.

78. See Song of Songs, 1:3: "Therefore, young girls love you . . ."

79. See Boyarin, *Intertextuality,* chapter 8, for a brilliant discussion of this and related texts.

80. See Nehemia Polen, "Miriam's Dance: Radical Egalitarianism in Hassidic Thought," in *Modern Judaism* 12, 1 (1992): 1–21.

81. Cavell, *Pitch,* 146.

82. See B. Eruvin 54b: "From here we learn that everywhere it says *va'ed*—for ever—eternally, there will be no discontinuity."

83. See Ramban to 15:18.

84. This midrash appears in B. Pesachim 118b. Rashi's version, on 14:31, begins: "So that the Israelites *should not say,* 'Just as we have emerged . . .' " God engages in preemptive activity, to *prevent* the expected counter-narrative from developing. Cf. Rashi on Ps 106:7—the proof-text for the midrash: "There were some people of little faith who said . . ." A compromise solution?

85. Cavell, *Pitch,* 144.

86. It is interesting to note that Miriam's son, Hur, is one of the men who support Moses' hands at Rephidim, in the battle against Amalek (17:10). Yet again, Miriam is associated with the problem of "rising and falling" (Moses' hands) and with the sense of faith as constancy.

87. See B. Ta'anit 9a; Tanchuma Bamidbar 2.

88. See Num 20:1–2.

89. William Wordsworth, "Essay upon Epitaphs," *The Prose Works,* vol. 2, ed. W. J. B. Owen and Jane Wothington Smyser (Oxford University Press/Clarendon Press, 1974), 53.

90. Tanchuma Beshallach 24.

91. Adam Phillips, *On Kissing, Tickling, and Being Bored* (Cambridge, Mass.: Harvard, 1993), 68–69.

92. Ibid., 74.

93. Ibid., 73.

94. Ibid., 72.

95. Ten tests, according to the midrash (Arachin 15a), based on Num 14:22.

96. *On Kissing,* 75.

97. B. Sanhedrin 56b.

98. John Keats, *Letters,* February 19, 1818.

99. The word for "song" (*shira)* can be associated with *shura*—"a straight line."

100. See, e.g., Chatwin, *Songlines.* The songlines are the "labyrinth of invisible pathways which meander all over Australia and are known to Europeans as 'Dreaming-tracks' or 'Songlines'; to the Aboriginals as the 'Footprints of the Ancestors' or the 'Way of the Law'" (p. 2). The Ancestors, who sang the world into existence, were poets "in the original sense of *poesis,* meaning 'creation': 'Providing you knew the song, you could always find your way across country' " (pp. 15–16).

101. A play on the words *riv* ("dispute")/*rav* ("master").

102. A play on the words *riv* ("dispute")/*ribui* ("bounty").

103. Shemoth Rabba 26:2.

104. See note 95.

105. Num 21:17–18.

106. Maharal, *Gevuroth Hashem,* chapter 7. It is significant that the blow to the rock is a reversion, even a regression, to Moses' original modality—*hitting* the Egyptian overseer (2:12), threatening with sticks the Israelite women who have offered mirrors to the Tabernacle. (See chapter 1).

107. See Ha-amek Davar to Numbers 20:8.

108. *The Selected Poetry of Rainer Maria Rilke,* ed. and trans. Stephen Mitchell (New York: Vintage, 1982), 231.

109. To Princess Marie von Thurn und Taxis-Hohenlohe, November 17, 1912.

110. Likkutei Moharan 1, 282.

111. Exod 17:11–12.

112. Mechilta Beshallach 1:11.

113. *Awakenings,* 60, note 45.

114. Tanchuma Beshallach 1. Here, of course, the forty-year desert journey is given as God's primary intention, not as the punishment for the sin of the Spies. Perhaps sin and punishment are only a human notation for the destinies of human beings; underlying these comprehensible models is the mystery of God's knowledge.

Yithro: "If a lion roars . . ."

1. B. Zevachim 116a. Rashi includes two of these views in his commentary on this verse.
2. See Ramban to 18:12; and his source in the Zohar VaYikra (9:1).
3. Jethro's world is, of course, the world of the nomadic shepherd and, as such, it is set in the wilderness. Before the intrusion of the Israelite rumor, however, it, like all worlds, displays the contours and stabilities of a constructed culture.
4. See Shemoth Rabba 27:5.
5. There is a midrashic tradition that places Jethro in Egypt as one of Pharaoh's advisers, at the beginning of the persecution. See, e.g., Shemoth Rabba 1:31.
6. See James Hillman, *Healing Fiction* (Spring Publications, 1983), chapter 1.
7. B. Baba Bathra 16a.

8. The fact that Jethro eventually leaves the Israelite camp and returns to his own people, while maintaining a special historical attachment to the Israelite destiny, is expressive of the unresolved nature of his ambivalence, in spite of the therapeutic narrative. In this sense, Bahya's discussion does not deal with the full complexity of the problem of the "sick soul."

9. See, e.g., the famous midrash that makes the survival of the world contingent on the successful accomplishment of this moment (B. Shabbat 88a).

10. A simile has a more precise and reductive effect than a metaphor. "Like a furnace," evoking a resemblance to a particular object, is more problematic than the open suggestiveness of "I bore you on eagles' wings . . ."; in the latter case, some undefined register of resemblance is evoked.

11. See Ibn Ezra, whose view Ramban is disputing.

12. See Rashi's source in the Mechilta (9:15), which adds: "not the angels alone but God, too, helped them to move in both directions."

13. One source (Mincha Belula) even associates this rocking motion with the traditional rocking stance of prayer (in Yiddish, "shockle"), citing the Psalmist's cry: "All my bones say, O God, who is like You?" Baal HaTurim associates to the rocking motion of one who learns Torah, "since the Torah was given 'in dread, and fear, and trembling, and shuddering' " (Berachoth 22a). See Torah Shelemah 20:449.

14. The proof-text is Deut 4:10: "You shall tell them [the experiences of Sinai] to your children and to your grandchildren. The day you stood before God your God at Chorev . . ." This serves as the basis for replicating the essence of the Sinai experience throughout history.

15. See Rashi to 3:22.

16. Shemoth Rabba 29:3.

17. Etz Yosef on Shemoth Rabba 29:3.

18. B. Shabbat 88b.

19. See Pachad Yitzhak, Shavuoth 8:10 for a discussion of the two dimensions of Revelation. R. Hutner cites the Beraita in the Haggadah, recited at the Seder on Passover: "If He had brought us to Mount Sinai, and not given us the Torah, it would have been sufficient for us!"

20. Shemoth Rabba 29:1.

21. Torah Shelemah 20:420.

22. B. Shabbat 88a.

23. Maimonides, *Guide for the Perplexed,* 2:33.

24. Shemoth Rabba 5:9.

25. See, e.g., the seven directions in which the lulav is shaken on Sukkoth. The seventh is toward one's own heart.

26. Shemoth Rabba 29:3.

27. Rosenzweig, *Star,* 4.

28. Torah Shelemah 20:231 (Mechilta d'Rabbi Shimeon bar Yochai).

29. Rosenzweig, *Star,* 151.

30. Rosa Newmarch, *The Life and Letters of Peter Ilich Tchaikovsky* (London: 1906), 274–275.

31. Abraham J. Heschel, *The Prophets* (New York: The Jewish Publication Society of America, 1962), 405.

32. Czeslaw Milosz, *"Ars Poetica?" The Collected Poems (1931–1987)* (Penguin Books, 1988), 211.

33. William Blake, "The Tyger," in "Songs of Experience," *The Poetical Works of William Blake* (London: Oxford University Press, 1961), 85.

34. B. Sanhedrin 89a.

35. The proof-text is 1Kings 22:7. Jehoshafat rejects the prophecy of the four hundred prophets of the Baal, and asks: "Is there not here another prophet of God?" The Talmudic comment, cited also by Rashi on Kings, reads the *unanimity* of the four hundred prophets as clear evidence that they are *not* prophets of God!

36. Bollas, *Cracking Up,* 42.

37. Ibid., 56.

38. Levinas, "Revelation," 194–195.

39. Emmanuel Levinas, *Ethique et infini: Dialogues avec Philippe Nemo* (Paris: Fayard, 1982), 115.

40. Mechilta to 19:11.

41. Levinas, "Revelation," 204–205.

42. Ibid., 209.

43. Winnicott, *Playing,* 96–97.

44. Winnicott inserts a footnote into his text about the reference to "objects": he notes that the title of his original paper was "Transitional Objects and Transitional Phenomena."

45. Ps 119:92.

46. Winnicott uses this as epigraph to chapter 7 (p. 95).

47. Winnicott, *Playing,* 98.

48. See Ha-amek Davar on 5:25.

49. B. Avoda Zara 5a–b.

50. This translation of the Hebrew terms I owe to an unpublished lecture by R. Matthis Weinberg.

51. D. W. Winnicott, "Primitive Emotional Development," in *Collected Papers: Through Pediatrics to Psycho-Analysis* (London: Tavistock; New York: Basic Books, 1958), 150.

52. B. Avoda Zara 5b.

53. Winnicott relates that he once made an interpretation in analysis—ten years too soon! (*Home Is Where We Start From* [New York: Norton, 1986], 84).

54. Sefath Emeth: VaYikra, p. 72.

55. See chapter 3.

56. Paul Celan, "Ashglory" ("Ashenglorie"). See John Felstiner's discussion in *Paul Celan, Poet, Survivor, Jew* (New Haven: Yale University Press, 1995), 223.

Mishpatim: Before Revelation: The Hearing Heart

1. See Mechilta 21:10. For other examples of this continuity principle, see Deut 4:13–14 and 5:28–6:17.

2. *The JPS Commentary, Exodus,* commentary by Nahum Sarna (JPS: 1991), 150.

3. Ibid., 150.

4. Ibid., 151–152.

5. Abarbanel notes that the *chachmei tzorfat*—the French school, led by Rashi—follow Mechilta, while the *chachmei sefarad*—the Spanish school, led by Ramban—follow the chronological order of the text.

6. B. Sanhedrin 56b.

7. See Rashi on 18:9. See chapter 5 (pp. 253–255) for a discussion of this episode.

8. See Ha'amek Davar on Gen 44:18.

9. See B. Gittin 60a for a discussion of whether the Torah was written down in segments ("scrolls") or as one unit. Meshech Chochma claims that this discussion has no direct bearing on his reading.

10. Maor VaShemesh on 24:3.

11. See Levinas, "Temptation," 47: "The Torah is given in the Light of a face."

12. Christopher Bollas, *The Shadow of the Object* (London: Free Association Books, 1987), 33.

13. Ibid., 35.

14. Ibid., 36.

15. Ibid., 38.

16. Shemoth Rabba 5:23. For another discussion of this midrash (in its Tanchuma form) see chapter 2 (pp. 114–117).

17. George Steiner, *After Babel* (Oxford: Oxford University Press, 1992), 228.

18. Ibid., 229.

19. Ibid., 242.

20. Ps 119:92.

21. Yalkut Shimeoni 1,764.

22. Felman, "Education and Crisis," in *Testimony: Crises of Witnessing,* 15.

23. Ibid., 16.

24. Felman, "Education and Crisis," *Testimony,* 24.

25. Shabbat 88a.

26. Levinas, "Temptation," 48.

27. Ibid., 45.

28. Ibid., 42.

29. Emmanuel Levinas, *Totality and Infinity* (Pittsburgh: Duquesne University Press, 1969), 24.

30. Levinas, *Temptation,* 32.

31. Ibid., 33.

32. Ibid., 43.

33. Ibid., 47–48.

34. Levinas, *Totality,* 24.

35. Ibid., 25.

36. Ibid., 27.

37. Ibid., 51.

38. Ibid., 171.

39. Tanchuma Yithro, 8.

40. Oliver Sacks, *The Man Who Mistook His Wife for a Hat* (London: Picador, 1985), 56–62.

41. Ibid., 62.
42. Tanchuma Yithro, 8.
43. Gen 48:14–19.
44. Rashi, Hizkuni, Rabbenu Bahya.
45. Seforno. See also the view of R. Nehemia in Pesikta Rabbati (83, 12a).
46. Sefath Emeth Shemoth, 121.
47. B. Kiddushin 22b.
48. Levinas, *Totality,* 51.
49. Levinas, *Temptation,* 48.
50. J. Kiddushin 1:2.
51. Levinas, *Temptation,* 43.
52. Likkutei Moharan 1, 22:9–10.
53. Arthur Green, *Tormented Master* (New York: Schocken Books, 1981), 292–93. The term *maqqif* is not used in our passage, but the circular image has a similar significance. Green notes: "The term is adapted from its frequent usage in Lurianic literature, where its meaning is quite different. The followers of Luria use the terms *'or maqqif* or *'orot maqqifin* with reference to the *sefirotic* world, not to the human mind" (331n.13).
54. Benjamin, "The Work of Art in the Age of Mechanical Reproduction," in *Illuminations,* 224–25.
55. Ibid., 228.
56. 1Kings 3:9.
57. Tanchuma Ki Tavo, 1.
58. Rosenzweig, *Star,* 175.

Teruma: The Sanctuary in Fire: Comedy and Tragedy

1. Ramban 25:1.
2. See Zohar Pikudei 229,1.
3. 24:16; Deut 5:21; Exod 40:34, 35.
4. Deut 4:36; Num 7:89.
5. Deut 4:36.
6. Exod 25:22; 29:42–43.
7. Cf. Jonathan Lear, *Open Minded: Working Out the Logic of the Soul* (Cambridge, Mass.: Harvard, 1998), 164–65: "This is the tragedy of the *Symposium.* For 2,500-odd years Western civilization has been trying to comprehend the demise of classical Greece. Plato seems to suggest that there is something in this undoing which must remain incomprehensible. Indeed, the *Symposium* is a dramatization in miniature of this disintegration. The party falls apart, as does Greece, because there is an intersection of the divine and human realms, the full meaning of which is incomprehensible in purely human terms." This passage appears at the end of Lear's discussion of the "undoing of the *Symposium*'s account of love."
8. Cassuto, *A Commentary,* 319.
9. Tanchuma Teruma 8.
10. See, e.g., Tanchuma Pekudei 2, 11; Shemoth Rabba 51:4; Tanchuma Tissa 4;

Midrash Tehillim 3. For a different midrashic view—that the commandment to build the Mishkan was given before the Golden Calf (as written) and only transmitted to the people after they had been forgiven—see: Lekah Tov 105; Seder Eliyahu Rabba 17; Tanchuma Yashan Bechukothai 65. See also the commentaries of Ramban and Ibn Ezra to 25:1; and Ramban to 35:1.

11. See Rashi to 31:18; 33:11. See also Seforno to 24:18.

12. Lear, *Open Minded,* 70.

13. Ibid., 65. The statue of the Commendatore appears at the end of Mozart's *Don Giovanni,* to pronounce doom on the hero; it is a figure of supernatural judgment, sorrowful but aloof.

14. Ibid., 62–63.

15. Ibid., 63.

16. Ibid., 73.

17. Ibid., 74.

18. In mystical literature, gold is the material representation of fire. See, e.g., Ramban on the gold cherubim as analogous to the fire out of which God speaks (25:1).

19. Tanchuma Yashan Tissa 3.

20. Cassuto, 321.

21. Bamidbar Rabba 12:10.

22. Sotah 11. See chapter 1, 37–41.

23. This is the meaning of the word, *Mishkan*—the interior of a tent, as opposed to its exterior surface (*Ohel*). See Cassuto, *A Commentary,* 345–48. Both terms emphasize the temporary, "unsettled" quality of the Mishkan modality; cf. 2 Samuel 7:6: "From the day that I brought the people of Israel out of Egypt to this day, I have not dwelt (*yashavti*) in a house, but have moved about in Tent (*ohel*) and Tabernacle (*mishkan*)."

24. See Don Handelman and David Shulman, *God Inside Out* (New York: Oxford University Press, 1997), 62–63: "The term *model* is common in English-language usage. In its dictionary rendition, for example, a model may refer to 'a standard, an example used as a canon,' and to 'a representation or pattern in miniature . . . of something to be made on a larger scale.' These definitions contain two aspects—thinking and doing—that often are attributed to the concept. A model is good for thinking with (a standard, a canon) or for doing with (a miniature of something to be made). This usage parallels the broad distinctions between 'knowing that' and 'knowing how,' which are made by Gilbert Ryle; and those between 'models of and models for,' which are made by Clifford Geertz, who based his usage on Ryle's." The Mishkan model deployed in these midrashic sources is obviously a "model for," and offered as an aid in "knowing how." In a less obvious sense, however, the other meaning emerges as the important one, as difficulties gather around the "practical" usage.

25. Tanchuma Yashan Shemini 11.

26. Gaston Bachelard, *The Psychoanalysis of Fire,* trans. Alan C. M. Ross (Boston: Beacon, 1964), 7.

27. Jacques Derrida, *Archive Fever* (Chicago: University of Chicago Press, 1996), 26.

28. Levinas, *Totality*, 257–258.
29. Ibid., 259.
30. Canetti, *Crowds*, 253.
31. Ibid., 255.
32. Ibid., 254.
33. Pirke d'Rabbi Eliezer, 44.
34. B. Rosh Hashana 29a.
35. Levinas, *Totality*, 257–258.
36. Ha-amek Davar suggests that the blatantly miraculous mode—the staff—is held in reserve, if the natural modality of prayer, the expressive body, replacing the destructive body, fails in its task.
37. Levinas, *Totality*, 257–258.
38. Ibid., 261.
39. B. Baba Bathra 15a.
40. The phrase is from the guidebook to the exhibit of Byzantine art at the Metropolitan Museum.
41. A classic Chasidic story tells of the Kotzker Rebbe's answer to the question, "Where is the place of His Glory?"—"Wherever we give Him room, where there is space for Him."
42. See Frank Kermode, *The Sense of an Ending* (New York: Oxford, 1996), 7. Sir Philip Sidney, in his *Apology for Poetry*, writes "a Poet thrusteth into the middest, euen where it most concerneth him, and there recoursing to the thinges forepast, and diuining of thinges to come, maketh a pleasing analysis of all."
43. Martin Heidegger, "Building Dwelling Thinking," in *Basic Writings*, edited by David Farrell Krell (San Francisco: Harper, 1977), 361. See also p. 356: "What the word for space, *Raum*, designates is said by its ancient meaning. *Raum, Rum*, means a place that is freed for settlement and lodging. A space is something that has been made room for, something that has been freed, namely, within a boundary, Greek *peras*. A boundary is not that at which something stops but, as the Greeks recognized, the boundary is that from which something *begins its essential unfolding*."
44. The exegetical point is made by Malbim (to 25:8) among many other commentaries.
45. Gaston Bachelard, *The Poetics of Space* (Boston: Beacon Press, 1969), 8.
46. Ibid., 14.
47. Or HaChaim to 25:8.
48. Shemoth Rabba 33:3.
49. See Marcus Jastrow, *A Dictionary of the Targumim . . . and the Midrashic Literature* (New York: Judaica Press, 1971), 1504.
50. Rashi relates the silver cord to the spinal cord which becomes hollow, desiccated, and twisted in old age.
51. Handelman and Shulman, *God Inside Out*, 54.
52. Ibid., 55–56.
53. Bachelard, *Poetics of Space*, 39.
54. Shemoth Rabba 33:1.
55. Sefath Emeth 136.
56. Hans Leowald, *Papers*, 62. Quoted in Lear, *Open Minded*, 124.

57. Winnicott, *Playing,* 103.

58. Ibid., 97.

59. Cf. Plato's *Symposium,* where eros is described as living in an intermediate region between the divine and human realms.

60. Bachelard, *Poetics of Space,* 8.

61. Deut 4:11.

62. Shemoth Rabba 2:8.

63. Antoine de Saint-Exupéry, *The Little Prince* (London: Pan Books, 1974), 66–68.

64. B. Yoma 54a.

65. Bachelard, *Poetics of Space,* 8.

66. Hamlet, III.ii. 371.

67. See Ps 18:11: "He rode on a cherub, and flew; yea, He came swiftly upon the wings of the wind."

68. Benjamin, *Understanding Brecht,* 73.

69. Blanchot, *L'Entretien Infini,* 74.

70. The debate about whether "the Testimony" refers to the Tablets or to the Scroll of the Law is summarized in Torah Shelemah 25 [123].

71. George Steiner, *Real Presences* (Chicago: University of Chicago Press, 1989), 94–95.

72. Ibid., 96.

73. Ibid., 121.

74. Ibid., 122.

75. J. Shekalim 6:1.

76. B. Chagiga 13a, b.

77. Steiner, *No Passion Spent,* 359.

78. John Felstiner, *Paul Celan* (New Haven: Yale University Press, 1995), 168.

79. Lear, *Open Minded,* 146–147.

80. 2Sam 7:6. See note 23.

81. See, e.g., Shemoth Rabba 45:3; Tanchuma Tissa 27. Also Rashi to 33:7.

82. See Pirke d'Rabbi Eliezer 46; Seder Eliahu Zutta 84, 180. See also Zohar 1:52b; 2:236a; 3:114a.

83. See Rashi to 33:11.

84. Gur Arye to 33:11.

85. Rashi to 33:8. There is an alternative, uglier scenario in Rashi's source, J. Bikkurim 3:3. This holds its own fascination but is not directly related to our theme.

86. See chapter 9, 440–441, for a discussion of this passage.

87. The dancing around the Calf that Moses witnesses as he comes down the mountain is described as *mecholoth,* circle-dancing (32:19).

88. Seder Elyahu Rabba 17.

89. The *ohel,* the tent, is the site of sexuality in the classic midrashic encoding. It represents the intimacy and complexity of nonrational experience.

90. See Beith Ya'acov Teruma 60. We remember that at the end of *The Symposium,* Socrates tries to prove to Aristophanes and Agathon that authors should be

able to write both comedy and tragedy. Jonathan Lear suggests that this must mean that "there is something important about the human condition that can be conveyed only in a drama which can be read both as tragedy and as a comedy" (p. 137). In the drama of Mishkan and Golden Calf, the comedy is the narrative as we have it in the Torah, with the Mishkan first. The tragedy is implicit in the midrashic reading, with the Golden Calf first.

91. B. Gittin 43a.

Tetzaveh: Loss and Gain

1. See Ha-amek Davar to 27:20.
2. See pp. 318–322.
3. One exception occurs during leap years, when Tetzaveh falls in Adar Rishon and Moses' *yahrzeit,* his death date, in Adar Sheni.
4. The cantillations on the word *ve-atta,* in all three cases, imply a pause (*gershayim, pazer, revi'i*) and indicate a dramatic focusing on the presence of Moses. The commentary of Alshikh suggests that the cantillation evokes for Moses a reassurance about his essential role, even in the issue of the priesthood.
5. Cassuto, *A Commentary,* 372.
6. Shemoth Rabba 37:4.
7. Shemoth Rabba 2:13.
8. Likkutim, Tetzaveh.
9. See, e.g., the initial barrenness of the marriages of Abraham and Sarah, Isaac and Rebecca, Jacob and Rachel (but not Leah, the "hated" wife), Elkanah and Hannah (but not Peninah).
10. The audacity is compounded by the slippage between the Psalmist's "I should have perished in my poverty" and God's "I should have lost My world"—with its implication of God's very life in relation to the world being at risk.
11. Tanchuma Shemini 3.
12. Rashi's main source is B. Zevachim 102a.
13. Adam Phillips, *On Flirtation* (Cambridge, Mass.: Harvard), 34.
14. Ibid., 34.
15. B. Megilla 31a.
16. B. Zevachim 17b.
17. See, e.g., the representative function of the sons of Eli the priest, who abuse their privileged position and are replaced. The expressive power of the robes is exposed in a condition of dissonance and the dynastic sanctity of Eli's line is rejected (1Sam 2:12–36).
18. *Hamlet* I.ii.76, 85–86.
19. *Hamlet* V.i.187.
20. *Lear* III.iv.105.
21. B. Menachoth 42b.
22. Benjamin, *Illuminations,* 72.
23. George Steiner, *The Steiner Reader* (Middlesex: Penguin, 1984), 384.

24. Ibid., 369.

25. B. Menachoth 8a.

26. Shemoth Rabba 52:2.

27. Kenneth Burke, *Permanence and Change* (Berkeley: University of California Press, 1984), 172.

28. Ibid., 173.

29. Ibid., 175.

30. *Walden,* ed. Owen Thomas (New York: Norton, 1966), 61.

31. Mark Edmundson, *Towards Reading Freud* (Princeton: Princeton University Press, 1990), 8.

32. Italo Calvino, "The Non-Existent Knight," in *Our Ancestors* (London: Picador, 1980), 289.

33. Ibid., 300.

34. Ibid., 322.

35. *Permanence,* 179.

36. The empty suit of armor figures in the Disney film, *Bedknobs and Broomsticks,* in a comic, surrealistic mode, to represent the invincibility of the fascist ideology. The sinister dimension of a total investment in a role is conveyed, also, in Brecht's *Galileo,* in the scene where Cardinal Barberinin is invested in his papal robes: as he takes on the form of Pope Urban VIII, he yields his moral autonomy, agreeing to threaten Galileo with the torture instruments.

37. Christopher Ricks, *The Force of Poetry* (Oxford: Oxford University Press, 1997), 279.

38. T. S. Eliot, "Marvell," in Ricks, 277.

39. Pirke d'Rabbi Eliezer, 20.

40. Bereshith Rabba 20:29.

41. Pirke, 14.

42. See RaDaL on Pirke, 14 [23].

43. See Gen 3:7.

44. Calvino, "Knight," 300.

45. See, however, the mysterious reference to a mask or veil that Moses assumes and removes, "dons and doffs," after the Golden Calf episode (34:33–35). For discussion of this passage, see chapter 9, 443–450.

46. Rashi to Num 20:26.

47. See Tanchuma Chukath 17.

48. Rashi to 20:25.

49. Rashi to Deut 34:6.

50. Burke, *Permanence,* 179.

51. See note 8.

52. Beit Yaakov Tetzaveh, 39.

53. J. Yoma 1:5.

54. This verse is often cited in Chasidic texts to refer to the spiritual condition of *kenosis* (personal emptiness in the presence of the divine).

55. B. Chagiga 27a.

56. VaYikra Rabba 21:11.

57. T. S. Eliot, "Marvell," in Ricks, *Force of Poetry.*

58. Burke, *Permanence*, 172.

59. I owe these examples to Murray M. Schwartz, "Where is Literature?" in *Transitional Objects and Potential Spaces: Literary Uses of D. W. Winnicott*, ed. Peter L. Rudnytsky (New York: Columbia University Press, 1993), 59.

60. Rashi to 10:2.

61. Yalkut Shimeoni 1:524.

62. VaYikra Rabba 20: 6, 7.

63. Jose Ortega, *The Revolt of the Masses* (New York: Norton, 1957), 157.

64. Kierkegaard, *Sickness*, 166, 170–172.

65. See above,

66. Kierkegaard, *Sickness*, 169.

67. Ibid., 164, 169.

68. Tanchuma Tetzaveh 1.

69. Winnicott, *Playing*, 95.

70. Ibid., 101.

71. For a further discussion of this midrash, see my *The Beginning of Desire*, 106–107.

72. William Wordsworth, note to "The Thorn, 1800," in *Poetry and Prose*, selected by W. M. Merchant (London: Rupert Hart-Davis, 1955), 236.

73. This concept of the surprise function of *ve-atta* can be used to interpret usages specifically in reference to Moses. See, e.g., Exod 4:16; 14:16; 30:23; 31:13.

74. Rashi, however, reads: "I will hope for Your salvation, and *when You do save me*, I shall praise You even more." He inserts the concept of fulfillment into the text. Ibn Ezra's reading is more faithful to the restrained tone of the text; it also relates to the larger context (see v. 12).

75. See Winnicott, *Playing*, 98.

76. André Neher, *The Exile of the Word*, trans. David Maisel (Philadelphia: Jewish Publication Society, 1981), 197.

77. Ibid., 198. Neher later refers to the use of this verse in *Sefer Chasidim*, where valiant trust in God is compared to the chivalric courage of knights in battle who fight to the end without thought of reward (231).

78. Keats, *Letters*, 53.

79. Ibid., 50.

80. Winnicott, *Playing*, 98.

81. Richard Rorty, *Contingency, Irony, and Solidarity* (Cambridge: Cambridge University Press, 1990), 39–40.

82. Harold Bloom, *The Anxiety of Influence* (Oxford: Oxford University Press, 1973), 94.

83. Ha-amek Davar to 27:20.

84. Bereshith Rabba 91:12.

85. B. Berachoth 57.

86. See VaYikra Rabba 31: "To you: for your use." See Ha-amek Davar 27:20.

87. *Laws of Talmud Torah*, 3:1.

88. Maimonides cites Deuteronomy 33:4: "Through me kings shall reign . . ."

89. Yalkut Shimeoni 941.

90. The sages of the Amoraic period had the custom of calling one another, generically, "Moses."

91. Likkutei Moharan, 64. See my discussion of this passage on pp. 190–192.

92. *Ethics of the Fathers,* 1:17.

93. I owe the analogy between the *chalal panui* and "potential space" to Rabbi Daniel Epstein.

94. Jessica Benjamin, *The Bonds of Love* (New York: Pantheon, 1988), 42.

95. See Benjamin, *Bonds of Love,* 44.

96. See Rashi to 4:14: "All anger narrated in the Torah *leaves a trace* . . ."

97. Tanchuma Devarim 1.

98. *Pri Tzaddik,* Tetzaveh, 2.

99. *The Exile of the Word,* 197.

100. *Towards Reading Freud,* 163.

101. Benjamin, *The Bonds of Love,* 48.

Ki Tissa: The Golden Calf: Fire in the Bones

1. See chapter 7, pp. 318–322.

2. B. Nedarim 38a.

3. See Ha-amek Davar to 31:18.

4. See Rashi and Ha-amek Davar to 31:18.

5. *Boshesh* is used twice in the Book of Judges: 3:25 and 5:28.

6. Ha-amek Davar suggests an unexpected connection between the pre-sin condition of Adam and Eve, naked and *unashamed* (*lo yithboshashu*), and the notion of lateness. Although shame (*bosh*) and lateness (*boshesh*) seem unrelated, the Hebrew word used in the Genesis narrative is, in fact, derived from the "lateness" root. Because of this anomaly, Ha-amek Davar explores the phenomenological connections of shame and lateness: locating the meaning of the sin in the genesis of consciousness, with its impediments to self-forgetful union, whether mystical or sexual. Here, too, one may suggest, the dependence of the people on the consciousness of time is a bathetic counterpoint to the Revelation.

7. Rashi to 32:1.

8. See Ha-amek Davar to 32:1.

9. B. Shabbath 89a.

10. See Maharal, Tiffereth Yisrael, 48.

11. Winnicott, *Playing,* 97.

12. Shemoth Rabba 41:10.

13. Meshech Chochma to 32:19.

14. See Winnicott, *Playing,* 97.

15. Ps 106:20.

16. Rashi to Deuteronomy 5:24. See my discussion of this crisis on pp. 283–284.

17. See C. S. Lewis, *Till We Have Faces* (San Diego: Harcourt Brace, 1957).

18. Beit Yaacov Yithro 114. I am grateful to R. Daniel Epstein, whose reference in a lecture alerted me to this passage.

19. "Circles," in Ralph Waldo Emerson, *Selected Essays,* ed. Larzer Ziff (New York: Penguin Classics, 1985), 226.

20. Freud 14:257. I am indebted to Mark Edmundson's discussion of Emerson and Freud in his *Towards Reading Freud.*

21. Emerson, "Circles," 227.

22. Emerson, "Threnody," in *The Portable Emerson* (Viking Press, 1962), 340.

23. Burke uses this expression to describe Freud's reformulation of the "old doctrine of original sin," in comprehensive sexual terms (*Permanence and Change,* 127).

24. B. Shabbat 88b.

25. There is a contrasting midrashic tradition that does minimize the people's sin; that, for instance, lays the blame on the *Erev rav,* the "mixed multitudes" (Exod 12:38), that left Egypt together with the Israelites. See, e.g., Tanchuma 19; Midrash HaGadol to 32:1; Zohar 2:191.

26. B. Sanhedrin 63a.

27. See chapter 2 for my discussion of the "autism" of Pharaoh, and of Moses and the Israelites: Egypt is constructed in midrashic language as the symbolic territory of insensibility, out of which the Israelites must be "born."

28. Burke, *Permanence,* 125.

29. Ibid., 71.

30. Ibid., 74.

31. Ibid., 129.

32. Freud 14:255.

33. Emerson, "Self-Reliance," in Ziff, *Selected Essays,* 190.

34. Edmundson, *Reading Freud,* 149.

35. Emerson, "Compensation," quoted in Edmundson, 135.

36. Freud, 14:255.

37. Emerson, "Self-Reliance," in *Selected Essays* (New York: Penguin, 1982), 181.

38. Philip Rieff, *The Mind of the Moralist* (Chicago: University of Chicago Press, 1979), 166.

39. Seforno to 32:9.

40. Tanchuma 22.

41. See Or HaChaim to 32:11.

42. B. Berachoth 32a.

43. Ps 106:23; used as a proof-text in midrashic descriptions of Moses' role as intercessor. See, e.g., Shemoth Rabba 43:1.

44. Adam Phillips, *The Beast in the Nursery* (London: Faber and Faber, 1998), 95.

45. Zohar 67b.

46. B. Berachoth 32a.

47. Heschel compares God's anger to that of parents who experience "spiritual dependence" in relation to their children: they "are in misery when unable to love" (*The Prophets,* 294).

48. See Ecclesiastes Rabba 5:13, which discusses the contributions of the three "partners" in the creation of the human being: God, the father, and the mother.

49. Meshech Chochma to 32:11.

50. 107–108.

51. See Rashi to 10:10. See also my discussion on pp. 159–164.

52. Lear, *Open Minded,* 79.

53. *Mecholoth*—"dancing"—indicates ring dancing. See my discussion of Miriam's dance on pp. 229–231.

54. See Pachad Yitzhak (Yom Kippur, 25) for a discussion of the relation between conflict and transformation.

55. Mei HaShiloach, 1: Tissa.

56. William Shakespeare, *Hamlet,* III.i.60–68.

57. See, e.g., the words of the Kaddish prayer where *be-agala* expresses a central motif of *immediate* and ultimate revelation of God's glory.

58. Seforno to 32:21.

59. See Immanuel Kant, "Idee zu einer allgemeinen Geschichte in welburgerlicher Absicht" (1784): "Out of timber so crooked as that from which man is made nothing entirely straight can be built." Isaiah Berlin's *Crooked Timber of Humanity* cites this as its epigraph.

60. See Tanchuma, 26.

61. Sefath Emeth, Thissa, 200.

62. See Brevard Childs, *Exodus, A Commentary* (SCM Press Ltd., 1974), 565–66. The bull represented Apis among the Egyptians and Baal among the Egyptians; as "a common Near Eastern reflex [it] has exerted a force even when it was unconscious to the biblical writer."

63. See Meshech Chochma to 32:19.

64. B. Shabbath 89a.

65. VaYikra Rabba 10:3.

66. Rashi to 32:5.

67. 24:14.

68. Freud 14:257.

69. Ibid., 14:255.

70. *Castle,* 37.

71. Ibid., 36.

72. Nietzsche, *The Gay Science,* quoted in Steiner, *Castle,* 40–41.

73. *Castle,* 41.

74. Ibid., 45.

75. *The Portage to San Cristobal of A. H.,* in *The Steiner Reader,* 275.

76. Steiner, *Castle,* 45–46.

77. Rieff, *Mind of the Moralist,* 166.

78. Freud, *Moses and Monotheism,* 128.

79. Yerushalmi, *Freud's Moses: Judaism Terminable and Interminable* (New Haven: Yale University Press, 1991), 33.

80. Ibid., 31. The reference is to Eliot's *Four Quartets.*

81. Freud, *Moses and Monotheism,* 88.

82. Yerushalmi, *Freud's Moses,* 85.

83. Ibid., 87.

84. Ibid., 86.

85. Derrida, *Archive Fever.*

86. Assmann, *Moses the Egyptian.*

87. Richard J. Bernstein, *Freud and the Legacy of Moses* (Cambridge: Cambridge University Press, 1998).

88. Ibid., 50.

89. Ibid., 59.

90. Assmann, *Moses the Egyptian,* 215.

91. See 17:10–12; 24:14.

92. Shemoth Rabbah 41:10.

93. All these examples are from Yerushalmi, 84–85.

94. Bamidbar Rabba 16:13.

95. Cf. Derrida's response to Yerushalmi's "exoneration" of the Israelites ["what counts is that the Israelites did not actually kill him."]. He makes two main points: first, that "*the intention to kill was effective, actual, and in truth accomplished* . . . The stones were thrown *in fact* . . . only divine intervention intercepted them." Second, invoking a psychoanalytic perspective, "the unconscious does not know the difference here [in the case of murder] between the intention and the action" (*Archive,* 65–66).

96. The version of the midrash in B. Sotah 35a makes this scenario more explicit.

97. Assmann comments on Freud's narrative of Moses—not God—as liberator from Egypt and creator of the Jewish nation (163). This construction of Moses, running counter to all historical probability, is represented even in the title of Freud's work, *The Man Moses and Monotheistic Religion.* Assmann suggests that this title is derived from Exod 11:3 ("Indeed, the man Moses was very great in the land of Egypt."), pointing out that this is "the only verse in the Hebrew Bible that alludes to Moses' important Egyptian position" (149). It seems to me, however, that Freud may well have drawn his title from Exod 32:1, where Moses is constructed by his people as the sole author of redemption (". . . this man Moses who brought us up from the land of Egypt . . .") Freud then identifies with this "fetishization" of Moses which goes against the classic religious intuition of the Jewish people which, as Assmann points out, tends to play down Moses' role in the Exodus. In the Passover Haggadah, Moses is not even mentioned.

98. 1Kgs 19:8–15.

99. Rashi to 19:16.

100. Rashi explicates: "That was the crevice in the rock where Moses stood. See Exodus 33:22."

101. Another midrashic example of this potent paradox is to be found in the strange observation in B. Sanhedrin 110a: "The people suspected him of committing adultery with their wives." The founder of the Chasidic movement, the Baal Shem Tov, reads this as the syndrome in which the charismatic leader becomes the screen for the projected fantasies of the crowd. This dynamic is portrayed in ex-

treme form in the suspicion, jealousy, and resentment projected onto the austere charisma of Moses. I am grateful to Mark Kirschbaum for pointing out this passage in the Baal Shem Tov (see Sefer Baal Shem Tov, Machon Da'at Yosef; 1993, "Korach").

102. See Beit Yaakov, 42.

103. Julia Kristeva, *Black Sun* (New York: Columbia University Press, 1989), 5.

104. Ibid., 40–41.

105. Ibid., 44.

106. Ibid., 3.

107. Ibid., 3.

108. See Beit Yaakov, 42, 45.

109. See pp. 345–347.

110. See Rashi to 33:8.

111. See Rashi to 33:7, 8. Rashi reads the whole passage as in the continuous mode.

112. Seder Eliyahu Rabba, chapter 17.

113. Rashi to 33:23. From B. Berachoth 7a.

114. Rashi to 33:19.

115. Wolfson, *Through a Speculum,* 392.

116. Shemoth Rabba 47:13.

117. Ibid., 47:12.

118. Rashi to 34:29. The source is Tanchuma, 37.

119. *Permanence*, 158.

120. Beit Yaacov, 68.

121. See Beit Yaacov, 69.

122. The Hebrew *be-dabro itho* is ambiguous, leaving unresolved whether God or Moses is the subject. The ambiguity reinforces the sense of Moses' total involvement.

123. Noam Elimelech, Ki Tissa (end).

124. Rashi to 34:30. The source is Sifrei Nasso, 1.

125. See Rashi to 32:5: "'And Aaron saw . . .' that there was a spirit of life in it . . . He saw that Satan's work had succeeded and he had no words to put them off."

126. Isa 30:20. See also B. Horayoth 12a, for a discussion of the pedagogical application of this verse.

127. This is Mark Edmundson's expression (144).

128. See Rabbenu Bahya to 34:30.

129. Tanchuma, 31.

130. See 34:3.

131. In *Otherwise than Being or Beyond Essence,* Levinas develops the distinction between *le dit* and *le dire:* the first plays the role of fetish, while the second deprives one of artificial supports and frees the spirit.

132. Eccl 8:1.

133. Likkutei Moharan, 230.

134. See B. Sukkah 28a.

135. Likkutei Yehuda, cited in Torah Shelemah, Ki Tissa, appendix 6 [8], 182. A similar notion is attributed to the Kotzker: the veil is simply the face that masks its inner fire.

136. Phillips, *Beast,* 39.

137. Ibid., 40.

138. *Twilight of the Idols,* cited in Harold Bloom, *Shakespeare: The Invention of the Human* (New York: Riverhead, 1998), 412.

139. *Hamlet* II.ii.589.

140. *Hamlet* I.ii.137ff.

141. Shemoth Rabba 42:6.

142. Phillips, *Flirtation,* 22.

143. Ibid., 24.

144. Cited in Ibid., 26.

145. Ibid., 25.

146. Bollas, *Cracking Up,* 141.

147. Freud, "Negation," cited in Phillips, *Flirtation,* 23.

148. Phillips, *Flirtation,* 23.

149. B. Avodah Zarah 44a.

150. Phillips, *Flirtation,* 37.

151. B. Eruvin 54.

152. B. Menachoth 99b.

153. This is the title of Adam Phillips's essay in *On Flirtation.* R. Hutner does not title his essay, which appears in *Chanukah,* 3.

154. B. Temura 16a.

155. B. Chagiga 16a.

156. Blanchot, *L'Entretien infini,* 74.

157. Benjamin, "On Some Motifs in Baudelaire," in *Illuminations,* 161.

158. Ps 78:37.

159. Benjamin, *Illuminations,* 161.

160. Phillips, *Flirtation,* 29–30.

161. Ibid., 31.

162. "The Image of Proust," in Benjamin, *Illuminations,* 204.

163. See B. Berachoth 32b for an evocative discussion of the paradoxes of remembering and forgetting.

Va-Yakhel—Pekudei: The Fiery Imagination

1. B. Shabbat 70a; 97b. The number 39 is obtained by a numerological count of *eileh (aleph=1 + lamed=30 + heh=5 = 36),* added to *devarim (=2 - representing the plural form) + ha- (=1 - the definite article).*

2. See, e.g., 31:3, 5; 35:28.

3. B. Shabbat 73b. This principle is, however, subject to much qualification and discussion.

4. See Rashi to 35:1.

5. See Ha-amek Davar to 35:1.

6. See Benno Jacob's comment in Leibowitz, *Studies in Shemot,* 538.

7. Seforno to 35:2.

8. Rashi to 31:13. There is no clear source for relating Rashi's comment to this verse. The idea that Shabbat overrides the building of the Mishkan is usually found in exegesis of 35:2. See Torah Shelemah to 31 [34].

9. Cf. 16:23 with its oblique reference to fire: "Bake what you would bake and boil what you would boil; and all that is left put aside to be kept until morning."

10. See, however, B. Shabbat 106a for a discussion of the different views on this subject.

11. Kli Yakar to 35:5. See also Ha-amek Davar: the donor must appear personally with his gift, so that the authenticity of his enthusiasm can be scrutinized. Inauthentic motives—social pressure or competition—disqualify the gift.

12. In midrashic readings, these camping points in the desert encode the history of the forty-year journey: *Dizahav*—"enough gold"—is a cryptic reference to the people's excessive generosity.

13. Shemoth Rabba 51:6.

14. This is Rashi's reading of Deuteronomy 1:1, based on B. Berachoth 32a. Moses is rebuking the people precisely for their passionate generosity in contributing to the Golden Calf; a more moderate response might have delayed the production of the idol till Moses' return (Etz Yosef).

15. See pp. 319–322.

16. Jerome Bruner, *Actual Minds, Possible Worlds* (Cambridge, Mass.: Harvard University Press, 1986), 102–103.

17. Bruner, *Actual Minds,* 105. Research has found that seven-month-old North American infants are able to discriminate between English and non-English phonemes (such as English and Hindi alveolar and dental consonants), but lose this ability some time later as they are increasingly exposed only to English. Making a particular world obscures many features of other possible worlds.

18. See Ramban to 25:1: gold is the symbolic structural equivalent of fire in the Mishkan.

19. Shemoth Rabba 48:7.

20. This is Rashi's translation. See 31:3. His translation for *da'at* is "the holy spirit."

21. See, e.g., Brevard Childs, *Exodus,* 570.

22. Rashi to 32:5.

23. Shemoth Rabba 43:7.

24. B. Megilla 25b

25. Shemoth Rabba 43:7.

26. See Rashi to 32:24. In Aaron's version of the narrative, his practical instructions to the people—"Break off your gold rings from your wives' ears and from your sons' and daughters' and bring them to me"—are reconstituted as a bare question: "One word only—'Who has gold?' " releases an avalanche of gifts.

27. Arthur Koestler, *The Ghost in the Machine* (Picador, 1975), 183.

28. "Henri Poincaré . . . explained scientific discovery as the happy meeting of 'hooked atoms of thought' in the unconscious mind" (Ibid., 184–185).

29. Ramban to 35:21.

30. The expression, *nessa'o libo*—"whose heart exalts him"—may well be translated as "inspired," in the Latin sense: *in-spirare,* inflated by the Spirit, is equivalent to *nessa'o libo,* the heart buoyed up by filled lungs.

31. B. Berachoth 55a.

32. Ramban to 31:2.

33. Rashi to 38:22. See J. Peah 1:1; Bereshith Rabba 1:20.

34. Rashi ibid. See B. Berachoth 55a.

35. Ha-amek Davar to 39:43.

36. See, e.g., the use of leitmotivs such as "seeing," "blessing," and "finishing the work" (39:43; 40:33; Gen 1:31–2:1–3) in the Mishkan and Creation narratives.

37. Bezalel's riposte to Moses about the "way of the world"—entailing building a house before making the furnishings—might seem to fit this description. See Rashi to 38:22.

38. Bamidbar Rabba 12:10. See my discussion of this midrash, 323–324.

39. See Rashi to 25:9.

40. Kedushath Levi, 143–144.

41. B. Sanhedrin 89a.

42. Bachelard, *On Poetic Imagination,* xxxvii.

43. Gaston Bachelard, *Air and Dreams* (Dallas: Dallas Institute Publications, 1988), 1.

44. See Rashi to 32:5. His sources are VaYikra Rabbah 10:3 and B. Sanhedrin 7a.

45. Meshech Chochma (35:31) points to this connection between Hur and his grandson, Bezalel. It is striking that Bezalel's precise genealogy, going back to Hur, is repeated in Moses' transmission of God's instructions to the people.

46. This is a literal translation of the phrase *melecheth machsheveth,* which is idiomatically translated, "designer's craft" (JPS).

47. Rashi to 26:1, 31. The source is B. Yoma 72b.

48. See Seforno and Ramban to 36:8.

49. Shemoth Rabba 42:5.

50. See Ramban to 32:1.

51. Bachelard, *Air and Dreams,* 1–2.

52. Ibn Ezra to 25:20.

53. See chapter 7, 339–343.

54. See Tanchuma Tissa, 26.

55. Handelman, *God Inside Out,* 149.

56. Ibid., 161.

57. Ibid., 186.

58. Ibid., 199.

59. *Psychoanalysis of Fire,* 56.

60. Empedocles was an eloquent philosopher in Sicily ca. 460 B.C.E. He was also a doctor and considered a magician. One tradition relates that he threw himself into the flames of Mount Aetna, so that by his sudden disappearance he might be believed to be a god.

61. Bachelard, *Psychoanalysis of Fire,* 16.

62. Shemoth Rabba 2:8.

63. Rashi to 3:12.

64. Bachelard, *Psychoanalysis of Fire,* 57.

65. Ibid., 58.

66. J. Berachoth 5:2. See Pachad Yitzhak Shavuoth, 18 [5] for a discussion of this paradox.

67. Keats, *Letters,* 53.

68. Marion Milner, *On Not Being Able to Paint,* cited in Phillips, *Beast,* 86.

69. Phillips, *Beast,* 66.

70. Ibid., 67.

71. Ibid., 71.

72. Ibid., 69.

73. Tanchuma VaYakhel, 2.

74. Bollas, *Cracking Up,* 53.

75. Cf. Phillips, *Beast,* 76: "Language, one might say, is like perfume; it circulates to unpredictable effect."

76. Shemoth Rabba 51:6.

77. This enigmatic quality is evoked also by the anomaly that the midrash narrates divine forgiveness for the Golden Calf by citing the verse signifying forgiveness *in the narrative of the Spies.* This conveys the mysteriously pervasive nature of the rupture, as well as of the reunion, which is the midrashic counter-emphasis to the lucid definition of the biblical narratives.

78. See chapter 7.

79. Ramban to 35:1.

80. Rashi to 38:21.

81. See Mizrahi to 31:18.

82. Pirkei Avoth 3:18.

83. The proof-text in Pirkei Avoth about the human being *informed* that he is in God's image is this verse—and not the more famous "Let us make man in our image and after our likeness" (1:26).

84. 40:33–38.

85. See Rashi to 40:35.

86. Midrash HaGadol 40:38.

87. D'Annunzio in Bachelard, *Psychoanalysis of Fire,* 19–20.

88. Rashi to Song of Songs, 2:3, citing Song of Songs Rabba 2:10.

89. Song of Songs Rabba 2:11.

90. Bachelard, *Psychoanalysis of Fire,* 56.

91. See B. Shabbath 97b.

92. Phillips, *Beast,* 86.

93. Phillips, *Beast,* 68.

94. In the most obvious sense, v. 2 is a general statement of the law, followed by the work-rest sequence. My interest is in a conceptual reading of the order in the text.

95. See Or HaChaim to this verse. He links the *gift* of the Land to its *observing a sabbath of God:* God's gift is not absolute but contains the Shabbat idea as a foundational aspect.

96. A classic play on words shows that *ish* (man) and *isha* (woman) have as their common factor *esh* (fire). The remaining letters—*yod* in the one case, and *heh* in the other—combine to compose the Name of God. Emblematically, the fire that may unite with fire is mediated by God's presence in the relationship.

97. See *Tzeror HaMor* in Torah Shelemah 40 [82]; and Sifrei BeHa'alothcha, 83.

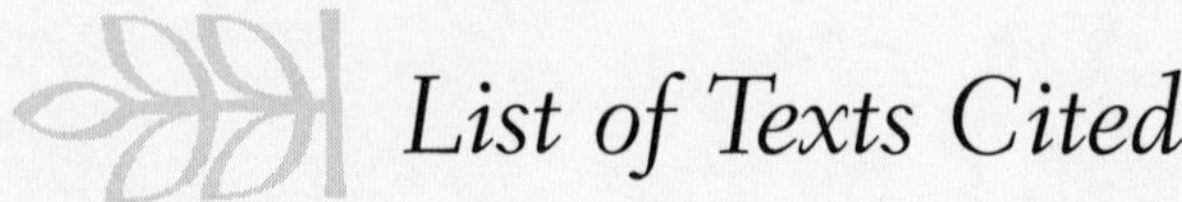

List of Texts Cited

Biblical

Tanach - The Holy Scriptures

Rabbinic

Babylonian Talmud
Bereshith Rabbati
Jerusalem Talmud
Mechilta
Mechilta d'Rabbi Shimeon bar Yochai
Midrash Chemdat Yamim
Midrash Hagadol
Midrash Lekach Tov
Midrash Rabba
Midrash Tehillim
Pesikta d'Rav Kahana
Pesikta Rabbati
Pirkei Avoth
Pirke d'Rabbi Eliezer
Seder Eliahu Rabba
Seder Eliahu Zuta
Sifrei
Tanchuma
Tanchuma Yashan
Targum Jonathan
Targum Onkelos
Torah Shelemah
Yalkut Shimeoni

Medieval and Later

Abarbanel
Baal Shem Tov
Beit Yaacov
Cassuto
Ha-amek Davar
Hizkuni
Kedushat Levi
Kli Yakar
Likkutei Moharan
Maharal - Commentary on the Torah (Gur Arye)
- Gevuroth Hashem
Maimonides - Guide for the Perplexed
- Hilchoth Yesodei HaTorah
Malbim
Ma'or Va-Shemesh
Mei HaShiloach
Mizrahi
Noam Elimelech
Olat Re'iyah (R. Kook)
Or HaChaim
Pachad Yitzhak
Pri Zaddik
Rabbenu Bahya
Radal
Ramban
Rashbam
Rashi
Sefat Emet
Seforno
Shadal
Zohar

Bibliography

Alvarez, A. *Night* (New York: W.W. Norton and Company, 1996).

Assmann, Jan. *Moses the Egyptian: The Memory of Egypt in Western Monotheism* (Cambridge, Mass.: Harvard University Press, 1997).

Auden, W. H. *Poems* (New York: Everyman's Library, 1995).

Bachelard, Gaston. *On Poetic Imagination and Reverie.* Selected, translated, and introduced by Gaudin Colette (Dallas: Spring Publications, Inc., 1987).

———. *The Poetics of Space* (Boston: Beacon Press, 1969).

———. *Air and Dreams* (Dallas: Dallas Institute Publications, 1988).

———. *The Psychoanalysis of Fire.* Translated by Alan C. M. Ross (Boston: Beacon, 1964).

Bataille, Georges. *The Accursed Share.* Translated by Robert Hurley (New York: Zone Books, 1993), Vol. 2.

Becker, Ernest. *The Denial of Death* (New York: Free Press, 1973).

Benjamin, Jessica. *The Bonds of Love* (New York: Pantheon, 1988).

Benjamin, Walter. *Illuminations* (London: Fontana, 1973).

———. *Understanding Brecht* (London: 1977).

Berger, John. *Keeping a Rendezvous* (New York: Vintage International, 1992).

———. *The Sense of Sight* (New York: Vintage International, 1985).

Berlin, Isaiah. *The Crooked Timber of Humanity* (New York: Knopf, 1991).

Bernstein, Richard J. *Freud and the Legacy of Moses* (Cambridge: Cambridge University Press, 1998).

Bion, W. R. *Cogitations* (London: Karnac Books, 1992).

Blake, William. *The Poetical Works* (London: Oxford University Press, 1961).

Blanchot, Maurice. *The Space of Literature.* Translated by Ann Smock (Lincoln: University of Nebraska, 1982).
———. *L'Entretien infini* (Paris: Gallimard, 1969).
Bloom, Harold. *Shakespeare: The Invention of the Human* (New York: Riverhead, 1998).
———. *The Anxiety of Influence.* (Oxford: Oxford University Press, 1973).
Bodenheimer, Aron. *Why? On the Obscenity of Questioning* (Stuttgart: 1984).
Bollas, Christopher. *Cracking Up* (New York: Hill and Wang, 1996).
———. *The Shadow of the Object* (London: Free Association Books, 1987).
Boyarin, Daniel. *Intertextuality and the Reading of Midrash* (Bloomington: Indiana University Press, 1990).
Brown, Norman O. *Life Against Death* (Middleton, Conn.: Wesleyan University, 1959).
Bruner, Jerome. *Actual Minds, Possible Worlds* (Cambridge, Mass.: Harvard University Press, 1986).
Bruns, Gerald. *Hermeneutics Ancient and Modern* (New Haven: Yale University Press, 1992).
Buber, Martin. "Prophecy, Apocalyptic, and the Historical Hour," in *On the Bible* (New York: Schocken, 1982).
Burke, Kenneth. *Language as Symbolic Action* (Berkeley: University of California Press, 1966).
———. *Permanence and Change* (Berkeley: University of California Press, 1984).
Calvino, Italo. "The Non-Existent Knight," in *Our Ancestors* (London: Picador, 1980).
Canetti, Elias. *Crowds and Power* (Middlesex: Penguin, 1973).
Cassuto, U. *A Commentary on the Book of Exodus* (Jerusalem: Magnes Press, 1967).
Cavell, Stanley. *A Pitch of Philosophy* (Cambridge, Mass.: Harvard University Press, 1994).
Chatwin, Bruce. *The Songlines* (London: Picador, 1988).
Childs, Brevard. *Exodus, A Commentary* (SCM Press Ltd., 1974).
Clement, Catherine. *Syncope.* Translated by Sally O'Driscoll (University of Minnesota Press, 1994).
———. *Opera, or the Undoing of Women.* Translated by Betsy Wing (Minneapolis: University of Minnesota Press, 1988).
Cover, Robert M. "Nomos and Narrative," in *Harvard Law Review* (November 1983).
Derrida, Jacques. *Archive Fever.* Translated by Eric Prenowitz (Chicago: University of Chicago Press, 1995).
Dickens, Charles. *Hard Times* (New York: Signet Classics, 1961).
———. *Bleak House* (New York: Signet Classics, 1964).
Douglas, Mary. *Purity and Danger* (London: Routledge, 1994).
Edmundson, Mark. *Towards Reading Freud* (Princeton: Princeton University Press, 1990).
Emerson, Ralph Waldo. "Self-Reliance," in *Selected Essays* (New York: Penguin, 1982).
———. "Threnody," in *The Portable Emerson* (Viking Press, 1962).
———. *Walden.* Edited by Owen Thomas (New York: Norton, 1966).
———. *Selected Essays.* Edited by Larzer Ziff (New York: Penguin Classics, 1985).
Felman, Shoshana and Dori Laub. *Testimony: Crises of Witnessing in Literature, Psychoanalysis, and History* (New York and London: Routledge, Chapman and Hall, 1992).
Felstiner, John. *Paul Celan: Poet, Survivor, Jew* (New Haven: Yale University Press, 1995).

Fingarette, Herbert. *The Self in Transformation* (New York: Harper Torchbooks, 1965).

Freud, Sigmund. *The Standard Edition of the Complete Psychological Works.* Translated by James Strachey, et al. (London: Hogarth Press, 1953).

———. *Moses and Monotheism* (New York: Vintage, 1939).

Gallop, Jane. *Reading Lacan* (Ithaca: Cornell University Press, 1985).

Green, Arthur. *Tormented Master* (New York: Schocken Books, 1981).

Handelman, Don, and David Shulman. *God Inside Out* (New York: Oxford University Press, 1997).

Handelman, Susan. "The 'Torah' of Criticism and the Criticism of Torah: Recuperating the Pedagogical Moment," in *Interpreting Judaism in a Postmodern Age.* Edited by Steven Kepnes (New York and London: New York University Press, 1996).

Harrison, Robert Pogue. *Forests: The Shadow of Civilization* (Chicago: University of Chicago Press, 1992).

Havel, Vaclav. *The Power of the Powerless* (New York: Palach Press, 1985).

Heidegger, Martin. *Basic Writings* (San Francisco: Harper, 1977).

Heschel, Abraham J. *The Prophets* (New York: The Jewish Publication Society of America, 1962).

Hillman, James. *Healing Fiction* (Spring Publications, 1983).

James, William. *The Varieties of Religious Experience* (London: Fontana Library, 1960).

The JPS Commentary, Exodus. Commentary by Nahum Sarna (JPS, 1991).

Kafka, Franz. *The Trial* (Middlesex: Penguin, 1970).

———. *Parables and Paradoxes* (New York: Schocken Books, 1975).

Keats, John. *Letters.* Selected by Frederick Page (Oxford: Oxford University Press, 1965).

Kermode, Frank. *The Sense of an Ending* (New York: Oxford, 1966).

Kierkegaard, Soren. *The Sickness unto Death.* Translated by Howard V. Hong and Edna H. Hong (Princeton: Princeton University Press, 1980).

Koestler, Arthur. *The Ghost in the Machine* (Picador, 1975).

Kristeva, Julia. *Black Sun* (New York: Columbia University Press, 1989).

Kundera, Milan. *The Unbearable Lightness of Being* (London: Faber and Faber, 1985).

Lacan, Jacques. *Écrits* (New York: W.W. Norton, 1977).

Lear, Jonathan. *Open Minded: Working Out the Logic of the Soul* (Cambridge, Mass.: Harvard University Press, 1998).

Leibowitz, Nehama. *Studies in Shemot* (Jerusalem: World Zionist Organization, 1981).

Levinas, Emmanuel. "Revelation in the Jewish Tradition," in *The Levinas Reader.* Edited by Sean Hand (Oxford: Blackwell, 1989).

———. *Ethique et infini: Dialogues avec Philippe Nemo* (Paris: Fayard, 1982).

———. *Difficult Freedom: Essays on Judaism.* Translated by Sean Hand (Baltimore: Johns Hopkins University Press, 1990).

———. "The Temptation of Temptation," in *Nine Talmudic Readings.* Translated by Annette Aronowicz (Bloomington: Indiana University Press, 1990).

———. *Totality and Infinity* (Pittsburgh: Duquesne University Press, 1969).

Lewis, C. S. *Till We Have Faces* (San Diego: Harcourt Brace, 1957).

Mandelstam, Nadezhda. *Hope Against Hope* (New York: Atheneum, 1970).

Mann, Thomas. *Dr. Faustus* (Middlesex: Penguin, 1949).

Milosz, Czeslaw. *The Collected Poems (1931–1987).* (Penguin Books, 1988).

Mitchell, Stephen. *Hope and Dread in Psychoanalysis* (New York: Basic Books, 1993).
Muffs, Yochanan. *Conservative Judaism* xxxiii, no. 3 (spring 1980): 25–37.
———. *Love and Joy: Law, Language and Religion in Ancient Israel* (New York: The Jewish Theological Seminary of America, 1992).
Neher, André. *The Exile of the Word.* Translated by David Maisel (Philadelphia: Jewish Publication Society, 1981).
Neumann, Erich. *The Origins and History of Consciousness* (New Jersey: Princeton University Press, 1973).
Newmarch, Rosa. *The Life and Letters of Peter Ilich Tchaikowsky* (London: 1906).
Ortega, José. *The Revolt of the Masses* (New York: Norton, 1957).
Ouaknine, Marc-Alain. *The Burnt Book.* Translated by Llewellyn Brown (Princeton: Princeton University Press, 1995).
Paul, Robert A. *Moses and Civilization* (New Haven: Yale University Press, 1996).
Phillips, Adam. *The Beast in the Nursery* (London: Faber and Faber, 1998).
———. *On Flirtation* (Cambridge, Mass.: Harvard University Press, 1994).
———. *On Kissing, Tickling, and Being Bored* (Cambridge, Mass.: Harvard University Press, 1993).
———. *Terrors and Experts* (Cambridge, Mass.: Harvard University Press, 1996).
Polen, Nehemia. "Miriam's Dance: Radical Egalitarianism in Hassidic Thought," in *Modern Judaism* 12, 1 (1992): 1–21.
Porten, Gary. "Defining Midrash," in *The Study of Ancient Judaism.* Edited by J. Neusner (New York, 1981), 59–60.
Raphael, Max. *Prehistoric Pottery and Civilization in Egypt* (Pantheon, 1947).
Read, Herbert. *Icon and Idea* (New York: Schocken, 1965).
Ricks, Christopher. *The Force of Poetry* (Oxford: Oxford University Press, 1997).
Ricoeur, Paul. *History and Truth* (Northwestern University Press, 1965).
Rieff, Philip. *The Mind of the Moralist* (Chicago: University of Chicago Press, 1979).
Rilke, Rainer Maria. *The Selected Poetry of Rainer Maria Rilke.* Edited and translated by Stephen Mitchell (New York: Vintage, 1982).
Rorty, Richard. *Contingency, Irony, and Solidarity* (Cambridge: Cambridge University Press, 1990).
Rosenzweig, Franz. *The Star of Redemption.* Translated by William W. Hallo (Notre Dame: University of Notre Dame Press, 1985).
Rudnytsky, Peter L. ed. *Transitional Objects and Potential Spaces: Literary Uses of D. W. Winnicott* (New York: Columbia University Press, 1993).
Sacks, Oliver. *Awakenings* (New York: HarperPerennial, 1990).
———. *The Man Who Mistook His Wife for a Hat* (Picador, 1985).
Saint-Exupery, Antoine de. *The Little Prince* (London: Pan Books, 1974).
Sarna, Nahum. *Exploring Exodus* (New York: Schocken Books, 1987).
Scarry, Elaine. *The Body in Pain: The Making and Unmaking of the World* (New York: Oxford University Press, 1987).
Schwartz, Murray M. "Where is Literature?" in *Transitional Objects and Potential Spaces: Literary Uses of D. W. Winnicott.* Edited by Peter L. Rudnytsky (New York: Columbia University Press, 1993).
Semprun, Jorge. *The Long Voyage* (New York: Schocken, 1964).

Shakespeare, William. *Hamlet.* Edited by John Dover Wilson (London: Cambridge University Press, 1961).

Sontag, Susan. *Styles of Radical Will* (New York: Anchor, 1999).

Steiner, George. *After Babel* (Oxford: Oxford University Press, 1992).

———. *No Passion Spent* (New Haven: Yale University Press, 1996).

———. *Real Presences* (Chicago: University of Chicago Press, 1989).

———. *The Steiner Reader* (Middlesex: Penguin, 1984).

———. *In Bluebeard's Castle* (New Haven: Yale University Press, 1971).

Sternberg, Meir. *The Poetics of Biblical Narrative* (Bloomington: Indiana University Press, 1985).

Stevens, Wallace. "Notes Toward a Supreme Fiction," *Selected Poems* (London: Faber and Faber).

Thoreau, Henry David. *Walden*. Ed. Owen Thomas (New York: Norton, 1966).

Trilling, Lionel. *Sincerity and Authenticity* (Cambridge, Mass.: Harvard University Press, 1973).

Walzer, Michael. *Thick and Thin: Moral Argument at Home and Abroad* (Notre Dame: University of Notre Dame Press, 1994).

Weschler, Lawrence. *Calamities of Exile* (Chicago: University of Chicago Press, 1999).

Winnicott, D. W. *Playing and Reality* (London: Tavistock/Routledge, 1997).

———. "Primitive Emotional Development," in *Collected Papers: Through Pediatrics to Psycho-Analysis* (London: Tavistock; New York: Basic Books, 1958).

Wolfson, Elliot R. *Through a Speculum that Shines* (Princeton: Princeton University Press, 1994).

Wollheim, Richard. *Art and Its Objects* (Cambridge: Cambridge University Press, 1980).

Wordsworth, William. *Poetry and Prose.* Selected by W. M. Merchant (London: Rupert Hart-Davis, 1955).

———. *The Prose Works,* Vol. 2. Edited by W. J. B. Owen and Jane Wothington Smyser (Oxford University Press/Clarendon Press, 1974).

Yerushalmi, Yosef Hayim. *Freud's Moses: Judaism Terminable and Interminable* (New Haven: Yale University Press, 1991).

Zizek, Slavoj. *The Sublime Object of Ideology* (London, New York: Verso, 1989).

Zornberg, Avivah. *The Beginning of Desire: Reflections on Genesis* (New York: Doubleday, 2996).

Acknowledgments

I feel fortunate to be able to teach at several Jerusalem institutions where the atmosphere of vigorous and liberal Torah study has nurtured my thinking over the years. These chapters are based on lectures that I gave at Matan, Pardes, Jerusalem College for Adults, and Midreshet Lindenbaum. I am grateful to these institutions and to their students; because of them, my Torah study has intensified continuously.

I would like to dedicate this book to my first and most significant teacher, my father, Rabbi Dr. Ze'ev Gottlieb *z'l;* and to my mother, Bracha Rosen Gottlieb *z'l,* who communicated to me her sense of the beauty of life. In them, I felt the reality of "Torah and greatness in one place" (B. Gittin, 59a).

In very different ways, Rabbi Daniel Epstein's teachings in Torah and Adam Phillips's psychoanalytic essays have been generative for me, sharpening my awareness of the "particulars of rapture." This book also owes much to the encouragement of many people, whose belief in my work moved me through narrow places. David Shulman read a section and with his usual luminous intelligence inspired me to continue writing with new zest. Haym Soloveitchik encouraged me to undertake this project; and my agent, Sharon Friedman, volunteered assistance beyond the call of duty. My husband, Eric Zornberg, constantly helps me in more ways than I can tell.

I particularly want to thank those friends who have read parts of the manuscript and those with whom I have had fruitful conversations; often, too, they have made valuable bibliographical suggestions: Susan Shapiro, Betsy Rosenberg, Susan Handelman, Peter Pitzele, Mark Kirschbaum, Paul Slater, Chana Mann, Tamar Ross, Dina Kazhdan, Shaindy Rudoff, Arieh Strikowsky, Judy and Steve Klitzner, Danny Schwartz, Linda Zisquit, Bracha Zornberg. Their warmth, wisdom, and enthusiasm have contributed to my efforts to bring together disparate worlds. A special thanks to Arieh Supperstein, who rescued me from the vagaries of my computer; to Yvonne Heitner, who has been my faithful tape archivist; and to Adele and Ron Tauber for providing me with a home in the U.S. during my lecture tours.

I want to thank all those at Doubleday who had a share in this endeavor, especially my editors Mark Fretz and Andrew Corbin. I have had valuable editorial and technical help from Dean Curtis, Eric Schramm, Tali Stern, and Eben Weiss.

Glossary

Abarbanel, Don Isaac (1437–1508): Spanish Bible commentator as well as a philosopher and statesman.

Avot d' Rabbi Natan: tannaitic amplification on tractate Avot by R. Natan, an older contemporary of R. Judah Ha-Nasi.

Baal Shem Tov (1700–1760): Israel ben Eliezer Baal Shem Tov (usually referred to by initials BeShT). Most successful of originating leaders of the Hasidic movement.

Bahya: Spanish fourteenth-century commentator on the Torah.

Beit Yaacov: Hasidic commentary on the Torah, by Jacob Leiner (1814–1878), son of Mordecai Joseph Leiner, the Ishbitzer.

Cassutto, Umberto (1883–1951): Italian Jewish Bible commentator. Renowned for his critique of the documentary theories of Higher Criticism.

Chizkuni: mid-thirteenth-century commentary on the Torah of Hezekiah ben Manoah. Probably a member of the school of Rashi.

Gur Arye: supercommentary to Rashi of Judah Loew ben Bezalel, known as Maharal of Prague (1525–1609).

Ha-amek Davar: commentary on the Torah of Naftali Zvi Yehuda Berlin, known as the Netziv (1817–1893).

Hasidism: religious movement founded by Israel ben Eliezer, known as the Baal Shem Tov, in the eighteenth century.

Ibn Ezra, Abraham (1080–1164): Spanish Bible commentator, poet, and grammarian.

Ishbitzer: R. Modecai Josef Leiner (d. 1854), author of Mei HaShiloach, a collection of his writings on the Torah.

Kedushat Levi: Hasidic homilies on the Torah of Levi Isaac of Berditchev (1740–1810).

Kli Yakar: homiletic commentary on the Torah of Ephraim Solomon ben Hayyim of Luntshitz (1550–1619).

Kook, Avraham, Yitzhak HaKohen (1865–1935): author of monumental works on the Talmud, rabbinic law, and Jewish thought, as well as a commentary to the Prayer Book. First Chief Rabbi of Israel. His philosophy of religious nationhood outlined in poetic mystic language has profoundly influenced twentieth-century Jewish thought.

Likkutei Moharan: *see* Nahman of Bratzlav.

Maharal: Judah Loew ben Bezalel (1525–1609), author of philosophical, legal, and exegetical works, including Gur Arye, Gevuroth HaShem, Tiffereth Yisrael.

Malbim: initials of Meir Yehuda Leibush ben Yehiel Mikhal (1809–1880), Russian rabbi chiefly noted for his commentary on the Torah.

Maor VaShemesh: Hasidic commentary on the Torah of Kalonymos Kalman Epstein (d. 1823), disciple of Elimelech of Lizhensk.

Mechilta: tannaitic midrash on Exodus, both halachic and aggadic.

Mei HaShiloach: *see* Ishbitzer.

Meshech Chochma: commentary on the Torah of Meir Simha HaKohen of Dvinsk (1843–1926), Talmudist and rabbinic leader.

Midrash HaGadol: collection of midrashim on the Bible compiled from ancient tannaitic sources by David ben Amram Adani, a Yemenite scholar in the thirteenth century.

Midrash Lekach Tov: midrashic commentary to the Torah, compiled by Tobias ben Eliezer, a Balkans rabbinic scholar in the late eleventh century.

Midrash Rabba: collection of ten midrashim, from various periods, on the five books of the Pentateuch and on the Five Scrolls (Ruth, Esther, Lamentations, Ecclesiastes, and Song of Songs).

Mizrahi, Iliahu (1440–1525): author of supercommentary to Rashi on the Torah.

Nahman of Bratzlav (1772–1811): author of Likkutei Moharan, a collection of theological teachings in which he expounded a paradoxical concept of faith, the centrality of the tzaddik, and the importance of doubt and self-criticism, as well as of melody and dance, in the life of the spiritually aspiring.

Noam Elimelech: Hasidic sermons on the weekly Torah readings, of Elimelech of Lizhensk (1717–1787), one of the founders of Hasidism in Galicia.

Or HaChaim: commentary on the Torah of Chaim ibn Attar (1696–1743), Moroccan Kabbalist, Talmudist, and leader of Moroccan Jewish resettlement in Israel.

Pachad Yitzhak: collected discources of R. Yitzhak Hutner (b. 1907), representing a synthesis of Talmudic conciseness, Hasidic mysticism, and ethical sensitivity.

Pirke d'Rabbi Eliezer: a midrashic description of the workings of God in creation and in the oldest history of Israel. The book was probably written in Palestine, about the beginning of the ninth century.

Rambam: initials of Rabbi Moshe ben Maimon, or Maimonides (1135–1204), author of a master code of Jewish law, *Mishneh Torah*; a philosophical handbook to Judaism,

Guide of the Perplexed; and a compendium of the 613 commandments, *Sefer HaMitzvoth*.

Ramban: initials of Rabbi Moshe ben Nahman, or Nahmanides (1194–1270), Spanish biblical and Talmudic commentator.

Rashbam: initials of Rabbi Shmuel ben Meir (1080–1158), member of Tosafist school, grandson of Rashi, renowned for his *peshat*—plain sense—commentary on the Torah.

Rashi: initials of Rabbi Shelomo Yitzhaki, foremost commentator on the Torah (1049–1105). Lived in Troyes, France.

Sefat Emet: collected writings of Judah Aryeh Leib Alter (1847–1905), Polish Jewish leader and head of Hasidim of Gur. Characterized by wide scholarship, profundity of ideas, and clarity of exposition. Reflects the influence of Maharal.

Seforno, Ovadia ben Yaakov (1475–1550): Italian Talmudist, physician, and commentator on the Torah.

Shadal (1800–1865): Shmuel David Luzzatto, Italian Jewish scholar, poet, grammarian, and author of commentary on the Torah.

Siftei Chachamim: the most important of Rashi's supercommentaries, usually printed alongside Rashi. The author is Shabtai ben Yosef (1641–1718), usually known as Meshorrer Bass.

Talmud: code of Jewish law, lore, philosophy, and ethics, compiled between 200 and 500 C.E. in both Palestine and Babylon. Here, the two codices are referred to by J. and B.

Tanhuma: homiletic midrash on the Torah known in a number of collections.

Targum: Hebrew for "translation." Any of the Aramaic translations of the Torah done in the last centuries B.C.E. and the early centuries C.E. Often exegetical in nature.

Torah Shelemah: compendium of early rabbinic commentary of the Torah, by Rabbi Menahem Kasher, begun in 1924.

Torah Temimah: commentary on the Torah of Rabbi Baruch HaLevi Epstein, Russian Talmudist (1860–1942), in which he appended to the written text his own selection of the main dicta of Oral Tradition, selected from Talmudic literature, with his commentary explaining their relevance.

Yalkut Shimeoni: a midrashic thesaurus on the whole of the Bible compiled from more than fifty works. Probably compiled in the first half of the thirteenth century,

Zaddok HaCohen (1823–1900): author of Hasidic writings on the Torah (Pri Zaddik), combining knowledge of Kabbalah and of Halachah. Disciple of the Ishbitzer.

Zohar: the Book of Splendor, the most important text of Jewish mysticism, purportedly written by Shimeon bar Yohai, but in fact composed in Spain in the thirteenth century.

Index of Sources

Items marked [n.] indicate source affiliated with note number.

Bible

Rabbinic